INDEX OF DEATH LISTS APPEARING IN THE

CINCINNATIER ZEITUNG

1887–1901

Hamilton County Chapter of the Ohio Genealogical Society
P. O. Box 15865
Cincinnati, Ohio 45215-0865

INDEXED BY
Jeffrey G. Herbert

HERITAGE BOOKS
2010

HERITAGE BOOKS
AN IMPRINT OF HERITAGE BOOKS, INC.

Books, CDs, and more—Worldwide

For our listing of thousands of titles see our website
at
www.HeritageBooks.com

Published 2010 by
HERITAGE BOOKS, INC.
Publishing Division
100 Railroad Ave. #104
Westminster, Maryland 21157

International Standard Book Numbers
Paperbound: 978-0-7884-1206-6
Clothbound: 978-0-7884-8321-9

TABLE OF CONTENTS
***** ** ********

Introduction

Cincinnatier Zeitung was a newspaper published in German from July 1887 until September 1901 for German speaking immigrants of Cincinnati. Cincinnatier Zeitung, which simply means "Cincinnati newspaper" was published six days a week, and was a rather insignificant newspaper as far as subscription and influence is concerned. At its highest point, its circulation reached only about 6,000 readers, as opposed to a newspaper like the Cincinnati Volksblatt, which had a circulation of around 23,000 readers during its highest point. The newspaper can be classified as a specialty or niche newspaper since it catered mostly to union or organized labor issues. In fact, for several months, an endorsement appeared in the paper on a daily basis. The example, which follows appeared in the newspaper on 4, November 1896 on page 5, which stated "To whom it may concern: This is to certify that the Cincinnatier Zeitung has been endorsed and is regarded by the Central Labor Council of Cincinnati and vicinity as the one daily paper published in Ohio that advocates the rights of the members of labor organizations and is cordially recommended as a newspaper that will reach the trade unions."

What makes this newspaper of significant value and use to the family history researcher, is that a list of death records was published for fellow Germans who were reported to the Cincinnati Health Department on a daily basis. These death records are of great value, since many of these deaths were reported due to the fact that these individuals died in a city institution. These were typically people who lived in mental institutions, orphanages, the 'poor house', and homes for widows and the aged. These were people who normally could not afford to pay for a death notice to be published in a newspaper. While these death records do not contain much information about the deceased, they contain the name of the person, their age, their street address, and sometimes the disease from which they died.

Since not all this vital information can be contained in this index, the date(s) of the death notice is supplied after the person's name so that the reader may look for this additional information in the original notice if desired.

This index contains the full name of the deceased, sorted alphabetically by last name, the dates that the death notice appeared in the newspaper, and the actual date of death, if published. Also listed is the age of the person in (YY-MM-DD) format, the page on which the notice was printed, the maiden name of the woman, if listed, and if the city of birth was mentioned in the notice, an '*' appears before the page number. In the case where a death notice is published for more than two days, only the first two days are listed, or the two days which contain the most information about the deceased and their family.

The issues of Cincinnatier Zeitung covered by this index are the issues that are still in existence from July 1887 until September 1901. These issues are located in the Magazines and Newspapers Department of the Public Library of Cincinnati and Hamilton County located at 8th and Vine Street.

The death lists that were published in the paper can be identified rather easily since they had any of the following words in bold large print at the top of the list: 'TODESNACHRICHTEN', 'STERBEFÄLLE', 'TODTENLISTE', or 'DIE TODTEN DES TAGES'; which mean respectively: 'DEATH REPORTS', 'DEATH CASES', 'DEATH LISTS', or 'THE DEATHS OF THE DAY'. This index contains the names of over 20,000 people who died between 1887 and 1901.

In many cases, the names of the deceased were recorded in the original German spellings, however, sometimes they were also spelled using their English equivalents. To be certain that a particular name is not overlooked or missed, both spelling variations should be checked. There may be additional spelling variations to watch for, such as the frequent interchangeability of the letters 'C' and 'K' (e.g. Carl/Karl) and the use of double final letters in German (e.g. Horman/Hormann).

The unique German letters and their usual English equivalents are listed below as an aid to the reader.

'ä' translated into English as 'ae'
'ö' translated into English as 'oe'
'ü' translated into English as 'ue'
'ß' translated into English as 'sz' or 'ss'

Some examples are as follows: (Schäfer = Schaefer), (Schröder = Schroeder), (Müller = Mueller), (Bußmann = Bussmann). Letters with an umlaut are sorted alphabetically as if they came after the letter 'Z' (i.e. ... u,v,w,x,y,z,ä,ö,ü,ß).

CINCINNATIER ZEITUNG DEATH NOTICES --- 1887 - 1901

Name	Notice Date	Death Date	Age	Page	Maiden Name
Aarig, Johan	21, Oct. 1896	20, Oct.	73- 4m	5	
Abbes, Herman	8, Mar. 1888		27	1	
Abburg, Louise G.	30, Nov. 1887		55	4	
Abdes, Simon	9, Dec. 1887		20	1	
Abel, Emilie	8, Nov. 1887		31	1	
Abel, Joseph	12, Feb. 1891		46	4	
Abel, Lena	19, July 1887		29	1	
Abel, Michael	17, Apr. 1888		55	1	
Abeling, Louise	29, Aug. 1895	28, Aug.	28-1m	5	Cook
Abeling, Margaretha	22, Aug. 1895	21, Aug.	1- 2w	5	
Able, W.J.	31, July 1894		2m	5	
Abold, Adolph	28, May 1892		5m	5	
Abrahams, Bertha	17, Jan. 1893		31	5	
Abrams, Pauline	2, May 1901		73	8	
Abt, Magdalena	16, Apr. 1898	15, Apr.	39- -12d	5	Stoeser
Achten, Herman	3, Apr. 1891		49	4	
Achter, Georg Herman	24, June 1899	21, June	23-11m	4	
Achterkamp, Joseph	21, Jan. 1893		54	5	
Achtermeyer, Irwin	23, June 1894		9m	5	
Ackel, D.	30, Aug. 1890		77	2	
Ackenhauser, William	19, Jan. 1893		6m	5	
Acker, John	1, May 1888		2	2	
Acker, Nany	10, Apr. 1901		80	8	
Acker, Raymond	8, Feb. 1901		2	8	
Ackerland, Abraham	2, Dec. 1893		72	5	
Ackermann, Alexander	1, Feb. 1888		2-10m	4	
Ackermann, Anna Mary	22, Aug. 1892		6	5	
Ackermann, Edward	1, May 1895		6	5	
Ackermann, Elisabeth	24, July 1890		93	1	
Ackermann, Ferdinand	15, Apr. 1900			8	
Ackermann, George	12, May 1893		25	5	
Ackermann, Louis Joseph	10, Feb. 1900	8, Feb.	11m	5	
Ackermann, Mary	14, Apr. 1893		70	5	
Ackley, John L.	1, Oct. 1887		25	1	
Acomb, Harry	14, Aug. 1888		10	1	
Ada, Bertha	28, Apr. 1896	27, Apr.	15m	5	
Adae, Franklin R.	10, Apr. 1891		33	4	
Adam, Ada	19, July 1893		4m	5	
Adam, Elizabeth	8, July 1901		60	8	
Adam, Fritz	30, Mar. 1899	29, Mar.	29-11m	5	
Adam, Margaretha	7, Dec. 1898	7, Dec.	15- -14d	4	
Adam, Wilhelm	24, Aug. 1900		81	5	
Adams,	14, Feb. 1888		6d	4	
Adams, Alex.	13, Aug. 1888		44	1	
Adams, Alice	15, Jan. 1901		30	8	
Adams, Charles F.	7, Feb. 1901		22	8	
Adams, Edna	23, July 1901		5	8	
Adams, Elizabeth	16, Jan. 1892		11m	5	
Adams, Emma	29, Aug. 1900		5m	5	
Adams, Georg	2, Apr. 1896	1, Apr.	70- 5m	5	
Adams, Gustav	5, Dec. 1890		43	4	
Adams, Jesse	22, Nov. 1894		20	5	
Adams, Richard	12, June 1889		16m	1	
Adams, Sallie	26, Apr. 1895		49	5	
Adderley, Clara	6, Nov. 1900		36	8	
Addinger, Rudolph	1, Oct. 1901		59	1	
Ade, Margarethe	13, Mar. 1895		52	5	
Adel, Artline	18, Apr. 1893		26	5	
Adele, (Sr.)	13, Oct. 1892		56	5	
Adelmann, Wilhelm	4, Oct. 1897	1, Oct.	68	5	
Ader, Barbara	2, May 1890		64	1	
Ader, Charles	11, Jan. 1898	10, Jan.	37-11m-11d	5	
Ader, Elisabeth	8, Sept 1899	7, Sept	81- -20d	4	Awe
Ader, Eva	7, Sept 1888		56	1	
Ader, Franz	19, May 1900	18, May	70- 7m	8	
Ader, Henrietta A.	3, Feb. 1891		3	4	
Ader, Theresia	8, Mar. 1893		32	5	
Adler, Ad.	27, Oct. 1894		49	5	
Adler, Allie M.	18, Jan. 1901		32	8	
Adler, Isaac	2, June 1894		22	5	
Adler, John	31, Dec. 1888		52	1	

Name ****	Notice Date ****** ****	Death Date ***** ****	Age ***	Page ****	Maiden Name ****** ****
Adolph, Mary	17, Apr. 1901		45	8	
Adrian, Herbert	26, July 1900		7m	5	
Aebi, Maria Eva	12, Dec. 1899	11, Dec.	37- 3m	4	Rohr
Aefner, Charles	21, Nov. 1900		46	8	
Afsprung, Katharine	8, Apr. 1896	7, Apr.	69-11m	5	Hinkender
Agin, Harold	4, Jan. 1898	3, Jan.	5- 5m	5	
Agin, Oliver	8, Feb. 1896	7, Feb.	5m	5	
Agricola, Georg	30, Dec. 1892	29, Dec.	12- 9m	5	
Agricola, George	6, July 1901		10m	8	
Ahaus, John B.	19, Oct. 1892		30	5	
Ahaus, Mary	3, July 1894		3	5	
Ahaus, Mary	28, Dec. 1900		84	8	
Ahlborn, William	13, Apr. 1894		76	5	
Ahlbrandt, Dora A.	15, Nov. 1893		8m	5	
Ahlbrandt, John H.	18, Dec. 1889		79	1	
Ahlbrant, Eva	1, Nov. 1888		51	1	
Ahlenbach, John	25, Mar. 1893		34	5	
Ahlenstorf, Fred.	26, Feb. 1891		1	4	
Ahlenstorf, Hermine	18, Feb. 1891		71	4	
Ahlenstorp, John	12, Apr. 1892		38	5	
Ahlering, Katharina Elisabeth	16, Jan. 1899	14, Jan.	81- 3m	5	Stragegir
Ahlers, Arnold	11, Apr. 1891		57	4	
Ahlers, Charles Theodore	22, Feb. 1899	21, Feb.	72- -13d	5	
Ahlers, Henry	29, July 1887		12	1	
Ahlers, Henry W.	19, July 1895		66	5	
Ahlers, Herman W.H.	2, July 1895		6m	5	
Ahlers, Johan	27, Jan. 1890		23	1	
Ahlers, John F.	4, Apr. 1894		68	5	
Ahlers, Katharina Marie	2, Mar. 1897	28, Feb.	64- 9m	5	Brunnemeyer
Ahlers, Mary	17, Oct. 1900		45	8	
Ahlers, Sarah M.	8, June 1895		38	5	
Ahlert, Louisa	18, Jan. 1892		78	5	
Ahmann, Gertrud	3, Sept 1901		37	8	
Ahmann, Sibilla	16, July 1895		10m	5	
Ahnefeld, Friedrich C.	13, Mar. 1891		9m	4	
Ahnemann, Johan	4, Feb. 1888		58	4	
Ahr, Theodore	13, July 1887		6m	1	
Aichale, William F.	24, Mar. 1893		52	5	
Aichholz, Emma	15, Apr. 1899	14, Apr.	21	4	
Aker, Dora	14, Feb. 1895		12	5	
Aker, Gaudenz	4, Apr. 1895		41	5	
Aker, Mary L.	20, Feb. 1891		2	4	
Akers, Emma	7, June 1901		22	8	
Alaid, Mary	4, June 1901		1m	8	
Alben, Carolina	27, Apr. 1896	25, Apr.	31- 8m	5	
Alber, Joseph	28, June 1892		23	5	
Alberhard, Mamie	30, July 1892		21	5	
Albers, Catharine	7, Sept 1888		82	1	
Albers, Dora	25, Mar. 1891		25	4	
Albers, George	27, June 1895		3m	5	
Albers, Henry	17, Apr. 1890		79	1	
Albers, Henry	10, Oct. 1890		15	4	
Albers, Herman	1, May 1888		4m	2	
Albers, John	19, July 1901		1	8	
Albers, Leo	5, Dec. 1891		6	4	
Albers, Leonhard F.	19, Mar. 1891		15d	4	
Albers, Paul	7, Apr. 1897	6, Apr.	9m	5	
Albert, Charles	8, Sept 1898	6, Sept	68	4	
Albert, George F.	22, Feb. 1897	21, Feb.	41- 5m	5	
Albert, Louise	14, Feb. 1893		26	5	
Albert, Matilda	15, Apr. 1888		4m	5	
Albert, Prince	27, Apr. 1895		50	5	
Albert, Stella	16, Dec. 1891		4	4	
Albiez, Edward	26, Dec. 1900		53	8	
Albrecht, Emily	31, May 1892		24	5	
Albrecht, Frank	7, Dec. 1893		46	5	
Albrecht, Fred	2, Sept 1887		62	1	
Albrecht, Georg	12, Jan. 1897	11, Jan.	21- 3m	5	
Albrecht, J.	18, Nov. 1894		26	5	
Albrecht, Kate	17, Dec. 1900		33	8	
Albrecth, Frederick E.	5, Mar. 1891		3	4	

Name	Notice Date	Death Date	Age	Page	Maiden Name
****	****** ****	***** ****	***	****	****** ****
Albrick, B.	23, Dec. 1896	21, Dec.		5	
Albroes, Joseph	2, June 1891		42	4	
Alderson, Warren	11, Apr. 1901		17	8	
Aldhof, L.	13, Jan. 1897	11, Jan.	85	5	
Alening, Herman	11, Jan. 1888		7d	4	
Alexander, Anna	13, Dec. 1890		74	1	
Alexander, Belle	16, July 1888		26	1	
Alexander, Charles	3, Apr. 1888		3	4	
Alexander, David A.	27, Jan. 1891		38	4	
Alexander, Harry	30, Aug. 1887		62	1	
Alexander, Ida M.	10, Dec. 1891		22	4	
Alexander, Irving	6, June 1901		35	8	
Alexander, Julius	12, June 1901		70	8	
Alexander, Lena	7, Oct. 1890		7	1	
Alexander, Louisa	3, June 1901		40	8	
Alexander, Phil.	23, Dec. 1889		11	1	
Alexander, Raymond	24, Jan. 1901		5d	8	
Alf, Albert	25, July 1901		2	8	
Alf, Gerhard	24, Mar. 1888		7m	1	
Alf, John	2, Aug. 1887		27	1	
Alf, William	23, Oct. 1888		3m	1	
Alfing, Herman	25, Apr. 1897	22, Apr.	43- 2m	5	
Alfonso, Walter	27, Feb. 1888		4m	4	
Alich, Florentine	31, Jan. 1900	30, Jan.	18- - 9d	5	
Alich, John A.	3, Apr. 1888		68	4	
Allbright, J.	2, Mar. 1901		68	5	
Alled, Donald	11, Aug. 1900		4m	8	
Allen, Anna	28, Jan. 1901		49	8	
Allen, Annie	26, Mar. 1901		38	8	
Allen, H.C.	16, July 1900		78	8	
Allen, Lewis	31, July 1900		72	5	
Allen, Margaret	24, Oct. 1900		40	8	
Allen, Mary E.	30, Mar. 1901		45	8	
Allen, Washington	30, Mar. 1901		61	8	
Allen, William	27, Apr. 1895		39	5	
Allen, William	17, Aug. 1900		13d	5	
Allenberg, Ricka	9, July 1897	9, July	74	4	
Allender, Henrietta	2, Oct. 1900		55	8	
Allendorf, August	22, Apr. 1891		29	4	
Allendorf, Heinrich	10, Mar. 1899	9, Mar.	76- 3m	5	
Allendorf, Henry	18, Jan. 1901		7d	8	
Allgeier, Clemens	8, Feb. 1901		73	8	
Allgeyer, Alma	9, Sept 1893		4m	5	
Allgeyer, Bertha	27, Nov. 1899	26, Nov.		5	
Allinger, Friedricka D.	28, Dec. 1892		38	5	
Allison, Mary	23, May 1895		16	5	
Allius, Patrick	7, Sept 1887		29	1	
Allman, Florence	7, Nov. 1891		1d	1	
Allman, Grant	15, May 1901		62	8	
Allmann, Abraham F.	22, Nov. 1889		41	1	
Allmoslechner, Georg	23, Feb. 1898	22, Feb.	49- 6m	5	
Alms, Adelheid	23, Apr. 1898	22, Apr.	80	4	
Alms, Frederick H.	26, July 1898	25, July	59	5	
Alms, Gus J.	23, Jan. 1889	22, Jan.	35	2	
Alms, Margaretha Duhme	2, June 1896	30, May	74	5	
Alsfelder, Nellie	19, Sept 1891		1m	4	
Alsfelder, Samuel	23, June 1893		74	5	
Alsfelder, Sarah	20, Oct. 1891		65	1	
Alt, Edward	14, Sept 1899	13, Sept	22	5	
Alt, George G.	20, July 1895		31	5	
Alt, John	1, Nov. 1887		31	1	
Altemeyer, Annie	9, Sept 1892		1d	5	
Altemeyer, Mary	9, Sept 1892		1d	5	
Altenau, Henry G.	24, Nov. 1898	22, Nov.	42- 9m	5	
Altenau, J. Heinrich	21, Nov. 1895	20, Nov.	2- 3m	5	
Altenau, Katharina	9, July 1897	8, July	75	4	
Altenberg, Maria	25, May 1901		21	8	
Altenhevel, Anna	5, Nov. 1891		68	1	
Altenhoevel, Fred.	18, Sept 1900		84	5	
Altenhoff, Elisabeth	25, Aug. 1897	24, Aug.	75	4	
Alterschmidt, R.	7, Apr. 1900	4, Apr.	22- 2m	5	

Name	Notice Date	Death Date	Age	Page	Maiden Name
Altevers, Anna Maria	15, Jan. 1897	14, Jan.	72	5	Krieger
Althammer, Ernst	1, Mar. 1894		40	5	
Althammer, Gottfried	23, Apr. 1897	21, Apr.	80	5	
Althoff, Henry	29, Aug. 1892		22	5	
Althoff, Minnie	19, Jan. 1893		76	5	
Altig, Anna M.	1, Aug. 1888		68	2	
Altmeyer, Eva	15, Jan. 1892		10m	5	
Alvord, James	30, May 1895		43	5	
Alwes, Georg J.	20, June 1888		1	1	
Aman, Alma Elisabeth	18, Apr. 1900	17, Apr.	14m	8	
Aman, Johanna A.	18, Apr. 1893		1m	5	
Aman, Karl H.	18, Apr. 1893		1m	5	
Amann, Albert	8, Dec. 1900		3	8	
Amann, Mary	12, Jan. 1893		43	5	
Ambaun, Antonius	25, July 1899	24, July	15d	5	
Amberg, Eugene	24, Dec. 1893		6	5	
Amberg, Lizzie	26, Feb. 1900	24, Feb.	45- 8m	8	
Ambrose, Robert	14, July 1891		21d	4	
Amenskamp, Clemens A.	20, Mar. 1895		24	5	
Amenskamp, Mathilde	13, May 1901		40	8	
Amick, W.	3, Aug. 1887		37	1	
Amling, Harry	12, Sept 1901		19	5	
Amling, Jakob	17, May 1889		82	1	
Amlingmeier, H.R.	25, Apr. 1889		33	1	
Amlung, Adam	4, Sept 1890		34	1	
Amlung, Clara	20, Jan. 1890		5m	1	
Amlung, Elisabeth	4, Jan. 1897	1, Jan.	80	5	
Amman, Lizzie	11, Aug. 1890		10m	1	
Ammann, Joseph	25, Feb. 1901		73	8	
Ammann, Pearlie	6, July 1895		17m	5	
Ammann, Philipp	13, Apr. 1896	10, Apr.	64-11m	5	
Ammon, Coelestine	14, Dec. 1887		22	4	
Amon, Konrad	19, Jan. 1899	17, Jan.	86	5	
Ampthaur, Henry	5, June 1891		51	1	
Amrein, Edwin	15, Mar. 1898	13, Mar.	13	4	
Amrein, Henry	6, June 1889		54	1	
Amrein, John	2, May 1894		39	5	
Amrein, William	28, June 1893		9m	5	
Amrhein, G.E.	12, Sept 1899	11, Sept	3- 9m	5	
Amrhein, Toni	16, May 1893	16, May	7-10m-18d	5	
Amsbler, Walter M.	31, Dec. 1891		6m	1	
Amsler, Doretta M.	13, Apr. 1901		70	8	
Amster, Ellen	8, Dec. 1891		6	4	
Ana, Katharina	21, Oct. 1889		4m	1	
Anders, Augusta	19, May 1894		21	5	
Anderson,	22, Mar. 1901		19d	8	
Anderson, Bernard	16, Jan. 1890		19	1	
Anderson, Charles	8, May 1889		17	1	
Anderson, Charles	24, Apr. 1895		29	5	
Anderson, Josephine	5, Mar. 1888		6d	4	
Anderson, Laura W.	8, Aug. 1891		15	4	
Anderson, M.	21, Jan. 1889		29	1	
Anderson, Millie	4, Apr. 1895		30	5	
Andrae, Peter	30, May 1895		54	5	
Andre,	9, July 1891		2d	4	
Andres, Edwin	21, Feb. 1901		4	8	
Andres, Sophia	28, Nov. 1898	27, Nov.		5	
Andrew, Charles	10, May 1901		70	8	
Andrew, John S.	27, July 1892		4	5	
Andrews, Dolly	17, Aug. 1887		20m	1	
Angel, Naomi	29, Dec. 1900		4	8	
Ankenbauer, Franziska B.	20, Dec. 1893		19	5	
Ankenbauer, Fred.	15, Feb. 1895		5m	5	
Ankenbrock, Catharine	30, June 1896	28, June		5	
Ankenbrock, M.G.	25, Mar. 1901		80	8	
Ankenbrock, Wilhelm Anton	16, Apr. 1898	15, Apr.	32- 5m	5	
Anker, John F.	31, Oct. 1900		23	8	
Anmann, Friedrich	6, 7, Apr. 1896	5, Apr.	43- 1m	4	
Annento, Angeline	18, Jan. 1901		3	8	
Ansalm, John	18, Aug. 1892		2m	5	
Ansorg, Gunther	19, Jan. 1899	17, Jan.	49	5	

Name	Notice Date	Death Date	Age	Page	Maiden Name
****	****** ****	***** ****	***	****	****** ****
Ante, Harry	18, Aug. 1900			8	
Ante, Joseph	2, Apr. 1891		57	4	
Ante, Louise	26, Feb. 1898	25, Feb.	69-10m	5	Ewald
Anthe, Maria	28, Dec. 1899	27, Dec.	73- 6m	5	Brand
Anther, Katharina	4, Nov. 1899	3, Nov.	63- - 2d	5	Mathes
Anthony, August A.	20, Oct. 1900		6	8	
Anthony, John	22, May 1901		34	8	
Antram, Stewart L.	17, Mar. 1888		10m	4	
Apel, Wilhelm	23, Apr. 1895		59	5	
Apfel, Con.	10, July 1887		42	1	
Apfel, Ed.	21, July 1887		18m	1	
Apfel, Margaret	11, Dec. 1900		73	8	
Apffel, Jacob	24, May 1894		39	5	
Apking, Eva Marie	30, Dec. 1899	28, Dec.	68- 5m	5	
Appel, Alice	8, Jan. 1890		3	1	
Appel, Caroline	24, May 1894		39	5	
Appel, Emma	25, May 1889		18	1	
Appel, Emma	18, Apr. 1895		2	5	
Appel, Eva	11, Oct. 1899	10, Oct.	50- 2m	5	Daller
Apple, A.B.	13, Dec. 1900		61	8	
Arand, Emma	16, May 1894		28	5	
Arans, August	16, May 1893		69	5	
Araren, A.	19, Oct. 1901		22	8	
Arata, Rosa	10, Jan. 1888		46	4	
Arbra, Gertrude M.	4, Apr. 1891		14d	4	
Archinger, George A.	20, June 1898	19, June	42- 9m-22d	5	
Arenberg, Edna	2, May 1901		3m	8	
Arens, Cecilia	20, June 1901		3m	8	
Arens, Christian	19, Aug. 1895	17, Aug.		5	
Arey, Mary	22, Mar. 1901		46	8	
Aring, Georg Heinrich	18, Dec. 1899	15, Dec.	76- 6m	4	
Arldt, Fred.	28, July 1887		7m	1	
Arleth, Fred	10, Apr. 1901		40	8	
Arlinghaus, M.	17, Nov. 1888		30m	1	
Arlt, Anna Olinda	5, Apr. 1900	4, Apr.	3	5	
Armanin, Mary	28, May 1891		23	4	
Armbrust, Anton	7, Jan. 1891		52	4	
Armbruster, Franziska	22, Mar. 1893		32	5	
Armbruster, Josephine	10, Apr. 1901		27	8	
Armleder, Amelia	31, Jan. 1891			4	
Armleder, Maria	7, Oct. 1895	6, Oct.	63- 8m	5	
Arms, F.W.	30, Nov. 1887		79	4	
Armstroff, Adelheid	3, Oct. 1898	2, Oct.		5	
Armstroff, Gustav	21, Jan. 1896	20, Jan.	69- 1m	5	
Armstrong, Elisabeth	24, Dec. 1900		80	8	
Armstrong, Elizabeth	25, May 1901		89	8	
Armstrong, Leo	10, Aug. 1901		2m	8	
Armstrong, N.H.	29, Dec. 1887		21	4	
Armstrong, Patrick	23, Jan. 1901		65	8	
Arndt, Adolf	31, Dec. 1892		27	5	
Arnett, Sarah	25, Nov. 1887		75	1	
Arnhold, Henry	10, Mar. 1891		55	4	
Arnim, Frank	30, Jan. 1890		63	1	
Arnold, Adolph J.	4, Aug. 1891		2m	4	
Arnold, Anna	4, July 1901		59	8	
Arnold, Annie	28, Feb. 1889		29	2	
Arnold, Barbara	17, Aug. 1893		29	5	
Arnold, Carrie	22, Sept 1891		3	1	
Arnold, Catharina	23, Mar. 1893		2	5	
Arnold, Catharine	7, Mar. 1891		62	4	
Arnold, Charles	21, Mar. 1890		4m	1	
Arnold, Charles	28, Jan. 1893		28	5	
Arnold, Clara	9, Mar. 1889		26	1	
Arnold, Clara	4, June 1889		7m	1	
Arnold, Clark	16, June 1894		7m	5	
Arnold, H.	21, Nov. 1889		14	1	
Arnold, Helen	4, June 1901		5m	8	
Arnold, Irene C.	28, Dec. 1900		1m	8	
Arnold, Johan	20, Jan. 1899	19, Jan.	79- 6m	5	
Arnold, Joseph	4, Oct. 1888		90	4	
Arnold, Margaret	15, July 1887		5m	1	

CINCINNATIER ZEITUNG DEATH NOTICES --- 1887 - 1901

Name ****	Notice Date ****** ****	Death Date ***** ****	Age ***	Page ****	Maiden Name ****** ****
Arnold, Margaretha	7, June 1899	6, June	67- 2m	5	Becker
Arnold, Mary	17, Dec. 1900		44	8	
Arnold, Peter	1, Dec. 1896	29, Nov.	62- 1m	5	
Arnold, Philip	27, Feb. 1901		41	8	
Arnold, W.	30, Apr. 1896	29, Apr.	7m	5	
Arnoldi, Anna	24, Mar. 1898	23, Mar.	59- -23d	5	
Arnott, Elizabeth	17, Jan. 1894		83	5	
Arns, Anna	3, Dec. 1891		3	4	
Arsel, Sophia	2, Dec. 1887		44- 5m	4	
Arstingstall, Mary A.	3, Nov. 1891		82	4	
Art, John G.	17, Dec. 1891		41	4	
Artholthoff,	13, Aug. 1891		1d	4	
Artz, Julius	30, July 1898	29, July	14-11m	5	
Arzheimer, Henry	7, Nov. 1898	6, Nov.	57- 1m- 2d	5	
Asbery, Charles H.	30, June 1888		16m	1	
Asbury, William C.	5, Nov. 1900		2m	8	
Aschcraft, George H.	19, July 1887		45	1	
Aschenbach, Alfred G.	3, Jan. 1893		34	5	
Ashbrook, Joseph	6, Aug. 1901		13	8	
Ashcraft, William F.	16, Aug. 1901		2	8	
Ashorn,	24, Jan. 1901		7m	8	
Ashrech, Anton	27, Feb. 1901		66	8	
Ashton, Edna M.	3, July 1901		6	8	
Asinmus, Julia	28, Sept 1888		3w	2	
Asken, Nahala	25, Feb. 1901		75	8	
Aslum, Joseph	23, Oct. 1889		60	1	
Asmus, Karl	7, Sept 1899	5, Sept		5	
Aspden, Frank	1, Aug. 1901		47	8	
Assel, Emma	26, Mar. 1896	26, Mar.		5	
Asselboy, W.E.	12, Sept 1887		3w	1	
Assmann, Henry T.	16, Feb. 1894		71	5	
Assmus, Sigmund J.	8, Feb. 1894		65	5	
Astroth, Eduard F.	26, Oct. 1899	25, Oct.	27	8	
Astroth, Frank	15, Mar. 1892		27	5	
Atkeson, Clara L.	9, Jan. 1901		11	5	
Atkins, Mary	11, Dec. 1890		77	1	
Atkinson, Eliza Margaret	21, Feb. 1888			1	
Atkinson, Jane	16, Nov. 1900		40	8	
Atkinson, Verna	23, Apr. 1895		4m	5	
Attig, William	14, Aug. 1889		48	1	
Atzel, Elisabeth	4, Oct. 1895	3, Oct.	57	5	
Atzel, Margaretha	1, May 1900	28, Apr.	64	5	Morch
Aub, Samuel	7, May 1901		57	1	
Auberg, Maggie	2, Apr. 1891		32	4	
Auberger, Rosina	30, Dec. 1892		54	5	
Auckland, William	22, Aug. 1888		43	1	
Aue, William	19, Dec. 1891		43	4	
Auel, Adam	6, Sept 1900		79	5	
Auel, Emma	19, Apr. 1893		1	5	
Auel, Heinrich	30, Nov. 1897	29, Nov.	70	5	
Auel, Margaretha	15, May 1896	14, May	5-10m	5	
AufdemBerge, W.G.	3, Apr. 1888		68	4	
AufdemBrinke, Helene	29, Sept 1891		40- 7m	4	
AufdemBrinke, Regina	18, Aug. 1900		47	8	
AufdenBerg, F.W.	7, May 1888		51	1	
AufderHeide, Amanda	10, July 1887		5w	1	
AufderHeide, Anna M.	23, Dec. 1890		61	1	
AufderHeide, Ernst	26, Mar. 1901		57	8	
Aufderheide, Johan Wilhelm	7, Aug. 1894		54- 2m	5	
Aufdermarsch, Maria	28 Aug. 1899	27, Aug.	68- 5m	4	
Augenstein, Margarethe	16, Apr. 1901		40	8	
Augspurger, Charles	6, Mar. 1891		33	4	
August, Arthur	6, Oct. 1899	5, Oct.	2- 1m	5	
Aulbach, Theresia	24, June 1893		77	5	
Aull, Jacob	11, Apr. 1898	10, Apr.	82	5	
Aull, Margaretha	23, Aug. 1899	22, Aug.	80	5	
Aull, Marie	26, Feb. 1895		32	5	
Aumeldorf, John	18, Apr. 1890		7	1	
Aurger, Louis	15, Feb. 1901		59	8	
Ausdenmoore, Dorothea	24, Aug. 1897	21, Aug.	27	5	
Ausdenmoore, Joseph	30, Sept 1897	29, Sept	51-11m	5	

Name	Notice Date	Death Date	Age	Page	Maiden Name
****	****** ****	***** ****	***	****	****** ****
Ausdenmore, Harry	30, Nov. 1897	28, Nov.	26- 6m	5	
Aust, Emma	3, Aug. 1892		1- 6m	5	
Austermann, Johann	3, Jan. 1890		21d	1	
Austin, Fred.	31, Oct. 1894		3m	5	
Austin, Harry	6, Oct. 1900		65	5	
Austin, Theodore	3, June 1901		52	8	
Austing, Elizabeth	26, May 1892		40	5	
Austing, Theodor J.	5, Jan. 1901		6m	8	
Autenrieth, Margaretha	30, Sept 1899	28, Sept	73	4	Klein
Averdick, Ferd.	29, Oct. 1900		65	8	
Avermaat, Georg	31, Aug. 1896	30, Aug.	91	5	
Averwieser, Katharine	27, Mar. 1889		73	1	
Avery, Charles	5, July 1887		87	1	
Avery, Dock O.	18, Apr. 1895		42	5	
Axline, Jasper	23, Aug. 1900		51	8	
Axmann, Herman A.	6, Aug. 1896	5, Aug.	33	5	
Axmann, Mathilda	23, June 1888		1	1	
Axt, J.N.	18, Feb. 1897	16, Feb.	65-11m	5	
Ayers, George	5, July 1901		12	8	
Aylward, Lee	11, Nov. 1891		7m	1	
Ayres, Mary	31, July 1900		51	5	
Baade, Ida	31, Jan. 1901		50	8	
Baasch, Henry	22, Feb. 1898	19, Feb.	55- 6m	5	
Baasch, Oliver	5, Jan. 1897	3, Jan.	18- 3m	5	
Babel, August	2, Mar. 1894	28, Feb.	60	5	
Babka, Anna	27, Feb. 1888		83	4	
Babros, Frank	15, Jan. 1901		2m	8	
Babros, John	16, Apr. 1889		5m	1	
Bach, Adam C.	1, Feb. 1901		13	8	
Bach, Clara A.	22, Mar. 1893		2	5	
Bacharach, Max S.	16, Jan. 1890		48	1	
Bacharach, Theresa	14, Dec. 1897	13, Dec.	77	5	Schiele
Bachaus, Clarence	12, Sept 1887		3	1	
Bacher, Emil	2, July 1896	30, June	22- 5m	5	
Bacher, George	2, Mar. 1893		62	5	
Bacher, Magdalena	9, Oct. 1901		31	5	
Bachers, Henry	16, May 1891		5m	2	
Bachert, Rosa	2, Aug. 1893		20	5	
Bachherms, Emma	4, Nov. 1897	3, Nov.	27- 7m	5	Kohake
Bachmann, Adolph	27, June 1888		9m	1	
Bachmann, Catharine	1, Oct. 1887		60	1	
Bachmann, Henry	5, Jan. 1897	4, Jan.	66	5	
Bachmann, Joseph	1, Oct. 1887		16d	1	
Bachmann, Katharine	1, May 1900	30, Apr.	72	5	Kragler
Bachmann, Peter	20, July 1901		50	8	
Bachmeier, Charles	2, Apr. 1891			4	
Bachmeier, Margaret	7, Sept 1887		42	1	
Bachs, Herman	21, Sept 1894		10m	5	
Bachscheiter, Regina	2, Apr. 1900	29, Mar.	24	8	
Back, A.	11, Oct. 1901		75	5	
Back, Dorothea	22, July 1901		77	8	
Back, Edward	16, Dec. 1898	15, Dec.	29	5	
Back, J.H.	24, Feb. 1897	23, Feb.	72- 2m	5	
Back, Margaretha	31, July 1896	30, July	80	5	
Backas, Walter	18, June 1901		3m	8	
Backer, Ernestina	7, Aug. 1891		2m	4	
Backer, Henry	15, Nov. 1887		3	4	
Backer, William	17, Dec. 1887		1-10m	1	
Backhaus, G. Henry	4, Apr. 1899	2, Apr.	30- 9m	5	
Backhaus, Georg	24, Feb. 1888		49	4	
Backhaus, Herman	5, Nov. 1897	4, Nov.	58	5	
Backhaus, John C.	13, July 1894		1	5	
Backherms, Herman Heinrich	9, Oct. 1899	8, Oct.	34- 7m	5	
Backmeier, Charles A.W.	22, Apr. 1899	19, Apr.	24-10m	5	
Backmeier, Frederick	21, June 1894		68	5	
Backmeier, Lillie	28, Oct. 1893		25d	5	
Backmeier, W.H.	9, Mar. 1900	8, Mar.	21- 8m	8	
Backs, Josepha	17, Mar. 1888		36	4	
Backscheider, Charles A.	25, Jan. 1893		1	5	
Backus, Paul	2, July 1901		5m	8	

Name	Notice Date	Death Date	Age	Page	Maiden Name
****	****** ****	***** ****	***	****	****** ****
Backus, Rob. J.	19, July 1894		1	5	
Bade, Heinrich	5, May 1898	5, May	83- -16d	5	
Baden, Eugene	16, Apr. 1891		47	4	
Bader, Barbara	8, Jan. 1898	6, Jan.	78- 2m	4	Weitmann
Bader, Elisabeth	8, June 1893		47	5	
Bader, Ferdinand	17, May 1899	16, May	55	5	
Bader, Leonard	4, Aug. 1891		25	4	
Baechley, Bertha	27, Aug. 1901		2	1	
Baehr, John	24, Feb. 1893		1	5	
Baenninger, Alwine	6, June 1899	3, June	63	5	
Baer, Edgar	25, June 1895		6m	5	
Baer, Henry	11, Feb. 1898	10, Feb.	78	5	
Baer, Louisa	27, June 1898	25, June	64-11m	5	
Baerlocher, Carl	23, Apr. 1895		55	5	
Baffler, Emma	2, Jan. 1890		30m	1	
Bagby, Daniel	7, Jan. 1901		16	5	
Bagby, Elizabeth	21, Sept 1887		28	1	
Bager, J.M.	26, Mar. 1891		72	4	
Bahlmann, Amelia	14, Feb. 1891		37	4	
Bahlmann, Edward	22, July 1887		7m	1	
Bahlmann, Elisabeth	16, Dec. 1891		88	4	
Bahlmann, Elisabeth	11, Mar. 1893		58	5	
Bahlmann, Henry	24, Apr. 1901		45	8	
Bahlmann, Katharina	9, Feb. 1897	8, Feb.	36- - 3d	5	
Bahlmann, Regina	27, May 1901		47	8	
Bahlmann, Theodor	16, Dec. 1891		23	4	
Bahm, Margaret	12, Feb. 1890		60	1	
Bahmann, Carl	16, Aug. 1894		34	5	
Bahmann, Fred.	15, June 1889		67	1	
Bahrs, William	16, Apr. 1891		1d	4	
Baichle, William	9, Aug. 1892		1	5	
Baier, Alma	3, Mar. 1894		18m	5	
Baier, Charles C.	3, Aug. 1893		33	5	
Baier, Frida	14, May 1895		9m	5	
Bailer, Anna	13, Dec. 1893		48	5	
Bailer, Clara	16, Aug. 1890		2	1	
Bailer, Henry	15, Aug. 1891		37	4	
Bailey, Mary Ann	19, Oct. 1887		41	1	
Bailey, Mildred	11, Oct. 1900		21d	8	
Bailey, Robert B.	5, Jan. 1892		6m	5	
Baird, Lucille	6, Sept 1901		6m	8	
Baiter, Charles	17, Feb. 1891		48	4	
Baiter, William	10, Nov. 1900		39	8	
Baker, Clara	20, Nov. 1900		11	8	
Baker, David	19, Dec. 1891		69	4	
Baker, Fredie	21, Mar. 1891		5	4	
Baker, Herbert	12, Feb. 1901		18	8	
Baker, Jacob	27, Feb. 1888		18	4	
Baker, John A.	23, July 1901		73	8	
Baker, Lincoln	21, Sept 1901		38	8	
Baker, Louis	30, Sept 1887		34	1	
Baker, Margaretha	30, Apr. 1898	29, Apr.	72	4	Wolff
Baker, Martin	26, Feb. 1894		38	5	
Baker, Nathan F.	11, Feb. 1891		71	4	
Baker, Orlie	13, July 1900		1	8	
Baker, Samuel	12, Apr. 1892		58	5	
Baker, Sylvia	19, Aug. 1891		2m	4	
Baldauf, Louis Philip	1, Nov. 1897	31, Oct.	8	5	
Baldinger, Emma	7, Feb. 1890		1	1	
Balduine, A.	6, Jan. 1888		58	1	
Baldwin, Lawrence	13, July 1887		8m	1	
Baldwin, Mary	18, Aug. 1900			8	
Baldwin, Mary B.	20, Oct. 1900		29	8	
Baldwin, May	20, July 1887		9m	1	
Baldwin, Nellie	7, Mar. 1901		43	8	
Baldwin, Sophia	30, Aug. 1901		66	8	
Baldwin, William	6, July 1901		2m	8	
Baldwing, Sarah E.	14, Oct. 1901		66	5	
Balgenroth, Maria	10, May 1888		1d	1	
Balitzer, Abraham	4, Aug. 1888		5m	4	
Ball, Georg	9, June 1898	8, June	51	5	

Name	Notice Date	Death Date	Age	Page	Maiden Name
****	****** ****	***** ****	***	****	****** ****
Ball, William	22, Mar. 1901		17	8	
Ballance, C.H.	18, Apr. 1888		36	1	
Ballauf, Henrietta	5, July 1887		64	1	
Ballhauser, John	7, Oct. 1891		1- -15d	4	
Ballinger, Anna M.	18, Nov. 1894		80	5	
Ballmann, Eduard Gustav	20, Sept 1899	18, Sept	25- 2m	8	
Ballmann, Edward	19, July 1898	18, July	56	5	
Ballmann, Eliza	30, Jan. 1899	28, Jan.	70	4	Kottkamp
Ballmann, Elizabeth	12, Sept 1891		52	1	
Ballmann, Francis	15, July 1891		6m	1	
Ballmann, Heinrich	21, Nov. 1900		80	8	
Ballmann, Henry	16, Sept 1891		40	4	
Ballmann, Mary J.	21, Nov. 1893		2	5	
Ballmann, Wilhelm	20, Feb. 1897	17, Feb.	48- 3m	5	
Ballmeyer, Hannah	11, Aug. 1900		41	8	
Balon, Florence	23, Nov. 1900		7m	8	
Balser, Ed.	24, May 1892		42	5	
Baltenort, John	9, Apr. 1891		35	4	
Balton, Thomas	20, July 1887		4m	1	
Baltzer, John	2, June 1893		5	5	
Baltzer, Wilhelm	13, Sept 1899	12, Sept	32- 7m	4	
Balz, Margaretha	31, July 1899	28, July	73- -28d	4	Hinninger
Balzer, P.	24, July 1894		6	5	
Balzer, Peter	23, Oct. 1895	22, Oct.		5	
Bamberger, Adolf	16, Oct. 1895	15, Oct.	20- 2m	5	
Bamberger, Emanuel	13, Mar. 1897	12, Mar.	91- 2m	5	
Bamberger, Henry	27, Apr. 1901		36	8	
Bamberger, J.	26, Mar. 1888		51	4	
Bamberger, Johan	15, Sept 1897	13, Sept	36	5	
Bamberger, John	16, Sept 1897	13, Sept	36	5	
Bamberger, Regina	5, Sept 1895	3, Sept	5- 2m	5	
Bamberger, Regina	6, Sept 1895	3, Sept	56	5	
Bamberger, Wilhelm	1, Aug. 1896	30, July	30- 2m	5	
Bamkump, George	9, Sept 1891		2	4	
Bammerlin, Walter August	15, Mar. 1898	13, Mar.	6m- 7d	4	
Bang, Lewis	10, Jan. 1893		1	5	
Bange, Mary	27, Nov. 1889		15m	1	
Banger, Fred.	19, July 1887		8w	1	
Banke, Harry	17, Dec. 1891	15, Dec.	6- - 9d	1	
Banker, Fred.	30, Jan. 1901		37	8	
Bankerecht, Barbara	3, Aug. 1901		75	8	
Bann, Samuel	8, July 1901		57	8	
Bannahan, Patrick	29, June 1901		63	8	
Bannemeyer, Maria Agnes	20, Oct. 1899	19, Oct.	66- 9m	8	Wielenberg
Bantam, Mary	1, Oct. 1900		90	5	
Bante, Elisabeth	25, Mar. 1891		72	4	
Banteau, John	23, July 1901		77	8	
Bantel, Bertha	15, Aug. 1891		4- 6m	1	
Bantel, Mary	27, June 1891		1	1	
Bantley, Andreas	10, Aug. 1899	9, Aug.	44- 1m	5	
Bantlin, Julius J.	13, Jan. 1898	12, Jan.	71- 6m	5	
Bantly, Jacob	27, Aug. 1888		27	1	
Banumann, George W.E.	13, Feb. 1890		14m	1	
Banzhof, Flora	6, June 1900	5, June	3- 6m	8	
Bappert, Charles	14, Jan. 1901		33	8	
Barbar, Kate	8, Aug. 1900		40	8	
Barber, Alexander	15, Oct. 1900			5	
Barber, Amelia	5, Aug. 1892		46	5	
Barber, Julia	31, Jan. 1901		73	8	
Bardelmann, H.	30, Mar. 1901		45	8	
Bardelmann, Johan Anton	8, May 1899	6, May	75- - 5d	4	
Bardelmann, Maria Louisa	11, May 1897	9, May	69- 4m	5	Steffen
Barden, Julia	10, Jan. 1888		52	4	
Bardes, Christian	22, July 1893		3	5	
Bardes, F.	18, Apr. 1888		7	1	
Bardes, Henry	17, July 1891		71	1	
Bardes, Louis C.	4, 5, Nov. 1895	3, Nov.	70- 2m	5	
Bardes, Louisa Mary	22, Mar. 1897	21, Mar.	78- 1m	5	Wagner
Barelmann, Elisa	11, July 1893		46	5	
Barenstein, Esther	14, Sept 1894		80	5	
Barge, Edward	16, July 1892		3m	5	

Name	Notice Date	Death Date	Age	Page	Maiden Name
****	****** ****	***** ****	***	****	****** ****
Barge, Edwin	15, July 1892	15, July	4m	5	
Barger, Kate	23, Mar. 1895		50	5	
Bargmann, Mary	4, Mar. 1891		34	4	
Barhitt, Felicia	20, Feb. 1901		71	8	
Barington, Sam	14, Feb. 1888		65	4	
Barkau, Stella	7, July 1890		18m	4	
Barker, Henry B.	15, Oct. 1900		68	5	
Barker, Walter	13, Aug. 1901		8	8	
Barklay, Mary	10, Apr. 1888		13m	4	
Barkman, Harry	6, Jan. 1893		3	5	
Barlag, Theresia	15, July 1897	14, July	68	5	Hoecker
Barlage, Gertrude	28, Sept 1888		7	2	
Barlage, John F.	7, Mar. 1892		39	5	
Barlage, William	4, Dec. 1888		4m	1	
Barlogh,	7, Dec. 1887		1d	1	
Barman, Theodore	16, Mar. 1901		44	8	
Barme, Catharine	22, Apr. 1889		60	1	
Barmeyer, Catharine	6, Apr. 1894		67	5	
Barmeyer, Herman	2, Apr. 1897	1, Apr.	76	5	
Barnett, Edward	21, Sept 1901		31	8	
Barnett, Levi	23, June 1896	22, June		5	
Barnett, Polly	4, Aug. 1887		5w	1	
Barnett, Tillie	6, June 1888		3	1	
Barnhorn, Amelia	6, Mar. 1897	6, Mar.	26	5	Busse
Barnhorst, Anna	19, Sept 1888		2m	2	
Barnise, Ann.	10, Apr. 1888		49	4	
Barnitz, Mary	3, July 1901		64	8	
Barns, Mary	18, July 1895		38	5	
Barnstrop, Ernst	29, Aug. 1887		44	1	
Barrel, Patrick	7, Jan. 1901		69	5	
Barrett, Edward	8, Dec. 1891		65	4	
Barrett, Elisabeth	14, Jan. 1901		52	8	
Barrett, Minnie F.	29, Oct. 1900		43	8	
Barrett, Richard	17, Dec. 1900		69	8	
Barretta, Thomas	2, Aug. 1887		69	1	
Barringer, Mary	26, Aug. 1901		65	8	
Barrington, Glen	15, Jan. 1901		2m	8	
Barry, Anna	2, Feb. 1888		27	4	
Bart, Charles F.	25, Feb. 1891		3	4	
Bartel, M.E.	3, Apr. 1888		62	4	
Bartels, Georg	17, June 1897	15, June	70-10m	5	
Bartelsen, Henry	25, Mar. 1891		58	4	
Bartetzko, Victoria	17, Dec. 1900		54	8	
Barth, Henry	21, Aug. 1894		62	5	
Barth, John G.	26, Mar. 1891		6	4	
Barth, Margaretha	5, Nov. 1891		57	1	
Barth, Sophia	11, Apr. 1898	9, Apr.	66	5	Lipps
Barth, Sophie	3, Apr. 1897	2, Apr.	59	5	
Barthold, Christian	20, Mar. 1891		45	4	
Bartman, Eleanora	31, July 1900		70	5	
Barton, Amanda	3, July 1895		38	5	
Barton, John H.	17, Dec. 1900		60	8	
Bartrauff, Charles	21, Apr. 1895		66	5	
Bartridge, Bernard	29, Aug. 1901		65	8	
Bartsch, Emma	28, Jan. 1899	27, Jan.	42	5	
Bartsche, Johan Edward	14, Apr. 1897	13, Apr.	71- 5m	5	
Baruls, Joseph R.	1, May 1895		38	5	
Barwise, Elisa	12, May 1895		67	5	
Barwise, Robert A.	4, July 1887		4m	1	
Barz,	26, Sept 1887		1d	1	
Basch, Johanna	19, July 1887		46	1	
Basford, (Dr.)	9, Jan. 1889		57	1	
Basse, Catharine	26, Mar. 1895		79	5	
Bassenhorst, Wilhelm C.	19, June 1900	16, June	56- -17d	5	
Bassett, James A.	11, Jan. 1901		59	5	
Bastian, Phil.	27, Sept 1900		49	8	
Bastian, William	31, May 1892		1m	5	
Bateman, Edward	27, Nov. 1889		45	1	
Bateman, J.	1, Oct. 1901		59	1	
Bateman, L.A.	3, Dec. 1888		72	1	
Bates, Elizabeth	26, Mar. 1895		74	5	

Name	Notice Date	Death Date	Age	Page	Maiden Name
****	****** ****	***** ****	***	****	****** ****
Bates, Isaak	18, Feb. 1888		5	1	
Batsche, Henry F.	10, Dec. 1900		87	8	
Batschmann, Louisa B.	14, Mar. 1893		7m	5	
Baudendistel, Blanche	19, Oct. 1900		4m	5	
Bauer,	12, June 1891		1d	4	
Bauer, Adele	1, Nov. 1893		3	5	
Bauer, Albert	13, Apr. 1901		36	8	
Bauer, Alberta Sadie	14, Feb. 1900	13, Feb.	1- 8m	8	
Bauer, Andreas	19, Dec. 1895	18, Dec.	39	5	
Bauer, Andreas (Mrs)	16, July 1895		36	5	
Bauer, Andy	25, Sept 1891		3m-10d	4	
Bauer, Anna	23, Sept 1893		53	5	
Bauer, Anna Maria	15, Dec. 1896	14, Dec.	79-10m	5	Mager
Bauer, August	20, June 1892		66	5	
Bauer, Carrie	20, Feb. 1900	12, Feb.	38- 1m	5	
Bauer, Carrie A.	23, Apr. 1891		29	4	
Bauer, Casper	14, May 1895		78	5	
Bauer, Charles	13, Sept 1890		32	1	
Bauer, Charles	29, Apr. 1891		16	4	
Bauer, Charles	25, Aug. 1900		37	5	
Bauer, Charles J.	11, Jan. 1890		19	1	
Bauer, Christ.	24, Jan. 1901		42	8	
Bauer, Christian L.	17, May 1900	16, May	28- 7m	5	
Bauer, Clara	14, Jan. 1892		119	1	
Bauer, Clarence	12, Sept 1887		5w	1	
Bauer, Clarence	29, Mar. 1888		1- 9m- 7d	1	
Bauer, Conrad	17, Oct. 1887		67	1	
Bauer, David	17, Jan. 1894		59	5	
Bauer, Eddie	7, July 1888		7m	4	
Bauer, Edward	8, Aug. 1891		2	4	
Bauer, Elenore	27, June 1889		52	1	
Bauer, Elisabeth	8, May 1888		33	1	
Bauer, Elisabeth	28, June 1893		54	5	
Bauer, Emilia	5, June 1888		54	4	
Bauer, George	21, May 1901		3m	8	
Bauer, Harry	16, Apr. 1891		4	4	
Bauer, Henry	22, June 1889		14	1	
Bauer, Henry	17, July 1890		62	1	
Bauer, Herbert	1, May 1901		8m	8	
Bauer, J.	21, Feb. 1888		69	1	
Bauer, J.C.	3, Sept 1889		6	1	
Bauer, Jacob	5, Apr. 1890		61	1	
Bauer, Jacob	14, Aug. 1897	11, Aug.	41- 7m	5	
Bauer, Jacobina	3, Feb. 1900	2, Feb.	84	5	
Bauer, Jessie	1, Feb. 1894		23m	5	
Bauer, Johanna	9, Apr. 1890		33	1	
Bauer, Johanna	3, Mar. 1892		2	5	
Bauer, Johanna	23, Sept 1893		74	5	
Bauer, John	21, June 1895		34	5	
Bauer, John	2, 3, Dec. 1895	1, Dec.	47- 1m	5	
Bauer, Joseph	6, Nov. 1896	3, Nov.	37- 6m	5	
Bauer, Joseph	10, May 1901		45	8	
Bauer, Julia	31, Dec. 1895	29, Dec.	24- 1m	5	Melber
Bauer, Katharine	19, Feb. 1891		72	4	
Bauer, Kunigunde	9, Feb. 1897	8, Feb.	81- 1m	5	Popp
Bauer, Lena	25, Aug. 1899	24, Aug.	33-10m	5	Meyer
Bauer, Lillian	18, Apr. 1893		24d	5	
Bauer, Louise	2, Dec. 1894		69	4	
Bauer, Margaret	6, Nov. 1891		61	4	
Bauer, Maria	21, Jan. 1893		3m	5	
Bauer, Maria	29, July 1897	27, July	71- 5m	5	Kramer
Bauer, Mary	3, Sept 1901		70	8	
Bauer, Michael	20, Mar. 1891		64	4	
Bauer, Michael	5, 6, Apr. 1897	3, Apr.	60- 4m	5	
Bauer, Minnie	5, May 1894		60	5	
Bauer, Robert William	19, Jan. 1893		4	5	
Bauer, Sophia	4, Dec. 1888		73	1	
Bauer, Tredene H.	8, Nov. 1900		9	8	
Bauer, Val.	26, July 1888		43	2	
Bauer, Willie C.	29, Sept 1887		22m	4	
Bauers, E.	3, Dec. 1888		21m	1	

Name ****	Notice Date ****** ****	Death Date ***** ****	Age ***	Page ****	Maiden Name ****** ****
Bauers, Maria D.	2, Sept 1887		17m	1	
Baum, Anna	1, Oct. 1887		9	1	
Baum, Charles	18, Sept 1891		3m	1	
Baum, Elisabeth	29, Apr. 1897	28, Apr.	64- 2m-25d	5	Bikel
Baum, Eva	10, Aug. 1895	8, Aug.		5	Cawein
Baum, Evalyn	11, Oct. 1901		19	5	
Baum, G.	19, Dec. 1896	16, Dec.	78- 3m	5	
Baum, Jacob	5, Sept 1898	3, Sept	65	5	
Baum, Louisa	7, July 1891		1	1	
Baum, Mary	29, Mar. 1895		57	5	
Baum, Mollie	7, July 1887		87	1	
Bauman, Fred	22, Feb. 1893		39	5	
Baumann, Andreas	26, Mar. 1900	24, Mar.	51- 9m	8	
Baumann, Caroline	14, Jan. 1901		71	8	
Baumann, Elise	20, July 1889		1w	1	
Baumann, Henry	25, Mar. 1889		54	1	
Baumann, Kunigunde	2, Feb. 1893		62	5	
Baumann, Loatje	7, Mar. 1890		30	1	
Baumann, Louise	30, May 1894		6	5	
Baumann, Mary	15, July 1893		7d	5	
Baumann, Mary	16, Aug. 1894		62	5	
Baumann, Phil	9, Aug. 1900		14	8	
Baumann, Wilhelm	10, Oct. 1898	9, Oct.	21-11m- 8d	4	
Baumann, William	17, Aug. 1901		7m	8	
Baumbusch, Charles	29, Aug. 1887		21	1	
Baumeister, Bernard Henry	7, July 1898	6, July	79- 2m	5	
Baumeler, Nicolaus	2, June 1891		56	4	
Baumer, Albert	23, June 1894		2	5	
Baumer, Engelbert	19, June 1895		82	5	
Baumer, Louis	23, Sept 1891		8m	4	
Baumer, Theodore	2, Feb. 1892		68	5	
Baumer, William E.	10, Oct. 1891		17d	4	
Baumgardner, Hildegard	30, Mar. 1894		11m	5	
Baumgartner, Benjamin E.	18, Feb. 1891		2	4	
Baumgraß, Jane	26, Sept 1901		90	8	
Baumgärtner, Mary	14, Feb. 1893		2m	5	
Baumhar, Gertrude	18, Feb. 1901		89	8	
Baur, Barbara Magdalena	7, Oct. 1899	6, Oct.	67-11m	8	Hettinger
Baur, Elmer W.	12, May 1895		1m	5	
Baur, Felicitas	1, June 1901		78	8	
Baur, Johan	5, Mar. 1896	4, Mar.	73- 2m	5	
Baurichter, Catharine	21, Apr. 1893		14	5	
Baurittel, Emil	7, Oct. 1895	5, Oct.	18	5	
Baurittel, Emilia	21, May 1901		43	8	
Baurittel, Karolina	23, Sept 1899	22, Sept	71-10m	5	Pfeiffer
Bausch, Anna	23, Dec. 1889		25	1	
Bause, Dora	17, Oct. 1891		81	4	
Baust, Hilda	15, Nov. 1893		7m	5	
Bautz, Adam (Mrs)	10, Feb. 1896	9, Feb.	39-11m	5	Rover
Bautz, Christine	12, Feb. 1896	9, Feb.	39	5	Rover
Baußhof, Friedrich	5, Jan. 1888		1- 2m	1	
Baverdick, Stanislaus	23, July 1895		21m	5	
Baxter, Gertie	14, Aug. 1888		7m	1	
Baxter, Mary	26, Mar. 1901		71	8	
Bayden, John F.	14, Nov. 1893		63	5	
Bayer, Alma	2, Feb. 1894		6	5	
Bayer, Charles	21, Mar. 1890		1w	1	
Bayer, Charles	15, Mar. 1901		61	8	
Bayer, Chester	28, Feb. 1891		1	4	
Bayer, Emerich	23, Oct. 1888		2	1	
Bayer, Maria	24, July 1895		1	5	
Bayer, Phil.	25, Feb. 1891		31	4	
Bayes, William H.	9, Jan. 1901		81	5	
Bayliß, Ed.	17, Sept 1901		44	8	
Bazeley, Katie	14, Feb. 1901		33	8	
Baßmann, Anna	19, Mar. 1895		35	5	
Bean, W.W.	6, Jan. 1888		26	1	
Beard, Lotta S.	11, Aug. 1887		5	1	
Beasley, Mary	5, Sept 1901		46	8	
Beaton, Mary	24, Oct. 1900		75	8	
Beatty, Mary V.	17, Oct. 1900		50	8	

Name	Notice Date	Death Date	Age	Page	Maiden Name
****	****** ****	***** ****	***	****	****** ****
Beaver, Catharine	2, Feb. 1901		37	8	
Bechler, Elizabeth	18, Mar. 1890		68	1	
Bechler, John	24, Dec. 1900			8	
Becht, Herold	11, July 1888		7m	1	
Becht, John E.	9, Aug. 1894		1	5	
Becht, Lizzie	3, Sept 1901		36	8	
Becht, Norma	16, May 1893		10m	5	
Bechtold, Elizabeth	15, Sept 1900		40	5	
Bechtold, R.	20, Aug. 1901		54	8	
Bechtold, Rosa	21, July 1888		11m	1	
Beck, August	27, Jan. 1895		15	5	
Beck, Barney	22, Dec. 1893		34	5	
Beck, Catharine	3, Feb. 1893		14	5	
Beck, Charles A.	7, July 1888		5m	4	
Beck, Christian	30, Apr. 1897	29, Apr.	43-10m	5	
Beck, Edmund B.	10, Jan. 1893		9d	5	
Beck, Elisabeth	24, May 1893		74	5	
Beck, George	30, June 1888		6m	1	
Beck, Henry	1, July 1901		43	8	
Beck, Johan Jacob	6, May 1901	4, May	59- 8m -7d	* 5	
Beck, John B.	30, July 1891		1	4	
Beck, Joseph	17, Dec. 1895	16, Dec.	69	4	
Beck, Kate	2, Dec. 1893		47	5	
Beck, Leonard	10, Aug. 1893		13m	5	
Beck, Ludwig	13, Jan. 1890		66	1	
Beck, Maria Theresia	19, Mar. 1900	18, Mar.	66	5	Schaettle
Beck, Martha	30, Nov. 1892		6m	5	
Beck, W.S.	18, Jan. 1898	16, Jan.	76	5	
Beck, Willie	28, Apr. 1891		11d	4	
Beckel, Adelheid	1, July 1901		56	8	
Beckel, W.	19, Aug. 1895	18, Aug.	47	5	
Beckemeyer, August	27, Apr. 1896	25, Apr.	46-10m	5	
Beckenhaupt, J.	1, Mar. 1888		60	4	
Beckenhaupt, J.W.	20, Aug. 1895	17, Aug.	44-11m	5	
Beckenhaupt, John H.	14, Jan. 1896	11, Jan.	47	5	
Becker, Adam Robison	14, Aug. 1890		89	1	
Becker, Anna	10, Mar. 1891		46	4	
Becker, Anna	7, Nov. 1891		9m	1	
Becker, Anna	26, Mar. 1897	24, Mar.	40-11m	5	
Becker, Anna M.	18, Nov. 1895	17, Nov.	45- 6m	5	Schneider
Becker, Anton	2, Apr. 1896	1, Apr.	73- 2m	5	
Becker, Anton Rudolf	18, Feb. 1899	17, Feb.	7- 1m- 2d	5	
Becker, Augusta	23, July 1889		65	1	
Becker, Augusta	15, Feb. 1901		67	8	
Becker, Bernardina Maria	8, Aug. 1898	6, Aug.	63- 3m	5	Kruse
Becker, Catharina M.	31, July 1893	30, July	60- 6m	* 5	
Becker, Catharine	14, Jan. 1891		75	4	
Becker, Catharine	26, Apr. 1901		80	8	
Becker, Charles	28, Sept 1898	27, Sept	61	4	
Becker, Christian Anton	7, 11, Dec. 1893	7, Dec.	70- 5m	5	
Becker, Christine	27, Apr. 1901		65	8	
Becker, Clifford	22, Oct. 1894		2	5	
Becker, Dorothea	10, May 1899	8, May		5	
Becker, Edward Ch.	11, Jan. 1890		56	1	
Becker, Edwin	4, Feb. 1891		7m	4	
Becker, Ellen	12, Aug. 1890		5m	1	
Becker, Emilie	9, Mar. 1896	8, Mar.		5	
Becker, F.	8, Nov. 1887		39	1	
Becker, Fred	6, Apr. 1898	4, Apr.	62	5	
Becker, Fred. W.	4, Apr. 1893		66	5	
Becker, Friedrich A.	26, Jan. 1897	25, Jan.	26- 9m	5	
Becker, George	6, Mar. 1889		4	1	
Becker, George	25, Feb. 1891		4m	4	
Becker, Gretchen	7, June 1895		6	5	
Becker, Helena	19, Jan. 1892		74	5	
Becker, Helena	26, Dec. 1900		60	8	
Becker, Helene	19, Dec. 1891		48	4	
Becker, Henry	28, Jan. 1891		32	4	
Becker, Henry	9, Sept 1891		34	4	
Becker, Henry	6, Mar. 1895		66	5	
Becker, Henry	17, Jan. 1899	16, Jan.	55	5	

Name ****	Notice Date ****** ****	Death Date ***** ****	Age ***	Page ****	Maiden Name ****** ****
Becker, Herman H.	9, July 1900	7, July	49	8	
Becker, Jacob	25, Apr. 1889		84	1	
Becker, John	5, May 1892		69	5	
Becker, John	1, Aug. 1901		72	8	
Becker, Katharine	27, Aug. 1890		72	1	
Becker, Katharine	31, May 1901		4	8	
Becker, Katharine M.	2, Aug. 1893		60	5	
Becker, Laura	31, Jan. 1891		2	4	
Becker, Louis	10, Mar. 1891		66	4	
Becker, Louis	20, Dec. 1893		3m	5	
Becker, Margareth	8, Jan. 1901		28	8	
Becker, Margaretha	23, Aug. 1887		38	1	
Becker, Margaretha K.	18, Dec. 1893		1	5	
Becker, Maria	12, Jan. 1892		75	5	
Becker, Maria	10, May 1894		31	5	
Becker, Mathaus	27, Mar. 1900	26, Mar.	73	5	
Becker, Peter	8, June 1889		8m	1	
Becker, Robert	2, Mar. 1888		32	1	
Becker, Robert	5, June 1890			4	
Becker, Sarah	11, Aug. 1900		56	8	
Becker, Seb.	5, Dec. 1888		78	1	
Becker, Simon	14, Apr. 1891		62	4	
Becker, Thomas	10, Jan. 1891		6m	4	
Becker, Wilhelm	18, Jan. 1894		79	5	
Becker, Wilhelm	26, Sept 1896	24, Sept	36- 9m	5	
Becker, Wilhelm Henry	30, Nov. 1897	29, Nov.	6- 1m	5	
Becker, Wilhelmina	16, Apr. 1895		7m	5	
Becker, William	10, Dec. 1891		20	4	
Becket, Wilford	21, Feb. 1901		17	8	
Beckett, Louis	26, Mar. 1901		42	8	
Beckett, Norman	13, Oct. 1900		5m	8	
Beckham, Ed.	5, Sept 1900		1	5	
Beckhop, Anna M.	6, Nov. 1889		79	1	
Beckle, Clara	3, Nov. 1891		20	4	
Beckler, Michael	20, Apr. 1899		61	4	
Beckman, Elisabeth	4, Dec. 1891		9	4	
Beckmann, Anton	14, Oct. 1894		11	5	
Beckmann, August	4, Oct. 1894		72	5	
Beckmann, Elisabeth	1, Dec. 1897	29, Nov.	67-10m	4	Middendorf
Beckmann, Elizabeth	15, Jan. 1901		68	8	
Beckmann, Frank	23, Jan. 1894		1	5	
Beckmann, Frieda Lillie	1, June 1893		10m	5	
Beckmann, Gerhard H.	9, Feb. 1894		72	5	
Beckmann, Henry	21, Feb. 1894		21	5	
Beckmann, Henry	20, July 1895		55	5	
Beckmann, John F.	28, Dec. 1900		74	8	
Beckmann, John H.	19, Apr. 1895		72	5	
Beckmann, Joseph Heinrich	13, Aug. 1896	11, Aug.	34- 6m	5	
Beckmann, Nettie	22, Oct. 1894		54	5	
Beckmann, Rudolph	9, Dec. 1891		4	2	
Beckmann, Theodor	25, Mar. 1891		81	4	
Beckmann, Wilhelm Heinrich	12, May 1898	10, May	23- 9m	5	
Beckmann, William	18, June 1895		13m	5	
Beckroeger, Elisabeth	7, Aug. 1899	5, Aug.	82	5	Stickworth
Becksmith, Frankie	26, Feb. 1900	25, Feb.	11- 6m	8	
Becksmith, Theresa	28, Sept 1896	27, Sept	67- 9m	5	
Beckwege, Harold	26, Jan. 1901		3	8	
Bedeker, Frederick	27, Jan. 1894		24	5	
Bedel, John	10, Jan. 1894		36	5	
Bedinghaus, Antoinette	20, Apr. 1899	18, Apr.	32	4	Classen
Bedinghaus, Bernard	28, Jan. 1901		49	8	
Bedinghaus, Bernard Theodore	31, Aug. 1896	30, Aug.	69- 4m	5	
Bedinghaus, Helena	19, Jan. 1899	17, Jan.	70- 6m	5	Heidt
Bedinghaus, John	12, May 1892		4	5	
Bedinghaus, Joseph	5, Feb. 1901		26	8	
Bedinghaus, Mary	25, Mar. 1901		51	8	
Bedoit, Florence L.	29, Sept 1900		29	8	
Bee, Rebecca	18, Sept 1900		57	5	
Beebe, Earl	22, June 1901		2	8	
Beebe, Lucy	2, Oct. 1891		9	4	
Beekmann, Charles	18, June 1895		22	5	

Name	Notice Date	Death Date	Age	Page	Maiden Name
****	****** ****	***** ****	***	****	****** ****
Beel, Frank	23, Sept 1901			8	
Beelmann, Louise	6, Feb. 1899	5, Feb.	40	4	Benecke
Beelser, Emma	27, Mar. 1891		25	4	
Beer, Catharine	31, Dec. 1890		33	4	
Beerle, August	9, Aug. 1888		5m	1	
Beerle, Eugene	27, June 1891		6m	1	
Beerle, Louisa	27, June 1891		6m	1	
Beerlein, Nora	21, Apr. 1888		9m	1	
Beermann, Maria	3, Feb. 1893		1d	5	
Beermann, Wilhelm Joseph	19, July 1898	18, July	34- 4m-22d	5	
Beesten, Theodor	18, Dec. 1888		4m	2	
Beeston, Caroline	7, Aug. 1901		76	8	
Beh, Caroline	5, Sept 1891		64	1	
Beh, Friedrich	20, Jan. 1891		69	4	
Behan, Anna	5, Feb. 1901		24	8	
Beher, Konrad	20, Mar. 1897	18, Mar.	33-11m	4	
Beheymer, William E.	5, Jan. 1892		3m	5	
Behle, Alice	12, Feb. 1891		21	4	
Behle, Fred.	1, Apr. 1890		67	1	
Behle, Maggie	7, Feb. 1891		1d	4	
Behlen, Charles	26, June 1889		61	1	
Behlendorf, Hartwig Wilhelm	8, 9, Jan. 1896	7, Jan.	74- 9m	5	
Behlendorf, Sophia	8, Aug. 1898	6, Aug.	70-10m	5	Freers
Behler, Johanna	8, Mar. 1894		5m	5	
Behler, Lawrence	14, Aug. 1900		1	5	
Behling, Katharine	22, 23, July 1896	22, July	54- 3m-14d	4	Wolfer
Behmer, Henry	13, Jan. 1891		1d	1	
Behne, August	16, July 1901		60	8	
Behr, August	18, Nov. 1891		58	4	
Behr, Theresa	25, Feb. 1891		66	4	
Behrens, Eddie	15, Sept 1888		14m	2	
Behrens, Gustav	2, Oct. 1899	1, Oct.	44- 6m	4	
Behrens, Wilhelmine	17, Dec. 1900		79	8	
Behringer, J.	30, Mar. 1889		33	1	
Behrmann, Charles	17, Feb. 1895		40	5	
Behymer, Mabel G.	25, Dec. 1891		2	2	
Behymer, Myrtle E.	27, Apr. 1894		34	5	
Beidenbach, George	27, June 1895		46	5	
Beiderkellen, Louis	28, Dec. 1896		40- 5m	5	
Beier, Nicholaus	22, Apr. 1896	21, Apr.	71- 7m	5	
Beierbach, Valentin	16, Feb. 1897	15, Feb.	59-10m	5	
Beierlein, Elizabeth	16, Nov. 1894		2w	5	
Beierlein, Martha	2, Aug. 1900		6w	8	
Beifling, William	8, Aug. 1893		9m	5	
Beifuss, Charles	5, June 1895		4m	5	
Beifuß, George	7, Jan. 1893		35	5	
Beigel, Leonhard	15, Feb. 1889		62	1	
Beigel, Leonhard	27, May 1889		10m	1	
Beil, Elizabeth	5, May 1895		52	5	
Beil, Lizzie	5, May 1895		52	5	
Beile, Carl F.	18, Oct. 1897	14, Oct.	73- 6m-14d	5	
Beile, Mary	23, May 1900	22, May		8	
Beiler, Charles	8, May 1889		20	1	
Beimish, Herman	21, Mar. 1893		42	5	
Beineke, Rudolf	12, Oct. 1897	10, Oct.	78	4	
Beiner, Peter	25, 26, Sept 1895	24, Sept	60- 7m	5	
Beising, Mary	22, June 1895		58	5	
Beisinger, Mary	5, May 1891		72	1	
Beiting, Elisabeth	29, Jan. 1900	27, Jan.	21-11m	5	
Beiting, Elizabeth	23, Feb. 1889		36	1	
Beitling, George A.	24, July 1889		40	1	
Beitmann, Franziska	17, May 1900	16, May	55	5	
Beitmann, Karl	1, July 1896	30, June	80	5	
Belding, Mila W.	23, Oct. 1900		40	8	
Bell,	16, July 1895		19d	5	
Bell, Charles	19, Oct. 1901		27	8	
Bell, Edward	21, Apr. 1888		16m	1	
Bell, George G.	17, Apr. 1895		55	5	
Bell, H.L.	11, Jan. 1888		3m	4	
Bell, Henry	3, June 1901		81	8	
Bell, Herman	10, May 1895		49	5	

Name	Notice Date	Death Date	Age	Page	Maiden Name
****	****** ****	***** ****	***	****	****** ****
Bell, Josephine	5, Jan. 1888		47	1	
Bell, William O.	28, Nov. 1900		78	8	
Bellem, Eva	27, 28, Nov. 1893	26, Nov.	37-10m-24d	* 5	Lergenmüller
Beller, Andrew	3, Apr. 1890		47	1	
Bellmann, Barney	20, July 1887		72	1	
Bellstedt, Alvin	30, July 1890		11m	1	
Bellstedt, Anna C.	5, Dec. 1889		52	1	
Bellstedt, Norma	10, Apr. 1889		16m	1	
Belte, Loola	6, June 1895		13d	5	
Beltemann, Friederika D.	28, Mar. 1900	26, Mar.	81	8	
Beltinger, M.	23, May 1888		66	1	
Beltzhower, John D.	1, May 1894		36	5	
Belvens, Henry	18, Jan. 1892		38	5	
Belzel, Caroline	20, July 1893		8m	5	
Belzel, Marie	18, Aug. 1887		16m	1	
Belzhuber, Josephine	18, June 1901		42	8	
Bembeneck, Ch.	5, Jan. 1888		4	1	
Bemmes, Clemens	27, Feb. 1892		31	5	
Bendel, Fanny	25, Jan. 1894		20	5	
Bender, August	20, Jan. 1890		2	1	
Bender, Bernhard	16, Oct. 1891		58	1	
Bender, Christ.	8, Aug. 1890		62	1	
Bender, Fred. August	3, Nov. 1893		18d	5	
Bender, Freddie A.	3, July 1894		3d	5	
Bender, George	21, Dec. 1898	20, Dec.	63- 1m	5	
Bender, Henry	23, May 1888		37	1	
Bender, Ida	9, July 1895		3m	5	
Bender, Katie	8, Aug. 1889		63	1	
Bender, Louisa	28, Feb. 1900	27, Feb.	43- 3m	5	
Bender, M.L.	27, Aug. 1889		9m	1	
Bender, Max H.	29, Sept 1897	28, Sept	53	5	
Bender, William	19, July 1887		26	1	
Bender, Willie	23, July 1887		16	1	
Benders, Philomena	10, Sept 1890		50	1	
Bendren, John H.	14, Mar. 1891		60	4	
Bene, Gerhard Henry	22, Feb. 1893		70	5	
Bengel, Mathilda	4, July 1887		53	1	
Bengert, Helena	7, Mar. 1900	5, Mar.	1-10m	5	
Beninghaus, Georg	10, Aug. 1898	9, Aug.		5	
Benjamin, Charles H.	10, Feb. 1891		4m	4	
Benjamin, Joseph S.	8, May 1891		10m	4	
Benkenstein, Elmer C.	28, Mar. 1893		1	5	
Benker, Bernard	20, June 1892		5m	5	
Benkert, Charles	21, July 1900		5m	8	
Benndorf, And.	26, Feb. 1895		75	5	
Benne, Adelheid	17, June 1888		9m	1	
Bennemeyer, Samuel	13, Aug. 1891		5	4	
Benner, F.	21, July 1897	20, July	43	5	
Benner, Pedro G.	9, Mar. 1894		36	5	
Bennett, John	17, Sept 1901		61	8	
Bennett, Neal	24, May 1901		40	8	
Bennett, Peter	12, May 1895		71	5	
Bennett, William	2, July 1901		2	8	
Benninger, Fred.	10, Dec. 1888		7	1	
Benninger, Jacob	16, Sept 1898	15, Sept	64	5	
Benninger, William H.	26, June 1891		7	4	
Benninghaus, Maria	11, Apr. 1890		73	1	
Benninghaus, Rich.	27, Mar. 1888		78	4	
Benny, Margaret	23, Oct. 1888		67	1	
Bens, Carrie	20, Oct. 1891		26	1	
Bensmann, Emma	9, Aug. 1887		5m	1	
Benson, Thomas	8, Apr. 1901		60	8	
Bente, Carrie	18, May 1898	17, May	1- 2m- 2d	4	
Benten, Bernard	12, Oct. 1897	12, Oct.	49	4	
Benten, Fred.	18, Sept 1894		8d	5	
Benten, R.	25, Jan. 1888		40	1	
Benter, Monika	15, Jan. 1897	13, Jan.	64	5	
Bentley, Milton	1, May 1901		74	8	
Benton, George H.	10, Feb. 1891		22	4	
Benton, Solomon E. (Mrs)	12, Feb. 1891		60	4	
Bentz, J.	25, Nov. 1887		4w	1	

Name ****	Notice Date ****** ****	Death Date ***** ****	Age ***	Page ****	Maiden Name ****** ****
Bentz, Johan	30, July 1898	29, July	41- 3m	5	
Bentz, John	13, June 1891		1	4	
Bentz, Peter	17, Aug. 1901		18	8	
Bentzinger, Christ.	8, Aug. 1895	7, Aug.	69- 7m	5	
Benz, Clara	18, Nov. 1893		3	5	
Benz, Gustav A.	23, Jan. 1894		32	5	
Benz, Harry	21, Feb. 1894		3	5	
Benzenger, Christ	26, Nov. 1892		73	5	
Benziger, Carrie	18, June 1895		2	5	
Benzing, Christine	7, Mar. 1893		73	5	
Bènzing, George	18, Apr. 1895		23	5	
Benzing, Maria	12, Feb. 1901		45	8	
Benzinger, Fred. C.	26, Jan. 1901		77	8	
Benzinger, Luella	24, Aug. 1900		1	5	
Bepler, Maria	8, Aug. 1895	6, Aug.	78-11m	5	Manzer
Berberich, Abner	10, Dec. 1892		11	5	
Berberich, Florence K.	12, Apr. 1893		1	5	
Berchtold, Elizabeth	4, Feb. 1901		78	8	
Berdeck, Bernardine	5, Mar. 1901		68	5	
Berding, Josephine	26, Aug. 1898	25, Aug.	69- 6m	4	Niehaus
Berdis, Annie	6, Apr. 1889		33	1	
Berends, Louise	17, Apr. 1901		66	8	
Berendson, Emma	27, Nov. 1889		2m	1	
Berens, Fred.	22, Mar. 1895		40	5	
Beresford, F.M.	14, Dec. 1887		26	4	
Beresford, Helen	13, Mar. 1901		21	8	
Beresford, Roll	16, Feb. 1901		23	8	
Beresford, Sam	10, Dec. 1888		56	1	
Berg, Anthony B.	10, Jan. 1894		24	5	
Berg, Eliza	15, Mar. 1893		62	5	
Berg, Henry	13, July 1900		35	8	
Berg, Philomena	13, Feb. 1901		69	8	
Bergelt, Charles T.A.	13, Sept 1901		59	8	
Bergen, Alvina	21, Apr. 1895		5	5	
Bergen, Dora A.	4, Dec. 1891		2	4	
Berger, Adelia	28, Aug. 1901		18	8	
Berger, Alois	8, June 1901		1	8	
Berger, Andrea Emilie Christin e	30, Apr. 1891	29, Apr.	59- 1m- 2d	4	Wermuth
Berger, Clifford	15, Aug. 1891		4	4	
Berger, Frank	5, Feb. 1901		75	8	
Berger, Helena	22, Oct. 1894		68	5	
Berger, Joseph	16, Apr. 1891		13d	4	
Berger, Margaret	3, Mar. 1892		66	5	
Berger, Mary	30, Jan. 1891		38	4	
Berger, Mary	18, Dec. 1893		48	5	
Berger, William	15, Jan. 1890		42	1	
Bergerle, Theresia	28, Mar. 1892		46	5	
Bergermann, Henry A.	13, Jan. 1890		4d	1	
Bergfeld, Henry	6, May 1892		38	5	
Berghaus, Georg	25, Sept 1896	23, Sept	68	5	
Bergheger, Edward H.	10, Feb. 1898	9, Feb.	17- 3w	5	
Bergheger, Francis	28, May 1901		26	8	
Bergmann, Anna	31, July 1901		24	8	
Bergmann, Annie M.	11, Jan. 1890		29	1	
Bergmann, Bernard	14, Mar. 1901		66	8	
Bergmann, Charles	20, Apr. 1894		8m	5	
Bergmann, Elisabeth	16, Dec. 1893		73	5	
Bergmann, Gustave	3, June 1901		63	8	
Bergmann, Margaret	5, June 1895		3d	5	
Bergmann, Maud	15, July 1890		13m	1	
Bergmann, Minnie	9, Oct. 1894		20	5	
Bergmann, Ruby	6, Nov. 1891		1	4	
Bergmann, Sophia	14, Aug. 1900		78	5	
Bergmann, W.F.	24, Dec. 1895	23, Dec.	39- 3m	5	
Bergmann, Wilhelm	5, Dec. 1899	2, Dec.	46- 1m	4	
Bergmann, Wilhelm B.	1, Sept 1896	30, Aug.	64	5	
Bergsieker, Clara	20, Oct. 1898	18, Oct.	73-10m	5	
Bering, Mary	9, Oct. 1889		53	1	
Beringer, Theresa	30, Apr. 1901		78	8	
Berkemeier, Catharine M.	14, Nov. 1893		78	5	
Berkemeier, Mary	9, Mar. 1901		5	8	

Name ****	Notice Date ****** ****	Death Date ***** ****	Age ***	Page ****	Maiden Name ****** ****
Berkemeyer, Henry	25, Mar. 1901		33	8	
Berkenkamp, Henry	6, July 1889		59	1	
Berker, Maggie	30, Dec. 1890		83	4	
Berkhöfer, George H.	12, May 1895		47	5	
Berkle, Jacob	4, June 1891		7w	4	
Berlage, James	4, June 1895		52	5	
Berlemann, Christina	14, Feb. 1901		67	8	
Berlin, Dorothea	26, July 1887		64	1	
Berlin, Henry	29, Jan. 1892		61	5	
Berling, Elisabeth	30, Dec. 1893		57	5	
Bermann, David	23, May 1901		86	8	
Bernadin, George P.	23, July 1891		2m	4	
Bernard, B.J.	12, Feb. 1900	11, Feb.	48	5	
Bernard, Clarence	16, June 1893		9	5	
Bernard, W.	7, Nov. 1899	6, Nov.	2m	5	
Bernardini, Theo.	12, Sept 1900		52	5	
Bernart, Marie	24, Sept 1901		62	1	
Bernauer, Elisabeth	5, May 1898	4, May	33- 2m	5	Frey
Bernd, Jacob	11, July 1891		21	1	
Berne, Emma	28, Oct. 1891		18	4	
Bernens, Anna Mary	16, Dec. 1891		78	4	
Bernens, Joseph	19, Mar. 1891		78	4	
Bernens, Maria Gertrude	17, Oct. 1899	15, Oct.	73-11m	8	
Berner, Alma	23, Feb. 1891		1	4	
Berner, Rachel	13, Aug. 1891		15	4	
Bernet, Charles	14, Nov. 1894		11d	5	
Bernett, Cornelia	16, Aug. 1887		37	1	
Bernhard, Albert	4, Oct. 1894		6	5	
Bernhard, Elisabeth	2, Apr. 1897	31, Mar.	59- 3m	5	Gehring
Bernhard, Joseph	10, Mar. 1891		1d	4	
Bernhard, L.	21, Feb. 1888		21	1	
Bernhard, Mary	18, Nov. 1891		29	4	
Bernhardt, Amalia	10, June 1889		21	1	
Bernhardt, F.A.	19, Dec. 1888		76	1	
Bernhardt, Frank	23, Mar. 1895		49	5	
Bernhardt, Marie	10, Jan. 1899	8, Jan.		5	
Bernhart, Margaretha	25, 27, Mar. 1897	24, Mar.	76- 9m	5	Hollstein
Berning, Andrew	25, July 1900		10	5	
Berning, Anna M.	25, Jan. 1894		72	5	
Berning, Henry	26, Nov. 1891		80	1	
Berningham, Edward	28, Oct. 1891		64	4	
Berninghaus, Milton D.	23, June 1888		6m	1	
Berninghaus, Thusnelda	20, Apr. 1900	19, Apr.	84	5	
Bernings, Dora	16, May 1892		67	5	
Bernke, Maria T.	14, Mar. 1891		60	4	
Bernreuther, Ernst	8, Dec. 1891		72	4	
Bernstein, August	23, Feb. 1892		7m	5	
Bero, Peter Paul	6, July 1901		63	8	
Berold, Johann	12, Oct. 1898	11, Oct.	70- 1m-14d	5	
Berry, John	3, July 1901		42	8	
Berser, Martin	28, Sept 1901		56	5	
Bert, Dorothea	21, Oct. 1895	20, Oct.	38	5	
Berte, Clara	19, Oct. 1892		8m	5	
Berte, Nellie	21, Nov. 1891		3d	4	
Bertelt, Frank	1, Sept 1891		64	4	
Berter, Lawrence	27, Jan. 1891		1	4	
Berther, Ida	17, Mar. 1891		3	4	
Berting, Karolina Antonette	8, Jan. 1898	7, Jan.		4	Henke
Berting, Katharina	21, Dec. 1897	20, Dec.	82- 1m	5	Blömer
Berting, Lizzie M.	16, May 1893		2	5	
Bertling, Bernhard H.	23, Aug. 1888		13	1	
Bertman, Wheeler	12, Sept 1890		2w	1	
Bertram, Joseph	3, Jan. 1901		68	5	
Bertram, Mary	27, Apr. 1901		22	8	
Bertram, William	29, May 1901		22	8	
Bertsch, Jonas	6, Nov. 1896	5, Nov.	81	5	
Bertsch, Rosine	4, May 1898	3, May	84	5	Banner
Bertsche, John H.	31, Dec. 1892		1	5	
Bertschinger, Rosa	17, Dec. 1900		18	8	
Berwanger, Amalie	3, Nov. 1892		84	5	
Berwanger, Barbara	16, June 1891		3	4	

Name ****	Notice Date ****** ****	Death Date ***** ****	Age ***	Page ****	Maiden Name ****** ****
Berzel, William	19, Feb. 1895		40	5	
Besel, Henriette	1, Feb. 1901		21	8	
Besel, Johanna	11, July 1893		1	5	
Besh, Eugene	27, July 1887		1	1	
Besler, Lizzie	28, Jan. 1893		37	5	
Bessenkamp, Fred.	22, June 1892		50	5	
Besser, John V.	23, Mar. 1893		5w	5	
Besser, Phillipine	28, Feb. 1901		62	8	
Bessinger, Charles J.	1, Sept 1887		33	1	
Besson, Charlotte	4, Feb. 1888		79	4	
Best, Anna M.	27, Apr. 1901		84	8	
Best, Apollonia	14, Apr. 1898	13, Apr.	76- 6m	5	
Best, Benjamin	28, Dec. 1892		62	5	
Best, Clifford	19, July 1895		5m	5	
Best, Conrad	13, Dec. 1897	11, Dec.	69	5	
Best, Emilie	9, June 1898	7, June	61	5	
Best, Julia	11, Apr. 1892		2m	5	
Best, Margaretha	23, Oct. 1897	22, Oct.	76	4	
Bestin, Joseph	25, Sept 1890		11m	1	
Besuden, John	23, Aug. 1900		46	8	
Betker, John F.	17, July 1895		32	5	
Betman, Alice	29, June 1892		9m	5	
Betscher, Adelheid	5, Oct. 1898	4, Oct.	70-10m- 6d	5	
Betscher, Maria	26, May 1897	24, May	27	5	
Bettinger, Charles	5, May 1896	4, May	17	5	
Bettinger, Elisabeth	29, Nov. 1895	28, Nov.	73	5	Dieringer
Bettinger, Elisabeth	6, Aug. 1896	4, Aug.	77- 4m	5	Schmidt
Bettinger, Herbert H.	22, Mar. 1894		4m	5	
Bettinhaus, John H.	5, Mar. 1895		28	5	
Bettler, Elisabeth	25, May 1894		7	5	
Bettmann, James	20, Dec. 1897		33	5	
Bettmann, Mamie	29, Mar. 1897	24, Mar.		5	
Bettmann, Meyer	16, Oct. 1894		61	5	
Bettner, Charles	15, Mar. 1894		40	5	
Betts, Cynthia	4, Apr. 1901		75	8	
Betts, Edwin	3, Apr. 1888		31	4	
Betts, Elmer	6, July 1901		18m	8	
Betts, H. Louisa	30, Mar. 1895		54	5	
Betty, Lulu	7, Sept 1887		5d	1	
Betz, August	22, Jan. 1888	21, Jan.	41- 7m	* 4,5	
Betz, Emma K.	24, Feb. 1890		9m	1	
Betz, F.T.	22, Aug. 1895	20, Aug.	3-11m	5	
Betz, Fred.	4, Jan. 1893		21	5	
Betz, Harry R.	3, May 1888		7m	1	
Betz, Louise	20, July 1889		22	1	
Betz, Rosa	6, Feb. 1894		8m	5	
Betzing, Anna Elisabeth	10, May 1898	8, May	68- 2m	5	Schneider
Betzing, George	15, Mar. 1888		2- 6m	4	
Betzing, Henry	20, Nov. 1900		57	8	
Betzing, Konrad	16, Apr. 1897	14, Apr.	71	5	
Betzner, Cora L.	3, Aug. 1893		19	5	
Beuerlein, Catharine	15, July 1901		3	8	
Beulley, Martha	10, Feb. 1891		58	4	
Beutelschieß, Catharine	24, Sept 1900		40	5	
Beuttel, (Mrs)	14, Aug. 1895	13, Aug.	24- 9m	5	
Beuttel, Amanda	6, Oct. 1899	5, Oct.		5	Seiter
Beverdick, Herman	22, Jan. 1898	20, Jan.	75- 8m	5	
Beverdick, Josephine	27, Mar. 1890		2	1	
Beyer, Frances	5, Dec. 1890		7	4	
Beyer, H.E.	8, Aug. 1896	8, Aug.	60	5	
Beyer, Philipp	28, Dec. 1892		14	5	
Beyer, Phillip	27, Jan. 1891		43	4	
Beyerhofer, John	20, July 1889		64	1	
Beyerlein, Charles	26, June 1891		7w	4	
Beyerlein, Emma	17, Sept 1891		6	1	
Beyerlein, Louis	1, Apr. 1889		16m	1	
Beyley, Mary	23, Jan. 1901		28	8	
Beyrer, Franzis	1, Sept 1887		21m	1	
Bezold, Catharine W.	5, June 1895		2m	5	
Bfein, Sam.	13, Jan. 1891		72	1	
Bibbe, Nicholas	16, Nov. 1896	14, Nov.	66- 1m	5	

Name ****	Notice Date ****** ****	Death Date ***** ****	Age ***	Page ****	Maiden Name ****** ****
Bichard, Amelia	30, Dec. 1898	29, Dec.	23	5	
Bichard, Joseph C.	20, Dec. 1893		28	5	
Bichard, Louis C.	22, Oct. 1894		26	5	
Bichwine, William	21, Apr. 1893		14d	5	
Bickard, William	6, Apr. 1895		26	5	
Bickel, Anna M.	22, June 1895		65	5	
Bickel, Eduard P.	27, 29, Jan. 1896	26, Jan.	37	5	
Bickeler, Charlotte	23, Sept 1887		5	2	
Bickhaus, Barney	18, July 1893		60	5	
Bickwell, Walter A.	14, Aug. 1896	13, Aug.	38	5	
Biddle, Rosa	4, Mar. 1898	1, Mar.	64	5	
Bidlingmeyer, John	29, Jan. 1901		80	8	
Bieber, Maria Johanna	20, Jan. 1897	19, Jan.	1- 8m	5	
Biedenbender, Lulu B.	11, Nov. 1895	10, Nov.	5-11m	5	
Biedenharn, Herman Heinrich	4, Aug. 1898	2, Aug.	63- 3m	5	
Biedenharn, Leonhard	14, Nov. 1900		7d	8	
Biedenholz, Helene	27, May 1901		3m	8	
Biedinger, Alice	15, Feb. 1889		18	1	
Biedinger, Peter	21, Feb. 1893		65	5	
Biedinger, Robert	25, Dec. 1891		8	2	
Biegert, Katharine	10, Mar. 1895		90	5	
Biegler, Leonhard	10, July 1888		30	1	
Biegler, Robert	29, Aug. 1892		11	5	
Biehl, Fred. W.	6, Apr. 1892		20m	5	
Biehl, Freddie G.	10, May 1895		1	5	
Biehl, Joseph	16, Mar. 1899	14, Mar.	37	5	
Biehle, Arthur J.	6, Nov. 1891		2d	4	
Bieker, Emma	25, Feb. 1898	24, Feb.	15	5	
Bieker, Leopold	13, Mar. 1901		60	8	
Bielefeld, Charles W.	22, Dec. 1893		55	5	
Bieler, George	12, Feb. 1889		47	1	
Bieman, Frank	24, Jan. 1888		30	1	
Biemann, Louis	11, Oct. 1900		42	8	
Biemann, Margaretha	3, Oct. 1898	1, Oct.	77- 9m	5	
Biemesche, Herman	23, Nov. 1888		32	1	
Bien, C.	25, Jan. 1888		33	1	
Bien, Kate	3, Feb. 1894		54	5	
Bienenstein, Andreas	21, Feb. 1900	20, Feb.	41- 8m	5	
Bienne, Lillie A.	9, Dec. 1892		6m	5	
Bierbaum, Cleopa	27, Aug. 1891		69	1	
Bierbaum, Henry	6, June 1891		54	4	
Biere, Wilhelmine	13, June 1899	11, June	83- 8m-27d	4	VonDalkmann
Bierkotte, Gertrude	14, Mar. 1891		76	4	
Bierlein, Dennis	21, Mar. 1893		58	5	
Bierman, Adolf	23, May 1901		45	8	
Bierman, Goldy	4, June 1895		20m	5	
Bierman, Ida E.	17, Feb. 1891		1m	4	
Biermann, Adolph	7, Dec. 1889	6, Dec.	3	4	
Biermann, Sarah	9, Dec. 1892		38	5	
Biermann, Wilhelm G.	15, July 1897	14, July		5	
Biesang, Annie	5, May 1891		52	1	
Biesten, Joseph	1, Nov. 1895	31, Oct.	74	5	
Bigler, Daniel M.	9, Mar. 1889		66	1	
Bigler, Mary	26, Aug. 1891		4m	4	
Bigney, P.M.	9, May 1895		61	5	
Bihn, Katharine	11, Mar. 1891		38	4	
Bihr, Anna	16, Dec. 1891		54	4	
Bilger, John	11, Aug. 1887		11m	1	
Bilger, Justina	10, Jan. 1899	8, Jan.	72	5	
Bill, Edward J.	10, Mar. 1896	9, Mar.	3	5	
Bill, Mildred M.	18, Sept 1900		2	5	
Billan, Louise W.	14, Apr. 1894		31	5	
Billermann, Th.	11, Aug. 1888		17	1	
Billet, Annie	8, Apr. 1890		40	1	
Billiani, Pauline	29, May 1888		48	2	
Billingheimer, Sophie	19, July 1894		72	5	
Billington, Martha	6, Sept 1900		2d	5	
Billman, Rosella	5, June 1901		2	8	
Billmann, Friedrich	9, Apr. 1900	7, Apr.	18- 2m	4	
Bimmerle, David	27, Oct. 1888		2	1	
Bimser, William	3, Apr. 1888		17	4	

Name	Notice Date	Death Date	Age	Page	Maiden Name
****	****** ****	***** ****	***	****	****** ****
Bindemann, Anna M.	28, Dec. 1893		34	5	
Binder, Conrad	29, Mar. 1894		49	5	
Binder, Franz Xavier	26, Sept 1896	25, Sept	70- 9m	5	
Binder, George J.	20, Dec. 1893		4	5	
Binder, Louise	5, Dec. 1893		29	5	
Bindheim, Frederika	2, June 1894		53	5	
Bing, Clifford S.	3, May 1888		9	1	
Bingeman, George	11, July 1893		31	5	
Binges, Dominick	3, Oct. 1891		72- 3m	1	
Bingmeyer, Kat.	20, Jan. 1888		68	4	
Binhert, Joseph	14, Feb. 1891		53	4	
Binker, Elizabeth	4, May 1892		28	5	
Binne, Anna	5, July 1899	4, July	49- 2m	4	Reche
Binne, Henry	9, Dec. 1893		69	5	
Binner, Susanna	10, Jan. 1888		4m	4	
Bird, Clara	6, Sept 1901		1m	8	
Bird, James C.	3, Jan. 1901		45	5	
Bird, Sarah	5, Mar. 1901		6	5	
Birk, Jakobine	14, June 1889		63	1	
Birkemeyer, Frank	5, May 1896	3, May	55	5	
Birkenbusch, Minna	16, Sept 1895	14, Sept	17	5	
Birkenkamp, Henry	10, Aug. 1894		2m	5	
Birkhofer, Katharine	10, Apr. 1901		61	8	
Birkle, Marcel	13, July 1901		1	8	
Birkler, John	23, Aug. 1900		32	8	
Birnbryer, Adolph	31, Dec. 1891		55	1	
Birr, August	1, Aug. 1893		3m	5	
Birrer, Mary	15, Apr. 1893		35	5	
Birt, William	10, Dec. 1900		67	8	
Birth, Fred.	27, Feb. 1889		39	1	
Bisack, B.H.	3, July 1894		20	5	
Bisack, Mary	10, Oct. 1891		50	4	
Bischof, Anna W.	12, Nov. 1891			4	
Bischof, Anton	3, Apr. 1889		46	2	
Bischof, Charlotte	30, Nov. 1887		19	4	
Bischoff, Catharina	16, Aug. 1899	14, Aug.	71- 7m	5	Thels
Bischoff, G.	13, Sept 1900		68	5	
Bischoff, Georg	23, Jan. 1899	21, Jan.	50-10m	5	
Bischoff, Louis	7, Oct. 1891		44	4	
Bischoff, Margaretha	12, May 1893		58	5	
Bischoff, William	21, Jan. 1901		29	8	
Bischopp, Wilhelm	26, Apr. 1893		29	5	
Bishop, A.E.	21, Feb. 1888		2m	1	
Bishop, May	24, Feb. 1888		50	4	
Bissing, August	7, Feb. 1896	6, Feb.	77	5	
Bitte, Charles	11, Apr. 1901			8	
Bitter, Henriette	20, July 1887		4m	1	
Bitter, Henry	5, Dec. 1888		52	1	
Bitter, John	22, Apr. 1891		86	4	
Bittler, Rudolph	18, Mar. 1899	17, Mar.	79	5	
Bittlinger, Anna	17, Sept 1901		31	8	
Bittlinger, Catharine	19, June 1895		67	5	
Bittlinger, Charles	22, Feb. 1890		64	4	
Bittner, Clara	14, Dec. 1893		17m	5	
Bittner, George	9, July 1887		1d	1	
Bittner, Martha	26, Mar. 1901		17	8	
Bittner, Martin	16, May 1893		87	5	
Bittner, Michael	14, Feb. 1888		7w	4	
Bitzer, Charles	15, Dec. 1892		3	5	
Bitzer, Cresentia	27, Mar. 1896	26, Mar.	73	5	
Bitzer, Eva	18, Apr. 1899	17, Apr.	70- 1m	4	Postel
Bitzer, George	3, Mar. 1888		19d	1	
Bitzer, John	9, Mar. 1893		67	5	
Bißmeyer, Katharine	28, Dec. 1895	27, Dec.	63- 4m	5	
Black, Annie	18, Apr. 1890		19	1	
Black, Edward	21, Aug. 1887		29	5	
Black, Luella	31, July 1900		28	5	
Blackburn, Grace	15, July 1901		1	8	
Blackburn, Robert	21, Sept 1887		10m	1	
Blackburne, G.	28, Feb. 1888		58	1	
Blackman, Carrie	15, Feb. 1901		38	8	

Name ****	Notice Date ****** ****	Death Date ***** ****	Age ***	Page ****	Maiden Name ****** ****
Blackmann, Ester	3, Aug. 1887		12m	1	
Blair, Bryston	15, Mar. 1901		3w	8	
Blair, Herman E.	4, Jan. 1899	3, Jan.		5	
Blair, James	22, Sept 1900		59	5	
Blake, Patrick	9, May 1895		59	5	
Bland, F.	13, July 1900		20	8	
Bland, George	16, July 1901		60	8	
Bland, Lizzie	27, Dec. 1890		6m	2	
Blandow, Caroline	21, Sept 1895	20, Sept	70- 4m	5	Fischer
Blangy, H.	5, May 1895		57	5	
Blank, Frank H.	4, Apr. 1891		76	4	
Blank, Jake	23, Sept 1891		3m	4	
Blank, Joseph	13, Dec. 1890		2	1	
Blank, Pearl	28, June 1895		75	5	
Blank, Ralph J.	15, Sept 1888		46	2	
Blanken, Johan Hendrikus	6, Apr. 1899	4, Apr.	38	4	
Blanken, Sabina	11, Apr. 1899	10, Apr.	34	5	Häring
Blankenbuehler, John F.	20, Jan. 1891		70	4	
Blankenmeyer, Joseph	31, Jan. 1901		76	8	
Blankmeyer, August	28, Mar. 1892		2	5	
Blasch, Lauretta	24, May 1901		5	8	
Blase, Julia C.	25, May 1900	24, May	19- 8m	8	
Blase, Louisa	19, Feb. 1895		45	5	
Blase, Louise	5, Apr. 1897	2, Apr.	26- 3m	5	Westerkamp
Blase, Maria E.	6, Oct. 1899	3, Oct.	75- 9m	5	Heckert
Blase, Oscar	2, Feb. 1894		18m	5	
Blasing, Scholastia	24, Jan. 1891		80	4	
Blasse, Charles	13, Oct. 1891		35	4	
Blatten, John	2, June 1891		26	4	
Blatter, (girl)	25, Nov. 1887		1d	1	
Blattman, Charles	23, June 1888		42	1	
Blattner, Paul	18, Dec. 1900		43	8	
Blaurock, Katie	4, Oct. 1900		20	8	
Blautz, John	26, Jan. 1889		5m	1	
Blaß, Joseph	4, Oct. 1888		50	4	
Blech, Martin	17, Oct. 1889		8m	1	
Blechschmidt, Fr.	1, Oct. 1895	30, Sept	45	5	
Blechschmidt, Johanna	20, May 1890		16	1	
Blechschmidt, Louis	31, July 1888	30, July	14m	4	
Bleh, Johan	20, Oct. 1898	18, Oct.	59- 1m	5	
Bleichner, Margaret	26, 27, Sept 1895	25, Sept	85- 1m	5	Brunett
Bleichstein, Katharina	4, Oct. 1887		67	1	
Bleil, Charles H.	6, May 1889		18m	1	
Bleinke, (Sr.)	27, Dec. 1890		23	2	
Blesch, Emanuel T.	22, Feb. 1895		39	5	
Blesi, Margaret	15, Mar. 1901		65	8	
Blesi, Mortiz	24, Jan. 1899	23, Jan.	20- 5m	4	
Blevins, Neil	10, Apr. 1901		65	8	
Bley, Doloris	23, Mar. 1901		16	8	
Bley, Louise	10, Sept 1895	8, Sept		5	
Bley, Mary E.	14, Sept 1901		14d	1	
Bley, Theresia Karolina	14, July 1896	13, July	62- 7m	5	Trickler
Bleyer, Moritz	27, Feb. 1901		79	8	
Bleymeyer, Robert	8, Apr. 1891		35d	4	
Blinn, Alpheus W.	2, Dec. 1894		85	4	
Bliß, Flora	21, Feb. 1888		16	1	
Bliß, John	3, June 1901		66	8	
Bloch, Grace	22, Jan. 1892		21	5	
Bloch, Hannah	9, Nov. 1897	8, Nov.		5	
Block, Elias	27, July 1894		76	5	
Block, Ephraim	5, Mar. 1900	3, Mar.		8	
Block, George	14, Nov. 1893		4	5	
Block, H.	22, July 1897	21, July	78	5	
Blockmann, Richard J.W.	14, Mar. 1893		6m	5	
Bloebaum, Carl	12, June 1901		5d	8	
Bloebaum, Henry	31, July 1901		38	8	
Bloem, Ida	26, Mar. 1888		3m	4	
Bloemker, Fred J.	6, Mar. 1899	5, Mar.		4	
Blom, Gertrud	20, July 1898	19, July	9- 4m-16d	5	
Blome, Bertha J.	6, Oct. 1900		5	5	
Blome, Louis	21, Mar. 1888		6	1	

Name ****	Notice Date ****** ****	Death Date ***** ****	Age ***	Page ****	Maiden Name ****** ****
Blomer, Sophia	30, Jan. 1894		1	5	
Blomken, Johan Hendrikus	5, Apr. 1899	3, Apr.	38	4	
Bloom, Elmira	4, Apr. 1895		70	5	
Bloom, Fred.	2, Oct. 1888		6w	1	
Bloom, Solomon	10, Mar. 1891		68	4	
Bloomer, Henry	30, Oct. 1891		3m	4	
Blopp, Margaretha	10, July 1891		63	4	
Bluche, Augustin	3, Apr. 1888		77	4	
Bludau, Johanna	13, Oct. 1892		46	5	
Bluener, Henry	18, Apr. 1890		28	1	
Bluet, J.	24, Feb. 1888		48	4	
Blum, Anna	29, Jan. 1897	27, Jan.	6m- 6d	5	
Blum, August	19, May 1897	18, May	70	5	
Blum, Charles	26, June 1889		6	1	
Blum, Charles L.	17, July 1894		23	5	
Blum, Edwin	4, Feb. 1901		1d	8	
Blum, Elisabeth	13, Apr. 1896	12, Apr.	56	5	Bohler
Blum, Elizabeth	5, Aug. 1887		10m	1	
Blum, Frank	16, Sept 1897	14, Sept		5	
Blum, George P.	3, July 1895		9m	5	
Blum, Ida	1, Aug. 1887		10m	1	
Blum, John G.	18, Jan. 1894		37	5	
Blum, Katharine	26, Sept 1894		15	5	
Blum, Loretta	17, July 1895		11m	5	
Blum, Louis	2, Feb. 1895		41	5	
Blum, Margaretha	17, Jan. 1898	15, Jan.	75	5	
Blum, Mary	7, Apr. 1891		65	4	
Blum, Michael	8, Feb. 1901		57	8	
Blum, William R.	15, May 1895		38	5	
Blume, Lucia	12, Sept 1891		19	1	
Blumenbach, Emma	2, Mar. 1896	29, Feb.	28	5	
Blumenbach, Henriette	13, Sept 1895	12, Sept	58- - 1d	5	Kappel
Blumer, Kate	12, Jan. 1894		14m	5	
Blumer, Katie	7, Feb. 1889		52	1	
Blust, August	1, Jan. 1888	27, Dec.	43- 1m	* 5	
Blust, John	23, Mar. 1895		6	5	
Blömer, Harry	15, Aug. 1893		1	5	
Blömker, Marie	4, July 1895		4d	5	
Boader, Kasper	24, May 1898	23, May	64-10m	4	
Boalt, Charles	18, June 1901		3	8	
Bobe, Maria A.	20, July 1897	19, July	47	5	Eichenlaub
Boberg, Gerhard Heinrich	17, May 1900	15, May	75- 2m	5	
Bobisch, Carrie	17, Aug. 1892		7m	5	
Bock, Casper	31, Mar. 1891		82	4	
Bockelmann, Anna	12, Dec. 1900		67	8	
Bockelmann, Charles	16, Mar. 1899	14, Mar.	33- 7m	5	
Bockenstette, John J.	23, July 1887		5	1	
Bockerstette, August	29, Sept 1893		32	5	
Bockerstette, John	13, Sept 1900		41	5	
Bockharfer, Herman	29, Sept 1894		69	5	
Bockhorst, Bernardina	30, May 1898	28, May	68	4	Wilke
Bockhorst, Herman	16, July 1895		4d	5	
Bockhorst, J.H.	27, Nov. 1896	25, Nov.	68	5	
Bockhorst, Joseph	26, Mar. 1901		64	8	
Bockhorst, Katie	28, Dec. 1896	27, Dec.		5	
Bockhorst, Maria Katharina	4, Feb. 1900	4, Feb.	79- 3m	5	Blömer
Bocklage, Anna	25, Jan. 1898	22, Jan.	65- 1m	4	
Bocklage, Catharina	24, Feb. 1892		59	5	
Bocklage, John	29, June 1893		1d	5	
Bocklage, Wilhelm	25, Mar. 1901		30	8	
Bocock, Mary	19, June 1901		6	8	
Bode, Albert	5, Mar. 1895		42	5	
Bode, Anna	13, June 1900	12, June		8	
Bode, Christian	15, Feb. 1896	14, Feb.	42	5	
Bode, Louis A.	16, Feb. 1895		1	5	
Bode, William	26, Dec. 1900		44	8	
Bodemer, Elisabeth	15, Jan. 1890		83	1	
Bodemer, Jordan E.	7, Apr. 1897	6, Apr.	60- 8m	5	
Boden, A.	21, Mar. 1888		63- 3m	1	
Boden, Kate	12, Sept 1900		39	5	
Bodenstein, C.	7, Aug. 1894		27	5	

Name ****	Notice Date ****** ****	Death Date ***** ****	Age ***	Page ****	Maiden Name ****** ****
Boebing, Mary	10, Oct. 1891		38	4	
Boebinger, Charles	24, Dec. 1900		42	8	
Boebinger, Jakob	7, Dec. 1889		15- 6m	1	
Boebinger, Margaretha	15, Sept 1890	15, Sept	36	1	Lorenz
Boeck, Friedericka	28, May 1896	26, May	34-11m	5	Winkelmann
Boeckelmann, Anna	5, Oct. 1889		5	1	
Boeckelmann, Heinrich	17, Aug. 1900		57	5	
Boeckle, Anna	25, Feb. 1901		78	8	
Boeckmann, Gertrude	23, Jan. 1894		90	5	
Boeckmann, Kurt	26, Aug. 1892		8	5	
Boeckmann, Mary	16, May 1901		19	5	
Boedecker, Charles	7, June 1890		9	1	
Boedeker, Catharine M.E.	7, Dec. 1893		82	5	
Boedker, Arthur Andrew	11, July 1891		7m	1	
Boedker, Caroline	20, Nov. 1899	19, Nov.	65	5	Schumacher
Boegel, J.H.	1, Mar. 1888		96	4	
Boegel, William	7, Mar. 1892		27	5	
Boegemann, Marie	20, Nov. 1900		68	8	
Boeh, Wilhelmina	28, Nov. 1893		36	5	
Boehle, F.W.	6, Aug. 1895	5, Aug.	2m-15d	5	
Boehle, Fred.	28, Dec. 1893		66	5	
Boehm, Anton	18, July 1887		64	1	
Boehm, Daniel H.	14, Jan. 1901		33	8	
Boehm, Elisabeth	6, Jan. 1893		43	5	
Boehm, Fred.	31, Oct. 1894		3m	5	
Boehm, Henriette	28, Nov. 1899	28, Nov.	56- 1m	8	Heger
Boehm, Marie	12, Dec. 1900		43	8	
Boehmer, Alice	5, Sept 1894		4m	5	
Boehmer, H.	27, Dec. 1887		1	1	
Boehmer, John T.	10, Dec. 1900		42	8	
Boehmer, Maria A.	31, Mar. 1896	30, Mar.	63-10m	5	Krimpelbach
Boehmlein, Kasper	14, June 1901		40	5	
Boehnlein, Emilie	15, Aug. 1891		48	4	
Boehnlein, Joseph	11, Apr. 1893		52	5	
Boehnlein, Mike	2, Feb. 1893		65	5	
Boehringer, Adam	20, June 1891		60	1	
Boehringer, Charles	6, May 1896	5, May	53- 2m	5	
Boelemer, Margaretha	11, July 1887		36	1	
Boelicke, Katharine	8, June 1901			8	
Boelike, Auguste	27, June 1900	27, June		8	Fink
Boelscher, Franziska Elisabeth	21, Sept 1898	20, Sept	4-11m- 8d	4	
Boelscher, Theresa	20, Mar. 1894		53	5	
Boeman, Katharine	6, July 1901		71	8	
Boemann, Anna	4, Nov. 1891		5	1	
Boemer, Emma	10, July 1891		8m	4	
Boemmich, Michael	3, Sept 1890		78	1	
Boeracker, Johan Heinrich	24, Mar. 1896	23, Mar.	68- 8m	5	
Boeres, Edmund	6, Feb. 1894		2- 6m	5	
Boeres, Jakob	13, Sept 1893		36	5	
Boeres, Milton	6, Feb. 1894		2m	5	
Boerschig, Stephen	26, May 1898	24, May	60- 6m	5	
Boes, Maria Antoinette	12, Sept 1895	11, Sept	2m-29d	5	
Boese, Frederick W.	2, Jan. 1901		68	5	
Boese, Sophie	1, Nov. 1898	29, Oct.	43	5	
Boesherz, Mary	15, Apr. 1893		59	5	
Boetcher, Mamie	5, May 1895		3m	5	
Boettcher, Otto	16, July 1892		10m	5	
Boettcher, Robert	8, June 1893		4m	5	
Boettcher, Robert	15, May 1894		18	5	
Boetticher, Hans	25, June 1888		7w	1	
Boex, William	8, July 1901		5m	8	
Bogart, Cornelius	6, June 1901		73	8	
Bogart, Mildred	30, Aug. 1900		3m	5	
Bogen, Amelia	27, May 1896	26, May	56- - 4d	5	
Bogen, Mary	30, Aug. 1900		23	5	
Bogen, Oskar	5, Feb. 1895		8m	5	
Bogenreif, Lillie	21, July 1887		6w	1	
Bogenschütz, Francis	15, Aug. 1891		74	4	
Bogenschütz, Walter Ernst	11, May 1896	9, May	2- 6m	5	
Boger, Georg	26, Aug. 1897	25, Aug.		5	
Boger, Michael	24, Feb. 1897	22, Feb.	75- 7m	5	

Name ****	Notice Date ****** ****	Death Date ***** ****	Age ***	Page ****	Maiden Name ****** ****
Boger, R.	2, Aug. 1900		38	8	
Boher, Eleonora	10, Oct. 1891		3	4	
Bohl, Elizabeth	27, Aug. 1901		58	1	
Bohland, Fred.	9, Apr. 1890		9	1	
Bohlander, Dina	17, June 1888		68	1	
Bohlander, J.G.	30, Sept 1888		50	4	
Bohlander, Jacob	27, Apr. 1898	26, Apr.	58	5	
Bohlender, Maggie	4, Oct. 1894		35	5	
Bohlson, Henry	3, May 1901		25	8	
Bohländer, Clara Katharina	13, Feb. 1896	12, Feb.	6	5	
Bohm, Joseph	13, Jan. 1896	11, Jan.	61	5	
Bohmann, Francisca	6, May 1893		42	5	
Bohmann, Joseph	2, Aug. 1901		20	8	
Bohme, Theresa	4, Dec. 1891		79	4	
Bohmer, Frederick J.	24, Apr. 1891		3	4	
Bohn, Charlotte	29, Nov. 1899	28, Nov.	72	8	Stegemüller
Bohn, George Johan	30, Apr. 1896	29, Apr.	77-10m	5	
Bohn, John H.	11, Apr. 1891		1d	4	
Bohn, Samuel	24, Sept 1900		22	5	
Bohne, Ferd F. Wilhelm	4, Apr. 1900	2, Apr.	27-10m	8	
Bohne, Fred.	12, Aug. 1901		3w	8	
Bohne, Henry	19, July 1893		46	5	
Bohnen, Katharine	25, Jan. 1896	23, Jan.	7- 3m	5	
Bohnenkamp, Louis	14, Aug. 1887		82	1	
Bohnert, Albert S.	17, Sept 1891		17m	1	
Bohnert, Anna	13, Nov. 1899	12, Nov.	34	5	Felix
Bohnert, Bernard	1, Sept 1896	31, Aug.	71	5	
Bohnert, Mary	20, Mar. 1901		73	1	
Bohnett, L.P.	16, Mar. 1888		5w- 4d	1	
Bohr, Joseph	5, Dec. 1900		57	8	
Bohrer, Bernhard	28, Jan. 1901		12	8	
Bohrer, Theresa	24, Jan. 1891		34	4	
Bohsancurt, Carolina	14, July 1892		45	5	
Bohsancurt, Jacob	11, Mar. 1898	10, Mar.	56- - 1d	5	
Boiles, Margaret (Mrs)	8, Apr. 1891		48	4	
Bolan, Sarah	11, Aug. 1900		85	8	
Boland, Elisabeth	27, Oct. 1899	26, Oct.	63- 1m	8	Steimer
Boland, Herman	17, Jan. 1901		44	8	
Boland, John	9, Nov. 1893		55	5	
Boland, Mary	4, May 1895		46	5	
Bold, Clara	25, Jan. 1888		22	1	
Bold, Julia D.	5, Jan. 1901		40	8	
Bolger, Annie	28, July 1893		1	5	
Bolger, Edwin	16, July 1900		13m	8	
Bolia, Anna	3, June 1897	2, June	45- 7m	5	
Bolia, Charles	29, Aug. 1900		75	5	
Bolison, Walter	13, Dec. 1890		3	1	
Bolke, Anna	28, Nov. 1891		58	1	
Boll, Catharina	27, Feb. 1892		27	5	
Boll, John	23, Sept 1901			8	
Bolle, Conrad	30, Nov. 1900		65	8	
Boller, Elmore	8, Feb. 1895		2m	5	
Bolles, Bernard	28, Sept 1898	26, Sept	62	4	
Bollhauer, Anna	16, Aug. 1901		45	8	
Bollinger, Marie M.	10, Mar. 1897	9, Mar.	80- -19d	5	Stephan
Bollkard, Magdalena	24, Dec. 1900		33	8	
Bollmann, Anthony	18, Jan. 1894		5	5	
Bollmann, Elisabeth Maria	2, Nov. 1898	1, Nov.	40- 6m	5	Alf
Bollmann, Eva	28, Dec. 1891		5	4	
Bollmann, F.	22, Sept 1888		1m	1	
Bollmann, K.E.	26, Mar. 1888		1m	4	
Bollmann, William	11, Jan. 1892		45	4	
Bolmer, Ann	10, Mar. 1895		67	5	
Bolmer, Cecilia	14, Oct. 1888		87	4	
Bolmer, Lizzie	14, Oct. 1894		20	5	
Bolofoha, Marie	24, Nov. 1896	23, Nov.	67	5	Steinecke
Bolt, Mary	24, June 1901		4	8	
Bolte, Clara	27, Aug. 1890		82	1	
Bolte, Conrad	18, Mar. 1890		42	1	
Bolte, Edwin	28, Feb. 1901		8m	8	
Bolte, Eleonore Catharine	11, July 1891		25d	1	

Name	Notice Date	Death Date	Age	Page	Maiden Name
****	****** ****	***** ****	***	****	****** ****
Bolte, Kasper Heinrich	29, Mar. 1898	28, Mar.	59- 1m	5	
Bolte, Maria	22, Aug. 1888		62	1	
Bombach, Edward	31, Jan. 1890		33	1	
Bomkamp, Emma	25, Aug. 1892		6	5	
Bommer, Christian	21, Feb. 1900	18, Feb.	89- 7m	5	
BonHajo, Mildred	3, Dec. 1900		14m	8	
Bonde, Rudolph	2, Apr. 1895		10m	5	
Bondich, Elisabeth	10, Jan. 1889		44	1	
Bonkamp, Henry	6, July 1893		7m	5	
Bonmeier, Kate	13, Oct. 1892		3	5	
Bonner, Joseph	19, Dec. 1891		54	4	
Bonner, Mary	8, Mar. 1888		67	1	
Bonner, Mary	19, Sept 1888		42	2	
Bonomi, Caroline	19, Aug. 1889		54	1	
Bonte, Bernard	21, Feb. 1898	20, Feb.		5	
Book, Jennie	28, Aug. 1901			8	
Boon, Jane	28, Nov. 1900		80	8	
Boone, Serena	2, Mar. 1901		37	5	
Boos, Eva M.	6, Mar. 1889		3m	1	
Boos, Joseph A.	18, July 1887		30	1	
Bopfi, Henry	26, Aug. 1901		74	8	
Bora, Frances	15, Mar. 1888		38	4	
Borch, Agnes	13, Aug. 1891		1	4	
Borcher, Edward	22, Aug. 1891		1	4	
Borcherding, Conr.	9, Mar. 1895		67	5	
Borchers, Irene	2, Aug. 1893		10m	5	
Borchers, John	4, June 1901		66	8	
Borches, William	13, Sept 1888	12, Sept	5	4	
Borck, John	15, Oct. 1891		32	4	
Borge, Christ.	21, Mar. 1892		18	4	
Borgeding, Alois	17, Mar. 1890		8m	1	
Borgelt, Casper	21, Oct. 1896	20, Oct.	35- 9m	5	
Borgelt, Gertrude	16, Mar. 1892		4	1	
Borgemenke, Maria	1, 2, Nov. 1895	31, Oct.	65- 2m	5	Lücken
Borger, August	23, Aug. 1901		50	8	
Borger, Bernard	4, Mar. 1890		5m	1	
Borger, John	11, Mar. 1889		75	1	
Borger, Julie	26, Aug. 1896	25, Aug.	31	5	
Borger, Louis A.	26, July 1893		5m	5	
Borger, Mary	22, Jan. 1889		19	1	
Borgerding, Flora	15, Jan. 1901		1m	8	
Borgerding, Franz B.	4, Feb. 1896	3, Feb.	16- 9m	5	
Borgman, Mary	19, Mar. 1889		76	1	
Borgmann, Albert	18, Feb. 1898	17, Feb.	2- 6m	5	
Borgmann, Edward	12, Dec. 1891		70	4	
Borjes, Bernard	5, Aug. 1901		41	8	
Bork, Elizabeth	1, June 1893		41	5	
Borker, Johan G.	4, Nov. 1894		5m	5	
Borkhart, Anton	3, Oct. 1887		3d	1	
Borkowsky, Martius	15, Dec. 1893		62	5	
Borle, Peter	22, May 1890		10m	1	
Bormann, Fred.	9, Aug. 1901		33	8	
Borneman, Minnie	24, Apr. 1895		29	5	
Bornemann, Christian	8, May 1889		46	1	
Bornemann, Lena	26, Mar. 1898	25, Mar.	34	5	
Bornemann, Lillie	18, June 1895		8m	5	
Bornhäuser, Sophia	28, May 1891		64	4	
Borning, Bernard	31, Dec. 1892		60	5	
Borns, Herman	19, Feb. 1891		50	4	
Bornschein, Edward	22, Apr. 1891		65	4	
Bornszki, Andrew	30, Jan. 1901		2m	8	
Borntraeger, Matt.	16, Jan. 1894		39	5	
Bornträger, Clara	8, Feb. 1889		6	1	
Boroff, Jared F.	10, Feb. 1891		34	4	
Bortholochen, Helen	22, Aug. 1900		3	5	
Borucki, Marie	22, Aug. 1900		40	5	
Bosandick, Anna	9, Dec. 1897	8, Dec.	78	5	Mese
Bosch, Friedrich	8, 10, Jan. 1896	7, Jan.	60-11m	5	
Bosch, Walter	18, Jan. 1892		1m	5	
Bosche, Carolina	10, Mar. 1891		85	4	
Bose, Maselle Emilie	11, Apr. 1896	10, Apr.		5	

Name	Notice Date	Death Date	Age	Page	Maiden Name
****	****** ****	***** ****	***	****	****** ****
Bosken, Kate L.	8, June 1894		42d	5	
Bosse, Alma M.	14, July 1900	13, July	29- 1m	8	Schaffstall
Bosse, Bernard	28, Apr. 1896	27, Apr.	83- 4m	5	
Bosse, Henry	23, Feb. 1893		47	5	
Bosse, Marie Engel	13, Oct. 1899	11, Oct.	77	5	
Bossenberger, Robert	19, Sept 1900		2	8	
Bossert, Friedrich	12, Nov. 1888		77	2	
Bostick, Alice	7, Feb. 1891		21	4	
Bottenhorn, Malinda	3, July 1897	2, July	32	5	Haehn
Botter, Bernhard	16, Apr. 1889		72	1	
Bottler, Phillip	19, Apr. 1889		45	1	
Boullia, John	9, Apr. 1890		46	1	
Bowden, Albert	29, Aug. 1901		59	8	
Bowen, Emma	20, Dec. 1900		70	8	
Bowers, Louise G.	18, June 1895		54	5	
Bowers, Mary	27, Mar. 1891		1d	4	
Bowls, Bettie	1, July 1901		82	8	
Bowman, Clyde S.	10, Sept 1901		26	1	
Bowman, M.J.	23, Apr. 1895		42	5	
Bowman, Margaret	5, Mar. 1901		27	5	
Boyd, Mary	21, Jan. 1901		49	8	
Boyer, Mary	26, Apr. 1901		78	8	
Boyle, Joseph	5, Aug. 1892		14d	5	
Boö, Joseph	12, Feb. 1890		58	1	
Boß, George	20, July 1901		33	8	
Boß, Joseph	31, Aug. 1900		42	5	
Boßhardt, Dora	17, Aug. 1893		3	5	
Braam, Johanna	21, Oct. 1887		28-10m	1	
Braam, Johanna	5, Mar. 1892		55	5	
Braam, Joost	17, June 1888		65	1	
Brabender, Ida	2, Mar. 1893		1	5	
Brabender, John	25, Apr. 1901		38	8	
Brach, Louis	8, Feb. 1889		2	1	
Bracher, Albertina	4, June 1900	1, June	85	5	Zwick
Bracher, Emilie	27, Aug. 1890		40	1	
Brachle, C.	21, Mar. 1892		66	4	
Brachmann, Ernst	7, Sept 1887		80	1	
Brachmann, William	1, Feb. 1901		63	8	
Brackemeyer, Fred.	8, Oct. 1900		84	8	
Bracken, Mary	13, May 1901		40	8	
Brackenmann, Adelheid	13, Mar. 1900	12, Mar.	73- 5m	5	
Bracker, Louis H.	22, July 1893	21, July	48- 9m-20d	5	
Brackland, Harry	18, Apr. 1900	17, Apr.	70	8	
Brackmann, Stanley	23, Feb. 1893		4	5	
Bracton, H.	27, Dec. 1887		53	1	
Braddock,	25, Jan. 1901		8d	8	
Brademeyer, Fred.	22, Dec. 1900		43	8	
Braden, George M.	7, Jan. 1893		32	5	
Bradfish, Clara	22, Dec. 1900		24	8	
Bradford, Elmer	4, Apr. 1895		19	5	
Bradford, James	7, Apr. 1888		39	4	
Bradford, John	28, Aug. 1901		47	8	
Bradley, Annie	18, July 1887		5w	1	
Bradley, Cath. L.	23, July 1887		23	1	
Bradley, J.	27, Dec. 1887		40	1	
Bradley, John	25, Mar. 1901			8	
Bradley, John	5, Apr. 1901		81	8	
Bradley, Mary	5, June 1888		3m	4	
Bradley, O.A.	23, Aug. 1888		75	1	
Brady, Alice	22, May 1888		1m	1	
Brady, Annie	11, Apr. 1895		42	5	
Brady, Francis	10, Aug. 1901		3	8	
Brady, Mary	3, Apr. 1889		100	2	
Braering, Phillipina	28, Jan. 1894		70	5	
Brahm,	4, Aug. 1887		3w	1	
Brahm, Henry	3, Apr. 1901		63	8	
Brahm, Johan Herman	2, Nov. 1898	1, Nov.	62-11m	5	
Brahm, Louis B.	21, Dec. 1896	20, Dec.	36	5	
Braithwaite, E.	4, Jan. 1901		50	5	
Brake, Ralph	26, Jan. 1901		3m	8	
Brakenmann, Herman	17, Nov. 1896	16, Nov.	74	5	

Name ****	Notice Date ****** ****	Death Date ***** ****	Age ***	Page ****	Maiden Name ****** ****
Braker, Josephine	28, Dec. 1900		47	8	
Braking, Johanna	14, July 1892		8m	5	
Bramble, Alfred F.	25, July 1893			5	
Bramble, Ella	27, Apr. 1892		25	5	
Bramble, May	9, Oct. 1901		57	5	
Bramkamp, Alvina	21, June 1900	18, June	17-10m	6	
Bramkamp, Mary C.	8, June 1895		77	5	
Bramkamp, Wilhelm	27, Apr. 1899	25, Apr.	24-10m	5	
Bramsche, Anna	28, Dec. 1899	26, Dec.		5	Koehnken
Branan, P.	27, Dec. 1887		73	1	
Brancamp, Elizabeth	5, Aug. 1901		54	8	
Brand, Alma	26, Jan. 1893		6m	5	
Brand, Charles	1, Feb. 1893		55	5	
Brand, George	12, Sept 1900		67	5	
Brand, John	26, July 1888		71	2	
Brand, Maggie	2, Aug. 1899	1, Aug.		5	
Brand, Margaretha Josephina	15, June 1896	14, June	25- 5m	5	Kostermann
Brand, Maria	1, Oct. 1895	30, Sept	62	5	Koehler
Brand, Mary	20, May 1893		37	5	
Brand, Rosa E.	29, July 1887		3	1	
Brandau, Matilda	27, Mar. 1901		70	8	
Brande, Rosina	21, Oct. 1890	21, Oct.	30	1	Möller
Brandenburg, Mamie	5, June 1894		10	5	
Brandeweide, Mary G.	18, Nov. 1891		80	4	
Brandhorst, Friedrich	24, Sept 1896	22, Sept	69- -27d	5	
Brandis, Henry	23, July 1889		9m	1	
Branditz, Walter	26, Oct. 1894		2	5	
Branditz, Willie	25, Mar. 1889		10m	1	
Brandle, Louis	13, Apr. 1901		57	8	
Brandon, Lizzie	13, Mar. 1888		1- 4m	1	
Brandt, Gerhard H.	8, July 1891		56	4	
Brandt, Gottlieb	6, May 1892		61	5	
Brandt, John	8, Feb. 1895		69	5	
Brane, J.F.	19, Aug. 1895	17, Aug.	44	5	
Brannagan, Thomas	11, Aug. 1887		23	1	
Bransson, James Henry	25, July 1888		7m	4	
Brant, Theresa	20, June 1888		43	1	
Brash, Belle	9, Jan. 1901		23	5	
Brauch, Albert	30, July 1890		1	1	
Brauch, Bertha	17, Jan. 1893		16	5	
Brauch, Ed.	15, Dec. 1892		19d	5	
Brauch, Frank	4, Feb. 1900	4, Feb.	13- 1m	5	
Brauch, Henry	28, Nov. 1891		4d	1	
Brauchle, W.	15, Feb. 1892		62	5	
Brauer,	14, Nov. 1900			8	
Brauer, Arthur	7, Sept 1901		1	8	
Brauerle, Eleonore	23, Aug. 1887		14m	1	
Braun, Andreas	1, July 1889	1, July	1- -20d	1	
Braun, Anna	29, Apr. 1891		9	4	
Braun, Anna	1, Sept 1891		67	4	
Braun, Anna Maria	2, Oct. 1894		63	5	
Braun, Annie C.	10, Nov. 1891		1	1	
Braun, Barbara	19, Aug. 1896	17, Aug.	63	5	Daiker
Braun, Caroline	23, Aug. 1901		62	8	
Braun, Charles	31, Mar. 1888		1m-24d	4	
Braun, Christ.	22, Apr. 1890	22, Apr.	57- 4m- 1d	4	
Braun, Elisabeth	11, May 1896	10, May	63- 5m	5	Rapp
Braun, Elsie	18, Aug. 1897	17, Aug.	1- 5m	5	
Braun, Flora	27, July 1893		6m	5	
Braun, Franziska	28, Mar. 1898	25, Mar.	21-11m	5	
Braun, Joseph	16, Aug. 1894		74	5	
Braun, Konrad	20, June 1898	18, June	71-11m	5	
Braun, Leopold	1, May 1900	30, Apr.	71- 5m	5	
Braun, Lorenz	30, Nov. 1888		5	1	
Braun, Margaretha	23, Dec. 1893		75	5	
Braun, Margaretha	29, Nov. 1898	28, Nov.	72- 3m	5	Mundorf
Braun, Mary	14, Mar. 1888		23	1	
Braun, R.C.	27, Dec. 1895	26, Dec.	30- 6m	5	
Braun, Rosa A.	7, Feb. 1891		26	4	
Braun, Stella	8, June 1889		4-11m	4	
Braun, Wilhelm	23, Jan. 1892	22, Jan.	1- 7m-22d	5	

Name ****	Notice Date ****** ****	Death Date ***** ****	Age ***	Page ****	Maiden Name ****** ****
Brauner, Emilia	7, June 1899	5, June	38- 7m	5	Woerner
Braunschweiger, Adolph	12, July 1890		29	1	
Brauntz, Catharina	6, May 1892		88	5	
Brawley, Anna M.	26, Dec. 1900		80	8	
Bray, John	10, Dec. 1900		58	8	
Breaker, Bessie	11, Jan. 1888		7m	4	
Brecherding, C.	26, Feb. 1901		70	8	
Brechli, Walter Stephen	22, Aug. 1890		1	1	
Brecker, Cora	5, June 1890		5	4	
Brecker, Peter	26, June 1894		1	5	
Breckheimer, Paul	4, Mar. 1896	3, Mar.	58	5	
Breckmann, Elizabeth	7, Mar. 1892		1m	5	
Bredding, Charles	17, Feb. 1892		5d	5	
Bredemaier, Mary	29, July 1888		30	1	
Brederlow, Caroline	30, Dec. 1895	29, Dec.	56- 6m	5	
Breed, Nellie	18, Sept 1894		5m	5	
Breehne, Theresia	5, Sept 1899	3, Sept	71	5	
Breen, Daniel	24, Apr. 1901		74	8	
Breen, Flora	17, July 1891		12	1	
Breen, Patrick	10, May 1888		22	1	
Breetlove, Edna	1, Dec. 1900		2	8	
Bregen, Albert	6, July 1889		4	1	
Brehm, Eva	14, May 1900	12, May	73- 7m	8	Thein
Brehme, Martha	7, June 1890		7m	1	
Brehmer, Henry	23, Sept 1901			8	
Breiling, Frank	7, May 1891		60	4	
Breilung, John	13, May 1891		66	2	
Breimer, Joseph William	9, July 1887		3m	1	
Breining, Anna E.	25, Feb. 1891		62	4	
Breining, Max	25, Apr. 1889		31	1	
Breinling, Albert	12, Apr. 1893		1	5	
Breisacher, Lewis	20, July 1887		10m	1	
Breitbeil, Fred F.	25, June 1897	23, June	52	5	
Breitbeil, George	17, Sept 1896	15, Sept	87- 5m	5	
Breitenbach, George E.	1, May 1888		28	2	
Breitenbach, Theresa	24, July 1901		15	8	
Breitenbecker, Bertha	21, July 1900		16	8	
Breitfeld, Annie	23, Apr. 1895		7	5	
Breitfeld, Hulda	11, Aug. 1892		1	5	
Breitfeld, Wilhelmina	17, Sept 1901		90	8	
Breitfelder, Anna	2, Nov. 1888		2	1	
Breitheil, Elisabeth	9, Aug. 1894		1	5	
Breitholle, William	17, Mar. 1890		7	1	
Breitner, Eva	16, June 1894		63	5	
Breitner, Martin	5, Mar. 1901		85	5	
Breman, Elisabeth	5, Oct. 1889		1- 9m	1	
Breman, Willie	8, July 1888		6m	1	
Bremer, Dorothea	31, July 1894		69	5	
Bremer, Elisabeth	8, Nov. 1887		34	1	
Bremer, Georg	5, Sept 1895	3, Sept	40- 2m	5	
Bremer, J.H.	9, July 1887		1m	1	
Bremer, Joseph	9, June 1891		27	4	
Bremerschenke, H.	21, Feb. 1888		52	1	
Bremke, Anna	18, Sept 1891		27	1	
Brendel, Frank J.	21, Feb. 1898		15- 5m	5	
Brendel, John	29, Sept 1887		10m	4	
Brennan, Bessie	17, Dec. 1887		27	1	
Brennan, Ella K.	15, Jan. 1901		12d	8	
Brennan, Hannah	12, Sept 1888		56	1	
Brennan, Joseph M.	7, Aug. 1888		9	1	
Brennan, Josephine	26, Sept 1899	24, Sept	68- 6m	5	Bold
Brennan, Mary	13, Jan. 1888		32	1	
Brennen, Victor	30, Nov. 1900		2	8	
Brenner, Charles J.	13, Oct. 1896	12, Oct.	69- 9m	5	
Brenner, Emma	6, Dec. 1892		21	5	
Brenner, Jessie	5, Dec. 1890		1m	4	
Brenner, Johan	21, 22, Mar. 1890	18, Mar.	57- 4m-22d	4	
Brenner, Katharina	23, June 1898	21, June	64- 7m	5	Blymer
Brenner, Katharine	4, 5, Aug. 1897	3, Aug.	44- - 8d	5	Schwarzkopf
Brenner, Louisa	21, June 1895		20m	5	
Brenner, Lucy	8, June 1894		2	5	

Name	Notice Date	Death Date	Age	Page	Maiden Name
****	****** ****	***** ****	***	****	****** ****
Brenner, Mary E.	14, Nov. 1893		27	5	
Brenner, Philipp	9, Jan. 1899	7, Jan.	66	5	
Brenner, William	16, Dec. 1893		45	5	
Brent, C.P.	23, Aug. 1901		68	8	
Brerman, Anna	13, May 1901		29	8	
Breslin, Thomas	17, Apr. 1895		6d	5	
Bresnan, Margarethe	17, May 1901		60	8	
Bresser, Anna	13, Oct. 1891		5d	4	
Bresser, Gerhard H.	15, Oct. 1900		72	5	
Bresser, Henry	17, May 1894		33	5	
Brestel, Albert	22, Dec. 1892		9	5	
Brestel, B.	27, Dec. 1887		86	1	
Brestel, Frederick	2, July 1895		2m	5	
Bretz, Lizzie (Sr. Alvera)	26, Oct. 1894		23	5	
Breuber, John	27, Aug. 1889		35	1	
Breuer, Florentine	5, Sept 1894		79	5	
Breuer, Emma	9, Mar. 1894		2	5	
Breuer, Kate G.	20, Mar. 1896	19, Mar.	36	5	
Breuer, Louise	7, Aug. 1900			8	
Breuer, W.	2, Nov. 1895	31, Oct.	35- 1m	5	
Breumer, Henry	16, Feb. 1895		49	5	
Breuninger, Carl	3, Mar. 1890		15	1	
Brewe, Herman	9, Jan. 1891		40	4	
Brewer, Elisabeth	10, Feb. 1891		26	4	
Brewer, Marie	19, July 1900		4m	8	
Brewster, J.	19, Nov. 1900		14	8	
Breyer, Charles	17, Mar. 1896	16, Mar.	38-10m	5	
Breyer, Laura	5, Mar. 1888		46	4	
Breßler, Barbara	31, Oct. 1900		76	8	
Breßler, Elisabeth	6, Mar. 1900	5, Mar.	70- 6m	8	
Brick, Frederick	30, Aug. 1900		56	5	
Bricka, Friedrich	31, July 1896	30, July	30-11m	5	
Brickelhouse, Simon	4, Feb. 1891		2m	4	
Bricker, David	3, June 1889		8m	1	
Brickley, Fred.	21, Oct. 1891		42	4	
Brickmann, Philipp	29, Dec. 1896	26, Dec.	71- 1m	5	
Bridges, Ellen	9, Aug. 1900		3	8	
Bridges, Ida May	3, Apr. 1888		3w	4	
Briede, Selma Margaret	24, Feb. 1888		7m	4	
Briehl, Magdalena	8, Apr. 1891		57	4	
Brigatte, Antoian	30, Jan. 1901		81	8	
Brigel, Conrad D.	9, Nov. 1897	8, Nov.	87	5	
Brigel, Stella	5, July 1888		5	1	
Briggemann, Francisca	1, Nov. 1887		29- 3m	1	
Briggie, Mary	27, Sept 1900		23	8	
Briggs, Margaret	20, Feb. 1901		84	8	
Brill, Anna M.	4, Feb. 1889		68	1	
Brill, Catharina	20, Sept 1898	19, Sept		5	
Brill, Edna	18, Sept 1901		15	8	
Brill, Georg	19, Oct. 1887		2w	1	
Brill, Helen	18, May 1901		1	1	
Brill, Jacob	2, Oct. 1896	1, Oct.	72	5	
Brill, Verona	15, June 1901		7	8	
Bringelmann, Anna	29, Jan. 1892		64	5	
Bringelmann, Katharine	28, June 1894		77	5	
Brink, August	15, June 1895		47	5	
Brink, Elmer	30, June 1888		7m	1	
Brink, M.E.	1, Mar. 1888		70	4	
Brink, Marie	15, Dec. 1899	14, Dec.		5	Lemmel
Brinker, Adelheid	26, Mar. 1896	24, Mar.	65- 6m	5	Lampke
Brinker, Bernardina	8, July 1891		3	4	
Brinker, George	19, Jan. 1893		50	5	
Brinker, Mary	26, Dec. 1900		85	8	
Brinker, Mathilda	20, June 1889		4	1	
Brinkers, J.B.	1, Sept 1899	31, Aug.	28	5	
Brinkhaus, F.	1, Feb. 1888		19m	4	
Brinkman, Clara	14, Jan. 1892		4m	1	
Brinkman, John B.	11, Dec. 1891		74	4	
Brinkman, Maria Elisabeth	12, Mar. 1896	10, Mar.	77-10m	5	Ruhe
Brinkman, Ralph	14, June 1901		8m	5	
Brinkmann, Alfred	24, Sept 1890		18m	4	

Name	Notice Date	Death Date	Age	Page	Maiden Name
****	****** ****	***** ****	***	****	****** ****
Brinkmann, Bernard	27, Mar. 1895		42	5	
Brinkmann, Bernardina	28, Jan. 1892		75	5	
Brinkmann, C.F.	6, June 1895		86	5	
Brinkmann, Elisabeth	28, Jan. 1894	27, Jan.	41-10m- 9d	5	
Brinkmann, Frank	2, Feb. 1901		38	8	
Brinkmann, Franz	4, Jan. 1899	3, Jan.	58- 4m	5	
Brinkmann, Friedrich W.	5, June 1897	4, June	69- 4m	5	
Brinkmann, George E.	4, Apr. 1895		15	5	
Brinkmann, Heinrich	20, Apr. 1897	17, Apr.	73- 1m	5	
Brinkmann, Hermine	21, Feb. 1896	20, Feb.	1-11m	5	
Brinkmann, Johan C.	23, Dec. 1896	22, Dec.	67	5	
Brinkmann, Johan Clemens	16, Feb. 1900	15, Feb.	75- 6m	5	
Brinkmann, John	14, July 1891		31	4	
Brinkmann, John B.	22, Mar. 1894		10d	5	
Brinkmann, John L.	31, Jan. 1891		2	4	
Brinkmann, Katharine	16, Mar. 1895		71	5	
Brinkmann, Louis	17, July 1890		34	1	
Brinkmann, Louis	10, July 1901		60	5	
Brinkmann, Margaretha	21, Apr. 1898	20, Apr.	69	5	
Brinkmann, Mary	1, Apr. 1889		50	1	
Brinkmann, Mary	27, July 1892		59	5	
Brinkmann, Mary	1, May 1901		54	8	
Brinkmann, Mathes	25, Mar. 1897	24, Mar.	22	5	
Brinkmann, Willi	20, Aug. 1889		6	1	
Brinkmauer, Elisabeth	25, Mar. 1891		73	4	
Brinkmeier, Bernhard	28, Nov. 1891		29	1	
Brinkroege, Louise	17, Aug. 1900		76	5	
Brisker, Robert	10, Apr. 1894		22	5	
Britscher, Jean	19, Apr. 1895		45	5	
Britt, Elizabeth	18, Dec. 1893		76	5	
Britt, Margaret	9, Dec. 1887		7- 9m	1	
Britta, Anna	16, July 1888		4m	1	
Brittenbuecher, William B.	24, June 1891		1	4	
Brittenham, John	25, Apr. 1890		31	1	
Britting, Anna	22, May 1891		63	1	
Britting, Ellen	30, July 1890		45	1	
Britting, Sabina M.	6, Mar. 1890		83	1	
Brittor, Eva	16, Mar. 1892		72	1	
Brock,	1, Dec. 1900		1d	8	
Brock, Katharina Margaretha	19, Dec. 1898	17, Dec.	61- 9m	4	Koske
Brockamp, Heinrich	26, Dec. 1898	25, Dec.	56	5	
Brockeny, W.	18, Nov. 1899	17, Nov.		4	
Brockharde, Tillie	25, Sept 1891		9m	4	
Brockhoff, Johan	30, Nov. 1895	30, Nov.	76	5	
Brockhoff, Johan A.	28, Aug. 1899	27, Aug.		4	
Brockland, Henry	6, Mar. 1895		22	5	
Brockland, Joseph	7, Aug. 1901		26	8	
Brockman, G.	14, Oct. 1901		89	5	
Brockman, Herman	27, Aug. 1891		57	1	
Brockman, Richard	21, Mar. 1893		79	5	
Brockmann, Catharine	24, Sept 1894		67	5	
Brockmann, Charles	19, Dec. 1890		32	1	
Brockmann, Emilie	7, Sept 1899	6, Sept	30- 5m	5	
Brockmann, Frank	28, Mar. 1901		50	8	
Brockmann, Fritz	19, Mar. 1890			1	
Brockmann, Gilbert	23, Aug. 1887		39	1	
Brockmann, H.	16, Sept 1895	14, Sept	63	5	
Brockmann, Henry T.	25, Sept 1891		31- 6m	4	
Brockmann, Herman Heinrich	23, Dec. 1899	21, Dec.	73- 3m-10d	5	
Brockmann, Johanna L.W.	11, Nov. 1892		36	4	
Brockmann, John H.	26, Aug. 1891		44	2	
Brockmann, Kate	10, Nov. 1896	8, Nov.	39	4	
Brockmann, Maria	6, July 1897	3, July	69- 9m	5	
Brockmeier, Fanny G.	31, Jan. 1896	29, Jan.	75-10m	5	
Brockmeier, Fritz	9, 10, Apr. 1894	8, Apr.	48	5	
Brockmeier, H.	30, Oct. 1896	29, Oct.	55- 5m	5	
Brockmeier, Henry	29, Aug. 1891		67	4	
Brockmeyer, Charles	4, July 1891		7	4	
Brockschmidt, Amelia	10, June 1891		19	4	
Brockschmidt, Anna	13, May 1901		78	8	
Brockschmidt, Wilhelmina	21, Jan. 1901			8	

Name ****	Notice Date ****** ****	Death Date ***** ****	Age ***	Page ****	Maiden Name ****** ****
Brode, Henry	26, June 1891		39	4	
Broderick, Ella	25, Sept 1888		30	1	
Broderick, Mamie	21, Aug. 1890		20	1	
Broderick, Mary B.	20, Feb. 1895		58	5	
Brodhag, Wilhelmine	15, May 1889		27	1	
Broegel, Anna	1, July 1901		8	8	
Broenner, Rosa	19, Nov. 1900		37	8	
Broenning, Maximillian	19, Apr. 1898	18, Apr.	48	5	
Broermann, Bernard	21, Apr. 1892		65	5	
Broermann, Henry	10, Dec. 1892		66	5	
Broesamle, Fred.	15, May 1901		43	8	
Brogelmann, Friedrich	26, Sept 1898	24, Sept	70- 5m- 8d	4	
Broiles, Phyllis	23, May 1895		57	5	
Brokamp, Elisabeth	18, Nov. 1891		71	4	
Brokamp, Fred.	30, Apr. 1901		14	8	
Brokamp, George	24, Apr. 1895		54	5	
Brokamp, Kate	2, Aug. 1900		40	8	
Brokate, Emma	16, Oct. 1895	14, Oct.	37	5	Schreick
Brokus, Mary	16, July 1891		1m	4	
Brommer, George	15, Apr. 1888		9d	5	
Bromoitsch, Henry	20, July 1887		55	1	
Bronetrup, Lina	7, Mar. 1898	5, Mar.	16- 4m	5	
Bronner, Cornelia	16, June 1893		13d	5	
Bronson, Sabina	28, Aug. 1901		51	8	
Bronston, Rose	10, Sept 1887		48	2	
Bronstrup, Amelia	29, Aug. 1901		35	8	
Bronstrup, H.R.	29, Oct. 1888		75	1	
Bronstrup, Wilhelm	7, Apr. 1896	5, Apr.	24- 9m	5	
Brood, Everett R.	30, May 1895		47	5	
Brookers, Elmer	26, Jan. 1894		3w	5	
Brooks, Daniel	20, July 1901		55	8	
Brooks, Doc.	23, Apr. 1895		22	5	
Brooks, G.	24, Sept 1888		55	1	
Brooks, George	26, Feb. 1901		54	8	
Brooks, Ruth	24, Apr. 1901		3m	8	
Brophil, William	13, Nov. 1900		39	8	
Brophy, John L.	4, June 1895		20	5	
Brose, William Albert	14, Feb. 1890		19	1	
Brosemer, Ben	31, July 1900		2	5	
Brosman,	25, Feb. 1891		1d	4	
Brosmann, Joseph E.	27, Feb. 1894		1m	5	
Brossart, Charles T.	14, Nov. 1899	13, Nov.	64- 1m	4	
Brossart, Kasper	9, Oct. 1889		26- 6m	1	
Broster, Robert	2, June 1892		5m	5	
Brotherton, Anna	28, July 1888		61	1	
Browing, Richard (Rev)	2, Feb. 1888		50	4	
Brown,	4, July 1887		2w	1	
Brown, Adolph L.	10, Apr. 1901			8	
Brown, Annie M.	5, Sept 1901		24	8	
Brown, Caroline	6, June 1895		63	5	
Brown, Charles	16, Feb. 1901		38	8	
Brown, Charlotte	14, May 1896	13, May	55	5	
Brown, Cornelia	5, Dec. 1900		74	8	
Brown, Della	2, May 1895		2m	5	
Brown, Edward	23, Oct. 1900		25	8	
Brown, Ellen	27, July 1892		5m	5	
Brown, Eva	30, Apr. 1901		42	8	
Brown, Folding	17, Dec. 1900		67	8	
Brown, George	14, Aug. 1900		26	5	
Brown, Hazel	1, Aug. 1888		5m	2	
Brown, J.S.	10, July 1901		48	5	
Brown, James	27, Jan. 1898	26, Jan.	64	5	
Brown, John	20, June 1901		49	8	
Brown, Joseph	8, Dec. 1900		59	8	
Brown, Larus	2, Aug. 1888		45	2	
Brown, Lillian A.	1, Feb. 1900			5	Wolf
Brown, Louisa	24, Dec. 1900		12	8	
Brown, M.	6, Feb. 1901		80	8	
Brown, Margaretha	27, Mar. 1899	26, Mar.		4	Mundorff
Brown, Marnus	2, Aug. 1887		65	1	
Brown, Mary	28, Nov. 1900			8	

Name	Notice Date	Death Date	Age	Page	Maiden Name
****	****** ****	***** ****	***	****	****** ****
Brown, Max	4, Dec. 1900		78	8	
Brown, Peter	3, Apr. 1901		58	8	
Brown, R.	26, Dec. 1900		11d	8	
Brown, Raymond	12, May 1895		27	5	
Brown, Robert E.	26, July 1887		9m	1	
Brown, Stella	29, Sept 1900		21	8	
Brown, Walter	4, Apr. 1888		25	1	
Browne, Sam.	10, Apr. 1888		40	4	
Browning, Robert	31, Oct. 1900		43	8	
Broxtermann, Ed.	19, Aug. 1901		2	8	
Broß, George	19, Apr. 1895		8	5	
Brubacker, Homer	23, May 1894		1m	5	
Bruch, Emil	1, Dec. 1892		48	5	
Bruchard, Eva	10, Dec. 1900		65	8	
Brucker, Adolphena	23, Sept 1887		42	2	
Brucker, Bernard	27, July 1887		17m	1	
Brucker, Charles	1, Sept 1888		3	1	
Brucker, Eduard	30, Apr. 1892	29, Apr.	4-11m- 7d	5	
Brucker, Elisabeth	15, Oct. 1889		86	1	
Brucker, John G.	27, Oct. 1888		53	1	
Bruckman, Henry	25, Apr. 1901		37	8	
Bruckmann, Anna	18, Dec. 1891		5m	2	
Bruckmann, Friedrich	15, May 1897	14, May	66	4	
Bruckmann, Michael	11, Apr. 1890		26	1	
Bruckmann, Philipp	22, Mar. 1895		41	5	
Bruckmann, Sophie	9, Dec. 1896	6, Dec.	28-11m	5	Kukelhau
Bruder, Georg	22, Aug. 1899	19, Aug.	76- 4m	5	
Brueckmann, Johan C.	14, Aug. 1887	12, Aug.	57-11m-25d	5	
Bruecknmayer, Cornelia	21, Mar. 1901			8	
Brueggemann, Gottfrieda	7, Aug. 1891		2	4	
Brueggemann, Mary A.	19, May 1894		72	5	
Bruening, Catharina A.	10, Apr. 1899	9, Apr.	41- 1m	5	Hauger
Bruesch, Ella	28, June 1895		5m	5	
Bruestle, R.G.	19, May 1897	18, May	31	5	
Bruetting, Margaretha	21, Apr. 1898	19, Apr.	82- -16d	5	Burkard
Brugger, Louis	30, May 1901		55	8	
Bruhe, Anna	27, Sept 1890		60	1	
Bruhl, Margaret	24, Sept 1888		55	1	
Brummer, Edna	12, Aug. 1901		5	8	
Brummer, Fred.	8, Mar. 1890		22m	1	
Brune, Bernard J.	12, Aug. 1887		9d	1	
Brune, Elisabeth	26, Aug. 1891		59	2	
Brune, Henrietta	19, July 1893		9m	5	
Brune, J.B.	3, Feb. 1897	2, Feb.	60	5	
Brune, Johan Bernard	2, Feb. 1897	1, Feb.	80	5	
Brune, Joseph	17, May 1899	16, May	43- 5m-16d	5	
Brune, Marie A.	12, Feb. 1901		80	8	
Brune, Mary	15, Apr. 1888		24	5	
Brunemann, John C.	6, Mar. 1895		60	5	
Bruner, Anna	10, June 1901		24	8	
Bruner, John	18, Mar. 1890		58	1	
Bruning, Henry Herman	9, Mar. 1896	6, Mar.	68	5	
Brunk, Leo	2, July 1891		6m	4	
Brunnemann, Marie	10, May 1895		9m	5	
Brunner, Eva	3, July 1901		2	8	
Brunner, Howard	26, July 1895		4	5	
Brunner, Joseph	11, July 1895		27	5	
Bruno, Louis	8, Mar. 1894		20	5	
Bruns, Anna	21, Nov. 1894		27	5	
Bruns, Anna M.	18, Apr. 1893		46	5	
Bruns, Carolina	31, Jan. 1898	28, Jan.		5	Teipe
Bruns, Casper	21, Dec. 1892		66	5	
Bruns, Christian	9, Feb. 1897	7, Feb.	21- 7m	5	
Bruns, H.H.	23, Dec. 1893		80	5	
Bruns, Henry	9, Dec. 1896	8, Dec.	49- 9m	5	
Bruns, Katharine	27, Sept 1900		85	8	
Bruns, Lambert	9, June 1892		57	5	
Bruns, Ludwig	21, July 1887		46	1	
Brunsbach, John H.	24, Dec. 1892		1m	5	
Brunsbach, Joseph	29, Dec. 1896	28, Dec.	12- 2m	5	
Brunsh, Clara	11, July 1887		8m	1	

Name ****	Notice Date ****** ****	Death Date ***** ****	Age ***	Page ****	Maiden Name ****** ****
Brunsmann, Elisabeth	2, Sept 1898	31, Aug.	68	4	
Brunsmann, Harriet	23, Nov. 1900		28	8	
Brunsmann, Hattie	20, July 1896	18, July	18-10m	5	
Brunsmann, J.H.	16, May 1894		64	5	
Brunsmann, Maria L.	3, May 1897	2, May	62	5	
Brunswick, Wilhelmine	20, Feb. 1897		80- 3m	5	Bohne
Brunte, Carrie	16, Jan. 1893		1	5	
Bruntlaus, Louis Andrew	28, Jan. 1896	27, Jan.	1- 1m	5	
Bruschie, Catharine M.	6, Mar. 1895		6m	5	
Brusenne, Henry	29, July 1888		11m	1	
Bruske, Frank	18, Jan. 1894		38	5	
Brusnan, Thom.	16, Mar. 1888		26	1	
Brusse, Martin	17, Feb. 1892		72	5	
Brutsche, Fred.	7, Oct. 1893		69	5	
Bryant, Willis	4, June 1901		53	8	
Bryce, Tennice	25, July 1888		23	4	
Bryler, John	20, Sept 1887		51	1	
Bräuchle, Christ.	7, Jan. 1888		43	1	
Brönstrup, G.	16, Oct. 1895	14, Oct.	35- - 2d	5	
Brörmann, Bernard	6, Aug. 1896	5, Aug.	40	5	
Brückner, Anna M.	23, Aug. 1899	22, Aug.	78- 2m	5	Bruch
Brüggemann, Herman	18, Aug. 1900		39	8	
Brünemann, Friedrich	1, Aug. 1896	31, July	59- 1m	5	
Brünich, Nellie	11, Dec. 1891		5	4	
Brüning, Katharine	7, Dec. 1887		79	1	
Brütting, Augustine	8, July 1889	7, July	3m	1	
Buarmann, Clara Elisa	20, Apr. 1898	19, Apr.	74- 2m	4	Buermeier
Buch, Joseph A.	3, May 1893		56	5	
Buchanan, Joseph	12, Nov. 1887		49	1	
Buchanan, Katie	28, Mar. 1901		33	8	
Buchanan, Laura	19, July 1887		14m	1	
Buchanan, Lillie	21, Feb. 1888		7- 8m	1	
Buchanan, Margaret	25, Oct. 1900		59	8	
Buchelmann, J.	25, Jan. 1888		2	1	
Bucher, Franz	27, May 1889		32	1	
Bucher, John	27, Aug. 1890		74	1	
Bucher, Theodore	15, Sept 1892		45	5	
Buchheit, E.	11, Dec. 1888		4	1	
Buchholz, Carl	17, Jan. 1899	14, Jan.	67	5	
Buchholz, George F.	9, Mar. 1895		32	5	
Buchholz, Josephine	22, Dec. 1893		73	5	
Buchholz, Theresia	29, Apr. 1898	28, Apr.	29	5	
Buchmann, Flora E.	5, Dec. 1891		2m	4	
Buchmann, Nich.	2, Oct. 1900		77	8	
Buchmann, Richard	23, July 1887		6m	1	
Buchmann, William	23, July 1887		16m	1	
Buchner, Simon	1, Sept 1891		52	4	
Buchriegel, John	28, Mar. 1890		12	1	
Buchwald, Charles	7, Mar. 1901		60	8	
Buck, August	15, 16, Oct. 1888	13, Oct.	46	4	
Buck, Elisabeth	8, Jan. 1901		69	8	
Buck, Henry	5, Jan. 1888		69	1	
Buck, Rebeka	28, Apr. 1890		3	1	
Buck, Regina	18, Oct. 1894		48	5	
Buck, Walter J.	19, July 1893		3m	5	
Buck, Wilhelm F.	13, Jan. 1896	12, Jan.	38- 7m	5	
Buckel, Daniel	30, Dec. 1891		23	4	
Buckel, Peter	22, July 1901		12	8	
Buckenberger, Louis H.	21, Jan. 1901		40	8	
Bucker, Eugene	26, Dec. 1900		71	8	
Buckheart, Mary	12, Feb. 1891		39	4	
Buckle, John George	4, Nov. 1887		35	1	
Buckles, Frank M.	12, Sept 1901		65	5	
Buckley, E.	18, Feb. 1888		67	1	
Buckley, Julia	15, Nov. 1887		24	4	
Buckley, Katharine	21, Apr. 1888		58	1	
Buckman, Thomas	23, June 1888		5m	1	
Buckner, Jake	8, Apr. 1889		50	1	
Buckner, Jane	5, May 1892		56	5	
Buckner, M.	25, Feb. 1901		67	8	
Buckner, William	20, Apr. 1895		56	5	

Name	Notice Date	Death Date	Age	Page	Maiden Name
****	****** ****	***** ****	***	****	****** ****
Budd, Jesse	26, Feb. 1891		10	4	
Budde, Edward	25, Apr. 1901		1	8	
Budde, Fred.	16, May 1891		36	2	
Budde, Maria Elisa	8, Jan. 1897	7, Jan.	70- 4m	5	Steffen
Budde, Mary A.	30, Dec. 1891		67	4	
Buddeke, Joseph G.	27, Mar. 1895		53	5	
Buddeke, Mary K.	4, July 1891		13m	4	
Buddeke, Walter	15, Nov. 1894		3m	5	
Buddelmann, Katie	23, Jan. 1899	21, Jan.	44- 3m	5	Bode
Bude, Lizzie	29, Dec. 1891		6	4	
Budke, Ernst	1, Aug. 1887		56	1	
Budke, Kate	30, Aug. 1888		23	1	
Budke, Wilhelm Friedrich	19, Sept 1896	16, Sept	72- 8m- 2d	5	
Bue, Lizzie	15, May 1895		22	5	
Buebler, Mary	11, Nov. 1891		52	1	
Bueche, Julia Catharina	27, Nov. 1899	25, Nov.	17-10m	5	
Bueche, Maria	3, Feb. 1900	2, Feb.	81- 2m	5	
Buecker, Ernst	25, 27, Apr. 1896	24, Apr.	76- 8m	5	
Buecker, Wilhelmina J.	11, July 1893		24	5	
Bueckle, Christina	5, Mar. 1897	4, Mar.	69- 5m	5	Schaible
Bueckner, Charles	4, June 1892	3, June	54	5	
Buehler, Maria	25, Feb. 1896	23, Feb.	10	5	
Buehren, Charles	15, June 1894		25	5	
Buehrle, Henry	31, July 1894		20	5	
Buehrwein, Walter W.	10, May 1888		2	1	
Bueltee, M.	22, Dec. 1887		2- 6m	4	
Bueltel, Charles	18, July 1895		22	5	
Bueltel, Herman	23, Aug. 1887		4m	1	
Bueltel, John B.	27, Mar. 1895		70	5	
Bueltman, Henry	28, Dec. 1888		15	1	
Buening, Alice Elizabeth	11, May 1899	9, May	42	4	Wills
Buenker, Bernard Gerhard	24, Nov. 1891		5d	4	
Buerck, Henry	12, July 1889			1	
Buerckle, E.W.	11, Mar. 1896	10, Mar.	55	5	
Buerger, Mat. J.	11, Oct. 1900		4	8	
Buerk, Francisca	9, Apr. 1891		74	4	
Buermann, M.	20, Apr. 1888		68- 6m	4	
Buescher, Leo	6, Dec. 1900		2	8	
Buesmann, Otilla	28, Jan. 1893		14d	5	
Buettinger, Adam	5, Nov. 1900		70	8	
Buettinger, Esther	22, Mar. 1901		23d	8	
Buettner, Clara A.	14, Feb. 1891		9m	4	
Buettner, Henriette	29, Dec. 1891		5	4	
Buffington, Hannah	25, May 1901		27	8	
Bugganer, Dominick	4, Jan. 1901		49	5	
Buhlmann, Katharine	8, Sept 1897	6, Sept	61- 1m	5	
Buhr, Regina	15, Jan. 1901		84	8	
Buhr, W.	8, Sept 1900		31	5	
Buhr, Walter H.	15, Nov. 1893		1m	5	
Buhrlage, Carrie Louise	27, Feb. 1888		27	4	
Buhrmann, Gerhard L.	12, May 1891		73	1	
Buhrmann, Hildegard	26, Jan. 1893		11d	5	
Buler, Pearle	22, Mar. 1889		2	1	
Bulger, Gooham	22, May 1891		40	1	
Bullerdick, Henry	17, Oct. 1894		7m	5	
Bullerdieck, Elizabeth	22, Oct. 1900		65	8	
Bullitt, George	13, Feb. 1901		44	8	
Bulmer, John H.	15, July 1901		1	8	
Bultemeyer, B.	27, Dec. 1888		1	2	
Bulzer, August	13, Sept 1889		53	1	
Bumb, Jak.	20, Feb. 1889		75	1	
Bunch, Joseph	20, Oct. 1887		2d	1	
Bunche, August	15, Apr. 1892		63	5	
Bund, Charles	10, Oct. 1891		3m	4	
Bund, Louis	14, Jan. 1892		31	1	
Bungenstock, Karl	5, Apr. 1899	3, Apr.	43- 8m	4	
Bunke, Aloysius	18, Feb. 1890		2- 3m	2	
Bunker, Anna	16, Aug. 1887		18m	1	
Bunker, Anna Maria	27, Mar. 1900	26, Mar.	62- 2m	5	Dodt
Bunker, Anna Maria Theresia	7, Aug. 1897	5, Aug.	66- 7m	4	Kobbe
Bunker, George	30, Nov. 1899	28, Nov.	36	5	

Name ****	Notice Date ****** ****	Death Date ***** ****	Age ***	Page ****	Maiden Name ****** ****
Bunker, Harry	23, Aug. 1887		3m	1	
Bunker, Joseph P.	24, Dec. 1900		1m	8	
Bunker, Kate	26, July 1895		78	5	
Bunnemeyer, Aloysius B.	5, Apr. 1895		14	5	
Buns, Elisabeth	28, Mar. 1898	25, Mar.	70- 2m	5	Bansing
Buns, Friedrich Wilhelm	3, Feb. 1896	31, Jan.	53- 9m	5	
Buns, Heinrich	4, Apr. 1899	1, Apr.	55- 8m	5	
Buns, Sophia	23, Sept 1891		64	4	
Bunselmeier, Anna	23, June 1897	22, June	58- 8m	5	Heins
Bunte, Clarence	15, Feb. 1900	14, Feb.	1- - 7d	5	
Bunthoff, Bernhard	20, July 1899	19, July	15- 3m	5	
Bunting, Barbara	5, Sept 1894		29d	5	
Buob, Anna	14, Sept 1893		66	5	
Burbacher, George	28, Mar. 1898	26, Mar.	34-11m	5	
Burbacher, Robert	28, June 1893		5m	5	
Burch, Ellen M.	14, Nov. 1893		8	5	
Burch, Kate	22, July 1887		44	1	
Burch, Mary E.	20, Sept 1887		1	1	
Burchard, Charles G.	14, Sept 1887		3	1	
Burchard, Gustav	11, June 1895		38	5	
Burchard, Henry	14, Mar. 1896	12, Mar.	67- 6m	5	
Burchill, Mary	15, Jan. 1901		80	8	
Burck, Catharina	5, July 1890		66	1	
Burck, Nora	11, Jan. 1888		7	4	
Burckey, Sarah	9, Sept 1900		45	5	
Burckhard, Frank	27, Dec. 1888		2	2	
Burckhardt, Carrie	25, May 1897	24, May	28	5	Cahn
Burckhardt, Frank	27, Mar. 1901		76	8	
Burckhardt, William	9, July 1895		7m	5	
Burden, Maggie	25, June 1901		34	8	
Burdick, B.	6, Mar. 1901		68	5	
Burdick, John	19, Aug. 1901		40	8	
Burdick, William	19, June 1895		11m	5	
Burdsal, Charles A.	25, Oct. 1887		19- -21d	1	
Burduck, Bernard	12, Nov. 1890	11, Nov.		1	
Bure, C.	20, Apr. 1896	18, Apr.	36-10m	5	
Bures, Mary	17, Apr. 1901		73	8	
Burg, Barbara	29, Nov. 1893		81	5	
Burg, Louisa	9, Jan. 1899	8, Jan.	62- 4m-13d	5	Schönefeld
Burg, Margaret	9, Sept 1891		78	4	
Burg, Ottilie	24, July 1901		70	8	
Burger, Albert L.	19, Sept 1891		4	4	
Burger, Cletus	1, Nov. 1887		71- 7m	1	
Burger, Emma	16, Mar. 1895		56	5	
Burger, Joseph	8, May 1901		61	8	
Burger, Katharina	29, Nov. 1895	28, Nov.	44-10m-12d	5	
Burger, Laura E.	1, Feb. 1894		2	5	
Burger, Mamy	4, June 1889		1	1	
Burger, Sophia	27, Nov. 1897	25, Nov.	64- 2m	4	Lindauer
Burger, Valentin	13, Oct. 1900		69	8	
Burges, Laura	14, Mar. 1891		86	4	
Burgeß, G.G.	14, Sept 1901		59	1	
Burggraf, Lucas	11, Apr. 1893		60	5	
Burghardt, Cecilia	8, Nov. 1897	7, Nov.	56	4	
Burghardt, Dorothea	4, May 1896	3, May	66-11m	5	Lebening
Burgheim, Agnes	14, Nov. 1900		43	8	
Burgheim, Rudolph	19, July 1893	18, July	51	5	
Burgraf, Eliza	26, Feb. 1895		65	5	
Burhen, Reinhard	18, Oct. 1897	17, Oct.	62- -18d	5	
Burk, John	16, Oct. 1889		62	1	
Burk, Maria	1, Oct. 1890		83	1	
Burkardt, Elizabeth	8, July 1891		35	4	
Burkardt, Mary	25, Jan. 1901		43	8	
Burkart, Luise	27, June 1894	27, June	44- 3m	5	
Burke, Ann	8, Apr. 1901		75	8	
Burke, Bridget	18, July 1891		49	1	
Burke, Catharine	6, July 1893		30	5	
Burke, Edmund	8, Nov. 1887		3m	1	
Burke, Edward	20, Aug. 1901		67	8	
Burke, Elisabeth	9, Dec. 1891		26	2	
Burke, James	8, Oct. 1891		2	4	

Name ****	Notice Date ****** ****	Death Date ***** ****	Age ***	Page ****	Maiden Name ****** ****
Burke, James F.	7, Sept 1894		65	5	
Burke, Jennie	14, Apr. 1891		36	4	
Burke, Jennie	5, Dec. 1900		18	8	
Burke, Juliet	11, Mar. 1891		22	4	
Burke, Katharine	25, July 1888		58	4	
Burke, Katie	13, Aug. 1901		42	8	
Burke, Maria	10, Mar. 1895		5m	5	
Burke, Mary	18, June 1891		50	4	
Burke, Michael	28, Apr. 1888		61	1	
Burke, Michael V.	17, Oct. 1900		56	8	
Burke, Robert	1, July 1891		19m	1	
Burke, Thomas C.	22, July 1887		8m	1	
Burke, Thomas F.	16, Nov. 1900		45	8	
Burkhard, John A.	18, Feb. 1890		24	2	
Burkhard, Joseph	14, Sept 1893		62	5	
Burkhard, Stella	16, Mar. 1889		2	1	
Burkhardt, Caroline	15, Nov. 1894		46	5	
Burkhardt, Edward	12, June 1891		5m	4	
Burkhardt, Margaret	14, Aug. 1888		66	1	
Burkhauser, Conrad	24, May 1892		6d	5	
Burkhold, Willie	14, Dec. 1900		10	8	
Burlage, Gertie	11, July 1887		5m	1	
Burling, Lulu	16, Aug. 1894		8	5	
Burmann, Catharine	19, Sept 1896	18, Sept	81- - 3d	5	
Burmann, Maria Anna	25, Mar. 1899	23, Mar.	72	5	Brandhove
Burnett, Elizabeth J.	14, Feb. 1901		27	8	
Burnett, Roxand	12, Mar. 1901		85	8	
Burney, Agnes	29, Sept 1887		9m	4	
Burns, Arthur	28, July 1887		16	1	
Burns, Bridget	11, Aug. 1887		28	1	
Burns, G.	27, Aug. 1889		7	1	
Burns, Kate	19, June 1889			1	
Burns, Katie	20, Oct. 1887		5w	1	
Burns, Maggie	9, Aug. 1900		40	8	
Burns, Thomas	14, Aug. 1887		49	1	
Burns, Thomas	14, Jan. 1893		5	5	
Burns, Thomas	5, May 1895		34	5	
Burr, Bessie	3, Mar. 1894		26	5	
Burr, Edna Lona	14, 15, Sept 1900		1- 6m	5	
Burrichter, Josephine	19, June 1896	18, June	52	5	Schoppe
Burrmann, Bernard	5, Feb. 1901		83	8	
Burst, Alma	6, Mar. 1894		9m	5	
Burtaus, Sarah	29, June 1892		76	5	
Burton, Mary	22, Oct. 1900		2m	8	
Burwinkel, Frank	2, Aug. 1887		1- 6m	1	
Busam, John	5, Oct. 1888		2	1	
Busam, John	30, Apr. 1901		29	8	
Busam, Magdalena	18, Aug. 1896	17, Aug.	45-10m	5	Krans
Busam, W.	26, Jan. 1893		28	5	
Busch, Anna M.	8, Dec. 1891		83	4	
Busch, C.	24, July 1901		78	8	
Busch, Emil	24, Oct. 1891		45	4	
Busch, Ernst August	8, Nov. 1897	6, Nov.	61	4	
Busch, Frank	28, June 1899	27, June	50- 2m	4	
Busch, Friedrich	29, May 1889		21	1	
Busch, H. Ferdinand	23, Oct. 1897	22, Oct.	37	4	
Busch, Henry	17, Mar. 1891		50	4	
Busch, Jakob	16, Apr. 1891		4	4	
Busch, Joseph W.	19, Oct. 1894		63	5	
Busch, Susie	21, Apr. 1891		6w	4	
Busch, Walburga Lutz	21, Aug. 1896	20, Aug.	70- 6m	5	Schmit
Busch, Wilhelm	28, Oct. 1893		11m	5	
Busche, Adolph	14, Feb. 1901		8m	8	
Busche, W.	10, Sept 1895	9, Sept	28- 2m	5	
Buscher, Kate	22, June 1889		2	1	
Buschle, Charles R.	6, Jan. 1899	4, Jan.	54- 4m	4	
Buschle, Joseph	1, June 1901		5	8	
Buschle, Nicholas	15, July 1893		32	5	
Buschmiller, Bernardina	23, Dec. 1898	21, Dec.	54- 9m	5	Schmidt
Buse, George	6, Aug. 1890		18	1	
Buse, Louis	9, Dec. 1893		45	5	

Name	Notice Date	Death Date	Age	Page	Maiden Name
****	****** ****	***** ****	***	****	****** ****
Bush, Flora	7, Mar. 1901		1	8	
Bush, Thornton	1, Sept 1887		44	1	
Bushelman, William	30, Nov. 1887		61	4	
Busker, Maria	9, Dec. 1893		69	5	
Busse, Catharine	7, May 1891		74	4	
Busse, Charles	28, June 1895		39	5	
Busse, Conrad	16, Mar. 1895		73	5	
Busse, Fred. C.	27, May 1899	26, May	60- 4m	4	
Busse, Sophia	19, Mar. 1890		74	1	
Busse, William	15, Sept 1888		27	2	
Bussieck, Kate	11, Apr. 1901		43	8	
Busten, Bernard	16, Feb. 1894		17m	5	
Buten, Anton	4, Jan. 1898	2, Jan.	54- 8m	5	
Buthen, Henry	16, Aug. 1887		31	1	
Butke, John H.	3, Nov. 1891		72	4	
Butler, David	4, July 1887		23	1	
Butler, John	5, Sept 1900		35	5	
Butler, Julia	4, Sept 1891		57	4	
Butler, Kate	21, June 1888		25	1	
Butler, Mary	22, June 1901		57	8	
Butler, Sam.	23, Apr. 1895		53	5	
Butler, William	27, Sept 1889		15m	1	
Buttemeyer, Elizabeth	17, Jan. 1894		67	5	
Butter, Konrad	18, June 1895		60	5	
Butterfan, Philip	15, July 1891		32	1	
Butz, Barbara	13, Jan. 1896	10, Jan.	51- 6m- 7d	5	Jochers
Butz, William	28, Feb. 1890		42	1	
Buxer, Mary	30, Dec. 1890		55	4	
Buß, Margaret	15, July 1893		48	5	
Bußmann, Henry W.	30, Sept 1888		18	4	
Bußmann, Lizzie	31, Dec. 1888		7w	1	
Bußmann, Minnie	12, Jan. 1893		1d	5	
Byas, Lindsey	25, July 1901		36	8	
Bybee, Edna	21, Mar. 1901		7w	8	
Byers, Charles	23, Mar. 1901		84	8	
Byrard, Suluth E.	29, Dec. 1900		16	8	
Byrne, Honora	10, Apr. 1895		63	5	
Byrne, John J.	30, Nov. 1900		40	8	
Byrne, Julia	8, May 1901		81	8	
Byrne, Katie	10, June 1901		47	8	
Byrne, Mary	10, Aug. 1887		2- 6m	1	
Byrne, Stephen	4, Feb. 1888		63	4	
Byrnes, Margaret	11, Aug. 1900		34	8	
Byron, Rebecca	8, Dec. 1891		71	4	
Bäckler, John	29, Sept 1893		52	5	
Bär, Emma	18, Oct. 1895	17, Oct.	39	5	
Bäuerlein, Barbara	25, Mar. 1899	24, Mar.	69- 5m	5	
Böbinger, Maria	20, Dec. 1895	19, Dec.		5	Knauber
Böbinger, Regina	24, Apr. 1889		63	1	
Böcker, Wilhelm	2, Sept 1890		67	1	
Böckle, Georg	26, Mar. 1896	24, Mar.	39- 6m	5	
Böckmann, Emma	28, Mar. 1889		20	1	
Böckmann, Katharina	20, Feb. 1897	18, Feb.	54- 6m	5	Grapperhaus
Böhm, Charles	8, Feb. 1889		44	1	
Böhm, Ernestina	2, Sept 1898	1, Sept	80- 5m-16d	4	
Böhm, Leo	1, Sept 1891		5w	4	
Böhm, Oscar	22, June 1889		18m	1	
Böhm, Rosa	10, May 1889		60	1	
Böhme, Flora	14, Sept 1889	13, Dec.	10	4	
Böhmer, Charlotte	10, Jan. 1898	8, Jan.	60- 4m	5	Höveler
Böhmer, Katharina	30, Aug. 1895	29, Aug.	75	5	
Böhmer, Mary	11, Mar. 1890		58	1	
Böhn, J.	14, Jan. 1889		81	1	
Bölerick, Emma	23, Mar. 1895		34	5	
Bölscher, Gerhard Heinrich	6, Feb. 1899	5, Feb.	65	4	
Bömmel, John	11, Apr. 1895		41	5	
Böniker, Christ	4, July 1891		60	4	
Böning, J.	11, Nov. 1892		1	4	
Börger, Fr. C.	22, June 1889		77	1	
Börger, Henry Joseph	1, Sept 1891		41	4	
Börger, Maria	22, Sept 1899	21, Sept	56- 7m	5	Steineman

Name ****	Notice Date ****** ****	Death Date ***** ****	Age ***	Page ****	Maiden Name ****** ****
Böse, Albert	18, July 1890	17, July	79- 9m	1	
Böwer, Mary E.	16, May 1893		33	5	
Büche, Leopoldina	10, Dec. 1895	8, Dec.	67- 9m	5	
Büchel, Theresa	9, Aug. 1894		15- 8m	5	
Bücher, Frank	27, Jan. 1891		1	4	
Büchle, Franz Xaver	22, Mar. 1897	20, Mar.	80- 8m	5	
Bücker, Henry	4, May 1893		57	5	
Bügel, M. Emma	25, Sept 1900		18d	5	
Bühler, Anna S.	5, Aug. 1887		10	1	
Bühler, Elisabeth	10, Mar. 1899	9, Mar.	37- 1m	5	Grammer
Bührmann, Margaretha	3, Apr. 1899	2, Apr.	82	5	
Bültel, Philomena	22, June 1889		5m	1	
Büncker, Elisabeth	13, Feb. 1897	11, Feb.		5	Torner
Büning, Anton	5, May 1897	4, May	33-11m	5	
Bürck, Martin	22, Oct. 1891		39	1	
Bürger, Jakob	15, Dec. 1899	13, Dec.	82- 3m	5	
Bürger, Johan	24, Aug. 1898	23, Aug.	57	5	
Bürkel, Charles	8, Mar. 1889		35	1	
Bürkle, Joseph	2, Apr. 1891		66	4	
Bürkle, Joseph F.	28, Jan. 1889		4	1	
Bürkle, Martin	18, Jan. 1896	17, Jan.	77- 6m	5	
Büscher, Gerhard Heinrich	23, Nov. 1896	22, Nov.	82	5	
Büscher, Maria	27, Dec. 1893		62	5	
Büttner, Bernard	3, Aug. 1893		2m	5	
Caatmann, Anna B.	18, Oct. 1895	16, Oct.		5	
Cabot, John A.	18, Nov. 1891		2m	4	
Cadee, Albert	5, Nov. 1897	3, Nov.	57- -12d	5	
Cady, Charles	8, Nov. 1887		4m- 5d	1	
Cagney, James	25, Mar. 1901		34	8	
Cahill, Ann	23, Aug. 1901		80	8	
Cahill, Mary F.	23, July 1887		19m	1	
Cahill, W.R.	15, Dec. 1900		40	8	
Cahn, Herman	7, Aug. 1900		45	8	
Cahn, Ruth	20, Dec. 1893		1	5	
Cahro, Louis	21, Oct. 1887		1- 3m	1	
Cain, Dean	9, June 1892		3m	5	
Cain, Julia	5, Sept 1900		36	5	
Cair, Hattie	30, Aug. 1900		34	5	
Caldwell, Betsy	9, May 1895		78	5	
Caldwell, William	5, Mar. 1901		19	5	
Caldwell, William L.	26, Sept 1887		37	1	
Caldwell, William T.	18, Oct. 1900		45	8	
Callahan, Catharine	5, Nov. 1900		67	8	
Callahan, James	27, Oct. 1900		68	8	
Callahan, Laura	28, May 1901		35	8	
Callahan, Natalie	14, Jan. 1901		26	8	
Callahan, Patrick	10, Mar. 1888		60	1	
Callahan, Robert	19, Aug. 1901		16	8	
Callahan, Robert C.	6, June 1888		45	1	
Callahan, William	30, May 1901		36	8	
Calleghan, John	13, July 1887		45	1	
Callis, Albrecht	24, Apr. 1896			5	
Callmann, Joseph	31, Aug. 1889		6- 5m	1	
Calvin, Anna	8, Oct. 1901		25	1	
Cameron, Eliza St.	22, Oct. 1900		80	8	
Cameron, John	10, May 1895		44	5	
Camilla, (Sr.)	14, Dec. 1900		32	8	
Campaert, Johanna L.	2, July 1895		3m	5	
Campbell, Benjamin	14, Oct. 1901		65	5	
Campbell, Catharine	2, May 1901		41	8	
Campbell, Clara	28, Mar. 1888		3- 6m	1	
Campbell, Grace M.	2, May 1895		7m	5	
Campbell, Harry	14, Oct. 1901		28	5	
Campbell, James	14, Sept 1901		6m	1	
Campbell, John	5, Jan. 1901		48	8	
Campbell, Mary	8, Feb. 1901		74	8	
Campbell, Ursula	12, June 1901		3m	8	
Canady, Julian A.	2, Aug. 1901		1	8	
Canary, Catharine	31, Jan. 1901		44	8	
Cann, Bernard	20, Feb. 1897	19, Feb.	62	5	

Name ****	Notice Date ****** ****	Death Date ***** ****	Age ***	Page ****	Maiden Name ****** ****
Cannon, E. (Mrs)	13, Jan. 1888		78	1	
Capelle, Ludwig	2, June 1898	1, June	74-10m	4	
Capello, Emma	30, Nov. 1887		18	4	
Capp, George	16, Sept 1891		40	4	
Cappel, Carl	15, June 1901		3d	8	
Cappel, Heinrich	3, Aug. 1897	2, Aug.	70- 6m	5	
Cappel, Mary	20, Feb. 1901		40	8	
Carberg, B.H.	8, May 1896	4, May	73- 9m	5	
Cardwell, Henry	17, Sept 1901		22	8	
Carey, Edw.	10, Jan. 1888		32	4	
Carey, John	19, June 1901		37	8	
Carey, William	12, July 1901		34	8	
Carle, Carrie	7, Jan. 1893		24	5	
Carle, Magdalena	29, June 1901		52	8	
Carlin, James	11, Dec. 1891		1	4	
Carlin, Margaret	11, Dec. 1891		3	4	
Carly, Lows	26, July 1887		7m	1	
Carnahan, Amanda	31, Aug. 1901		73	8	
Carnal, George	24, Jan. 1901		34	8	
Carnal, Ida	10, Apr. 1901		22	8	
Carnest, V.A.	19, Jan. 1888		5d	4	
Carney, Hugh	21, Sept 1887		32	1	
Carney, M.	25, Jan. 1888		87	1	
Carney, Steven	17, Aug. 1900		32	5	
Carpenter, Emma C.	13, Sept 1890		5	1	
Carpenter, Lillie	12, Feb. 1897	11, Feb.	24- 6m	5	Rabbe
Carr, James	30, Nov. 1900		70	8	
Carr, Mary	8, Nov. 1900		85	8	
Carrigan, Rob.	11, Jan. 1888		3	4	
Carrol, Henrietta	7, Sept 1900		19	5	
Carroll, Charles	19, July 1901		21	8	
Carroll, Henry	11, July 1887		3w	1	
Carroll, John	3, May 1901		46	8	
Carroll, Michael	15, Jan. 1901		42	8	
Carroll, Patrick	25, June 1888		67	1	
Carson, Lucille	14, July 1900		1	8	
Carsten, Friedrich	6, July 1889		47	1	
Carstens, Anna Dorothea	22, Sept 1898	21, Sept	76	4	Bollstedt
Carter, Anna	30, Apr. 1901		32	8	
Carter, Hattie	17, Oct. 1900		22	8	
Carter, Lillian W.	31, Aug. 1887		6m	1	
Carter, William	27, May 1901		28	8	
Carter, William	26, June 1901		22	8	
Cartigan, Catharine	25, Mar. 1901		61	8	
Carver, George W.	22, Nov. 1893		39	5	
Carvill, Agnes	17, Sept 1901		2	8	
Cary, Martin	17, May 1901		83	8	
Case, James	27, Feb. 1901		4d	8	
Casey, Joseph	5, Nov. 1900		3m	8	
Cashmann, Mary	18, Dec. 1900		41	8	
Caslay, Marg.	23, July 1887		69	1	
Casper, Anna	1, June 1894		7m	5	
Casper, Friedrich	24, 26, Sept 1900		3m	5	
Casper, J.H.	6, Jan. 1888		1d	1	
Cassair, Frank	17, Oct. 1901		50	8	
Cassander, Jacob	8, Jan. 1896	7, Jan.	81- 3m	5	
Cassel, William B.	23, Mar. 1893		37	5	
Cassidy, Elizabeth	14, Mar. 1895		36	5	
Cassidy, Katie	18, Dec. 1900		2	8	
Cast, Robert B.	31, Jan. 1896	29, Jan.	6- 4m	5	
Catharine, Flora	24, Sept 1901		2	1	
Catley, Frank	5, July 1887		40	1	
Cattam, Johan	12, Oct. 1893	11, Oct.	39- 3m-17d	* 5	
Cattani, Fannie	22, Nov. 1899	20, Nov.	45- 5m	5	
Cattein, Leopold	21, Nov. 1899	20, Nov.	45- 1m	5	
Cautlin, Katharine	28, Apr. 1888		2d	1	
Cauz, Ida Paulina	15, Feb. 1890		14m	4	
Cavanaugh, Sarah J.	28, July 1887		3	1	
Cawein, Daniel	11, July 1898	9, July	67- 3m	5	
Ceck, Katie	9, Apr. 1897	8, Apr.	28- 7m-16d	5	Laubner
Center, Ralph	18, Dec. 1900		2	8	

Name ****	Notice Date ****** ****	Death Date ***** ****	Age ***	Page ****	Maiden Name ****** ****
Centner, Ch.	1, Nov. 1888		38	1	
Centnet, Frank	27, Aug. 1889		66	1	
Certel, Elizabeth	1, Mar. 1893		64	5	
Chain, Leslie	8, Dec. 1900		5m	8	
Chalfant, F.	29, Aug. 1900		25d	5	
Chaliff, Esther	17, Oct. 1900		14d	8	
Chamberlain, John R.	26, Dec. 1900		71	8	
Chambers, Elizabeth	10, Mar. 1891		97	4	
Chaney, Christina	4, June 1895		73	5	
Chaney, Robert	29, Oct. 1900		22	8	
Chapman,	29, Dec. 1887		1d	4	
Cheesemann, F.	1, Oct. 1900		1m	5	
Cheevers, James	23, July 1887		5m	1	
Cherdon, Cora	8, July 1891		1m	4	
Cherdron, Amelia L.W.	2, Apr. 1898	1, Apr.	35- 5m- 3d	5	Nordmann
Cherdron, David	22, Feb. 1898	21, Feb.	36- 3m	5	
Chesman, Nellie	2, June 1891		4	4	
Chills, Jac.	3, Sept 1890		4	1	
Chisman, H.F.	4, Jan. 1901		4m	5	
Choate, Leo W.	19, Apr. 1895		8	5	
Chrat, Mary	11, May 1889		51	1	
Chrisman, Anna E.	6, June 1895		75	5	
Chrisman, Laura	31, Mar. 1891		5d	4	
Christ, Barbara	16, Dec. 1889		62	1	
Christ, Emilie	25, Feb. 1896	23, Feb.	38	5	
Christ, Margaret	23, Aug. 1901		63	8	
Christian, Bridget	18, Apr. 1895		61	5	
Christian, M.	19, Aug. 1901		13	8	
Christie, Elizabeth	15, Mar. 1901		78	8	
Christie, Frank	6, Mar. 1891		40	4	
Christmann, Elisabeth	13, Feb. 1899	11, Feb.	68- 9m	5	Feil
Christmann, M.	3, Dec. 1888		8	1	
Christmann, Mary	29, Dec. 1888		23	1	
Christoffel, L.	6, Sept 1901		63	8	
Christophel, Barbara	14, Jan. 1896	12, Jan.	86	5	Steiner
Christopher, Harry	2, Sept 1887		4	1	
Christopher, John	21, Nov. 1891		60	4	
Christopher, John	20, Mar. 1901		45	1	
Christopher, Marg.	22, Feb. 1895		73	5	
Christopher, Stella	6, Apr. 1892		5m	5	
Cisco, Mary	15, May 1901		63	8	
Claassen, Elmer	5, June 1897	2, June	2- 4m	5	
Clancey, James	12, Mar. 1901		64	8	
Clancy, Ann	3, Nov. 1887		80	4	
Clara, Annie	1, May 1888		17m	2	
Clark,	10, Apr. 1888		1d	4	
Clark,	8, Nov. 1900		4d	8	
Clark, Alex	18, Feb. 1901		67	8	
Clark, Alexander	3, Feb. 1888		61	4	
Clark, Alice	4, Aug. 1900		18	8	
Clark, Anna	5, June 1901		51	8	
Clark, Anton	10, May 1895		85	5	
Clark, Charles	28, Jan. 1901		32	8	
Clark, Charlotte	11, Apr. 1901			8	
Clark, Edith	14, Mar. 1901		6	8	
Clark, Edward	8, Mar. 1901		7	8	
Clark, Eugene	8, Dec. 1900		29	8	
Clark, Francis	2, July 1901		3m	8	
Clark, Genevieve	26, Sept 1887		2m	1	
Clark, Marie	30, Mar. 1901		1m	8	
Clark, Mary	2, Oct. 1900		83	8	
Clark, Robert	12, Nov. 1900		3m	5	
Clark, Sam. M.	22, June 1895		49	5	
Clark, Winifrede	5, June 1901		50	8	
Clarke, William H.	25, July 1900		62	5	
Claude, Samuel	14, May 1891		45	4	
Clauder, Martha W.	3, Feb. 1891		14	4	
Claus, B.	24, Feb. 1888		21	4	
Clause, Maggie	31, May 1901		31	8	
Claussen, Louisa	18, Jan. 1892		51	5	
Claussen, Mary	9, July 1887		68	1	

Name ****	Notice Date ****** ****	Death Date ***** ****	Age ***	Page ****	Maiden Name ****** ****
Clavey, B.	30, Jan. 1888		67	1	
Clavis, Bernhard	31, May 1890		3m	1	
Claybon, Mary	18, Sept 1900		22	5	
Clayborne, May	11, Apr. 1901		76	8	
Claybrook, Jane	8, Aug. 1900		80	8	
Clayton, Elmer	24, May 1901		1	8	
Claß, Carolina	7, Dec. 1897	4, Dec.	62- 9m	5	Mang
Claß, Edward	18, Nov. 1893		4m	5	
Clem, William	9, July 1891		13	4	
Clemens, Anselm (Rev)	22, 24, Sept 1900		37	5	
Clemens, Elisabeth	25, Feb. 1893		51	5	
Clemens, John	10, Apr. 1895		35	5	
Clemens, Loraine P.	16, Feb. 1901		1m	8	
Clemens, Marie	27, Mar. 1896	25, Mar.	64- 3m	5	Kirschner
Clemm, William	19, Oct. 1892		28	5	
Clemmens, William	9, Feb. 1901		25	8	
Clendenmug, Mary S.	29, Aug. 1887		54	1	
Clendenning, T.W.	14, Feb. 1901		63	8	
Clermont, C.	28, Nov. 1900		45	8	
Clifford, Beatrice A.	11, Aug. 1887		11m	1	
Clifford, Elizabeth	11, June 1901		65	8	
Clifford, Honora	11, July 1887		78	1	
Clifford, J.	25, Nov. 1887		27	1	
Clifford, Michael	12, July 1895		17	5	
Clifford, Sarah	30, Nov. 1900		35	8	
Clingmann, Clara	26, Nov. 1900		75	8	
Clive, George	10, Mar. 1888		38	1	
Clobes, Katharine	9, June 1898	7, June		5	
Clodius, Henriette	23, 24, Aug. 1895	22, Aug.	71	5	Schmit
Clover, Elisabeth	3, May 1901		65	8	
Cloves, John	22, Mar. 1901		53	8	
Clymer, Isaac D.	10, Dec. 1900		55	8	
Coblentz, John J.	24, July 1895		58	5	
Coburn, Eduard	8, Aug. 1901		34	8	
Cochnowcz, Ch. W.	7, May 1888		3	1	
Cochran, Sam.	2, Mar. 1901		78	5	
Cochrane, Lottie	6, Sept 1901		40	8	
Cody, James	15, July 1887		85	1	
Coffey, K.	6, Jan. 1888		60	1	
Coffin, H.	4, Feb. 1888		62	4	
Coffman, Tasso R.	22, Dec. 1892		36	5	
Cogan, Catharine	3, Jan. 1901		62	5	
Cogan, James	16, Oct. 1901		60	1	
Cogin, John	4, July 1887		6d	1	
Cohen, Abraham	27, Apr. 1901		47	8	
Cohen, Amelia	18, June 1901		1m	8	
Cohen, Isadore	30, Jan. 1901		2	8	
Cohen, Louis	12, Jan. 1894		67	5	
Cohen, Ray	15, Oct. 1900		25	5	
Cohen, Rebecca	19, Mar. 1895		38	5	
Cohl, Frank	1, June 1894		2m	5	
Cohn, Barbara	7, Dec. 1893		69	5	
Cohn, Charles	18, Apr. 1889		19	1	
Cohn, Ruth	20, Jan. 1891		46	4	
Cohn, Sardna	14, Dec. 1893		65	5	
Cohn, William	13, July 1887		26	1	
Cohnen, Leo	7, Sept 1893		50	5	
Cohoon, Gasie	8, Dec. 1900		41	8	
Cohrs, Wilhelm E.	2, Oct. 1897	1, Oct.	36	4	
Cohs, Joseph	14, Jan. 1893		1m	5	
Coin, William	23, May 1895		7w	5	
Cokill, Thomas	30, Sept 1901		25	8	
Colby, Lucius	19, Sept 1888		62	2	
Coldehoff, Charles J.	5, May 1891		10m	1	
Cole, Elizabeth	10, Sept 1901		50	1	
Cole, Granville	26, Feb. 1888		27	4	
Cole, Hiram	14, Feb. 1901		55	8	
Cole, Kate	8, Oct. 1901		59	1	
Cole, Lucy A.	30, Apr. 1895		59	5	
Cole, Mary	28, Mar. 1901		23	8	
Coleman, C.H.	22, Apr. 1897	21, Apr.	49	5	

Name ****	Notice Date ****** ****	Death Date ***** ****	Age ***	Page ****	Maiden Name ****** ****
Coleman, Edward	7, Sept 1888		42	1	
Coleman, Francis	3, July 1901		32	8	
Coleman, John	19, Apr. 1895		19	5	
Coleman, Julia	8, Aug. 1891		52	4	
Coleman, Michael	2, July 1895		68	5	
Coleman, Sarah	17, Apr. 1895		4m	5	
Coleman, Thomas	31, Jan. 1901		34	8	
Coleman, William	8, June 1901		71	8	
Collingham, Elisabeth	14, Jan. 1901		39	8	
Collins, Celia	11, Apr. 1901		78	8	
Collins, Emma	13, Nov. 1893		11	5	
Collins, George	19, July 1887		10m	1	
Collins, Harrold	15, June 1901		1m	8	
Collins, Hilda	8, Jan. 1901		21	8	
Collins, Margaret	8, Nov. 1887		51	1	
Collins, Margaret	2, Aug. 1901		2m	8	
Collins, Marie D.	24, Apr. 1895		12d	5	
Collins, Mary	26, Jan. 1901		31	8	
Collins, Mary A.	13, July 1887		41	1	
Collins, Thomas	30, Nov. 1887		27	4	
Collison, Katharine	17, Oct. 1900		36	8	
Colvin, Emma	20, Sept 1901		20	1	
Colvin, Ralph	11, July 1901		3m	5	
Combs, Vena	21, Feb. 1901		27	8	
Comer, Mary	8, Jan. 1901		10	8	
Comer, Thomas	10, Jan. 1893		20	5	
Commicer, Elizabeth	15, May 1895		60	5	
Commisser, Joseph	13, June 1901		75	8	
Conden, Mary	21, Jan. 1901		67	8	
Condermann, Pauline	20, July 1898	20, July	21	5	
Conklin, Andrew C.	4, Apr. 1895		68	5	
Conklin, John	5, June 1888		67	4	
Conklin, Samuel	12, Dec. 1900		73	8	
Conlan, May	21, Oct. 1887		52	1	
Conley, George E.	11, Aug. 1887		32	1	
Conley, Joseph	20, Mar. 1901		4	1	
Conley, Maggie	4, Feb. 1888		20	4	
Conley, Margaret	19, Dec. 1900		81	8	
Conley, William	16, Oct. 1900		42	8	
Conlon, Anna	12, Feb. 1901		57	8	
Conn, John	4, Sept 1901		56	8	
Connell, Eliza	5, July 1887		83	1	
Connelly, Nellie	17, Aug. 1887		3w	1	
Conner, Mary	4, Oct. 1901		65	8	
Conners, John	11, Jan. 1901		32	5	
Conners, Pat.	7, May 1888		1d	1	
Conners, Winifred	12, Sept 1900		6m	5	
Connor, Patrick	5, Apr. 1901		83	8	
Conover, Diana S.	27, Mar. 1888		80	4	
Conrad, Clara	7, June 1888		5m	1	
Conrad, Dorothea	4, Jan. 1893		63	5	
Conrad, Henry	30, Jan. 1888		42	1	
Conradi, Anna Maria	30, May 1898	29, May	59	4	Schroeck
Conradi, Charles	10, Feb. 1890		53	1	
Conradi, Charles	31, Mar. 1896	30, Mar.	28	5	
Conradi, Elizabeth	27, June 1888		57	1	
Conradi, Emma S.	26, Nov. 1892		27	5	
Conradi, Lizzie	1, May 1901		30	8	
Conradi, Margaret L.	10, Oct. 1891		34	4	
Conradi, Margaretha	20, Jan. 1899	20, Jan.	60	5	
Conradi, Mary	3, Feb. 1897	1, Feb.	7m	5	
Conradi, Wilhelm	18, Jan. 1896	17, Jan.	36-10m	5	
Conradi, Wilhelm	18, Feb. 1899	17, Feb.	67- 5m	5	
Conroy, Ellen	19, Oct. 1887		2	1	
Conroy, John	25, June 1895		41	5	
Conway, Harry A.	28, Apr. 1888		4m	1	
Conway, Pat.	14, Nov. 1900		39	8	
Coogin, John	5, July 1887		6d	1	
Cook, A.J.	13, Mar. 1895		65	5	
Cook, Anthony	1, Feb. 1898	31, Jan.	64	5	
Cook, Bertha	24, Aug. 1900		29	5	

Name	Notice Date	Death Date	Age	Page	Maiden Name
****	****** ****	***** ****	***	****	****** ****
Cook, Gertrude	13, Aug. 1901		15	8	
Cook, J.B.	28, May 1896	27, May	70- 2m	5	
Cook, J.B.	12, Mar. 1900	11, Mar.	3- 11m	8	
Cook, John	8, Oct. 1900		42	8	
Cook, Lydia	5, June 1901		28	8	
Cook, Margaretha	13, Jan. 1896	10, Jan.	68- 2m	5	Beelmann
Cook, W. Howar	3, Jan. 1888		9m	1	
Cooke, Augustus	4, Dec. 1900		71	8	
Coombs, Elizabeth	5, Apr. 1900	4, Apr.	26	5	Fern
Cooper, Allen	30, Aug. 1900		80	5	
Coors, By.	14, July 1900		1d	8	
Cope, William	8, Feb. 1901		2	8	
Coper,	15, Oct. 1900		1d	5	
Corbett, Edward F.	4, Sept 1901		37	8	
Corbett, Millie	1, Sept 1887		28	1	
Corbly, Emilia	23, Apr. 1897	21, Apr.		5	Aufderheide
Corcoran, Elisabeth	9, Jan. 1901		81	5	
Corcoran, John	26, Nov. 1900		36	8	
Corcoran, Mary	30, May 1895		30	5	
Cordes, Emma	30, Mar. 1898	28, Mar.	9- 7m	5	
Corey, Emma	5, Sept 1900		34	5	
Corf, Sarah	14, June 1895		20	5	
Cornberger, Gustav	12, Dec. 1900		74	8	
Cornelius, Frank	11, Aug. 1888		1	1	
Correvont, Andreas	22, May 1888		42	1	
Corsmeier, J.B.	25, Nov. 1896	24, Nov.	74- 4m	5	
Cosgrove, William	10, July 1901		63	5	
Cosgrove, Willie	20, July 1887		7m	1	
Costello, Florence	13, July 1901		26	8	
Costello, Mary	26, June 1901		1	8	
Costello, Minnie	27, May 1901		40	8	
Costen, Mollie	13, Apr. 1895		37	4	
Cottrell, George	27, Feb. 1901		76	8	
Cotts, Lizzie	4, Jan. 1901		30	5	
Couchman, Mary	3, Oct. 1887		39	1	
Coughlin, John	20, June 1901		70	8	
Coughlin, Mary	27, Aug. 1901		23	1	
Courtney, Jane	11, Apr. 1895		47	5	
Covert, Nobert B.	8, Dec. 1891		46	4	
Cowen, James	24, Nov. 1900		60	8	
Cowen, John	22, July 1901		40	8	
Cowman, Elizabeth	20, Apr. 1895		63	5	
Cox, A.	8, Oct. 1901		72	1	
Cox, Arthur	20, July 1887		7m	1	
Cox, Beverly	14, Aug. 1900		35	5	
Cox, Isaac	9, July 1887		7m	1	
Cox, Malinda	29, Dec. 1900		42	8	
Craig, Ellen	12, Dec. 1900		30	8	
Craig, James	6, Mar. 1901		51	5	
Craig, Jennie	21, Oct. 1887		23	1	
Craig, Marie	21, Mar. 1901		57	8	
Craig, Mary	20, Mar. 1901		47	1	
Crambert, Charles	20, June 1892		8	5	
Cramer, Carol	3, Jan. 1888		70	1	
Cramer, Christian F.	28, Jan. 1894		79	5	
Cramer, Friedricka	12, Mar. 1901		55	8	
Cramer, Mary A.	30, May 1895		76	5	
Cramer, Salome	18, Sept 1895	17, Sept	71	5	
Cramer, Wilhelm C.	6, Feb. 1896	3, Feb.	47- 9m	5	
Cramerding, Christ.	8, Dec. 1900		57	8	
Cramin, Rose	15, Aug. 1891		40	4	
Crane, Sarah	16, Mar. 1901		75	8	
Crarack, Adolph H.	20, Sept 1901		69	1	
Crary, William	18, Feb. 1901		4	8	
Craut, Ella	30, Dec. 1890		22	4	
Crawford, George	9, Aug. 1887		83	1	
Creden, Mary	11, July 1901		77	5	
Creed, Thomas J.	28, June 1898	27, June	37- 6m	5	
Creed, Wilhelm C.	5, Mar. 1897	3, Mar.	31- 9m	5	
Creelman, James	13, Nov. 1896	12, Nov.	56	5	
Creelmann, B.	29, Aug. 1895	27, Aug.	31- 8m	5	

Name ****	Notice Date ****** ****	Death Date ***** ****	Age ***	Page ****	Maiden Name ****** ****
Creemer, Ellen	22, Dec. 1900		56	8	
Cremens, Philip G.	20, Oct. 1891		34	1	
Cremering, Anna	31, Aug. 1901		73	8	
Cremering, B.	7, Mar. 1900	6, Mar.	75	5	
Cremering, Charles	4, Apr. 1901		9m	8	
Cremering, William	26, Feb. 1895		1	5	
Creppel, Charles	31, May 1890		19	1	
Creppel, Fr.	12, Nov. 1888		66	2	
Creskamp, Christina	14, June 1895		70	5	
Crevers, John N.	6, July 1893		90	5	
Criddle, Andrew	7, Oct. 1901		44	1	
Crommer, Harry	26, Mar. 1901		2	8	
Crone, Catharine	30, Apr. 1897	28, Apr.	63- 6m	5	Bocklage
Crone, Joseph J.	1, Feb. 1899	30, Jan.	56- 6m	5	
Cronin, James	17, Apr. 1888		42	1	
Cronin, Margaret	10, Dec. 1900		80	8	
Cronin, Tim. F.	2, July 1901		35	8	
Croom, Fred.	13, Nov. 1893		44	5	
Croons, Emma	30, Jan. 1901		24	8	
Crosby, Irene V.	4, July 1887		33	1	
Croswell, Clara	28, Nov. 1900		30	8	
Crotty, Michael R.	6, June 1888		8m	1	
Crotty, Robert E.	3, Nov. 1887		3- 2m	4	
Crout, George	6, Nov. 1900		79	8	
Crow, Simon	25, Mar. 1901		60	8	
Crowley, Margaret	8, Jan. 1901		75	8	
Crowton, Edward C.	17, Feb. 1891		52	4	
Croß, Belle	22, July 1901		31	8	
Crugar, Nettie M.	10, Apr. 1895		24	5	
Cruntcher, James	12, Nov. 1900		75	5	
Cruse, Clara C.	14, May 1895		21m	5	
Culberston, William	8, Nov. 1887		25	1	
Culbertson, John	11, Oct. 1901		9	5	
Cullen, Hannah	30, May 1895		65	5	
Cullin, Edwin W.	17, Apr. 1895		38	5	
Cullmann, Charles	23, Feb. 1889		39	1	
Cullmann, J.G.	4, Dec. 1895	3, Dec.		5	
Cullmann, Martha	21, Mar. 1895		67	5	
Culver, Anna F.	5, Aug. 1887		59	1	
Culver, Clara	28, Mar. 1901		59	8	
Cummings, John	3, Mar. 1888		7w	1	
Cummings, Marietta	24, May 1901		48	8	
Cunningham, Charles	26, June 1901		26	8	
Cunningham, Ed.	17, Oct. 1901		16	8	
Cunningham, Ella	21, Oct. 1887		6w	1	
Cunningham, J.	6, Sept 1901		38	8	
Cunningham, James	2, Feb. 1888		41	4	
Cunningham, Katie	1, Mar. 1901		35	8	
Cunningham, R.	14, Aug. 1887		16m	1	
Curley, Bridget	18, Feb. 1888		95	1	
Curley, Owen	13, May 1901			8	
Curley, Peter	10, Sept 1901		26	1	
Curran, Catharine	14, Dec. 1900		27	8	
Curran, Margaret	11, Dec. 1900		40	8	
Curran, Mary	13, Oct. 1900		60	8	
Curran, Patrick F.	15, Dec. 1887		42	1	
Curran, William F.	29, Mar. 1888		73	1	
Currus, Catharina	4, Apr. 1901		87	8	
Curry, Michael	28, May 1901		53	8	
Curry, Ruth	27, June 1888		4	1	
Curtin, Alice	12, June 1901		1m	8	
Curtis, Alexander	18, July 1887		58	1	
Curtis, Elisabeth	14, Dec. 1900		73	8	
Curtis, Emma	26, July 1900		54	5	
Curtis, Virginia L.	6, Apr. 1895		3w	5	
Cusack, Catharine	5, Mar. 1901		55	5	
Cusick, Joseph	9, Aug. 1900		33	8	
Cuthbert, Daisey	28, Jan. 1901		58	8	
Czaikowsky, Vincenz	13, Aug. 1896	12, Aug.	63- 1m	5	
Czerwinski, Edw.	1, June 1898	31, May		5	

Name ****	Notice Date ****** ****	Death Date ***** ****	Age ***	Page ****	Maiden Name ****** ****
Dabney, William Hope	29, Aug. 1887		73	1	
Dacey, Michael	22, June 1901		56	8	
Dacey, Susan	25, July 1888		34	4	
Daeny, J.	9, Oct. 1901		72	5	
Daeriger, Ernst	29, Jan. 1891		72	4	
Dagauer, Annette	30, Sept 1891		20	4	
Dagner, Mathilda A.	6, Apr. 1895		44	5	
Dahle, Frederick	2, Apr. 1891		59	4	
Dahle, William	27, Dec. 1893		36	5	
Dahling, Alma Cora	25, Jan. 1889		5d	1	
Dahlman, Anna	7, Oct. 1901		58	1	
Dahlmann, Katharine	27, Apr. 1894		3	5	
Dahlmann, Louis	2, Apr. 1901		25	8	
Dahms, Franziska	1, Feb. 1900	31, Jan.	55-10m-18d	5	Auzinger
Daiber, Anna Maria	3, June 1899	2, June	72	5	
Daiber, Caroline	21, Mar. 1901		28	8	
Daiber, Christiana	5, Feb. 1898	3, Feb.	65	5	Koenig
Daiber, H.	21, Jan. 1898	19, Jan.	73	5	
Daigger, Franz A.	7, Sept 1893		5	5	
Daiker, Albert	1, July 1901		3m	8	
Daiker, Mary	5, Oct. 1888		8	1	
Daiker, Olga	27, July 1889		1d	1	
Daiker, Wilhelm	11, May 1889	10, May		1	
Dailey, Michael E.	17, Apr. 1888		35	1	
Dakr, Annie	11, July 1901		53	5	
Dale, Joseph	22, Mar. 1901		50	8	
Daley, Joseph	22, Oct. 1900		27	8	
Dallas, A.	6, Jan. 1888		73	1	
Dallmann, Herman	21, Nov. 1889		72	1	
Dallmann, Oskar	1, Feb. 1899	31, Jan.	2- 6m	5	
Dalrymple, Bell	14, Feb. 1891		24	4	
Dalton, James	8, July 1901		49	8	
Dalton, Martha T.	7, July 1887		72	1	
Daly, Mary	29, July 1888		6w	1	
Damert, Mary	3, May 1901		87	8	
Damm, Friedricka	4, Oct. 1888		78	4	
Damm, Sadie	5, Apr. 1890		6	1	
Dammann, Ernst	3, Dec. 1895	2, Dec.	31	5	
Dammeier, Amalie	29, Mar. 1889		62	1	
Dammert, M.	29, Dec. 1887		33	4	
Damus,	7, July 1891		1d	1	
Damus, Hugo	6, Oct. 1891		28	4	
Danberbis, Jacob	24, May 1895		52	5	
Danemeier, August	25, Feb. 1893		15d	5	
Dangenfoehr, William	6, Nov. 1894		53	5	
Daniels, Julie Everett	1, Nov. 1887		24	1	
Dankel, Henry	16, Nov. 1889		33	1	
Dankowicz, Alex.	30, Apr. 1895		42	5	
Danmann, Henry	27, Aug. 1901		61	1	
Dannecker, John	20, Nov. 1900		84	8	
Dannenhauer, Georg	9, Mar. 1895		62	5	
Danner, Anna	4, Nov. 1887		61	1	
Danner, Joseph	6, May 1889		37	1	
Danner, Joseph	13, Dec. 1900		48	8	
Dannhausen, Henry	3, Aug. 1899	2, Aug.	24	5	
Dans, Mary	9, June 1893		2	5	
Dappen, Ed.	26, Sept 1901		70	8	
Dappen, Ophelia	8, Aug. 1891		9m	4	
Darfmann, Herman	29, Apr. 1891		30	4	
Darmody, James	8, Jan. 1901		32	8	
Darmody, May	28, June 1888		6m	1	
Darusmont, Maria Louisa	7, Jan. 1893		1	5	
Dase, Harry	7, Feb. 1901		15d	8	
Dasen, Lillie	15, Feb. 1890		2- 6m	4	
Dassell, Fred. A.	7, Aug. 1894		63	5	
Dattilo, Maria	8, July 1888		5m	1	
Daub, Johan	1, Nov. 1898	29, Oct.	22- 8m-16d	5	
Dauer, Anna M.	6, Mar. 1891		2	4	
Dauer, Frank	2, Jan. 1889		16	1	
Daughty, Parvin	26, July 1887		4	1	
Daum, Christ.	28, Dec. 1897	27, Dec.	37- 3m- 1d	4	

Name ****	Notice Date ****** ****	Death Date ***** ****	Age ***	Page ****	Maiden Name ****** ****
Daum, George	18, Apr. 1891	18, Apr.		4	
Daum, Margaretha	1, Dec. 1896	29, Nov.	64	5	
Daumann, Jacob	13, Dec. 1892		41	5	
Daun, Jennie	10, Jan. 1893		32	5	
Dautzauer, Katie	25, Oct. 1887		2m	1	
Dauwalter, Katharina	23, Apr. 1898	22, Apr.	69- 8m	4	Greiner
Davenport, Floyd	18, Feb. 1901		24	8	
Daveron, Peter	3, Aug. 1887		6m	1	
David, Joseph	19, July 1887		11m	1	
Davidson, William A.	10, Dec. 1900		47	8	
Davies, James	21, July 1900		4m	8	
Davis, Abraham D.	23, May 1895		71	5	
Davis, Annabelle	15, Jan. 1901		75	8	
Davis, Charles	19, Dec. 1900		5d	8	
Davis, Charles F.	27, Apr. 1895		52	5	
Davis, Cornelius	11, Aug. 1891		71	4	
Davis, Daniel F.	20, June 1888		72	1	
Davis, David	11, Jan. 1888		8	4	
Davis, Eli	17, Dec. 1900		74	8	
Davis, Eliza	23, May 1901		78	8	
Davis, Elizabeth	22, Oct. 1900		71	8	
Davis, Elizabeth G.	23, Oct. 1887		83	4	
Davis, Esther	29, May 1895		38	5	
Davis, Freda	15, Sept 1900		9m	5	
Davis, Goldie	17, Oct. 1900		2	8	
Davis, Helen	11, Apr. 1895		8m	5	
Davis, James A.	13, Apr. 1901		60	8	
Davis, John	19, July 1901		13d	8	
Davis, Josephine	12, Aug. 1901		48	8	
Davis, Joshua	14, Jan. 1893		71	5	
Davis, Marie	12, May 1898	10, May		5	
Davis, Mary	1, Oct. 1890		65	1	
Davis, Mary	5, May 1895		39	5	
Davis, Mary	6, Oct. 1900		6	5	
Davis, Mary	10, Oct. 1900		5	8	
Davis, May	16, July 1888		4w	1	
Davis, S.M.	14, Feb. 1888		78	4	
Davis, Sarah P.	4, May 1889		68	1	
Dawidoff, Leo.	7, July 1888		3m	4	
Dawns, James	19, July 1887		35	1	
Dawson, Jane M.	29, Dec. 1900		67	8	
Day, Absalom	25, Mar. 1901		1	8	
Day, Edna	19, July 1901		2	8	
Day, Harry	11, Jan. 1901		24	5	
Day, Katharine	8, Mar. 1888		75	1	
Day, Rebecca	18, May 1901		85	1	
Day, William F.	27, Aug. 1901		36	1	
Dayhoff, Albert	30, Apr. 1901		2	8	
DeBoor, Cornelius A.	16, Sept 1891		3	4	
DeBra, Lena Hofling	11, Jan. 1901		25	5	
DeBrunn, Katharine	11, Feb. 1889		77	1	
DeCorevant, Franz	30, July 1896	28, July	63- 7m	5	
DeGraff, Harry	3, Mar. 1891		65	4	
DeHahn, Sophie	4, Feb. 1891		87	4	
DeKloe, Elisabeth	3, Mar. 1888		3	1	
DeMitt, L.F.	6, Jan. 1888		4	1	
DeRaay, Alexander	10, Mar. 1898	9, Mar.	19- 1m	5	
DeRaay, Magdalena	22, Sept 1898	21, Sept	73	4	Schorle
DeRonde, Stephan	21, Nov. 1900		53	8	
DeRuiter, Elisabeth	6, Feb. 1896	4, Feb.	83	5	
DeWay, Henry	21, Mar. 1891		38	4	
Deaken, Harry	8, July 1901		3m	8	
Dean, Anna	1, Mar. 1888		27	4	
Dean, Catharine	28, May 1901		70	8	
Dean, Charles	8, Jan. 1901		60	8	
Dean, Ed. A.	13, Nov. 1893		33	5	
Dean, F.	3, Feb. 1888		44	4	
Dean, John	11, Dec. 1900		41	8	
Dean, Michael	5, Aug. 1901		25	8	
Deane, Dana	16, May 1901		58	5	
Deans, Mary	18, Oct. 1900		77	8	

Name ****	Notice Date ****** ****	Death Date ***** ****	Age ***	Page ****	Maiden Name ****** ****
Dear, Louis	25, Oct. 1900		2	8	
Dearing, David	24, Oct. 1900		35	8	
Dearing, Thomas	24, Jan. 1888		54	1	
Dearwester, Henry E.	19, Feb. 1891		1	4	
Debrinker, Bernard	22, Dec. 1891		11d	4	
Dech, Jakob	11, Feb. 1891		42	4	
Deck, Edward	11, Mar. 1891		40	4	
Deck, Georg	2, Aug. 1898	1, Aug.	18- 6m	4	
Deck, Jacob J.	8, June 1895		19	5	
Decke, Maria Elisabeth	30, Apr. 1898	29, Apr.	70- 7m	4	Ruwe
Deckebach,	26, Mar. 1891		1d	4	
Deckebach, Friedrich Christian	1, Mar. 1899	28, Feb.	38-11m	5	
Deckebach, Margaret	5, Mar. 1901		38	5	
Deckebach, Philip	7, Aug. 1900		40	8	
Decker, Amelia	25, Sept 1889		53	1	
Decker, G.A.	9, June 1897	7, June	70	5	
Decker, George H.	25, Apr. 1889		2	1	
Decker, George T.	3, Mar. 1891		54	4	
Decker, Gerhard	10, Sept 1896	8, Sept	66	5	
Decker, Hilda Dorothea	17, Feb. 1896	16, Feb.	3- 6m	5	
Decker, John	28, Feb. 1901		67	8	
Decker, Lorine	22, Mar. 1895		3	5	
Decker, Norma	6, July 1895		3	5	
Dedmerel, Martha	2, Oct. 1888		2	1	
Dee, James	4, June 1895		2	5	
Deeke, George	10, Jan. 1894		66	5	
Deeken, Heinrich	31, Jan. 1896	29, Jan.	50- 3m	5	
Deffinger, F.	18, Aug. 1900		3m	8	
Deffinger, Henry	14, Sept 1897	13, Sept	58- 2m	5	
Deffren, Louise	24, Apr. 1900	23, Apr.	34- 9m	8	Wiegand
Deffruges, Christ.	30, Jan. 1888		18	1	
Defle, Katharine	14, June 1901		83	5	
Degan, A.E.	21, Feb. 1888		45	1	
Degenhardt, Otto	31, July 1894		40	5	
Degenhart, August	24, Aug. 1900		78	5	
Degenhart, Ph.	26, Sept 1895	25, Sept	61- 4m	5	
Degenhorst, Wilhelmine	22, Nov. 1895	21, Nov.	72- 4m	5	Bollicke
Degginger, F.	29, Apr. 1899	28, Apr.	59	5	
Degischer, Frank	9, Aug. 1901		1	8	
Deglow, Georg H.	24, Sept 1898	23, Sept	35	5	
Degnan, Laura A.	23, July 1895		35	5	
Degnan, Mary	11, July 1901		70	5	
Dehler, Clara	23, Apr. 1890		1	4	
Dehne, Dora	1, June 1893		14m	5	
Dehne, Joseph F.	15, July 1890		15m	1	
Dehner, John	20, Dec. 1892		46	5	
Dehner, Joseph	19, Nov. 1895	18, Nov.	6- 7m	5	
Dehner, Joseph A.	22, Oct. 1900		37	8	
Deibert, John	30, July 1901		74	8	
Deichman, Marie Elisabeth	2, Nov. 1899	31, Oct.	86-10m	8	Schneidhorst
Deichmann, Walter	1, July 1891		1	1	
Deicke, Karl G.	13, Jan. 1894		1	5	
Deinlein, Dora	3, Apr. 1890		66	1	
Deirsing, Clara	5, Feb. 1892		10m	5	
Deischer, Ludwig	26, July 1888		10m	2	
Deisenroth, Anna B.	28, Dec. 1891		68	4	
Deisenroth, John	26, Nov. 1892		37	5	
Deiters, John	6, July 1901		65	8	
Deiters, Wilhelm H.	27, June 1898	25, June	37- 6m	5	
Deklemann, Barbara	15, Oct. 1891		-8	4	
Delaney, Bridget	4, Nov. 1887		65	1	
Delaney, Catharine	9, Sept 1889		44	1	
Delaney, Johanna	19, July 1887		6m	1	
Delaney, Martin	14, Dec. 1900		33	8	
Delaney, Thomas	26, Sept 1900		24	5	
Delaney, Thomas	28, May 1901		64	8	
Delano, Anna	15, Nov. 1887		1d	4	
Delbruegge, Henry N.	27, July 1894		45	5	
Delbrügge, Bertha	27, Oct. 1888		6	1	
Delbrügge, Nora	12, Aug. 1893		20	5	
Delehanty, M.J.	12, July 1895		25	5	

Name ****	Notice Date ****** ****	Death Date ***** ****	Age ***	Page ****	Maiden Name ****** ****
Delehanty, Rob	23, Aug. 1887		17m	1	
Delfendahl, Annie	11, Jan. 1888		18	4	
Delfendahl, Arthur A.	8, Mar. 1899	6, Mar.	21- 1m- 9d	5	
Delfendahl, George	22, June 1897	20, June	25	5	
Delfendahl, William	17, Aug. 1887		42	1	
Dell, Barbara	27, Aug. 1891		79	1	
Dellbruegge, Friedrich Wilhelm	18, Feb. 1890		77	1	
Dellbrügge, Lizzie	27, Mar. 1895		24	5	
Dellenback, Eliza	19, Nov. 1900		60	8	
Deller, Andrew	21, May 1901		33	8	
Deller, Francis	28, May 1891		57	4	
Deller, Magdalena	19, Mar. 1895		78	5	
Demand, Frances	14, Feb. 1901		71	8	
Demauer, William	14, May 1891		14d	4	
Demmers, Eddie	9, July 1895		5m	5	
Demmler, Johan Andreas	26, Aug. 1899	24, Aug.	75	4	
Dempsey, Harriet	18, Sept 1900		40	5	
Dempsey, Hattie	15, Sept 1900			5	
Demuth, Bertha	6, Dec. 1888		8	1	
Demuth, Matth.	22, Nov. 1898	20, Nov.	60- 9m	5	
Denglen, Robert	6, July 1897	5, July		5	
Dengler, Lorentz	22, Jan. 1891		50	4	
Denker, Edna	6, July 1895		15m	5	
Denker, Lena	7, Nov. 1896	6, Nov.	26-10m	5	
Denker, T.	22, Dec. 1887		20	4	
Denman, Isabel	15, Nov. 1900		78	8	
Denning, Maria	11, Feb. 1889		48	1	
Denning, Theodor	13, Sept 1899	12, Sept	46- 3m	4	
Denninger, Jul.	21, Feb. 1889		43	1	
Densler, Rosa	7, June 1890		31	1	
Dentmeyer, Harry V.	28, July 1891		1	4	
Depenbrock, Anna	9, Dec. 1892		47	5	
Depenbrock, Mary E.	1, Nov. 1893		9m	5	
Depew, Julia	16, Mar. 1901		34	8	
Depler, Walter	5, Mar. 1888		11m	4	
Depp, Lizzie	5, May 1893		63	5	
Deppe, Catharine	19, Oct. 1891		54	1	
Deppe, Marie	8, Feb. 1895		28	5	
Deppen, Theresa	28, Mar. 1890		12	1	
Deppermann, E.	25, Feb. 1901		70	8	
Depweg, Herman	30, Nov. 1900		23	8	
Deramo, J.	19, Aug. 1901		17	8	
Deramo, Karoline	27, Dec. 1895	26, Dec.	30	5	Zinck
Deranney, Patrick	13, July 1887		63	1	
Dereke, Johanna	11, Dec. 1893		77	5	
Derflinger, Caroline	16, Nov. 1889		72	1	
Derfus, Penelope	13, Oct. 1892		61	5	
Dering, Johanna	27, July 1889		5w	1	
Dering, William	15, Mar. 1894		48	5	
Derr, Charles	4, May 1895		18m	5	
Derrich, Walter	26, Jan. 1892		1	5	
Derrmann, Lillian	31, Aug. 1887		6m	1	
DesLourier, Hattie	1, Feb. 1901		66	8	
Desch, Amanda	22, Mar. 1895		1m	5	
Desch, Christina	26, Jan. 1893		56	5	
Descherer, Fred.	16, June 1893		4m	5	
Deschli, Willie	20, July 1887		7m	1	
Deschner, Charles	5, July 1887		18	1	
Deschner, Michael	27, Apr. 1901		30	8	
Deschser, Louisa	28, Jan. 1899	26, Jan.	39-10m	5	Adam
Desemo, A.M.	3, May 1888		68	1	
Desmond, John	22, July 1901		27	8	
Desmond, Sarah	15, Mar. 1901		30	8	
Desmond, William	10, Apr. 1901		5m	8	
Dester, John	4, Mar. 1890		55	1	
Detars, George	11, Feb. 1889		16m	1	
Deterlin, Paul A.	2, Sept 1891		30- 5m	4	
Determann, Henry	28, Dec. 1892		36	5	
Deters, Anna M.E.	27, Mar. 1891		72	4	
Deters, Elizabeth	5, Apr. 1901		65	8	
Deters, Franz A.	17, Dec. 1891		21d	4	

Name	Notice Date	Death Date	Age	Page	Maiden Name
****	****** ****	***** ****	***	****	****** ****
Deters, H.C.	5, May 1893		52	5	
Deters, John H.	8, Dec. 1891		74	4	
Deters, Louis H.	21, Sept 1894		29	5	
Deters, Maggie	15, Sept 1888		1d	2	
Deters, Nicholas	12, May 1891		79	1	
Detert, John	23, July 1889		17m	1	
Dethless, Alvina	16, May 1892	15, May	25- 9m-24d	5	
Dethless, Claus	25, Sept 1888		54	1	
Detleft, Mary	25, Aug. 1890		3m	1	
Detman, Frederick	15, May 1889		62	1	
Detmer, Fren	11, Dec. 1891		31	4	
Dette, Anna M.	23, Sept 1887		23	2	
Dette, Elisa	1, Aug. 1890		2m	1	
Dette, Francis	29, June 1894		6m	5	
Dette, Frank	10, July 1889		9m	1	
Dette, Franziska	13, Sept 1889	13, Dec.	8m	1	
Dettermann, Bernhard	19, July 1900		52	8	
Dettmer, Charles	17, Apr. 1894		58	5	
Detwiler, John	3, Apr. 1888		28	4	
Detzel, Ben.	21, Mar. 1889		2m	1	
Detzel, Elizabeth	27, Oct. 1891		34	1	
Detzel, Fred.	11, Feb. 1893		22	5	
Detzel, Ruth	30, Nov. 1892		4m	5	
Detzel, William	23, June 1894		6m	5	
Deubel, Theresia	13, Apr. 1898	12, Apr.	53- 7m	5	Ziegler
Deurer, Charles	5, Nov. 1889		29	1	
Deurn, May	10, Mar. 1895		61	5	
Deuschle, Elisabeth	2, Aug. 1895	1, Aug.	30	5	
Deusel, Sophia	15, Feb. 1898	14, Feb.	20-11m	5	
Deuser, Willie	8, Jan. 1888	6, Jan.	4-11m-21d	5	
Deuterlein, Casper	26, Feb. 1889		41	1	
Deutsch, Friedrich	4, Nov. 1887		43	1	
Deutschbein, Fred. C.	20, Mar. 1895		40	5	
Deutschbein, Friedricka	5, Apr. 1895		29	5	
Deutschle, Elizabeth	16, May 1894		6m	5	
Devaney, Lacky	20, July 1887		35	1	
Devanney, Bridget	8, Aug. 1901		64	8	
Devare, Mary S.	30, Sept 1887		28	1	
Devoto, Elizabeth	6, June 1888		28	1	
Devow, Martin R. (Mrs)	5, Feb. 1891		55	4	
Dewald, Emma	4, Oct. 1887		27	1	
Dewald, G.	27, Apr. 1889		45	1	
Dewar, David	13, Oct. 1900		79	8	
Dexter, Harrison	21, May 1901		84	8	
Dhonau, Emma	20, Nov. 1900		34	8	
Dhonau, Jakob	21, Apr. 1897	20, Apr.	41-10m	5	
Dibowski, Ferdinand Gottfried	2, June 1900	2, JUne	53- 5m- 6d	5	
Dichhauer, Mary	26, Jan. 1892		22	5	
Dichtner, John	10, Jan. 1888		27	4	
Dick, Charles	25, Sept 1890		25	1	
Dick, Georg	20, Sept 1895	19, Sept	33- -27d	5	
Dick, Lillie	22, Apr. 1891		8	4	
Dickerson, Lillie	2, Aug. 1888		28	2	
Dickescheid, Maria	11, Jan. 1899	9, Jan.	46- 6m	5	Dorrmann
Dickescheid, Wendelin	31, Mar. 1896	30, Mar.	72- 7m	5	
Dickhaus, Catharine	15, Feb. 1901		85	8	
Dickhaus, Gastie	4, July 1887		5m	1	
Dickhaus, Johan	13, June 1900	11, June	78	8	
Dickhaus, John H.	3, Dec. 1891		1	4	
Dickhoff, August	2, May 1899	1, May	66- 1m	5	
Dickhoff, Carrie	4, Feb. 1901		41	8	
Dickman, Carrie	1, Aug. 1888		26d	2	
Dickman, Eugene	3, Mar. 1891		4	4	
Dickman, Katie	3, Mar. 1891		6	4	
Dickmann, Anna Maria	17, Mar. 1897	16, Mar.	60- 6m	5	Apries
Dickmann, Ernst W.	24, Apr. 1894		72	5	
Dickmann, F.H.	16, Oct. 1896	15, Oct.	82- 8m	5	
Dickmann, Kate	8, Oct. 1901		30	1	
Dickmann, Louise	25, July 1899	24, July	48- 5m	5	Stolz
Dickon, William	18, May 1894		36	5	
Dickop, Louise	29, Oct. 1891		4- 6m	4	

Name ****	Notice Date ****** ****	Death Date ***** ****	Age ***	Page ****	Maiden Name ****** ****
Dickow, Ida	9, Mar. 1896	6, Mar.	7	5	
Dickruger, Louis	19, Feb. 1895		37	5	
Dickson, James	30, Aug. 1901		59	8	
Didden, J.B.	4, June 1898	2, June	64- 3m	5	
Didie, Anna Babette	15, Nov. 1897	14, Nov.	30-10m-12d	5	Römmler
Diebenhorn, John	22, Aug. 1889		2d	1	
Diebold, Clara H.	8, July 1891		14d	4	
Diebold, Louis	17, Dec. 1900		74	8	
Diebold, Matthew	4, Apr. 1895		49	5	
Diebold, Tillie	14, Sept 1894		10m	5	
Dieckmann, Ben J.	1, Aug. 1887		29	1	
Dieckmann, Bernardina	11, June 1891		36	4	
Dieckmann, Elizabeth	25, July 1891		31	4	
Dieckmann, Ferdinand	19, Dec. 1896	18, Dec.	32	5	
Dieckmann, Herman	4, Jan. 1897	3, Jan.	63	5	
Dieckmann, Herman	21, Aug. 1899	20, Aug.	59- 9m	4	
Dieckmann, Joseph	14, July 1891		2	4	
Dieckmann, Maria Sophia	2, June 1897	31, May	66- 9m	5	Brehe
Dieckmeier, Fred.	5, June 1895		17	5	
Diedling, Harry	25, Aug. 1900		1	5	
Diedrich, Lena	25, Sept 1890		21	1	
Diegle, Jacob	13, July 1894		40	5	
Diehl, Adam	22, July 1889		63	1	
Diehl, Alice	10, Oct. 1901		11m	8	
Diehl, Anna M.	30, July 1892		73	5	
Diehl, Conrad	29, Aug. 1891		67	4	
Diehl, Eliza J.	13, July 1894		53	5	
Diehl, George	24, Feb. 1894		38	5	
Diehl, J.A.	31, Mar. 1900	30, Mar.	53-11m	5	
Diehl, Jacob	10, Jan. 1893		82	5	
Diehl, Josephine	30, Dec. 1896	29, Dec.	44- 8m	5	Butscha
Diehl, Margaret A.	16, July 1895		47	5	
Diehl, Mary W.	24, Dec. 1893		23	5	
Diehl, Nellie	13, Oct. 1892		28	5	
Diehlmann, Adam	10, Aug. 1897	8, Aug.	55	5	
Diehm, Franz	11, Jan. 1899	10, Jan.	82-11m	5	
Diehm, Henry	10, May 1901		56	8	
Diehm, Margaretha	2, June 1897	1, June	71- 6m	5	Pinger
Diehner, Adolf	15, Sept 1900		48	5	
Diekmeyer, Herman	24, Sept 1895	22, Sept	40-11m	5	
Diel, George	3, June 1892		58	5	
Dielhof, George	5, Sept 1889		7	1	
Dienst, Charles	24, May 1892		12d	5	
Dienst, Elise	21, Apr. 1898	20, Apr.	65- 3m-27d	5	
Dierckes, H.B.	13, Apr. 1896	11, Apr.	68	5	
Dierheimer, Julia	19, Aug. 1901		83	8	
Diering, Mary Ann	12, June 1891		58	4	
Dieringer, August D.	8, 9, Sept 1891	6, Sept	46- - 3d	* 1	
Dieringer, Emma	23, 24, Oct. 1890	22, Oct.	12- 9m- 3d	1	
Dierken, Clara	25, May 1899	22, May	10-10m	5	
Dierken, Helena	13, Oct. 1900		67	8	
Dierken, Henrietta	28, Apr. 1896	27, Apr.	1- 8m	5	
Dierken, John H.	21, Apr. 1888		13m	1	
Dierker, Carolina	24, June 1901		71	8	
Dierker, Georg	2, Feb. 1899	1, Feb.	48- 7m	5	
Dierkes, Elisabeth	2, Apr. 1900	1, Apr.	81- 8m	8	Nagel
Diersing, Bernard	4, Jan. 1901		50	5	
Diersing, Bernard	6, July 1901		86	8	
Dieschburg, John	13, Sept 1889		31	1	
Diesel, Emil	9, Dec. 1887		2m	1	
Diesel, Herbert	4, June 1901		1d	8	
Dieterle, Anton	1, Oct. 1887		3m	1	
Dieterle, John	1, June 1892		64	5	
Dieterle, John	29, June 1894		61	5	
Dietheim, John	30, Nov. 1887		4	4	
Diether, Johan	17, Oct. 1898	16, Oct.	67	4	
Dietlein, Joseph	22, July 1887		39	1	
Dietlein, R.	14, Feb. 1888		11m	4	
Dietrich, Alois	30, Sept 1893		3m	5	
Dietrich, Bertha C.	6, May 1889		6m	1	
Dietrich, Charles	1, Dec. 1888		31	4	

Name ****	Notice Date ****** ****	Death Date ***** ****	Age ***	Page ****	Maiden Name ****** ****
Dietrich, E.F.	13, Jan. 1888		11m	1	
Dietrich, Elisabeth	18, Sept 1895	16, Sept	53- 4m	5	
Dietrich, Frank	21, Feb. 1901		68	8	
Dietrich, Gustav	10, Jan. 1899	8, Jan.	21	5	
Dietrich, Jacob	13, Sept 1899	10, Sept	39- 5m	4	
Dietrich, Louise	11, Mar. 1898	10, Mar.	67- 1m	5	Beinert
Dietrich, Michael	2, Mar. 1896	29, Feb.	88	5	
Dietrich, Peter	22, Aug. 1898	20, Aug.	68	5	
Diettrich, Louisa	8, Aug. 1892		2m	5	
Dietz, Casper	23, Feb. 1893		42	5	
Dietz, Eliza	20, Dec. 1892		4	5	
Dietz, Johan	12, May 1899	10, May	67- 2m	5	
Dietz, Louis E.	13, Oct. 1892		4m	5	
Dietz, Mamie	4, Apr. 1901		28	8	
Dietz, Oswald	10, Mar. 1898	9, Mar.	75	5	
Dietz, Paulina	7, Sept 1887		28	1	
Dietz, Sarah A.	30, July 1901		67	8	
Dietz, Stella M.	23, July 1887		18m	1	
Dietz, Theresa	23, Dec. 1891		74	4	
Dietz, Walter	19, Aug. 1889		11	1	
Dietzgen, Joseph	18, Aug. 1891		21	4	
Diez, Friedrich	3, July 1888	2, July	1- 1m- 5d	1	
Dießlin, Barbara	18, Nov. 1896	16, Nov.	40- 7m	5	Bill
Dießlin, Charles	1, Aug. 1894		38	5	
Dihlmann, Sophie	28, Mar. 1892			5	
Dilbad, Henry	24, Sept 1894		2m	5	
Dildim, H.	3, Sept 1889		7	1	
Dilg, Christian	16, June 1891		4m	4	
Dilg, Eva E.	28, Nov. 1893		62	5	
Dilg, George	11, June 1900	9, June	36- 8m	5	
Dilg, John	26, Dec. 1900		39	8	
Dilg, W.	20, Dec. 1895	19, Dec.	52	5	
Dilger, Emma L.	5, Nov. 1891		3	1	
Dilges, Lizzie	26, Feb. 1888		29	4	
Dillaby, Mary J.	10, Sept 1887		61	2	
Diller, Albert	26, Apr. 1893		2	5	
Dillerd,	20, June 1895		3d	5	
Dillhoff, Johan Heinrich	27, Nov. 1896	27, Nov.	27- 9m	5	
Dillhoff, John H.	2, May 1895		58	5	
Dillhoff, Louise Josephine	24, Oct. 1898	23, Oct.	18-10m	5	
Dillinger, Flora	18, Nov. 1894		1	5	
Dillon, Nellie	15, June 1895		3	5	
Dillon, William	29, May 1895		8	5	
Dilner, Frank	7, Feb. 1891		35	4	
Dimerding, Anthony	7, Mar. 1894		7m	5	
Dingen, Maria Magdalena	17, Feb. 1888		4	4	
Dinger,	13, Feb. 1901		19d	8	
Dinger, Anna	5, June 1890		2m	4	
Dinger, Bertha	23, Nov. 1891		4	1	
Dinger, John	7, May 1895		6m	5	
Dinger, Joseph W.	18, June 1889		1	1	
Dinger, Leopold	15, June 1898	14, June	41-10m	4	
Dingfelden, Johan	2, Mar. 1897		78	5	
Dinkel, John	17, Mar. 1890		34	1	
Dinkelacker, Anna M.	10, July 1888		11m	1	
Dinkelacker, Caroline	1, June 1898	31, May	27-10m	5	
Dinkelaker, Friedrich	10, June 1896	8, June	62	5	
Dinkelaker, Henry	26, Jan. 1901		33	8	
Dinkelmann, Adelheid	30, 31, Jan. 1896	29, Jan.	73	5	Pape
Dinkelmann, Sophia C.	25, June 1897	24, June	51- 6m	5	
Dinnies, Jacob	6, Mar. 1890		29	1	
Dinnies, Margaretha	24, Oct. 1896	23, Oct.	59- 4m	5	Wagner
Dinser, Franz X.	16, July 1896	14, July	48	5	
Dinsmore, Mary	18, Apr. 1895		2m	5	
Dirken, J.B.	19, July 1887		67	1	
Dirr, Agatha	7, June 1890		77	1	
Dirr, Clarence N.	26, Jan. 1893		3d	5	
Dirr, Eva C.	17, Jan. 1888		4w	4	
Dirrheimer, Mary	5, Mar. 1891		30	4	
Dischbourn, Louis	10, Aug. 1901		41	8	
Dischinger, Georg Gottlieb	15, July 1899	14, July	49	4	

Name ****	Notice Date ****** ****	Death Date ***** ****	Age ***	Page ****	Maiden Name ****** ****
Diserens, Anna	18, Aug. 1900		87	8	
Dishmore, Eliza	11, July 1901		43	5	
Disser, Peter	23, Jan. 1900	22, Jan.	81- 4m	4	
Distler, Anna Cath.	24, July 1890		66	1	
Distler, Johan G.	2, Apr. 1895		83	5	
Ditmars, Elizabeth	6, Sept 1901		76	8	
Ditrich, John A.	22, July 1893		32	5	
Ditschler, Anna	21, Nov. 1900		76	8	
Dittes, August	26, Mar. 1895		51	5	
Dittmann, Caroline	16, Jan. 1894		70	5	
Dittmann, Jakob	23, June 1896	22, June	71- 8m	5	
Dittmeyer, Joseph	3, June 1901		69	8	
Dittus, Fred.	3, July 1901		6m	8	
Ditzel, Florian	15, Oct. 1891		42	4	
Diven, Julia	29, Dec. 1900		70	8	
Divings, Laura	4, Aug. 1887		11m	1	
Dixon, Elizabeth	27, Nov. 1900		24	8	
Dixon, Hula	15, Oct. 1900		8m	5	
Diß, G.C.	7, Dec. 1895	6, Dec.	6w.	5	
Diß, Katharina Annabelle	21, Feb. 1898	21, Feb.	5-10m	5	
Doag, Catharine	25, Jan. 1901		40	8	
Dobbeling, Katie E.	23, Aug. 1887		35	1	
Dobrowatsky, Frank	29, Nov. 1888		3	1	
Dodd, Spencer B.	19, Nov. 1900		46	8	
Dodson, George	12, Nov. 1887		38	1	
Dodson, Jennie	30, Nov. 1900		34	8	
Dodsworth, Caleb	21, Jan. 1901			8	
Dodt, Henrietta	21, July 1893		4	5	
Doeker, Bernard	2, Feb. 1899	31, Jan.	35- 6m	5	
Doelling, Linda	1, Sept 1900		7m	5	
Doelling, Willie	16, Sept 1889		4m	1	
Doepke, Anna Katharina	13, Dec. 1898	12, Dec.	81	5	Behrens
Doepke, Frederick	3, Nov. 1891		18	4	
Doepke, John H.	2, Oct. 1894		66	5	
Doepke, Louis	8, May 1889		34	1	
Doepke, Norma	6, Jan. 1894		1	5	
Doerger, Anna	12, Feb. 1896	11, Feb.	39- 1m	5	Kotz
Doerger, Anna Cacilia	21, Apr. 1899	20, Apr.	4m	5	
Doerger, Anthony	8, Jan. 1892		8m	5	
Doerger, Maria	28, Oct. 1889		1m	1	
Doering, Peter M.	4, Jan. 1893		30	5	
Doerler, Christina	10, June 1897	9, June	72	5	Aman
Doerler, Johan	21, Aug. 1899	19, Aug.	74	4	
Doermann, Annie	26, Nov. 1900		3	8	
Doerper, John	3, Oct. 1900		2m	5	
Doerr, John	1, Dec. 1900		54	8	
Doerr, John H.	9, Nov. 1894		64	4	
Doerr, Kunigunda	15, Oct. 1896	14, Oct.	68	5	Appel
Doerr, Rosa	23, June 1893		29	5	
Doerr, Rosina	10, Mar. 1891		68	4	
Doeschel, Rudolph	15, Feb. 1895		1	5	
Doescher, Barbara	23, 24, Oct. 1896	22, Oct.	62-10m	5	Eiserle
Doettker, Henry	13, Apr. 1892		31	5	
Doeß, Friedrich	9, Sept 1896	8, Sept	62- 8m	5	
Doeß, George Philipp	8, July 1893	7, July	23- 7m-28d	5	
Doffenbach, Katharine	8, July 1897	6, July	76	4	
Doherty, James	2, May 1901		45	8	
Doherty, Sarah	1, Aug. 1887		7	1	
Doherty, Terrence M.	30, Sept 1887		2w	1	
Dohme, Ferdinand	14, Jan. 1899	13, Jan.	71- 6m	5	
Dohme, Ida	27, Mar. 1895		3	5	
Dokin, Charles H.	21, Apr. 1895		50	5	
Dolan, James	10, July 1901		28	5	
Dolan, Joseph	5, Aug. 1887		30	1	
Dolch, Christian	20, Mar. 1891		72	4	
Dold, Bertha	29, Aug. 1901		21	8	
Dold, Mathaeus	28, Jan. 1891		16	4	
Dold, Melvin	31, July 1901		7m	8	
Dolf, Peter J.	4, Jan. 1901		70	5	
Doll, Charles B.	4, May 1897	3, May	58	5	
Doll, Johan	24, Apr. 1896	23, Apr.	46-10m	5	

Name	Notice Date	Death Date	Age	Page	Maiden Name
****	****** ****	***** ****	***	****	****** ****
Doll, Joseph	24, July 1891		62	1	
Doll, Samuel	6, Oct. 1898	4, Oct.		5	
Doll, Thelma	25, June 1901		8d	8	
Dollar, Mathilda	5, May 1891		2	1	
Dollenmeyer, Catharine	29, May 1894		12	5	
Doller, Max	9, June 1897	8, June	43	5	
Dollman, Mary	21, July 1887		7w	1	
Dollmann, Florence	29, Sept 1893		11m	5	
Dollmann, Johan A.	17, Mar. 1896	16, Mar.	68- 7m	5	
Dollmann, John E.	19, Apr. 1895		36	5	
Dollries, John	23, Nov. 1900		1m	8	
Domis, Josephine	6, Dec. 1898	4, Dec.	34- 9m	5	
Domscher, Ethel	9, Oct. 1894		5m	5	
Donahue, William	16, Mar. 1901		71	8	
Donavan, Mary	8, Oct. 1901		49	1	
Donelly, Maggie E.	3, Oct. 1887		4	1	
Donelly, William A.	25, Apr. 1888		18	1	
Donnelly, Charles	24, Mar. 1888		7m	1	
Donnelly, Frank	7, July 1887		3m	1	
Donnelly, Mary	7, July 1887		3m	1	
Donnelly, Mary	28, Dec. 1900		64	8	
Donnelly, Nellie	29, May 1901		39	8	
Donnelon, Ellen	16, Feb. 1901		76	8	
Donnewald, Christopher	30, Mar. 1895		74	5	
Donohue, Elisabeth	8, Oct. 1900		52	8	
Donohue, Thomas J.	21, July 1888		31	1	
Donovan, Edward	26, Apr. 1895		58	5	
Donovan, Jeremiah	25, Apr. 1901		76	8	
Donovan, T.S.	25, Jan. 1888		40	1	
Doodey, John	10, Mar. 1891		17	4	
Dooglag, Walter	15, Nov. 1887		3m	4	
Dooley, Mary	18, Aug. 1900			8	
Door, Rosa	22, July 1887		10m	1	
Doppe, Herman	6, June 1895		49	5	
Doppelmann, Joseph	8, Jan. 1890		28	1	
Doppes, Klara	18, May 1900	17, May	83	5	Kordes
Dora, Monice	29, Nov. 1889		40	1	
Doran, Felix	5, Dec. 1887		80	1	
Doran, Joseph	13, July 1901		11m	8	
Dorawitz, Joseph	18, July 1890		6m	1	
Dore, William J.	20, Sept 1887		27	1	
Dorenbusch, Maria	23, Sept 1896	21, Sept	39- 5m	5	Volck
Dorenbusch, Maria	19, July 1898	18, July	43	5	
Doring, George	9, Sept 1891		38	4	
Doring, Henrietta	7, Oct. 1893		63	5	
Dorman, Fred.	26, Feb. 1890		68	1	
Dorman, Matt	5, May 1891		40	1	
Dormann, Christian	15, June 1895		75	5	
Dormer, Max	10, June 1896	8, June	55	5	
Dornbusch, Barbara	6, Dec. 1899	5, Dec.	67- 6m	5	Knorr
Dorner, D.	7, Dec. 1887		11	1	
Dornette, Wilhelmina	5, Oct. 1896	4, Oct.	54- 9m	5	Bierbaum
Dornhegge, Johan Friedrich	25, Apr. 1899	23, Apr.	58- 8m	4	
Dornseifer, Charlotte	8, Nov. 1900		71	8	
Dornsey, Peter L.	2, Nov. 1888		2m	1	
Dorsch, Friedrich	9, Feb. 1899	8, Feb.	74	5	
Dorsch, Kunigunde	28, Feb. 1896	27, Feb.	71- 8m	5	Bezold
Dorse, Anna Maria	9, 11, Nov. 1895	8, Nov.	62	5	Butler
Dorse, Jacob	30, May 1895		63	5	
Dorsey, Edward	16, Mar. 1901		59	8	
Dorsey, Willie	11, Dec. 1891		3	4	
Dorst, Louis	26, Jan. 1892		49	5	
Dorst, Magdalena	23, Sept 1891		50	4	
Dorst, Valentin	30, May 1898	28, May	66- - 8d	4	
Dosenbach, Therese	10, May 1889		22	1	
Dosterkamp, Mary	14, Aug. 1887		16d	1	
Dotschengall, Margaretha	7, Oct. 1898	6, Oct.	57	5	
Dott, Bernard	27, Dec. 1888		31	2	
Dottmann, B.H.	12, Sept 1895	11, Sept	65	5	
Dotz, C.G.	31, Oct. 1894		5	5	
Dotzauer, Charles	19, Dec. 1900		59	8	

Name ****	Notice Date ****** ****	Death Date ***** ****	Age ***	Page ****	Maiden Name ****** ****
Dotzauer, Frank	31, Aug. 1901		43	8	
Dotzauer, Frank A.	24, Dec. 1893		2	5	
Dotzauer, Helene	25, Aug. 1898	23, Aug.	1- -19d	4	
Dotzauer, Joseph	7, May 1895		10	5	
Dotzauer, Maria	12, Mar. 1897	11, Mar.	61	5	
Dougherty, A. May	21, Feb. 1888			1	
Dougherty, Letitia	1, Aug. 1888		46	2	
Dougherty, William	11, Aug. 1900		2m	8	
Douglas, Julia M.	17, June 1888		4m	1	
Dowd, Dennis	14, Mar. 1901		55	8	
Doyle, James	20, Mar. 1901		5m	1	
Doyle, Mary	5, Aug. 1901		35	8	
Doyle, Mary	5, Sept 1901		2	8	
Doyle, Thomas	4, Aug. 1888		21	4	
Doyle, Thomas	7, Jan. 1901		26	5	
Doß, Mary	11, June 1901		60	8	
Drach, Adolph C.	6, May 1896	4, May		5	
Drach, Felicia	6, May 1896	5, May	5	5	
Drach, Martha	3, May 1895		11m	5	
Drach, Rosa	25, Dec. 1894		18	5	
Drach, Senta	13, July 1897	12, July	7	5	
Drahmann, Bernardina	16, Oct. 1900		54	8	
Drahmann, John	26, Apr. 1901			8	
Drain, Joseph	15, Aug. 1901		71	8	
Drake, Adelaide	9, Jan. 1901		20	5	
Draper, John	13, July 1887		13	1	
Draper, Martha S. (Mrs)	3, Feb. 1891		80	4	
Draude, Edmund C.	24, Mar. 1896	23, Mar.	2- - 3d	5	
Draude, Gertrud	23, Mar. 1899	21, Mar.	63	5	Kunkel
Draur, Grace M.	28, July 1887		7	1	
Drees, Alphons J.	10, July 1901		2m	5	
Drees, Anna	5, Dec. 1888		2m	1	
Drees, Elisabeth	7, Mar. 1898	6, Mar.	25- 1m	5	Dornberger
Drees, Henrietta	26, Dec. 1900		74	8	
Drees, Maria Teckla	20, Nov. 1899	19, Nov.	70- 5m	5	Stevens
Drees, William	26, May 1892		67	5	
Drees, William	5, Apr. 1901		28	8	
Dreger, Elizabeth	15, July 1890		65	1	
Dreher, Anna	14, May 1895		22	5	
Dreher, Fred.	16, Dec. 1892		30	5	
Dreher, George	14, June 1901		41	5	
Dreher, Katharine	23, Mar. 1900	21, Mar.	52	8	
Dreier, Anna	20, Jan. 1894		61	5	
Dreier, Franz	13, Mar. 1890		70	4	
Dreier, Katharina	29, Jan. 1890		34	1	
Dreifus, Meyer	21, Sept 1897	20, Sept	41	5	
Dreihs, Fred. A.	25, Sept 1900		2	5	
Dreis, H.H.	11, Apr. 1895		62	5	
Dresch, Christina	10, May 1895		51	5	
Dressel, Fred.	8, Jan. 1890		46	1	
Dressel, William	16, Aug. 1887		59	1	
Dresselhaus, Henry	22, Aug. 1899	21, Aug.	42- 4m	5	
Dresser, Ira S.	9, June 1891		60	4	
Drew, Shirley J.	2, Aug. 1901		6d	8	
Drexilius, Edward	23, Mar. 1895		4	5	
Dreyer, Herman Bernard	4, Mar. 1898	3, Mar.	73- 1m	5	
Dreyer, Mary	2, May 1901		34	8	
Dreß, Henrietta C.	5, Sept 1891		10m	1	
Driehaus, Henry	5, Mar. 1901		54	5	
Driemeyer, Mildred	27, Feb. 1896	26, Feb.	7m	5	
Driemeyer, Rosina	14, Mar. 1895		60	5	
Dries, Bertha	28, Aug. 1890		7m	1	
Drinkard, Kittie	21, June 1895		33	5	
Drischel, Willie	24, Sept 1889		10m	1	
Driscoll, William	3, Apr. 1901		2	8	
Driskell, Wesley	14, Feb. 1891		80	4	
Driver, William	21, Feb. 1901		40	8	
Droege, John H.	3, Nov. 1893		54	5	
Droege, Wilhelm Karl	13, Nov. 1893		62	5	
Droesch, Joseph	26, Nov. 1892		3	5	
Droeßler, Willie	6, Jan. 1892		5	5	

Name ****	Notice Date ****** ****	Death Date ***** ****	Age ***	Page ****	Maiden Name ****** ****
Droger, August	5, July 1888		48	1	
Droll, Edward	23, Feb. 1901		29	8	
Droop, William	17, Dec. 1900		58	8	
Droppelmann, Elisabeth	26, May 1896	24, May	66- 7m	5	
Drosch, Katharine	24, July 1894		8m	5	
Droste, Blanch	24, Oct. 1891		1	4	
Droste, John F.	31, May 1890		74	1	
Drout, Nellie	2, Aug. 1900		17	8	
Drouyhard, Simon	28, May 1891		2	4	
Droyer, Julia	31, Jan. 1901		50	8	
Drucher, Mary	16, Apr. 1891		52	4	
Druck, Katharine	23, Mar. 1891	22, Mar.	81	1	
Drucker, Gertrude	8, May 1896	7, May	5	5	
Drury, Michael	4, Oct. 1900		50	8	
Drury, Winnie	4, July 1901		24	8	
Dryhaus,	14, Nov. 1900		1d	8	
Dubach, Christ. H.	23, Nov. 1900		74	8	
Duboski, William	17, Apr. 1891		42	4	
Duck, B.	12, Oct. 1895	11, Oct.	66	5	
Duebel, (Mrs. Heinrich)	2, Aug. 1899	1, Aug.		5	Fels
Duem, Heinrich	1, Mar. 1888		56	4	
Duerholter, Gottfried	31, Jan. 1901		75	8	
Duernbach, Joseph	8, Oct. 1900		50	8	
Duesing, Gerhard	26, Mar. 1901		62	8	
Dufficy, Margaret	29, Oct. 1900		27	8	
Duffs, Jakob	4, June 1900	2, June	53	8	
Duffy, A.M.	24, Jan. 1888		1m	1	
Duffy, Catharine	11, Oct. 1901		6	5	
Dufner, Leonda	5, Mar. 1892		51	5	
Dugan, John	2, Aug. 1900		26	8	
Dugan, W.F.	29, Dec. 1887		31	4	
Duhlmeier, John Henry	19, Feb. 1900	17, Feb.	32- 9m	4	
Duhlmeier, Martha	30, Nov. 1887		5- 6m	4	
Duhme, Herman Heinrich	6, June 1900	4, June	24- 6m	8	
Duhme, Margaretha	8, Apr. 1899	7, Apr.	86	5	
Duitschreiber, Henry	27, Sept 1889		56	1	
Dulach, Joseph	4, Apr. 1901		39	8	
Dulicks, John	16, July 1901		37	8	
Dulitz, Fred	26, Jan. 1892		95	5	
Dullmeier, Amelia	28, Oct. 1891		5	4	
Dullweber, Frieda	29, 30, May 1901		2m	8	
Dullweber, Mary	24, June 1901		81	8	
Dulweber, Frank	23, May 1894		12	5	
Dulweber, Johan	13, Dec. 1897	12, Dec.	39- 9m	5	
Dulweber, Theodore	12, Feb. 1901		51	8	
Dumbacher, Maria Susana	10, Nov. 1898	8, Nov.	66- 2m	4	Grimm
Dumler, George	13, Mar. 1901		75	8	
Dumler, Martin C.	8, Aug. 1893		63	5	
Dumont, Katie G.	30, May 1895		36	5	
Dumont, Philipp M.	3, July 1895		2	5	
Dunbar, H.J.	13, Aug. 1888		5m	1	
Dunbar, John D.	14, Feb. 1901		38	8	
Dunbar, Marie	7, July 1887		45	1	
Duncan, Aettie	29, Dec. 1900		34	8	
Duncan, Margaret	17, Apr. 1888		60	1	
Duncanson, Antonia	8, Dec. 1891		14m	4	
Dunhoft, Anna Maria	1, Mar. 1898	28, Feb.	54- 8m	5	Sander
Dunholter, W.H.	5, Dec. 1899	3, Dec.		4	
Dunken, Elizabeth	20, Oct. 1888		27	1	
Dunker, Maria	26, Feb. 1896	24, Feb.	78	5	Beckschmidt
Dunkie, Hattie	2, July 1901		17	8	
Dunkle, John	22, Mar. 1901		50	8	
Dunkmann, Bernard	26, Dec. 1898	25, Dec.	67	5	
Dunkmann, Frank W.	28, July 1891		4	4	
Dunkmann, Mary	16, May 1894		59	5	
Dunlap, Charles	15, Dec. 1900		26	8	
Dunlap, Edgar	6, Dec. 1900		33	8	
Dunlap, Mary	23, Mar. 1893		42	5	
Dunn, Moses	21, Apr. 1888			1	
Dunn, Peter	31, July 1901		27	8	
Dunn, William	23, Oct. 1900		71	8	

Name	Notice Date	Death Date	Age	Page	Maiden Name
****	****** ****	***** ****	***	****	****** ****
Dunn, William	13, Aug. 1901		54	8	
Dunn, William P.	2, Oct. 1888		27	1	
Dunnemeier, Carrie	20, Oct. 1893		22	8	
Dunnican, James	27, Nov. 1900		6	8	
Dunphy, John	22, Mar. 1901		1	8	
Duntz, Catharine	13, Dec. 1900		73	8	
Dupree, Ellen	1, July 1901		5m	8	
Dupuis, Wilhelm	26, Dec. 1896	25, Dec.	70- 1m	5	
Durand, Dora	22, Aug. 1889	22, Aug.	2- 9m	1	
Durandt, Edward Paul	15, July 1889	15, July	5m-15d	4	
Durham, Ed.	5, Aug. 1890		1	1	
Durham, Emma J.	13, July 1887		9	1	
Durham, Ida	16, Apr. 1890		22	1	
Durham, Louis	5, Mar. 1888		37	4	
Durner, Joseph	23, July 1887		13m	1	
Dusterberg, Mary E.	23, Feb. 1893		85	5	
Duwel, Karl	7, Aug. 1895	6, Aug.	61- 8m	5	
Duweling, Mary	3, Dec. 1900		36	8	
Dwyer, James	13, May 1901		30	8	
Dwyer, Mary	6, Dec. 1900		53	8	
Dwyer, William	24, 25, Sept 1900		23	5	
Dyer, Annie	20, June 1901		70	8	
Döcker, Franz	10, Mar. 1897	8, Mar.	87	5	
Döllmann, Maria	19, Dec. 1896	18, Dec.	69	5	
Döllmann, Theodor	2, June 1898	1, June	45	4	
Döpke, Bertha Barbara	26, Dec. 1896	24, Dec.		5	Wolf
Dören, Frank	28, Jan. 1893		52	5	
Dörger, Margaretha	29, Dec. 1896	28, Dec.	81- 8m	5	Klostermann
Döring, Martin	16, Oct. 1897	15, Oct.	61- 3m	5	
Dörmann, Heinrich	15, Aug. 1898	13, Aug.	69- 6m	5	
Dörr, Leo	11, July 1888		3m	1	
Dücker, H.H.	30, Oct. 1895	29, Oct.	50	5	
Düringen, Marie	11, Mar. 1889		62	1	
Dürstock, Karoline	8, May 1894		33	5	
Düsing, Bernardina Elisabeth	4, Feb. 1900	3, Feb.	18- 1m	5	
Düsterberg, Herman	3, July 1897	2, July	53- 3m	5	
Eagers, Caroline	22, Nov. 1893		73	5	
Early, Andrew	14, Jan. 1893		53	5	
Early, Armsted	15, Dec. 1900		60	8	
Early, S.A.	11, Apr. 1895		45	5	
Eaton, Edward W.	23, Aug. 1887		48	1	
Ebbrecht, Adolph	13, Sept 1893		21	5	
Ebenhack, Margaret	24, July 1901		61	8	
Eberanz, John	17, July 1890		26	1	
Eberhard, Adam	7, Oct. 1890		41	1	
Eberhardt, Fannie	15, June 1901		47	8	
Eberhardt, Lena	8, Aug. 1895	7, Aug.	42- 9m	5	Schuler
Eberhorst, Raymond	15, Feb. 1892		5	5	
Eberle, C.J.	4, Nov. 1895	2, Nov.	57- 9m	5	
Eberle, Ernst M.	14, Sept 1897	13, Sept	27	4,5	
Eberle, Jakob V.	23, Oct. 1897	22, Oct.	33-10m	4	
Eberle, Johan	14, June 1897	12, June	67- 2m	5	
Eberle, Mabel	3, June 1891		6	4	
Eberle, Martin	10, Aug. 1900		65	8	
Eberle, Martin	11, Aug. 1900	10, Aug.	58	5	
Eberle, Stephanie	19, July 1887		27	1	
Eberling, Edward	3, May 1893		8	5	
Ebert, Alma	10, Nov. 1896	9, Nov.	31	5	Sohn
Ebert, Louis P.	1, May 1895		53	5	
Ebert, Regina	18, May 1894		9m	5	
Ebinger, Mary	27, Nov. 1900		62	8	
Ebner, Ferdinand A.	18, May 1894		5	5	
Eby, Artemus J.	5, Feb. 1901		70	8	
Echert, Harry	8, July 1891		3m	4	
Echtermann, Anna	15, Feb. 1895		1	5	
Eck, Albert C.	19, July 1895		27	5	
Eck, George Jacob	30, Apr. 1898	29, Apr.	67- 3m	4	
Eck, Jacob	27, Oct. 1888		4	1	
Eckel, George	14, June 1898	13, June	48- 2m	5	
Eckel, George T.	17, Dec. 1900		13	8	

Name ****	Notice Date ****** ****	Death Date ***** ****	Age ***	Page ****	Maiden Name ****** ****
Eckelmann, Mary E.	6, Nov. 1891		67	4	
Eckenroad, Ernst	21, June 1894		9	5	
Eckenroth, Bessie	9, July 1891		6m	4	
Eckenroth, Frank P.	5, Jan. 1888		4m	1	
Eckenroth, Grace	19, Jan. 1894		2	5	
Eckenroth, William	28, July 1893		8d	5	
Eckerle, Bertha	11, July 1895		37	5	
Eckerle, Franziska	12, Aug. 1899	11, Aug.	68- 7m	5	Nageleisen
Eckerle, Johan F.	22, Jan. 1890		2	1	
Eckerle, Joseph	5, Feb. 1901		7	8	
Eckerle, Rosa M.	30, Sept 1891		1m	4	
Eckerle, Tillie	11, Oct. 1895	10, Oct.	4- 6m	5	
Eckert, August	9, July 1890		1	1	
Eckert, August	14, Sept 1893		46	5	
Eckert, Carolina	30, July 1896	28, July	54	5	
Eckert, Charles W.	24, Jan. 1888		46	1	
Eckert, Elisabeth	2, May 1889	1, May	64	* 1	Veit
Eckert, Elisabeth	15, Feb. 1897	13, Feb.	60- 5m	5	Ehrhardt
Eckert, Emma	30, Mar. 1893		16	5	
Eckert, John	11, June 1901		83	8	
Eckert, Lorenz	23, Oct. 1889		67	1	
Eckert, Rosa	15, Oct. 1891		3	4	
Eckert, Sunno	31, Dec. 1890		62	4	
Eckhard, Bruno	12, Mar. 1901		32	8	
Eckhardt, Theresa	25, Feb. 1896	24, Feb.	64- 7m	5	Jakob
Eckhoff, Aloysius J.B.	5, May 1893			5	
Eckler,	30, Jan. 1891		1d	4	
Eckles, Ursula	14, June 1901		3m	5	
Eckmann, Johan Heinrich	8, Mar. 1898	6, Mar.	34- 8m	5	
Eckmann, Magdalena	31, Dec. 1891		72	1	
Eckstein, Fred.	11, Apr. 1893		72	5	
Eckstein, Frederick C.	13, Apr. 1895		84	4	
Eckstein, M.A.	1, Mar. 1888		3m	4	
Edelmann, John	10, May 1889		51	1	
Edelstein, Kate	14, Aug. 1889		45	1	
Eden, L.R.	30, Oct. 1891		41	4	
Edenburgh, W.E.	27, Apr. 1889		20	1	
Eder, Dorothea	27, Apr. 1892		3m	5	
Eder, Ernst	1, Sept 1900		35	5	
Eder, John	4, Mar. 1889		3m	1	
Eder, Norma	4, Apr. 1895		1	5	
Eder, Phil.	7, June 1890		49	1	
Edgar, Raymond	14, Sept 1900		2m	5	
Eding, Mary	18, Nov. 1891		36	4	
Edrich, Mary	16, July 1901		5	8	
Edward, Mary	21, Mar. 1888		34	1	
Edward, William S.	20, June 1888		31	1	
Edwards, Florence	17, Sept 1890		4	1	
Edwards, J.H.	19, Aug. 1895	18, Aug.	42- 4m	5	
Edwards, John	1, Aug. 1887		79	1	
Edwards, Laima May	2, Dec. 1887		6- 3m	4	
Edwards, Lucy	7, Aug. 1901		49	8	
Edwards, O.	4, Dec. 1900		1d	8	
Edwards, W.	27, June 1888		49	1	
Effinger, Francis Xavier	30, Nov. 1898	29, Nov.	79	4	
Effinger, Frank A.	7, Mar. 1891		10m	4	
Efland, Lilly	14, Aug. 1900		10	5	
Egan, H.	30, Jan. 1888		10d	1	
Egan, James	15, Nov. 1900		49	8	
Egan, Kate	4, Jan. 1901		54	5	
Egan, Mary	4, Feb. 1901		16	8	
Egbers, Emilie	22, July 1901		39	8	
Egbers, Georg	14, Jan. 1897	12, Jan.	70- 2m	5	
Egbers, Helena Adelheid	4, Apr. 1899	3, Apr.	66	5	Pohl
Egbers, Joseph	14, June 1897	13, June	38- 1m	5	
Egbers, Maria	2, Aug. 1900		58	8	
Eger, Elisabeth	19, Mar. 1890		66	1	
Eger, John	1, Aug. 1887		7m	1	
Eggebrecht, Gustav	11, June 1895		5	5	
Eggebrecht, Jakob	13, June 1894		42	5	
Eggen, Albert	22, Sept 1891		46	1	

Name ****	Notice Date ****** ****	Death Date ***** ****	Age ***	Page ****	Maiden Name ****** ****
Eggers, August	10, Aug. 1887		45	1	
Eggers, Henry	15, Nov. 1894		24	5	
Eggler, J.	8, Dec. 1900		1	8	
Eggleston, B.	10, Feb. 1888		72	1	
Egle, Angelina	24, May 1895		4	5	
Egleman, John F.	4, June 1891		71	4	
Egli, Johan	29, Mar. 1900	28, Mar.	87	4	
Egloff, Herman	9, Sept 1893		3m	5	
Egner, Ada E.	18, July 1893		1	5	
Egner, Christian	24, Apr. 1891		91	4	
Egner, Maria	4, July 1891	3, July	55- 6m-27d	4	Becker
Eha, Barbara	20, June 1895		43	5	
Ehert, Emma	9, Oct. 1900		2m	8	
Ehlen, Frida	24, Apr. 1891		4m	4	
Ehlerding, Karl	21, July 1893		49	5	
Ehlerding, Louise	4, Dec. 1897	2, Dec.	72- 6m	5	
Ehlers, August	25, July 1900			5	
Ehlers, Louis	21, Nov. 1891		13m	4	
Ehman, Lizzie	6, Mar. 1891		1	4	
Ehmann, Christoph	14, Dec. 1898	13, Dec.	83	5	
Ehmer, Friedricka	15, May 1901		63	8	
Ehrensperger, Elizabeth	10, May 1901		81	8	
Ehrer, Sebastian	28, July 1888		53	1	
Ehret, Catharine	2, Jan. 1901		1d	5	
Ehretsmann, Arthur	18, May 1894		8m	5	
Ehrhardt, Catharine	6, Sept 1901		77	8	
Ehrhardt, Kate A.	17, July 1901		45	8	
Ehrhardt, Wilhelm	10, Jan. 1894		51	5	
Ehrlich, Selma	30, Sept 1895	28, Sept	4- 1m	5	
Ehrmann, Sarah B.	27, July 1893		39	5	
Ehrmantraut, Th.	26, Nov. 1888		66	1	
Ehrmsperger, Elise	18, Jan. 1893		43	5	
Eibeck, Elisabeth	1, Oct. 1895	30, Sept	80- 6m	5	Frie
Eich, Anna Margaretha	29, 30, Dec. 1894	27, Dec.	32- 9m-13d	5	Poggendick
Eich, Catharine	19, July 1900		73	8	
Eich, Charlotte	7, July 1891		70	1	
Eich, Georg	5, Feb. 1895		15m	5	
Eichbaum, Fred.	21, Jan. 1901		61	8	
Eichel, Ed. G.	12, July 1890		4m	1	
Eichel, Oscar	17, Dec. 1895	14, Dec.	8m-15d	4	
Eichelberger, Clifford	23, May 1894		1	5	
Eichelberger, Frank	12, Mar. 1901		42	8	
Eichelberger, Peter	13, Oct. 1892		52	5	
Eichele, A.R.	17, May 1894		6m	5	
Eichenlaub, Anton E.	13, July 1895		2	5	
Eichenlaub, Marie Josephine	19, Oct. 1888	18, Oct.	17-11m	1	
Eichenlaub, Theresa	17, Feb. 1899	16, Feb.	69- -25d	5	Rhein
Eicher, Anna Maria	2, Jan. 1897	1, Jan.	25- 7m	5	
Eicher, Anthony	5, Nov. 1891		44	1	
Eicher, Barbara	13, Jan. 1894		70	5	
Eichert, Katharine	6, Sept 1895	5, Sept	98- 1m	5	
Eichhold, Samuel	7, Oct. 1891		71- -29d	4	
Eichholz, August	24, July 1890		27	1	
Eichholzer, Agnes	14, Jan. 1892		7	1	
Eichhorn, Catharina	27, Oct. 1891		59	1	
Eichhorn, Franziska	6, July 1896	5, July	52-10m	5	Hartke
Eichhorn, Harry	6, July 1901		11m	8	
Eichhorn, Heinrich	21, Feb. 1898	20, Feb.	28- 6m	5	
Eichhorn, Joseph	3, Nov. 1887		6	4	
Eichhorn, Salome	12, July 1893		63	5	
Eichhorn, Theresa	8, July 1901		52	8	
Eichler, Alma	18, Jan. 1894		4m	5	
Eichler, Catharine	7, June 1901		41	8	
Eichler, Edward	4, Jan. 1893		1	5	
Eichler, Friedrich	29, Dec. 1893		8m	5	
Eichler, H.	20, Jan. 1888		4	4	
Eichler, Heinrich	13, Sept 1900		55	5	
Eichner, Alma	12, May 1893		1	5	
Eichner, Elisabeth	4, Aug. 1890		76	1	
Eickenhorst, Herman	23, Jan. 1900	22, Jan.	2- -23d	4	
Eickerling, Herman	10, Mar. 1888		1d	1	

Name	Notice Date	Death Date	Age	Page	Maiden Name
****	****** ****	***** ****	***	****	****** ****
Eickhoff, John	7, July 1887		21m	1	
Eiden, Jacob E.	19, Feb. 1897	18, Feb.	2- 5m	5	
Eikel, Henry	29, Jan. 1896	28, Jan.	70- 3m- 9d	5	
Eikens, Johanna	13, Oct. 1900		28	8	
Eilermann, Henry	28, Dec. 1892		1	5	
Eilermann, John	13, Jan. 1891		12d	1	
Eilers, Anna M.	2, Dec. 1892		79	5	
Eilers, Bernard F.	26, Jan. 1899	25, Jan.	39-11m	5	
Eilers, Gerhard	25, Nov. 1895	23, Nov.	82- 4m	5	
Eilers, Henry	24, Jan. 1894		57	5	
Eilers, Sophie	22, Mar. 1895		72	5	
Einhaus, Katharina	19, Jan. 1897		53	5	
Einsecke, Joseph	24, Dec. 1895	23, Dec.	42	5	
Einspanner, Francis	14, June 1901		1	5	
Eiseberg, Mary	10, Dec. 1891		51	4	
Eisele, Albert	27, Dec. 1893		3m	5	
Eisele, Katie	20, July 1887		5m	1	
Eisele, Sophia	25, Mar. 1891		24	4	
Eiselein, Albert	6, Apr. 1900	5, Apr.	29	4	
Eisemann, Fred.	27, Aug. 1890		6	1	
Eisen, Anna	14, June 1889		3	1	
Eisenhardt, Anna	3, Jan. 1901		72	5	
Eisenhardt, Dorothea	17, Feb. 1895		71	5	
Eisenhardt, Georg	6, Feb. 1894		30	5	
Eisenhart, Karolina	8, Apr. 1897	7, Apr.	51- 4m	5	Winter
Eisenhauer, Joseph	4, Oct. 1887		5d	1	
Eisenmann, Annie	2, Feb. 1888		2- 8m	4	
Eisenmann, Eduard	27, Oct. 1887		7m	1	
Eisenmann, Mabel	16, July 1892		6m	5	
Eisenschmidt, Fredericka	16, Dec. 1892		53	5	
Eisenschmidt, Herman	26, July 1899	25, July	61	5	
Eisenschmitt, Lester	2, July 1901		3m	8	
Eisert, Emma	21, Aug. 1891		21d	4	
Eisker, Berthold	4, Dec. 1891		56	4	
Eisman, Francis	5, Jan. 1901		37	8	
Eismann, Anna	13, July 1899	12, July	46- 8m	5	Meyer
Ekardt, Louis	11, July 1896	9, July	36-11m	5	
Ekemeyer, William (Rev.)	20, May 1897	18, May	72	5	
Elbent, Ermina	6, June 1893		1	5	
Elbert, Alma K.	23, July 1887		12	1	
Elbin, John F.	19, Apr. 1895		38	5	
Elder, Nido	28, May 1892		90	5	
Elder, William	8, Sept 1900		56	5	
Eldering, Anna	5, Apr. 1895		25	5	
Elfaring, H.	14, Oct. 1901		43	5	
Elfers, Catharine	19, Dec. 1891		68	4	
Elfers, Clara	9, Jan. 1889		8m	1	
Elfner, L.M.	25, Jan. 1888		31	1	
Elfring, Anna M.	16, Dec. 1891		70	4	
Elgert, Charles F.	25, Jan. 1901		60	8	
Elies, Mary	8, Apr. 1901		8	8	
Elitzer, John	2, Apr. 1890		58	1	
Elk, Joseph	12, Jan. 1892		1m	5	
Elk, Marie	19, July 1889		69	1	
Ellaback, Veronica	18, Dec. 1891		76	2	
Ellas, Anna	28, Mar. 1901		32	8	
Ellebrecht, August	12, Feb. 1891		4	4	
Ellenbrock, Henry	19, Aug. 1891		24	4	
Ellenmein, Barbara	12, May 1891		34	1	
Ellerding, William	23, Nov. 1888		57	1	
Ellerhorst, H.	1, Feb. 1888		14m	4	
Ellermann, Amelia	15, Feb. 1895		25	5	
Ellermann, Anna	14, Mar. 1901		37	8	
Ellermann, B.H.	26, Mar. 1897	26, Mar.	14-11m	5	
Ellermann, Bernard	12, 13, Oct. 1893	11, Oct.	67- 9m- 1d	5	
Ellermann, Carrie	8, Mar. 1901		3	8	
Ellermann, Catherina	5, Dec. 1893		76	5	
Ellermann, Clara	31, July 1890		1	1	
Ellermann, Emilie	12, 13, Feb. 1895	11, Feb.	25- 3m-10d	5	
Ellermann, Eva	15, Nov. 1887		48	4	
Ellig, Mathew	8, Apr. 1891		57	4	

Name	Notice Date	Death Date	Age	Page	Maiden Name
****	****** ****	***** ****	***	****	****** ****
Elliot, Frank	3, Mar. 1888		30	1	
Elliot, William	19, Oct. 1887		4m	1	
Ellis, John	13, Aug. 1901		52	8	
Ellis, Robert	28, Mar. 1888		65	1	
Ellison, Rees	5, Sept 1900		2	5	
Ellmann, Clem	31, July 1899	30, July	70- 9m	4	
Elsasser, George	3, 4, Sept 1890	2, Sept	48	1	
Elsbernd, Gerhard H.	5, Nov. 1900		78	8	
Elsen, Franz X.	10, Dec. 1898	9, Dec.	44- 1m	5	
Elsener, Johan Baptiste	7, Aug. 1899	5, Aug.		5	
Elsenheimer, Johan Georg	28, Dec. 1897	27, Dec.	78	4	
Elsenheimer, Maggie	16, Mar. 1893		2m	5	
Elshof, Josephina	22, May 1891		1d	1	
Elshoff, Anna	22, Nov. 1893		18	5	
Elshoff, Anton	21, Jan. 1898	20, Jan.	64- 3m	5	
Elsing, Francis	21, Nov. 1900		59	8	
Elstein, Esther	14, Aug. 1887		40	1	
Elsässer, George	4, Sept 1890		49	1	
Eltins, William	11, May 1901		33	8	
Emanuel, Joseph	25, Mar. 1891		6	4	
Embshoff, Catharine	31, July 1901		73	8	
Embshoff, Emilie	26, Nov. 1895	25, Nov.	30-10m	5	Renzelmann
Embshoff, George F.	2, Feb. 1901		67	8	
Embshoff, Lillian	7, Sept 1895	5, Sept	13-10m	5	
Embshoff, Mary G.	22, Nov. 1893		17	5	
Emders, W.J.	19, Oct. 1901		51	8	
Emerson, M.J.	6, Jan. 1888		8	1	
Emge, O.	4, Dec. 1888		50	1	
Emig, Celia	5, June 1895		2	5	
Emig, Elisabeth	11, Apr. 1898	10, Apr.	83	5	
Emig, John J.	3, Jan. 1893		24	5	
Emig, Philipp	9, Nov. 1896	8, Nov.	55- 7m	5	
Emigholz, W.	10, 12, Mar. 1898	9, Mar.	41- 9m	5	
Emlich, Bernardina	29, Feb. 1896	27, Feb.	78- 9m	5	
Emme, Cash	13, Dec. 1900		80	8	
Emmel, Georg	13, Jan. 1898	12, Jan.	63- 6m	5	
Emmerhorst, Dora	23, Dec. 1893		2m	5	
Emmerich, Arnold	7, June 1888		53	1	
Emmert, Augusta	9, June 1891		42	4	
Emmert, Elisa	23, Apr. 1891		39	4	
Emmert, Henry	12, May 1895		27	5	
Emmert, Louis	19, Aug. 1892		32	5	
Emmich, Bernard	26, Aug. 1896	25, Aug.	81	5	
Emmick, Louise	14, Oct. 1901		44	5	
Emos, Eva	14, Feb. 1901		80	8	
Emrich, Jacob	10, Oct. 1900		76	8	
Emrich, Louis G.	6, June 1895		38	5	
Emshoff, J.A.	16, Nov. 1895	14, Nov.	21- 2m	5	
Emsicke, Cecilia M.	22, July 1891		9m	4	
Emsieke, Anna Maria	10, Nov. 1899	9, Nov.	77- 8m	4	Enneking
Emwalle, H.	5, June 1894		10m	5	
Endebrock, Louisa	21, Aug. 1888		9m	1	
Endebrock, Wilhelm	17, Dec. 1898	16, Dec.	73	5	
Ender, Norma H.	4, July 1891		3	4	
Enderle, Mary	23, Sept 1889		5	1	
Endmann, Emma	10, Oct. 1890		2	4	
Endres, Barbara	21, Jan. 1896	20, Jan.	28- 2m	5	Gruener
Endres, Barbara	2, Aug. 1901		70	8	
Endres, Clara	10, Jan. 1888		2	4	
Endres, Ellen	10, Jan. 1888		44	4	
Endreß, Louis	1, Nov. 1888		28	1	
Engbers, B.H. (Fr.)	25, Sept 1895	24, Sept	40	5	
Engbersen, B.H.	22, June 1889		33	1	
Engbert, August	1, June 1901		2m	8	
Engel, Anna R.	7, Apr. 1895		69	5	
Engel, Henry	6, Apr. 1893		46	5	
Engel, Jacob G.	9, June 1899	7, June	38	5	
Engel, John	25, Sept 1894		89	5	
Engel, Lena	11, July 1895		21m	5	
Engel, Margaret	20, Oct. 1891		70	1	
Engel, Robert P.	4, Feb. 1891		9	4	

Name ****	Notice Date ****** ****	Death Date ***** ****	Age ***	Page ****	Maiden Name ****** ****
Engel, Sarah	8, Aug. 1896	7, Aug.	68- 2m	5	
Engelbeck, Gus.	8, June 1895		52	5	
Engelbert, H.	11, Dec. 1888		5m	1	
Engelbrecht, Amanda	18, Nov. 1891		11m	4	
Engelbrecht, William	5, July 1887		47	1	
Engelbrink, H.	21, Nov. 1898	18, Nov.		5	
Engelhard, John	8, Mar. 1889	7, Mar.	46- 4m-26d	1	
Engelhard, Walter	27, Dec. 1888		5m	2	
Engelhardt, John	8, Mar. 1889		46	1	
Engelhart, John	5, Mar. 1901		68	5	
Engelhen, Anna Margaretha	4, Oct. 1897	3, Oct.	74-10m	5	
Engelke, Clarence	1, July 1901		6m	8	
Engelke, George F.	20, Feb. 1894		57	5	
Engelke, Henriette	9, July 1890		59	1	
Engelke, Maria Elisabeth	4, Apr. 1900	3, Apr.	86- 6m	8	Meyer
Engelmann, Heinrich	11, Jan. 1899	10, Jan.	39- 8m	5	
Engelmann, Johan G.	25, 26, June 1890	25, June	34	1	
Engelmeier, John	29, Jan. 1890		48	1	
Engels, Christ.	21, June 1894		70	5	
Enghauser, Josephine	10, Mar. 1893		1d	5	
Enginger, Ignatz	27, May 1901		47	8	
Engle, Francis	16, Oct. 1901		60	1	
Englehardt, Friedrich	16, June 1898	15, June	56	5	
Englender, Philip	11, Mar. 1890		8m	1	
Engler, Nettie	27, Feb. 1896	26, Feb.	32- 1m	5	
Englert, Edward	9, July 1895		2	5	
Englert, Eva	17, Apr. 1901		69	8	
Englert, Magdalena	19, Dec. 1891		76	4	
Englert, Maria Emma	4, Apr. 1899	3, Apr.	44- 4m	5	Lischer
English, James	17, May 1901		67	8	
Enke, Wilhelm	10, Mar. 1897	9, Mar.	29- 1m	5	
Ennebrock, Dora	13, Sept 1899	12, Sept	29- 1m	4	Wulf
Ennebrock, Friedrich	27, Feb. 1899	25, Feb.	34	5	
Enneking, Elisabeth	23, Apr. 1891		58	4	
Enneking, Gahan B.	4, Apr. 1891		50	4	
Enneking, Henry	25, Apr. 1889		4	1	
Enneking, J.B.	2, Dec. 1895	30, Nov.	64	5	
Enneking, Johanna	20, Feb. 1900	19, Feb.	76	5	Thiemann
Enneking, Maria Agnes	22, June 1896	21, June	72	5	Heidlage
Ennen, Alma E.	19, Jan. 1888		6m	4	
Ennen, Herman	19, Mar. 1889		31	1	
Ensert, Charles	9, Feb. 1893		37	5	
Enslein, Frank	18, Aug. 1893		2	5	
Enslin, Phillipine	17, Feb. 1892		90	5	
Entrup, Lizette	16, Feb. 1901		45	8	
Entwhistle, John	1, Mar. 1901		69	8	
Enzinger, Joseph	3, Oct. 1894		35	5	
Enzinger, L.	14, Aug. 1887		2m	1	
Eoff, Margaret	14, Mar. 1901		70	8	
Eperlein, Gustav	14, Jan. 1889		1	1	
Eppenetter, Elisa C.	28, Mar. 1890		6	1	
Eppens, Bernard	1, Dec. 1896	29, Nov.	78	5	
Eppens, Elise Margaretha	13, Apr. 1896	11, Apr.		5	Dallmann
Eppens, Wilhelmine	13, Dec. 1897	11, Dec.	71	5	
Eppensteiner, Bertha	21, Jan. 1889		2m	1	
Eppich, Frank	29, Dec. 1892		29	5	
Epping, Margaret	26, Feb. 1894		12	5	
Eppinger, Eva	26, June 1901		67	8	
Epple, Christian	10, Nov. 1891		23	1	
Eppstein, Rosalind	12, June 1891		4	4	
Eppzy, Flora	26, Mar. 1888		33	4	
Eprtein, J.	30, Jan. 1888		3m	1	
Epstein, Herman	12, May 1895		64	5	
Erbacher, Minnie Rosa	9, Mar. 1900	8, Mar.	17- 2m	8	
Erbacher, William	1, Feb. 1892		1	5	
Erbeck, Anna Catharina	26, May 1896	24, May	71- 3m	5	Noeding
Erbersdobler, Ambrosius	9, 10, Dec. 1890	8, Dec.	23	1	
Erbersdobler, Joseph	18, 20, Dec. 1893	17, Dec.	48- 9m-18d	5	
Erbs, Joseph	7, Feb. 1896	5, Feb.	27- 4m	5	
Erdhaus, Johan Philip	15, Dec. 1899	14, Dec.	61	5	
Erdhaus, Lena	23, Mar. 1893		82	5	

Name	Notice Date	Death Date	Age	Page	Maiden Name
****	****** ****	***** ****	***	****	****** ****
Erdmann, Frankie	27, Aug. 1897	26, Aug.	12	4	
Erdmann, Wilhelmina	2, Oct. 1897	1, Oct.	28- 1m	4	
Erfenbeck, August	22, July 1901		9	8	
Erhard, Otto	10, Jan. 1896	8, Jan.	78	5	
Erhardt, G.A.	17, Dec. 1895	16, Dec.	8m-21d	4	
Erhardt, Jac.	23, Nov. 1888		77	1	
Erhardt, Lizzie	10, July 1889		1	1	
Erhardt, Louisa	11, July 1901		71	5	
Erhardt, Minnie	24, June 1901			8	
Erhardt, William	2, Jan. 1901		7	5	
Erhart, Carl	12, May 1893	10, May		5	
Erhart, Katie L.	7, Apr. 1893		3	5	
Erickson, Stella	21, Sept 1900		30	5	
Erke, Frank	8, Jan. 1898	6, Jan.	28- 1m	4	
Erke, Minnie	18, Oct. 1900		59	8	
Erkenbrecher, Emma	19, July 1898	18, July	46	5	
Erkenbrecher, Friedrich O.	12, Oct. 1897	11, Oct.	38- 3m	4	
Erker, George	14, June 1894		35	5	
Ermen, Regina	16, May 1891		45	2	
Erminok, Herman	28, July 1893		50	5	
Erninger, Carrie	31, Mar. 1891		37	4	
Ernst, Ad.	27, Oct. 1891		63	1	
Ernst, Agnes	16, July 1896	14, July	65-10m	5	Fuchs
Ernst, Charles	26, July 1888		54	2	
Ernst, Elise	28, Oct. 1893		52	5	
Ernst, Elizabeth	16, Jan. 1889		47	1	
Ernst, Freddie	22, Aug. 1888		1	1	
Ernst, Heinrich	29, May 1894		46	5	
Ernst, Joseph	25, Jan. 1901		20d	8	
Ernst, Katie	8, Aug. 1889		6w	1	
Ernst, Lincoln	9, Jan. 1901		5	5	
Ernst, Mary	1, Feb. 1893		23	5	
Ernst, Otto	5, Apr. 1892		4m	4	
Ernst, Thomas	25, Apr. 1901		70	8	
Ernst, Viola	17, Apr. 1894		2	5	
Ernst, William D	3, Oct. 1894		7m	5	
Ernst, William H.	23, Feb. 1893		5m	5	
Ernsting, Wilhelm	19, Sept 1895	17, Sept	14- 7m	5	
Erpenbeck, Matilde	5, Oct. 1896	5, Oct.	13m	5	
Erser, Annie M.	5, Jan. 1892		51	5	
Erst, Louisa	4, Apr. 1894		9m	5	
Ertel, Edward	18, Aug. 1887		16m	1	
Ertler, Friedricka	10, July 1888		3	1	
Ertz, Friedrich	4, May 1894		55	5	
Esberger, Herbert	23, Oct. 1896	22, Oct.	8- 2m	5	
Esch, Susanna M.	30, Dec. 1889		3m	1	
Eschelbach, Henry	7, May 1895		16	5	
Eschelbach, Ludwig	13, July 1887		4m	1	
Eschen, August	22, Jan. 1899	20, Jan.	60- 2m	5	
Eschenbach, Ed.	11, Apr. 1892		8d	5	
Eschenbrenner, Johanna	19, Aug. 1898	17, Aug.	69-11m	5	Metzger
Eschenbrenner, Peter	21, Aug. 1887		31	5	
Eschmann, Adelaide	21, July 1888		3m	1	
Eschmann, Jacob	15, Feb. 1889			1	
Esel, John	12, Aug. 1901		34	8	
Eshbach, Jakob	21, May 1889		59	1	
Eshelbach,	24, July 1891		1d	1	
Eslun, Clarence	4, Aug. 1890		12	1	
Esmann, Elisabeth	13, July 1896	11, July	66- 5m	5	Gärtner
Esmond, Gladys	29, Dec. 1900		30	8	
Espel, August H.	27, Feb. 1894		2d	5	
Espelage, Joseph	22, Mar. 1901		60	8	
Espenscheid, Anna Barbara	21, June 1898	20, June	67	4	Legner
Essel, Anna E.	30, Sept 1891		2m	4	
Essel, Elisa Amalia	7, Jan. 1899	6, Jan.	43	5	Bauer
Essel, Hulda	4, Aug. 1890		5m	1	
Essel, Paul	17, Oct. 1900		20	8	
Essel, Susanna B.	5, Feb. 1891		70	4	
Esselborn, Julius	7, May 1900		64	8	
Esselman, Albert	4, Aug. 1893		1d	5	
Esselmann, Heinrich	16, Nov. 1897	15, Nov.	44	4	

Name ****	Notice Date ****** ****	Death Date ***** ****	Age ***	Page ****	Maiden Name ****** ****
Esselmann, Maria	18, Oct. 1899	17, Oct.		7	
Essen, Bernard	8, Dec. 1891		48	4	
Essen, Francisca	14, Aug. 1900		21	5	
Estep, Johan	21, June 1897	20, June		5	
Estep, Richard T.	14, Mar. 1891		71	4	
Estermann, Bernardina Angela	2, Mar. 1900	28, Feb.	26- 5m	4	
Estermann, Herman B.	12, Jan. 1893		59	5	
Estermann, J.A.	23, Sept 1895	22, Sept	51- -28d	5	
Ethel, Gertrude	4, Apr. 1893		35d	5	
Etter, Edward	31, Jan. 1893		11m	5	
Etter, Louis	12, Aug. 1887		74	1	
Etter, Mary	23, Oct. 1888		21	1	
Etter, Peter	15, July 1891		2	1	
Etter, Wilhelm	28, Nov. 1893		67	5	
Etterer, Philomena Josephina	1, July 1898	29, June	39- 5m	5	Helmig
Ettis, Mary	7, May 1888		21	1	
Ettlinger, Michael	15, Jan. 1901		73	8	
Etzel, Anna B.	16, Mar. 1889		14m	1	
Euchler, Andreas	2, Oct. 1894		60	5	
Euxel, Mary	12, Sept 1891		7m	1	
Evans, Arthur	27, July 1892		10d	5	
Evans, Horace	8, July 1888		31	1	
Evans, John	25, July 1901		35	8	
Evans, Lillian	29, Sept 1900		2m	8	
Evans, Mary	9, Oct. 1900		41	8	
Evans, Maud	10, Aug. 1900		19d	8	
Evans, Richard	15, June 1895		48	5	
Evarling, John F.	27, Sept 1888		35	2	
Evel, Charles	15, Mar. 1900	13, Mar.	38-10m-14d	5	
Evermann, Emma	14, Apr. 1891		53	4	
Evers, Anna	15, Apr. 1899	13, Apr.	74- 6m	4	Müller
Evers, Elisabeth	16, July 1900	15, July	63- 3m- 3d	8	Reusing
Evers, H.A.	2, Aug. 1895	1, Aug.	19- 2m	5	
Evers, Henry	6, Oct. 1900		34	5	
Eversfield, Ellen	5, Mar. 1901		76	5	
Eversmann, Maria Engel	14, Apr. 1896	13, Apr.	70- 1m	5	Wellmer
Everson, Mary	8, July 1888		35	1	
Eversull, Josephine	6, Sept 1900		60	5	
Eveslage, Anna H.C.	7, May 1891		17	4	
Eveslage, Bridget	8, Sept 1887		40	1	
Eveslage, Maria G.	16, Sept 1887		91	1	
Eveslage, Thomas	21, Oct. 1899	20, Oct.	28-11m- 6d	5	
Ewald, Elisabeth	24, Nov. 1898	23, Nov.	10- 5m-21d	5	
Ewert, Heinrich	30, Mar. 1899	28, Mar.	66- - 6d	5	
Ewing, Blanche	11, May 1892		23	5	
Exter, Karoline	4, Feb. 1899	3, Feb.	70	4	Uphues
Eyer,	7, Oct. 1901		1d	1	
Eyman, Charles	22, Feb. 1895		73	5	
Eyman, Louis	21, Feb. 1901		68	8	
Eyrich, Caroline	22, Dec. 1887		54	4	
Faber,	2, Apr. 1891		1d	4	
Faber, Charles	29, Dec. 1891		69	4	
Fachler, Maria Anna	3, May 1900	2, May	83- 8m	5	Boeh
Fachles, Henry M.	16, May 1891		8m	2	
Fachser, Michael	26, July 1895		41	5	
Fackler, Henry	19, Apr. 1894		1m	5	
Fackler, John E.	20, Oct. 1888		69	1	
Fackler, Margaretha	14, June 1894		30	5	
Fagans, George	22, July 1887		26	1	
Fagin, Kate	4, Oct. 1900		32	8	
Faherty, Delia	3, Mar. 1888		10w	1	
Fahr, August	29, Dec. 1891		27	4	
Fahrenbruck, Lisetta	24, June 1901		82	8	
Fahrenholtz, Bessie	7, Aug. 1901		3	8	
Fahrwein, Frieda	28, Dec. 1900		6	8	
Failharer, Frank	2, June 1891		8	4	
Faith, Louise	18, July 1898	17, July	33-10m	5	Görlich
Falk, Henriette	7, Oct. 1896	6, Oct.	61- 2m	5	Gottschalk
Falk, J.E.	28, Dec. 1891		5m	4	
Falk, Rosa	11, Mar. 1889		16	1	

Name	Notice Date	Death Date	Age	Page	Maiden Name
****	****** ****	***** ****	***	****	****** ****
Falke, Dorothea	7, Feb. 1899	6, Feb.		5	Rennecke
Falke, Frank H.	17, Aug. 1894		62	5	
Fallis, Anna E.	11, Aug. 1890		66	1	
Fallon, Mary	4, Oct. 1888		31	4	
Fallon, Pat C.	1, Oct. 1900		71	5	
Falls, James	1, Mar. 1901		56	8	
Faltenstein, Henry	31, Jan. 1901		49	8	
Falthaus, Joseph	24, Jan. 1888		10m	1	
Falvey, Margaret	25, Oct. 1900		38	8	
Fanged, Elizabeth	12, July 1889		70	1	
Fangman, Joseph	22, Nov. 1887		62	1	
Fangman, Mary	22, Aug. 1900			5	
Fangmann, Karl Bernard	22, June 1896	20, June	22- 5m	5	
Fangmann, Lillie	12, Mar. 1901		24	8	
Fangmann, Maria K.	28, Feb. 1900	27, Feb.	61- 1m	5	Scheeta
Fangmann, Mary	18, Aug. 1891		70	4	
Fangmann, Theodor F.	23, Oct. 1900		2	8	
Fanner, Ida J.	30, Dec. 1890		1d	4	
Fanning, Margaret	24, Oct. 1891		42	4	
Fantz, M.	9, Aug. 1888		10m	1	
Fanwest, August	16, Jan. 1893		40	5	
Farbach, Willard	20, July 1901		2m	8	
Farber, Mary	6, Sept 1894		32	5	
Farber, Sarah	23, May 1894		60	5	
Fardele, Frank	4, July 1895		2m	5	
Farfsing, Frank	11, Nov. 1892		23	4	
Farfsing, Johan Wilhelm	26, July 1898	24, July	24- 7m	5	
Farley, Isaac	29, Aug. 1887		16m	1	
Farley, John J.	26, July 1887		32	1	
Farmann, Anna	19, Oct. 1896	17, Oct.	25- 9m	5	Kruse
Farmer, Rosanna	5, Mar. 1901		83	5	
Farr, Ethel	10, Sept 1887		14m	2	
Farrankopf, Albert	2, Dec. 1889		6m	1	
Farrel, Ellen	22, Mar. 1901		58	8	
Farrell,	23, May 1888		2d	1	
Farrell, Myrtle	21, Sept 1900		6	5	
Farrell, Pat.	13, Oct. 1900		38	8	
Farrell, Patrick	9, Aug. 1887		54	1	
Farret, Sarah J.	12, Nov. 1887		32	1	
Farsing, Francis	1, Aug. 1887		6m	1	
Farwick, Johanna	2, Aug. 1901		69	8	
Farwick, Sophie	19, Apr. 1900	18, Apr.	26- 5m	4	Kowener
Farwick, Theodor R.	14, Jan. 1898	13, Jan.	59- 3m	4	
Farwig, Katie	12, Oct. 1894		9m	5	
Fasse, H.	14, Dec. 1896	12, Dec.	64- 3m	5	
Fasse, Minnie	12, Feb. 1891		23	4	
Fassett, Peter F.	7, Jan. 1901		84	5	
Fassnacht, Gertrude	19, Mar. 1900	18, Mar.		5	
Fath, Catharine	7, Mar. 1900	5, Mar.	32-10m	5	
Fatten, Patrick	5, Sept 1900		80	5	
Fatthauer, Fred.	22, Nov. 1893		70	5	
Faubel, Lillie	9, Aug. 1887		12m	1	
Faulhaber, Elizabeth	12, May 1891		10m	1	
Faulhaber, Marie	26, Aug. 1893		3	5	
Faust, Frederika	15, Oct. 1896	14, Oct.	53	5	Schoell
Faust, William	24, Feb. 1891		62	4	
Fay, Elizabeth	9, Feb. 1901		78	8	
Fay, John	8, Dec. 1891		28	4	
Fay, John	16, Dec. 1891		35	4	
Fay, Thomas	4, Nov. 1887		29	1	
Fay, Thomas	17, Dec. 1900		22	8	
Fayne, Louisa	8, Apr. 1901		45	8	
Faße, Conrad Heinrich	28, Oct. 1887	26, Oct.	90- -26d	4	
Feakins, Mary	11, Jan. 1888		85	4	
Feber, Minna	18, Aug. 1890		7m	1	
Fecher, Rosie	13, May 1891		3	2	
Fechheimer, May	30, May 1898	28, May	52	4	
Feck, Charles	17, Sept 1901		50	8	
Fecker, Margaret	12, Feb. 1901		50	8	
Feder, John	23, May 1894		36	5	
Federle, J.	17, Jan. 1888			4	

Name ****	Notice Date ****** ****	Death Date ***** ****	Age ***	Page ****	Maiden Name ****** ****
Feed, John	29, Aug. 1892		73	5	
Feeley, Hannah	2, May 1901		60	8	
Feeley, Johanna	2, May 1901		75	8	
Feeters, Alberta	29, Dec. 1900		6	8	
Fehl, Edward F.	22, Oct. 1900		3	8	
Fehr, Christina	3, Oct. 1896	2, Oct.	69	5	
Fehr, Joseph	26, Feb. 1896	25, Feb.	52-11m	5	
Fehrenbach, Bertha	27, June 1891		1	1	
Fehring, Herman	17, May 1901		44	8	
Fehring, Marie	8, Mar. 1894		79	5	
Fehring, Russell	30, Nov. 1900		1d	8	
Fehrmann, Clifford Heinrich	15, Dec. 1896	14, Dec.	3- 7m-11d	5	
Feht, Herman	8, Apr. 1891		52	4	
Feick, Valentin	10, Jan. 1898	9, Jan.	83	5	
Feid, Susanna	11, Apr. 1890		71	1	
Feiertag, Helena Barbara	29, July 1896	27, July	27- 8m-19d	5	Becker
Feiertag-Hetzner, Sophia	18, Dec. 1888		19	2	
Feige, Charles	26, Feb. 1895		3	5	
Feigenspan, Maria Johanna	24, Oct. 1898	21, Oct.	21- 7m-21d	5	
Feigler, Amelia	28, July 1893		1	5	
Feiler, Charles	15, Aug. 1901		33	8	
Feiler, John G.	31, Mar. 1891		3m	4	
Feinstein, Joseph	20, June 1889		6m	1	
Feishen, Ida	19, July 1894		16m	5	
Feist, Mary	27, June 1895		30	5	
Feith, Annie M.	5, Jan. 1892		68	5	
Feitig, Katharina	31, July 1899	30, July	38	4	McGregor
Feitig, Margartha	21, June 1894		61	5	
Feiß, John	9, Mar. 1894		7m	5	
Feiß, Leopold	5, Apr. 1901		68	8	
Feißler, Rosa	21, Sept 1900		20	5	
Felbin, Francis	12, Feb. 1890		68	1	
Felchmann, William	27, Mar. 1901		45	8	
Feld, Anna Maria	21, Jan. 1892		65	5	
Feld, Henry	1, Nov. 1892		66	5	
Feld, Marie	23, Jan. 1891		37	4	
Feld, Mary H.	17, Mar. 1890		4	1	
Feld, Theodor A.	24, May 1893		1	5	
Feldhaus, Harry	26, Feb. 1896	25, Feb.	14- 2m	5	
Feldhaus, Henry	24, Feb. 1890		18	1	
Feldhaus, Henry	8, Feb. 1894		54	5	
Feldhaus, Julia	4, Mar. 1891		71	4	
Feldkamp, Anna M.	25, Jan. 1890		4w	1	
Feldkamp, Anton	28, June 1889		2	1	
Feldkamp, Beatrice	4, May 1894		10m	5	
Feldkamp, Flora	9, Jan. 1896	8, Jan.		5	
Feldkamp, Herman	30, Oct. 1889		59	1	
Feldkamp, Sophia Christina	17, Jan. 1899	16, Jan.	63- 8m	5	Ahlers
Feldmann, Alma	28, Dec. 1891		3m	4	
Feldmann, Amelia	3, June 1892		38	5	
Feldmann, August	27, Oct. 1900		37	8	
Feldmann, B. Joseph	23, Jan. 1896	22, Jan.	20m-12d	5	
Feldmann, Catharine	7, Aug. 1891		11m	4	
Feldmann, Christina	6, July 1897	4, July	65- -24d	5	Whetoter
Feldmann, Christine	11, June 1895		17	5	
Feldmann, Elisabeth	19, 20, Oct. 1896	17, Oct.	4- 5m	5	
Feldmann, Frank	18, Oct. 1893		62	5	
Feldmann, Franz	30, Mar. 1897	29, Mar.	60	5	
Feldmann, Herman	10, Jan. 1899	8, Jan.	87- - 2d	5	
Feldmann, John	5, June 1891		65	1	
Feldmann, John H.	18, July 1893		42	5	
Feldmann, John W.	15, Feb. 1895		75	5	
Feldmann, M.R.	25, June 1888		4	1	
Feldmann, Martin	31, Dec. 1888		24	1	
Feldmann, Tezillia	26, Sept 1887		5m	1	
Feldner, Rebekka	13, Mar. 1891		51	4	
Felipe, Leon	23, Mar. 1893		5m	5	
Felix, Charles P.	22, Feb. 1895		15m	5	
Felix, Edith	10, Nov. 1896	8, Nov.	11m	4	
Felix, Georg J.	23, Jan. 1900	21, Jan.	78- 2m	4	
Felix, George L.	1, Mar. 1893		18m	5	

Name ****	Notice Date ****** ****	Death Date ***** ****	Age ***	Page ****	Maiden Name ****** ****
Fell, Christopher	26, Nov. 1892		29	5	
Feller, David	23, July 1890		81	1	
Fellermann, Wilhelmine	28, Dec. 1893		65	5	
Felock, Edward Albert	11, Mar. 1893		1	5	
Fels, Albert	17, June 1899	16, June	19- 7m	5	
Fels, Jacob	28, Dec. 1891		38	4	
Felsenthal, Yetta	18, Nov. 1891		61	4	
Felter, A.	16, Sept 1887		15m	1	
Feltrup, Bernard	1, Nov. 1888		82	1	
Feltrup, William	29, Oct. 1891		50	4	
Felzer, Anton	2, Sept 1891		74	4	
Femeyer, John W.	17, Dec. 1891		3m	4	
Femm, Elisabeth	3, Dec. 1892		83	5	
Fender, Lorenna	3, July 1887		5	4	
Fenker, Frederick	18, Aug. 1891		30	4	
Fennekol, Christine	11, Aug. 1888	10, Aug.	7m-13d	5	
Fennel, Anna	9, Aug. 1901		60	8	
Fennel, Fanny	12, Aug. 1901		35	8	
Fennel, Sophie	15, May 1894		40	5	
Fennell, William	5, July 1887		35	1	
Fennemann, Annie	28, Dec. 1891		1	4	
Fennemann, Johan H.	13, Jan. 1899	12, Jan.	83	4	
Fennemeyer, John H.	7, Feb. 1894		24d	5	
Fenning, Mary	7, Apr. 1895		74	5	
Fenton, Catharine	30, Aug. 1900		73	5	
Fenton, Mary	7, Sept 1887		61	1	
Fenzer, John G.	12, Aug. 1887		65	1	
Ferbach, John	5, Dec. 1893		27	5	
Ferber, Charlotte M.	29, July 1893		4m	5	
Ferdelmann, John	14, July 1890		74	1	
Ferguson, Anna	1, Oct. 1890		66	1	
Ferguson, Earl	13, June 1901		1	8	
Ferguson, James	17, Jan. 1901			8	
Ferguson, John A.	16, Feb. 1901		62	8	
Ferhalle, Catharine	28, Jan. 1901		55	8	
Ferheiden, Anna F.	21, Aug. 1894		4m	5	
Ferkel, Charles	14, Jan. 1892		2	1	
Fermann, Bernard	10, Nov. 1900		43	8	
Fern, Ida	8, Apr. 1891		1d	4	
Fern, Jacob	5, Dec. 1893		3	5	
Fern, Jacob	12, June 1899	10, June	54	4	
Fernberg, Louis	15, Sept 1888		67	2	
Ferneding, Catharine	31, Jan. 1901		88	8	
Ferneding, Henry (Rev.)	26, Feb. 1895		59	5	
Ferntheil, Ida	19, Feb. 1890		4	1	
Ferree, Helen	2, Jan. 1901		8	5	
Ferrick, Theresa	16, Dec. 1891		56	4	
Ferris, Abner	18, Dec. 1900		51	8	
Ferris, Edward	21, Aug. 1887		30	5	
Ferris, M.	27, Dec. 1887		70	1	
Ferrmann, Bernard H.	18, Feb. 1891		62	4	
Ferry, Walter	19, Jan. 1888		14m	4	
Fesker, Emma	3, Mar. 1897	1, Mar.	26	5	Tag
Fester, Catharine	4, Dec. 1891		74	4	
Fetch, Josephine	3, Jan. 1901		37	5	
Feth, Louis	24, Nov. 1900		78	8	
Fetick, Margaret	1, Feb. 1901		53	8	
Fetman, Henry	28, Apr. 1890		6	1	
Fett, John	24, Jan. 1901		27	8	
Fetter, August	24, Dec. 1893		33	5	
Fettig, Gabriel	17, Mar. 1897	16, Mar.	35	5	
Fettig, Louise	6, June 1889		2	1	
Feuchter, Barbara	29, Jan. 1897	28, Jan.	44- 3m	5	
Feuchtinger, George	1, Feb. 1889		1	1	
Feuersanger, Fred.	16, Apr. 1891		34	4	
Feuerstein, Josephine	22, Dec. 1892		55	5	
Feuerstein, Lena W.	8, Sept 1887		14m	1	
Feuerstein, Margaretha	23, Dec. 1897	22, Dec.	50- 9m	5	Gressel
Feuger, Elisabeth	16, Aug. 1890		69	1	
Feut, Anna	1, Feb. 1889		68	1	
Feuß, Mary E.	25, July 1891		3	4	

Name ****	Notice Date ****** ****	Death Date ***** ****	Age ***	Page ****	Maiden Name ****** ****
Fey, Anna Marie	25, Dec. 1891		70	2	
Fey, Catharina	10, Feb. 1891		20	4	
Fey, Elisabeth	20, July 1896	18, July	83- 1m	5	
Fey, Elizabeth	8, Oct. 1901		76	1	
Fey, Frank	13, Apr. 1901		1	8	
Fey, Henry	1, Mar. 1900	27, Feb.		5	
Fey, John	16, Dec. 1891		63	4	
Fey, Nikolaus	8, Apr. 1896	7, Apr.	73	5	
Feye, Joseph H.G.	25, Oct. 1900		54	8	
Feßler, Gertie	28, Dec. 1892		4	5	
Fick, John	16, Mar. 1888		20	1	
Ficke, Herman	31, Mar. 1892		63	5	
Ficker, Bernard	30, Dec. 1893		29	5	
Ficker, Mary	14, July 1900	13, July	24- 6m	8	
Ficker, Theresa	21, Aug. 1896	18, Aug.	49- 2m	5	Deppen
Fiebersyser, Christian	2, Dec. 1893		75	5	
Fiedeldey, Albert	20, June 1889		5m	1	
Fiedeldey, George	22, Oct. 1900		3	8	
Fiedler, Amelia	21, Mar. 1893		70	5	
Fiedler, Anna Maria	15, July 1897	13, July	56-10m	5	Glöckler
Fiedler, Julius	21, July 1894		53	5	
Fiedler, Katie	13, Oct. 1894		27	5	
Fiedler, Sarah	4, Sept 1901		62	8	
Fiege, John C.	23, Aug. 1894		3d	5	
Fieke, Marie	16, Aug. 1890		12	1	
Fields, Pauline	24, May 1901		28	8	
Figalist, Conrad	6, Mar. 1891		60	4	
Filger, John	10, May 1892		3	5	
Filges, Katharina	5, Aug. 1889		27	1	
Fillrath, Ed.	15, July 1901		38	8	
Filser, Charles	20, Apr. 1889		2	1	
Filser, Theresa	9, Feb. 1899	8, Feb.	76- 4m	5	Braun
Filser, Willie	27, July 1889		5	1	
Filzer, Josephine	26, Apr. 1901		44	8	
Fincke, Henry	10, Oct. 1901		55	8	
Findlater, William E.	2, Mar. 1893		25	5	
Findley, Marshall	14, Aug. 1900		20	5	
Findling,	18, Feb. 1891		3m	4	
Findly, Frank	29, July 1891		43	1	
Finerty, Joseph	21, Mar. 1895		30	5	
Fingel, John	22, Sept 1888		2	1	
Fink, Carl	26, Mar. 1900	25, Mar.	50- 7m	8	
Fink, Emma	15, Apr. 1893		2	5	
Fink, Franziska	23, Aug. 1887		23	1	
Fink, Friedrich	26, Feb. 1897		76	5	
Fink, Helen	23, July 1895		5m	5	
Fink, Jakob	13, Jan. 1890		67	1	
Fink, Joseph	16, July 1888		1d	1	
Finke, Charles	18, Sept 1891		22	1	
Finke, Ernst	21, Aug. 1888		1	1	
Finke, Marie	5, Apr. 1892		6m	4	
Finke, Sophia M.	4, July 1895		11d	5	
Finke, Willie	2, Jan. 1889		6	1	
Finkel, Alexander H.	14, Apr. 1894		16m	5	
Finkelstein, Aaron	4, Mar. 1897	3, Mar.	64	5	
Finkelstein, Rose	7, Aug. 1891		60	4	
Finkenstedt, Fred.	26, Jan. 1899	24, Jan.	81- 1m	5	
Finkhaus, Anna M.	23, Nov. 1891		28	1	
Finkler, Martin	29, Sept 1900		43	8	
Finley, Ed.	2, Mar. 1888		22	1	
Finley, James	19, Dec. 1900		13	8	
Finley, Margaret	5, Apr. 1895		89	5	
Finn, Lizzie	14, Mar. 1895		51	5	
Finnerty, John	11, June 1901		58	8	
Finnismann, Philipp	21, Nov. 1894		73	5	
Fiox, Henry	10, Sept 1887		17m	2	
Firman, Benjamin	13, June 1891		50	4	
Firmbach, Albert	19, May 1896	17, May	17- 8m	5	
Firnstein, Cyril	16, Jan. 1899	14, Jan.	7-10m	5	
Firsching, John	4, Sept 1888		47	2	
Firsching, Michael	16, July 1895		26	5	

Name ****	Notice Date ****** ****	Death Date ***** ****	Age ***	Page ****	Maiden Name ****** ****
First, Mary L.	13, Nov. 1900		38	8	
Firth, B.	27, Dec. 1887		55	1	
Firth, George	11, May 1901		37	8	
Fischbein, John M.	3, Aug. 1901		2m	8	
Fischer, Adam	7, Oct. 1897	5, Oct.	65- 5m	5	
Fischer, Anna Barbara	24, May 1897	22, May	65- 4m	5	Wintz
Fischer, Anthony	23, Dec. 1893		3	5	
Fischer, Anton H.	12, Sept 1901		53	5	
Fischer, Apollonia	20, Mar. 1889		75	1	
Fischer, Auguste	9, Oct. 1897	8, Oct.	45	5	
Fischer, Caroline	5, Mar. 1901		78	5	
Fischer, Carrie L.	7, Mar. 1894		23	5	
Fischer, Charles F.	13, July 1894		31	5	
Fischer, David	24, Feb. 1891		5m	4	
Fischer, David	13, Oct. 1891		96	4	
Fischer, Elisabeth	10, May 1889		39	1	
Fischer, Elisabeth F.	11, Jan. 1893		24	5	
Fischer, Elizabeth	3, Feb. 1892		1	5	
Fischer, Frank	11, Nov. 1894		1- 3m	5	
Fischer, Friedricka	8, Jan. 1890		33	1	
Fischer, G.W.	16, Aug. 1899	13, Aug.	29- 2m	5	
Fischer, Gerhard	29, Nov. 1898	28, Nov.	72- 5m	5	
Fischer, H.W.	8, Oct. 1895	7, Oct.	11m-27d	5	
Fischer, Harry	22, July 1887		14m	1	
Fischer, Harry	28, Jan. 1901		9	8	
Fischer, Jacob	9, Aug. 1887		67	1	
Fischer, Johan	10, Feb. 1898	9, Feb.	18- 1m	5	
Fischer, John	6, Aug. 1890		44	1	
Fischer, John	2, May 1895		56	5	
Fischer, John T.	15, Dec. 1893		70	5	
Fischer, Joseph	1, Dec. 1892		1	5	
Fischer, Josephine	8, June 1889		28	1	
Fischer, Lena	1, May 1900	30, Apr.	23- 3m	5	Rohling
Fischer, Leonhard	24, Aug. 1900		3	5	
Fischer, Lorenz	11, Jan. 1892		83	4	
Fischer, Louis	26, Aug. 1895	25, Aug.	77	5	
Fischer, M.E. (Mrs)	31, Mar. 1891		52	4	
Fischer, Margaretha	17, June 1897	16, June	57	5	Geiger
Fischer, Maria Gertrude	15, Sept 1898	13, Sept	70- 1w	5	Frone
Fischer, Marie	31, July 1900		1	5	
Fischer, Martin	7, Oct. 1891		32	4	
Fischer, Martin	8, Feb. 1894		71	5	
Fischer, Michael	19, Sept 1895	18, Sept	81	5	
Fischer, Mina	8, July 1888		10	1	
Fischer, Paul	4, Apr. 1901		3d	8	
Fischer, Pauline	26, June 1894		53- 9m-14d	5	Mäding
Fischer, Peter	28, Dec. 1893		82	5	
Fischer, Ph.	12, Mar. 1892		67	5	
Fischer, Phene	30, Oct. 1891		49	4	
Fischer, Robert Lee	17, June 1888		67	1	
Fischer, Theodor	6, July 1901		51	8	
Fischer, Valentin	11, Mar. 1899	10, Mar.	33- -30d	5	
Fischer, Valentine	8, Aug. 1891		78	4	
Fischer, Wilhelm	8, Nov. 1898	7, Nov.	58	4	
Fischer, William	30, Sept 1887		18	1	
Fischer, William	25, Apr. 1901			8	
Fischmann, August F.A.	19, Nov. 1897	19, Nov.	71- 2m-14d	5	
Fischmann, Charles	31, Jan. 1893		87	5	
Fischmann, Isaac	5, Oct. 1894		18d	5	
Fish, George R.	21, Aug. 1887		13m	5	
Fishburn, Cyrus D.	29, Aug. 1892		60	5	
Fisher, Albert G.	26, Dec. 1890		4	1	
Fisher, Anton	11, Apr. 1898	10, Apr.	40	5	
Fisher, August	11, Oct. 1901		49	5	
Fisher, Barbara R.	18, Feb. 1901		26	8	
Fisher, Catharine M.	24, Dec. 1900		46	8	
Fisher, Charles	26, June 1891		20	4	
Fisher, Ella	17, June 1891		21	4	
Fisher, James	25, Mar. 1891		4m	4	
Fisher, John	20, Apr. 1893		65	5	
Fisher, John	8, Mar. 1901		42	8	

Name ****	Notice Date ****** ****	Death Date ***** ****	Age ***	Page ****	Maiden Name ****** ****
Fisher, K.	3, Apr. 1888		82	4	
Fisher, Katharine	28, Apr. 1890		53	1	
Fisher, Lillie	30, Mar. 1894		19m	5	
Fisher, Walter	2, May 1901		44	8	
Fisk, Lester	19, Sept 1894		54	5	
Fisse, Catharine Adelheid	9, Apr. 1896	8, Apr.	6- 5m	5	
Fisse, Christina	6, July 1897	4, July	76- 1m	5	Overberg
Fisse, Harry	7, Sept 1893		8m	5	
Fisse, Louise	14, Feb. 1889		26	1	
Fister, Lena	15, Oct. 1898	13, Oct.		4	
Fithen, Sarah	10, June 1901		21	8	
Fitsch, Maria	15, Sept 1898	14, Sept	25	5	Lang
Fitzgerald, David	28, Feb. 1888		50	1	
Fitzharris, Andrew	16, Aug. 1887		50	1	
Fitzpatrick Katharine	25, Nov. 1887		2	1	
Fitzpatrick, Anna	30, July 1901		64	8	
Fitzpatrick, Cora	10, Jan. 1888		28	4	
Fitzpatrick, J.	27, Dec. 1887		2w	1	
Fitzpatrick, James	21, Nov. 1900		35d	8	
Fitzpatrick, Kryan	2, Dec. 1887		67	4	
Fitzpatrick, Kyran	2, Aug. 1888		18m	2	
Fitzpatrick, Nora	7, Sept 1887		54	1	
Fix, Elisabeth	17, Dec. 1895	15, Dec.	18- 2m	4	
Fix, Johan	23, Dec. 1896	22, Dec.	74- 4m	5	
Fix, Louise	27, Apr. 1894			5	
Fißler, Jakob	11, Feb. 1892		58	4	
Flack, John	7, May 1891		10m	4	
Flack, John	14, Sept 1900		77	5	
Fladdermann, Anna	7, Jan. 1901			5	
Flagge, Charles H.	9, July 1891		1m	4	
Flaherty, Annie	24, Aug. 1900			5	
Flaherty, Ed	21, July 1900		40	8	
Flaig, Augustine	26, Nov. 1891		30	1	
Flaig, Caroline	7, Sept 1901		69	8	
Flaig, Harry	24, Mar. 1897	23, Mar.	26-10m	5	
Flaig, J.G.	21, May 1897	19, May	71	5	
Flamm, Mamie	4, Feb. 1901		7	8	
Flanagan, James	30, Sept 1901		54	8	
Flanery, Bernard	21, July 1887		7m	1	
Flannery, Catharine	28, July 1888		48	1	
Flannigan, Dennis	22, June 1901		34	8	
Flasch, Lottie	27, July 1895		2	5	
Flautz, Gottlieb	13, Oct. 1891		50	4	
Flechter, Simon	16, Dec. 1892		70	5	
Fleck, Casper	18, July 1890		68	1	
Fleck, Elisabeth	19, July 1898	18, July		5	
Fleck, Jakob	24, Apr. 1901		22	8	
Fleckenstein, Henry	17, June 1891		58	4	
Fledderjohann, Wilhelm Herman	8, Nov. 1897	7, Nov.	69- 1m	4	
Fleddermann, Emma	12, Jan. 1894		9m	5	
Flegmann, Henry	19, Apr. 1894		6w	5	
Flehming, Hattie	22, 24, Oct. 1894	22, Oct.		5	
Fleischer, Anna	8, May 1889		27	1	
Fleischmann, Henry	3, June 1889		14	1	
Fleischmann, Israel	19, Aug. 1901		67	8	
Fleischmann, Samuel	27, Feb. 1896	26, Feb.	72	5	
Fleming, Mary	29, Mar. 1894		3	5	
Flemming, E.	24, Sept 1888		17	1	
Flenck, James	26, Mar. 1895		7d	5	
Flesch, Joseph	1, Aug. 1893		2m	5	
Fletcher, Frank	18, Apr. 1893		6	5	
Fletcher, Mary G.	1, Nov. 1892		85	5	
Fletcher, Walter	5, Sept 1900		15d	5	
Flick, Edward	19, July 1894		3m	5	
Flick, Emma Margaret	11, July 1891		1	1	
Flick, Franz	22, Aug. 1898	21, Aug.	78	5	
Flick, Helene	6, July 1898	5, July	70- 3m	5	
Flick, Kate	20, Nov. 1889		5	1	
Flick, Lulu	14, Feb. 1901		1	8	
Flicker, Andrew	28, Jan. 1901		59	8	
Flinn, Joseph	22, Aug. 1900		79	5	

Name	Notice Date	Death Date	Age	Page	Maiden Name
****	****** ****	***** ****	***	****	****** ****
Floch, Emma	13, Feb. 1894		39	5	
Flock, D.	16, Mar. 1888		94	1	
Flocken, Margaretha	16, Feb. 1898	15, Feb.	67- 3m	5	
Floehr, Jakob	4, Sept 1897	3, Sept	67- 7m	4	
Floerken, Harry	31, July 1901		11m	8	
Flohr, Barbara	26, Nov. 1892		65	5	
Flonn, Annie	11, Feb. 1891		35	4	
Flood, Martha A.	16, Feb. 1901		64	8	
Florence, M.	10, Aug. 1901		6m	8	
Floth, Margareth	8, Feb. 1895		60	5	
Flotmann, J.B.	28, Mar. 1898	27, Mar.		5	
Flower, John	14, Mar. 1901		82	8	
Floyd, Elsie	2, Mar. 1901		26	5	
Floyd, Frank	8, Jan. 1901		60	8	
Fluch, Francisca F.	14, Feb. 1891		41	4	
Fluck, Elizabeth	7, Sept 1887		1	1	
Fluck, Emma	11, Aug. 1891		3m	4	
Fluck, Martin	29, Dec. 1891		47	4	
Flueck, Henry	1, Aug. 1893		11m	5	
Fluhrer, Anna M.	18, Jan. 1901		75	8	
Fly, Mary	17, Apr. 1888		30	1	
Flyan, Chris.	22, Mar. 1901		35	8	
Flynn, Annie	8, Aug. 1891		4	4	
Flynn, Frank	14, Mar. 1901		4	8	
Flynn, Katie	17, May 1901		14d	8	
Foellger, Anna	10, Dec. 1895	8, Dec.	42	5	
Foerner, Ella	26, Nov. 1888		26	1	
Foerster, Edward C.	23, Nov. 1893		10	5	
Foertmeyer, Ottilie	30, Dec. 1897	29, Dec.		5	
Fogle, George E.	23, Nov. 1892		44	5	
Folan, Hannah	7, June 1901		41	8	
Folck, Joseph	17, Dec. 1900		21	8	
Folger, Anna G.	29, Jan. 1901		79	8	
Folger, Jane D.	24, Feb. 1891		72	4	
Follmer, Charles C.	16, June 1894		25	5	
Follmor, Mary	16, Dec. 1891		40	4	
Follner, Frank	7, Dec. 1893		75	5	
Folz, David	29, July 1897	26, July		5	
Folz, Joseph	9, Apr. 1896	8, Apr.	43- 5m	5	
Folzenlogel, Joseph	14, Aug. 1889		36	1	
Folzenlogel, Josephine	25, Feb. 1891		24	4	
Food, Amanda	2, Aug. 1887		103	1	
Fooley, J.P.	23, May 1895		44	5	
Foote, Mattie F.	24, Jan. 1901		21	8	
Foradzinsky, Joseph	7, Feb. 1891		4w	4	
Foraker, Corrine D.	21, June 1888		1	1	
Foran, James	4, Feb. 1901		56	8	
Forberg, George W.	4, Apr. 1893		1	5	
Forbes, M.C.	24, Jan. 1888		29	1	
Forbes, Mary	1, Sept 1887		3d	1	
Forbriger, Karl Friedrich	26, Apr. 1898	25, Apr.		5	
Forbus, Catharine	19, Oct. 1892		87	5	
Ford, George	24, Aug. 1887		61	1	
Fordelmann, William A.	10, Aug. 1894		1m	5	
Forest, Emma	22, Mar. 1901		2m	8	
Forg, Mary	13, July 1895		13d	5	
Forman, Rebecca	19, Dec. 1893		22	5	
Forn, Victor	13, 14, Feb. 1893	12, Feb.	21-11m-11d	5	
Forrest, W.	14, Dec. 1887		42	4	
Forster, Abraham	10, May 1888		52	1	
Forster, Frank	29, Aug. 1901		74	8	
Forster, Paul A.	28, Sept 1899	27, Sept	45	5	
Forstlechner, Cornelius	23, Aug. 1887		1- 6m	1	
Fortman, A.	25, Sept 1890		18m	1	
Fortman, Charles	16, Dec. 1892		4	5	
Fortman, Henry	24, Dec. 1900		34	8	
Fortmann, Catharine	4, Oct. 1888		59	4	
Fortmann, H.	19, Nov. 1888		3m	1	
Fortmann, Louis A.	14, July 1898	13, July	32- 8m	5	
Fortwangler, Lena	29, Dec. 1892		2	5	
Foss, N.A.	7, Aug. 1901		70	8	

Name ****	Notice Date ****** ****	Death Date ***** ****	Age ***	Page ****	Maiden Name ****** ****
Fossett, William B.	13, Aug. 1901		76	8	
Foster, Alaphair	2, Oct. 1900		70	8	
Foster, Viola	21, June 1901		2m	8	
Foster, William B.	10, July 1901		50	5	
Fosthoff, Theodor	16, May 1893		59	5	
Fountain, Peter	13, July 1901		65	8	
Fournell, Johanna	20, Sept 1901		3	1	
Fowler, G.	25, Jan. 1888		36	1	
Fowler, George A.	24, Nov. 1900		49	8	
Fowler, Mary	20, Apr. 1888		42	4	
Fox, Abraham	18, July 1891		89	1	
Fox, Barbara	22, Apr. 1889		65	1	
Fox, Ben. J.	28, May 1890		31	1	
Fox, Carmen	18, Dec. 1900		20	8	
Fox, Catharine	2, Mar. 1901		59	5	
Fox, E.C.	15, Dec. 1887		21	1	
Fox, Emma	3, Mar. 1899	2, Mar.		4	
Fox, Frank R.	18, Feb. 1899	14, Feb.	26	5	
Fox, George	22, Aug. 1896		25	5	
Fox, George	29, May 1901		24	8	
Fox, Johanna Margaretha	29, Apr. 1896	28, Apr.	75	5	
Fox, Joseph	5, Mar. 1891		69	4	
Fox, Margaret	17, Mar. 1888		55	4	
Fox, Simon	7, May 1901		83	1	
Fox, William	8, Oct. 1901		22	1	
Foy, William	6, Apr. 1888		5m	4	
Foß, Catharina Maria	26, Aug. 1893	15, Aug.	29-11m	* 5	Moormann
Fraesdorf, Albert	21, Aug. 1894		20	5	
Fralier, Frank	21, June 1888		7m	1	
Francis, George	25, June 1888		1d	1	
Frank, Al.	21, July 1890		7m	1	
Frank, Albert	12, May 1891		26	1	
Frank, Albert	14, May 1895		1	5	
Frank, Anna	23, July 1887		22	1	
Frank, Anna	12, Oct. 1895	11, Oct.		5	
Frank, Bertha	8, Aug. 1900			8	
Frank, Bruno	10, Sept 1901		2	1	
Frank, Casper C.	11, Nov. 1892		38	4	
Frank, Christian	29, Jan. 1892		27	5	
Frank, F.R.	29, Nov. 1888		3	1	
Frank, Franziska	27, Aug. 1889		1	1	
Frank, George	28, Feb. 1889		9d	2	
Frank, George	4, Dec. 1891		56	4	
Frank, George	27, June 1895		58	5	
Frank, George D.	6, Feb. 1894		29	5	
Frank, Gustave	25, July 1901		58	8	
Frank, Harry	20, June 1895		21	5	
Frank, Hattie	22, Aug. 1888		3w	1	
Frank, Henry	18, Sept 1891		40	1	
Frank, Henry	22, Jan. 1892		5m	5	
Frank, Hubert	25, Jan. 1901		3	8	
Frank, Mabel	11, July 1895		10d	5	
Frank, Maria	25, Aug. 1890		72	1	
Frank, Mary B.	24, May 1893		51	5	
Frank, Nicolaus	11, July 1887		49	1	
Frank, Rosina	24, Jan. 1899	23, Jan.	72-11m	4	
Frank, Tillie	19, Mar. 1889		12	1	
Frank, William	25, Sept 1889		17- 6m	1	
Franke, August	22, Mar. 1901		27	8	
Franke, Lorain	4, July 1901		5m	8	
Franke, Wilhelm	18, Feb. 1890		29	1	
Franke, Wilhelmine	1, Aug. 1896	31, July	53	5	Kruse
Frankel, Moses	5, July 1888		70	1	
Franken, Henry	7, Sept 1888		6w	1	
Franken, Rosalie	19, Mar. 1901		71	8	
Frankenberg, Fred.	14, June 1889		65	1	
Frankenberger, J.	18, Aug. 1900		71	8	
Frankenhoff, Lorenz	20, Apr. 1889		2	1	
Frankenstein, Gustavus	14, Dec. 1893		64	5	
Franklin, Elizabeth	15, Feb. 1901		39	8	
Franklin, Isabella	9, Dec. 1887		19	1	

Name	Notice Date	Death Date	Age	Page	Maiden Name
****	****** ****	***** ****	***	****	****** ****
Franklin, Jennie	1, Sept 1888		3	1	
Franklin, Thomas	1, Dec. 1900		38	8	
Franks, Richard D.	8, Dec. 1891		5	4	
Frantz, Friedrich	29, Apr. 1898		70	5	
Franz, Augustus	28, Oct. 1893		50	5	
Franz, Carrie	23, Mar. 1901		33	8	
Franz, Celia	10, Aug. 1894		11m	5	
Franz, George H.	21, June 1895		22m	5	
Franz, Joseph F.	22, Oct. 1900		64	8	
Franz, Margaretha	28, Feb. 1896	26, Feb.	88- 2m	5	
Franzel, Joseph	2, July 1892		27	5	
Franzmeier, Friedrich	15, Mar. 1898	14, Mar.	67-11m	4	
Franzmeier, Maria	14, June 1894		59	5	
Franzreb, Ed.	24, June 1901		3	8	
Franzreb, Jakob	13, Apr. 1901		71	8	
Fraser, Thomas K.	4, Oct. 1900		68	8	
Fratz, Helena	7, Feb. 1896	6, Feb.	87	5	Sandroh
Fratzie, Mollie	12, July 1895		27	5	
Frazer, Abner L.	18, Feb. 1901		80	8	
Frazer, Edwin	8, Aug. 1901		19	8	
Frazier, Edward	11, Dec. 1900		40	8	
Frazier, Martin	5, Sept 1890		85	4	
Frazier, Mary E.	30, Apr. 1901		37	8	
Frech, Anna	16, Oct. 1891		3d	1	
Frech, Charles	14, Dec. 1893		4m	5	
Frech, Friedrich	2, Sept 1897	1, Sept	72- 8m	5	
Frech, Georg J.	24, Jan. 1900	23, Jan.	32	4	
Frech, Julia	16, Oct. 1891		3d	1	
Frech, K.	1, Mar. 1888		53- 3m	4	
Frech, William	24, Oct. 1887		20- 6m	1	
Frecher, Crecentia	11, Dec. 1891		34	4	
Fredland, Violet	18, July 1887		13m	1	
Fredricks, Caroline	17, Apr. 1901		84	8	
Freeman, Dorothy	15, Feb. 1901		2	8	
Freeman, Leon	26, Apr. 1901		2	8	
Freeman, Maggie	7, July 1888		21	4	
Freemann, Dan.	3, Oct. 1900		58	5	
Freese, Johanna	16, Jan. 1894		8m	5	
Freese, Margaret	23, Aug. 1900		1	8	
Freese, Rudolph	22, July 1887		3m	1	
Frehlinger, Margaret	14, Nov. 1891		3m	4	
Frehse, Betty Regina	4, May 1900	3, May	68	8	Kroeger
Frei, Dora	24, May 1892		43	5	
Frei, Elisabeth	28, Apr. 1900	27, Apr.		5	
Frei, Karolina	9, Aug. 1897	7, Aug.		5	
Freiberg, Amalia	15, Sept 1900		77	5	
Freiberg, Milton	15, Oct. 1891		6	4	
Freiberg, Stella	11, Jan. 1889		7m	1	
Freiheit, Roy	29, June 1901		2	8	
Freiling, John	2, Dec. 1893		82	5	
Freisens, Johan	6, July 1900	5, July	80- 6m	8	
Freisens, Magdalena	1, May 1901		77	8	
Freitag, Ambrose	14, Feb. 1891		56	4	
Freitag, Frank	15, Feb. 1890		40	4	
Freitag, Georg	31, Mar. 1890		66	1	
Freitag, M.	29, Dec. 1887		45	4	
Freitag, Sophia	13, June 1900	13, June	64-11m	8	
Freitag, Sophia	12, June 1901		52	8	
Freitag, William	24, Nov. 1896	23, Nov.	17	5	
Freking, Albert	24, Dec. 1892		1m	5	
French, O.	14, Feb. 1888		4	4	
French, William	16, Oct. 1890		32	1	
Frenkel, Ernestine	3, Dec. 1900		80	8	
Frenkhaus, Matilda	10, Mar. 1888		2	1	
Frensch, Matthias	12, May 1897	10, May	82- 2m	5	
Frenzel, Elmer Oscar Wilhelm	11, Oct. 1897	9, Oct.	2- 9m	5	
Frerking, Willy	11, Jan. 1888		14- 6m	4	
Frersing, Henry	17, June 1889		33	1	
Frersing, Lizetta	25, June 1901		77	8	
Frese, Heinrich	31, Mar. 1896	30, Mar.	43	5	
Freudiger, Johan	1, June 1889	31, May	38	* 1	

Name ****	Notice Date ****** ****	Death Date ***** ****	Age ***	Page ****	Maiden Name ****** ****
Freund, Catharine	11, Dec. 1891		66	4	
Freund, Ernst A.	30, Sept 1891		5	4	
Freund, Francis L.	25, Mar. 1901		27	8	
Freund, Frank	30, July 1896	19, July	32	5	
Freund, Helena	1, Feb. 1888		27	4	
Freund, Leonhard	8, Apr. 1897	7, Apr.	70- 6m	5	
Freund, Willie	2, July 1892		6	5	
Frey, Alma	8, Feb. 1901		16	8	
Frey, Caroline	27, Mar. 1894		67	5	
Frey, Charles	18, Dec. 1889		3	1	
Frey, Edward	17, Mar. 1890		2m	1	
Frey, Elise	13, May 1891		3m	2	
Frey, Fred.	1, Nov. 1893		41	5	
Frey, Fred.	13, Apr. 1895		41	4	
Frey, George	19, Apr. 1893		50	5	
Frey, Gilbert	17, Apr. 1894		5m	5	
Frey, Gottfried	24, Sept 1895	22, Sept	71- 7m	5	
Frey, Johan	20, Apr. 1899	18, Apr.	37	4	
Frey, John	4, June 1901		36	8	
Frey, Katharina	2, Apr. 1900	31, Mar.	39- 9m	8	Susinger
Frey, Lillie B.	23, Oct. 1888		3w	1	
Frey, Louise	16, Oct. 1900		43	8	
Frey, Philomena	25, Jan. 1893		24	5	
Frey, Sophia	28, Dec. 1897	25, Dec.	76-11m	4	
Freybler, Michael	24, July 1901		45	8	
Freytag, Barbara	17, Mar. 1894		67	5	
Freytag, Elisabeth	17, Oct. 1893	15, Oct.	65- 7m-28d	5	Freytag
Freytag, Elisabeth	15, June 1900	13, June	39-11m	8	Dornbusch
Freytag, Ella	18, Aug. 1891		5m	4	
Freytag, George Valentin	6, Mar. 1897	5, Mar.	30- 9m	5	
Freytag, Johan	27, Apr. 1897	25, Apr.	24- 6m	5	
Freytag, Philip L.	28, Jan. 1889		22	1	
Frichelstein, Rosa	14, Sept 1894		7m	5	
Frick, John	19, July 1887		34	1	
Frick, Karoline	7, July 1891		65	1	
Fricke, Anna	17, Oct. 1887		11- 3m-18d	1	
Fricke, Augusta	27, Nov. 1894		29	5	
Fricke, Herman	19, Jan. 1888		73	4	
Fricke, Jacobina	24, Oct. 1899	23, Oct.	57- 6m	5	
Fricke, Maria	26, Nov. 1888		40	1	
Fricker, Mary E.	26, Nov. 1892		40	5	
Frickert, Katharine	25, May 1901		70	8	
Frickmann, Emma	11, Jan. 1901		9	5	
Friechold, Thekla	11, Feb. 1892		14	4	
Friedeborn, William	12, June 1889		30	1	
Friedeborn, William	11, Dec. 1893		67	5	
Friedel, Mary	4, Aug. 1891		36	4	
Friedemann, Frederick	22, June 1895		23m	5	
Friedhoff, Lorenz	14, Sept 1900		4m	5	
Friedhoff, W.	15, Sept 1900		4	5	
Friedland, Johan	28, Oct. 1889	26, Oct.	62	* 1	
Friedlander, S.	11, Jan. 1888		28	4	
Friedman, Philipp	3, Dec. 1892		14d	5	
Friedmann, Anton	20, Feb. 1901		75	8	
Friedmann, Crescentia	17, Aug. 1899	16, Aug.	72	4	Bucher
Friedmann, Fanny	26, Dec. 1895	25, Dec.	75- 1m	4	
Friedmann, Harry F.	16, Aug. 1887		4	1	
Friedmann, Morris	11, Dec. 1888		3	1	
Friedrich,	17, July 1891		1d	1	
Friedrich, Eloi	3, May 1893		53	5	
Friedrich, Ignatz	13, Apr. 1898	12, Apr.		5	
Friedrich, Sophia	11, July 1893		1	5	
Friehmelt, Louise Koch	7, Sept 1899	6, Sept	44	5	
Friend, Annie	5, July 1887		35	1	
Friend, Jakob	8, Apr. 1901		45	8	
Friends, Stella	26, July 1888		2	2	
Fries, Albert	6, Feb. 1894		9	5	
Fries, Balthasar	25, Feb. 1897	24, Feb.	70- 3m	5	
Fries, Clifford	6, Apr. 1893		9m	5	
Fries, Ed. W.	28, Feb. 1901		8m	8	
Fries, Edward	28, Oct. 1891		1m	4	

Name ****	Notice Date ****** ****	Death Date ***** ****	Age ***	Page ****	Maiden Name ****** ****
Fries, Fridolin	7, Mar. 1890		5	1	
Fries, George	23, Aug. 1901		1	8	
Fries, Harry	30, Aug. 1890		72	2	
Fries, Hermina	3, Feb. 1888		3- 6m	4	
Fries, Joseph Georg	21, Feb. 1893		54	5	
Fries, Magdalena	13, June 1888		2	1	
Fries, Magdalena	15, Aug. 1891		70	4	
Fries, Mary A.	7, Jan. 1891			4	
Fries, Rosa	11, Mar. 1893		71	5	
Friese, Julius H.	28, July 1891		7	4	
Frietsch, Bernhard	21, Mar. 1890		46	1	
Frietsch, Lena	28, May 1901		71	8	
Frietsch, Mathias	3, Dec. 1900		67	8	
Frieß, Joseph	5, Mar. 1901		66	5	
Frilling, Gertrud	15, May 1900	13, May	69- 8m	8	
Frische, Charles	17, Jan. 1901		32	8	
Frische, William	24, Sept 1891		8d	1	
Frischknecht, Rudolph	19, Jan. 1897	10, Jan.	70	5	
Fritsch, Alice	26, June 1895		6	5	
Fritsch, Dorothea	29, Mar. 1889		55	1	
Fritsch, Emil	26, Mar. 1901		37	8	
Fritsch, Francis	9, Jan. 1894		30	5	
Fritsch, Henry	19, July 1900		68	8	
Fritsch, Rudolph	8, Sept 1898	6, Sept	42	4	
Fritsch, Sybilla	4, Feb. 1893		65	5	
Fritsch, William	31, Oct. 1894		36	5	
Fritsche, Barbara	27, Nov. 1900		76	8	
Fritsche, Louis	9, Mar. 1900	7, Mar.	32- 9m	8	
Fritschler, Sophia	30, July 1901		71	8	
Fritz,	14, Nov. 1891		1d	4	
Fritz, Anna	5, June 1893		48	5	
Fritz, Catharine	11, Nov. 1892			4	
Fritz, John A.	11, Nov. 1892		57	4	
Fritz, Josephine	17, Mar. 1888		10	4	
Fritz, Katharina	28, Feb. 1900	26, Feb.	65	5	Klein
Fritz, Maria Magdalena	24, Oct. 1898	23, Oct.	63	5	Binder
Fritz, Mary	10, Feb. 1893		1	5	
Fritz, Michael	5, Jan. 1889		82	1	
Frizzel, Edith	10, Apr. 1894		40d	5	
Frobeck, Fannie A.	7, Mar. 1891		2	4	
Froehlich, Charles	11, Apr. 1901		74	8	
Froehlich, Henry	13, Jan. 1896		33	5	
Froehlich, Margaretha	25, Apr. 1897	23, Apr.	56-11m	5	Boheim
Froehlich, Melusine	17, May 1899	15, May	66	5	
Froehlich, Philipp	15, Nov. 1900		32	8	
Froelich, Frederick J.	27, Feb. 1894		1	5	
Froelking, August	1, Oct. 1887		59	1	
Froelking, Florence	19, May 1899	18, May	36- 7m	4	
Froendhoff, Herman	28, Oct. 1895	27, Oct.	73- 9m	5	
Frohle, Joseph	10, 11, Dec. 1896	8, Dec.	62-11m	5	
Frohle, Regina	20, Dec. 1897	19, Dec.	60- 3m	5	Koch
Frohm, Bernardina	11, Jan. 1890		47	1	
Frohman, George	3, Dec. 1892		2m	5	
Frohmiller, Mary	22, Sept 1888		18m	1	
Frohoff, Eugen	22, Mar. 1901		7m	8	
Frohoff, Lawrence	30, Dec. 1891		4m	4	
Fromeyer, Elisabeth	12, Oct. 1899	11, Oct.	76	5	Fideldey
Fromhold, Ida	25, Feb. 1893		5m	5	
Fromie, Sophie	25, Jan. 1892		65	5	
Fromiller, Rose	31, Dec. 1890		21	4	
Fromm, Auguste	2, Nov. 1895	1, Nov.	56	5	Gottschalk
Frommann, Elizabeth	3, June 1901		56	8	
Frommeyer, John F.	16, Dec. 1892		47	5	
Frommeyer, Kate	3, June 1901			8	
Frooks, Walter	30, Mar. 1901		13d	8	
Froschauer, Eduard	4, Jan. 1896	4, Jan.	9- 7m-24d	5	
Frosdidier, Theodor	23, May 1901		2	8	
Frosedale, Anna E.	23, Apr. 1890		36	4	
Frueh, Joseph	10, July 1901		56	5	
Fruehe, Louisa	2, Mar. 1901		73	5	
Fruemann, Amanda	21, Mar. 1901		7	8	

Name ****	Notice Date ****** ****	Death Date ***** ****	Age ***	Page ****	Maiden Name ****** ****
Fruschel, Ph.	15, Feb. 1897	14, Feb.		5	
Fry, Maggie	29, July 1888		38	1	
Frytag, Arthur	8, Dec. 1891		3	4	
Frölke, Maria	30, Jan. 1896	29, Jan.	78- 1m-14d	5	Hünemeier
Fuchs, Anna H.	26, Dec. 1890		7m	1	
Fuchs, Anna Maria	6, May 1899	3, May	72	4	Werey
Fuchs, Conrad	22, Dec. 1897	20, Dec.	35- 9m	5	
Fuchs, Emil	25, 26, Mar. 1897	23, Mar.		5	
Fuchs, Frederick H.	11, Nov. 1894		1	5	
Fuchs, Friedricka	26, June 1901		64	8	
Fuchs, George M.	28, June 1888		2	1	
Fuchs, Jacob	3, Feb. 1891		65	4	
Fuchs, John	20, July 1889		6m	1	
Fuchs, John	6, June 1891		50	4	
Fuchs, Louisa	1, Aug. 1887		10m	1	
Fuchs, Nora	29, Oct. 1896	27, Oct.	11m	5	
Fuchs, Peter	29, June 1899	20, June	78	4	
Fuchs, Ruth	11, Apr. 1893		7m	5	
Fuchs, Walburga	7, Sept 1893		71	5	
Fuchs, Wilhelm Friedrich	5, Apr. 1900	4, Apr.	74-11m	5	
Fuchsberger, Robert	14, Jan. 1892		82	1	
Fuchsberger, Theresa	21, July 1887		78	1	
Fuerer, Erwin	25, June 1901		5	8	
Fuerst, Minna	4, Aug. 1891		3d	4	
Fuerste, Fred.	12, Aug. 1901		68	8	
Fugazzi, Mary	18, Feb. 1888		10m	1	
Fuhrmann, Albert	7, Mar. 1896	5, Mar.	61	5	
Fuhrmann, Katharine	15, Oct. 1895	14, Oct.	19	5	
Fuhrmann, Nellie	11, May 1901		2	8	
Fuian, James	26, July 1887		3- 6m	1	
Fuldner,	10, Sept 1891		1d	4	
Fuldner, Jakob	1, Aug. 1896	31, July	68- 6m	5	
Fuldner, Mitcehl H.	1, June 1893		10	5	
Fuller, Ada	6, Aug. 1901		44	8	
Fuller, Mary	27, Dec. 1895	26, Dec.		5	
Fullerton, George W.	28, Sept 1896	28, Sept	34	5	
Fullerton, Thomas	9, Jan. 1901		66	5	
Fully, Hannah	15, Aug. 1901		58	8	
Fuls, Meta	15, Feb. 1890		47	4	
Fulscher,	4, Feb. 1891		2m	4	
Fulton, Levi S.	16, Apr. 1895		75	5	
Fulton, Ray	22, Dec. 1887		6m	4	
Funck, Emilie	13, Feb. 1901		72	8	
Funck, John	5, July 1887		44	1	
Funck, William	16, July 1896	15, July	3- 4m-14d	5	
Funk, Augusta	11, May 1900	10, May	57	5	Anschutz
Funk, Charles	2, 4, Nov. 1895	1, Nov.	21- 5m	5	
Funk, D.	1, Dec. 1888		5	4	
Funk, Eduard	8, Sept 1890		9m	4	
Funk, Frank H.	6, Nov. 1891		3	4	
Funk, Fred.	28, Sept 1901		71	5	
Funk, John H.	24, May 1901		71	8	
Funk, Joseph	7, June 1901		8	8	
Funke, Catharine	20, Sept 1901		81	1	
Funke, Ferdinand T.	26, Aug. 1893		65	5	
Funke, Martha	10, Feb. 1892		5m	5	
Funte, Emma	19, Nov. 1895	18, NOv.	16m	5	
Furey, Peter	8, Apr. 1901		80	8	
Furio, Lucy	28, Mar. 1901		6	8	
Furlong, James H.	4, Aug. 1887		1m	1	
Furry, Lucy	14, Sept 1887		9	1	
Furschulte, Louis	25, July 1901		44	8	
Fusshippel, Eugen	30, Apr. 1900	28, Apr.		4	
Fussner, John A.	18, Aug. 1894		68	5	
Fuß, Joseph	2, July 1901		26	8	
Fuß, Rosina	18, May 1894		26	5	
Fußhippel, Marie	6, Apr. 1896	5, Apr.	37	4	Zehndick
Fußner, Anna	6, Jan. 1892		25	5	
Fußner, Anna E.	12, Feb. 1901		8m	8	
Fußner, Johan Amor	17, 18, Aug. 1894	16, Aug.	68- 6m	5	
Fußnicker, John	8, Oct. 1888		36	1	

Name ****	Notice Date ****** ****	Death Date ***** ****	Age ***	Page ****	Maiden Name ****** ****
Förstel, Albert	4, Aug. 1900		1	8	
Fügel, Willie	17, June 1889		17m	1	
Fürst, August	21, Oct. 1887		20	1	
Füsser, Maria	22, Dec. 1897	21, Dec.	62- 1m	5	Beyer
Gabel, Arthur	17, July 1894		4m	5	
Gabel, Caroline	29, July 1888		63	1	
Gabel, Charles	18, Aug. 1891		31d	4	
Gabel, Charlotte	21, Apr. 1891		9m	4	
Gabel, Elisabeth	6, Mar. 1889		4d	1	
Gabel, Jakob	6, Mar. 1889		5d	1	
Gabel, S. Bertha	26, Nov. 1892		4	5	
Gabelmann, Maggie	22, Sept 1896	21, Sept	33	5	
Gabennet, Clara	11, Oct. 1900		15	8	
Gabriel, Charles	11, Dec. 1893		28	5	
Gabriel, Julia	10, Aug. 1887		66	1	
Gabriel, Karl	13, June 1888		10m	1	
Gabriel, Pearl K.	25, Feb. 1891		3	4	
Gaddum, Clarence A.	30, Apr. 1895		9m	5	
Gaebe, Henry	12, Mar. 1901		8	8	
Gaebel, Wilhelm	26, Oct. 1897	24, Oct.	38- 6m	5	
Gaefe, Fred.	25, Jan. 1901		28	8	
Gaefe, Wilhelmina	21, Sept 1901		71	8	
Gaffey, Marguerite L.	1, Oct. 1900		2	5	
Gaffney, John	15, Feb. 1901		6	8	
Gafford, Marion	28, Aug. 1901		9	8	
Gahm, Margaret	20, Jan. 1891		81	4	
Gaile, Samuel	11, Feb. 1889		44	1	
Gaisser, Katharine	8, Aug. 1900		67	8	
Gal, Elisabeth	26, Dec. 1900		28	8	
Galdi, Jakob	15, Sept 1896	14, Sept	64	5	
Gale, Hannah	1, Oct. 1887		76	1	
Gall, Caroline	11, Apr. 1896	9, Apr.	68	5	Stein
Galla, Joseph	28, Mar. 1888		35	1	
Gallagher, George H.	12, Sept 1901		32	5	
Gallagher, Margaret	10, Apr. 1901		55	8	
Galle, Henry J.	5, June 1891		36	1	
Galle, William Henry	28, Dec. 1891		3m	4	
Gallenkamp,	6, Feb. 1890		3	1	
Gallenkamp, Olga	2, Mar. 1888		8	1	
Galler, Arthur	31, Dec. 1890		4	4	
Gallman, Marcellus	4, Aug. 1887		44	1	
Galti, Josephine	12, Feb. 1891		3m	4	
Galvagni, Justine Katharina	9, Mar. 1900	8, Mar.	75	8	Stengel
Galvin, Michael	21, July 1887		66	1	
Galvin, Rodrich	17, Apr. 1888		33	1	
Gamber, Elisabeth	5, Dec. 1893			5	
Gamble, Elizabeth A.	27, Sept 1888		77	2	
Gamm, Gaspard	30, Apr. 1895		69	5	
Gampfer, Peter	14, Aug. 1900		63	5	
Gams, John	23, Sept 1887		9	2	
Gamster, Elizabeth	6, Apr. 1895		43	5	
Gandenberger, Louis	12, July 1901		36	8	
Gander, Julia	12, Mar. 1892		4	5	
Gander, Mary	9, June 1893		3	5	
Gandolfo, Peter	19, Dec. 1898	16, Dec.	74	4	
Gang, John	10, Feb. 1888		2m	1	
Gansel, Enno	7, Jan. 1901		1	5	
Ganselmann, Albert	15, Aug. 1892		1	5	
Ganselmann, Bernard Heinrich	16, Mar. 1897	15, Mar.	64	5	
Ganter, Leopold	3, Sept 1898	2, Sept	31	4	
Ganter, Lida	5, Mar. 1891		35	4	
Gantz, Louise	2, Dec. 1895	30, Nov.	34	5	
Ganz, Amalia	23, Dec. 1891		54	4	
Ganz, Fred.	25, Jan. 1894		31	5	
Ganzer, Mary	25, Feb. 1893		23	5	
Ganzler, Joseph	23, May 1888		26	1	
Garber, Fred.	28, Feb. 1891		53	4	
Garber, Mary	14, Jan. 1892		49	1	
Garber, W.	30, Aug. 1898	29, Aug.	23- 4m	4	
Garbow, L.	27, Dec. 1887		23	1	

Name ****	Notice Date ****** ****	Death Date ***** ****	Age ***	Page ****	Maiden Name ****** ****
Garde, Joseph	21, Jan. 1901			8	
Gardi, John	9, Aug. 1887		13d	1	
Gardi, Mary	9, Aug. 1887		12d	1	
Gardner, F.	25, June 1888		7w	1	
Gardner, Francis	11, Sept 1901		61	8	
Gardner, Fred W.	1, Oct. 1900		60	5	
Gardner, John	22, July 1887		39	1	
Gardner, John P.	2, Oct. 1888		7m	1	
Gardner, Karl	8, Oct. 1896	7, Oct.	49	5	
Gardner, Louis	10, Oct. 1901		18	8	
Gardner, Martha Katharine	31, Mar. 1888		1- 9m	4	
Gardner, Philomena	5, June 1890		65	4	
Gardner, S.M.	7, Aug. 1888		2m	1	
Gardner, Samuel	8, Dec. 1900		22	8	
Gardner, Samuel B.	8, Feb. 1901		22	8	
Garens, Otto	3, Apr. 1891		54	4	
Garlich, Clemence	11, July 1892		32	5	
Garmhausen, Louisa	26, Jan. 1892		74	5	
Garner, Joseph	17, July 1895		50	5	
Garnet, Mary	28, Apr. 1888		67	1	
Garnon, Mary	8, Feb. 1901			8	
Garold, Amelia	10, Aug. 1889		30m	1	
Garr, John	30, Nov. 1887		1- 8m	4	
Garrard, Raymond	15, Mar. 1901		8m	8	
Garret, Mary	2, July 1895		72	5	
Garretson, J. (Dr)	22, Jan. 1889		81	1	
Garrette, Clarence A.	27, July 1895		39	5	
Garrity, Nellie	1, Dec. 1900		28	8	
Gartheffner, Mary	15, May 1889		26	1	
Garthlein, George	4, Mar. 1890		35	1	
Garthmann, Anton Herman	20, Nov. 1897	19, Nov.	48- 6m- 8d	5	
Gartner, William C.	21, Mar. 1891		37	4	
Garttner, Fred.	26, Aug. 1892		8m	5	
Garver, Jennie	8, Apr. 1901		48	8	
Gassner, Franziska	4, July 1887		15- 6m	1	
Gastdorf, Albert	26, May 1892		7	5	
Gastinger, Edward	30, Aug. 1888		20	1	
Gates, America A.	2, May 1895		45	5	
Gates, Mary A.	28, June 1895		83	5	
Gatewood, Joseph	16, Oct. 1901		33	1	
Gatto, John B.	21, Mar. 1891		52	4	
Gatto, Lillian	26, June 1901		13	8	
Gaug, Emma	10, Apr. 1888		11m-28d	4	
Gauggel, Anselm	10, Sept 1887		25	2	
Gauggel, Edward H.	27, Mar. 1894		2	5	
Gaugh, Katharine	25, Aug. 1900		82	5	
Gaul, John	13, Sept 1893		28d	5	
Gault, George	15, June 1901		57	8	
Gaus, J.J.	13, Nov. 1899	10, Nov.	84- 5m	5	
Gauselmann, Heinrich	3, Oct. 1896	2, Oct.	31	5	
Gauselmann, W.	16, July 1901		1	8	
Gausling, Katie	20, July 1887		15m	1	
Gausmann, Harry J.	30, June 1897	29, June	31	5	
Gausmann, J.	7, July 1888		56	4	
Gautschi, Nancy	21, June 1888		47	1	
Gauß, Amalia	4, Aug. 1896	3, Aug.	76	5	Sonne
Gavin, William	9, Oct. 1900		51	8	
Gaynor, Margarite	30, Aug. 1900		1	5	
Gaytree, J.D.	21, Feb. 1888		34	1	
Gazzolo, Frank	24, Dec. 1900		38	8	
Gaßman, Stella H.	18, Feb. 1890		18	1	
Gaßner, Andreas	24, Apr. 1900	23, Apr.	72- 4m	8	
Gaßner, Bertha Elisabeth	4, Aug. 1896	3, Aug.	23-11m	5	Winn
Gaßner, Eva	17, Apr. 1900	16, Apr.	26- 4m	5	Bickel
Gaßner, Regina	26, May 1898	24, May	72- - 2d	5	Boni
Geary, George H.	5, July 1887		20m	1	
Gebel,	31, July 1900		2m	5	
Gebhard, A.J.	29, Oct. 1894		67	5	
Gebhard, Magdalena	18, July 1887		76	1	
Gebhardt, Angela	31, May 1901		1	8	
Gebhardt, Clifford	8, Aug. 1901		9d	8	

Name ****	Notice Date ****** ****	Death Date ***** ****	Age ***	Page ****	Maiden Name ****** ****
Gebhardt, Edward	19, Feb. 1890		66	1	
Gebhardt, Theodor J.H.	6, Sept 1895	4, Sept	17- 1m	5	
Gebhart, Annie L.	23, Aug. 1887		16	1	
Gebhart, Joe	1, Feb. 1889		2m	1	
Gebhart, Johan	20, Feb. 1896	19, Feb.	80- 8m	5	
Gebhart, Mathilda	22, Mar. 1901		18	8	
Gecks, Adolph	11, July 1893		4m	5	
Gecks, Julia	4, Oct. 1901		36	8	
Gecks, Julia A.	4, Mar. 1893		22d	5	
Geering, Bernard	3, Dec. 1892		27	5	
Geers, Anton	26, Sept 1887		15m	1	
Geers, Custina	21, Apr. 1892		64	5	
Geers, Flora	23, Sept 1887		14m	2	
Geers, John	16, May 1891		50	2	
Geesen, Henriette	26, Aug. 1899	25, Aug.	9m-20d	4	
Gehefer, Cornelius	7, Jan. 1901		71	5	
Gehle, John Henry	29, July 1897	26, July	60- 4m	5	
Gehlert, Olga	23, Aug. 1887		11m	1	
Gehre, Katharina	14, Jan. 1901		54	8	
Gehred, Casper	13, Nov. 1899	12, Nov.		5	
Gehret, Margaretha	5, Oct. 1896	3, Oct.	56	5	Freibert
Gehring, Frank H.	20, Apr. 1889		6m	1	
Gehring, Gesina	29, Mar. 1897	26, Mar.	64- 4m	5	Klostermann
Gehring, Henriette	20, Mar. 1894		63	5	
Gehring, John	15, Apr. 1888		59	5	
Gehring, John	21, Mar. 1901		16	8	
Gehring, Josephine	3, Jan. 1893		18	5	
Gehrlein, Lizzie	5, May 1893		4	5	
Gehrlich, Resine	18, Dec. 1895	17, Dec.	70- 3m	5	
Gehrum, Andrew	1, July 1901		44	8	
Gehrum, John	5, May 1893		35	5	
Geier, Amanda Virginia M.	21, July 1898	20, July		5	
Geier, Barbara	19, Dec. 1891		29	4	
Geier, Jacob	17, Jan. 1899	15, Jan.	63	5	
Geier, Margaretha	9, Nov. 1898	8, Nov.		4	Ueschel
Geier, Peter	24, Apr. 1894		4	5	
Geiger, Anna	14, Aug. 1900		50	5	
Geiger, Anton	7, Mar. 1894		1d	5	
Geiger, Edith M.	24, Jan. 1901		1m	8	
Geiger, Herman	23, Feb. 1901			8	
Geiger, James	12, Sept 1891		1	1	
Geiger, John	7, Feb. 1901		69	8	
Geiger, K.	3, May 1888		26	1	
Geiger, Lambert	30, Sept 1896	29, Sept	33- 1m	4	
Geiger, Lawrence	27, Sept 1893		4m	5	
Geiger, Martin	17, Apr. 1891		7m	4	
Geiger, Mary	7, Sept 1894		57	5	
Geiger, Norma	27, Dec. 1890	26, Dec.	4	1	
Geiger, Theresa	17, Dec. 1888		3w	1	
Geil, Mary A.	20, Mar. 1891		1	4	
Geiler, Jak.	4, Sept 1888		36	2	
Geilfuß, Ivanora	23, Jan. 1891		9	4	
Geimeier, Johan	16, Feb. 1898	15, Feb.	83	5	
Geis, Edward	26, June 1894		6m	5	
Geis, Jacob	12, Dec. 1891		63	4	
Geis, Theresa	6, Apr. 1894		23	5	
Geise, Henriette	16, Dec. 1889		4	1	
Geise, Margaretha	25, Mar. 1890		65	1	
Geise, Mary	20, July 1901		7m	8	
Geisendorf, Mary	14, Jan. 1892		62	1	
Geisendorfer, John	1, Mar. 1892		60	5	
Geiser, August	21, Feb. 1888		41	1	
Geiser, Caroline	25, May 1895		83	5	
Geiser, Leonard	20, Feb. 1894		47	5	
Geisler, August	18, Dec. 1891		71	2	
Geisler, Caroline	17, Oct. 1887		62	1	
Geisler, Friedrich	14, 15, July 1887	12, July	62-11m- 4d	* 1	
Geisler, Johanna	4, Feb. 1893	4, Feb.	32- 4m-21d	5	Günther
Geist, Caroline	12, Sept 1900		46	5	
Geist, Heinrich	15, Apr. 1900	11, Apr.	80- 6m	8	
Geisting, Anna L.	24, June 1891		35	4	

Name ****	Notice Date ****** ****	Death Date ***** ****	Age ***	Page ****	Maiden Name ****** ****
Geiß, John	21, Jan. 1894		22m	5	
Geiß, Louise	6, Feb. 1896	4, Feb.	28- 8m	5	Keller
Geiß, Theodor	9, Mar. 1895		8m	5	
Gelb, Hazel B.	4, Jan. 1893		3m	5	
Gelbert, Norma	17, Jan. 1893		4	5	
Gelbricht, Paul	28, June 1894		2	5	
Gelchhoffsky, Belle	16, Mar. 1901		21d	8	
Geldreich, Jacobine	26, Dec. 1889		62	1	
Gellenbeck, G.	19, Nov. 1888		79	1	
Gellenbeck, Henry	23, Aug. 1888		28	1	
Gellhaus, Henry H.	27, Oct. 1899	26, Oct.	40- 7m	8	
Gellhaus, Katharina	4, June 1900	3, June	77- 5m	8	Rohr
Gellhaus, Otto	23, Nov. 1895	22, Nov.	74- 4m	5	
Gels, Frank	8, Nov. 1889		3	1	
Gels, Henry	16, July 1895		20	5	
Gels, Herman	18, Oct. 1899	15, Oct.	51	7	
Geltmann, Mary	21, Dec. 1891		22	4	
Gemehle, Anna	11, Dec. 1890		66	1	
Geming, Louisa	26, Jan. 1892		37	5	
Gemm, Katharine	18, Feb. 1888		40	1	
Genau, Joseph	29, Sept 1897	26, Sept	7m-18d	5	
Genau, Mary	3, Dec. 1888		69	1	
Geneceo, Theresa	8, Feb. 1895		1d	5	
Genge, Robert	17, Jan. 1893		71	5	
Gennett, Loraine	3, May 1901		1m	8	
Genslinger, Stephen	22, Oct. 1900		13	8	
Genter, Louisa	25, July 1890		19	1	
Gentrup, Mildred	17, July 1895		6m	5	
Genve, Anna	30, Nov. 1887		36	4	
George,	26, Jan. 1888		38	4	
George, Adam George	8, Oct. 1900		77	8	
George, Amelie Philomena	20, Nov. 1897	17, Nov.	43- 5m	5	Drill
George, Margarethe	28, Jan. 1901		73	8	
George, Richard	23, Sept 1887		73	2	
Gerbach, Magdalena	1, June 1901		72	8	
Gerber, Elisabeth	16, May 1894		21	5	
Gerber, Francis	27, Apr. 1894		4	5	
Gerber, Heinrich	1, Oct. 1901		62	1	
Gerber, Theresa	12, Feb. 1900	11, Feb.	63- 1m	5	Leick
Gerbhardt, Friedrich	15, Nov. 1899	13, Nov.	52	5	
Gerbus, Katharina	20, Sept 1899	18, Sept	53- 3m	8	Victor
Gerde, Casper	23, Feb. 1901		63	8	
Gerdes, Elizabeth	8, Dec. 1891		18	4	
Gerdes, Joseph T.	28, Jan. 1889		4	1	
Gerding, Franz	8, Apr. 1889		47	1	
Gerding, Margaretha	25, Jan. 1893		57	5	
Gerdsen,	16, Nov. 1900			8	
Gerdsen, Georg Herman	30, Mar. 1899	28, Mar.	44- 7m-10d	5	
Gerdsen, Margaret	4, July 1901		77	8	
Gerdt, E.G.	11, Nov. 1892		1d	4	
Gerdt, Mary	25, Mar. 1892		2	5	
Gerhard, Anna	9, May 1894		62	5	
Gerhard, Louis A.	20, Nov. 1891		1	4	
Gerhardstein, Albert	5, Nov. 1900		2	8	
Gerhardt, Barbara	24, Oct. 1898	23, Oct.		5	
Gerhardt, Clara	28, Feb. 1891		3	4	
Gerhardt, Henry	25, Sept 1890		50	1	
Gerhardt, Johan	14, Mar. 1896	12, Mar.	60	5	
Gerhardt, Katharina	21, July 1897	20, July	56	5	Hahn
Gerhardt, Louis	28, May 1892		15	5	
Gerhardt, Willie	29, Jan. 1891		4	4	
Gerichten, Clara K.	22, June 1895		1	5	
Gericke, Bernhard	21, Mar. 1892		65	4	
Geringer, Robert A.	8, May 1891		5	4	
Geritz, Katie	8, July 1891		8	4	
Gerke, Bettie	4, May 1894		42	5	
Gerke, Mathilda	22, June 1892		1	5	
Gerkens, Katharina	17, Apr. 1890		75	1	
Gerlach, John	23, Sept 1901			8	
Gerlacher, A.	16, July 1901		6m	8	
Gerland, Elisabeth	26, Sept 1900		70	5	

Name ****	Notice Date ****** ****	Death Date ***** ****	Age ***	Page ****	Maiden Name ****** ****
Gerland, Frederick	3, Aug. 1901		78	8	
Gerleman, B.H.	27, Aug. 1889		62	1	
Gerling, Margaret	11, Sept 1894		1	5	
Gerling, Mary	5, Aug. 1887		11m	1	
German, Mary	30, Aug. 1888		74	1	
German, William	25, Mar. 1890			1	
Germann, Elenora	19, Mar. 1891		3	4	
Germer, Frederick	7, Mar. 1891		76	4	
Gerna, Christ	19, Oct. 1892		43	5	
Gerold, Albert H.	24, Aug. 1896	22, Aug.	28- 3m	5	
Geroschi, Bode	29, June 1892		4	5	
Gerrard, Steph.	20, Aug. 1888		10m	1	
Gerrein, Maria	5, Aug. 1898	4, Aug.	21- 7m	5	
Gerrmann, Augusta	5, Dec. 1896	5, Dec.	35- 8m-23d	5	Luebke
Gersmad, Anna	28, June 1894		86	5	
Gersmann, August	28, Dec. 1892		56	5	
Gersmann, Carrie	27, Feb. 1888		2	4	
Gersmann, George	11, Feb. 1893		61	5	
Gersmann, Lizzie	3, Oct. 1891		19	1	
Gerst, August	13, May 1891		34	2	
Gerstle, Friedrich Wilhelm	22, Dec. 1892	21, Dec.	74	5	
Gerten, Theresa	17, Apr. 1894		66	5	
Gerth, Annie M.	9, Mar. 1893		32	5	
Gerth, Friedrich	27, Oct. 1900		57	8	
Gerth, Gustav H.	18, June 1895		5m	5	
Gervers, George	13, July 1887		5m	1	
Gerversmann, Maria	15, Feb. 1900	14, Feb.	50-11m	5	Schwierjohann
Gerves, Johan	20, Sept 1898	19, Sept	45	5	
Gerwe, Clara	26, Jan. 1901		4	8	
Gerwe, Ellen M.	16, Aug. 1894		29	5	
Gerwig, Albert	10, Dec. 1892		80	5	
Gerwing, Adelheid	30, July 1898	29, July	65- 7m	5	Schwietert
Gerwing, Henry	26, Aug. 1892		42	5	
Geschwind, Constantine	4, Jan. 1898	2, Jan.	60- 6m	5	
Geschwind, John	7, Jan. 1888		86	1	
Geselbracht, Charles	23, Feb. 1889		7	1	
Geselbracht, Henry	11, May 1897	9, May		5	
Geselbrecht, Edward	23, Nov. 1891		1d	1	
Gesner, Emma	18, July 1891		18	1	
Gessert, George H.	17, Feb. 1891		19	4	
Gessert, Henry	18, May 1900	18, May	77	5	
Gessert, Lillie M.	11, Dec. 1891		22	4	
Gessert, Theresa	4, June 1901			8	
Gest, John	5, Jan. 1901		50	8	
Gester, Valentin	4, Dec. 1894		68	5	
Gettler, Mary	15, Feb. 1895		70	5	
Getz, Joseph	5, Apr. 1901		40	8	
Geyer, Catharine C.	22, July 1893		27	5	
Geyer, Dorothea	14, Jan. 1899	12, Jan.	39- 6m	5	
Geyer, Emma	22, May 1899	20, May	25- 5m	4	Burbacher
Geyer, Frederick	23, Apr. 1895		52	5	
Geyer, Georg L.	16, Apr. 1890		4m	1	
Geyer, George A.	28, June 1888		8d	1	
Geyer, Jakob	3, Mar. 1892		3	5	
Geyer, Johan	6, Mar. 1894		75	5	
Geyer, John	25, 26, Feb. 1901		78	8	
Geyer, Julius	3, Apr. 1895		64	5	
Geyer, Katie M.	3, Mar. 1899	1, Mar.	16- 6m	4	
Geyer, Lena	27, Nov. 1900		36	8	
Geyer, Lizzie	11, Nov. 1892		23	4	
Geyser, Anna M.	12, May 1891		60	1	
Geßner, Sophia	16, Sept 1889		69	1	
Gfreir, Matthew	2, Apr. 1895		53	5	
Gibbons, William	9, Oct. 1900		29	8	
Gibbs, Forest H.	17, Oct. 1900		1	8	
Gibbs, Shelby	29, Dec. 1900		67	8	
Gibing, Alvin	28, Jan. 1889		21m	1	
Giblin, Michael	2, July 1901		58	8	
Gibner, Georg	11, Jan. 1892		16	4	
Gibney, Charles	4, June 1901		67	8	
Gibney, George A.	28, Jan. 1901		65	8	

Name ****	Notice Date ****** ****	Death Date ***** ****	Age ***	Page ****	Maiden Name ****** ****
Gibson,	29, Oct. 1900		18d	8	
Gibson, Hugh	26, Aug. 1901		72	8	
Gibson, Thomas	11, Apr. 1901		54	8	
Gick, Barbara	21, Jan. 1890		64	1	
Gick, Elisabeth	9, Sept 1896	8, Sept	39-11m	5	Beck
Gick, Emma L.	8, May 1889		3	1	
Giebel, Adam	3, Feb. 1893		35	5	
Giebelmeier, C.	14, Dec. 1887		19	4	
Giering, John	20, Aug. 1901		1	8	
Gieschen, Albert	29, Jan. 1891		1	4	
Giese, Amelia S.	26, Aug. 1901		36	8	
Giese, Charles	7, Mar. 1889		59	1	
Giese, Idella	18, Apr. 1895		18	5	
Giese, Joseph	1, Nov. 1892		67	5	
Giese, Louise	27, Aug. 1892		54	5	
Giese, Stella	16, July 1895		2	5	
Giese, Wilhelm	5, July 1890		5m	1	
Giese, Wilhelm	19, May 1900	18, May	46-10m	8	
Giesecke, Sophia	8, Aug. 1901		67	8	
Gieseke, William	31, Oct. 1891		57	4	
Gieseking, Caroline	17, Feb. 1895		59	5	
Gieseking, Heinrich	19, Aug. 1898	17, Aug.	70	5	
Gieske, Kate	14, Oct. 1901		24	5	
Giesken, C.	5, Oct. 1888		13m	1	
Giesken, George	10, June 1889		3w	1	
Giesken, Herman	20, Jan. 1890		69	1	
Giesker, Louisa G.	11, Dec. 1893		4	5	
Giesler, Victoria	4, Dec. 1891		86	4	
Giesling, Herman	14, Feb. 1891		5m	4	
Giessler, Sophie	15, Dec. 1896	14, Dec.		5	Kuhlmann
Giffin,	15, Jan. 1901		4d	8	
Giffin, Lena	2, Feb. 1888		3- 3m	4	
Gilb, Charles	12, July 1893		25	5	
Gilb, Gussie	29, May 1895		4	5	
Gilb, Rosa	12, July 1890		53	1	
Gilbert, Kunigunda	1, Mar. 1888		75	4	
Gilbert, Wilhelmine	26, Jan. 1898	25, Jan.	68- -23d	5	Kuhlmann
Gilday, Bridget	10, Mar. 1888		60	1	
Gilday, Honora	22, Sept 1888		56	1	
Gilday, John	14, Aug. 1887		64	1	
Gildea, Charles	10, Apr. 1901		28	8	
Gildea, Mary	23, Aug. 1900			8	
Gildehaus, Maggie	4, Aug. 1888		33	4	
Gildehaus, Mina	16, Oct. 1897	14, Oct.	62	5	Kemper
Gilden, Robert	25, July 1893		5m	5	
Gildlein, Albert	10, July 1887		4w	1	
Gilett, William H.	20, Sept 1901		55	1	
Gilks, Clifford	11, Feb. 1891		2	4	
Gill, Annie	14, Jan. 1901		54	8	
Gill, Charles	26, Aug. 1887		17	1	
Gill, James	5, Aug. 1901		69	8	
Gill, John	13, Oct. 1892		49	5	
Gill, Katharine	9, Mar. 1901		64	8	
Gillen, Mary	25, Feb. 1901		15	8	
Gillespie, Ebed. W.	29, Oct. 1900		10	8	
Gilligan, Annie	23, Aug. 1900		34	8	
Gilling, William	27, July 1888		34	1	
Gillispie, Lenora	24, Dec. 1900		1	8	
Gillmann, Patrick	20, Mar. 1901		55	1	
Gilpin, Charles C.	19, Sept 1900		4	8	
Gilroy, John	1, June 1901		42	8	
Gilsey, Nettie	14, Apr. 1897	13, Apr.	23	5	
Gilsey, Peter	1, June 1901		72	8	
Giltz, Lulu	15, Sept 1892		1	5	
Gimsley, Clyde	17, Dec. 1900		4	8	
Ginandt, Eva	13, Oct. 1892		75	5	
Ginber, Xavier	4, June 1895		4m	5	
Ginter, Anna	30, Aug. 1890		62	2	
Gipner, Percival	4, June 1891		1d	4	
Girten, Amanda	8, May 1889		1	1	
Giseke, Emma	3, May 1897	2, May	28- 8m	5	

Name	Notice Date	Death Date	Age	Page	Maiden Name
****	****** ****	***** ****	***	****	****** ****
Giseke, Wilhelm	18, Feb. 1897	17, Feb.	56- 5m	5	
Gisker, Georg H.	14, June 1897	14, June	79	5	
Glaab, J. Adam	20, Apr. 1900	19, Apr.	67- 1m	5	
Glacken, John	30, Nov. 1892		37	5	
Gladen, Friedrich	13, Nov. 1900		29	8	
Gladwisch, John	30, July 1889		44	1	
Gladwisch, John F.	17, Oct. 1900		32	8	
Glaescher, Clara	5, Mar. 1892		3	5	
Glaeser, Michael	6, May 1897	4, May	46	5	
Glandorf, Anna G.	3, Apr. 1891		2	4	
Glandorf, Annie	8, Oct. 1891		32	4	
Glandorf, Josephine E.	20, July 1896	18, July		5	Waldapfel
Glankler, John	2, Aug. 1898	31, July	76	4	
Glanz, Jacob	16, Oct. 1900		32	8	
Glasmeyer, Friedrich	2, Apr. 1900	30, Mar.	1	8	
Glatz, Pauline	8, Feb. 1896	6, Feb.		5	Brucker
Glaub, Gertrude	15, Apr. 1893		74	5	
Glazell, Hazel	24, Mar. 1898	22, Mar.	2- 9m	5	
Glaß, Gertie	24, Feb. 1894		7w	5	
Glaß, Henry	4, Oct. 1888		60	4	
Glaß, Karoline	11, Feb. 1889		58	1	
Glaß, William	18, Nov. 1894		18	5	
Glaßmeyer, Frederick	9, May 1899	7, May	66	5	
Glaßmeyer, Gerhard Heinrich	6, July 1898	5, July	84	5	
Glaßner, Charles	21, Nov. 1900		33	8	
Gleason, Dennis	24, Apr. 1895		47	5	
Gleason, Michael	2, Nov. 1900		20	8	
Gleich, Balthasar	9, May 1895		80	5	
Gleis, Frank	14, July 1891		6m	4	
Glemser, Christiana	30, Aug. 1900		65	5	
Glemser, Clara H.	6, Feb. 1889		5w	1	
Glemser, Edith M.	16, Aug. 1887		2	1	
Glenn, Amanda	29, Oct. 1888		70	1	
Glenn, John J.	16, Nov. 1900		73	8	
Glockner, Ludwina	3, Nov. 1892		34	5	
Glodwell, Kat.	24, Jan. 1888		59	1	
Gloner, Lettie	27, June 1891		4m	1	
Gloner, William	2, Apr. 1891		17	4	
Glore, Mary	1, Aug. 1888		33	2	
Glore, William	24, Dec. 1900		28	8	
Glover, Emma	23, May 1901		39	8	
Glover, George	3, Mar. 1888		47	1	
Glover, Mary E.	23, Sept 1887		22	2	
Glozer, Anna	5, June 1893		15	5	
Gloßmeyer, K.	24, Feb. 1888		66	4	
Glucker, Flora	24, Oct. 1890		25	1	
Gluckler, Louise	12, June 1889		2	1	
Glunz, Anna	31, Dec. 1892		73	5	
Glunz, Gertrud	12, Feb. 1890		7	1	
Glunz, Herman	19, Nov. 1900		27	8	
Glunz, Jessie	7, June 1890		3	1	
Glynn, Anna	8, Dec. 1900		65	8	
Gläscher, M.A.	26, Jan. 1889		7w	1	
Gläser, Andreas	31, Jan. 1893		52	5	
Glöckler, Karl	5, 6, Dec. 1887	3, Dec.	34- 1m- 5d	4	
Gnoose, Maria	22, Dec. 1900		11d	8	
Goarham, James	1, May 1901		68	8	
Gobelman, Louise H.	10, July 1891		2	4	
Goblet, Jennie	20, Nov. 1900		52	8	
Gobrecht, August	6, Feb. 1889		56	1	
Gobrecht, G.A.	14, July 1899	12, July	60	4	
Gock, John Bernard	5, Oct. 1889		66	1	
Gockel, Charles	28, July 1893		10m	5	
Goda, August	7, Dec. 1898	5, Dec.	23- 5m	4	
Goda, Edward A.	11, Oct. 1900		13d	8	
Goda, Herman Heinrich	7, July 1897	6, July	54-10m	5	
Goddel, Raymond	10, Apr. 1901		7d	8	
Godemann, Joseph	11, June 1895		38	5	
Godfrey, Sarah	21, Jan. 1901		6m	8	
Godman, Fred.	3, Feb. 1892		38	5	
Godsey, Lizzie	12, May 1895		75	5	

Name ****	Notice Date ****** ****	Death Date ***** ****	Age ***	Page ****	Maiden Name ****** ****
Goebel, Christine	28, June 1893		63	5	
Goebel, George J.	24, July 1895		1	5	
Goebel, Gertrude S.	4, Aug. 1893		18m	5	
Goebel, Jacob	23, Jan. 1894		66	5	
Goebel, Joseph	8, Aug. 1892		44	5	
Goebel, Maria Louise	12, Apr. 1898	11, Apr.		5	
Goecke, Henry	26, Feb. 1901		53	8	
Goecke, Vincent	6, June 1901		1m	8	
Goeckler, Andreas	6, Oct. 1891		60	4	
Goedecke, John	15, Apr. 1892		1	5	
Goedicke, Wilhelm	22, July 1891		13m	4	
Goeft, Joseph	7, Apr. 1893		4	5	
Goehring, Martin	5, Feb. 1895		62	5	
Goeking, George	28, Jan. 1901		73	8	
Goels, Eddie	5, Nov. 1889		1- 6m	1	
Goepf, Louisa	10, Jan. 1893		34	5	
Goepfert, Maria Theresia	11, June 1897	9, June	60- 7m	5	Millern
Goepper, Herman	22, Oct. 1900		53	8	
Goepper, William H.	27, Nov. 1900		39	8	
Goeppinger, Frida	19, Aug. 1901		2m	8	
Goering, William H.	20, June 1895		12d	5	
Goerlich, William	7, Mar. 1892		65	5	
Goerner, Karl	5, June 1901		58	8	
Goers, V.	29, June 1893		52	5	
Goertemoeller, Margarethe	21, Dec. 1899	20, Dec.	65- 6m	4	Leonard
Goesling, Joseph	20, June 1896	19, June	35-10m	5	
Goettelmann, Elizabeth	2, July 1892		1m	5	
Goettle, Leona	21, Mar. 1892		3	4	
Goetz, Caroline	3, Nov. 1891		20	4	
Goetz, Christina	25, Apr. 1898	23, Apr.	62	5	Schwarz
Goetz, Fr.	1, Dec. 1888		10m	4	
Goetz, Johan	24, 25, Jan. 1899	23, Jan.	43- 1m-26d	5	
Goetz, Johann	23, Mar. 1900	22, Mar.	77- -11d	8	
Goetz, Karolina	25, Nov. 1899	24, Nov.		5	
Goetz, Louisa	11, Dec. 1896	10, Dec.	45	5	Korzenborn
Goetz, Mary	5, Dec. 1891		2	4	
Goetz, Minnie	9, Aug. 1900		42	8	
Goetz, Rosina	28, 29, Nov. 1896	26, Nov.	83- 1m-15d	5	Feick
Goetze, August	15, Dec. 1899	14, Dec.	69	5	
Goetze, Gustav	7, May 1901		41	1	
Goetzer, Gustav	27, July 1888		2	1	
Goetzinger, Andreas	26, Dec. 1896	25, Dec.	68-10m	5	
Goetzl, Otto	7, Aug. 1891		9	4	
Gogreve, Wilhelm H.	21, June 1900	20, June	40- 8m	6	
Gogrieve, C.H.	24, Dec. 1898	22, Dec.	79	5	
Gohm, Leary	21, Jan. 1892		11m	5	
Gohr, Alice	25, May 1901		40	8	
Gohr, Edmund	11, Sept 1888		2	1	
Gohs, Joseph H.	17, June 1896	16, June	28- 9m	5	
Going, Angela	16, Oct. 1891		30	1	
Goins, Robert	23, Feb. 1901		67	8	
Goke, Georgina Seraphina	19, Jan. 1897	18, Jan.	23- 7m	5	
Gold, Hannah	11, Apr. 1901		63	8	
Gold, Mary	24, Jan. 1889		72	1	
Gold, William	7, Aug. 1901		71	8	
Goldberg, Joseph	4, Sept 1891		79	4	
Golde, Charles	26, Feb. 1891		69	4	
Golden, Margaret	12, Feb. 1901		46	8	
Golden, William	10, July 1888		32	1	
Goldfogel, Henrietta	13, Jan. 1896	11, Jan.	70	5	
Goldfogel, Moses	11, July 1887		91	1	
Goldfuß, Carl W.	17, Jan. 1893		68	5	
Goldfuß, Elisabeth	20, Aug. 1897	19, Aug.	29- 4m-14d	5	
Goldfuß, John	4, Oct. 1901		47	8	
Goldhammer, Julius	30, Sept 1887		57	1	
Golding, Katie	22, Sept 1900		29	5	
Goldman, Ella May	10, Nov. 1900		43	8	
Goldmeier, Louisa	25, June 1896	23, June	46- 8m	5	
Goldner, Alfred	21, Mar. 1893		7w	5	
Goldner, Bertha	27, Mar. 1890		18m	1	
Goldschmidt, Alma	16, Dec. 1891		6	4	

Name ****	Notice Date ****** ****	Death Date ***** ****	Age ***	Page ****	Maiden Name ****** ****
Goldschmidt, Alma	29, May 1901		2	8	
Goldschmidt, Heinrich	22, July 1891		48	4	
Goldschmidt, Rosina	18, Feb. 1896	17, Feb.	55	5	Riederhauser
Goldsmith, Adolf J.	8, Dec. 1896	8, Dec.	46	5	
Goldsmith, Benjamin	1, Aug. 1887		68	1	
Goldsmith, Joseph	30, Apr. 1901		60	8	
Goldstein, Otto	9, Feb. 1895		14m	5	
Goldstein, Robert	3, Sept 1901		44	8	
Goldstone, Clara	5, Mar. 1901		39	5	
Gollmer, Hugo	18, Jan. 1889	17, Jan.		* 1	
Gomersall, Bruce	21, Feb. 1901		53	8	
Gonzales, (Sr.)	1, Mar. 1901		35	8	
Good, Elisabeth	28, Mar. 1898	27, Mar.	60-10m	5	Schwarz
Good, Louis A.	16, Feb. 1901		1	8	
Good, Marcella	22, June 1901		8m	8	
Good, Vera	7, June 1901		16	8	
Goodbar, Flora	8, Dec. 1900		50	8	
Gooder, Joseph	16, July 1895		35	5	
Goodin, C.	25, Nov. 1887		33	1	
Goodlow, Samuel	4, Apr. 1901		26	8	
Goodman, Margaret A.	24, Dec. 1900		95	8	
Goodpastor, Thomas	11, Aug. 1891		20	4	
Goosman, Emma	19, Feb. 1891		1	4	
Goosmann, Fr.	12, July 1899	11, July	80	5	
Goosmann, Marianne	26, July 1898	25, July	75	5	
Gorbach, Theodore	30, Apr. 1896	29, Apr.	25- 6m	5	
Gordon, Harry	6, Feb. 1901		18	8	
Gordon, Joseph	18, June 1889		11m	1	
Gorien, Daniel	26, Apr. 1901		27	8	
Gorman, Anna	29, Aug. 1900			5	
Gorman, M.	3, Oct. 1901		60	8	
Gorman, Maggie	17, Dec. 1887		18	1	
Gorman, Thomas	16, July 1895		78	5	
Gorris, Earl C.	28, Dec. 1900		10	8	
Gorrmann, Frank	26, July 1895		10m	5	
Gosemeyer, Maria	24, Nov. 1898	23, Nov.		5	
Goshorn, Nicholas	27, Sept 1893		6d	5	
Goshorn, Thomas	1, June 1894		44	5	
Gosling, William J.	6, Mar. 1889		35	1	
Gossin, Maria	8, Dec. 1900		80	8	
Gothmann, Elizabeth	20, Nov. 1900		76	8	
Gott, Anna Maria	26, July 1899	24, July		5	Haarmeyer
Gott, Maria	19, Dec. 1891		44	4	
Gottlieb, Clara	10, Jan. 1891		37	4	
Gottlieb, Emma	11, Aug. 1892		3	5	
Gottlieb, Flora	10, Aug. 1894		64	5	
Gottlieb, Joseph	19, Aug. 1891		58	4	
Gottlieb, Margarethe	16, Mar. 1901		15d	8	
Gottlieb, Simon	19, Jan. 1898	18, Jan.	73	5	
Gottman, Emma	12, Sept 1891		36	1	
Gottman, Karoline	2, Apr. 1900	31, Mar.	73	8	Fischer
Gottschalk, Conrad	23, Feb. 1889		79	1	
Gottschlich, Paul	17, Feb. 1891		47	4	
Goßman, John S.	27, Dec. 1890		54	2	
Goßney, Effice	19, Mar. 1901		1m	8	
Grabel, William	8, May 1894		62	5	
Grabenstetter, Michael	3, May 1895		68	5	
Graber, Carrie	31, Jan. 1893		16	5	
Grabing, Gertrude	20, June 1901		1	8	
Grabmann, Frank	29, July 1899	28, July	31- 1m	5	
Grabo, Henriette	28, Nov. 1898	26, Nov.	58- 8m	5	Hoelscher
Grabon, Mabel	18, Aug. 1887		3m	1	
Grace, John	22, May 1901		6m	8	
Grace, Marie	24, Dec. 1900		16d	8	
Gradel, John	6, Sept 1889		64	1	
Gradel, Louisa	7, July 1891		36	1	
Gradolf, John	9, Aug. 1887		6m	1	
Gradsky, Samuel	29, Jan. 1891		6m	4	
Grady, Bernard	23, Apr. 1895		45	5	
Grady, Daniel J.	4, June 1895		39	5	
Grady, Ed.	1, Oct. 1900		2	5	

Name ****	Notice Date ****** ****	Death Date ***** ****	Age ***	Page ****	Maiden Name ****** ****
Grady, Kate	4, Feb. 1901		28	8	
Grady, Patrick	22, June 1901		57	8	
Graef, Friedrich	22, Aug. 1896	21, Aug.	38	5	
Graef, Henry	20, Mar. 1894		3	5	
Graeff, Joseph	6, July 1889		57	1	
Graefle, Albert	14, Feb. 1901		62	8	
Graeger, Sarah	16, Feb. 1894		56	5	
Graeling, Joseph	13, 14, July 1893	12, July	12- 3m-12d	* 5	
Graeser, Martin	15, May 1901		30	8	
Graeser, William	29, Jan. 1891		42	4	
Graf, Ada L.	18, July 1893		12	5	
Graf, Alfred	14, July 1892		2m	5	
Graf, Barbara	7, Mar. 1898	6, Mar.	31- 4m	5	Zimmermann
Graf, Elisabeth	18, Jan. 1898	17, Jan.	57- 2m	5	Heidelmann
Graf, Frank	9, Jan. 1894		34	5	
Graf, Heinrich	21, June 1901		33	8	
Graf, Ignatz	4, Dec. 1891		40	4	
Graf, John L.	28, Mar. 1888		2- 6m	1	
Graf, Margaretha	10, Jan. 1898	8, Jan.	74	5	
Graf, William H.	9, Jan. 1890	9, Jan.	25	1	
Graff, Don. O.	19, July 1895		3d	5	
Graff, Flora	12, Nov. 1888		3	2	
Graff, Joseph	12, Nov. 1900		57	5	
Graff, Maria	13, July 1894		43	5	
Graff, Wilhelmina	16, Dec. 1892		77	5	
Graffe, John	20, Sept 1887		71	1	
Graffenbacher, Edward	7, Apr. 1891		3	4	
Grah, John	17, Feb. 1892		17m	5	
Graham, Grafton	19, Mar. 1901		30	8	
Graham, W.P.	11, Jan. 1888		4	4	
Grahams, Mary	17, Oct. 1887		1d	1	
Graichen, Anthony F.	2, Mar. 1893		45	5	
Grainey, Thomas	22, Mar. 1901		20	8	
Gramann, Anna	18, Dec. 1888		24	2	
Gramann, Bernard	23, Apr. 1895		69	5	
Gramann, Caroline	30, Dec. 1898	28, Dec.	79	5	Brinkmann
Gramann, Clarence	16, Feb. 1901		4	8	
Gramann, Frederick	21, July 1893		1	5	
Gramke, Joseph	8, Oct. 1901		72	1	
Grammer, Ada	7, Mar. 1891		1	4	
Gramp, Michael	3, Apr. 1891		74	4	
Gramp, Michael	22, July 1895	21, July	59- 9m- 7d	5	
Gramp, Una	17, Apr. 1894		5m	5	
Grandison, Cyrus	9, Jan. 1901		29	5	
Grandme, Charles	9, Aug. 1890		41	1	
Granfield, Franz Joseph	17, Feb. 1888		14m	4	
Granger, Carrie	31, Dec. 1893		52	5	
Granger, Lillian B.	1, June 1893		9m	5	
Granger, Martha	13, July 1901		51	8	
Granger, Sarah	16, Apr. 1901		82	8	
Graninger, Peter Joseph	22, Apr. 1891		66	4	
Grannon, Mary	20, Mar. 1901		78	1	
Grant, Charles	15, May 1901		39	8	
Grant, John	19, Nov. 1900		47	8	
Grant, Kate	5, July 1887		32	1	
Grant, Maria	4, Jan. 1901		48	5	
Grant, Mary E.	12, Sept 1901		67	5	
Grant, Maud	28, June 1888		2m	1	
Graperin,	25, Oct. 1887		1d	1	
Grappenbecker, Ida	7, Jan. 1891		9m	4	
Grasser, Catharine	19, Sept 1894		54	5	
Grastner, William	11, Mar. 1891		50	4	
Gratz, Carrie	1, Oct. 1900		56	5	
Grau, C.C.	12, Mar. 1897	11, Mar.	54	5	
Grau, Ernst	12, Oct. 1894		69	5	
Grau, Margaretha	8, Mar. 1899	7, Mar.	65	5	
Grau, Max	31, Aug. 1901		36	8	
Grauer, Otto	21, July 1887		43	1	
Grause, J.	2, Mar. 1901		56	5	
Grautmann, C.F.	6, Mar. 1891		76	4	
Grautmann, Elisabeth C.	16, Aug. 1899	15, Aug.	81-11m	5	

Name ****	Notice Date ****** ****	Death Date ***** ****	Age ***	Page ****	Maiden Name ****** ****
Grave, Joseph	19, Feb. 1890		54	1	
Gravel, Bernard	1, Feb. 1901		37	8	
Graves, Florence M.	16, July 1888		8m	1	
Graves, Herbert	21, Nov. 1900		6	8	
Graveston, Julia	8, Apr. 1901		76	8	
Grawe, Heinrich	25, Oct. 1899	24, Oct.	67- - 9d	5	
Gray,	15, Aug. 1901		2d	8	
Gray, Louisa N.	3, Sept 1895	2, Sept	27	5	
Gray, Solomon	15, May 1901		16	8	
Grayson, Margaret	29, June 1901		31	8	
Graßmann, Henry	21, Feb. 1901		78	8	
Grear, Inez	14, Feb. 1888		29d	4	
Grebe, Mary	8, Jan. 1901		12d	8	
Gred, Henry W.	9, Nov. 1893		22d	5	
Green, Charles	23, July 1887		3m	1	
Green, George	11, Oct. 1901		16	5	
Green, Kitty	24, Dec. 1900		25	8	
Green, Millie	17, Apr. 1890		70	1	
Green, Osborne	28, Apr. 1888		39	1	
Greenbaum, L.	5, July 1888		1d	1	
Greenberg, Rosa	15, Jan. 1901		1	8	
Greenfelder, Fred.	16, Mar. 1889		34	1	
Greenfelder, J.	3, Jan. 1888		5	1	
Greenfelter, Carrie	1, Feb. 1888		3- 6m	4	
Greenfielder, Henry	28, July 1887		2w	1	
Greenloh, Katharina	28, Feb. 1901		75	8	
Greenwald, Elisabeth	13, Jan. 1896	11, Jan.	52	5	
Greenwood, Mabel	24, Feb. 1888		37	4	
Greer, Ella	4, Mar. 1892		35	1	
Grees, Josephine	16, Dec. 1891		38	4	
Greff, Henrietta	30, Nov. 1888		57	1	
Gregory, Fred.	23, Mar. 1895		4	5	
Gregory, George	3, Mar. 1891		18	4	
Gregory, Richard	21, Oct. 1891		19	4	
Greichen, William F.	12, Nov. 1900		28	5	
Greifenkamp, Ella	15, Aug. 1901		29	8	
Greifenkamp, Johan Bernard	27, Nov. 1899	25, Nov.	32- 8m	5	
Greilich, Amanda	4, Aug. 1896	2, Aug.	3-10m	5	
Greime, Herman	6, Feb. 1901		54	8	
Greiner, Anna	6, June 1888		1m	1	
Greiner, Eva	15, Jan. 1901		2m	8	
Greisenbrocker, Claire	3, Aug. 1892		20	5	
Greiwe, Alma	18, July 1887		20m	1	
Greiwe, Catherine	3, Sept 1891		20	4	
Greiwe, Edward	20, Nov. 1900		79	8	
Greiwe, Elisabeth	23, Apr. 1900	22, Apr.	72	8	Lietemeyer
Greiwe, Gerhard	25, Nov. 1895	23, Nov.	72- 9m	5	
Greiwe, Herbert	14, July 1898	12, July	5m-12d	5	
Greiwe, Josephine	10, Jan. 1889		32	1	
Greiwe, Maria	17, June 1897	15, June	33- 2m	5	
Greiwe, Mary E.	7, Dec. 1893		66	5	
Greiwe, Sophia	23, Dec. 1891		60	4	
Greißmann, Elisabeth	4, Apr. 1894		20	5	
Gresger, Josephine	30, Sept 1888		3w	4	
Greskamp, M. Theresa	27, Sept 1900		69	8	
Gressi, Maria	28, Jan. 1896	26, Jan.	80	5	Froehly
Greszkiewig, Mathilda	11, Dec. 1893		41	5	
Grether, Harry	16, July 1895		51	5	
Greulich, John	23, Aug. 1901		67	8	
Greve, Ida	8, July 1891		21d	4	
Grevenkemper, Carl	24, Feb. 1898	23, Feb.	33- -18d	5	
Grey, Kitty	28, July 1887		51	1	
Greßle, Herman	29, Jan. 1892		3	5	
Gribi, Fritz	4, Feb. 1891		6	4	
Gridley, Mary A.	11, Feb. 1891		27	4	
Grieme, Clemens	12, Sept 1899	10, Sept	50- 8m	5	
Grier, Mary	21, Mar. 1893			5	
Gries, Catharine	9, Feb. 1895		68	5	
Gries, Karl	11, Jan. 1899	10, Jan.	77- 1m	5	
Griese, Stella	11, July 1891		1	1	
Grieser, Joseph	10, May 1894		4	5	

Name ****	Notice Date ****** ****	Death Date ***** ****	Age ***	Page ****	Maiden Name ****** ****
Griesse, Theodor	30, Mar. 1895		24	5	
Griesser, Bonus	28, Jan. 1894		43	5	
Griesser, Mary	8, Nov. 1888		2	1	
Griewe, Gustav	1, July 1891		1	1	
Grieß, May	22, Dec. 1887		48	4	
Grießman, Louise	13, July 1894		6m	5	
Griffen, Mary	6, Aug. 1901		43	8	
Griffeth, Helen	30, Nov. 1900		6d	8	
Griffig, Florence	2, July 1895		3	5	
Griffin, Ed.	15, Aug. 1901		3	8	
Griffin, Mary	1, Aug. 1888		5m	2	
Griffith, Jane	15, June 1901		82	8	
Griffiths, H.R.	22, Jan. 1889		35	1	
Grigegeis, Christoph	18, Nov. 1893		34	5	
Grigg,	19, Oct. 1892		1d	5	
Grim, Theodor	10, Oct. 1890		1	4	
Grimes, Nancy	10, Mar. 1888		18	1	
Grimkemper, John A.	3, May 1893		2	5	
Grimm, Albert G.	8, Mar. 1889		5	1	
Grimm, Charles	18, Aug. 1887		9m	1	
Grimm, Frank	5, Apr. 1901		44	8	
Grimm, Fred.	7, Feb. 1901		3m	8	
Grimm, Gallus	2, Aug. 1897	1, Aug.	70	5	
Grimm, Gottlieb	19, Oct. 1887		48	1	
Grimm, Margaretha	2, May 1894		56	5	
Grimm, Nicholas	3, Aug. 1895	2, Aug.	60	4	
Grimm, Ralph	7, Jan. 1901		5	5	
Grimme, Franz	25, July 1896	24, July	69	5	
Grimmelsmann, John F.	6, Mar. 1895		2	5	
Grimmelsmann, Marie	11, Sept 1900		17	5	
Grimmer, Dorothea	10, Sept 1896	8, Sept	75- 2m	5	Ludwig
Grimwiez, Andreas	16, Jan. 1899	14, Jan.	79	5	
Grininger, Margaretha	4, Mar. 1891		3m	4	
Grinkemeyer, Andreas	7, May 1891		2	4	
Grischy, Friedrich Wilhelm	18, Apr. 1900	16, Apr.	8- 6m	8	
Grischy, Louis	7, Aug. 1897	6, Aug.	39- 4m	4	
Griter, Belzarer	16, May 1892		84	5	
Grob, Louise R.	1, Apr. 1889			1	
Grob, Mamie	11, July 1892		1	5	
Grob, Peter	12, Mar. 1901		43	8	
Grockley, Elizabeth	25, Oct. 1894		70	5	
Groen, J.	17, Jan. 1888		41	4	
Groene, Anna Maria	15, Nov. 1895	14, Nov.	65- 8m	5	Redder
Groene, John	22, Nov. 1894		69	5	
Groene, Lucy M.	3, Sept 1891		4	4	
Grofer, Lizzie	10, July 1888		11m	1	
Grofer, Rosa	22, Aug. 1889		9m	1	
Grogan, Mary	9, July 1887		50	1	
Grogan, Michael	8, Apr. 1901		64	8	
Grogan, Peter	21, June 1901		67	8	
Groh, Dora F.	23, July 1887		18d	1	
Groh, John B.	11, Jan. 1894		65	5	
Groh, Stella	18, Apr. 1889		3	1	
Groll, Katharine	4, Aug. 1890		15	1	
Groll, Oscar D.	24, Jan. 1896	22, Jan.	16- 2m	5	
Grolle, Martha A.	3, June 1889		44	1	
Grolling, Theodor	25, Aug. 1900		80	5	
Grome, Florence	28, June 1895		3m	5	
Gronauer, Milton	28, June 1889		9m	1	
Gronauer, William	26, July 1887		6d	1	
Gronemann, Anna	5, June 1895		80	5	
Gronemann, Johan	17, May 1898	15, May	82- 7m-10d	4	
Groneweg, Fritz	20, Feb. 1896	16, Feb.	67	5	
Groninger, John G.	16, Apr. 1895		1m	5	
Gropenbacher, Lena	7, Feb. 1894		1	5	
Groppenbecker, Edwin H.	17, July 1895		3	5	
Gros, Julius	27, Dec. 1899	26, Dec.	5- 3m	4	
Grosch, H.E.	25, Nov. 1887		4	1	
Grosche, Christopher	26, July 1893		76	5	
Grose, Amelia M.	28, Feb. 1891		1	4	
Grose, John	1, Mar. 1901		47	8	

Name ****	Notice Date ****** ****	Death Date ***** ****	Age ***	Page ****	Maiden Name ****** ****
Grosquade, Anna	5, Oct. 1896	4, Oct.	47- - 4d	5	Kamphaus
Grosser, Louis	11, Jan. 1893		40	5	
Grossius, Heinrich	1, Nov. 1897	30, Oct.	52	5	
Grossmann, Margaretha	25, May 1894		1	5	
Grossmann, Mary Anna	11, Sept 1894		48	5	
Grot, Mary	29, Aug. 1901		55	8	
Grote, Benny	23, July 1887		7m	1	
Grote, Bernard	21, 23, Oct. 1895	20, Oct.	67	5	
Grote, Carrie	7, Mar. 1891		2	4	
Grote, Frank	24, May 1893		50	5	
Grote, George W.	4, Nov. 1891		5	1	
Grote, H.	8, Oct. 1895	7, Oct.	20	5	
Grote, Herman Henry	2, Mar. 1897	1, Mar.	35- 5m	5	
Grote, J.	6, Feb. 1901		41	8	
Grote, J.A.F.	9, Nov. 1898	8, Nov.	68- 1m	4	
Grote, John B.	31, Jan. 1893		45	5	
Grote, Joseph	16, Apr. 1895		46	5	
Grote, Maria	28, Mar. 1901		83	8	
Grote, Mina	4, May 1893		22	5	
Grotenkemper, Henry	29, Dec. 1891		76	4	
Groth, Ernst	1, June 1901		3	8	
Groth, Mary	24, Oct. 1900		44	8	
Grothaus, Henrietta	8, Aug. 1893		6m	5	
Grothaus, Irene	16, Feb. 1894		4	5	
Grothaus, Minnie	27, Apr. 1894		17	5	
Grothause, Cillie	29, Aug. 1892		4- 6m	5	
Grothe, John H.	27, Sept 1900		53	8	
Grotlisch, Wilhelm J.	4, Jan. 1896	3, Jan.		5	
Grotty, Frank	3, July 1894		13	5	
Grove, Charles	20, 21, June 1901		31	8	
Grover, John	12, Apr. 1889		84	1	
Groves, Harriet	29, Mar. 1888		65	1	
Grow, John A.	3, June 1891		63	4	
Grower, Elizabeth	20, Oct. 1900		64	8	
Groz, Frank	17, Sept 1890		6	1	
Groß, Albert	2, Feb. 1892		40	5	
Groß, Albert	8, Aug. 1900		64	8	
Groß, Andreas	19, Aug. 1889		29	1	
Groß, B.	7, Feb. 1899	6, Feb.		5	
Groß, E.	30, Jan. 1888		1	1	
Groß, Katharine	1, May 1895		52	5	
Groß, Louisa	5, July 1901		42	8	
Groß, Lousina K.	21, Oct. 1891		13	4	
Großheim, Eug.	11, Nov. 1892		3m	4	
Großheim, Joseph	22, May 1890		64	1	
Großkopf, Carrie	19, Oct. 1888		59	1	
Großmann,	14, Mar. 1891		7d	4	
Großmann, Katharine	21, Jan. 1888		70	4	
Großmann, W.A.	21, Feb. 1889		29	1	
Grube, Augustus	24, Mar. 1893		42	5	
Grube, Katie	26, Nov. 1900		39	8	
Gruber, Emma	4, Dec. 1891		2	4	
Gruber, John	7, Mar. 1890		69	1	
Gruber, John	27, Aug. 1891		4	1	
Gruber, Margaret	6, Dec. 1900		80	8	
Gruber, Minnie	29, Oct. 1900		82	8	
Gruener, Barbara	28, Mar. 1898	27, Mar.	52-10m	5	Hammer
Gruener, Frank	21, Nov. 1900		59	8	
Grueninger, Christ.	4, Jan. 1901		70	5	
Grueninger, Friedricka	29, Mar. 1897	28, Mar.	41	5	
Grueninger, Fritz	29, Mar. 1897	28, Mar.	43	5	
Gruenland, Julia	12, Feb. 1901		80	8	
Grueter, Herman	21, Nov. 1900		48	8	
Grumberg, Anna Clara	12, Sept 1890		4m	1	
Grunder, Emma	16, Aug. 1887		1	1	
Grunder, Genefefa	15, Oct. 1900		84	5	
Grunecker, Fred.	11, June 1901		16	8	
Grunert, Ed.	31, Aug. 1900		5m	5	
Grunewald, Louise	8, June 1899	7, June	65	4	Salzmann
Grupenhof, Hilda	4, May 1895		4m	5	
Grupenhoff, Harry	2, Apr. 1900	31, Mar.	23- 6m	8	

Name ****	Notice Date ****** ****	Death Date ***** ****	Age ***	Page ****	Maiden Name ****** ****
Grusbaum, Christine	2, Aug. 1887		35	1	
Grusse, Josephine	5, Mar. 1901		37	5	
Gräser, Elenore	1, Aug. 1898	29, July		5	
Gröne, Anna	29, May 1900	28, May		5	
Grönefeld, J.H.	30, Dec. 1893		15	5	
Grönemann, Mathias	17, May 1889		39	1	
Gröneweg, Amelia	23, June 1894		77	5	
Gröschel, Barbara	15, Feb. 1889		66	1	
Grötzer, Frank	5, Aug. 1892		28	5	
Grünewald, Kunigunde	23, Mar. 1895		74	5	
Grünewein, Louis	24, Oct. 1887		3m	1	
Grüninger, George	3, Dec. 1891		66	4	
Grüntkemeier, Henry	10, Aug. 1894		66	5	
Grützner, Arno Bruno	19, Feb. 1897	17, Feb.	22-11m	5	
Grüßer, Maria	21, Jan. 1897	20, Jan.	68	5	Kaemmerling
Gschwind, Emma	30, July 1890		11	1	
Gubbins, Mary	19, Apr. 1895		31	5	
Guckenberger, Eugen F.	20, May 1893		5m	5	
Guckenberger, George	10, Apr. 1888		49- 6m	4	
Guckenberger, Leonora	14, Jan. 1892		8m	1	
Gude, Elisabeth	1, Dec. 1891		52	4	
Gude, Herman	8, Mar. 1889		5m	1	
Guelker, Louise	27, Feb. 1901		70	8	
Guellig, John	10, Apr. 1901		8m	8	
Guenbeck, Lena	1, Feb. 1894		33	5	
Guenther, Charles	6, Jan. 1892		6m	5	
Guenther, Ellen C.	2, Nov. 1894		5	5	
Guenther, Henry	28, Dec. 1900		43	8	
Guenther, Johan	1, July 1897	30, June	60- 6m	5	
Guenther, Lena	15, Mar. 1901		1m	8	
Guenther, William	1, Mar. 1901		70	8	
Guenthner, Agnes	18, Feb. 1901		4	8	
Guese, Maggie	22, Dec. 1891		21m	4	
Guesterman, Agnes	8, Oct. 1889		2	1	
Guethlein, Kate	14, Feb. 1901		45	8	
Guethlein, Katharine	11, July 1901		27	5	
Gueting, John G.	26, Mar. 1892		61	1	
Guetlein, Mary	9, Nov. 1893		20	5	
Gueß, Thomas	4, May 1895		46	5	
Guffey, Michael	4, Nov. 1887		28	1	
Gugel, Philipp	19, Dec. 1891		79	4	
Gugel, Sophie	8, Oct. 1891		47	4	
Guhe, Margaretha	10, Nov. 1900		60	8	
Guhl, Willie	9, Aug. 1887		3m	1	
Guhmann, Robert	25, Jan. 1890		36	1	
Guilford, Eliza W.	26, Feb. 1888		86	4	
Guinaes, Homer	14, Aug. 1900		3	5	
Guinn, Leonora	26, Feb. 1901		5d	8	
Gulden, George O.	7, Aug. 1888		1w	1	
Gulker, Edward	25, June 1891		52	4	
Gullner, Augusta	26, Apr. 1899	25, Apr.	72- 2m	5	Spengler
Gulow, Minna	4, May 1900	3, May	33- 3m	8	
Gultermann, Elisabeth	30, Jan. 1894		47	5	
Guminski, John	16, Apr. 1891		2	4	
Guminsky, Charles	14, Apr. 1891		59	4	
Gumminsky, Joseph A.	21, Jan. 1901		22	8	
Gundermann, Wilhelmine	6, Sept 1889		46	1	
Gundlach, August H.	6, May 1893		2	5	
Gundmann, Clara	24, Mar. 1888		3w	1	
Gunkel, Caroline	5, June 1899	3, June	72-11m	5	Hammlert
Gunkel, Elisabeth	27, Jan. 1891		42	4	
Gunkel, Ernst	13, Aug. 1891		73	4	
Gunkel, Henry Charles (Dr.)	2, May 1899	1, May	33	5	
Gunklach, Barbara	15, Mar. 1892		60	5	
Gunklach, Lewis	10, Nov. 1891		4	1	
Gunklach, William	28, Apr. 1891		10m	4	
Gunkle, W.A.	22, Nov. 1893		40	5	
Gunmers, Georg	17, May 1897	15, May	38- 6m	5	
Gunn, Herbert	1, Mar. 1893		2m	5	
Gunselmann, Louise	23, Feb. 1899	22, Feb.	51	5	Deiering
Gunther, Louis C.	23, May 1895		4	5	

Name	Notice Date	Death Date	Age	Page	Maiden Name
****	****** ****	***** ****	***	****	****** ****
Gunthner, Christina	3, June 1891		76	4	
Guntrum, Albert	5, Aug. 1889		26	1	
Guntrum, Ernst (Pastor)	2, Apr. 1897	1, Apr.	73	5	
Guntz, Louise	31, May 1889		51	1	
Gurski, Gregor	1, Aug. 1887		7m	1	
Gurth, Lenora	16, Feb. 1895		4	5	
Gusemann, Willard	2, July 1895		5m	5	
Gute, George	1, Nov. 1892		6	5	
Gutekunst, W.	6, July 1901		5m	8	
Gutfleisch, Christina	19, Dec. 1893		1	5	
Guthardt, Anna M.	8, Nov. 1899	5, Nov.	33- 9m	5	
Guthardt, Herman M.	28, Oct. 1899	26, Oct.	62	5	
Gutknecht, Maria	20, June 1891		4m	1	
Gutknecht, W.	14, Aug. 1895	13, Aug.	39- 3m	5	
Gutmann, Louis	4, Feb. 1901		62	8	
Gutmann, Robert M.	20, Sept 1901		6m	1	
Gutzwiller, Frank	29, Dec. 1900			8	
Göbel, Amalie	11, Sept 1894		58	5	
Göbel, Leonard	3, July 1894		8m	5	
Göduke, Johanna	6, Mar. 1895		67	5	
Göhring, Louise	24, Feb. 1890		71	1	
Göppenger, Frieda	3, Sept 1901		26	8	
Görka, John B.	1, Nov. 1888		51	1	
Göttle, Walter	9, Feb. 1894		1	5	
Götz, Eduard	25, Mar. 1896	23, Mar.	2- 6m	5	
Götz, J. Jacob	31, July 1899	30, July	69	4	
Götz, Jacob	28, June 1893		68	5	
Götz, John	14, Apr. 1894		39	5	
Götz, Kunigunda	16, July 1890		84	1	
Götz, Philipp	8, Dec. 1887		77	1	
Götz, Tobias	7, July 1897	6, July	74- 7m	5	
Götzl, Carl	7, May 1896		41	5	
Göyert, Louise	25, Jan. 1896	24, Jan.	10m-18d	5	
Güntert, Eduard	21, Apr. 1900	20, Apr.	25- -29d	5	
Günther, Conrad	19, Apr. 1888		58	1	
Günther, Elizabeth	29, Oct. 1891		48	4	
Günther, Karoline	13, Dec. 1895	11, Dec.	61-10m	5	
Günther, Margaret J.	23, Apr. 1891		33	4	
Günthner,	15, Sept 1900		2d	5	
Güthlein, Barbara	22, Jan. 1897	21, Jan.	65-11m	5	Hoffmann
Güthlein, George	3, Mar. 1890	2, Mar.	35	1	
Haack, Charles	1, Sept 1894	30, Aug.	57- 5m	5	
Haacke, Andrew	3, Jan. 1901		27	5	
Haacke, Maria	4, Feb. 1891		34	4	
Haag, Franz Xavier	16, Aug. 1892	15, Aug.	45-10m-23d	* 5	
Haag, Jeneva	28, Mar. 1891		2d	4	
Haake, Margaretha	19, May 1896	17, May	65- 8m	5	Kassel
Haake, Rosa	14, Feb. 1888		2m	4	
Haap, Anna M.	17, Jan. 1893		23	5	
Haarmeier, A.M.	30, Oct. 1889		77- 9m	1	
Haarmeier, Gertrud	16, Apr. 1895		72	5	
Haarmeier, Henry	25, Apr. 1892		38	5	
Haarmeyer, Irene	13, July 1900		1	8	
Haas, Annie B.	13, Nov. 1893		1	5	
Haas, Ernst	12, Apr. 1889		2	1	
Haas, Frank	11, Apr. 1890		3m	1	
Haas, Fred.	11, Feb. 1892		31	4	
Haas, Harry	16, Apr. 1891		48	4	
Haas, John	17, Apr. 1900	15, Apr.		5	
Haas, Joseph	17, May 1901		2	8	
Haas, Lazarus	1, Aug. 1890		52	1	
Haas, Maria	19, June 1891		17	1	
Haas, Mary	28, Aug. 1901		7d	8	
Haase, Otto	2, May 1890		9m	1	
Haass, Jacob A.	21, Jan. 1888	20, Jan.	47- 2m	* 1	
Habe, Louis	16, July 1888		20	1	
Habedank, Bertha	10, Apr. 1891		19	4	
Habedank, William	20, June 1888		85	1	
Haber, Christian	11, Jan. 1893		32	5	
Haberkorn, Peter	8, July 1893		42	5	

Name	Notice Date	Death Date	Age	Page	Maiden Name
****	****** ****	***** ****	***	****	****** ****
Habethier, Catharine	23, Nov. 1900		66	8	
Habig, Cora	20, Nov. 1888		63	1	
Habig, Johan B.	4, May 1898	3, May	52- 1m-15d	5	
Hachman, John	17, Jan. 1888		46	4	
Hack, Charles	7, Aug. 1900		32	8	
Hackathorn, Blanche	30, Jan. 1901		14	8	
Hackberry, L.W.	1, Oct. 1887		45	1	
Hackdorn, Blanche C.	27, Mar. 1891		37	4	
Hackemeyer, Dorothea	21, Nov. 1889		68	1	
Hacker, Konrad	18, Jan. 1892		40	5	
Hackett, Irene	12, July 1895		2m	5	
Hackford, Eliza	15, Oct. 1891		67	4	
Hackle, Othomer	21, Mar. 1901		1	8	
Hackman, Ellen	12, Sept 1890		52	1	
Hackmann, August	6, Jan. 1892		52	5	
Hackmann, David	7, Feb. 1891		26	4	
Hackmann, Maria A.	31, Mar. 1890		73	1	
Hackmann, William	1, May 1895		34	5	
Hackwelder, Henry	6, June 1895		63	5	
Haders, Gertrud	5, July 1898	4, July		5	Kochmann
Haders, Walter	14, Dec. 1893		3	5	
Haebe, Charles	25, July 1890		18	1	
Haefer, John H.	28, Mar. 1893		71	5	
Haeffner, John	17, Oct. 1898	15, Oct.		4	
Haefling, George	22, Apr. 1891		77	4	
Haelscher, Ben.	25, Jan. 1892		1m	5	
Hafen, Gertrud	10, Feb. 1895			5	
Hafer, Carl	23, Apr. 1895		3	5	
Hafer, Joseph	19, Oct. 1889		5- 6m	1	
Hafer, Mary	21, Apr. 1888		38	1	
Hafer, Sophia	2, Aug. 1900		1	8	
Haffler, George	26, Mar. 1901		1	8	
Hafner, Fred.	26, Feb. 1888		25	4	
Hafner, Freda	1, Feb. 1893		2	5	
Hagaen, Louis	26, Feb. 1895		78	5	
Hagan, John G.	22, Apr. 1891		23	4	
Hagedorn, Bernard	18, May 1894		48	5	
Hagedorn, Charles	18, Dec. 1891		1	2	
Hagedorn, John	17, Jan. 1901		43	8	
Hagedorn, Mary	1, Aug. 1898	31, July	70- 6m	5	Paust
Hagedorn, Minnie	1, May 1901		39	8	
Hagel, Margaretha	31, Jan. 1891		33	4	
Hageman, Conrad	28, Aug. 1889		40	1	
Hagemann, A. Sabina	4, Feb. 1900	4, Feb.		5	
Hagemann, Adam	24, Aug. 1892		73	5	
Hagemann, Andreas	21, Aug. 1896	20, Aug.	59-11m	5	
Hagemann, Elmira	16, May 1894		58	5	
Hagemann, Henry	21, Mar. 1895		38	5	
Hagemann, Jas. H.	21, Nov. 1893		32	5	
Hagemann, Johan	23, Nov. 1899	21, Nov.	61- 4m- 4d	5	
Hagemann, Joseph	22, June 1901		60	8	
Hagemeier, Jakob	20, Apr. 1897	19, Apr.	39	5	
Hagemeyer, Lizette	14, Apr. 1898	12, Apr.	67-11m	5	Eilermann
Hagemeyer, Mary C.	12, Jan. 1889		2w	1	
Hagen, Caroline	21, 22, Oct. 1896	20, Oct.	81- 6m	5	
Hagen, Charles	25, Apr. 1888		17	1	
Hagen, William	8, Nov. 1887		61	1	
Hagenbarth, Alma	20, Nov. 1889		27	1	
Hageney, William A.	21, Mar. 1889		68	1	
Hager, Clara	20, Apr. 1888		7m	4	
Hager, Emma	1, Nov. 1887		3m	1	
Hager, Mary	24, Apr. 1901		50	8	
Hager, Williard	28, Dec. 1892		9	5	
Hagermann, Eva	3, Jan. 1888		1w	1	
Hagerty, Cornelius	7, Sept 1900		10d	5	
Hagerty, Hugh	5, Mar. 1901		42	5	
Hagerty, John	27, May 1901		30	8	
Haggerty, William	29, Oct. 1900		35	8	
Haglage, Emma	8, Feb. 1894		14	5	
Hagler, Rhode	27, Feb. 1901		31	8	
Hagmann, Laura Elizabeth	22, Apr. 1891		3m	4	

Name ****	Notice Date ****** ****	Death Date ***** ****	Age ***	Page ****	Maiden Name ****** ****
Hahn, Alfred	27, Oct. 1891		23d	1	
Hahn, Alvin	23, July 1895		6m	5	
Hahn, Arlina	24, Oct. 1891		21d	4	
Hahn, Carolina	7, May 1891		46	4	
Hahn, Caroline	5, Apr. 1893		60	5	
Hahn, Caroline	6, Apr. 1893		33	5	
Hahn, Elizabeth	28, Dec. 1893		76	5	
Hahn, Harry	18, Feb. 1890		5- 6m	2	
Hahn, John	10, Dec. 1892		79	5	
Hahn, John P.	20, Oct. 1891		1d	1	
Hahn, Joseph	30, Oct. 1891		76	4	
Hahn, Louis	4, Sept 1901		53	8	
Hahn, Louise Mathilda	6, June 1893		16	5	
Hahn, Sarah	3, June 1891		80	4	
Hahn, Sophia	19, July 1900		40	8	
Hahn, Wilhelm	31, Mar. 1898	28, Mar.		5	
Hahner, Amelia	19, May 1896	18, May	36- 2m	5	Becker
Hahnewinkel, Anna	10, Dec. 1891		25	4	
Haigh, Ellen	1, Dec. 1900		50	8	
Hain, Mary	31, May 1889		46	1	
Haines, Abener	22, Jan. 1892		51	5	
Haines, Elizabeth	30, Sept 1901		55	8	
Haisch, Karoline	28, Jan. 1899	27, Jan.	78	5	
Hake, Edith G.	23, Dec. 1891		6d	4	
Hake, Elsie	2, May 1890		1	1	
Halberstadt, A.C.	26, Apr. 1889		33	1	
Halden, Howard	10, Mar. 1896	9, Mar.	2	5	
Halder, Joseph	11, Nov. 1891		62	1	
Hale, George	30, Jan. 1901		67	8	
Hale, Thomas L.	21, Jan. 1901		23	8	
Hales, Florence	8, May 1888		9d	1	
Haley, Dennis	22, July 1887		45	1	
Haley, Thomas	18, June 1901		57	8	
Halin, Ed.	17, Aug. 1892		2	5	
Halker, Frank X.	20, Mar. 1894		68	5	
Halker, Mary A.	23, Apr. 1895		13m	5	
Hall,	3, Jan. 1888		5d	1	
Hall,	11, Jan. 1888		7w	4	
Hall, Andrew	5, Mar. 1901		66	5	
Hall, Floy	6, Sept 1900		34	5	
Hall, George	26, Dec. 1900		7	8	
Hall, Hortense E.	11, Nov. 1891		26	1	
Hall, Joseph William	25, Oct. 1887		13m	1	
Hall, Levitia	28, July 1887		17	1	
Hall, Margaret	18, Feb. 1888		38	1	
Hall, Martin	22, June 1901		35	8	
Hall, Mercy	3, June 1901		79	8	
Hall, Robert	11, Oct. 1901		6	5	
Halle, Suse H.	26, June 1889		4m	1	
Haller, Andreas	20, Aug. 1898	18, Aug.	63- 2m	5	
Haller, Anna M.	22, Mar. 1895		19	5	
Haller, Bertha	27, Feb. 1892		59	5	
Haller, Catharina	14, Jan. 1892		91	1	
Haller, Charles	8, Aug. 1898	6, Aug.		5	
Haller, Clara Elisabeth	26, Sept 1896	25, Sept	5- 5m	5	
Haller, Edward	6, Feb. 1901		19	8	
Haller, J.M.	13, Aug. 1888		50	1	
Haller, Jacob	4, Dec. 1900		4	8	
Haller, Ralph	24, Oct. 1900		2	8	
Haller, Susanna	27, Jan. 1890		39	1	
Haller, Susanna	12, Oct. 1898	11, Oct.	70- 9m-14d	5	Weyler
Haller, W.	9, Aug. 1887		24	1	
Hallermann, Emma	26, Jan. 1898	25, Jan.		5	Armleder
Halliday, Frank	7, Jan. 1888			1	
Halm, Johan C.	16, Mar. 1896	15, Mar.	55- 1m	5	
Halpin, Ella	11, June 1901		5	8	
Halpin, Mary	24, Sept 1901		70	1	
Halsema, Lucifer	20, Mar. 1901		20	1	
Halsey, Harnet	4, Dec. 1900		67	8	
Halsey, Julia	2, Sept 1887		27	1	
Halstead, B.C.	25, May 1901		24	8	

Name	Notice Date	Death Date	Age	Page	Maiden Name
****	****** ****	***** ****	***	****	****** ****
Halts, Lulu	15, Mar. 1901		8	8	
Halves, Emilie	23, Aug. 1887		8m	1	
Haman, Louisa	23, July 1895		66	5	
Hamann, August	16, Dec. 1897	15, Dec.	50- 2m	5	
Hamann, Augusta F.	21, July 1891		60	4	
Hamann, Emilie	9, Aug. 1901		55	8	
Hamann, Emory H.	23, Mar. 1899	22, Mar.	34	5	
Hamann, Eugenie	31, Aug. 1894	30, Aug.	22	5	
Hamann, F.	21, Dec. 1898	19, Dec.	72- 9m	5	
Hamann, Helen	17, Mar. 1894		9m	5	
Hamann, Leonora	27, Jan. 1894		7m	5	
Hamann, Mary	2, Aug. 1888		4m	2	
Hamberger, M.	29, Oct. 1895	28, Oct.	80	5	
Hambers, Maria Anna	3, Jan. 1898	1, Jan.	60-10m	5	Bene
Hambrock, Henry	7, Oct. 1891		37-11m	4	
Hamburger, Elisabeth	2, Aug. 1898	1, Aug.	75	4	
Hamburger, Jacob	25, Aug. 1897	24, Aug.	77	4	
Hamburger, Paul	23, July 1887		34	1	
Hamburger, Rosa	29, July 1890		29	1	
Hambzy, L.H.	7, Jan. 1888			1	
Hamel, Henry	14, July 1892		40	5	
Hamer, Celia C.	2, Jan. 1901		8m	5	
Hamer, Emily J.	1, Aug. 1888		54	2	
Hamer, Herman H.	29, Oct. 1900		80	8	
Hamer, Mary	18, Aug. 1894		1	5	
Hamer, Wilhelm Heinrich	11, Mar. 1898	10, Mar.	7- 4m	5	
Hamiger, Charles F.	2, Dec. 1887		11- 7m	4	
Hamilton, Anne	19, Nov. 1900		37	8	
Hamilton, James	25, Feb. 1901		53	8	
Hamilton, James E.	5, Aug. 1887		6m	1	
Hamilton, Oscar	5, Nov. 1900		39	8	
Hamman, Frank	23, Jan. 1889		2	2	
Hammann, Elisabeth	30, Nov. 1899	28, Nov.	36- 9m	5	Hammann
Hammann, Ernst	26, Feb. 1888		3	4	
Hammel, Charles	10, Dec. 1891		63	1	
Hammel, Emma	24, Feb. 1894		13	5	
Hammel, John	6, Nov. 1891		47	4	
Hammel, Magdalena	23, Feb. 1889		25	1	
Hammel, Magdalena	7, Oct. 1890		66	1	
Hammel, Margaretha	9, 10, Jan. 1896	8, Jan.	71	5	Johannes
Hammel, Marie Elisabeth	28, Feb. 1900	28, Feb.	39- 8m- 8d	4	
Hammell, Sarah S.N.	27, Feb. 1894		43	5	
Hammelmeier, Laura	13, July 1892		1m	5	
Hammelrath, Max	28, July 1887		44	1	
Hammer, Adolph	20, Feb. 1894		44	5	
Hammer, Emma F.	3, Dec. 1889		15	1	
Hammer, Fred. W.	10, Mar. 1894		19	5	
Hammer, Gustav F.	11, Sept 1900		75	5	
Hammer, John A.	10, Mar. 1894		3m	5	
Hammer, Katharine C.	8, Jan. 1891		21d	4	
Hammer, Maria	17, Dec. 1895	15, Dec.	31- 8m	4	Kattus
Hammer, Mary A.	4, June 1889		66	1	
Hammerle, Andreas	26, May 1900	24, May	54- 4m	8	
Hammersmith, Leonard	16, Apr. 1895		69	5	
Hammond, Ed.	16, Aug. 1901		6m	8	
Hammond, Edward	2, Jan. 1901		1	5	
Hammond, John	5, Aug. 1892		38	5	
Hampton, Howard	16, Oct. 1900		3d	8	
Hampton, James	8, Sept 1887		54	1	
Hanaughan, Richard	16, Apr. 1901		6m	8	
Hanche, Henry	7, May 1891		81	4	
Hancke, Ernst	26, Jan. 1892		2m	5	
Hancke, Mary	12, Sept 1901		45	5	
Hand, Joseph	30, Nov. 1887		74	4	
Hand, Mary M.	23, July 1887		42	1	
Hand, Sarah	11, Dec. 1891		92	4	
Handmann, Louis	25, June 1895		70	5	
Handmann, Mary	18, Sept 1900		2d	5	
Handrich, Anna	6, May 1899	5, May	33	4	Nagel
Handrich, Caroline	29, Jan. 1901		50	8	
Handtmann, Fred	9, June 1899	7, June	75- 4m-23d	5	

Name ****	Notice Date ****** ****	Death Date ***** ****	Age ***	Page ****	Maiden Name ****** ****
Haneberg, Gregory Anthony	8, May 1901		4m	8	
Hanekamp, Alma	17, Jan. 1894		11m	5	
Hanes, Diana	3, Apr. 1888		63	4	
Hanes, P.	24, Jan. 1888		83	1	
Haney, Martin	13, Dec. 1900		6d	8	
Hang, Martin	15, Jan. 1892		53	5	
Hanhart, Henry	1, Apr. 1890		75	1	
Hanhauser, Johan	14, July 1898	13, July	84- 6m	5	
Hanke, Clara	22, Oct. 1898	21, Oct.	15- 2m	4,5	
Hankinger, John	12, Sept 1901		32	5	
Hanks, Elizabeth	24, May 1901		81	8	
Hanks, Harry	18, Dec. 1891		6	2	
Hanks, William M.	13, Apr. 1893		56	5	
Hanley, Bartley	19, Oct. 1900		67	5	
Hanley, Patrick	26, Jan. 1901		46	8	
Hanlon, George	31, Mar. 1888		8d	4	
Hanlon, M.	4, Apr. 1888		68	1	
Hanlon, Stephen	3, June 1901		27	8	
Hanna, Charles	16, Oct. 1894		40	5	
Hannerow, Ignatius	21, July 1887		1- 6m	1	
Hanrahan, Edward	23, May 1888		30	1	
Hans, Ida	2, Oct. 1894		10m	5	
Hansche, Elisabeth Sophia	11, Dec. 1899	9, Dec.	77-11m-18d	4	
Hanschmidt, Arnold	4, Jan. 1893		67	5	
Hanselmann, Emma	11, Sept 1900		8	5	
Hansfeld, George	30, Sept 1901		39	8	
Hanson, James	7, Sept 1901		40	8	
Hanzelmann, John	6, Sept 1889		29	1	
Haos, Georg	9, Dec. 1893		27	5	
Happell, Joseph S.	24, July 1895		3	5	
Harber, Sarah	16, Oct. 1900		76	8	
Harbers, Herman	24, Mar. 1894		67	5	
Harcourt, Mamie	6, May 1893		2	5	
Hardebeck, Herman	22, June 1889		12	1	
Hardebeck, Ruth	20, Sept 1901		4	1	
Harden, Henry	10, June 1901		64	8	
Harden, Laura	24, Dec. 1900		26	8	
Harden, Nida	9, Jan. 1901		22	5	
Harders, Henry	10, June 1891		57	4	
Hardig, Anna	27, Apr. 1901		63	8	
Hardiman, Mamie	25, May 1901		3m	8	
Hardin, Clifford	23, Mar. 1892		2	5	
Hardin, W.R.	8, Oct. 1901		50	1	
Harding, Gusav	15, Mar. 1892		24	5	
Harding, John B.	4, June 1895		47	5	
Harding, John H.	3, Nov. 1891		27	4	
Harding, Laura	30, June 1888		9m	1	
Hardt, Heinrich P.	21, Oct. 1887		56- 1w	1	
Hardy, Gertrude	8, July 1888		76	1	
Hare, Charles	3, July 1897	2, July	26	5	
Harff, Barbara	29, July 1893		1m	5	
Harff, Josephine Albert	15, 17, Dec. 1888	14, Dec.	77	1	Schönefeld
Harfuser, Fred.	1, Mar. 1893		7m	5	
Haring, Martha	3, Jan. 1898	1, Jan.	4	5	
Harkett, Jerry	14, June 1895		44	5	
Harkins, Herbert	21, Sept 1900		18m	5	
Harkins, James	21, Sept 1900		39	5	
Harkins, Rhoda	21, Sept 1900		4	5	
Harley, Alex	27, Aug. 1901		29	1	
Harloff, Anna	25, June 1888		5m	1	
Harlowe, Annie	20, Nov. 1900		1	8	
Harmeling, Alwine	27, Dec. 1895	26, Dec.	2- 7m	5	
Harmens, John	7, Apr. 1893		25	5	
Harmeyer, Anna	30, Nov. 1892		32	5	
Harmeyer, J.	9, Apr. 1889		36	1	
Harmeyer, John F.	16, Dec. 1892		80	5	
Harmeyer, Julia F.	20, July 1893		2m	5	
Harmeyer, Louis	24, Feb. 1892		63	5	
Harmeyer, Louisa	6, Nov. 1896	5, Nov.		5	
Harmon, Lulu	21, July 1900		1	8	
Harms, Mary	21, Sept 1901		57	8	

Name	Notice Date	Death Date	Age	Page	Maiden Name
Harmuth,	29, Dec. 1892		1d	5	
Harnert, Fred.	3, Feb. 1888		50	4	
Harnisch, Paulina	5, Dec. 1890		20	4	
Harnish, Arthur	2, Mar. 1901			5	
Harnold, John	7, June 1890			1	
Harold, Robert	21, Jan. 1901		22	8	
Harper, Addie S.	4, Aug. 1887		47	1	
Harper, Charles	22, Oct. 1900		75	8	
Harper, James C.	26, July 1887		8m	1	
Harperink, Anna	24, Dec. 1893		69	5	
Harries, J.W.	9, Oct. 1901		52	5	
Harriett, Peter	30, Aug. 1890		1	2	
Harrington, Mary	30, Mar. 1901		32	8	
Harrington, Mary	31, May 1901		60	8	
Harris,	10, Dec. 1900		1d	8	
Harris, A.	20, Sept 1889		28	1	
Harris, Anna	1, Oct. 1887		40	1	
Harris, Anthony D.	17, Mar. 1888		28	4	
Harris, Clarence	23, Apr. 1895		38	5	
Harris, George	9, Aug. 1901		65	8	
Harris, James	4, Apr. 1888		26	1	
Harris, Leander B.	19, Oct. 1900		62	5	
Harris, Louis	23, Mar. 1893		28	5	
Harris, Lucinda	10, Aug. 1901		42	8	
Harris, R.	14, Dec. 1888		60	1	
Harris, Rebecca	9, Jan. 1889		62	1	
Harris, Sarah	24, Aug. 1887		2m	1	
Harris, Thomas B.	10, July 1901		13	5	
Harrison, Minnie	5, Nov. 1900		41	8	
Harrison, Thelma	15, Jan. 1901		5m	8	
Harrison, Tony	4, Apr. 1895		23	5	
Harrison, Zelma	11, Jan. 1901		4m	5	
Harrmann, F.	20, Sept 1889		20m	1	
Harrmeyer, Joseph B.	6, Apr. 1893		1m	5	
Harrold, Johanna	14, Nov. 1891		65	4	
Harsch, Walter G.	8, Feb. 1894		1	5	
Harsha, William	13, Aug. 1891		6	4	
Harsouph, Ollie	8, Mar. 1901		20	8	
Hart, Elsie	1, Feb. 1888		7m	4	
Hart, Emilie	24, Oct. 1896	22, Oct.	48- 5m	5	
Hart, Emma	24, Sept 1889		24	1	
Hart, Howard	12, Sept 1891		4m	1	
Hart, Isaak	14, June 1895		51	5	
Hart, James	23, Apr. 1895		56	5	
Hart, John	14, Sept 1901		38	1	
Hart, Louis	13, July 1901		45	8	
Hart, Richard G.	27, July 1888		6w	1	
Harte, Edward	23, Mar. 1889		20	1	
Harte, Louise	17, May 1900	16, May	8-11m	5	
Hartel, Herman A.	12, Feb. 1901		3m	8	
Harter, Dora	3, Feb. 1890		5	1	
Harter, Sophia	27, Apr. 1894		74	5	
Hartfinger, Anna Susanna	2, Dec. 1896	1, Dec.	69-11m	5	Martin
Hartgens, Henrietta	29, July 1890		2	1	
Hartgens, Mary	4, Dec. 1891		37	4	
Harthig, Ed.	18, Mar. 1893		4	5	
Harthorn, Anna	21, Sept 1901		33	8	
Harting, Fred.	2, Apr. 1891		54	4	
Hartjens, Helena	31, Jan. 1900	30, Jan.	78	5	
Hartke, Aloisia M.	11, July 1889		1	1	
Hartlaub, A.	24, June 1901		3	8	
Hartlaub, Ida E.	23, May 1894		1m	5	
Hartlaub, J.W.	18, Jan. 1897	15, Jan.	62- -15d	5	
Hartley, C.E.	25, June 1888		3m	1	
Hartlich, Christine	31, Mar. 1891		60	4	
Hartlieb, Anna	11, Sept 1900			5	
Hartmann, A.F.	11, Aug. 1888		5d	1	
Hartmann, A.W.	20, Aug. 1895	17, Aug.	80	5	
Hartmann, Anna	21, Dec. 1892		22	5	
Hartmann, Anna	19, Apr. 1898	17, Apr.	49- 7m	5	Schwenlein
Hartmann, Anton	21, Dec. 1899	20, Dec.	78- 7m	4	

Name ****	Notice Date ****** ****	Death Date ***** ****	Age ***	Page ****	Maiden Name ****** ****
Hartmann, Bernard	2, Aug. 1888		15m	2	
Hartmann, Carrie	17, Dec. 1900		20	8	
Hartmann, Catharina	7, Oct. 1890		76	1	
Hartmann, Catharina	2, Feb. 1900	1, Feb.	83- 2m	4	
Hartmann, Charles	16, Sept 1891		28	4	
Hartmann, Charles	27, July 1892		27d	5	
Hartmann, Charles J.	18, Mar. 1889		6	1	
Hartmann, Eleanora	31, July 1900		70	5	
Hartmann, Elisabeth	1, June 1894		63	5	
Hartmann, Emma	24, May 1893		2	5	
Hartmann, Ernst	22, May 1900	21, May	59- 1m	4	
Hartmann, George	29, Apr. 1898	28, Apr.	15- 9m	5	
Hartmann, Henry	8, July 1893		90	5	
Hartmann, Katharina	23, June 1896	21, June	66	5	Hammelmeyer
Hartmann, Mathilda	29, June 1894		4m	5	
Hartmann, William	4, May 1894		56	5	
Hartroch, Sallie	2, Apr. 1891		10	4	
Hartsmeyer, Georg	25, May 1900	23, May	43- 1m	8	
Hartung, A.C.	28, June 1888		8m	1	
Hartung, Catharine	17, July 1897	15, July	83	5	Engelhardt
Hartung, Georg	31, Jan. 1898	29, Jan.	73- 9m	5	
Hartung, J.	30, Aug. 1888		49	1	
Hartung, Louisa	31, Jan. 1901		33	8	
Hartung, Lulu	12, Sept 1891		19	1	
Hartwell, John	20, June 1901		31	8	
Hartye, George	6, 7, Feb. 1896	5, Feb.	43	5	
Hartz, Elisabeth	7, Jan. 1901		78	5	
Hartzig, Henry	3, June 1901		40	8	
Harvey, Andrew	10, Aug. 1901		40	8	
Hase, Charles	11, July 1889		28	1	
Haseleder, Joseph	27, Oct. 1900		54	8	
Haselwanter, Joseph	24, May 1889		49	1	
Hasemeier, Johan	15, Oct. 1895	13, Oct.	76- 7m	5	
Hasenkamp, Henry	14, Mar. 1893		64	5	
Hasenlohr, Anna	5, Mar. 1901			5	
Hasenohr, Bertha L.	8, Dec. 1887		4m	1	
Hasenpflug, Daniel	5, July 1887		68- 5m	1	
Hasenreiter, Frank	30, June 1893		43	5	
Hasenzahl, Anna Margaret	26, Dec. 1899	26, Dec.		4	
Haskamp, Clara	30, July 1901		1	8	
Haskell, Sallie	5, Dec. 1900		46	8	
Hasler, Anna	17, Mar. 1891		10m	4	
Hasler, Apollonia	23, Apr. 1896	22, Apr.	48	5	
Hasler, Dena	30, Dec. 1893		1	5	
Hasse, Charles F.	11, Nov. 1891		73	1	
Hassel, Carl	10, May 1895		5d	5	
Hasselbacher, Conrad	6, June 1900	4, June	41- 2m	8	
Hasselbeck, Katharine	20, Apr. 1894		70	5	
Hasselbeck, Nora	19, Aug. 1889		6	1	
Hasselbusch, Jacob	23, June 1896	22, June	74- 5m	5	
Hasselmann, Maria Anna	29, Jan. 1896	28, Jan.	59- 1m	5	Hüninghacke
Hassinger, Adelheid	10, Feb. 1900	7, Feb.	67- 5m	5	
Hassler, Alphons	8, Mar. 1898	6, Mar.	52- 7m	5	
Hassmann, Alfred	15, June 1894		6m	5	
Hastings, Fuller H.	26, July 1887		16m	1	
Hastings, John	20, Feb. 1901		45	8	
Hastings, Mary	27, Nov. 1900		26	8	
Hastings, Nelly	13, Aug. 1888		1d	1	
Hater, Anna	8, Mar. 1901		61	8	
Hater, John	13, June 1888		14	1	
Hatfield, W.	1, May 1888		44	2	
Hatke, Euphemia	16, May 1901		59	5	
Hatke, George F.	12, May 1893		23	5	
Hatke, Henry	16, Feb. 1894		64	5	
Hatmaker, Nellie	3, Feb. 1888		1-11m	4	
Hator, Sophia	19, Jan. 1888		43	4	
Hatz, Minnie	12, July 1890		8m	1	
Hauber, Nannie	18, Dec. 1891		55	2	
Haubner, Andy	22, May 1894		4	5	
Haubner, Margaretha	9, Nov. 1895	8, Nov.	38	5	
Haubrock, Carolina	27, Feb. 1897	26, Feb.	64- 3m	5	

Name ****	Notice Date ****** ****	Death Date ***** ****	Age ***	Page ****	Maiden Name ****** ****
Haubrock, Friedrich Wilhelm	4, Aug. 1898	3, Aug.	67- - 7d	5	
Hauck,	3, May 1888		3m	1	
Hauck, August	30, May 1895		33	5	
Hauck, Ed.	24, Sept 1888		11w	1	
Hauck, Ed.	11, Feb. 1892		5m	4	
Hauck, Eva	28, Aug. 1895	27, Aug.	57-11m	5	Pfisterer
Hauck, Johan	6, June 1896	4, June	66-10m	4	
Hauck, John	19, Mar. 1900	18, Mar.	44- 1m	5	
Hauck, John C.	16, May 1894		56	5	
Hauck, Katharina F.	5, Jan. 1892		13	5	
Hauck, Katie	23, Mar. 1893		24	5	
Hauck, Lawrence	28, Nov. 1891		65	1	
Hauck, Michael	24, Feb. 1891		45	4	
Hauck, Sol.	27, Feb. 1892		61	5	
Hauck, William	9, Aug. 1887		18m	1	
Hauck, eva	25, Dec. 1891		85	2	
Hauenschild, Fred.	24, Dec. 1900		1	8	
Hauenschild, Paul	7, Oct. 1891		4m	4	
Hauenstein, Helene	16, Jan. 1890		14m	1	
Hauenstein, Maria Catharina	24, Apr. 1900	23, Apr.	63	8	Risser
Hauer, Gottfried	5, Apr. 1901		85	8	
Hauer, Johannes	13, Feb. 1896	11, Feb.	78- 6m	5	
Hauer, Louise	25, Nov. 1887		3w	1	
Haufbauer, Konrad	4, Apr. 1893		62	5	
Hauff, Emma	17, June 1891		21	4	
Haufler, Carl G.	8, Sept 1897	7, Sept	5- 5m	5	
Hauft, John	7, July 1887		51	1	
Haug, Anna	19, Aug. 1889		5d	1	
Haug, George Johan	29, 30, July 1901		27- 3m-11d	5	
Haug, Karl	11, Jan. 1893		25	5	
Hauger, Karl Leopold	27, Sept 1898	26, Sept	28- 1m	4	
Hauk, Bertha	20, May 1890		4m	1	
Hauk, Mamie	1, June 1893		2	5	
Haule, Anna	24, Mar. 1888		6	1	
Haun, Anna	2, Dec. 1889		85	1	
Haunnell, Anna	26, Apr. 1901		35	8	
Haupt,	13, May 1891		2d	2	
Haus, Delia	24, Oct. 1890		32	1	
Haus, George F.	18, Nov. 1891		6w	4	
Haus, John	8, Jan. 1890		28	1	
Haus, Julia	30, Aug. 1898	29, Aug.	22	4	
Haus, Robert	18, Dec. 1900		12	8	
Hause, Mary	1, July 1891		54	1	
Hauser, Anna	22, May 1901		32	8	
Hauser, Arnold	2, Apr. 1901		26	8	
Hauser, Bessie	19, Mar. 1895		14d	5	
Hauser, David	14, Mar. 1896	11, Mar.	70-10m	5	
Hauser, Emma	4, Dec. 1891		3d	4	
Hauser, Ernst E.	24, July 1899	22, July	22	5	
Hauser, George O.	22, Nov. 1887		35- 6m	1	
Hauser, Jennie	29, May 1901		3m	8	
Hauser, John Ch.	25, Feb. 1889		6w	1	
Hauser, Margaret	15, Dec. 1892		48	5	
Hauser, Mary	27, Mar. 1895		34	5	
Hauser, Mathias	8, June 1898	6, June	80	5	
Hauser, Ottilie	23, May 1899	22, May	4- 6m	5	
Hauser, Sophia	12, Sept 1887		37	1	
Hauser, William	16, Jan. 1892		29	5	
Hausfeld, Johan	5, Sept 1900		36	5	
Hausmann, Fred.	31, Oct. 1900		76	8	
Hausmann, Henry	20, Aug. 1901		39	8	
Haussler, Fredericke	30, Dec. 1898	29, Dec.	80-10m	5	
Hautz, Catharine	25, Mar. 1901		49	8	
Hautz, Mary	2, Apr. 1891		10m	4	
Hautz, Rosalia	22, Feb. 1895		21d	5	
Hauß, Jakob	15, 16, Nov. 1896	14, Nov.	68	5	
Haußer, William	11, July 1887		14m	1	
Haußler, Bertha	24, July 1895		2	5	
Haven, William	24, Oct. 1900		38	8	
Haverbusch, Henry	24, Aug. 1887		20m	1	
Haverkamp, A.	6, Feb. 1901		5m	8	

Name ****	Notice Date ****** ****	Death Date ***** ****	Age ***	Page ****	Maiden Name ****** ****
Haverkamp, Elizabeth	8, Feb. 1894		60	5	
Haverkamp, Wilhelmine	19, Apr. 1898	18, Apr.	64- 3m	5	Schopmeier
Havermann, Catharina	13, Dec. 1893		70	5	
Havermann, Erma	23, Mar. 1889		26	1	
Havermann, Olga	14, June 1895		17m	5	
Havlin, Ella	15, Dec. 1900		11	8	
Hawekamp, Gertrude Maria	18, Aug. 1892		41	5	
Hawekotte, Mary	1, Sept 1891		57	4	
Hawes, L.M.	8, Nov. 1887		27	1	
Hawig, Amelia	3, Mar. 1890		58	1	
Hawkins, Edward	20, June 1888		56	1	
Hawkins, Julia	11, May 1901		1	8	
Hawkins, Mamie A.	23, May 1895		24	5	
Hawkins, Wanetta	2, Apr. 1901		8m	8	
Hawley, D.	19, Oct. 1901		51	8	
Hawley, Mary	20, Oct. 1888		6w	1	
Hay, Ellen	24, Jan. 1888		98	1	
Hayden, J.	31, May 1889		26	1	
Hayes, Carl	8, Nov. 1900		4	8	
Hayes, James S.	11, Oct. 1900		38	8	
Hayes, Mary	23, July 1901		45	8	
Hayes, Olive	28, Mar. 1901		19	8	
Hayes, Ruth	29, Aug. 1901		1m	8	
Hayes, Thomas	11, Apr. 1901		65	8	
Hayne, Anna	13, Oct. 1900		23	8	
Haynes, Blanche	23, July 1901		2m	8	
Hays, George Washington	28, Dec. 1900		75	8	
Hazard, Edward C.	23, Apr. 1895		6	5	
Hazard, Frank	14, Mar. 1901		33	8	
Hazenfelt, Ernst	16, Apr. 1901		9m	8	
Haß, John	13, June 1891			4	
Haßler, Helen E.	22, Mar. 1895		2	5	
Haßlocher, Christine Elis.	8, May 1894		68	5	Hick
Haßmann, Henry	16, Mar. 1893		67	5	
Haßmann, Lena	11, Jan. 1894		27	5	
Headman, Margareth	2, Dec. 1887		60	4	
Heagle, Elmer	25, Feb. 1901		7m	8	
Heale, Martha	14, Mar. 1901		62	8	
Healey, Barney	18, Feb. 1901		58	8	
Healey, Margaret	3, Oct. 1901		68	8	
Healion, Thomas	17, Oct. 1900		61	8	
Healy, Lulu	31, May 1901		23	8	
Heaney, Catharine	16, Aug. 1887		66	1	
Heasing, Gesche H.	29, Sept 1898	28, Sept	55- -18d	5	
Heath, Veronika	4, May 1899	3, May	73- 5m	5	
Hebbeler, Henry Johan	4, May 1898	2, May	75	5	
Hebbeler, Herman	25, Mar. 1901		74	8	
Hebbig, Margaretha	11, June 1896	10, June	78- 1m	5	Hersel
Heben, Thomas	7, Mar. 1892		74	5	
Hebestreit, Anna	14, Aug. 1900		4m	5	
Hebmer, Ada	13, Mar. 1901		1m	8	
Hechinger, Anna	20, July 1895		2	5	
Hecht, Bettie	16, Mar. 1895		56	5	
Hecht, Louise	20, Feb. 1894		37	5	
Hecht, R.E.	13, Jan. 1888		52	1	
Heck,	15, Aug. 1893		1d	5	
Heck, Catharina C.	24, Jan. 1894		54	5	
Heck, Christine	26, Sept 1899	25, Sept	57	5	Schmidt
Heck, Elisabeth	7, Jan. 1898	6, Jan.	71	5	Hauck
Heck, Jennie	19, May 1896	17, May	19-10m	5	Kappel
Heck, John C.	8, Aug. 1889		8m	1	
Heck, Joseph	3, Oct. 1888		20	1	
Heck, Maria	8, Jan. 1898	6, Jan.	71	4	Hauck
Heck, Michael	5, June 1899	3, June	64	5	
Heck, Wilhelmina	22, Mar. 1895		3d	5	
Heckendorn, Katie	23, Aug. 1890		5m	1	
Hecker, Albert	27, July 1887		33	1	
Hecker, Frank	24, Sept 1891		32	1	
Heckermann, George	2, Mar. 1901		18m	5	
Heckinger, Ollie L.	16, Nov. 1889		21	1	
Heckle, Helene	7, Mar. 1898	6, Mar.	32- 9m-19d	5	

Name ****	Notice Date ****** ****	Death Date ***** ****	Age ***	Page ****	Maiden Name ****** ****
Heckle, J.M.	4, May 1898	3, May	78- 3m	5	
Heckle, John S.	15, June 1889		43	1	
Heckle, William	11, June 1895		55	5	
Heckler, Annie	16, Apr. 1891		35	4	
Heckmann, Alma	26, Feb. 1901		16	8	
Heckmann, Anna	15, Mar. 1897	14, Mar.	31	5	Fehr
Heckmann, Peter	18, Dec. 1897	17, Dec.	75- 1m	5	
Heckmann, Samuel	15, Aug. 1901		32	8	
Hedden, Christine	29, Oct. 1900		76	8	
Heddergott, Joseph	18, July 1887		13m	1	
Heddlestone, Caroline	24, Jan. 1901		57	8	
Hedrich, Elizabeth	5, Feb. 1892		87	5	
Hedrick, Barbara	10, Feb. 1893		17	5	
Hedt, John	29, Aug. 1891		35	4	
Heeb, Annie	10, Aug. 1887		22m	1	
Heeg, Charles	23, Aug. 1888		6d	1	
Heeg, Conrad	3, Dec. 1900		42	8	
Heeg, Emma	21, May 1896	20, May	25	5	
Heeg, Esther	1, Sept 1900		3m	5	
Heehauser, Herman	12, May 1891		56	1	
Heeke, Catharine	18, July 1887		65	1	
Heel, Nellie	15, June 1895		19	5	
Heeman, Emma	15, July 1890		4	1	
Heeman, Ernst	2, Aug. 1890		47	1	
Heemann, Henry E.	31, Oct. 1899	29, Oct.	40	5	
Heemeyer, William	16, Dec. 1891		18	4	
Heenan, William	30, Apr. 1901		5m	8	
Heerding, Peter	6, Mar. 1889		74	1	
Heery, James	30, Nov. 1900		40	8	
Heetlage, Bernard	17, Jan. 1898	16, Jan.	54- 8m	5	
Heffermann, James T.	18, June 1895		40	5	
Hefner, Charles	29, Jan. 1892		37	5	
Heftlein, Martin	11, Apr. 1891		63	4	
Hegel, Jakob	27, Apr. 1901		58	8	
Hegemann, Elizabeth	3, Jan. 1890		31	1	
Hegemann, Franziska	19, Sept 1888		10m	2	
Hegemeier, Anna	5, Aug. 1901		61	8	
Hegener, Catharine	28, June 1901		71- 1m-16d	8	
Hegeny, Louisa	13, Sept 1894		32	5	
Hegermann, Gertrude	22, May 1901		62	8	
Hegner, B.S.	15, Dec. 1899	14, Dec.	50	5	
Hehemann, Antonette	2, May 1895		3	5	
Hehemann, Clara	28, Apr. 1894		13m	5	
Hehemann, Clifford	15, Aug. 1901		9	8	
Hehemann, Clifford Clemens	18, Sept 1900		9	5	
Hehemann, Katharina	1, Aug. 1896	31, July	90- 5m	5	Ostendorf
Hehemann, Wilhelm	28, Mar. 1898	26, Mar.	32-11m	5	
Hehfritz, John	12, May 1891		43	1	
Hehl, Michael	22, May 1901		76	8	
Hehmann, Henry	4, Jan. 1894		67	5	
Heiber, Frank	15, Aug. 1901		29	8	
Heiby, Amelia	30, Mar. 1897	29, Mar.	18	5	
Heid, Jakob	29, Aug. 1899	27, Aug.	87	4	
Heid, Marie	14, Dec. 1893		74	5	
Heid, Mary	8, July 1901		41	8	
Heidecker, Charles	30, Aug. 1890		22	2	
Heidecker, Robert	5, Sept 1895	3, Sept	40	5	
Heidekamp, Elisabeth	4, Aug. 1890		57	1	
Heidel, John	17, Jan. 1893		28	5	
Heidel, Joseph	2, Nov. 1896	1, Nov.	12- 8m	5	
Heidelman, Johannah	28, Jan. 1892		65	5	
Heidelmann, Phil.	17, Mar. 1891		7m	4	
Heidemeyer, Edith	8, Aug. 1890		1	1	
Heidenreich, Barbara Theresa	18, Oct. 1889		20	1	
Heidenreich, Marie	8, Aug. 1898	7, Aug.	60- 7m	5	Kruse
Heider, Michael	16, Jan. 1899	14, Jan.	71	5	
Heidkamp, Ferdinand	6, July 1895		67	5	
Heidkamp, Gerhard	30, Mar. 1894		49	5	
Heidkamp, Josephine Paulina	31, Mar. 1898	30, Mar.	35- 2m- 5d	5	
Heidler, Joseph	8, Aug. 1888	8, Aug.	27- 4m	4	
Heidt, Katharina	11, July 1896	10, July		5	

Name	Notice Date	Death Date	Age	Page	Maiden Name
****	****** ****	***** ****	***	****	****** ****
Heidtmann, William	17, Feb. 1891		3m	4	
Heidts, Maggie	2, Oct. 1888		6	1	
Heien, Henry	13, Mar. 1890		29	4	
Heil, Bernard	26, Mar. 1895		55	5	
Heil, Elizabeth	21, Nov. 1896	19, Nov.	40-11m	5	Gutzwiller
Heil, Katie	25, Mar. 1889		3m	1	
Heil, Wilhelm	10, May 1898	9, May	37	5	
Heilbronn, Amelia	22, Mar. 1893		77	5	
Heile, Elisabeth	29, May 1900	26, May	63	5	
Heile, Frank	8, Sept 1887		58	1	
Heilemann, John	27, May 1901		83	8	
Heilemann, Mary	8, Sept 1900		63	5	
Heiligenthal, F.	11, Aug. 1899	9, Aug.		5	
Heilman, Barbara	12, Sept 1891		1	1	
Heilmann, Adolph	31, Dec. 1888		17m	1	
Heilmann, Anna	27, Jan. 1891	26, Jan.	25	1	Hang
Heilmann, George J.	26, Jan. 1889		55	1	
Heilmann, Henry	3, Sept 1890		36	1	
Heilmann, J.G.	26, Sept 1891		1	4	
Heilth, Louis	23, Aug. 1887		9m	1	
Heim, Elisabeth	28, Aug. 1895	26, Aug.	65- 1m	5	Kaus
Heim, Frank	5, Jan. 1901		4	8	
Heim, John	15, Feb. 1889		10	1	
Heim, Louis	3, Mar. 1894		73	5	
Heim, Mary	6, Dec. 1888		3	1	
Heim, Peter	22, Jan. 1897	21, Jan.	50-10m	5	
Heim, William	31, Jan. 1901		16	8	
Heimann, Bertha	4, Nov. 1887		15- 6m	1	
Heimann, Henry	15, Jan. 1892		32	5	
Heimann, Timothy C.	24, Feb. 1894		7w	5	
Heimbold, Katharine	12, Feb. 1897	10, Feb.	24- 6m-10d	5	Wagner
Heimer, Clarence	16, June 1891		5	4	
Heimerdinger, Wilhelmina	17, Nov. 1893		29	5	
Heiming, Frederick	19, Dec. 1890		2w	1	
Hein, Ernst	31, Oct. 1899	29, Oct.	1	5	
Hein, Franziska	7, Oct. 1893		5m	5	
Heinbuch, Eugene	11, Feb. 1889		9w	1	
Heine, Bella	26, Apr. 1901		31	8	
Heine, Catharine	19, Apr. 1889		48	1	
Heine, Frank	9, Jan. 1889		48	1	
Heine, George	22, Aug. 1889		4m	1	
Heine, Margaret	5, Sept 1888		55	2	
Heine, Margaret	27, Dec. 1899	26, Dec.		4	Firnkoetz
Heine, Sophia	11, Nov. 1896	8, Nov.	73- 7m	5	Oberhellmann
Heinemann, Fred.	10, Sept 1887		26	2	
Heinen, Herman J.	21, Apr. 1891		64	4	
Heiner, Mabel M.	30, May 1894		1	5	
Heinert, Katie	3, Oct. 1887		21	1	
Heing, Adelheid	12, Aug. 1901		65	8	
Heink, Maria	15, Feb. 1898	14, Feb.		5	Wahoff
Heinleier, Pauline	26, Jan. 1888		33	4	
Heinlein, Henry	10, Apr. 1894		75	5	
Heinlein, Henry	20, Oct. 1900		60	8	
Heinrich, Charles	14, May 1895		35	5	
Heinrich, Elsie	9, Oct. 1900		12	8	
Heinrich, Magdalena	23, Aug. 1901		73	8	
Heinrich, Nicholas	29, May 1901		76	8	
Heinrichsdorfer,	19, July 1893		4m	5	
Heinsche, Robert A.	16, June 1891		8	4	
Heinsheimer, Louis	27, Apr. 1894		3	5	
Heintz, Christina	24, Oct. 1890		79	1	
Heintz, Clara	28, Jan. 1898	26, Jan.	16-11m	5	
Heintz, Josephine	31, Mar. 1890		33	1	
Heintzmann, Henry	13, Apr. 1895		75	4	
Heinze, Anna M.	28, Sept 1893		71	5	
Heinze, Charles	3, Aug. 1887		30	1	
Heinzelmann, Rosina	12, May 1896	11, May	6-11m	5	
Heinzelmann, Theresia	29, Feb. 1896	28, Feb.	31- 6m	5	Schuler
Heinzerling, Ninna	19, July 1887		13m	1	
Heinzmann, May	14, Apr. 1894		29	5	
Heinzmann, Ursula	6, 7, Sept 1895	5, Sept	55	5	Link

Name ****	Notice Date ****** ****	Death Date ***** ****	Age ***	Page ****	Maiden Name ****** ****
Heis, Catharina	30, Dec. 1898	29, Dec.	59- 2m	5	Becker
Heis, Margaretha	13, Nov. 1899	11, Nov.	50- 6m	5	Krämer
Heisch, Hannah J.	5, Dec. 1887		35	1	
Heischemeyer, Bernard	28, June 1900	27, June	50-11m	8	
Heisel, Helen	3, July 1895		5m	5	
Heisel, Jacob	16, Apr. 1895		62	5	
Heisel, Johan George	22, Sept 1896	21, Sept	93- - 4d	5	
Heisel, Sophia C.	11, June 1897	10, June		5	
Heiser, Anna	3, Oct. 1887		49	1	
Heiser, Theresa	6, Feb. 1891		77	4	
Heister, Anna	9, Oct. 1888		17m	1	
Heister, Gertrud	15, Mar. 1890		65	1	
Heister, Hannah S.	11, July 1898	9, July		8	
Heisterkamp, Elisabeth	10, Jan. 1888		53	4	
Heistermann, Anna	17, Feb. 1891		32	4	
Heitacker, Minna	6, Jan. 1890		65	1	
Heitbrink, Adam	9, Aug. 1900		77	8	
Heitbrink, Herbert	28, Jan. 1892		1	5	
Heitbrink, Katharina Elisabeth	16, Dec. 1898	15, Dec.	71-11m	5	
Heitfeld, Herman	15, Apr. 1900	11, Apr.	64- 9m	8	
Heithaus, Theodor	11, Sept 1900		46	5	
Heither, William	4, Feb. 1891		63	4	
Heithoff, Maria	14, Jan. 1898	12, Jan.	34- 6m	4	
Heitkamp, G.H.	15, Aug. 1893		21	5	
Heitker, Anna	25, Apr. 1892		35	5	
Heitmann, Anna B.	19, Dec. 1890		73	1	
Heitmann, Elenore	26, Jan. 1894		17	5	
Heitmann, William	2, May 1894		33	5	
Heitz, John	11, Feb. 1892		49	4	
Heitz, Lillian Margaretha	26, Mar. 1900	25, Mar.	3- 9m	8	
Heitzmann, Anna	25, Jan. 1889		57	1	
Heitzmann, Franziska	12, May 1895		79	5	
Heißmann, John	27, Apr. 1894		43	5	
Helble, Anna	9, May 1894		20	5	
Held, Kate	16, Dec. 1891		19	4	
Held, Paulina	30, Sept 1898	28, Sept	77- 6m	4	Alripp
Heldmann, Rose	29, Aug. 1901		19	8	
Helems, Philip R.	17, Jan. 1894		44	5	
Helferich, Lucas	27, Aug. 1901		47	1	
Helferig, Anton	25, Feb. 1901		62	8	
Helfferich, C.E.	17, Dec. 1895	16, Dec.	78	4	
Helfrich, Franz	5, June 1899	3, June	80- 8m	5	
Helle, Clara J.	23, Dec. 1890		6	1	
Hellebusch, Clemens	21, Jan. 1893		59	5	
Hellebusch, Lillie May	21, Aug. 1896	20, Aug.	26- 5m	5	
Heller, Adolf	11, Dec. 1900		25	8	
Heller, Carrie	12, Jan. 1894		61	5	
Heller, John B.	15, Jan. 1892		38	5	
Heller, Louis	24, Sept 1890		53	4	
Hellinghaus, Heinrich	28, Mar. 1898	26, Mar.	45- 5m	5	
Hellmann, Carol.	3, Feb. 1890		24	1	
Hellmann, Casper	11, Apr. 1891		9	4	
Hellmann, Friedrich	23, Nov. 1896	21, Nov.	68-10m	5	
Hellmann, Friedrich H.	8, May 1897	7, May	61- 2m	5	
Hellmann, George	18, Mar. 1898	17, Mar.	23- 2m	5	
Hellmann, George	16, Nov. 1900		65	8	
Hellmann, H. Anton	19, Aug. 1895	17, Aug.	80- 2m	5	
Hellmann, Henry	23, Nov. 1889		3m	1	
Hellmann, Susanna F.	3, Apr. 1895		33	5	
Hellmund, Clara B.	15, Jan. 1901		17	8	
Hellmuth, Johan	5, July 1899	4, July	63	4	
Hellstein, John	2, Mar. 1888		29	1	
Hellwig, Mary E.	28, Dec. 1900		80	8	
Helm, Gustav	23, Aug. 1900		55	8	
Helman, M.A.L.	25, June 1888		52	1	
Helmbold, Mary	5, July 1888		3	1	
Helmeier, Harry	21, July 1900		4m	8	
Helmers, Henry	24, Jan. 1894		67	5	
Helmes, Bernard	18, Feb. 1901		78	8	
Helmig, Carolina	24, Nov. 1898	23, Nov.	64- 1m-19d	5	Goas
Helmig, Elisabeth	11, Sept 1901		1	8	

Name ****	Notice Date ****** ****	Death Date ***** ****	Age ***	Page ****	Maiden Name ****** ****
Helming, Fred.	27, Apr. 1901		55	8	
Helmkamp, Frank	23, Nov. 1893		39	5	
Helmkamp, Maria Lisette	14, Apr. 1897	12, Apr.	72-10m	5	
Helms, Annie	23, Apr. 1888		29	1	
Helmsdörfer, Edna S.	24, Apr. 1889		6m	1	
Help, Ellen	9, May 1894		44	5	
Helt, Henry	30, Nov. 1887		13m	4	
Helt, Rosa	10, Mar. 1891		38	4	
Heluring, Cl-de	12, June 1891		5	4	
Helver, Walter	15, Mar. 1888		12d	4	
Helvering, Leo.	10, Dec. 1900		8m	8	
Helvey, Grace	13, June 1901		3m	8	
Helwig, Karoline	31, Mar. 1900	29, Mar.	70- 8m	5	Meier
Helwig, Susanna	18, June 1895		95	5	
Hemann, Frank	9, Nov. 1889		70	1	
Hemann, Mary	24, July 1901		83	8	
Hemele, Ferd.	18, Apr. 1890		35	1	
Hemesath, David	8, Aug. 1901		43	8	
Hemker, Katharina	4, May 1896	2, May	70	5	
Hemlinger, E.R.	17, Jan. 1888		3w	4	
Hemm, Elisabeth	27, Aug. 1895	26, Aug.	65- 1m	5	
Hemmeder, Arthur	26, Mar. 1895		6w	5	
Hemmel, Frank	29, Dec. 1891		25	4	
Hemmelmeyer, Lillie	16, May 1891		1	2	
Hemmester, Elizabeth	8, Sept 1890		7w	4	
Hempe, Herman H.	16, May 1893		58	5	
Hempe, L.H.	7, July 1888		6m	4	
Hempel, Margaretha	29, Mar. 1900	27, Mar.	69- 2m	4	Willer
Hempelmann, Joseph Anton	15, Feb. 1897	14, Feb.	28- 8m	5	
Hempfling, Clarence	31, Aug. 1900		1	5	
Hempfling, Lydia	9, Apr. 1896	8, Apr.	23- 2m	5	
Hempfling, Therese	24, Sept 1900		26	5	
Hemphill, Janet	8, Jan. 1901		23d	8	
Hemsath, Henry	30, Aug. 1887		57	1	
Hemsath, Theresa	5, Apr. 1901		62	8	
Hemsche, Henry	26, May 1892		22	5	
Hemsel, Margaretha	3, June 1901		85	8	
Hemsoth, Elisabeth	9, Aug. 1887		13m	1	
Hemsterfer, Michael	5, Dec. 1900		33	8	
Hendermann, Alois	9, Feb. 1894		1	5	
Henderson, Harriet	27, July 1895		50	5	
Hendker, Catharine	30, Jan. 1894		24	5	
Hendrick, A.S.	3, Oct. 1900		32	5	
Hendser, Elsie R.	23, Apr. 1891		1	4	
Heneghan, Martin	1, Feb. 1901		73	8	
Hener, Fritz	25, July 1888		9m	4	
Hener, Maria	1, Apr. 1897	31, Mar.	80-11m	5	Agnus
Henesmann, Henry	31, Oct. 1889		2m	1	
Hengel, Emily	19, Apr. 1893		1	5	
Hengler, Herman W.	31, Jan. 1893		23	5	
Hengstenberg, Julius	20, Nov. 1897	19, Nov.	58- 7m	5	
Henke, Alma	17, Jan. 1890		30m	1	
Henke, Charlotte	4, May 1896	2, May	60- 1m	5	
Henke, Edna	16, Aug. 1901		5m	8	
Henke, George	17, Apr. 1890		53	1	
Henke, Hattie	11, Apr. 1901		38	8	
Henke, Julia	8, Dec. 1900		75	8	
Henke, Mathilda	6, Sept 1893		5m	5	
Henke, Sophia	16, July 1892		62	5	
Henke, William T.	23, Feb. 1891		1	4	
Henkel, Elisabeth M.	19, Jan. 1893		6m	5	
Henkel, Johanna	24, Dec. 1898	23, Dec.	71- 7m-14d	5	
Henkenberens, Joseph	8, Apr. 1890		17m	1	
Henle, C.F.	8, July 1889		47	1	
Henle, Henrietta	6, Sept 1900		50	5	
Henline, Margaret	9, July 1895		55	5	
Henne, Charles W.	26, Feb. 1889		3	1	
Hennecke, Frank	12, Feb. 1890		48	1	
Henneke, Frank	4, Mar. 1889		2	1	
Hennemann, Anna C.	4, Aug. 1893		45	5	
Henner, Joseph	13, July 1901		32	8	

Name ****	Notice Date ****** ****	Death Date ***** ****	Age ***	Page ****	Maiden Name ****** ****
Hennesey, Michael	23, May 1901		37	8	
Hennessey, Matthew	8, July 1901		6	8	
Hennessey, William	2, Mar. 1901		47	5	
Henney, Anna	1, Aug. 1901		3m	8	
Hennies, Dora	21, Apr. 1888		21	1	
Henning, Christoph B.	10, Mar. 1891		57	4	
Henning, Eddie	4, Sept 1891		4m	4	
Henning, Eleanora	29, Aug. 1901		2	8	
Henning, Lena	16, Aug. 1890		20	1	
Henninger, Fred.	16, Dec. 1891		2	4	
Henrich, Charles	21, Feb. 1901		2m	8	
Henrich, Herman	25, Sept 1891		69	4	
Henrich, Lillian	19, Dec. 1900		2m	8	
Henrich, Maria Magdalena	3, Mar. 1900	1, Mar.	73	5	Kattus
Henrich, Michael	23, May 1894		73	5	
Henry, Catharine	15, Mar. 1901		77	8	
Henry, Fredie	31, Jan. 1890		25	1	
Henry, Helene	4, Aug. 1888		11m	4	
Henry, John B.	10, Oct. 1900		33	8	
Henry, Michael	7, Jan. 1901		45	5	
Henry, Patrick	19, July 1887		74	1	
Henschell, Fred	8, Jan. 1889		24	1	
Henscher, Henry	10, Apr. 1891		81	4	
Hensel, Herman	5, Mar. 1901		68	5	
Hensel, Louis	17, Oct. 1887		35	1	
Hensler, Mary	4, Aug. 1887		69	1	
Henson, Alfretta	13, July 1900		2m	8	
Henson, Elizabeth	16, Feb. 1901		60	8	
Henson, Henry	14, Nov. 1900		7	8	
Hentschel, Robert F.	27, Apr. 1895		7w	5	
Henz, Conrad	13, Mar. 1888		1m	1	
Henz, John	19, Jan. 1888		46	4	
Henzsche, Malvin H.	18, Mar. 1889		20m	1	
Hepp, Emil	29, Mar. 1895		33	5	
Heppes, Bertha	26, June 1891		34	4	
Herberding, Frank	22, Feb. 1895		45	5	
Herberding, Rosa	16, Jan. 1894		34	5	
Herberg, Friederike	26, Feb. 1898		82	5	
Herbermann, Anna	23, Dec. 1889		68	1	
Herbers, Joseph	12, Jan. 1893		33	5	
Herbert, Bernard	31, July 1900		73	5	
Herbert, Fred.	19, June 1901		43	8	
Herbert, Frieda	13, Oct. 1891		2	4	
Herbert, Howard	10, July 1901		4	5	
Herbert, John B.	8, May 1891		1	4	
Herbert, Margaret	12, Nov. 1891		11	4	
Herbert, Mary	13, Apr. 1896	12, Apr.		5	
Herbold, Carl	21, May 1901		8m	8	
Herbrich, Felix	28, Mar. 1891		80	4	
Herbst, Caroline	30, Jan. 1899	28, Jan.	41- 3m	4	
Herbst, Mathilda Minnie	17, Jan. 1893		22	5	
Herbst, Philippina	23, Apr. 1891		66	4	
Herbstetter, Katie	13, July 1887		30	1	
Herbstreit, Herman	28, June 1900	27, June	54- 1m	8	
Herbstreit, Nora	30, Jan. 1891		15m	4	
Herbstreit, Sarah	23, Jan. 1891		5	4	
Herbus, George	8, May 1901		75	8	
Hereth, John	1, Feb. 1892		3	5	
Herfort, Max	18, July 1887		1	1	
Herger, Carolina	20, Dec. 1893		59	5	
Hering, Anton	25, July 1901		46	8	
Hering, Ernst	11, Aug. 1896	9, Aug.	68- 6m	5	
Hering, Laura	11, Aug. 1896	7, Aug.	30- 6m	5	
Heringhaus, Mary	16, Apr. 1901		67	8	
Herkhof, Elisa	13, July 1892		68	5	
Herkins, Stith G.	7, July 1887		82	1	
Herlinger, Ida	15, June 1894		2	5	
Herlinger, Louis	11, Jan. 1888		2	4	
Herman, Franziska	19, Nov. 1896	18, Nov.	68- 1m	5	Schaefer
Herman, Fred	10, May 1899	8, May	71- 8m	5	
Herman, Isaac	24, Apr. 1901		55	8	

Name ****	Notice Date ****** ****	Death Date ***** ****	Age ***	Page ****	Maiden Name ****** ****
Herman, Jennetta	5, Dec. 1893		85	5	
Herman, John	2, May 1890		15	1	
Hermann, Jacob	27, July 1892		80	5	
Hermann, John	6, May 1893		64	5	
Hermann, John	26, June 1901		60	8	
Hermann, Joseph R.	16, Dec. 1892		47	5	
Hermann, Maria	13, Nov. 1893		15	5	
Hermann, Sophia D.	14, Apr. 1891		79	4	
Hermann, Susanna	16, Dec. 1889		88	1	
Hermann, William	23, July 1891		2	4	
Hermann, William	1, Oct. 1900		18	5	
Hermeling, William	22, July 1893		45	5	
Hermerding, Amalia	21, 22, Aug. 1893	20, Aug.	28	5	Jenisy
Hermersdörfer, Otto	29, June 1891	28, June	4m-15d	1	
Hermes, Anna B.	17, Apr. 1891		13m	4	
Hermes, Annie	17, Mar. 1891		39	4	
Hermes, Bernard	14, Sept 1901		60	1	
Hermes, Henrietta	3, Sept 1901		77	8	
Hermes, Johan H.	10, Apr. 1895		10m	5	
Hermling, Gerhard Herman	6, May 1897	5, May	29- 8m	5	
Hermsen, Bernard Herman	1, Feb. 1898	31, Jan.	70- 5m	5	
Hernes, Gertie	22, Mar. 1894		6	5	
Herning, Zerind	11, Feb. 1891		3	4	
Hernsing, Fred.	1, Nov. 1893		62	5	
Herold, Maria	3, May 1897	2, May	1- 9m	5	
Herper, Louis	3, Jan. 1901		40	5	
Herr, Louis	25, Feb. 1891		57	4	
Herrel,	1, Aug. 1887			1	
Herrel, Albert	11, Aug. 1887		10d	1	
Herrel, Sarah E.	16, Apr. 1891		57	4	
Herret, Minnie	9, Jan. 1891		4	4	
Herrgen, Harry	30, Aug. 1887		14	1	
Herrig, Barbara	26, Dec. 1900		54	8	
Herring, Augusta	24, May 1895		31	5	
Herring, C.	5, July 1888		68	1	
Herring, Henry E.	21, July 1893		1	5	
Herring, Johan	23, Sept 1897	22, Sept	46	5	
Herrlinger, Elmer	20, Dec. 1900		7	8	
Herrlinger, George	10, Dec. 1898	9, Dec.	70- 2m	5	
Herrlinger, Maria	30, Nov. 1898	29, Nov.	50	4	
Herrlinger, Rosina	30, Sept 1897	29, Sept	66- 4m	5	Schweigert
Herrmann, Anna Barbara	5, 6, Feb. 1896	4, Feb.	67- 3m	5	Rober
Herrmann, Charles	20, June 1891		9	1	
Herrmann, Christ.	27, Jan. 1895		77	5	
Herrmann, Conrad	13, Aug. 1896	11, Aug.	71- 6m	5	
Herrmann, Dora K.	5, June 1891		11m	1	
Herrmann, Franz Xavier	7, Aug. 1899	5, Aug.	73- 1m	5	
Herrmann, Georg	14, Dec. 1900		47	8	
Herrmann, Johanna	6, Jan. 1899	5, Jan.	65-10m	4	Henkel
Herrmann, Leopold	3, Mar. 1890		2	1	
Herrmann, Louisa C.	14, June 1895		23	5	
Hersch, Andreas	17, Feb. 1895		8m	5	
Hersch, Annie	8, Mar. 1892		26	5	
Herson, May	16, Oct. 1901		50	1	
Hertenstein, Amelia	7, Mar. 1894		43	5	
Hertenstein, Elizabeth	10, May 1901		69	8	
Hertenstein, Rosa	19, Apr. 1894		4m	5	
Herth, Froney	9, July 1895		21d	5	
Hertwig, Adolph	4, Apr. 1894		63	5	
Hertzog, Aloysius	2, Nov. 1898	1, Nov.	68- 6m	5	
Herweger, Friedricka	20, Apr. 1893		70	5	
Herwegh, William	6, Oct. 1891		28	4	
Herweh, Adam	28, Apr. 1891		60	4	
Herwig, Frederick	6, Sept 1895	5, Sept		5	
Herwig, Johan	9, Aug. 1888		18m	1	
Herwig, Maria	12, July 1890		10m	1	
Herwig, Robert	1, June 1898	31, May	33- 8m	5	
Herz, Albert	17, Dec. 1893	15, Dec.	27- 8m-15d	* 5	
Herz, George	17, Oct. 1891		56	4	
Herz, Herman	26, Feb. 1898	23, Feb.	35- 1m	5	
Herz, John B.	24, May 1895		56	5	

Name	Notice Date	Death Date	Age	Page	Maiden Name
****	****** ****	***** ****	***	****	****** ****
Herzberg, Robert	30, Dec. 1891			4	
Herzberger, John	17, Jan. 1901		82	8	
Herzberger, Margaretha	1, May 1888		8	2	
Herzfield,Ester	31, Jan. 1893		27	5	
Herzner,	6, July 1893		1d	5	
Herzog, Bernhard	24, Oct. 1887		44- 7m	1	
Herzog, Christina	13, Jan. 1899	11, Jan.	71- 1m	4	Pothoff
Herzog, Clara	16, Aug. 1887		18m	1	
Herzog, Ed.	14, Mar. 1891		4	4	
Herzog, Frank A.	5, June 1894		3	5	
Herzog, Laura J.	11, July 1895		6	5	
Herzog, Mary	6, Mar. 1889		48	1	
Herztam, (Mrs. Isaac)	27, Oct. 1887		75	1	
Hesch, Margaretha	5, June 1894		27	5	
Hescher, Adolph	19, Sept 1888		8m	2	
Heschong, A.N.	8, Oct. 1896	7, Oct.	40-10m	5	
Heskamp, Margaretha	13, Feb. 1896	12, Feb.	73- 9m	5	Bueter
Hesping, Elizabeth	2, Sept 1887		2m	1	
Hess, Harry A.	12, Aug. 1893		9	5	
Hesse, Alfred C.	29, Mar. 1895		21m	5	
Hesse, August Justus	11, Mar. 1891	10, Mar.	3- 3m-13d	1	
Hesse, Frank J.	21, Mar. 1891		75	4	
Hesse, George D.	3, Mar. 1891		1	4	
Hesse, Louise	30, Aug. 1895	28, Aug.	56	5	Apke
Hesselbach, Rose	11, Sept 1888		4	1	
Hesselbrock, Aloysius	29, July 1887		14m	1	
Hesselbrock, Herman	22, July 1889		2m	1	
Hesseler, Lena	3, June 1901		36	8	
Hesseling, Herman	27, Mar. 1895		67	5	
Hessemann, Adolph	3, Mar. 1897	1, Mar.	41-10m	5	
Hessler, Johan	19, Aug. 1896	17, Aug.	70- 6m	5	
Hester, Mary	23, May 1888		1	1	
Hettel, Ella E.	26, Dec. 1890		7	1	
Hettel, George	7, Jan. 1901		34	5	
Hettenbach, Christ.	30, Nov. 1887		36	4	
Hettenheimer, Louisa	30, Nov. 1892		1m	5	
Hettesheimer, Edward	24, Mar. 1897	22, Mar.	21	5	
Hettesheimer, Peter	6, Apr. 1893		31	5	
Hettlich, Julia	28, Dec. 1891		32	4	
Hettrich, E.	11, Jan. 1888		70	4	
Hetzel, Maria	2, Mar. 1893		52	5	
Heuberger, Franz	26, June 1889		54	1	
Heuckmann, Bernard Nicolas	30, Mar. 1898	28, Mar.	60- 3m	5	
Heuer, H.	7, Dec. 1898	6, Dec.	62	4	
Heuer, John	22, Dec. 1887		58	4	
Heuer, Wilhelmina	12, May 1899	11, May	84- 2m	5	Kuehne
Heuermann, Herman	5, July 1901		62	8	
Heun, Emil	9, Sept 1898	8, Sept	46	5	
Heun, Johan	31, May 1898	30, May	74	4	
Heupel, Rosanna	5, Mar. 1901		55	5	
Heurmann, Elizabeth	26, Sept 1891		2w	4	
Heurmann, John	25, Dec. 1891		76	2	
Heuschling, J.P.	27, Sept 1900		43	8	
Heuther, Elisabeth	6, Apr. 1893		32	5	
Heutle, Johan	23, Sept 1893		67	5	
Heutle, Veronika	5, May 1899	3, May	73- 5m	5	Hormiller
Heuttle, Joseph	16, Jan. 1894		9	5	
Hewitt, Helen	11, Oct. 1900		7d	8	
Hewitt, Maggie	31, July 1901		24	8	
Hexter, Herman	10, Dec. 1900		45	8	
Hexter, Selig	10, Aug. 1887		68	1	
Hey, Bernard	24, Oct. 1900		4	8	
Heyer, Augusta	5, Jan. 1892		61	5	
Heyker, Hilda	16, Aug. 1894		1	5	
Heyl, A.C.	7, Dec. 1895	6, Dec.	27- 3m	5	
Heymann, Alexander	24, May 1895		67	5	
Heymann, Heinrich Alexander	24, Oct. 1898	23, Oct.	33-10m	5	
Heyn, Gus	2, July 1898	1, July	44- 2m	5	
Heyne, Albert E.	17, May 1898	15, May	30	4	
Heß, Albert	27, Feb. 1888		3m	4	
Heß, Anna Christina	14, Apr. 1900	5, Apr.		5	

Name ****	Notice Date ****** ****	Death Date ***** ****	Age ***	Page ****	Maiden Name ****** ****
Heß, Carl	11, Jan. 1899	10, Jan.	52-11m	5	
Heß, Casper J.	26, Sept 1896	25, Sept	78	5	
Heß, Cassandra	8, Apr. 1901		43	8	
Heß, Christian	20, Mar. 1891		8	4	
Heß, Christina	27, Nov. 1900		52	8	
Heß, Ed.	2, May 1890		17	1	
Heß, Elisabeth	25, Dec. 1899	24, Dec.	70- 9m	5	Heimkreider
Heß, Emanuel	8, Apr. 1889		62	1	
Heß, Emma	9, June 1899	9, June		5	Mueller
Heß, Helena	17, Apr. 1896	16, Apr.	26-10m	5	Beck
Heß, Henriette	10, May 1889		59	1	
Heß, John	5, Sept 1890		2	4	
Heß, Lizzie	3, Sept 1890		11m	1	
Heß, Louise	16, Aug. 1887		2	1	
Heß, Maria Dorothea	18, Jan. 1899	15, Jan.	64- 8m-10d	5	Lanz
Heß, Marie	11, Apr. 1898	10, Apr.	20- 8m	5	
Heß, Minnie	12, May 1892		35	5	
Heß, Stella	17, June 1896	16, June	3- 8m	5	
Heß, Walter	21, Jan. 1890		2	1	
Heßler, Edward	17, Apr. 1895		9d	5	
Heßler, Frances	27, Mar. 1895		2	5	
Heßler, Fritz	28, Jan. 1889		1	1	
Heßler, Jacob	8, Jan. 1890		24	1	
Heßler, Lawrence	17, Apr. 1895		9d	5	
Heßler, Maria	2, Aug. 1893		1m	5	
Heßling, Eva	10, Feb. 1890		2	1	
Heßling, Kate	20, Feb. 1895		26	5	
Hibben, Patience	27, Oct. 1900		84	8	
Hibloltine, Rosa	12, Jan. 1892		87	5	
Hickel, Michael	29, Jan. 1891		24	4	
Hickerson, O.	23, Feb. 1889		38	1	
Hicks,	8, May 1888		1w	1	
Hicks, Charles	14, June 1894		29	5	
Hicks, E.M.	28, Apr. 1888		22	1	
Hicks, Mary	16, Mar. 1901		50	8	
Hicks, William	10, Aug. 1901		20	8	
Hieber, C.W.	23, Dec. 1896	21, Dec.	88- 1m	5	
Hiemer, Cornelius	9, Oct. 1899	7, Oct.	71	5	
Hienbuch, Theresa	12, Sept 1895	11, Sept	66-10m	5	Nees
Hiepert, Ida	8, Dec. 1891		11m	4	
Hier, Thomas B.	23, Aug. 1901		1	8	
Hieser, Isaac	16, May 1891		79	2	
Hiffle, Laura Clara	13, Oct. 1894		7m	5	
Higa, Elsa	4, July 1891		14m	4	
Higgins, Ella	27, Nov. 1900		34	8	
Higgins, Fredericke	9, July 1887		8m	1	
Higgins, Michael	16, May 1901		62	5	
Highway, Archibald E. (Dr)	26, Jan. 1888		68	4	
Higler, Anthony	8, Dec. 1887		2	1	
Higler, Barbara	23, Dec. 1893		30	5	
Higler, Franz Xaver	19, May 1896	18, May	76- 6m	5	
Higler, John	1, Dec. 1900		44	8	
Hilb, Sarah	25, Mar. 1898	24, Mar.		5	
Hilberg, John	19, May 1894		63	5	
Hilberg, William	30, July 1901		40	8	
Hilbers, Herman Heinrich	4, Nov. 1898	3, Nov.	50- 6m	5	
Hilbers, Maria	2, 3, Dec. 1895	1, Dec.	66	5	Reckers
Hilbers, Maria Carolina	14, Aug. 1899	13, Aug.		4	
Hilbert, C.B.	21, Apr. 1888		53	1	
Hilbert, John	9, Apr. 1890		63	1	
Hilbert, Robert	20, Dec. 1900		5	8	
Hilburger, Margaret	1, Mar. 1893		40	5	
Hild, Charles A.	23, July 1895		3	5	
Hild, Henry	23, Mar. 1889		90	1	
Hildebrand, August	30, Mar. 1889		75	1	
Hildebrand, Augusta	14, Apr. 1891		17m	4	
Hildebrandt, August Jonas	24, Feb. 1888		2w	4	
Hildebrandt, Henry	26, June 1889		49	1	
Hildebrandt, Joseph	11, May 1892		13d	5	
Hildebrandt, Julius	6, July 1899	5, July	56	5	
Hildebrecht, Robert	11, Oct. 1897	10, Oct.	73- 2m	5	

Name ****	Notice Date ****** ****	Death Date ***** ****	Age ***	Page ****	Maiden Name ****** ****
Hildebrecht, Theodor	19, Dec. 1900		78	8	
Hilderbach, Anton	15, June 1900	13, June	69	8	
Hildwein, Magdalena	23, Aug. 1897	20, Aug.	44	5	Diehl
Hilfinger, Emma	9, Jan. 1891		32	4	
Hilge, Katharina	14, May 1897	13, May	65- 3m	5	Vordermark
Hilgedick, Elisabeth	17, Jan. 1893		64	5	
Hilgeman, Henrietta	17, Dec. 1896	15, Dec.	75- 4m	5	Heemann
Hilgemann, Bernard	19, Mar. 1895		34	5	
Hilgemann, Ernst J.	16, May 1893		68	5	
Hilgemann, Friedricka	15, Nov. 1887		35	4	
Hilgemann, Mabel	21, Oct. 1891		1	4	
Hilgermann, William	3, Feb. 1888		18	4	
Hilker, Herman Heinrich	24, Dec. 1896	23, Dec.	77-10m	5	
Hilker, John B.	6, Oct. 1894		29	5	
Hilker, Louisa	16, May 1893		2d	5	
Hill, Alexander	8, June 1901		66	8	
Hill, Frank	10, Dec. 1900		5m	8	
Hill, George W.	29, Aug. 1887		38	1	
Hill, Laura	10, Oct. 1894		83	5	
Hill, Mary J.	29, June 1892		22	5	
Hill, Richard	28, July 1891		4	4	
Hill, S.	22, Dec. 1887		1- 8m	4	
Hillburger, B.	26, Apr. 1892		44	5	
Hille, Adolph	4, Oct. 1894		6	5	
Hille, Anna	31, Aug. 1900		11m	5	
Hillebrand, G. Henry	22, Apr. 1899	20, Apr.	65	5	
Hillebrand, Henry	11, Jan. 1888		42- 6m	4	
Hillebrand, John	8, Dec. 1891		40	4	
Hillebrandt, August	19, June 1891		1	1	
Hillebrant, Harry	4, Aug. 1900		1m	8	
Hillen, Henry A.	30, June 1888		10m	1	
Hillen, Joseph	12, Apr. 1889		3	1	
Hillenhemerick, Emilia	14, Aug. 1889		9d	1	
Hiller, Gustav	3, Nov. 1892		61	5	
Hiller, Jacob	6, Feb. 1899	4, Feb.	66	4	
Hiller, Johann	13, Nov. 1895	11, Nov.	63-11m	5	
Hiller, Louisa	19, Dec. 1891		32	4	
Hiller, Victoria	28, Aug. 1897	27, Aug.	62-11m	5	Molitor
Hilles, Katie	11, Feb. 1891		35	4	
Hilling, M.	28, Sept 1901		94	5	
Hilling, Walter	22, July 1901		52	8	
Hillkowitz, Samuel	15, Nov. 1887		19	4	
Hillmann, Harry	11, Aug. 1896	9, Aug.	32- 1m	5	
Hillmann, Meta	4, Aug. 1893		23	5	
Hills, Alex.	5, Nov. 1900		63	8	
Hilmiger, Michael	3, Jan. 1893		60	5	
Hiltenbeitel, A.	13, July 1900		24	8	
Hilterberkel, Charles	3, Feb. 1888		11	4	
Hiltinger, F.	18, Nov. 1895	17, Nov.		5	
Hilvers, Bernard	10, Jan. 1893		27	5	
Hilvert, J.H.	12, Mar. 1898	11, Mar.	44- 5m- 8d	5	
Himberg, Louise	11, May 1898	10, May	64- 5m	4	
Himburg, Susie E.	9, Jan. 1901		5	5	
Hinborn, Mary	10, Aug. 1893		35	5	
Hinderberger, Lillie	13, Mar. 1899	12, Mar.	24- 9m	5	Rusche
Hindersmann, Mathilde	22, 23, Jan. 1896	21, Jan.	37- 4m	5	Schwecke
Hinds, George W.	8, Feb. 1894		49	5	
Hines, John	14, Aug. 1900		30	5	
Hines, Margaret	24, Jan. 1901		85	8	
Hiney, William	30, May 1901		29	8	
Hinkel, Val.	5, Jan. 1888		74	1	
Hinker, Agnes	5, Aug. 1887		8m	1	
Hinkler, Elisabeth	8, Feb. 1898	6, Feb.	75	5	Huß
Hinnan, Lisette	2, Dec. 1889		56	1	
Hinner, Caroline	29, Mar. 1888			1	
Hinrichs, Barbara	10, Nov. 1900		61	8	
Hinsdale, Frank Corwin	3, Mar. 1888		9-10m	1	
Hintereck, Emma M.	3, May 1897	1, May	37- 9m	5	Bolland
Hinternesch, Catharine	4, Feb. 1891		79	4	
Hinternesch, Fred.	31, Dec. 1891		44	1	
Hinton, Mary E.	16, Sept 1887		13	1	

Name	Notice Date	Death Date	Age	Page	Maiden Name
****	****** ****	***** ****	***	****	****** ****
Hintz, Antonie	16, Dec. 1896	14, Dec.		5	
Hintzler, Johan	26, Feb. 1900	24, Feb.	76	8	
Hinz, Anna	20, July 1887		1	1	
Hinzhaus, Ed.	7, Mar. 1892		2	5	
Hiog, Minnie	5, June 1890		11	4	
Hipp, Elizabeth	23, Apr. 1895		73	5	
Hirsch, Anna	29, Jan. 1892		6m	5	
Hirsch, Anthony	9, Feb. 1895		40	5	
Hirsch, Bertha	20, June 1898	20, June	76	5	
Hirsch, Katharine	27, Oct. 1888		63	1	
Hirsch, Lizzie L.	31, Mar. 1891		1	4	
Hirsch, Theresa	1, June 1893		20	5	
Hirschauer, Elisabeth	30, Dec. 1891		69	4	
Hirschmann, A.	8, Oct. 1901		78	1	
Hirschmeyer, H.L.	14, Mar. 1891		44	4	
Hirse, Augusta	5, June 1888		1	4	
Hirst, George	27, May 1901		49	8	
Hirt, William	20, July 1901		2	8	
Hirtz, Ehrhardt	23, Aug. 1887		42	1	
Hirtz, Maria	1, Dec. 1899	30, Nov.	67- 6m-17d	* 5	
Hissem, W.T.	10, Aug. 1900		70	8	
Hitkar, Frank	23, Dec. 1889		84	1	
Hitzler, Frank	23, July 1901		33	8	
Hitzler, Joseph	31, Dec. 1888		15m	1	
Hitzler, Matthias	19, Aug. 1892		49	5	
Hitzmann, August	23, Mar. 1894		56	5	
Hixson, Isaac	13, Apr. 1901		56	8	
Hoban, Thomas	12, May 1895		82	5	
Hobelmann, Henry	26, Aug. 1891		68	4	
Hoberg, Emilie	30, May 1901		34	8	
Hobson, Thomas	25, Oct. 1900		52	8	
Hochhardt, William	23, Nov. 1893		55	5	
Hochholzer, Rosa	9, July 1891		8m	4	
Hochstrasser, Karolina	18, June 1896	17, June	34	5	Grüßer
Hochstuhl, Charles	24, Feb. 1891		14d	4	
Hock, George	18, Feb. 1896	17, Feb.		5	
Hock, Heinrich	17, Mar. 1896	15, Mar.	48- 9m	5	
Hock, Jacob Arthur	24, June 1896	23, June	3m	5	
Hock, Johan	14, Apr. 1897	12, Apr.	18- -14d	5	
Hock, John	19, Oct. 1887		31	1	
Hock, Leonard	5, June 1901		48	8	
Hocker, Johanna	30, Oct. 1894		68	5	
Hockmann, Catharine	17, Aug. 1896	15, Aug.	95	5	
Hockmann, Georg Henry	18, Jan. 1898	17, Jan.	69- 3m	5	
Hodacker, Robert	6, Sept 1895	5, Sept	40	5	
Hoderlein, Franz	27, Nov. 1900		3	8	
Hoe, Eliza	22, July 1887		35	1	
Hoeb, Charles	26, Mar. 1888		27	4	
Hoebell, Julius	27, July 1893		5	5	
Hoecker, Elisabeth	28, Mar. 1893		65	5	
Hoefer, Friedricka	26, Nov. 1891		54	1	
Hoefer, John	20, Feb. 1901		58	8	
Hoefer, John F.	17, Jan. 1889		5m	1	
Hoeffling, Anna	2, June 1897	31, May	71-11m	5	
Hoefle, Anna	20, Aug. 1901		48	8	
Hoefle, Frida	26, Feb. 1897	23, Feb.	20	5	
Hoefler, J.	11, Dec. 1893		64	5	
Hoeft, Casper	4, Dec. 1891		68	4	
Hoeft, Fritz	16, June 1894		71	5	
Hoeg, Viktoria	19, Mar. 1890		4	1	
Hoegel, Franz	8, Sept 1899	7, Sept	42	4	
Hoeger, Johan	20, May 1893	20, May	2- 1m-17d	5	
Hoehn, Addie R.	2, Apr. 1891		4m	4	
Hoehn, Aloysius	8, Apr. 1896	7, Apr.	76- 7m	5	
Hoehn, Katharina	23, Feb. 1898	22, Feb.	76	5	
Hoel, Franziska	9, Oct. 1896	8, Oct.	38-11m	5	Guenther
Hoelhus, William	21, June 1888		9	1	
Hoelker, Mary E.	17, May 1894		81	5	
Hoelscher, Henrietta	1, Feb. 1899	31, Jan.	71- 6m	5	Sauerland
Hoelscher, Henry	24, Feb. 1892		7	5	
Hoeltge, F.	30, Aug. 1895	29, Aug.		5	

Name	Notice Date	Death Date	Age	Page	Maiden Name
****	****** ****	***** ****	***	****	****** ****
Hoeltke, Anna	15, Dec. 1893		19	5	
Hoeltmann, Henry	21, Mar. 1901		54	8	
Hoelz, Gustav	11, Feb. 1893		14m	5	
Hoemeyer, William	23, July 1890		46	1	
Hoen, Peter	10, Sept 1887		37	2	
Hoene, Henry G.	27, Oct. 1891		3	1	
Hoene, Henry H.	20, Apr. 1895		60	5	
Hoenemeyer, Theo.	4, May 1894		54	5	
Hoenschemeyer, Albert	9, Sept 1893		3	5	
Hoepke, Robert	2, July 1898	1, July	35	5	
Hoerner, Charles A.	26, July 1895		21	5	
Hoerth, Joseph	29, Mar. 1895		26	5	
Hoesl, Barbara	26, Aug. 1901		41	8	
Hoetker, Emma	30, Aug. 1901		2	8	
Hoeß, Anton	23, Dec. 1897	22, Dec.	67	5	
Hoeß, Marie Lizzie	16, Mar. 1899	15, Mar.	47- 4m	5	
Hoeßli, Margarethe	2, May 1901		82	8	
Hoff, Anton C.C.	12, Jan. 1894		1	5	
Hoff, Lucy	13, Mar. 1895		64	5	
Hoff, Martin	20, July 1887		4	1	
Hoff, Willie	13, Dec. 1893		18d	5	
Hoffe, Johanna	9, Feb. 1897	6, Feb.	44- -13d	5	Whde
Hoffelder, Lewis W.	11, Dec. 1891		10w	4	
Hoffheimer, Abraham	10, July 1901		72	5	
Hoffheimer, Solomon	3, Dec. 1891		73	4	
Hoffhus, Elisabeth	3, May 1893		34	5	
Hoffhus, Mary	27, Oct. 1894		63	5	
Hoffman, Anna Marie	13, Jan. 1896	10, Jan.	70	5	Knauber
Hoffman, Catharine	6, July 1893		36	5	
Hoffman, Charles	23, Mar. 1893		48	5	
Hoffman, Elisabeth	17, Dec. 1891		85	4	
Hoffman, Ella	27, July 1893		2m	5	
Hoffman, Emma	15, Oct. 1898	14, Oct.	43	4	Niederhauser
Hoffman, John	7, June 1890		77	1	
Hoffman, John	1, Sept 1900		76	5	
Hoffmann, Adam	24, Dec. 1896	23, Dec.	74	5	
Hoffmann, Albert M.	23, July 1887		15m	1	
Hoffmann, Amelia	23, Nov. 1891		67	1	
Hoffmann, Anna	24, July 1901		38	8	
Hoffmann, Apollonia	4, May 1899	2, May		5	Schäfer
Hoffmann, August	17, Dec. 1895	14, Dec.	20- 4m	4	
Hoffmann, August	27, Sept 1898	26, Sept	54	4	
Hoffmann, Babetta	18, Feb. 1892		22	4	
Hoffmann, Barbara	14, Mar. 1891		86	4	
Hoffmann, C.	21, Apr. 1888		75	1	
Hoffmann, Carolina	14, July 1892		48	5	
Hoffmann, Catharine	9, Sept 1891		41	4	
Hoffmann, Catharine	21, Mar. 1893		63	5	
Hoffmann, Charles	25, June 1891		10m	4	
Hoffmann, Charles	24, Mar. 1893		48	5	
Hoffmann, Charles	31, Dec. 1893		33	5	
Hoffmann, Charles	4, Oct. 1894		44	5	
Hoffmann, Charles	23, July 1901		91	8	
Hoffmann, Christ.	10, May 1889		47	1	
Hoffmann, Christian	6, Nov. 1891		65	4	
Hoffmann, Christian	28, Dec. 1891		53	4	
Hoffmann, Dorothea	25, 26, Apr. 1898	24, Apr.	22- -22d	5	Müller
Hoffmann, Ed.	6, June 1893		10m	5	
Hoffmann, Edward	10, Jan. 1896		61	5	
Hoffmann, Elisabeth	7, Mar. 1900	5, Mar.		5	
Hoffmann, Elise	24, Feb. 1888		72	4	
Hoffmann, Elise	1, Dec. 1899	30, Nov.	69	5	
Hoffmann, Emma	14, 15, Nov. 1890	13, Nov.	20- 8m- 6d	1	
Hoffmann, Emma	12, July 1901		3	8	
Hoffmann, Ernst	30, Jan. 1897	30, Jan.	3m- 3d	5	
Hoffmann, Eva	20, Apr. 1897	19, Apr.	62- 2m	5	Bester
Hoffmann, Eva M.	4, Jan. 1893		29	5	
Hoffmann, Fanny	10, Oct. 1895	8, Oct.	38- 4m	5	Schoen
Hoffmann, Frank	2, May 1901		2m	8	
Hoffmann, Friedericka	13, Jan. 1896	9, Jan.	50	5	Clemens
Hoffmann, Friedrich	13, July 1895	13, July	19w	5	

Name ****	Notice Date ****** ****	Death Date ***** ****	Age ***	Page ****	Maiden Name ****** ****
Hoffmann, Fritz	8, June 1895		45	5	
Hoffmann, Georg	3, May 1889		7	1	
Hoffmann, George	20, June 1889		13m	1	
Hoffmann, George	3, Apr. 1891		7m	4	
Hoffmann, H.	27, Dec. 1893		67	5	
Hoffmann, Henry	11, Jan. 1894		57	5	
Hoffmann, Johan Baptist	29, June 1899	27, June	69- 8m	4	
Hoffmann, Johanna	20, Oct. 1891		1m	1	
Hoffmann, John	19, Dec. 1889		19	1	
Hoffmann, John	24, July 1890		6	1	
Hoffmann, John	18, Jan. 1892		25	5	
Hoffmann, John	26, Apr. 1892		62	5	
Hoffmann, John	17, Aug. 1892		7- 6m	5	
Hoffmann, Josephine	25, Mar. 1891		39	4	
Hoffmann, Julius	11, Apr. 1892		50	5	
Hoffmann, Karoline	11, May 1899	10, May	75	4	
Hoffmann, Louis (Mrs)	17, Aug. 1893		36	5	
Hoffmann, Margaret	18, Jan. 1894		86	5	
Hoffmann, Maria	31, July 1895	30, July	67	5	Feitmann
Hoffmann, Martin J.	24, July 1901		60	8	
Hoffmann, Mary	28, Mar. 1891		4	4	
Hoffmann, Mary	14, Feb. 1901		40	8	
Hoffmann, Mathilda	17, Apr. 1900	15, Apr.	37- 7m	5	Kaiper
Hoffmann, Matilda	28, Nov. 1891		27	1	
Hoffmann, Meyer	17, Dec. 1900		36	8	
Hoffmann, Michael	27, Apr. 1897	26, Apr.	63- 3m	5	
Hoffmann, Mildred	24, Sept 1900		2m	5	
Hoffmann, Milton	18, June 1901		5m	8	
Hoffmann, N.	29, Sept 1891		4d	4	
Hoffmann, Peter Jacob	28, Aug. 1896	26, Aug.	18-11m	5	
Hoffmann, Phil.	5, July 1901		55	8	
Hoffmann, Philipp	19, Nov. 1900		78	8	
Hoffmann, R.	25, Feb. 1901		7	8	
Hoffmann, Rosa A.	18, June 1895		19	5	
Hoffmann, Sanford	29, Jan. 1892		64	5	
Hoffmann, Theodor	25, Aug. 1890		1	1	
Hoffmann, Theodor W.	6, Nov. 1891		3	4	
Hoffmann, Walter W.	19, Feb. 1891		51d	4	
Hoffmann, Wilhelm	28, Jan. 1893	27, Jan.	5w- 1d	5	
Hoffmeister, Bernardine	19, Dec. 1891		2	4	
Hoffmeister, E.F.	18, Jan. 1897	16, Jan.	27	5	
Hoffmeister, Edwin	5, Feb. 1901		27	8	
Hoffmeister, Fred	31, July 1901		36	8	
Hoffmeister, Henry	10, Feb. 1893		30	5	
Hoffmeister, Rosalie	1, May 1897	30, Apr.	70	5	Klein
Hoffner, Hilda	4, Mar. 1893		5m	5	
Hoffner, James	25, July 1900		80	5	
Hoffroge, Alvine	12, Nov. 1888		10	2	
Hoffrogge, Bernard G.	1, Apr. 1898	30, Mar.	42- 4m	5	
Hoffstedte, Herman	28, Jan. 1893		37	5	
Hofhus, Theodore	13, Mar. 1891		29	4	
Hofiger, Maria Josephina	30, Mar. 1896	28, Mar.	39	5	Olberding
Hofmann, Clara	13, Aug. 1901		9	8	
Hofmann, Georg	1, Feb. 1897	30, Jan.	54	5	
Hofrogge, Henry	1, Aug. 1888		26m	2	
Hofschimsky, Simon	30, Sept 1887		63	1	
Hogan, Raymond	17, Dec. 1900		2	8	
Hogan, Thomas	19, Oct. 1900		29	5	
Hoge, Christine	10, Dec. 1900		60	8	
Hogge, Bernard	21, Jan. 1894		59	5	
Hogreve, W.	13, Oct. 1900		72	8	
Hogrewe, Louisa	5, Sept 1901		60	8	
Hogue, J.	4, June 1901		83	8	
Hohman, Joseph	15, Jan. 1901		83	8	
Hohmann, Anna	4, Aug. 1891		23	4	
Hohmann, Frank	18, Nov. 1894		62	5	
Hohmann, Herman	20, Jan. 1890		66	1	
Hohmann, Margaretha	8, Mar. 1893		61	5	
Hohmer, Johan	22, Nov. 1894		51	5	
Hohne, Charles B.	20, Feb. 1894		63	5	
Hohnhorst, Eleonore	13, July 1901		22	8	

Name	Notice Date	Death Date	Age	Page	Maiden Name
****	****** ****	***** ****	***	****	****** ****
Hohnhorst, Florence	14, May 1897	13, May	1- 6m	5	
Hohnstedt, Dorothea	20, July 1901		79	8	
Hohnstedt, Gustav	23, Apr. 1895		32	5	
Hohnstedt, H.L.	29, Sept 1898	28, Sept	76	5	
Hohr, Rosina	25, Nov. 1893		4m	5	
Hohweiler, Stella L.	19, July 1895		22m	5	
Hoisler, Sophie	13, Dec. 1892		2	5	
Holabird, Bruce	4, Sept 1901		45	8	
Holberg, Bertha	19, May 1894		61	5	
Holberg, Ferdinand	22, Sept 1900		78	5	
Holbrock, Catharina	20, Jan. 1890		3	1	
Holbrook, Katharine	30, Mar. 1901		53	8	
Holden,	3, Apr. 1901		2d	8	
Holden, Aurelia C.	20, July 1893		77	5	
Holderbach, Fraunega	31, Jan. 1893		10d	5	
Holderbach, Justina	17, Aug. 1898	16, Aug.	65	4	
Holderbach, Maria	23, Oct. 1897	22, Oct.	28- 4m	4	Philipp
Holdgreiwe, Elisabeth	17, Aug. 1894		25	5	
Holdgriewe, Catharine	22, Feb. 1895		71	5	
Holdvogt, Johanna M.	23, July 1887		34	1	
Holen, John	9, Feb. 1894		64	5	
Holft, Peter	15, Jan. 1901		32	8	
Holland, Alice	7, Mar. 1891		24	4	
Holland, Catharine	13, July 1887		49	1	
Holland, Daniel	23, Feb. 1891		48	4	
Holland, Ethel	13, Apr. 1895		5m	4	
Holland, John	11, Jan. 1901		3	5	
Holland, Martha	25, Apr. 1888		80	1	
Hollander, Herman	7, Jan. 1891		53	4	
Hollander, Kate	17, Dec. 1891		28	4	
Hollander, Margaretha	1, Feb. 1894		57	5	
Hollbrock, Johan J.	13, Dec. 1898	12, Dec.		5	
Hollein, H.A.	22, Dec. 1887		3m	4	
Hollen, Maria E.	12, Sept 1895	11, Sept	77	5	
Hollenbeck, Hannah Sophia	17, May 1900	16, May	77	5	Söllmann
Hollenbeck, Mart.	3, Dec. 1892		28	5	
Hollenbeck, Martin	14, Mar. 1893		78	5	
Hollenkamp, Elisabeth	8, Dec. 1893		74	5	
Hollenkamp, Gertrude	13, Mar. 1894		14d	5	
Hollenkamp, Johan G.	20, Apr. 1899	17, Apr.	50- 1m	4	
Hollenstein, David	30, Dec. 1891		29	4	
Holler, Magdalena	2, Feb. 1894		59	5	
Holleran, Annie L.	17, Oct. 1893		56	5	
Hollerbach, Rosa	10, Feb. 1893		31	5	
Holley,	17, Oct. 1900		10m	8	
Holliday, Adelia	14, May 1895		44	5	
Holliday, F.	6, Jan. 1888		3w	1	
Hollis, William	24, Oct. 1890		1	1	
Hollman, Benne	23, Dec. 1890		4	1	
Hollman, Willie	15, Nov. 1887		4	4	
Hollmann, Anton	30, Mar. 1898	29, Mar.	37	5	
Hollmann, David	29, Dec. 1887		68	4	
Hollmeyer, Joseph	21, Mar. 1901		45	8	
Holls, Marie	15, Sept 1892		47	5	
Hollstein, Louise	13, Feb. 1890		37	1	
Holmann, Carrie	15, July 1901		3	8	
Holmeier, Beda	15, Dec. 1900		58	8	
Holmer, Henriette	21, Aug. 1887		74	5	
Holmes, Bridget	22, June 1901		22	8	
Holmes, Carrie	27, Sept 1888		53	2	
Holmes, Ida	20, July 1895		27	5	
Holmes, Margaret	4, Jan. 1901		70	5	
Holmes, Robert	23, May 1901		27	8	
Holmes, William	27, Sept 1900		78	8	
Holms, A. (Mrs)	7, July 1887		73	1	
Holste, Charles	23, Mar. 1901		39	8	
Holstein, August B.	9, Mar. 1898	7, Mar.	78	5	
Holstermann, Louisa	27, Aug. 1890		1	1	
Holt, August	7, Sept 1901		52	8	
Holters, Catharine	9, Feb. 1901		77	8	
Holters, Dora	1, Feb. 1888		16w	4	

Name	Notice Date	Death Date	Age	Page	Maiden Name
****	****** ****	***** ****	***	****	****** ****
Holters, J.H.	7, Nov. 1895	6, Nov.	77	5	
Holtgraeve, Bernard	7, Mar. 1890	5, Mar.	83- 8m	* 4	
Holtgrewe, Clements	18, Dec. 1893		11d	5	
Holtgrieve, Henry	5, Dec. 1893		3	5	
Holthaus,	26, Oct. 1894		2d	5	
Holthaus, Anna M.	11, Aug. 1891		53	4	
Holthaus, Gustav	1, Oct. 1891		3m	1	
Holthaus, Louis	4, Mar. 1896	3, Mar.	49	* 5	
Holthaus, Marie	19, Apr. 1895		60	5	
Holthausen, Henrietta	10, Nov. 1898	9, Nov.		4	Hütte
Holthoefer, Fred.	22, Apr. 1891		57	4	
Holtkamp, Henriette	20, June 1892		51	5	
Holtmann, Gertrude	24, Apr. 1895		4	5	
Holtmann, Mary A.	6, Oct. 1891		71	4	
Holton, Alex. M.	27, Aug. 1888		64	1	
Holtvogt, Henry	16, Dec. 1889		65	1	
Holtz, Carl	7, June 1901		44	8	
Holweg, Johan	31, May 1898	29, May	59- 4m	4	
Holz, Alice	18, Feb. 1888		13	1	
Holz, Augusta	4, Aug. 1900		61	8	
Holzbach, Jacob P.	4, Oct. 1897	3, Oct.	31- 2m	5	
Holzbach, Josephine	13, Sept 1901		9d	8	
Holzbauer, George J.	22, Oct. 1891		36	1	
Holzer, Martin	16, Aug. 1894		10m	5	
Holzer, Martin J.	8, June 1895		2m	5	
Holzhauer, Herman	11, Mar. 1897	9, Mar.	50- - 4d	5	
Holzhauser, Gustav	23, Nov. 1895	22, Nov.	48- 3m	5	
Holzmann, Catharine	20, July 1895		2m	5	
Holzreuter, August	7, 9, Feb. 1894	7, Feb.	43	5	
Holzwart, Barbara	8, Sept 1898	7, Sept	76- 8m	4	Harsch
Homan, Albert	30, Aug. 1897	28, Aug.	83- 9m	5	
Homan, Katharina	29, Oct. 1898	27, Oct.	74- -17d	4	Benolken
Homan, Margaret	24, Oct. 1900		63	8	
Homan, Marie Josephine	12, Jan. 1897	11, Jan.	11	5	
Homan, Southard S.	1, May 1894		65	5	
Homann, Johannah	19, Oct. 1891		1m	1	
Homberg, Anna	28, June 1898	27, June	75	5	Kriemberg
Homberg, Anna E.	17, Sept 1891		86	1	
Homcop, Mary	10, May 1901		64	8	
Homer, Cora	11, Nov. 1891		1	1	
Homer, Mary	24, Sept 1891		88	1	
Hommolle, Mary	29, May 1894		9m	5	
Honegger, Fred.	25, Nov. 1887		9	1	
Honert, Henry	14, July 1890		27	1	
Honetter, E.	3, Jan. 1888		53	1	
Honhorst, E.F.	16, Sept 1887		3- 6m	1	
Honroth, Elisabeth	16, Feb. 1894		74	5	
Honschopp, Albert	24, Aug. 1889	24, Aug.	14m-18d	1	
Hood, Ida M.	23, Feb. 1901		21	8	
Hoogerland, Abraham	21, Mar. 1891		56	4	
Hoogerland, Jeanette	5, Mar. 1901		67	5	
Hook, Elisabetha	31, Oct. 1899	30, Oct.	54	5	
Hoolihan, William	20, July 1887		4m	1	
Hoomer, Ettie G.	15, May 1895		8	5	
Hooper, Elizabeth	26, Apr. 1901		57	8	
Hopf, Mary	4, Aug. 1900		74	8	
Hopf, Viola	1, June 1892		2m	5	
Hopfengärtner, John	25, Nov. 1887		25	1	
Hoping, Eddie	4, Apr. 1895		4	5	
Hopkins, Ella	7, June 1901		53	8	
Hopkins, H.P.	10, Mar. 1888		78	1	
Hopkins, John F.	3, Dec. 1900		35	8	
Hopkins, Julia	19, July 1900		60	8	
Hopmann, Eliza	14, Jan. 1896	12, Jan.	60	5	Kroeger
Hoppe, Bernard	27, Feb. 1890		80	1	
Hoppe, Charles	23, Dec. 1891		11m	4	
Hoppe, Clarence	23, Jan. 1894		7m	5	
Hoppe, Gustav Wilhelm	26, Dec. 1896	25, Dec.	74- 3m	5	
Hoppe, Lizzie	18, Jan. 1899	17, Jan.	23- 4m	5	
Hoppe, Mary C.	9, Jan. 1891		54	4	
Hoppe, Simon	12, July 1897	11, July	59- 7m	5	

Name	Notice Date	Death Date	Age	Page	Maiden Name
****	****** ****	***** ****	***	****	****** ****
Hopper, Emma	8, Feb. 1894		30	5	
Hopper, Harry	13, Feb. 1901		18	8	
Hopple, James	8, Sept 1891		77	4	
Horan, Annie	21, July 1900		66	8	
Horch, Louis	1, Aug. 1890		76	1	
Horgan, Dennis	8, Apr. 1901		52	8	
Horgan, Kate	26, Aug. 1892		5m	5	
Horman, Carrie	2, Aug. 1901		35	8	
Horman, Edna	14, Feb. 1901		11m	8	
Horn, Alice	22, Mar. 1894		55	5	
Horn, Anna Margaretha	20, Mar. 1900	19, Mar.	66- 6m	5	Hilf
Horn, Charles	28, Mar. 1893		26	5	
Horn, Constantin	13, Sept 1890		4m	1	
Horn, Elisabeth	28, Mar. 1893		68	5	
Horn, Henry	6, Mar. 1901		37	5	
Horn, John	29, Jan. 1891		41	4	
Horn, John	27, Mar. 1895		84	5	
Horn, Luella	14, Aug. 1900		1	5	
Hornaday, Jesse	31, Aug. 1900		28	5	
Hornbach, Clara	17, Mar. 1893		1d	5	
Hornbeck, Alois	1, Feb. 1894		69	5	
Horne, Catharine D.	15, Dec. 1893		5m	5	
Horne, Nellie	18, Dec. 1893		7m	5	
Horner, Anna B.	12, May 1895		43	5	
Horner, Charles	2, June 1893		14	5	
Horner, Emma J.	14, Nov. 1893		53	5	
Horner, Theodor	15, Oct. 1901		36	8	
Horning, August P.	16, May 1893		1	5	
Horns, Walter	16, Feb. 1901		4	8	
Horowitz, Eddy	14, Feb. 1890		12	1	
Horst, Albertine	20, Feb. 1899	19, Feb.	76	5	
Horst, Frederick	29, Dec. 1892		86	5	
Horst, Helena	17, July 1894		41	5	
Horst, Herman	7, June 1901		79	8	
Horst, Sophia	28, Dec. 1892		40	5	
Horsting, Hubert	4, Apr. 1895		14m	5	
Horstkamp, Henry	17, Aug. 1894		57	5	
Horstman, Richard	10, Aug. 1901		44	8	
Horstmann, Charles	21, Mar. 1893		1	5	
Horstmann, Frank	6, Feb. 1889		17	1	
Horstmann, Freddie W	3, Mar. 1894		17	5	
Horstmann, Henry	29, Oct. 1888		20	1	
Horstmann, Henry	15, Mar. 1894		72	5	
Horstmann, Lucy	17, Sept 1891		65	1	
Horstmann, William H.	28, Feb. 1891		6	4	
Horstmeier, Henry	30, Dec. 1891		43	4	
Horstmeier, Rose	14, Nov. 1894		1m	5	
Horstmeyer, George	26, Dec. 1889		21	1	
Hortmann, William	19, June 1891		18	1	
Horton, J.C.	19, Apr. 1895		55	5	
Horton, Nina M.	22, Sept 1888		18	1	
Hortzmann, Anna	29, Aug. 1892		3m	5	
Horwitz, L.	12, Sept 1894		53	5	
Hosacker, Christian	24, Feb. 1897	22, Feb.	32- 2m	5	
Hoskopf, Johanna	11, July 1892		13d	5	
Hosmer, George	26, Nov. 1888		49	1	
Hotsburg, Sophia	31, Oct. 1888		5m	1	
Houck, Edward	7, Jan. 1901		67	5	
Houk, Mary	30, Oct. 1891		8d	4	
Houseley, Sylvester	10, July 1901		16	5	
Houseman, Oscar	26, July 1887		5m	1	
Houston, Harriet	8, May 1901		53	8	
Houston, Harry	20, Nov. 1900		26	8	
Houston, Ida	6, Oct. 1900		49	5	
Houston, Lorenzo	27, Sept 1897	26, Sept	41	5	
Houtz, John	2, Aug. 1901		63	8	
Hovekamp, Joseph	6, June 1901		5	8	
Hoveler, Theresa	23, Sept 1893		18	5	
Hoverkamp, Louis E.	15, Nov. 1893		1	5	
Hovestadt, Harry	22, Apr. 1898	21, Apr.	37- 7m	5	
Howard, Eugene	26, Feb. 1889		32	1	

Name ****	Notice Date ****** ****	Death Date ***** ****	Age ***	Page ****	Maiden Name ****** ****
Howard, Jessie	5, Dec. 1887		18	1	
Howard, Mary	9, Aug. 1900		48	8	
Howard, Mathilda	19, July 1887		11	1	
Howe, Dena	6, July 1901		53	8	
Howe, Frank	7, Aug. 1900		2m	8	
Howe, Heinrich	5, Nov. 1897		47	5	
Howe, Jeanette S.	19, Sept 1900		12	8	
Howe, Sophia	18, Sept 1900		12	5	
Howell, Elisabeth	31, Mar. 1890		52	1	
Howells, Arthur	31, July 1901		28	8	
Howk, Barrett	3, Jan. 1901		19	5	
Hubbard, Charles	30, Aug. 1887		7w	1	
Hubbard, Julia	20, Feb. 1901		25	8	
Hubbard, Matilda	30, July 1901		56	8	
Hubel, Christine	10, Jan. 1893		61	5	
Huber, Andreas	23, Sept 1897	22, Sept	72-11m	5	
Huber, Anna	19, Oct. 1889		84	1	
Huber, Anna	8, May 1901		8m	8	
Huber, Anna M.	6, Apr. 1893		65	5	
Huber, Anton M.	13, Oct. 1892		18	5	
Huber, Arthur	2, Dec. 1887		11w	4	
Huber, August	5, Mar. 1888		87	4	
Huber, August	21, June 1888		1	1	
Huber, August	9, Feb. 1895		24	5	
Huber, Charles	18, Feb. 1892		6	4	
Huber, Dora	17, Nov. 1893		93	5	
Huber, Ed.	5, June 1890		2	4	
Huber, Edward	19, Aug. 1897	18, Aug.	18- 3m	5	
Huber, Elisabeth	1, Oct. 1892	29, Sept	47- 8m-21d	* 5	Munter
Huber, Elisabeth	16, June 1898	15, June	78	5	
Huber, Emma	14, July 1900		50	8	
Huber, Franz	7, Dec. 1899	6, Dec.	48- 1m	5	
Huber, Frida	29, Nov. 1895	29, Nov.	2	5	
Huber, Joseph	9, Mar. 1895		76	5	
Huber, Mamie	31, May 1889		2	1	
Huber, Mary	20, Mar. 1891		58	4	
Huber, Mary	18, Aug. 1893		1	5	
Huber, Mary	28, June 1895		44	5	
Huber, Matt.	7, Mar. 1901		31	8	
Huber, Otto	21, May 1901		1m	8	
Huber, Peter	21, Jan. 1893		77	5	
Huber, Rosa	14, July 1900		6m	8	
Huber, Theresa	30, Mar. 1901		25	8	
Huber, Theresia	12, Feb. 1898	11, Feb.	41- 4m	5	Faulhaber
Huber, Thomas	10, Aug. 1897	8, Aug.	75- 7m-18d	5	
Huber, Vesta	26, Mar. 1892		7m	1	
Huber, W.G.	26, Oct. 1898	25, Oct.	42	5	
Hubert, Viola	14, June 1894		5d	5	
Hubing, Anton	15, Apr. 1896	14, Apr.	40- 7m	5	
Hubing, Fred.	4, Oct. 1888		66	4	
Hubing, Joseph	16, Dec. 1893		1m	5	
Hubler, Ruth M.	5, Feb. 1901		17m	8	
Hubner, Adolph	24, Feb. 1892		1m	5	
Hubner, Adolph	19, Nov. 1900		47	8	
Hubner, Bertie	17, Aug. 1900		29	5	
Hubner, Lizzie	3, Nov. 1891		21	4	
Huch, Bernard	14, Oct. 1901		52	5	
Huck, Elizabeth	3, Aug. 1901		44	8	
Huck, Thomas	8, July 1891		35	4	
Hucke, Catharina	5, June 1889		16m	1	
Huddlestin, Eva Grace	20, Oct. 1887		3w	1	
Hudepohl, Anna	15, Aug. 1891		36	4	
Hudepohl, Norbert	9, Jan. 1901		17d	5	
Hudsfirth, Charles E.	15, Apr. 1888		11m	5	
Hudson, Mary	23, Oct. 1900		50	8	
Hueber, Mary	30, Nov. 1900		84	8	
Huedepohl, Elizabeth	2, Jan. 1901		65	5	
Huegel, Freda	17, Apr. 1901		12	8	
Huegel, Sophie	12, Sept 1901		45	5	
Huehlefeld, Adalbert	7, Jan. 1896	6, Jan.	20- 7m	5	
Huelsebuch, Antonia	7, May 1891		43	4	

Name ****	Notice Date ****** ****	Death Date ***** ****	Age ***	Page ****	Maiden Name ****** ****
Huelsemann, Eugen	18, Oct. 1897	17, Oct.	2- 5m	5	
Huelsmann, Ferd H. (Dr.)	25, Mar. 1898	24, Mar.	64	5	
Huelsmann, Ferdinand	7, Jan. 1901		18	5	
Huelsmann, Friedrich	17, Nov. 1896	15, Nov.	61- 1m	5	
Huelsmann, Gerhard	16, May 1892		49	5	
Huelsmann, Heinrich	11, June 1900	9, June	29-10m	5	
Huelsmann, Herman Heinrich	18, Oct. 1899	17, Oct.	66- -24d	7	
Huelsmeier, J.	28, Sept 1901		77	5	
Huemmer, John	13, Dec. 1900		45	8	
Huenemeyer, Adolph H.	14, Feb. 1890		2- 6m	1	
Hueppenden, K.M.F.	10, Oct. 1891		1m	4	
Huermann, Frank	19, Sept 1891		26	4	
Huermann, Maria Angela	24, Feb. 1900	23, Feb.	76	8	Enneking
Huesmann, Frank H.	8, May 1899	7, May		4	
Huesmann, George	16, May 1892		36	5	
Huesmann, Maria	24, July 1895		79	5	
Huesmann, Wilhelm Joseph	1, June 1898	31, May	37- 1m	5	
Huetter, Johan A.	9, July 1898	7, July	68- 6m	5	
Huettner, Anthony F.	7, Feb. 1901		74	8	
Huevelmann, Bernardina	31, Oct. 1899	29, Oct.	58-11m-16d	5	Hunsche
Huewe, George	5, July 1887		23	1	
Hueßler, Christine	25, Mar. 1892		63	5	
Huff, Francis	11, May 1901		48	8	
Huff, Lena	3, July 1894		54	5	
Huffmann, Rosie	20, Mar. 1895		28	5	
Hufford, Nanette	5, June 1888		13	4	
Hufford, William	29, Mar. 1892		29	5	
Hug, Frieda	14, Aug. 1899	12, Aug.	20	4	
Hug, Jacob	17, Jan. 1894		68	5	
Hug, Mary	21, Nov. 1894		3m	5	
Hug, Rudolph R.	5, Mar. 1900	4, Mar.	49	8	
Hug, Wilhelm	3, Nov. 1893		4	5	
Hugebeck, Edw.	8, July 1901		1	8	
Hugel, Rosina	2, Feb. 1895		69	5	
Hugenberg, Johan Friedrich	19, Apr. 1899	17, Apr.	65- 9m	4	
Hughes, Elisabeth	2, Feb. 1901		79	8	
Hughes, George	20, July 1901		35	8	
Hughes, John	10, Apr. 1901		3m	8	
Hughes, Lucinda	10, Aug. 1900		85	8	
Hughes, Thomas	28, Feb. 1888		80	1	
Hughes, William	3, Aug. 1887		28	1	
Hugie, Eva	1, May 1901		20	8	
Hugo, Conrad	9, Nov. 1893		34	5	
Hugo, Johan	15, Apr. 1900	12, Apr.	57- 4m	8	
Hugo, Louis	12, Sept 1887		71	1	
Hugo, Margaretha	18, May 1899	16, May	79- 5m	5	Becker
Hugo, Peter	29, Jan. 1892		3	5	
Huhn, Friedrich	13, Mar. 1888		37	1	
Huising, Herman	17, Feb. 1894		35	5	
Hukill, Mont. L.	8, Nov. 1887		53	1	
Hulbert, Sam.	22, Aug. 1900		83	5	
Hull, Elenora	25, Mar. 1901		6m	8	
Hulle, Louis	12, June 1901		35	8	
Hullen, Francis	22, Mar. 1888		33	1	
Huller, Eva	8, May 1894		15m	5	
Huller, Martin	24, Oct. 1890		3m	1	
Hullings, Florence	7, June 1890		5m	1	
Hulmann, Albert	8, Dec. 1893		10m	5	
Huls, George	11, May 1901		3	8	
Hulse, Harriet	6, May 1892		69	5	
Hulsmann, Anton	11, Apr. 1891		5m	4	
Hulsmann, Maria	18, Apr. 1895		35	5	
Hulzmeyer, F.R.	13, Jan. 1894		3m	5	
Human, Frank	25, Jan. 1893		65	5	
Humbers, Johan Gerhard	11, Nov. 1898	10, Nov.	84-11m- 2d	5	
Humbers, Johan Wilhelm	8, 9, Jan. 1896	7, Jan.	79-10m	5	
Humbrecht, Erasmus	20, June 1901		55	8	
Humbser, John	19, July 1887		64	1	
Humeldorf, Alma	7, Sept 1893		8m	5	
Humler, Anna	23, Feb. 1901		26	8	
Humm, Herbert	22, Jan. 1899	20, Jan.	14m-13d	5	

Name ****	Notice Date ****** ****	Death Date ***** ****	Age ***	Page ****	Maiden Name ****** ****
Humm, R.W.	21, July 1888		10m	1	
Hummel, Alma	15, Feb. 1889		3	1	
Hummel, Carol.	17, Jan. 1888		62	4	
Hummel, Ch. C.	20, June 1888		26	1	
Hummel, David	25, Sept 1894		73	5	
Hummel, Edward	9, Sept 1893		15	5	
Hummel, Florence F.	17, Nov. 1893		1	5	
Hummel, Frank	10, Jan. 1898	9, Jan.	7m	5	
Hummel, Hazel D.	23, Jan. 1894		9m	5	
Hummel, J.P.	18, May 1898	17, May	19	4	
Hummel, Johan	17, May 1900	16, May	65- 6m	5	
Hummel, Joseph	18, Nov. 1889		71	1	
Hummel, Julius	16, May 1893		28	5	
Hummel, Pius	10, 11, Jan. 1894	9, Jan.	41- 7m	5	
Hummer, Joseph	17, Aug. 1898	16, Aug.	77- 5m	4	
Hummins, John Art.	2, Mar. 1888		2	1	
Hummitsch, Regina	4, July 1900	3, July	65	8	
Hummler, Franz	30, Oct. 1899	29, Oct.	69	5	
Hummler, Josephina	9, Sept 1896	8, Sept	35- 5m	5	
Humphreys, T.	2, Feb. 1901		57	8	
Humsche, Edward	1, May 1891		51	4	
Hunefeld, Edward	1, Feb. 1890		2m	1	
Huneke, Eddie	5, Mar. 1890		18m	1	
Hunemein, Lizette	31, July 1900		60	5	
Hungler, Albert	13, Oct. 1900		3	8	
Hungler, Frank F.	5, June 1901		1	8	
Hunglinger, Michael	9, Apr. 1891		6	4	
Hunker, John M.	26, Dec. 1890		3	1	
Hunnewell, Daniel H.	7, July 1888		85	4	
Hunning, Stella	16, Jan. 1893		1m	5	
Hunsche, Ernst	23, Jan. 1901		65	8	
Hunsche, Sophia	6, May 1899	4, May	78	4	Henkender
Hunsche, William	11, Mar. 1893		24	5	
Hunsinger, Delta	16, Apr. 1891		2	4	
Hunsinger, Hazel	30, July 1891		8m	4	
Hunt, Ada	26, Dec. 1900		19	8	
Hunt, August	4, Feb. 1900	3, Feb.	22- 8m	5	
Hunt, Cora	10, Apr. 1895		30	5	
Hunt, Eleanor L.	2, Nov. 1900		58	8	
Hunt, Franz	31, May 1898	30, May	44- 5m-15d	4	
Hunt, James F.	14, Feb. 1889		30	1	
Hunt, Jesse P.	21, Jan. 1901		67	8	
Hunter, George J.	17, Feb. 1888		13m	4	
Hunter, Webster	4, May 1892		3m	5	
Huntermann, Anna	14, Oct. 1894		70	5	
Hupp, Arthur F.	29, July 1893		1	5	
Hupp, Frank	18, Dec. 1900		61	8	
Hupp, Johan	23, Sept 1896	22, Sept	65- 8m	5	
Hupp, Peter	17, Oct. 1891		58	4	
Huppe, Eliza	6, Jan. 1892		60	5	
Hurlander, F.W.	25, Mar. 1889		4m	1	
Hurlbut, Minnie	17, Feb. 1895		17	5	
Hurlemann, Pauline	21, Feb. 1894		9m	5	
Hurley, Honora	11, Jan. 1888		67	4	
Hurley, Michael	23, Oct. 1900		31	8	
Hurmey, Christian	9, Dec. 1893		73	5	
Hurrelbrink, William	16, Dec. 1891		49	4	
Hurst, John	6, Mar. 1894		4	5	
Hurst, Katharine	20, Dec. 1893		13m	5	
Hurtig, Robert	10, Sept 1901		53	1	
Hurty, Ann J.	12, July 1895		79	5	
Husemann, Katharine	18, Nov. 1899	17, Nov.	97- 5m	4	
Husemann, Marie	26, Nov. 1898	25, Nov.	50	4	
Husman, John	18, Apr. 1893		31	5	
Husmann, Ambrosius Frank (Br)	5, Aug. 1897	3, Aug.	43- 9m	5	
Husmann, Friedrich	19, Oct. 1887		52	1	
Husmann, Harry	1, Sept 1888		7m	1	
Husser, John	25, Oct. 1894		9	5	
Hussmann, Joseph A.	29, Sept 1894		49	5	
Hussmann, William	21, Sept 1894		29	5	
Hust, Adam E.	22, Feb. 1896	19, Feb.	35-10m	5	

Name ****	Notice Date ****** ****	Death Date ***** ****	Age ***	Page ****	Maiden Name ****** ****
Hust, Anna Otilie	23, 24, Feb. 1898	22, Feb.	58- 7m	5	Rößner
Hust, Fred.	10, Mar. 1895		30	5	
Hust, Henry A.	8, Jan. 1892		43	5	
Hust, Margaret	4, Oct. 1888		78	4	
Hustedde, Anna	13, Aug. 1888		60	1	
Hustein, Henry	9, Oct. 1889		54	1	
Huster, Maria Elisabeth	30, Mar. 1898	29, Mar.	63- 6m- 3d	5	
Hustes, Alma	1, July 1891		5m	1	
Hutchinson, Robert	19, Dec. 1900		71	8	
Huth, Anna	10, Sept 1895	7, Sept	11m- 3d	5	
Huth, Emil	16, May 1891		21	2	
Huth, Mary A.	18, May 1901		46	1	
Hutler, Joseph J.	14, July 1896	12, July	42- 1m	5	
Hutmann, Jakob	2, May 1899	30, Apr.	70- 4m	5	
Hutterer, Anna	3, Jan. 1901		25	5	
Hutton, Bathania A.	3, Sept 1901		78	8	
Hutton, John	31, July 1900		84	5	
Hutzelmann, Barbara	30, Mar. 1899	29, Mar.		5	
Hutzelmann, Catharine	22, Sept 1897	20, Sept	73- 1m	5	Diehl
Hutzelmann, John P.	25, May 1894		70	5	
Hutzelmann, Mary	10, Oct. 1891		32	4	
Hutzenlaub, Gustav	16, Dec. 1889		41	1	
Hutzler, Charles	12, May 1891		27	1	
Huvelmann, Emilie	28, Dec. 1899	26, Dec.	23-10m	5	
Huwe, Catharina	13, Jan. 1899	12, Jan.		4	
Hux, Anna Barbara	1, Aug. 1896	31, July		5	Wenzler
Huß, August	5, Sept 1899	2, Sept	42-11m	5	
Huß, Friedrich	3, Nov. 1890	1, Nov.	46-11m-19d	4	
Huß, Louise	17, Sept 1889		22	1	
Huß, Paulina K.	23, May 1899	22, Ma	77	5	Schopper
Hußmann, Edward	26, Aug. 1893		4m	5	
Hyde, Clarence	18, June 1895		21m	5	
Hyde, Edward P.	20, Aug. 1901		38	8	
Hyndman, Frank	28, July 1887		1m	1	
Hyser, Bertha	3, Sept 1889		2m	1	
Hyser, Fred. W.	24, Jan. 1894		2m	5	
Häckel, Christina	10, Mar. 1897	9, Mar.	41-10m	5	Mueller
Häckel, Louisa	9, July 1900	8, July	21	8	
Häfner, Johan Conrad	30, Dec. 1893		82	5	
Härtig, Emma Johanna	16, Oct. 1890	15, Oct.	34- 9m	1	Donner
Härtlein, George	5, July 1890		18	1	
Häveler, Joseph	23, Jan. 1889	22, Jan.		2	
Höckel, John G.	12, Oct. 1889		32	1	
Höfele, Louise	14, Aug. 1887		9w	1	
Höfer, Charles	5, Aug. 1889		4	1	
Höfinghoff, Charles	21, Nov. 1898	20, Nov.	65	5	
Höfle, Elisabeth	24, July 1894		70	5	
Höhlein, Paulina	27, Nov. 1896	26, Nov.	48- 1m	5	Grammer
Höhlein, Willie	15, June 1896	14, June	6-10m	5	
Höhne, Johan	21, Nov. 1899	20, Nov.	64- 9m	5	
Hölzer, Adam	23, 24, June 1892	22, June	39- 9m-24d	5	
Hölzer, Julius	5, Jan. 1894	3, Jan.	29- 6m-24d	5	
Hömmelmeier, Marie	9, Jan. 1889		76	1	
Höninger, Katie	21, Jan. 1890		6	1	
Hörner, Jakob	21, Jan. 1897	20, Jan.	17-10m	5	
Hörnle, Fred.	18, Mar. 1889		67	1	
Hörschemeyer, Anton	25, Feb. 1893		1	5	
Hösel, Anna	2, Sept 1891		1- 1m	4	
Hübbe, Fred.	8, Nov. 1889		50	1	
Hüdepohl, Maria Gertrud	9, July 1897	7, July	70- 7m	4	Flaspoehler
Hüls, Mary	18, Dec. 1888		3	2	
Hülsebusch, Ferdinand	31, Mar. 1891		8d	4	
Hülsemann, Heinrich	27, Sept 1900		44	8	
Hümmer, Maria	3, Feb. 1897	2, Feb.	65- 4m	5	Lurz
Hünefeld, Ed.	17, Oct. 1901		36	8	
Hünefeld, Elise	20, Feb. 1899	16, Feb.	62- 5m	5	Lachtrip
Hünefeld, Margaretha	29, Mar. 1895		69	5	
Hüpel, Anna Maria	21, June 1897	19, June	71	5	Griesinger
Hüpker, Klara	27, Nov. 1894		33	5	
Hürst, Mary	25, Mar. 1891		42	4	
Hürster, Gertrud	12, Jan. 1889		5m	1	

Name	Notice Date	Death Date	Age	Page	Maiden Name
****	****** ****	***** ****	***	****	****** ****
Hüskes, John H.	5, Aug. 1889		28	1	
Hüsman, Herman	14, June 1889		6m	1	
Hütten, Bernard	20, Apr. 1898	19, Apr.	64- 7m	4	
Hüwel, Heinrich	6, May 1889		50	1	
Idasocher, Jakob	31, Mar. 1891		29	4	
Iffland, Johan	28, Jan. 1897	27, Jan.	47	5	
Iffland, Nellie	8, Mar. 1894		32	5	
Iglauer, S.K.	24, Oct. 1894		91	5	
Ihle, Anna	13, Feb. 1894		66	5	
Ihle, Michael	7, Dec. 1889		66	1	
Ihli, Barbara	1, July 1901		72	8	
Iliff, George W.	15, Aug. 1900		42	5	
Iliff, Harold F.	6, July 1893		6m	5	
Ilmstead, George	5, Sept 1901		50	8	
Imbus, Bernard F.	1, Feb. 1901		25	8	
Imbusch, Heinrich	16, Dec. 1893		17m	5	
Imfeld, D.	14, Dec. 1887		15	4	
Imhoff,	25, Mar. 1891		1d	4	
Imholte, Eleanora	2, Mar. 1901		11	5	
Imig, William	5, May 1891		51	1	
Immenhorst, Charles	5, July 1890		3m	1	
Imming, Maria	25, Dec. 1891		64	2	
Imorde, Gertie	21, Mar. 1891		26m	4	
Imsande, Emma	14, Apr. 1891		1- 6m	4	
Imsiecke, Joseph	21, Jan. 1901		93	8	
Imwalle, Albert G.	10, Aug. 1894		7m	5	
Imwalle, Christopher Heinrich	30, Jan. 1896	29, Jan.	69	5	
Imwalle, Joseph	17, May 1901		62	8	
Imwalle, Maria	24, July 1895		28d	5	
Imwalls, George	2, Aug. 1887		7m	1	
Ingels, George	25, July 1901		77	8	
Ingram, John	4, Aug. 1900		5m	8	
Inneß, Edward	28, June 1895		17	5	
Intelhofer, John	13, Sept 1889		21	1	
Intelhofer, John	6, Mar. 1891		50	4	
Intelhofer, Louisa	13, Jan. 1891		16	1	
Ireland, Elizabeth	9, Feb. 1901		60	8	
Ireland, John J.	28, June 1888		6m	1	
Ireland, Susan	13, Aug. 1901		59	8	
Isaninger, George	3, May 1901		65	8	
Isford, Bernhard	18, June 1889		24	1	
Isler, Arnold H.	26, Feb. 1894		45	5	
Israel, John	27, June 1895		69	5	
Israel, Sarah	12, Mar. 1901		87	8	
Ittig, Richard	2, Mar. 1901		21	5	
Ittner, Wenzel	4, Apr. 1894		45	5	
Itzen, Wilhelm	27, Mar. 1891		48	4	
Jack, James Elsworth,	21, May 1901		6m	8	
Jackle, William	29, May 1901		35	8	
Jacklikowski, A.	20, Dec. 1900		85	8	
Jackmann, Charles E.	9, Sept 1893		40	5	
Jackmann, Julius	10, Aug. 1887		7w	1	
Jackson, Carrie	30, Sept 1901		32	8	
Jackson, Elizabeth	31, Oct. 1888		29	1	
Jackson, Field	21, Sept 1887		29	1	
Jackson, Ida	7, June 1901		32	8	
Jackson, James	30, June 1888		34	1	
Jackson, Lottie	1, Dec. 1888		1	4	
Jackson, Martha	10, May 1895		8m	5	
Jackson, Ralph	2, May 1901		89	8	
Jackson, Ralph	18, May 1901		1	1	
Jackson, Robert	28, Dec. 1900		68	8	
Jackson, Samuel	1, Aug. 1887		32	1	
Jackson, Sarah	19, July 1887		9m	1	
Jackson, Viola	22, Sept 1900		5m	5	
Jacob, Abraham	13, Dec. 1892		65	5	
Jacob, Elizabeth	23, Feb. 1891		66	4	
Jacob, Emma	27, Aug. 1888		2m	1	
Jacob, Frank	15, May 1894		37	5	

Name	Notice Date	Death Date	Age	Page	Maiden Name
****	****** ****	***** ****	***	****	****** ****
Jacob, Katharina	28, July 1891		80	4	
Jacob, Michael	14, June 1900	13, June	1- 6m	5	
Jacob, W.	30, Oct. 1896	28, Oct.	67- 3m	5	
Jacober, Hortensia	12, Feb. 1891		36	4	
Jacobi, Clara	27, July 1892		8m	5	
Jacobi, Kunigunde	18, Mar. 1899	16, Mar.	36	5	Markert
Jacobi, Moritz Albert	13, May 1899	12, May	65	4	
Jacobi, Wilhelm	15, Aug. 1893		1	5	
Jacobi, William	23, Mar. 1893		68	5	
Jacobs,	6, Nov. 1900		1d	8	
Jacobs, A.	4, May 1896	2, May	68	5	
Jacobs, August H.	10, Sept 1887		3d	2	
Jacobs, Caroline	12, Nov. 1900		65	5	
Jacobs, Clospie	20, Sept 1901		48	1	
Jacobs, Edward	17, Feb. 1891		1d	4	
Jacobs, Elisa	18, Jan. 1892		33	5	
Jacobs, Friedricka A.	12, Sept 1887		4d	1	
Jacobs, John	6, Oct. 1891		26	4	
Jacobs, John R.	22, Jan. 1891		6m	4	
Jacobs, Lizzie	20, Apr. 1893		7m	5	
Jacobs, Maria T.	11, Mar. 1899	9, Mar.	70- 4m	5	
Jacobs, Peter	20, Apr. 1895		60	5	
Jacobs, Richard	20, June 1892		36	5	
Jacobs, William	8, Feb. 1890		18m	4	
Jacobs, William	1, Feb. 1892		38	5	
Jacobson, Jacob	23, Nov. 1893		4	5	
Jacobson, Robert	11, Jan. 1893		59	5	
Jacoby, Alex	1, Dec. 1891		72	4	
Jaeger, Edna K.	28, Mar. 1893		4m	5	
Jaeger, Franz	7, Sept 1899	6, Sept	42	5	
Jaeger, Franziska	27, Nov. 1899	26, Nov.	73- 9m	5	
Jaeger, John	11, Feb. 1893		78	5	
Jaeger, Lena	23, Feb. 1892		32	5	
Jaeger, Lena	14, Mar. 1893		61	5	
Jaeger, Mary	23, May 1888		2w	1	
Jaeger, William	1, Feb. 1889		57	1	
Jaerg, Alma	11, July 1895		2m	5	
Jaering, Bennie	29, Mar. 1894		12	5	
Jahn, Emma	19, Aug. 1890	18, Aug.	24	1	Riley
Jahn, Joseph	28, Dec. 1891		1	4	
Jahn, Katharine	7, May 1896	3, May	72	5	Kruse
Jahn, Robert W.	9, Aug. 1887		31	1	
Jahn, Walter	10, 12, Feb. 1890	9, Feb.	5m	1	
Jahncke, Emma	21, July 1892	21, July	46	5	
Jahnke, Albert	20, Nov. 1896	19, Nov.	20- 8m	5	
Jahnke, Clara	9, Oct. 1894		4	5	
Jahnke, John	3, Aug. 1893		6	5	
Jahnke, Otto	17, Aug. 1900		18	5	
Jahr, Doris	16, Jan. 1899	15, Jan.	79	5	
Jahrus, John C.	23, Jan. 1901		69	8	
Jakes, Dora	3, July 1901		71	8	
Jakob, Helen	8, June 1901		1	8	
Jakob, Michael	8, July 1897	6, July	43-11m	4	
Jakob, Theresia M.	2, Sept 1891		16	4	
Jakobs, Amalia E.	22, Mar. 1889		74	1	
Jakobs, Ida	4, June 1889		3	1	
Jakobs, John	17, May 1889		4m	1	
James, Hugh	11, Aug. 1900		31	8	
James, Ida	11, Oct. 1900		14	8	
Jana, Frankie	4, June 1895		15m	5	
Janck, Lena	20, June 1901		24	8	
Jander, Fred. L.	31, July 1894		61	5	
Jander, Gustav	5, Mar. 1901		74	5	
Jander, Paul	26, June 1891		24	4	
Janning, Edith	24, July 1895		3	5	
Jansen, Gerhard	3, Mar. 1899	2, Mar.	50- 2m	4	
Jansen, Henry	9, Dec. 1891		1d	2	
Jansen, John	18, Dec. 1888		41	2	
Jansen, John	30, July 1891		37	4	
Jansen, Kate	9, Dec. 1891		1d	2	
Jansen, Lucas	4, Jan. 1893		50	5	

Name ****	Notice Date ****** ****	Death Date ***** ****	Age ***	Page ****	Maiden Name ****** ****
Jansen, Margaretha	12, Jan. 1894		40	5	
Jansen, Minnie	30, Aug. 1890		2	2	
Jansmann, Valentine	30, Jan. 1894		59	5	
Janson, Cornelius	8, Sept 1891		73	4	
Janson, Elisabeth	26, Apr. 1898	25, Apr.	79-11m	5	Richter
Janson, Jacob	6, Oct. 1900		53	5	
Janson, Lena	4, Aug. 1891		15	4	
Janson, M.	15, Dec. 1887		5m	1	
Janson, Martin	1, Nov. 1897	31, Oct.	76- 2m	5	
Janson, Sidney	15, Apr. 1888		4m	5	
Janson, Wilhelmina	12, Feb. 1901		80	8	
Janssen, Anna	3, Aug. 1887		30	1	
Janssen, Bernhard	10, Apr. 1896	8, Apr.	61- 7m	5	
Janszen, Elisabeth	11, Dec. 1899	9, Dec.	88- 8m	4	Schumacher
Janszen, Marie	5, Apr. 1895		35	5	
Janz, Anton	4, Apr. 1893		3m	5	
Janz, Clara	8, Mar. 1901		7	8	
Janz, Mary	26, Nov. 1892		5	5	
Janzen, Herman H.	22, Feb. 1899	19, Feb.	77- -20d	5	
Jarvis, Bertha	7, Dec. 1887		7- 8m	1	
Jasper, Elizabeth	24, Dec. 1900		15d	8	
Jasper, Howard	12, Dec. 1900		1	8	
Jasper, Marianne	24, Dec. 1900		15d	8	
Jasper, William	21, Mar. 1892		10	4	
Jaspers, Henry	10, Dec. 1891			4	
Jaspers, Margaret	11, Nov. 1894		78	5	
Jauch, Louise	21, Dec. 1895	19, Dec.	60- 3m	5	
Jaß, O.	19, Mar. 1895		48	5	
Jeckel, Jennie	24, Mar. 1897	24, Mar.	17- 6m	5	
Jelk, Anna	11, July 1901		3m	5	
Jelks, Robert	11, July 1887		5m	1	
Jencori, Andrea	23, Mar. 1901		2	8	
Jenkens, John	11, May 1901		57	8	
Jenkins, A.E.	26, Feb. 1888		18	4	
Jenkins, Helen J.	16, Feb. 1901		8	8	
Jenkins, R.C. (Mrs)	28, Sept 1897	27, Sept		5	Ahlers
Jenkmann, Antonetta	23, Apr. 1890		58	4	
Jennings, Edna	9, Apr. 1890		10m	1	
Jennings, Henry	5, Feb. 1891		13m	4	
Jennings, Lizzie	24, Oct. 1891		34	4	
Jennings, Mary	2, Apr. 1895		40	5	
Jennings, Mary	12, Aug. 1901		70	8	
Jennings, Winona M. (Dr)	14, Dec. 1900		32	8	
Jentz, Lulu	14, Sept 1900		26	5	
Jentz, Samuel	29, Jan. 1898	28, Jan.	75	4	
Jentzon, John L.	18, June 1895		1d	5	
Jergens, Magdalene	9, Oct. 1896	7, Oct.	74	5	
Jerke, John	9, Apr. 1891		8	4	
Jerling, Benjamin	28, Feb. 1891		28	4	
Jernigan, Maurice	7, May 1901		68	1	
Jers, Washington M.	17, Feb. 1888		29	4	
Jessus, Emma	13, Oct. 1892		4m	5	
Jester, Lydia	17, Sept 1891		33	1	
Jester, Ruth	8, July 1901		5m	8	
Jetter, Blana	24, Dec. 1892		2	5	
Jetter, Robert A.	6, July 1901		3	8	
Jewett, Thomas	30, May 1901		60	8	
Jeynes, Olive E.	23, Oct. 1900		16	8	
Jiles, Rossa	16, Feb. 1901		24	8	
Joah, Karoline	11, Mar. 1891		68	4	
Joas, George	15, June 1889		63	1	
Joas, Minnie	2, Aug. 1888		59	2	
Joasting, Phil.	19, Oct. 1901		29	8	
Jobe, Dora	10, Oct. 1891		2m	4	
Jobe, George	27, May 1901		42	8	
Jockers, Charles	6, Aug. 1896	4, Aug.	35	5	
Jockers, George	5, Nov. 1900		10m	8	
Joehnk, Hans Heinrich	7, Mar. 1901	6, Mar.	79- 7m-14d	5	
Joerden, C. Laura	18, Oct. 1893		7	5	
Joering, Alois	23, Aug. 1887		21m	1	
Joering, Elisabeth	30, Jan. 1894		55	5	

Name ****	Notice Date ****** ****	Death Date ***** ****	Age ***	Page ****	Maiden Name ****** ****
Joering, Elisabeth	6, Mar. 1900	5, Mar.	66-11m	8	Trenkamp
Joering, Fred.	4, Oct. 1894		70	5	
Joest, John	4, Mar. 1891		55	4	
Joesting, Mary	5, Aug. 1901		2	8	
Johannes, Amanda M.	5, Sept 1894		7	5	
Johannes, Barbara	15, Feb. 1896	14, Feb.	63	5	Kiechler
Johannes, George	22, Apr. 1889		3m	1	
Johanning, August	13, May 1901		45	8	
Johanning, Ed.	8, Dec. 1900		20	8	
Johanning, Heinrich	2, July 1897	30, June	55	5	
Johanning, Louis	20, Jan. 1890		37	1	
Johanning, Peter	12, Aug. 1887		5m	1	
Johanningmann, Herman (Fr.)	25, Aug. 1896	23, Aug.	64	5	
Johanningmann, John	16, May 1901		3m	5	
Johantges, Albert	17, Oct. 1898	15, Oct.	54- 8m	4	
Johantges, Emma	5, Sept 1900		57	5	
John, Arthur H.	4, Aug. 1888		11m	4	
Johnen, Atta	4, May 1895		11m	5	
Johnen, Louis	2, June 1893		8d	5	
Johns, Herman	29, May 1895		21	5	
Johns, Kate	4, June 1901		44	8	
Johns, Mary	13, July 1901		41	8	
Johnson, Alice	11, Dec. 1900		46	8	
Johnson, Allie	23, Mar. 1901		6d	8	
Johnson, Andrew	16, Mar. 1901		45	8	
Johnson, Benjamin	7, May 1895		40	5	
Johnson, Charles	31, Mar. 1888		19m	4	
Johnson, Charley	5, Apr. 1895		32	5	
Johnson, David H.	2, May 1895		49	5	
Johnson, Felix	4, Oct. 1901		3	8	
Johnson, George	6, Sept 1900		34	5	
Johnson, Harry	17, May 1901		55	8	
Johnson, Hattie	28, June 1888		4m	1	
Johnson, Howard	24, June 1901		2	8	
Johnson, James	26, Apr. 1901		9m	8	
Johnson, James W.	15, Nov. 1887		57	4	
Johnson, Jay C.	20, Sept 1887		19	1	
Johnson, John	25, Jan. 1901		70	8	
Johnson, Joseph	22, Aug. 1900		52	5	
Johnson, Joseph	20, Mar. 1901		50	1	
Johnson, Kate	1, June 1901		34	8	
Johnson, Lizzie	10, May 1888		19	1	
Johnson, Lucy	1, Sept 1900		27	5	
Johnson, Lucy J.	23, Apr. 1895		37	5	
Johnson, Mabel	23, July 1901		2d	8	
Johnson, Margaret	8, Dec. 1900		75	8	
Johnson, Mary	30, Apr. 1901		5d	8	
Johnson, Mary E.	8, Nov. 1900		2m	8	
Johnson, May	22, July 1901		17	8	
Johnson, Philip	24, Apr. 1895		66	5	
Johnson, Robert	3, Nov. 1892		48	5	
Johnson, Stanley	23, Apr. 1895		6m	5	
Johnson, Walter	20, Apr. 1895		10m	5	
Johnson, William W.	10, Oct. 1900		71	8	
Johnston, Hannah	3, Feb. 1888		73- 9m	4	
Johnston, John	17, Apr. 1895		70	5	
Johnston, Katie	11, July 1888		10m	1	
Johnston, Stella	14, June 1901		15	5	
Jokers, Marie	22, Aug. 1900		63	5	
Jonap, Abraham	29, May 1889		69	1	
Jonas, Jakob	21, Dec. 1896	20, Dec.	18	5	
Jonas, John	2, Sept 1887		8	1	
Jonas, Lina	15, Feb. 1889		17m	1	
Jones, Alfretta	29, Jan. 1901		45	8	
Jones, Anna	20, June 1901		39	8	
Jones, Charles	3, Apr. 1888		8	4	
Jones, Charles	19, June 1901		5	8	
Jones, D.F.	23, Aug. 1887		64	1	
Jones, Ella	4, Aug. 1887		35	1	
Jones, Fannie	5, Sept 1901		19	8	
Jones, Florence J.	7, Aug. 1888		4m	1	

Name ****	Notice Date ****** ****	Death Date ***** ****	Age ***	Page ****	Maiden Name ****** ****
Jones, George	15, Mar. 1901		3	8	
Jones, George	6, June 1901		4	8	
Jones, Harriet	26, Apr. 1895		51	5	
Jones, Henry	7, Aug. 1900		65	8	
Jones, Ida	19, July 1900		30	8	
Jones, Ida May	20, Sept 1901		21	1	
Jones, J.	25, Feb. 1901		58	8	
Jones, J. Robert	4, Jan. 1901		66	5	
Jones, Joseph	2, July 1892		4	5	
Jones, Lilly May	14, Aug. 1888		5w	1	
Jones, Lorena P.	31, Aug. 1887		22	1	
Jones, Louisa Walden	13, Dec. 1900		82	8	
Jones, Lucy	7, July 1888		41	4	
Jones, Margaret	14, Sept 1900			5	
Jones, Mary	6, Apr. 1895		75	5	
Jones, Mary	14, Sept 1900		31	5	
Jones, Mary E.	21, Sept 1900			5	
Jones, May	31, Jan. 1901		14	8	
Jones, Minnie	2, Sept 1887		14	1	
Jones, Missouri	13, July 1895		58	5	
Jones, N.R.	24, Jan. 1888		82	1	
Jones, Paul	14, Aug. 1900		22m	5	
Jones, Paul	26, Mar. 1901		1m	8	
Jones, Richard	2, May 1895		65	5	
Jones, Wilhelmine B.	3, Nov. 1887		41- 8m	4	
Jones, William E.	26, Dec. 1900		53	8	
Jones, Willie	6, June 1901		16d	8	
Jonitz, Carl	14, Mar. 1896	13, Mar.	15-11m	5	
Jonte, Alfred	4, Apr. 1895		66	5	
Jordan, Charles	22, Oct. 1891		21	1	
Jordan, Charles H.	19, Oct. 1900		44	5	
Jordan, Cora	18, July 1895		6m	5	
Jordan, John	16, Apr. 1901		31	8	
Jordan, Nathan	4, Aug. 1900		40	8	
Jordan, Richard	26, Dec. 1900		22	8	
Jordan, Theresa	18, Feb. 1891		35	4	
Jordan, Verua H.	25, Jan. 1901		3	8	
Jordan, W.L.	30, Mar. 1896	27, Mar.	39- 3m	5	
Jorg, Maria Anna	2, June 1896	30, May	48	5	
Joseph, A.A.	12, Jan. 1897	11, Jan.	3m-21d	5	
Joseph, Edna E.	25, Apr. 1898	24, Apr.	1- 8m	5	
Joseph, Elmer C.	24, Sept 1891		4m	1	
Joseph, George	15, Apr. 1889		8m	1	
Joseph, Gertie	11, July 1887		9	1	
Joseph, Leah	21, Oct. 1891		1m	4	
Joseph, Levy	16, Jan. 1891		75	4	
Josephia, (Sr.)	7, May 1891		54	4	
Joslin, Louis	28, Jan. 1893		91	5	
Joyce, Martin	20, July 1887		8m	1	
Jucht, August	30, Dec. 1897	29, Dec.	47	5	
Judah, Judah	20, Nov. 1895	20, Nov.	86	5	
Judge, Anna	6, June 1888		36	1	
Judge, William	10, June 1901		2	8	
Juelg, Lottie	20, Dec. 1893		9	5	
Juen, Frank	11, Aug. 1891		57	4	
Juengling, Gustav	3, Apr. 1901		1d	8	
Juengst, William	8, Feb. 1892		64	4	
Juergens, Charles F.	3, July 1901		64	8	
Juergens, Fred. J.	18, Nov. 1891		69	4	
Juergens, Val.	6, July 1901		8m	8	
Julian, John	7, May 1901		1	1	
Julicks, Nancy	20, Oct. 1887		66	1	
Julien, Maggie	23, Mar. 1901		56	8	
Julien, Mary E.	10, Mar. 1891		68	4	
Julier, Charles	11, July 1889		9m	1	
Jullig, Nellie	5, June 1890		2	4	
Juna, Karl	30, Sept 1899	28, Sept	68- 7m	4	
Jundt, John	13, June 1894		55	5	
Jung, Anna	20, Jan. 1888		4w	4	
Jung, Charles	21, May 1889		43	1	
Jung, Charles	30, July 1901			8	

Name ****	Notice Date ****** ****	Death Date ***** ****	Age ***	Page ****	Maiden Name ****** ****
Jung, Daniel	2, Dec. 1894		31	4	
Jung, Elisabeth	4, Oct. 1897	3, Oct.	70- 5m	5	Klein
Jung, Elmer	30, Mar. 1901		3	8	
Jung, George	5, Aug. 1901		45	8	
Jung, Jacob	23, Mar. 1899	21, Mar.	55	5	
Jung, Jakob	10, July 1887		32	1	
Jung, Johan	24, Nov. 1896	22, Nov.	26- 4m	5	
Jung, John	7, Jan. 1891		5m	4	
Jung, John	27, Sept 1893		16	5	
Jung, Katherine	1, June 1894		61	5	
Jung, Lilian	23, Apr. 1896	22, Apr.	2m-15d	5	
Jung, Margaretha	22, July 1887		6d	1	
Jung, Theodor	13, Jan. 1896	11, Jan.	39	5	
Jung, Violet	23, Apr. 1896	22, Apr.	2m-15d	5	
Jung, W.	23, Nov. 1896	21, Nov.	65- -20d	5	
Jung, William	22, May 1890		4w	1	
Jungbluth, Dora	30, July 1890		4m	1	
Jungbluth, Elizabeth	1, Mar. 1901		44	8	
Jungbluth, Freddie	4, May 1895		1d	5	
Junge, D.	19, Oct. 1901		54	8	
Junghanns, George	21, Nov. 1891	21, Nov.	33	1	
Junghaus, Peter	13, Mar. 1897	12, Mar.	43- 2m	5	
Jungling, H.E.	27, Aug. 1889		67	1	
Junk, August	2, Aug. 1887		18	1	
Junk, Charles	14, June 1895		3	5	
Junker, Conrad	22, Dec. 1892		59	5	
Junker, Edeltraut Katharina	31, Oct. 1898	20, Oct.		5	Lyer
Junker, Louise	16, July 1900	14, July	81	8	
Junkins, Lena	21, Jan. 1893		2m	5	
Juppenlotz, Jakob	7, July 1887		41	1	
Jurgens, Joseph	10, Jan. 1891		65	4	
Jurling, Elisabeth	20, Apr. 1899	19, Apr.	60	4	
Just, Peter	4, Sept 1889		49	1	
Justa, Mary E.	4, Aug. 1887		10m	1	
Justis, Thomas	29, June 1901		50	8	
Jutzi, Caroline	27, Apr. 1897	26, Apr.	33	5	Reiners
Jäger, Eve	1, May 1888		59	2	
Jäger, Henry	14, Apr. 1894		7m	5	
Jäsche, Martha	1, July 1891		26	1	
Jörg, Bertha	3, Mar. 1890		5m	1	
Jörg, Charles	1, Aug. 1888		14m	2	
Jörg, Marie	19, Oct. 1889	18, Oct.	33	1	Wasserfallen
Jörgens, Annie	25, July 1894		11m	5	
Jöring, Bernard	3, Feb. 1896	2, Feb.	80	5	
Jülg, John	31, Dec. 1888		9m	1	
Jürgens, Hermine	26, Sept 1894		37	5	
Jürgens, Wendeline	14, Feb. 1893		72	5	
Kabbes, Friedrich	8, May 1896		72- 1m	5	
Kabbes, Maria	17, Dec. 1895	16, Dec.	24-11m	4	
Kabbes, Maria Anna	3, Apr. 1899	31, Mar.	80- 9m	5	Zurliene
Kabel, Catharina	23, Mar. 1893		55	5	
Kaberlein, William	6, Apr. 1893		17	5	
Kachel, Augusta	4, June 1895		16m	5	
Kachula, Fr.	25, July 1890		80	1	
Kaehlin, Rosalia	17, Jan. 1890		39	1	
Kaehn, Charles	2, Feb. 1893		26	5	
Kaelin, Albert M.	6, July 1893		3	5	
Kaelin, Joseph F.	4, Jan. 1894		38	5	
Kaelin, Louisa M.	20, July 1893		4m	5	
Kaelin, Louise	3, Feb. 1896	2, Feb.	5-11m	5	
Kaelin, William	24, July 1890		5	1	
Kaerman, Theresa	11, July 1889		81	1	
Kaesperlein, Johan	9, Jan. 1899	8, Jan.	38	5	
Kahl, Elisabeth	11, Feb. 1893		67	5	
Kahle, Henry D.C.	27, Mar. 1894		3m	5	
Kahleis, Louis	5, Feb. 1898	4, Feb.	52	5	
Kahn, Bertha	7, July 1891		54	1	
Kahn, Bessie	13, July 1901		12	8	
Kahn, Dora	16, Jan. 1890		14	1	
Kahn, Elias	14, Nov. 1899	12, Nov.		4	

Name ****	Notice Date ****** ****	Death Date ***** ****	Age ***	Page ****	Maiden Name ****** ****
Kahn, Gertrud	4, Apr. 1890		61	1	
Kahn, Hannah	5, Aug. 1891		72	4	
Kahn, Hattie	4, Nov. 1887		20	1	
Kahn, Maria	9, July 1895		9m	5	
Kahn, Moses	30, Mar. 1894		83	5	
Kahn, Moses	10, Apr. 1895		63	5	
Kaiholz, Johan	11, Aug. 1898	9, Aug.	70- 1m	5	
Kain, Bridget	4, Aug. 1900		62	8	
Kain, Bridget	16, Apr. 1901		70	8	
Kain, Thomas	25, June 1901		4m	8	
Kaing, Andreas	12, Feb. 1889		69	1	
Kaiser, Anna	16, Dec. 1893		71	5	
Kaiser, Catharine	31, Oct. 1891		80	4	
Kaiser, Frank	9, Apr. 1900	8, Apr.	34- 8m	4	
Kaiser, Friedrich	17, Oct. 1898	15, Oct.	89- 1m	4	
Kaiser, George	1, Aug. 1888		37	2	
Kaiser, Heinrich	1, June 1896	31, May	50- 9m	5	
Kaiser, Henry	17, Aug. 1887		76	1	
Kaiser, Henry F.	21, Aug. 1894		22	5	
Kaiser, John	4, Apr. 1891		48	4	
Kaiser, John	2, Feb. 1894		6m	5	
Kaiser, Joseph	14, June 1898	12, June	17- 3m	5	
Kaiser, Klara Maria Agnes	24, July 1896	22, July	74- 3m	5	Schneider
Kaiser, Margaret	12, Nov. 1887		86	1	
Kaiser, Mathias	9, Apr. 1891		60	4	
Kaiser, Otto	6, Mar. 1894		36	5	
Kaiser, W.	12, Mar. 1896	12, Mar.	82- 2m	5	
Kaiser, W. (Mrs)	14, Jan. 1896	13, Jan.	36	5	
Kaiser, William	23, Sept 1893		1m	5	
Kalaher, Timothy	27, Apr. 1895		79	5	
Kallenberg, J.W.	7, Aug. 1888		51	1	
Kallendorf, Clem. D.	26, Nov. 1888		24	1	
Kallendorf, Friedrich Wilhelm	12, Nov. 1896	11, Nov.	73- 1m	5	
Kallmeyer, Edna Albertine	7, July 1896	6, July		4	
Kallmeyer, John W.	23, Feb. 1901			8	
Kallmeyer, Wilhelm B.	25, Dec. 1899	24, Dec.	50- 5m	5	
Kalm, Joseph	30, Sept 1887		14	1	
Kalnig, Mary	29, Mar. 1892		9m	5	
Kaltenbrink, Minnie	29, Apr. 1891		36	4	
Kaltwasser, Margaretha	7, Feb. 1894		81	5	
Kalvelage, Theresa	3, Jan. 1896	1, Jan.	51	5	Dickmann
Kameron, Rachel	30, Mar. 1893		84	5	
Kameth, Benjamin	11, June 1895		34	5	
Kamf, Edward	7, Aug. 1900		16	8	
Kamm, Joseph	11, Sept 1888		65	1	
Kammann, Wilhelmina	1, Aug. 1887		86	1	
Kammar, Rosa	20, Mar. 1891		28	4	
Kamme, Johan G.	20, Oct. 1899	19, Oct.	24	8	
Kammer, Achoda	16, Mar. 1888		9w	1	
Kammer, Ida	19, June 1901		21	8	
Kammer, Theresa	7, July 1888		38	4	
Kammerer, Stephen H.	30, Mar. 1899	28, Mar.	40	5	
Kammeron, Martha	18, Jan. 1892		2	5	
Kammeron, Martha L.	13, June 1894		3m	5	
Kammeyer, William	16, Mar. 1893		15m	5	
Kamp, Maria	26, Sept 1899	25, Sept	80	5	Mescher
Kampe, Gasena M.	2, Apr. 1901			8	
Kampe, George	8, Apr. 1891		40	4	
Kampel, Karolina	2, July 1898	1, July	64-10m	5	Bailer
Kampel, Wilhelm Leopold Joseph	28, Dec. 1897	27, Dec.	75	4	
Kamper, Walter	4, Aug. 1891		8	4	
Kampfmueller, Charles	30, Mar. 1894		58	5	
Kamphues, Joseph	22, Apr. 1897	21, Apr.	34-10m	5	
Kamping, Josephine	14, Feb. 1889		38	1	
Kamuf, Agnes	11, Apr. 1895		2	5	
Kane, Daniel	30, Apr. 1895		58	5	
Kane, Ellen	10, Jan. 1888		54	4	
Kane, Mary	10, Apr. 1901		2	8	
Kane, William	8, Apr. 1901		76	8	
Kaney, Wilhelmina	15, Feb. 1898	14, Feb.	29	5	Scheidt
Kanis, John	11, Feb. 1891		70	4	

Name	Notice Date	Death Date	Age	Page	Maiden Name
Kanisy, Henry	5, Mar. 1891		26	4	
Kaniznik, Elisabeth	25, Aug. 1900		67	5	
Kanne, Emma	7, July 1888		16m	4	
Kanrisch, Ella	7, Jan. 1901		4	5	
Kansal, Alfred	20, June 1901		1	8	
Kanther, Anna	27, July 1888		1d	1	
Kantz, Elisabeth	1, June 1898	30, May	31- 1m	5	Uelzhöffer
Kapauf, Sabina	23, Jan. 1899	21, Jan.	87	5	Benter
Kaper, Mary	7, Jan. 1893		55	5	
Kaperitz, Verda	8, Aug. 1901		2	8	
Kaplan, Johanna	12, Jan. 1889		55	1	
Kapp, Lulu	6, Feb. 1899	5, Feb.	23- 7m	4	Kichler
Kappel, Wilhelm	26, July 1896		20- 6m	5	
Kappen, Christine	9, Aug. 1892		73	5	
Kappen, Heinrich	23, May 1898	22, May	55- 9m	5	
Kappen, Lena	22, Jan. 1898	21, Jan.	1- 8m	5	
Kappenhaeffer, William G.	3, Feb. 1891		14	4	
Kappner, Katie	16, May 1901		24	5	
Karcher, George W.	23, Nov. 1897	21, Nov.	60	4	
Kareth, Henry	26, Aug. 1891		40	4	
Kareth, John Fred.	29, Mar. 1888			1	
Kareth, Louisa	6, Apr. 1895		21	5	
Kareth, Michael	31, July 1896	30, July	76- 1m	5	
Karette, Leonhard	27, June 1891		25	1	
Karg, John	3, June 1891		54	4	
Karge, Paul	29, Dec. 1891		38	4	
Karger, Albert	20, Dec. 1893		25	5	
Karhoff, Frank	3, Aug. 1887		28	1	
Karhoff, John	16, Oct. 1900		4	8	
Karl, Hans	16, June 1898	15, June	45	5	
Karney, C.	10, Mar. 1888		1d	1	
Karney, John	30, Nov. 1887		64	4	
Karrisch, Emma	9, Dec. 1893		21	5	
Karrman, Hilda G.	12, May 1891		25	1	
Karrmann, Louis	5, Feb. 1896	3, Feb.		5	
Karst, August	8, June 1895		52	5	
Karst, Minnie	2, Aug. 1893		5m	5	
Karte, Henry A.	23, Apr. 1891		31	4	
Karter, George H.	30, Sept 1893		84	5	
Kasekamp, H.H.	17, Apr. 1890		1	1	
Kasemeyer, Ferd.	22, Feb. 1895		41	5	
Kaser, Rose	12, Aug. 1901		10m	8	
Kasgoerde, Alexander	28, Nov. 1899	27, Nov.	28-11m	8	
Kasheimer, Herman	21, Sept 1900		5	5	
Kaspar, Konrad	19, Oct. 1889		5	1	
Kasper, Catharine	13, Feb. 1894		38	5	
Kasselmann, Anton	8, Feb. 1892		56	4	
Kasselmann, Josephine	8, Apr. 1901			8	
Kasselmann, Mary A.	7, Dec. 1893		21	5	
Kassimir, Augusta	23, Apr. 1890		1	4	
Kastelhun, David	14, Aug. 1899	13, Aug.	84- 5m	4	
Kasten, Friedrich	8, Aug. 1896	8, Aug.	59	5	
Kastenberger, Berney C.	27, Apr. 1898	20, Apr.	27- 7m	5	
Kaster, Katie	19, Sept 1888		47	2	
Kasting, Emma C.	16, Oct. 1890		2m	1	
Kastings, Dorothea	19, June 1891		67	1	
Katenbrink, Katharina Marie	4, Jan. 1899	3, Jan.	79	5	Pahlmann
Katenbrink, Margaretha	24, June 1896	23, June	71	5	
Kater, J.H.	9, Nov. 1894		72	4	
Kathmann, A.	21, Nov. 1894			5	
Kathmann, Anna	23, July 1896	22, July	12-10m	5	
Kathmann, August	7, Oct. 1893		60	5	
Kathmann, Christian	22, Jan. 1890	19, Jan.	40	4	
Kathmann, Lizzie	11, Jan. 1888		6	4	
Katker, Wilhelm	26, Mar. 1900	25, Mar.	47- 6m	8	
Kattelmann, Henry	1, Apr. 1889		76	1	
Kattenbach, Theodore	4, Nov. 1891		55	1	
Kattenhorn, Johan H.	11, Dec. 1893		75	5	
Kattmann, Maria	20, Nov. 1899	19, Nov.	51- 4m	5	Sprung
Kattus, Frank	28, Sept 1896	27, Sept	27- 9m	5	
Kattus, Johanna T.	25, Jan. 1894		8m	5	

Name ****	Notice Date ****** ****	Death Date ***** ****	Age ***	Page ****	Maiden Name ****** ****
Kattus, Katharina	29, Aug. 1899	27, Aug.	62-10m	4	Steidle
Kattus, Mary	19, Sept 1888		2	2	
Katz, Harvey	28, Nov. 1891		4	1	
Katz, Joseph	17, Dec. 1891		5d	4	
Katz, Moritz	26, Jan. 1901		12d	8	
Katz, Salomon	20, Apr. 1895		74	5	
Katzenstein, Hannah	18, May 1900	17, May		5	
Kauersmann, Dina	5, Apr. 1892		59	4	
Kauffmann, Anna Barbara	9, June 1897	7, June	84- 6m	5	Schmidt
Kauffmann, Franz	30, Mar. 1896	29, Mar.	57	5	
Kaufmann, Franz Wilhelm	1, Mar. 1900	28, Feb.	84	5	
Kaufmann, Jakob	13, Jan. 1897	12, Jan.	72	5	
Kaufmann, Jakob	25, Apr. 1899	24, Apr.	80	4	
Kaufmann, Lizzie	2, Mar. 1889		3	1	
Kaufmann, Mary	31, Dec. 1892		24	5	
Kaufmann, Solomon	12, July 1895		84	5	
Kauper, Clara	3, Feb. 1894		81	5	
Kauper, Elise	29, Jan. 1890		45	1	
Kauther, Anna	23, Mar. 1895		32	5	
Kauther, Christina	20, Sept 1898	18, Sept	75- 4m	5	
Kauther, Jacob	29, Dec. 1891		32	4	
Kauther, Louisa	22, Sept 1888		20	1	
Kautler, George	3, Jan. 1893		27	5	
Kautz, Margaret S.	2, May 1894		41	5	
Kautz, Philip	24, June 1901		41	8	
Kautz, Wilhelmina	24, Jan. 1899	23, Jan.	76	4	Brodbeck
Kautzmann, Mary	7, Mar. 1901		35	8	
Kaux, R.	3, Jan. 1888		43	1	
Kayer, Emma Anna	8, Aug. 1892		29- 2m- 1d	5	Tecklenburg
Kaylor, Daniel	30, Jan. 1891		39	4	
Kaß, Herman	5, Aug. 1889		75	1	
Kaßmann, Luella	26, May 1892		3m	5	
Keadin, Peter J.	5, June 1895		18	5	
Keal, Anna	17, Oct. 1891		5	4	
Kealing, Elsie	8, July 1890		1	4	
Keans, Edward	28, Nov. 1900		22	8	
Kearney, Andrew	24, Aug. 1887		27	1	
Kearney, Ed.	28, Jan. 1892			5	
Kearney, Geneva	15, Aug. 1900		20	5	
Kearns, Annie	6, Dec. 1900		57	8	
Kearsey, M.	14, July 1900		26	8	
Keating, Annie	5, June 1888		64	4	
Keating, Cornelius	10, July 1888		8m	1	
Keating, George	1, Aug. 1888		10m	2	
Keating, Kate	28, July 1887		4m	1	
Keating, Mamie	1, Aug. 1891		18	4	
Keber, John W.	3, May 1893		56	5	
Keber, Susanna	12, Dec. 1896	11, Dec.	60- 6m	5	Born
Kebler, C.	25, Nov. 1887		33	1	
Kechler, Lucinda	14, Feb. 1901		52	8	
Keck, Albert	8, Dec. 1887		27	1	
Keck, Alexander	13, Apr. 1895		32	4	
Keck, Amelia	19, Mar. 1901		38	8	
Keck, Clifford	4, Jan. 1901		1	5	
Keck, Conrad	30, Dec. 1892		68	5	
Keck, Edward	9, Jan. 1901		30	5	
Keck, Frederick	18, Jan. 1894		4m	5	
Keck, Hermina	21, Aug. 1888		22w	1	
Keck, Lee	16, July 1901		58	8	
Keck, Mary	23, Dec. 1891		70	4	
Keck, Rosetta	1, 2, Apr. 1894	31, Mar.		5	
Keefe, Jenny	17, June 1888		28	1	
Keefe, W.	3, Aug. 1887		49	1	
Keegan, Anna	19, July 1901		56	8	
Keegan, Matthew J.	9, Oct. 1900		24	8	
Keegan, Michael	3, Aug. 1901		2	8	
Keegan, William H.	26, Apr. 1895		21	5	
Keeher, John	28, June 1893		33	5	
Keenan, Thomas F.	8, Oct. 1891		28	4	
Keepe, A.	23, Feb. 1889		56	1	
Keerkeritz, Mary	25, Dec. 1891		64	2	

Name	Notice Date	Death Date	Age	Page	Maiden Name
****	****** ****	***** ****	***	****	****** ****
Keesham, John P. (Dr.)	21, Mar. 1895		35	5	
Keeshan, Kate	10, Jan. 1888		55	4	
Keheal, Owen	30, Sept 1901		83	8	
Kehkohr, Ludwig	28, Aug. 1889		36	1	
Kehling, Helen	7, Dec. 1893		2	5	
Kehling, Wilhelm	1, Nov. 1892		2	5	
Kehoe, Eliza	5, Dec. 1900		47	8	
Kehoe, John	9, Oct. 1900		22	8	
Kehoe, William	22, May 1888		55	1	
Kehrer, George	7, Oct. 1899	4, Oct.	24	8	
Keiber, Louis	8, June 1895		42	5	
Keible, Annie	15, Aug. 1892		71	5	
Keidel, Lena	7, Feb. 1901		37	8	
Keidel, M.E.	29, July 1887		7w	1	
Keifer, Georg	6, Oct. 1899	5, Oct.	36- - 6d	5	
Keifer, John	6, Aug. 1901		44	8	
Keifer, Rosa	26, Mar. 1901		44	8	
Keil, Johan	6, Oct. 1899	4, Oct.	78- 9m	5	
Keil, Nicolaus	15, June 1889		16	1	
Keil, Peter	14, Jan. 1891		40	4	
Keil, Sophie	9, Mar. 1895		69	5	
Keim, Albert W.	25, June 1895		9m	5	
Keim, Anna Christine	25, July 1899	24, July	60-10m- 8d	5	Beerens
Keinath, Celia	31, Aug. 1901		2	8	
Keiring, Avena	21, July 1890		9m	1	
Kelch, William E.	31, Dec. 1888		2m	1	
Kelche, Ida	5, Dec. 1890		22	4	
Kelgenberg, Sophia	23, Aug. 1887		18	1	
Kelleher, Abbie	6, Jan. 1892		62	5	
Kellemann, Julia	6, Sept 1901		62	8	
Keller, Annie M.	26, Feb. 1894		53	5	
Keller, Barbara	13, May 1889		52	1	
Keller, Benjamin B.	27, July 1892		31	5	
Keller, Charles	7, Aug. 1895	5, Aug.	51	5	
Keller, Charles	8, Aug. 1895	7, Aug.	34	5	
Keller, Edward	31, Oct. 1900		50	8	
Keller, Edward W.	14, Mar. 1891		6	4	
Keller, Eliza	22, Jan. 1898	20, Jan.	46- 1m	5	
Keller, Friedricke	27, Dec. 1895	26, Dec.	65- 8m	5	
Keller, Jak.	4, Sept 1888		20	2	
Keller, John	8, Apr. 1901		1	8	
Keller, Joseph	19, June 1889		19m	1	
Keller, Joseph	11, Feb. 1893		17	5	
Keller, Leopold	1, June 1899	31, May	36	4	
Keller, Margaretha	8, Feb. 1896	7, Feb.	60	5	
Keller, Margaretha	22, May 1899	20, May	76- 5m	4	Pfeiffer
Keller, Maria	4, Jan. 1898	2, Jan.		5	
Keller, Martha	22, Feb. 1892	21, Feb.	28- 5m	5	
Keller, Mary H.	3, Dec. 1891		1m	4	
Keller, Raimond	28, Sept 1896	26, Sept	33- 5m	5	
Keller, Rosalia	12, Feb. 1901		78	8	
Keller, Tillie	25, June 1895		19m	5	
Kellermann, Andrew	12, May 1891		44	1	
Kellermann, Grover H.	28, Mar. 1893		3m	5	
Kellermann, Lena	27, Nov. 1894		18	5	
Kelley, Thomas	9, Aug. 1900		8m	8	
Kelley, William	2, Aug. 1901		3m	8	
Kelly, Bridget	11, July 1888		74	1	
Kelly, Bridget	7, Sept 1901		58	8	
Kelly, Catharine	20, Mar. 1901		72	1	
Kelly, Charles	25, Jan. 1901		1	8	
Kelly, Edward	11, Dec. 1891		20	4	
Kelly, Edward	16, Feb. 1901		65	8	
Kelly, Ellen	19, Oct. 1887		50	1	
Kelly, Margaret	19, Nov. 1900		66	8	
Kelly, Margaret	7, Mar. 1901		3d	8	
Kelly, Mary	18, Sept 1900		28	5	
Kelly, Mary	27, May 1901		65	8	
Kelly, Mathilda	23, Sept 1887		55	2	
Kelly, Michael	5, Mar. 1901		46	5	
Kelly, Michael J.	13, Dec. 1900		65	8	

Name ****	Notice Date ****** ****	Death Date ***** ****	Age ***	Page ****	Maiden Name ****** ****
Kelly, Owen	5, Apr. 1901		66	8	
Kelly, Pat	6, July 1901		60	8	
Kelly, Thomas	14, July 1900		60	8	
Kelson, Emma	4, Aug. 1900		9m	8	
Kelsor, James	11, Jan. 1892		46	4	
Kelum, Louisa	12, Feb. 1891		101	4	
Kemme, Bernardina	25, Apr. 1897	23, Apr.	50	5	
Kemme, Charles	12, June 1889		1	1	
Kemme, Francisca	12, Sept 1901		73	5	
Kemme, Heinrich	30, Mar. 1897	29, Mar.	71- 3m	5	
Kemme, Theodor	20, Apr. 1897	19, Apr.	66- 9m	5	
Kemmel, Anna	8, June 1894		33	5	
Kemmerer, Anna Maria	21, June 1899	20, June	67- 1m	4	Gerlach
Kemmerer, Salome A.	14, Feb. 1895		8m	5	
Kemmeser, Frank	10, Oct. 1901		44	8	
Kemp, Maria	9, July 1887		63	1	
Kempe, Elizabeth	20, Apr. 1899	18, Apr.	48- 6m	4	Brink
Kemper, Elisabeth	9, Apr. 1891		75	4	
Kemper, Flora S.H.	11, Dec. 1893		8m	5	
Kemper, Fred.	3, Jan. 1890		9	1	
Kemper, Georg	7, Aug. 1895	6, Aug.		5	
Kemper, Hugh F.	5, Aug. 1887		63	1	
Kemper, John	7, Mar. 1901		9	8	
Kemper, Margaret	12, Jan. 1893		20	5	
Kemper, William	30, Dec. 1893		63	5	
Kempf, Eva	13, Aug. 1895	11, Aug.	58-7m	5	Frank
Kempfer, Elisabeth	11, Mar. 1898	9, Mar.	38- 5m	5	Meimann
Kemphaus, Maria	16, May 1900	15, May	24-10m	5	
Kempker, Joseph	31, Jan. 1901		76	8	
Kemsedy, B.	17, June 1888		40	1	
Kendall, Thomas H.	18, Feb. 1901		83	8	
Kendle, George W.	11, May 1901		63	8	
Kendle, Phoebe	7, May 1901		46	1	
Kendrick, Eliza J.	10, Dec. 1900		79	8	
Kendrick, John L.	18, May 1901		57	1	
Kenkel, Casper Heinrich	8, Sept 1897	5, Sept	67- 5m	5	
Kenkel, Frederick	22, May 1894		17	5	
Kennach, Barbara	25, May 1894		64	5	
Kennedy, Annie	31, July 1900		70	5	
Kennedy, Catharine	18, May 1901		68	1	
Kennedy, Daniel	17, May 1901		13	8	
Kennedy, James	13, June 1901		43	8	
Kennedy, Mary	5, July 1901		62	8	
Kennedy, Michael	20, Mar. 1901		38	1	
Kennedy, Phillip	30, Apr. 1901		18	8	
Kennedy, Thomas	11, Aug. 1888		7m	1	
Kennedy, Walter	1, Sept 1887		17m	1	
Kennedy, William	27, July 1887		8	1	
Kenner, Katharine	14, Oct. 1901		50	5	
Kenney, Bridget	24, Jan. 1901		74	8	
Kenney, Lizzie	27, Apr. 1895		26	5	
Kenning, Clemens	30, Dec. 1895	29, Dec.	49-11m	5	
Kenning, Maria	6, Aug. 1898	4, Aug.	48	4	
Kenniston, Wilson	20, July 1901		24	8	
Kennon, Francis	29, June 1893		3m	5	
Kenny, Gertie	8, Dec. 1891		3w	4	
Kentner, C.	28, Jan. 1889		23	1	
Kenz, Louisa	22, Nov. 1887		30	1	
Keoghen, Ed.	3, Apr. 1888		30	4	
Keppen, Helen	17, Aug. 1893		1	5	
Keppler, Edward	1, May 1901		27	8	
Keppler, Louis	21, July 1891		63	4	
Keppler, Mary	18, Sept 1900		70	5	
Kerber, Nicholas	24, July 1895		44	5	
Kerl, William	10, Apr. 1889		7	1	
Kerler, William	15, Sept 1888	14, Sept		* 1	
Kerley, Jacob	18, Dec. 1900		71	8	
Kermeter, George	24, May 1894		28	5	
Kern, Anna L.	6, July 1893		1	5	
Kern, Barbara	23, Dec. 1891		43	4	
Kern, Bertha	2, July 1892		11m	5	

Name ****	Notice Date ****** ****	Death Date ***** ****	Age ***	Page ****	Maiden Name ****** ****
Kern, Charles	21, Sept 1901		7	8	
Kern, Christian	31, Dec. 1891		66	1	
Kern, Elizabeth	10, July 1889		69	1	
Kern, Lena	4, Apr. 1888		10m	1	
Kern, Leonard A.	6, Jan. 1892		2m	5	
Kern, Mary A.	16, July 1895		5m	5	
Kern, Willaim	3, Nov. 1892		64	5	
Kernan, Albert F.	7, July 1891		50	1	
Kernen, Christian	6, May 1896	4, May	65- 3m	5	
Kerns, Florentine	8, June 1901		13	8	
Kerr, Eliza	3, Sept 1890		72	1	
Kerrick, James	27, July 1889		76	1	
Kerser, Laura	16, Apr. 1901		18	8	
Kersker, Henry	8, Jan. 1890		57	1	
Kersteins, G.T.	1, 2, Aug. 1895	31, July	63-10m	5	
Kerstiens, Anna Maria	18, Feb. 1897	16, Feb.	70	5	Schneiders
Kersting, Wilhelm	27, Nov. 1899	24, Nov.	30- 7m	5	
Kerwick, Edith	7, Jan. 1901		25	5	
Kesel, Anna	21, July 1890		23	1	
Kesler, Constantin	29, Jan. 1897	28, Jan.	57- 1m	5	
Kessel, Christian	27, Nov. 1894		66	5	
Kessel, G.N.	18, July 1890		2	1	
Kessel, Henry	22, Dec. 1887		40	4	
Kessel, Katie	18, July 1890		6	1	
Kessens, Anna	27, Aug. 1901		25	1	
Kessing, Franz	23, Dec. 1898	22, Dec.	73	5	
Kessler, John	5, Aug. 1901		56	8	
Kessler, Maria	16, Oct. 1901		47	1	
Kessler, Mary	28, Nov. 1893		66	5	
Kester, J.	8, June 1889		4m	1	
Kestermann, John	5, July 1890		5	1	
Keterlinus, William	8, May 1889		16	1	
Ketscher, Harry	9, Nov. 1897	7, Nov.	18- 4m	5	
Ketser, Robert	21, Aug. 1887		8m	5	
Kettelmann, Frank	20, July 1887		1d	1	
Kettenacker, Ettie	12, Sept 1900			5	
Ketterling, Heinrich	3, May 1894	2, May	32	5	
Kettler, Carl	26, Apr. 1893		62	5	
Kettler, Edward H.	11, Dec. 1893		57	5	
Kettman, Cecilia	3, Oct. 1888		17m	1	
Kettmann, Anna Maria	30, Mar. 1898	29, Mar.	81	5	Geers
Kettner, Juliana	20, Oct. 1898	18, Oct.	68- - 8d	5	Schoenauer
Keuck, Margaretha	5, Jan. 1892		69	5	
Keutz, Bernard H.	13, Nov. 1899	12, Nov.	72- 7m	5	
Keyer, Emma Anna	9, Aug. 1892		29	5	
Keyes, Edward A.	5, Apr. 1901		2d	8	
Keyler, Anna P.	27, Mar. 1891		37	4	
Keys, Belle E.	13, Nov. 1900		22	8	
Keßheimer, Franziska	17, Aug. 1899	16, Aug.	31	4	Obert
Keßler, Anna	11, Sept 1900		58	5	
Keßler, Anna M.	26, July 1887		8m	1	
Keßler, Friedrich	7, July 1898	6, July	41	5	
Keßling, Joseph A.	9, Dec. 1892		24	5	
Keßner, Peter	23, Apr. 1898	22, Apr.	49- 7m	4	
Kibby, Lillie T.	10, Mar. 1888		13- 6m	1	
Kichler, Ella	28, Apr. 1890		69	1	
Kick, Johanna	16, July 1891		1d	4	
Kickbusch, Mary	2, Oct. 1894		4	5	
Kidd, Thomas	31, July 1901		35	8	
Kidwell, James	19, Mar. 1901		53	8	
Kieborth, Karolina	9, Nov. 1889		43- 3m	1	
Kiechler, Anna Maria	19, Jan. 1893		84	5	
Kiechler, Emmet C.	28, Dec. 1900		36	8	
Kiechler, Margaretha	28, Dec. 1899	26, Dec.	57- 4m	5	
Kieckbusch, Martha	18, Dec. 1891		3m	2	
Kieckousch, Catharina	1, Apr. 1890		52	1	
Kief, Lauretta	12, July 1901		2	8	
Kiefer, A.	7, Mar. 1889			1	
Kiefer, Andreas	24, Sept 1888		48	1	
Kiefer, Frank X.	4, Oct. 1894		69	5	
Kiefer, Franz	9, Dec. 1891	8, Dec.	2- 1m-15d	1	

Name	Notice Date	Death Date	Age	Page	Maiden Name
****	****** ****	***** ****	***	****	****** ****
Kiefer, Joseph	22, Sept 1898	21, Sept	18- 8m	4	
Kiefer, Katharina	17, Jan. 1898	15, Jan.		5	Druck
Kiefer, Peter	23, Oct. 1897	21, Oct.	71	4	
Kiefer, Peter	28, Nov. 1898	25, Nov.	41- 3m	5	
Kiefer, William C.	19, Dec. 1890		20	1	
Kiefert, August	27, Oct. 1887		53	1	
Kiefler, Clara	9, Dec. 1892		26	5	
Kiehborth, Harlam	19, July 1901		10m	8	
Kiehe, Joseph	18, Dec. 1900		10	8	
Kiehfuß, Francis	11, Dec. 1900		38	8	
Kiehm, Harry	7, Feb. 1889		6	1	
Kiel, Anna	11, Aug. 1887		2w	1	
Kiel, Walter H.W.	6, Dec. 1892		3	5	
Kielhold, Catharine	20, Oct. 1900		71	8	
Kiene, Ernest	18, Sept 1900		8	5	
Kiene, John	28, May 1894	26, May	39	5	
Kiensley, Annie	1, Oct. 1900		52	5	
Kienzle, Jacob	28, Jan. 1901		77	8	
Kienzle, Nettie	3, May 1888		4	1	
Kierstead, Hesekiah	6, Jan. 1892		82	5	
Kiersted, Leonora	20, June 1891		71	1	
Kiese, Louis	12, May 1891		24	1	
Kiesel, Allie May	10, Apr. 1888		2	4	
Kiesel, Friederika	15, Apr. 1896	13, Apr.	59-11m	5	Fehrenbach
Kiesel, Sophia	10, Aug. 1900		42	8	
Kieseler, Clara	17, Oct. 1899	16, Oct.		8	
Kiesewetter, Emma K.	20, July 1893		19	5	
Kiesewetter, Franz	9, May 1900	8, May		5	
Kiffner, Frederick	11, Jan. 1890		40	1	
Kihn, Amanda	31, Jan. 1901		17	8	
Kihn, Valentin	14, Aug. 1900		77	5	
Kilb, Katharine	11, Nov. 1894		65	5	
Kilbert, Ethel	5, Aug. 1901		5m	8	
Kilday, John	28, Nov. 1900		37	8	
Kildea, Albert	17, July 1895		18m	5	
Kilgarroff, James	21, Feb. 1901		35	8	
Kilgenstein, Maria	19, Nov. 1895	18, Nov.	39- 1m	5	Berwanger
Kilgoyne, Mary	29, June 1901		75	8	
Kilgus, Robert	27, Mar. 1897	25, Mar.	35- -22d	5	
Kille, Anna Maria	9, Jan. 1894		63-11m	5	Gimpel
Kille, Anton	28, Dec. 1887	27, Dec.	21- 5m	4	
Killgallon, Katharine	2, May 1901		77	8	
Killion, J.G.	21, Sept 1895	20, Sept	48	5	
Killschaff, Mary	5, Apr. 1892		39	4	
Kimball, William	8, Mar. 1901		57	8	
Kimble, Samuel	22, July 1901		35	8	
Kimmich, Ch.	13, Aug. 1888		1d	1	
Kimmich, Jacob	8, Sept 1891		6m	4	
Kimmich, Rosina	3, Aug. 1897	2, Aug.	66	5	Weis
Kimmich, Rosina	25, July 1898	24, July	84- 6m	4	Schmidt
Kimmich, T.	31, July 1901		84	8	
Kindelberger, William	24, Sept 1894		4	5	
Kinderman, William	7, Jan. 1901		11d	5	
Kindermann, Mary	18, Oct. 1893		30	5	
Kindt, F.	29, Aug. 1895	28, Aug.	18- 4m	5	
Kindt, Maria	24, Mar. 1896	23, Mar.	30	5	Lamping
King,	2, Feb. 1901		2m	8	
King, Adam	21, May 1901		64	8	
King, Belle	25, Sept 1900		60	5	
King, Benjamin	31, July 1901		78	8	
King, Catharine	10, Nov. 1900		24	8	
King, John H.	28, Feb. 1901		57	8	
King, Julia	20, Nov. 1895	18, Nov.	3	5	
King, Julius	15, Dec. 1900		30	8	
King, Myrtle R.	24, May 1895		2	5	
King, Patrick	26, Dec. 1900		74	8	
King, William A.	8, Nov. 1900		51	8	
Kinker, Herman A.	13, June 1891		28	4	
Kinker, Lillie	2, Mar. 1888		14	1	
Kinker, Louise	9, Dec. 1891		31	2	
Kinker, Mary	20, June 1895		59	5	

Name	Notice Date	Death Date	Age	Page	Maiden Name
****	****** ****	***** ****	***	****	****** ****
Kinker, Willie	7, May 1891		4	4	
Kinkhorst, Mary	27, Apr. 1901		92	8	
Kinnealy, Edward	6, June 1901		38	8	
Kinney, Mary	11, July 1887		46	1	
Kinney, Richard	4, Aug. 1888		46	4	
Kinscherff, Eva K.	4, Jan. 1893		49	5	
Kinscherff, Lorenz	26, Mar. 1892		22	1	
Kinsey, Louis P.	28, Feb. 1901			8	
Kinsherff, Frank	24, Feb. 1888		49	4	
Kinsilla, Katharine	5, Apr. 1895		42	5	
Kinsley, Mary	27, Apr. 1895		75	5	
Kinz, Mary K.	2, Apr. 1895		4m	5	
Kinz, Rose	4, Dec. 1891		45	4	
Kioken, Caroline	29, Sept 1891		37-10m	4	
Kipgen, William	29, May 1901		3d	8	
Kipp, August	11, June 1898	10, June	61- 1m	5	
Kipp, Elisa	31, Dec. 1891		49	1	
Kipp, Henry	20, Apr. 1897	19, Apr.	72- 3m	5	
Kipp, Johan	9, Jan. 1899	7, Jan.	79	5	
Kipp, Maggie	19, Mar. 1901		54	8	
Kipp, Martha	2, July 1897	1, July	4m-11d	5	
Kipp, Mary	15, Aug. 1891		1d	4	
Kipp, Wilhelm	10, Dec. 1898	8, Dec.	67- 9m	5	
Kippenbrock, Bernardina	16, May 1892		60	5	
Kirbert, Friedrich	26, July 1897	24, July	55	5	
Kirby, Ella	2, Aug. 1890		2m	1	
Kirch,	20, Apr. 1888		1d	4	
Kircher, Alwina	29, Aug. 1892		1	5	
Kircher, Charles	8, Apr. 1901		12	8	
Kircher, Karl	14, June 1897	12, June	72	5	
Kircher, Lilly	30, July 1892		3m	5	
Kirchheimer, August	30, Sept 1895	29, Sept	56	5	
Kirchhof, Elisabeth	4, Aug. 1897	2, Aug.	54- - 5d	5	
Kirchler, Ella	11, May 1892		8m	5	
Kirchner, Albert	21, Jan. 1894		19	5	
Kirchner, August	15, Oct. 1898	13, Oct.	42- 8m	4	
Kirchner, Frank	30, May 1899	28, May	68	4	
Kirchner, John	25, Mar. 1891		72	4	
Kirchner, Margaret	21, Jan. 1888		76	4	
Kirk, Virginia	23, Aug. 1901		2	8	
Kirker, John	28, Sept 1888		7w	2	
Kirkpatrick, Nellie	10, May 1901		49	8	
Kirman, Ruth J.	30, Nov. 1892		86	5	
Kirschner, Clara	16, Sept 1887		15m	1	
Kirstein, Henry E.	26, July 1895		24d	5	
Kirton, William	28, Mar. 1892		21d	5	
Kirwan, Caroline	8, Sept 1887		62	1	
Kisker, Annie	5, Apr. 1892		4	4	
Kisker, Charles H.	28, Jan. 1889		30	1	
Kisker, Henrietta	4, Jan. 1893		38	5	
Kisker, John	30, Jan. 1890		61	1	
Kismeier, Elsie	27, July 1893		10m	5	
Kissel, Dora	8, Mar. 1894		27	5	
Kissel, Elise	11, Feb. 1892		14d	4	
Kissel, John	25, July 1900			5	
Kissel, Lorenz	22, Jan. 1897	21, Jan.	50- 4m	5	
Kissinger, Carrie	1, June 1892		22	5	
Kist, Joseph	23, Nov. 1889		73	1	
Kist, Julia	24, Feb. 1890		16m	1	
Kist, Reinhardt	12, July 1895		60	5	
Kistenberger, George	19, Nov. 1896	18, Nov.	50	5	
Kistenmacher, Martha	5, Dec. 1893		18m	5	
Kister, Elizabeth	7, Mar. 1898	6, Mar.	68	5	Zier
Kistner, Anna	15, Feb. 1889		12d	1	
Kistner, Antoinette	25, Feb. 1893		8m	5	
Kistner, Clara	21, Mar. 1901		3	8	
Kistner, Daniel	5, Jan. 1892		36	5	
Kistner, Frederick	24, Nov. 1900		51	8	
Kistner, Jacob	10, Mar. 1891		27	4	
Kistner, Josephine	1, Aug. 1901		17	8	
Kistner, Lawrence	7, May 1891		26d	4	

Name ****	Notice Date ****** ****	Death Date ***** ****	Age ***	Page ****	Maiden Name ****** ****
Kistner, Lorenz	12, Mar. 1896	10, Mar.	1- 6m	5	
Kistner, Louisa	10, Jan. 1896	9, Jan.	18	5	
Kistner, Margaret	9, Jan. 1901		19	5	
Kistner, Rufina Agnes	29, Dec. 1891		66	4	
Kistowska, Mary	30, Jan. 1891		2	4	
Kitt, Ed.	29, Aug. 1900		17	5	
Kittel, Herman	3, June 1896	1, June	53- 8m	5	
Kittinger, Charles	3, Jan. 1888		8m	1	
Kizer, Martha	7, Feb. 1891		19	4	
Kißling, Julius	3, Apr. 1897	2, Apr.	56- -13d	5	
Klaiber, John A.	5, July 1887		8w	1	
Klaker, Joseph	16, Mar. 1895		59	5	
Klanke, Adeline	4, July 1901		44	8	
Klanke, Minnie	13, Oct. 1898	10, Oct.	24- 1m	5	
Klanke, Sophia	29, Oct. 1896	28, Oct.	62	5	
Klaphacke, Katharina	6, Aug. 1895	5, Aug.	69	5	
Klaphake, Catharine	21, May 1901			8	
Klapper, Wilhelm	18, Jan. 1896	16, Jan.	71	5	
Klas, Auguste	23, Apr. 1898	22, Apr.	43	4	
Klas, Gustav	12, Apr. 1898	11, Apr.	44	5	
Klasmann, Emma	26, Apr. 1893		33	5	
Klasmeier, Ed.	27, May 1889		20	1	
Klasmeier, Laura M.	27, June 1895		22	5	
Klasmeyer, Carrie	23, Apr. 1889		28	1	
Klassing, William	20, July 1901		14d	8	
Klaus, Adolph	13, Mar. 1894		7	5	
Klaus, Anna M.	7, July 1891		11m	1	
Klaus, J.H. Clemens	2, May 1899	1, May	60- 1m	5	
Klaus, John	23, Aug. 1901		47	8	
Klaus, Katharine	4, Feb. 1901		77	8	
Klausing, Joseph C.	6, July 1900	5, July	43-10m	8	
Klausing, Karl	3, Sept 1898	1, Sept	69-10m	4	
Klausing, Philomena	24, May 1901		46	8	
Klausmeyer, David C.	26, May 1896	23, May	58	5	
Klausmeyer, Wilhelm	28, Nov. 1893		76	5	
Klawest, Elizabeth	18, 19, July 1899	17, July	49- 7m-16d	5	Zurborg
Klawitter, Hans	23, Oct. 1899	22, Oct.	41	5	
Klawitter, John	19, Oct. 1887		2m	1	
Klawitter, L.H.	14, July 1897	13, July		5	
Klayer, Catharine	5, June 1895		72	5	
Klayer, Charles C.	4, Mar. 1891		9w	4	
Klayer, George	20, June 1891		1	1	
Klayer, Stella E.	28, Apr. 1888		5w	1	
Klayere, Anna L.	10, Oct. 1900		30	8	
Klaßmeier, L.A.	16, Aug. 1887			1	
Kleb, Jacobina	31, Dec. 1896	29, Dec.	86- 8m	5	
Klebecker, Kennon	13, June 1901		2m	8	
Klebecker, Mary	3, Feb. 1888		25	4	
Kleedoerfer, Nicholas	14, Sept 1887		36	1	
Kleeme, Annie B.	11, Dec. 1893		33	5	
Kleemeier, Albert	24, Oct. 1894		7m	5	
Kleemeier, H.	21, Sept 1895	20, Sept	78- 3m	5	
Kleemeier, Walter	22, Dec. 1891		1	4	
Klei, Conrad	10, Mar. 1895		64	5	
Klei, Valentin	19, Sept 1894		31	5	
Kleibecker, George	2, May 1895		28	5	
Kleibecker, Heinrich Gerhard	8, Apr. 1899	6, Apr.	44- 9m	5	
Kleider, Anna	30, Sept 1887		49	1	
Kleimann, Florence	1, Nov. 1887		3m- 7d	1	
Klein,	18, Sept 1891		1d	1	
Klein, A.H. (Dr.)	23, Jan. 1900	22, Jan.	59	4	
Klein, Aaron	6, Oct. 1899	4, Oct.		5	
Klein, Annie	7, Mar. 1890		6	1	
Klein, August	23, July 1901		13	8	
Klein, Babette	8, Feb. 1901		62	8	
Klein, Carl	25, Aug. 1899	25, Aug.	59- 6m- 4d	4	
Klein, Catharina	27, Nov. 1894		59	5	
Klein, Christian	31, Jan. 1898		70	5	
Klein, Clara M.	2, July 1891		8m	4	
Klein, Clifford	10, May 1892		3m	5	
Klein, Edwin B.	12, Jan. 1889		31	1	

Name	Notice Date	Death Date	Age	Page	Maiden Name
****	****** ****	***** ****	***	****	****** ****
Klein, Elsie	3, Oct. 1891		2- 3m	1	
Klein, Ernie	14, Feb. 1895		1	5	
Klein, Franziska	25, Oct. 1899	23, Oct.	73- 4m	5	Dater
Klein, Frederick S.	9, Sept 1891		2	4	
Klein, Friedrich	22, Aug. 1898	20, Aug.	30	5	
Klein, Friedrich	22, May 1899	20, May	53	4	
Klein, Harry	17, July 1891		5	1	
Klein, Heinrich S.	17, Dec. 1897	16, Dec.	6m	5	
Klein, Henry	21, May 1897	20, May	47- 2m	5	
Klein, Jacob	9, Oct. 1900		40	8	
Klein, Jacob	14, Sept 1901		41	1	
Klein, Jette	28, Jan. 1892		2	5	
Klein, Johannah J.	12, Aug. 1889		49	1	
Klein, John	23, Feb. 1891		2m	4	
Klein, John	14, Sept 1893		53	5	
Klein, John	5, June 1894		46	5	
Klein, Karl	25, Aug. 1899	15, Aug.	59- 6m	5	
Klein, Katharina	20, Aug. 1898	18, Aug.	60	5	
Klein, Louis	27, Oct. 1891		23	1	
Klein, Louis	17, Mar. 1897	16, Mar.	59- 1m	5	
Klein, Louise	9, Nov. 1899	8, Nov.	61- 9m	5	Staiber
Klein, Margaretha	11, Dec. 1891		69	4	
Klein, Maria	22, Oct. 1894		74	5	
Klein, Marie	5, Sept 1891		6m	1	
Klein, Nathan	18, Nov. 1894		1m	5	
Klein, Salomon	21, Aug. 1890		51	1	
Klein, William	13, May 1901		53	8	
Kleine, Agnes	3, Mar. 1899	1, Mar.	85	4	
Kleine, B.C.	18, Nov. 1895	16, Nov.	32- 3m	5	Elsenheimer
Kleine, Charles	20, July 1901		74	8	
Kleine, Fannie M.	13, Oct. 1892		10m	5	
Kleine, Frederick	22, Apr. 1899	21, Apr.	79	5	
Kleine, Victor Harry	14, Nov. 1898	13, Nov.	14m	5	
Kleineberg, Theodor	25, Sept 1889		63	1	
Kleinfelder, Elisabeth	9, Apr. 1898	9, Apr.	67- 7m	1	
Kleinfelter, Bessie	24, Dec. 1900		6	8	
Kleinhaus, Francis	10, Oct. 1900		42	8	
Kleinhaus, Franziska	8, Oct. 1900		31	8	
Kleinheinz, Harry T.	21, June 1888		15m	1	
Kleinmann, Amalia	8, July 1889		29	1	
Kleinmann, Magdalena	23, July 1896	22, July	69- 8m	5	Wolff
Kleinmann, Wilhelm E.	24, Feb. 1896	22, Feb.	23- 3m	5	
Kleinschmidt, E.F.	20, Mar. 1891		76	4	
Kleintank, Adelheid	25, June 1895		59	5	
Kleintank, John	7, Feb. 1889		64	1	
Kleinwächter, Mathilda	11, Sept 1889	10, Sept		1	
Kleisker, G.	13, June 1900	12, June	61	8	
Klemm, Dora	25, Sept 1889		60	1	
Klemm, Edward	19, Aug. 1891		34	4	
Klemm, Louisa H.	5, Jan. 1901		76	8	
Klench, Lena	15, July 1891		29	1	
Klenk, Alma F.	30, Jan. 1890		10m	1	
Klenk, Fritz	2, Dec. 1888	30, Nov.		2	
Klenk, Henry	19, July 1893		4m	5	
Klensch, Henriette	20, Aug. 1888		9m	1	
Klensch, Louis L.	26, Mar. 1891		24	4	
Klett, Ernst	28, Feb. 1891		3	4	
Klett, Ernst	28, Feb. 1891	27, Feb.	8- 5m	1	
Klewing, Philomena	22, May 1890		26	1	
Kleyoth, Benjamin	18, Apr. 1895		45	5	
Klie, Jakob	16, July 1891		52	4	
Klieber, Philipp	19, Apr. 1893		34	5	
Klinckhammer, Elisabeth	6, July 1899	5, July	73- 8m	5	Feldmann
Kline, Charles	6, Mar. 1897	4, Mar.	57- 2m	5	
Kline, Elsie M.	14, Jan. 1891		10	4	
Kline, Frank	26, June 1891		6	4	
Kline, Henry	18, Aug. 1900		55	8	
Kline, Peter	26, Feb. 1891		45	4	
Kline, Roy	21, Mar. 1901		14d	8	
Kline, S.	27, Dec. 1887		16m	1	
Kling, Jacob	3, Nov. 1891		41	4	

Name	Notice Date	Death Date	Age	Page	Maiden Name
****	****** ****	***** ****	***	****	****** ****
Kling, Jacob	10, Oct. 1893		61	5	
Kling, Mary	10, Mar. 1891		41	4	
Kling, Mary L.	30, Nov. 1887		1w	4	
Klinge, Martha E.	17, Sept 1891		16d	1	
Klingelberg, Sus.	28, Dec. 1888		76	1	
Klinger, Anna	15, July 1893		68	5	
Klinger, Mina	23, Feb. 1891		60	4	
Klingler, Mary	15, Jan. 1901		58	8	
Klink, Albert August	26, May 1889	25, May	2- 6m	5	
Klink, George	28, July 1891		4d	4	
Klinker, Johanna	20, June 1888		24	1	
Klinkicht, Arthur H.	13, Mar. 1894		7m	5	
Klinkiewitz, Adam T.	12, May 1893		5m	5	
Klintvort, Henry	4, Oct. 1900		43	8	
Kllemeyer, Louise	24, July 1890		1	1	
Kloak, Josephine	2, Aug. 1890		26	1	
Kloane, John	18, Dec. 1891		40	2	
Klob, John	18, June 1895		54	5	
Klockar, Henry	25, Jan. 1894		19	5	
Klocke, Amalie A.	25, June 1888		3m	1	
Klocke, Henry W.	6, Apr. 1895		48	5	
Klocke, Louis	19, Aug. 1891		3m	4	
Klocke, Margaret	18, Aug. 1900		42	8	
Kloene, Elisa	23, Apr. 1890		6	4	
Kloene, Herman	17, Nov. 1896	14, Nov.	51	5	
Kloenne, B.H.	21, Apr. 1897	20, Apr.		5	
Kloeppel, Lena	25, Aug. 1892		31	5	
Klogf, John	24, Feb. 1888		85	4	
Klohs, Julia	29, Aug. 1889	28, Aug.	4	1	
Kloman, Katie	17, Feb. 1888		18	4	
Klomann, Fred	21, May 1901		35	8	
Klomann, John	10, July 1888		4w	1	
Klonne, Mary E.	8, Feb. 1894		80	5	
Klopper, Frank	18, Sept 1891		18	1	
Klostermann, Bernard H.	3, July 1896	2, July	60-11m	5	
Klostermann, Gerhard	26, Jan. 1893		46	5	
Klostermann, Harry	24, Jan. 1891		17	4	
Klostermann, Henry M.	12, Dec. 1891		27	4	
Klostermann, Katharina	27, Dec. 1898	25, Dec.	73	5	Wulfert
Klostermann, Lizzie	11, Dec. 1893		62	5	
Klostermann, Maria Magdalena	24, Mar. 1896	23, Mar.	56-11m	5	Eilers
Klostermayer, Karl W.	28, Apr. 1900	27, Apr.	86	5	
Klotte, Bernard	15, Nov. 1900		36	8	
Klotter, George F.	21, Feb. 1894		75	5	
Klotter, Minnie	3, Aug. 1901		48	8	
Klotz,	5, Mar. 1891		1d	4	
Klotz, Christina	23, May 1888		58	1	
Klotz, Georg	10, May 1898	9, May	24- 2m	5	
Klotz, Maria	19, Jan. 1892		24	5	
Kluber, C.	13, July 1900		10	8	
Kluber, Joseph	8, Mar. 1888		57	1	
Kluesener, Gottlieb	9, May 1900	7, May	56- 9m	5	
Klug, Catharina	1, Oct. 1890		65	1	
Klug, Francis	24, May 1901		2	8	
Klug, Johan Valentin	15, Apr. 1896	13, Apr.	79- 2m	5	
Klug, Margaretha	7, July 1891		1	1	
Klug, Mina	15, June 1889		18m	1	
Klug, William	9, Aug. 1887		5w	1	
Kluge, Edward A.	16, July 1895		8m	5	
Klum, Jacob	22, Mar. 1889		50	1	
Klumb, Charles	4, May 1895		19	5	
Klumb, Frank	17, Dec. 1896	16, Dec.	29- 7m	5	
Klumb, Stephen	16, July 1891		5m	4	
Klumpp, Dina	29, Mar. 1888		2	1	
Klundt, John	31, Aug. 1887		20m	1	
Klus, Joseph	10, May 1901		59	8	
Kluse, Flora	2, Sept 1887		6d	1	
Klusmann, Heinrich Gottlieb	28, May 1896	27, May	77-11m	5	
Klusmann, Louis	26, Aug. 1891		36	4	
Klusmann, Mary	14, May 1895		55	5	
Klusmann, William	23, Aug. 1890		40	1	

Name ****	Notice Date ****** ****	Death Date ***** ****	Age ***	Page ****	Maiden Name ****** ****
Klöckner, Johan Heinrich	18, Oct. 1899	17, Oct.	59- 1m	7	
Klöning, Wilhelm	9, Mar. 1897	8, Mar.	3- 4m	5	
Klümper, Mary Elisabeth	24, Sept 1894		82	5	
Klüner, Ignatz	30, Aug. 1897	28, Aug.	67	5	
Klüsener, Wilhelm	24, Aug. 1900		20m	5	
Klüsner, Louise	7, Feb. 1889		1	1	
Knabe, Albert Johan	14, July 1899	12, July	88-10m	4	
Knabe, Johan Gottlieb	20, Apr. 1900	19, Apr.	73-10m	5	
Knabe, Louisa K.	9, Jan. 1899	8, Jan.	32	5	Backer
Knabel, George	14, Oct. 1888		68	4	
Knaeuper, John	11, May 1901		53	8	
Knaggs, Thomas P.	18, July 1891		66	1	
Knapke, Francis	18, Feb. 1901		21	8	
Knapke, J.B.	29, Oct. 1896	28, Oct.	55	5	
Knapke, Maria Adelma	12, May 1897	11, May	26- 9m	5	Schildmeyer
Knapmann, Frederike	17, Feb. 1899	15, Feb.	61	5	Heinemann
Knapmann, John H.	23, Feb. 1893		65	5	
Knapp, Alma	2, July 1895		5m	5	
Knapp, Elizabeth	1, Feb. 1894		93	5	
Knapp, Gus. A.	4, Aug. 1893		7m	5	
Knapp, Karl	11, 12, Oct. 1893	10, Oct.	36- - 4d	5	
Knapp, Margaretha	18, July 1893			5	
Knappmeier, John	14, Feb. 1891		51	4	
Knarr, Carrie	2, Dec. 1893		36	5	
Knarr, Mary	25, May 1894		11m	5	
Knau, Joseph	26, Nov. 1900		2	8	
Knauber, Marie	8, Aug. 1901		2	8	
Knauber, William	27, Apr. 1901		35	8	
Knauft, Lizzie	28, Mar. 1893		28	5	
Knauß, Henry	26, June 1895		45	5	
Knecht,	9, Feb. 1894		1d	5	
Knecht,	7, Sept 1894		1d	5	
Knecht, Edward	1, Sept 1888		19m	1	
Knecht, G. Wilhelm	1, June 1894		9	5	
Knecht, Irene Marie	29, Dec. 1899	28, Dec.	2- 7m	5	
Knecht, Katie	5, Nov. 1900		17	8	
Knecht, Laura C.	7, Sept 1894		28	5	
Knecht, Pearl	30, Mar. 1894		8m	5	
Knedler, Max	13, Jan. 1891		42	1	
Kneff, John	5, Jan. 1888		2- 6m	1	
Kneisle, Louis	8, Mar. 1889		19	1	
Kneiß, Michael	18, Oct. 1889		59- 6m	1	
Knertz,	24, July 1891		1d	1	
Knese, Caroline	28, Mar. 1889		72	1	
Knesser, Konrad	7, May 1895		2d	5	
Kneup, Valentin	8, Apr. 1896	6, Apr.	44- 9m	5	
Knicker, Fred	11, Feb. 1889		6m	1	
Knickmeyer, Lucy	10, June 1901		84	8	
Knieriehm, Louis	9, Feb. 1894		28	5	
Knifer, Daniel	18, June 1891		7m	4	
Knight, Vada	15, Mar. 1901		30	8	
Knille, Wilhelm Joseph	30, Nov. 1899	29, Nov.	28- 9m	5	
Knipper, Jakob	31, July 1900			5	
Knipper, Lullu	9, Mar. 1898	7, Mar.	18- 9m- 7d	5	
Knips, Alinis	7, Aug. 1891		1	4	
Knips, Elenora	16, Mar. 1892		3m	1	
Knoblauch, William	19, May 1894		69	5	
Knobloch, Franz	1, Nov. 1897	30, Oct.	71- -21d	5	
Knoche, Mary E.	28, Feb. 1891		13	4	
Knockeweisel, Olga	29, Mar. 1900	28, Mar.		4	Otten
Knoepel, William	25, Jan. 1888		2	1	
Knoll, Edward	19, July 1887		13m	1	
Knoll, Ellen J.	28, Apr. 1894		39	5	
Knoll, Joseph	8, June 1895		19	5	
Knoll, Lena	22, Feb. 1890		47- 6m	4	
Knoll, Wilhelm	25, 27, Nov. 1889		4- 6m	1	
Knolle, Henry	24, Jan. 1894		7d	5	
Knollmann, Flora K.	14, Nov. 1893		3m	5	
Knollmann, Gerhard	10, Apr. 1901		74	8	
Knollmann, Theresia	25, Mar. 1897	24, Mar.	89	5	Attermeier
Knorr, Henry	11, May 1892		52	5	

Name ****	Notice Date ****** ****	Death Date ***** ****	Age ***	Page ****	Maiden Name ****** ****
Knost, Henry	3, Aug. 1901		9d	8	
Knost, Wilhelm F.	28, Sept 1899	27, Sept	22- 2m-29d	5	
Knotsch, Clarence Richard	10, Oct. 1890		2m	4	
Knott, Ernst	8, June 1895		32	5	
Knott, Thomas	9, Mar. 1901		85	8	
Knueven, Anton	14, Aug. 1900		64	5	
Knuwen, Bernard Heinrich	2, Feb. 1899	1, Feb.	58	5	
Knüttel, Charles	8, May 1894		1m	5	
Koatz, Johan	30, Dec. 1895	29, Dec.	52- 6m	5	
Kobmann, John	26, Aug. 1887		26	1	
Kobmann, Philippina	16, Jan. 1889		55	1	
Koch,	30, June 1888		3d	1	
Koch,	3, Mar. 1891		1d	4	
Koch, Adele	18, Aug. 1892		32	5	
Koch, Anna Maria	12, July 1897	11, July	66- 3m	5	
Koch, Anna Maria	24, Oct. 1899	23, Oct.	69- 4m	5	
Koch, Bertha	22, Mar. 1888		6m	1	
Koch, Charles	17, Jan. 1896	16, Jan.	71	5	
Koch, Charlotte	17, Dec. 1888		56	1	
Koch, Christ.	18, Aug. 1890		7m	1	
Koch, Clara Alma	4, Dec. 1891		4	4	
Koch, Dora	29, Mar. 1892		50	5	
Koch, Elisa	21, May 1889		43	1	
Koch, Elizabeth	20, Aug. 1901		1	8	
Koch, Ernst C.	17, Jan. 1901		66	8	
Koch, Frank H.B.	1, Sept 1891		13	4	
Koch, Franziskus	18, July 1887		1	1	
Koch, Fred. A.	22, Aug. 1888		71	1	
Koch, George	13, Jan. 1896	10, Jan.	3- 8m	5	
Koch, Heinrich Wilhelm	8, June 1898	6, June	76	5	
Koch, Henry	7, Feb. 1891		59	4	
Koch, Henry	2, June 1891		3m	4	
Koch, Ida	8, May 1889		7	1	
Koch, Isa W.H.	10, Feb. 1893		72	5	
Koch, J.	14, Aug. 1888		1m	1	
Koch, Johan D.	8, May 1897	7, May	75	5	
Koch, John	27, Dec. 1890		2	2	
Koch, John	13, Mar. 1891		51	4	
Koch, Josephine	8, Oct. 1891		25	4	
Koch, Juliane	14, Apr. 1888	13, Apr.		1	Kudel
Koch, Lizzie	15, Oct. 1891		8m	4	
Koch, Louis	23, Jan. 1891		43	4	
Koch, Louise	25, Feb. 1897	23, Feb.	64- -16d	5	
Koch, Ludwig	12, Jan. 1892		41	5	
Koch, Magdalena	30, Dec. 1892		81	5	
Koch, Magdalena	19, July 1900	18, July	70- 5m	8	Deibert
Koch, Marcus	7, July 1898	6, July	67	5	
Koch, Margaretha	11, Aug. 1899	10, Aug.	39- 3m	5	Schmurr
Koch, Margaretha Gesina	6, Mar. 1897	5, Mar.	66- 3m	5	Gerding
Koch, Mary	26, June 1891		1	4	
Koch, Melchior	29, Apr. 1893		65	5	
Koch, Oliver	18, July 1887		4w	1	
Koch, Phil.	24, Feb. 1888		52	4	
Koch, Rudolph	14, Oct. 1891	14, Oct.	4m	1	
Koch, Salomea	1, 2, Nov. 1897	1, Nov.	58- 6m-11d	5	
Koch, Sophia	24, Apr. 1895		59	5	
Koch, Wilhelm	28, Sept 1888		21	2	
Koch, Wilhelm	23, Dec. 1893		45	5	
Koch, William	14, Dec. 1888		31	1	
Kocher, Elisabeth	29, 30, Oct. 1896	28, Oct.	20- 6m	5	
Kocher, Magdalena	1, June 1896	31, May	49- 7m	5	
Kochler, Johan	19, Mar. 1901			8	
Kock, Hen.	24, Feb. 1894		49	5	
Koebel, David	4, Oct. 1900		41	8	
Koebel, George	4, Apr. 1890		73	1	
Koebel, Johan	7, June 1899	6, June	25- 5m-27d	4	
Koebel, Magdalena	22, Dec. 1893		64	5	
Koebele, Johan	11, Apr. 1899	9, Apr.	42-10m	5	
Koebing, John	19, Jan. 1893		21	5	
Koeffler, Walter	24, Nov. 1900		3	8	
Koehl , Johan G.	25, Aug. 1898	23, Aug.	60-11m	4	

Name	Notice Date	Death Date	Age	Page	Maiden Name
****	****** ****	***** ****	***	****	****** ****
Koehle, Ed.	31, Aug. 1901		2	8	
Koehler, A.A.	16, Oct. 1901		53	1	
Koehler, Charles	13, May 1901		24	8	
Koehler, Ed.	21, Mar. 1892		18d	4	
Koehler, Ed.	30, Aug. 1901		2	8	
Koehler, Edward	12, Dec. 1900		38	8	
Koehler, Elizabeth	31, July 1900		55	5	
Koehler, Fred.	27, Dec. 1888		52	2	
Koehler, Jakob	28, June 1895		1	5	
Koehler, John	2, Aug. 1890		4m	1	
Koehler, John	20, Oct. 1893		43	8	
Koehler, John Ph.	28, Apr. 1888		53	1	
Koehler, Kasper	17, May 1894		15	5	
Koehler, Lucy	16, June 1894		8	5	
Koehler, Ludwig	6, June 1893		1	5	
Koehlke, Anna Maria Engel	13, June 1899	12, June	32- 8m-26d	4	Holtmeier
Koehn, August	22, Sept 1897	20, Sept	83	5	
Koehn, Fritz	27, Oct. 1887		72	1	
Koehnke, Louis	15, Apr. 1893		30	5	
Koehnken, Anna C.	4, Jan. 1901		74	5	
Koehnken, Johan H.	24, Feb. 1897	23, Feb.	77- 6m	5	
Koellner, Elisabeth	21, Nov. 1895	20, Nov.	70	5	Popp
Koellner, Gregor	1, Apr. 1897	30, Mar.	72- 1m	5	
Koeme, M.C.	24, Feb. 1888		46	4	
Koenermann, Henry	1, May 1891		39	4	
Koenig, Anna	8, Feb. 1894		74	5	
Koenig, Emilie	10, Feb. 1888		14	1	
Koenig, Joseph	12, Feb. 1898	11, Feb.	76- 3m	5	
Koenig, Marie	4, July 1887		10m	1	
Koenig, Paul L.	1, Nov. 1893		19m	5	
Koepke, Joachim	10, Sept 1901		1	1	
Koepke, John	1, Aug. 1901		47	8	
Koeppen, Elsa	10, Aug. 1887		15	1	
Koerkel, Jacob	2, Mar. 1897	1, Mar.	63- 5m	5	
Koester, Amea	13, Aug. 1901		2	8	
Koester, Bertha	7, Oct. 1891		36- 7m	4	
Koester, Bertha	1, Nov. 1893		33	5	
Koester, Doris	9, Apr. 1900	8, Apr.	79	4	
Koester, Fred. C.	28, July 1887		3- 6m	1	
Koester, Herman	21, July 1887		39	1	
Koester, Louise	13, Dec. 1893		75	5	
Koester, William	26, Apr. 1893		66	5	
Koetkemeier, George A.	18, Mar. 1890		13	1	
Koettkemeyer, Minnie	17, Aug. 1901		54	8	
Kofler, J. Henry	15, Nov. 1900		51	8	
Koger, Franz Xavier	29, Aug. 1890		28	* 1	
Koger, Karl	13, Sept 1897	12, Sept	33- 3m	5	
Kogg, Friedricka	1, July 1899	29, June	53- 2m	5	
Kohake, Johan F.	31, July 1899	30, July	24- -28d	4	
Kohake, William	8, July 1901		17	8	
Kohl, Anna M.	28, July 1888		3	1	
Kohl, Franz	10, Dec. 1895	9, Dec.	42	5	
Kohl, Friedrich	27, Mar. 1896	26, Mar.	65- 6m	5	
Kohl, John	10, May 1894		39	5	
Kohl, Walter	26, June 1894		1	5	
Kohlbrand, Elisa	10, 11, Mar. 1892	9, Mar.	70	5	
Kohlbrand, Julia	13, July 1900		36	8	
Kohlbrand, Louise	7, Dec. 1889		26	1	
Kohlbrandt, Ella	14, Sept 1897	13, Sept	19	5	
Kohlefrath, Emanuel	15, June 1889		84	1	
Kohler, Alfred	16, Aug. 1887		16m	1	
Kohler, Frederika	18, Sept 1901		54	8	
Kohler, George	23, Mar. 1901		83	8	
Kohler, Joseph	16, Mar. 1901		49	8	
Kohler, Max	27, Jan. 1889	26, Jan.	40	* 4	
Kohler, Robert	24, June 1901		33	8	
Kohlhaas, Fred	10, Oct. 1891		17m	4	
Kohlhoff, Mary	7, June 1901		25	8	
Kohlmann, Henry	14, Feb. 1891		44	4	
Kohlmann, Joseph	25, Oct. 1894		61	5	
Kohlmann, Lillie	19, May 1894		7m	5	

Name ****	Notice Date ****** ****	Death Date ***** ****	Age ***	Page ****	Maiden Name ****** ****
Kohlmeyer, Catharine	21, Mar. 1893		72	5	
Kohlmeyer, George	17, June 1891		2m	4	
Kohlmeyer, Herm.	24, Mar. 1894		5m	5	
Kohlrieser, Ernst	29, Aug. 1899	26, Aug.	79- 4m	4	
Kohlsdorf, Florian	21, Apr. 1895		20	5	
Kohlsdorf, Frank	24, Sept 1901		27	1	
Kohlsdorf, Mary E.	23, Nov. 1891		66	1	
Kohlsdorf, Peter	1, May 1891		19	4	
Kohlsdorff, Anna Theresia	2, July 1897	30, June	36- 1m	5	
Kohmescher, Anna Maria	11, July 1891		69	1	
Kohmesher, Joseph	24, Apr. 1901		54	8	
Kohne, Joseph	3, May 1901		36	8	
Kohnen, Elisabeth	3, Nov. 1898	1, Nov.	77	5	
Kohnen, Emma	28, Nov. 1900		4m	8	
Kohner, Caroline	13, Mar. 1901		64	8	
Kohns, William E.	23, Feb. 1893		3m	5	
Kohrs, Maria	26, July 1900		3m	5	
Kolb, Philipp	26, Jan. 1901		76	8	
Kolb, Sophia	10, Oct. 1893		11	5	
Kolbe, Joseph	19, Aug. 1890		43	1	
Kolbus, Heinrich H.	8, May 1900	5, May	70- 7m	5	
Kolbus, Louisa	28, June 1894		62	5	
Kolbus, Marie	23, Apr. 1895		83	5	
Kolen, Rosa	10, Oct. 1895	9, Oct.		5	Erpenstein
Kolise, Gertie	10, Sept 1887		8m	2	
Kolkee, John J.	2, Jan. 1890		69	1	
Koll, Edna J.	16, Aug. 1887		10m	1	
Koll, Emma	9, Sept 1900		30	5	
Koller, John	1, June 1897	28, May	43- 9m	5	
Kollmann, Anna	5, Apr. 1901		43	8	
Kolmel, Frank J.	20, Feb. 1894		34	5	
Kols, Rudolph	17, Apr. 1895		24	5	
Koltenbrock, Josephine	14, July 1892		6d	5	
Kolthoff, W.	31, Oct. 1896	30, Oct.	51	5	
Koltmann, Henry	23, Aug. 1887		4d	1	
Kolwes, Heinrich	23, Feb. 1899	21, Feb.	48- 1m	5	
Komburg, Louisa	26, May 1892		66	5	
Konba, Cäcilia	19, Sept 1900		1	8	
Kondering, Theodore	19, Jan. 1899	18, Jan.	78- 2m	5	
Kondz, Bernard L.	19, June 1895		5m	5	
Konermann, Charlotte	11, Jan. 1894		68	5	
Konermann, Robert	11, Dec. 1893		1m	5	
Koniger, Philipp	19, Sept 1888		72	2	
Konnermann, John H.F.	1, Dec. 1892		3m	5	
Konnersmann, H.	31, Oct. 1896	30, Oct.	74	5	
Konnors, Joseph	8, May 1888		2d	1	
Konrad, Joseph Christian	15, 16, Mar. 1893	14, Mar.	9m-20d	5	
Konsag, Annie	24, Feb. 1888		4	4	
Konschuetzky, Frieda	15, June 1901		3	8	
Konsheim, August	6, Apr. 1893		34	5	
Konsheim, Edward	26, Jan. 1901		33	8	
Konsheim, Edward W.	16, Jan. 1894		4m	5	
Konsheim, Kate	2, May 1895		24	5	
Konsheim, Oscar	29, July 1887		7m	1	
Konsheim, William	30, Nov. 1887		27	4	
Koob, H.H.	3, Oct. 1895	2, Oct.	68- -27d	5	
Kooman, Lagiestie	26, Aug. 1891		83	2	
Koons, Lulu Catharina	17, Sept 1887	16, Sept	3m	1	
Koopmann, Anna	14, Feb. 1899	12, Feb.	6- 5m	5	
Koopmann, Emilie	12, Apr. 1892		12	5	
Koors, Lawrence	11, June 1891		3	4	
Kopelent, Charles	26, Dec. 1900		92	8	
Kopelent, Harry	31, Jan. 1891		7- 3m	1	
Kopf, Margaretha	3, July 1894		77	5	
Kopf, Mary A.	25, Nov. 1893		55	5	
Kopfmann, And.	18, Apr. 1889		37	1	
Kopfmann, George	17, May 1889		68	1	
Kopman, John	5, Sept 1900		1	5	
Kopp, Johan	26, Apr. 1899	25, Apr.	83	5	
Kopp, Laura	20, Nov. 1900		4m	8	
Kopp, Marie	31, July 1901		1m	8	

Name	Notice Date	Death Date	Age	Page	Maiden Name
****	****** ****	***** ****	***	****	****** ****
Kopp, Rosina	2, July 1901		90	8	
Koppe, Fred.	13, Aug. 1891		66	4	
Koppe, Frederick	31, Oct. 1891		63	4	
Kopriva, John	30, Apr. 1895		82	5	
Korb, Cl.	19, Jan. 1888		2	4	
Korb, Rob E.	9, Aug. 1887		1	1	
Kore, Frank	28, Aug. 1889		61	1	
Koring, Sophia Louise	2, Mar. 1897	1, Mar.	81-	5	Balster
Kormann, George	21, Mar. 1893		3	5	
Korn, Ella F.	8, Jan. 1901		18d	8	
Kornbluth, J.	28, Nov. 1900		74	8	
Kort, Charles	10, Nov. 1891		1	1	
Korte, Anna	21, Nov. 1893		63	5	
Korte, Anna Christina	22, Jan. 1896	21, Jan.	20-10m	5	Schrage
Korte, E.	2, Aug. 1893		10m	5	
Korte, F. Harry	16, Mar. 1889		18	1	
Korte, Gerhard H.	4, Apr. 1893		72	5	
Korte, Henry	1, Dec. 1900		2	8	
Korte, J.F.	23, Aug. 1899	22, Aug.	75- 9m	5	
Korte, James	18, June 1891		16	4	
Korte, John G.	8, June 1895		77	5	
Korte, Joseph	26, Oct. 1894		3	5	
Korte, Mary	6, Apr. 1893		73	5	
Kortenbrock, Christina	27, Sept 1893		8m	5	
Korthaus, Johan	13, Apr. 1898	11, Apr.	53- -14d	5	
Kortkamp, Henry	20, Feb. 1895		67	5	
Kortkamp, Rosa	14, Jan. 1889		45	1	
Kortmann, E.	4, Jan. 1898	2, Jan.	88	5	
Kosbahn, Fred.	25, Jan. 1890		33	1	
Kose, Richard	16, Mar. 1893		30	5	
Kosker, Adelaide	6, July 1893		51	5	
Kosse, Elma	5, June 1893		2	5	
Kost, George	16, Feb. 1897	15, Feb.	37- 2m	5	
Kost, Henrietta	27, Mar. 1895		61	5	
Kost, Mary	11, May 1889		79	1	
Koster, Fred.	25, Feb. 1901		53	8	
Kostermann, C.	5, Sept 1901		4m	8	
Kothe, Charlotte	20, Nov. 1889		85	1	
Kotte, Bernard	11, May 1896	9, May	43-11m	5	
Kotte, Joseph	21, July 1890		2	1	
Kotte, Katharina	9, Nov. 1899	8, Nov.	47- 6m	5	Taphorn
Kottenbrink, Margaretha	25, June 1896	22, June	71- 2m	5	
Kotter, Anna Maria Elisabeth	14, Apr. 1900	13, Apr.	59- 9m	5	Knapke
Kottig, John	16, June 1894		6	5	
Kottmann, Louise	27, Apr. 1898	26, Apr.	72-11m-17d	5	Rietmann
Kottmanns, Theresa	1, Dec. 1892		65	5	
Kottmeyer, Wilhelm	3, Apr. 1899	2, Apr.	2	5	
Kotz, Johanna	18, May 1894		71	5	
Koucher, Othelia	3, Oct. 1887		23	1	
Kouger, Elma	23, Mar. 1892		6	5	
Kouschuetzky, Elisa	1, Dec. 1888		9m	4	
Koutze, George	19, Oct. 1892		36	5	
Kovermann, Bernhardt	30, Oct. 1891		3-	4	
Kowalski, Emil	16, May 1901		44	5	
Kowalski, Emma	19, Apr. 1897	17, Apr.	2- 5m	5	
Kowalski, Flora	13, Nov. 1893		4	5	
Koßmann, Philipp	11, Jan. 1898	10, Jan.	78	5	
Krabacher, Mary	15, July 1901		5	8	
Kracke, Dietrich	11, Oct. 1900		60	8	
Kracke, Elisabeth	30, Nov. 1900		76	8	
Kracke, Frank	27, Apr. 1895		42	5	
Kracke, Heinrich	26, Mar. 1896	25, Mar.	68	5	
Kracke, Mary	12, July 1893		8m	5	
Kracke, Minnie	8, Mar. 1901		58	8	
Kraemer, Annie	28, Feb. 1901		57	8	
Kraemer, Elisabeth	26, Mar. 1897	23, Mar.	33-10m	5	Hock
Kraemer, Katharine	11, July 1887		65	1	
Kraft, Angele	5, July 1887		1- 6m	1	
Kraft, Caroline	1, Feb. 1888		61	4	
Kraft, Elenora	24, June 1901		41	8	
Kraft, George	11, Jan. 1888		27	4	

Name	Notice Date	Death Date	Age	Page	Maiden Name
****	****** ****	***** ****	***	****	****** ****
Kraft, Ignatz	17, Aug. 1892		65	5	
Kraft, Karl	1, Mar. 1898	28, Feb.	14	5	
Kraft, Minnie	10, May 1889		1	1	
Krais, Bertha	4, Sept 1897	4, Sept	69	4	
Kramer,	21, Sept 1887		1d	1	
Kramer, Anna Helena	28, Nov. 1891		21d	1	
Kramer, Anna M.	18, Nov. 1893		55	5	
Kramer, Barbara	11, Oct. 1889		77	1	
Kramer, Bernard	16, July 1890		38	1	
Kramer, Bernhard	23, Feb. 1898	21, Feb.	58- 8m	5	
Kramer, E.W.	29, Nov. 1888		9m	1	
Kramer, Eduard	30, Sept 1895	29, Sept	53- 5m	5	
Kramer, Edward	23, Feb. 1889		14	1	
Kramer, Edward	1, July 1891		10m	1	
Kramer, Elsa F.	4, May 1893		5m	5	
Kramer, Ferdinand	14, Feb. 1891		74	4	
Kramer, Ferdinand H.	6, Apr. 1896	3, Apr.	48	4	
Kramer, Florence	21, Jan. 1901		2	8	
Kramer, Frank	1, June 1893		51	5	
Kramer, Fred.	16, Dec. 1891		46	4	
Kramer, Friedericka	13, Mar. 1896	12, Mar.	78- 4m	5	
Kramer, George	15, Mar. 1894		19	5	
Kramer, Gertrud	31, Jan. 1893		66	5	
Kramer, Gidius	9, Aug. 1888		2	1	
Kramer, H.	19, May 1896	18, May	82	5	
Kramer, Herman	5, Feb. 1895		21	5	
Kramer, John	12, June 1891		6d	4	
Kramer, Joseph	5, June 1894		77	5	
Kramer, Joseph	14, Apr. 1898	13, Apr.	65	5	
Kramer, Katie	20, Jan. 1890		3	1	
Kramer, L.	27, Aug. 1901		16d	1	
Kramer, Leo	9, Mar. 1893		5	5	
Kramer, Louise	23, June 1888		64	1	
Kramer, Magdalena	26, Feb. 1890		74	1	
Kramer, Margaretha	4, May 1894		65	5	
Kramer, Maria	4, Feb. 1897	2, Feb.	37	5	Greiwe
Kramer, Maria Katharina	25, July 1899	24, July	63- 9m	5	Schönhoff
Kramer, Marie Anna	15, July 1897	14, July	31- 1m	5	Sickmann
Kramer, Mary	8, May 1891		67	4	
Kramer, Mary	10, Mar. 1895		59	5	
Kramer, Mary	1, May 1901		46	8	
Kramer, Ottilia	28, Dec. 1891		14m	4	
Kramer, Rosa	25, July 1894		18	5	
Kramer, Rosa	5, Nov. 1896	4, Nov.	26- 8m	5	Herzog
Kramer, William	31, May 1889		20	1	
Kramer, William	1, Nov. 1892		37	5	
Kramer, Xavier	26, Apr. 1899	25, Apr.	70	5	
Krames, Katie	2, Oct. 1888		27	1	
Kramig, Edward C.	29, Aug. 1891		30	4	
Kramig, John	25, Oct. 1900		31	8	
Kramig, Kate	2, July 1895		49	5	
Krampe, Frederick	1, May 1891		5	4	
Krampe, Friedrich	28, Feb. 1890		57	1	
Krampe, Lizzie	25, Mar. 1891		53	4	
Kramschuster, Emilie	11, Apr. 1901		9m	8	
Kranbacher,	13, July 1900		1d	8	
Kranz, Eduard	28, Oct. 1898			4	
Kranz, Katharine	5, July 1888		2	1	
Kranz, Peter	17, Mar. 1890		3	1	
Kraper, Anton	1, Apr. 1889		61	1	
Krapp, Elisabeth	8, Apr. 1901		68	8	
Krapp, Friedrich	8, May 1900	7, May	70	5	
Kraus, Ben	19, Dec. 1891		1	4	
Kraus, Ernst H.	29, 30, Oct. 1896	29, Oct.	13d	5	
Kraus, Flora	14, Apr. 1891		11	4	
Kraus, Fred. W.	21, June 1888		2	1	
Kraus, Georg	5, Mar. 1901		42	5	
Kraus, J.A.	10, Dec. 1895	8, Dec.	36- 3m	5	
Kraus, Pauline	3, Aug. 1887		30	1	
Kraus, Sylvester	30, Nov. 1888		3	1	
Kraus, Theresia	8, May 1896	6, May	59- 8m	5	Dotzauer

Name ****	Notice Date ****** ****	Death Date ***** ****	Age ***	Page ****	Maiden Name ****** ****
Krause, Augusta	25, Aug. 1899	23, Aug.	61- 4m	5	
Krauter, Charles	10, July 1888		38	1	
Krauß, Gottlieb	11, Mar. 1899	9, Mar.	35	5	
Krauß, Sylvia	6, June 1901		2	8	
Krayer, Carl Rudolph	24, Mar. 1896	23, Mar.	4	5	
Krebs, Anna M.	6, Mar. 1894		67	5	
Krebs, Charles	31, May 1897	31, May		5	
Krebs, Christina	17, Aug. 1894		70	5	
Krebs, Edna	10, Mar. 1895		7m	5	
Krebs, Johan J.	13, Dec. 1899	12, Dec.	65	5	
Krebs, Julia	23, Oct. 1888		42	1	
Krebs, Maria	25, Oct. 1897	24, Oct.	62- 2m	5	Hahn
Krebs, Mary	29, May 1894		12d	5	
Krebsfanger, Alvina	11, Sept 1894		16m	5	
Kreegan, Maggie	23, June 1888		20	1	
Kreg, Mary	23, Nov. 1894		11m	5	
Kreh, Minnie Olga	16, July 1897	15, July	18	5	
Krehbiel, Anna M.	7, Mar. 1898	6, Mar.		5	
Krehe, George	5, Sept 1901		54	8	
Krehe, Wilhelm Albert	10, Nov. 1896	9, Nov.	2- -27d	4	
Krehm, Ed.	21, Apr. 1892		30	5	
Krehnbrink, Edna	28, May 1891		8d	4	
Kreider, George	13, Mar. 1888			1	
Kreidler, Evan D.	31, Dec. 1892		6d	5	
Kreidler, Johannes P.	14, June 1895		2m	5	
Kreidler, Mathias	16, Feb. 1900	15, Feb.	65	5	
Kreidler, Walburga	10, Apr. 1899	7, Apr.	90- 6m	5	Rupp
Kreidler, William J.	9, Jan. 1894		1	5	
Kreihenbaum, Henry	13, May 1891		39	2	
Kreil, Robert	8, Dec. 1893		75	5	
Kreimburg, John	11, June 1901		82	8	
Kreimer, Elsie	13, Mar. 1901		22	8	
Kreimer, Louise	23, Feb. 1898	22, Feb.		5	
Kreiner, Frieda	19, July 1887		21	1	
Kreis, Frank	5, Apr. 1889		42	1	
Kreis, Herman	7, May 1895		9d	5	
Kreis, Maria C.	2, Aug. 1901		90	8	
Kreiser, Katharine	21, Jan. 1893		84	5	
Krekeler, Ed.	12, June 1901		3m	8	
Krell, Albert	6, Jan. 1900	5, Jan.	68	* 5	
Krell, Alexander	18, Dec. 1895	15, Dec.		5	
Kremer, John	19, Oct. 1892		1d	5	
Krentz, Frank	26, July 1893		9m	5	
Kreppel, Barbara	12, Sept 1891		61	1	
Kresling, Robert H.	17, Jan. 1893		3	5	
Kretschmar, Adelaide	18, Feb. 1889		1m	1	
Kretschmar, Charles	7, Oct. 1896	6, Oct.	57	5	
Kretschner, Catharina	11, Feb. 1892		51	4	
Kreutz, Catharina	25, Oct. 1899	23, Oct.	79	5	
Kreutz, Fritz	25, Oct. 1897	22, Oct.		5	
Kreutz, Mary	18, Feb. 1891		50	4	
Kreutzer, Elisabeth	8, Dec. 1891	6, Dec.	59	1	
Kreutzer, Elisabeth	21, Jan. 1901			8	
Kreyenhagen, Ed.	7, June 1901		6m	8	
Kreß, William	11, July 1895		31	5	
Krieg, Ernst	29, Jan. 1892		1m	5	
Krieg, Henry	15, 18, Sept 1900		2d	5	
Kriege, Philomena	12, Mar. 1896	10, Mar.	11- 2m	5	
Krieger, Alma	27, Oct. 1891		1	1	
Krieger, Amelia	17, May 1899	16, May	75	5	
Krieger, Bernard	27, Jan. 1896	26, Jan.	53	5	
Krieger, Fred	11, May 1901		69	8	
Krieger, Henrietta A.	8, Aug. 1892		72	5	
Krieger, Johan	25, June 1898	22, June	71-11m	5	
Krieger, Johan Chr.	18, 21, Dec. 1895	18, Dec.	63	5	
Krieger, Johan Georg	30, Mar. 1896	29, Mar.	36- 6m	5	
Krieger, Magdalena	3, Nov. 1887		9- 7m	4	
Krieger, Otto	10, 12, Aug. 1893	9, Aug.	28	5	
Krieger, Phil.	24, Apr. 1889		62	1	
Kriesenberg, Maria	16, Nov. 1900			8	
Krimmel, Wilhelm Louis	8, June 1894		69	5	

Name	Notice Date	Death Date	Age	Page	Maiden Name
****	****** ****	***** ****	***	****	****** ****
Krimmel, Wilhelmine Caroline	22, Mar. 1898	21, Mar.	70	5	
Krinke, Richard	1, Aug. 1894		45	5	
Krinke, Richard	30, July 1894	29, July	4- 9m- 7d	5	
Krinke, Wilhelm	11, 12, Aug. 1890	10, Aug.	66- 6m	1	
Krinnel, Franz	18, Dec. 1897	16, Dec.	61-11m	5	
Krippner, Add.	11, Nov. 1897	10, Nov.	38-10m	4	
Krippner, Anton	11, Feb. 1898			5	
Krischler, Wilhelm H.	24, June 1899	23, June	15- 7m	4	
Krist, Ben.	8, July 1901		30	8	
Krocke, Elisabeth	26, Nov. 1892		4	5	
Kroeger, Albert G.	5, Aug. 1891		4	4	
Kroeger, Freddie	13, July 1899	12, July	3-10m	5	
Kroeger, Harry	12, July 1901		9	8	
Kroeger, Johann	23, June 1898	22, June	72	5	
Kroeger, Marga	12, Aug. 1901		16d	8	
Kroeger, Wilhelmine	14, Aug. 1895	13, Aug.	28- 6m	5	Intlekoffer
Kroell, Julia Anne	10, Aug. 1892		3m	5	
Krog, Vincent'	17, Oct. 1893		29	5	
Kroger, Bernard Joseph	24, Feb. 1896	22, Feb.	5- 3m	5	
Kroger, Caroline	24, June 1901		40	8	
Kroger, Frank	27, July 1894		5d	5	
Kroger, George	29, Aug. 1901		1	8	
Kroger, Raymond F.	17, Apr. 1895		16m	5	
Kroherr, George	31, Aug. 1887		22	1	
Krolage, H.	27, Apr. 1897	25, Apr.	41	5	
Kroll, Anthony	16, May 1894		27	5	
Kroll, Henry	20, July 1893		63	5	
Krollmann, Margaretha	24, July 1894		78	5	
Kron, Gottfried	11, Nov. 1892		56	4	
Krone, Catharine	5, Dec. 1891		53	1	
Krone, George	8, Oct. 1897	8, Oct.	64-10m	5	
Kroneis, Wilhelmina	23, Mar. 1892	23, Mar.		5	
Kronemeier, Albert	25, May 1901		6m	8	
Kroner, Elizabeth	26, Dec. 1900		64	8	
Kroner, Margaret	21, Feb. 1889		48	1	
Kronlage, Dora	16, Jan. 1894		82	5	
Kronlage, Heinrich	5, May 1898	4, May	58- 7m	5	
Krotmann, Frank	10, Aug. 1893		55	5	
Krouer, Harry M.	14, June 1894		11m	5	
Krouse, Friedricke	26, Dec. 1895	25, Dec.		4	
Kruckemeier, Gustav	9, Mar. 1889		49	1	
Kruckemeyer, Mary	25, June 1895		59	5	
Krucker, Susan M.	6, Feb. 1896	3, Feb.		5	
Krucker, T.M. (Mrs)	5, Feb. 1896	3, Feb.		5	
Krueger, Alfred	9, Aug. 1901		24	8	
Krueger, Anna	4, May 1892		25	5	
Krueger, Emma	28, July 1887		4	1	
Krueger, Fritz	28, July 1887		1	1	
Kruep, Anna	15, Feb. 1892		52	5	
Kruessel, John G.	17, June 1891		14	4	
Kruesser, C.F.	22, Dec. 1887		6m	4	
Krug, Louise	27, Nov. 1889		38	1	
Krug, Mary	24, Aug. 1887		45	1	
Kruger, Wilhelm	5, Nov. 1897	4, Nov.	40- - 2d	5	
Krull, Maggie	9, Jan. 1901		20	5	
Krumberg, Herman	14, Jan. 1899	13, Jan.	45- 6m	5	
Krumdick, Alma	20, July 1895		19d	5	
Krumdick, Flora	13, July 1895		2	5	
Krumdick, Irene	28, Apr. 1894		3	5	
Krumm, Henry	15, Jan. 1890		77	1	
Krumme, Phoebe M.	2, July 1901		2	8	
Krummen, Herman	20, Dec. 1892		67	5	
Krumpe, Mathilde	14, Sept 1901		27	1	
Krumpelmann, Mary F.	2, Dec. 1887		16- 6m	4	
Kruppling, Charles	31, May 1892		26	5	
Krusch, D.M.	21, Mar. 1888		54	1	
Kruse, Anna Maria Katharina	31, Aug. 1896	30, Aug.	81- 7m	5	Meiburg
Kruse, Bernard	2, Nov. 1894		60	5	
Kruse, Charles	25, June 1895		18m	5	
Kruse, Charlotte	11, Apr. 1899	10, Apr.	68-10m	5	Hagemeister
Kruse, Christina	16, Feb. 1895		2	5	

Name	Notice Date	Death Date	Age	Page	Maiden Name
****	****** ****	***** ****	***	****	****** ****
Kruse, Edward	19, Feb. 1891		14m	4	
Kruse, Elizabeth	10, July 1901		61	5	
Kruse, Ernst W.	2, Apr. 1890		65	1	
Kruse, Frances	29, May 1901		38	8	
Kruse, Gertrude	15, Aug. 1892		1- 6m	5	
Kruse, H.H.	13, Apr. 1898	12, Apr.		5	
Kruse, Henry	10, Oct. 1891		3m	4	
Kruse, Henry	12, Nov. 1891		70	4	
Kruse, Herman	6, Dec. 1900		30	8	
Kruse, Katharine	4, Oct. 1894		72	5	
Kruse, Lulu	27, June 1891		15	1	
Kruse, Magdalena C.	27, July 1895		4m	5	
Kruse, Mary E.	2, Dec. 1893		45	5	
Kruse, Sophia	21, Apr. 1899	20, Apr.	79- 3m	5	
Kruse, Sophie	11, Sept 1900		46	5	
Kruse, Theresa	21, July 1888		11m	1	
Kruse, Vincent	14, Aug. 1900		9m	5	
Kruse, William	18, Aug. 1894		77	5	
Krusekopsky, Henry	21, Feb. 1901		48	8	
Krusemeier, Henry	3, Sept 1891		27	4	
Krusemeier, Lawrence	3, Nov. 1893		5	5	
Krusemeier, Leo H.	18, Jan. 1893		9m	5	
Krusemeyer,	25, Feb. 1891		1d	4	
Krusemeyer, Maria	26, Oct. 1897	25, Oct.	73- 2m	5	Eilermann
Krusling, Johan Albert	28, Jan. 1898	27, Jan.	57- 1m	5	
Kruthaup, G. August	20, Jan. 1897	19, Jan.	28	5	
Kruthaup, L. Bernardina	15, Apr. 1897	14, Apr.	64	5	Laing
Kruthaup, Maria Anna	12, May 1900	10, May	81- 6m	5	Lange
Kruthaup, Sophie	17, Dec. 1900		17	8	
Krämer, Felix	19, Nov. 1888		65	1	
Krämer, Jacobina	2, Apr. 1895		41	5	
Kröger, Albert G.	13, Sept 1893		2m	5	
Kröger, Joseph	13, Aug. 1891		7m	4	
Kröger, Oskar	4, Mar. 1889		5w	1	
Krüger, Alma	9, Aug. 1892		13d	5	
Krüger, Aloice	16, Dec. 1892		18	5	
Krüger, Fred.	13, Apr. 1893		3m	5	
Krüsling, Maria	22, Oct. 1895	21, Oct.	76	5	
Krüssel, L.	16, Mar. 1893		18m	5	
Kuball, Julius	5, Sept 1888		1	2	
Kubbes, Johan Heinrich	23, Jan. 1896	22, Jan.	66- 3m	5	
Kube, George	23, Nov. 1891		16m	1	
Kuchenbeißer, Johan Adam	13, Dec. 1899	11, Dec.		5	
Kuchenbuch, Katharine	4, Nov. 1891		3	1	
Kuchenbuck, Theresa M.	18, June 1891		5m	4	
Kuchendorfer, Theresa	11, Apr. 1892		4m	5	
Kuchmeier, William	11, Apr. 1891		39	4	
Kuchner, Paul	1, June 1893		42	5	
Kuck, Dora	15, Apr. 1900	12, Apr.	70- 5m	8	
Kuck, John H.	28, Nov. 1891		10m	1	
Kuck, Minnie F.	28, Mar. 1894		14	5	
Kuckmeyer, Bertha	20, July 1893		35	5	
Kuckmeyer, Henry	5, Dec. 1887		72	1	
Kuddecke, William	7, Dec. 1893		37	5	
Kuechler, Rosalia	31, Jan. 1901		71	8	
Kueck, George	28, Mar. 1901		38	8	
Kueff, August	13, Oct. 1894		11	5	
Kuehling, Heinrich Clemens	6, Aug. 1898	4, Aug.	68- 9m	4	
Kuehner, Christopher	17, Aug. 1887		38	1	
Kuehnle, Elisabeth	22, Nov. 1899	21, Nov.	59- 8m	5	Horn
Kuehnle, Mary	13, May 1891		2m	2	
Kuehnle, Theresa	14, Jan. 1901		10	8	
Kuehte, Elisabeth	18, Nov. 1898	16, Nov.	61	5	Lampe
Kuemen, Minnie	4, Jan. 1893		2	5	
Kuemmerling, Friedrich	26, Oct. 1897	25, Oct.	67- 9m	5	
Kueneke, Frederick	24, Dec. 1892		56	5	
Kuenz, John	18, July 1890		16	1	
Kues, Ida	24, July 1894		4m	5	
Kuethe, Henry	3, Apr. 1901		72	8	
Kuhborth, Maria	19, Aug. 1899	17, Aug.	82-11m	5	Merz
Kuhfuß, William	25, July 1891		32	4	

Name	Notice Date	Death Date	Age	Page	Maiden Name
****	****** ****	***** ****	***	****	****** ****
Kuhl, Elizabeth	23, Feb. 1889		73	1	
Kuhl, Johan Heinrich	24, May 1897	21, May	47	5	
Kuhl, Joseph	28, Nov. 1891		23	1	
Kuhl, Wilhelmina	8, Nov. 1897	6, Nov.	65	4	Kuhl
Kuhlemann, John	27, Mar. 1891		54	4	
Kuhlenberg,	6, Mar. 1894		12d	5	
Kuhlenberg, Henry	13, Mar. 1891		50	4	
Kuhlenberg, Mary	21, June 1897	20, June	60	5	
Kuhlmann, B.	18, Dec. 1895	17, Dec.		5	
Kuhlmann, Emma	29, May 1895		11	5	
Kuhlmann, Fred	2, Aug. 1887		52	1	
Kuhlmann, Heinrich August	20, Feb. 1896	19, Feb.	72- 7m	5	
Kuhlmann, Helena	31, Dec. 1890		2	4	
Kuhlmann, Henry	3, Apr. 1891		32	4	
Kuhlmann, Henry	17, Oct. 1891		66	4	
Kuhlmann, Henry	7, Nov. 1891		26	1	
Kuhlmann, Jerome H.	30, Dec. 1889		44	1	
Kuhlmann, Julia R.T.	3, July 1895		3	5	
Kuhlmann, Louis	22, Sept 1891		55	1	
Kuhlmann, Mary	21, May 1889		22m	1	
Kuhlmann, Mary A.	25, Feb. 1891		38	4	
Kuhlmann, Mary A.	4, Apr. 1893		2	5	
Kuhlmann, Mathilda	18, June 1901		10	8	
Kuhlmann, Wilhlem Heinrich	18, Feb. 1899	16, Feb.	27- 6m	5	
Kuhn, Aaron	1, Apr. 1890		58	1	
Kuhn, Adam	8, Apr. 1891		72	4	
Kuhn, Amelia	19, Oct. 1901		49	8	
Kuhn, Barbara	12, Dec. 1891		22	4	
Kuhn, Christine	28, July 1899	27, July		5	
Kuhn, Edwin	24, Sept 1900		5d	5	
Kuhn, Ernst	15, Sept 1900		8	5	
Kuhn, Frank S.	13, Nov. 1893		28	5	
Kuhn, Fred. J.	11, Jan. 1889		12	1	
Kuhn, Helen	13, May 1901		23	8	
Kuhn, Jakobine	1, Nov. 1898	31, Oct.	68-11m	5	Dietinger
Kuhn, Jennie	11, June 1895		22	5	
Kuhn, Johan Nikolaus	16, May 1899	14, May	25- 3m	5	
Kuhn, M.	21, Jan. 1894		15	5	
Kuhn, M.E.	12, Sept 1895	11, Sept	57	5	
Kuhn, Magdalene	22, Oct. 1900		2m	8	
Kuhn, May	20, May 1890		22	1	
Kuhn, Regina	26, Jan. 1899	25, Jan.	70	5	
Kuhnell, Magdalena	13, Feb. 1900	12, Feb.	58	8	Newdorfer
Kuhr, Gerhardt H.	8, Aug. 1893		65	5	
Kuhr, Johan Herman	24, May 1897	22, May	67- 5m	5	
Kuhr, Mary A.	16, Oct. 1900		64	8	
Kuhrmann, Sophie	30, Dec. 1896	28, Dec.	68- 4m	5	
Kuinzel, Martha Frida	15, Feb. 1892		1d	5	
Kukehan, Henriette	25, Oct. 1897	23, Oct.	67- 3m	5	Fürste
Kukelhan, Fred	1, Oct. 1891		3d	1	
Kukelhau, Friedrich	29, Aug. 1896	28, Aug.	74- 9m	5	
Kulenberg, Herman	3, Apr. 1895		62	5	
Kulkink, Johan	13, Mar. 1899	10, Mar.	74- 8m	5	
Kumemann, Charles	29, Dec. 1900		3m	8	
Kumer, Andrew	14, Dec. 1893		68	5	
Kummuk, Barbara	30, Apr. 1891		52	4	
Kump, Bennie	26, Sept 1891		4	4	
Kumpel, Amelia	17, Apr. 1900	15, Apr.	20-10m	5	Müller
Kumstat, Frank	2, Mar. 1898	2, Mar.	3- 5m-15d	4	
Kundemüller, Clara	7, July 1890		2m	4	
Kunkel, Ferdinand	6, Jan. 1893		20	5	
Kunkel, John	31, Dec. 1891		38	1	
Kunkel, Kate	13, Apr. 1901		2d	8	
Kunkel, Katie	15, Oct. 1900		60	5	
Kunkel, Margaretha	31, Dec. 1897	30, Dec.	63- 6m	5	Stephens
Kunkel, Regine	24, Feb. 1897	22, Feb.	76	5	
Kunkel, William	2, Apr. 1901		26	8	
Kunkemoeller, Heinrich	13, Sept 1897	12, Sept	72- -19d	5	
Kunkemüller, Henry	3, Jan. 1889		15m	1	
Kunkermoeller, William	21, Feb. 1901		33	8	
Kunkler, Emma M.	12, May 1891		30	1	

Name ****	Notice Date ****** ****	Death Date ***** ****	Age ***	Page ****	Maiden Name ****** ****
Kunnen, Lucinda	16, Mar. 1888		2m	1	
Kunstmann, Seb.	5, Sept 1888		57	2	
Kunter, Henriette Maria Engel	8, Mar. 1898	6, Mar.	44- 4m	5	Lehde
Kuntz, Ella	5, July 1887		15m	1	
Kuntz, Johan	5, Apr. 1898	4, Apr.	48- 1m	5	
Kuntz, Jonas	22, July 1889		18	1	
Kuntz, Mary	6, Aug. 1890		83	1	
Kuntz, Philippina	6, Apr. 1899	5, Apr.		4	
Kuntz, Rosa	28, Feb. 1896	27, Feb.	13d	5	
Kuntzler, Lorenz	22, June 1901		2	8	
Kuntzmann, Gustav	23, Nov. 1894			5	
Kuntzmann, Sarah	1, Mar. 1901		47	8	
Kunz, Elizabeth	31, Jan. 1900	28, Jan.	42- 4m	5	
Kunz, Margaret	11, Feb. 1889		47	1	
Kunz, Peter	19, July 1900		44	8	
Kunze, H.F.	2, Oct. 1895	29, Sept	45-11m	5	
Kunze, William	3, Jan. 1901		57	5	
Kunzel, Charles	29, Mar. 1894		54	5	
Kunzler, Edward L.	15, Dec. 1893		1	5	
Kunzler, Nikolaus	6, Apr. 1888		66	4	
Kupferschmidt, Emil	10, Dec. 1898	9, Dec.		5	
Kupferschmidt, Jacob	16, Mar. 1895		54	5	
Kuppel, Felix	3, Apr. 1890		5	1	
Kuppel, Felix	10, Jan. 1893		51	5	
Kupper, (Mrs. Frank)	22, Jan. 1900	21, Jan.		5	Lenz
Kuriger, T.M.	24, Sept 1896	19, Sept	52	5	
Kurmer, F.	15, Apr. 1897	13, Apr.		5	
Kurrus, August	2, June 1897	31, May	24- 6m	5	
Kurrus, Francis	24, May 1895		14	5	
Kurrus, Katharina	4, Oct. 1897	3, Oct.	48- 2m	5	Buntschuh
Kurrus, Sophia	22, Jan. 1891		1d	4	
Kurtz, Clara	14, Apr. 1897	12, Apr.	76- 3m	5	Hanes
Kurtz, Joseph	31, Dec. 1888		7	1	
Kurtz, Maria Anna	13, July 1899	12, July	42- 4m	5	Exner
Kurwick, Loretta	15, June 1894		7m	5	
Kurzyski, H.	6, Oct. 1899	5, Oct.	64	5	
Kushman, S. Jane	17, Apr. 1888		62	1	
Kushmann, George Cox	10, Jan. 1893		5m	5	
Kuter, Joseph	18, Feb. 1892		47	4	
Kutschkowsky, Catharine	20, Apr. 1899	19, Apr.	38	4	Lütti
Kutz, Ida E.	26, July 1887		33	1	
Kutzberger, Frank	6, Mar. 1895		1m	5	
Kyle, Carl	31, Aug. 1887		22m	1	
Kyler, Cynthia	27, Mar. 1888		70	4	
Kyler, M.	15, Jan. 1901		59	8	
Käfer, Frank G.	11, Mar. 1889		1w	1	
Kästel, Elisabeth Maria	11, July 1893	10, July	20- 2m-23d	5	
Käter, Anna Maria	14, July 1898	13, July	80- 9m	5	Grefenkamp
Köble, Josephine	5, Aug. 1889		3	1	
Köhler, Albert	1, Feb. 1890		6m	1	
Köhler, Anna Mary	22, Feb. 1897	20, Feb.	78- 6m	5	Rinck
Köhler, Katharina	17, Nov. 1899	16, Nov.	80- - 4d	4	Folbert
Köhler, Philipp	25, Jan. 1890		2	1	
Kölblin, Karl A.	10, Mar. 1897	10, Mar.	43- 7m	5	
Köllmann, Wilhelm	2, June 1896	29, May	37	5	
Könemann, Heinrich	15, Feb. 1900	12, Feb.	70- 6m	5	
König, Anna G.	7, Mar. 1891		70	4	
König, Anna M.	5, Apr. 1898	4, Apr.	79	5	
König, Antoinette	31, Mar. 1896	29, Mar.	56	5	
König, Caecilia	12, Sept 1890		8	1	
König, Elisabeth	30, Jan. 1896	29, Jan.		5	
König, Elisabeth	11, June 1897	8, June	72- 2m	5	Hasselbacher
König, Henry	1, Mar. 1889		59	1	
König, Max	25, Feb. 1891		1	4	
König, Valentin	18, Nov. 1898	16, Nov.	88	5	
Königkramer, Caroline	13, July 1887		47	1	
Königkramer, Hermine L.	24, Jan. 1899	22, Jan.	25- 1m	4	Boulnois
Königs, George	21, Mar. 1892		46	4	
Köppel, Herman	9, Apr. 1889	8, Apr.	2	4	
Köppel, Maria	17, Dec. 1893	16, Dec.		1	
Körner, Johan	13, Mar. 1893	11, Mar.	70	* 5	

Name	Notice Date	Death Date	Age	Page	Maiden Name
****	****** ****	***** ****	***	****	****** ****
Körner, John	15, Mar. 1893		69	5	
Kösner, George	29, Aug. 1887		2	1	
Köster, Emilie	1, Sept 1891		3w	4	
Kötemeyer, Clemens	11, Aug. 1900		54	8	
Kötter, Catharine	22, Oct. 1891		66	1	
Kötter, Edward	21, Jan. 1890		1m	1	
Kötter, Wilhelmine	26, Apr. 1892		1	5	
Kötterheinrich, Johan Georg	25, Mar. 1896	22, Mar.	30- 8m	5	
Kötterjohn, Anna M.	19, Mar. 1889		5m	1	
Kübesch, Barbara	1, Apr. 1890		66	1	
Kübler, Maria	29, Dec. 1892		45	5	
Künzel, Sophia	27, May 1889		43	1	
LItz, Elmora	27, Aug. 1890		3m	1	
Labech, John R.	27, Jan. 1891		33	4	
Lacey, Miles	4, Sept 1901		56	8	
Lacher, Clara K.	16, Jan. 1891		12	4	
Lachtrupp, Carrie	27, Dec. 1893		1	5	
Lack, Emil	18, Dec. 1900		16	8	
Lack, Emilie	5, July 1901		23d	8	
Lack, Marie	16, Aug. 1901		2	8	
Lacker, Theresia	23, Apr. 1897	22, Apr.	57	5	
Lackman, Edward	21, Mar. 1893		23	5	
Lackmann, Herman	13, Oct. 1894		27	5	
Lackmann, Johan	9, Nov. 1896	6, Nov.	51- 9m	5	
Lackmann, Joseph	18, Dec. 1891		54	2	
Lackmann, Maria	13, Mar. 1896	12, Mar.	69	5	Breddermann
Lackner, Frank	4, May 1896	2, May	59-10m	5	
Lackner, Josephine Franziska	18, Aug. 1896	16, Aug.	24- 9m	5	
Lacy, Helen C.	26, Apr. 1895		24	5	
Ladenkoetler, Mary A.	16, Jan. 1894		81	5	
Ladewig, Lulu	23, Jan. 1894		2	5	
Ladley, Ellen	8, Nov. 1900		67	8	
Laesche, Maria	19, Apr. 1894		5m	5	
Laffey, Thomas	13, Oct. 1900		60	8	
Lage, Margaret	4, Dec. 1891		39	4	
Lageman, Fred.	2, Dec. 1892		3	5	
Lagemann, Bernard	7, Mar. 1901		31	8	
Lagemann, Joseph	5, Dec. 1900		40	8	
Lagemann, William	12, Aug. 1901		2	8	
Lagnia, Treisa	26, Feb. 1897	26, Feb.	21	5	Dunker
Lago, Mary	2, July 1891		26	4	
Lagory, Albert	24, May 1895		21m	5	
Laham, Paul	4, Oct. 1900		62	8	
Lahman, Amelia	7, Dec. 1889		23	1	
Lahmann, W.	7, Nov. 1895	6, Nov.	79-10m	5	
Lahnsen, Fred	20, Nov. 1899	19, Nov.		5	
Laibly, Hannah	22, Sept 1888		24	1	
Laile, Charles	8, Jan. 1890		2	1	
Laile, Edwin	23, July 1895		6m	5	
Laing, August H.	11, May 1896	9, May	50	5	
Laing, Christina	27, Dec. 1899	26, Dec.	52	4	Schulte
Lakamp, John C.	6, Nov. 1891		3	4	
Lakamp, Margaretha Caroline	16, Sept 1897	15, Sept	58-10m	5	Placke
Lake, Charles	2, June 1892		23	5	
Lake, G.J.	7, July 1897	6, July	21- 7m	5	
Lakin, Anthony C.	1, May 1895		2	5	
Lamade, Louis	27, Feb. 1892		62	5	
Lamanick, Yetta	25, Aug. 1890		28	1	
Lamb, Albert	2, June 1893		39	5	
Lamb, Sophia	21, Dec. 1891		11	4	
Lamber, Phil.	30, Aug. 1890		30	2	
Lambernds, John	23, May 1888		4m	1	
Lambers, Clara	29, Jan. 1901		2	8	
Lambers, Francis	27, Oct. 1894		21m	5	
Lambers, J.	14, July 1900		41	8	
Lambers, Louisa	10, Jan. 1898	9, Jan.	36	5	Stemann
Lambers, Mary	11, Nov. 1894		4	5	
Lambers, Nicholas	26, June 1891		7d	4	
Lambert, Assonia	24, Nov. 1891		9m	4	
Lambert, Christopher	29, Nov. 1893		66	5	

Name	Notice Date	Death Date	Age	Page	Maiden Name
****	****** ****	***** ****	***	****	****** ****
Lambert, Frank R.	29, Aug. 1887		5- 6m	1	
Lambert, Louis	20, Nov. 1888		40	1	
Lambert, Marcus	31, Dec. 1893		31	5	
Lambert, Margaret	8, May 1891		53	4	
Lambert, Margarethe	12, Sept 1900			5	
Lambert, Mary A.	4, Jan. 1894		22	5	
Lambert, Thomas J.	27, Mar. 1895		54	5	
Lamberz, Mary	26, Feb. 1901		56	8	
Lambfrit, Adam	31, Mar. 1891		57	4	
Lambing, Joseph	31, May 1890		74	1	
Lamburg, Leona	5, May 1895		3m	5	
Lammeier, Maria Angela	1, Aug. 1896	31, July	69-11m	5	Brinkmann
Lammerding, Frank	19, June 1901		13	8	
Lammers, Angela	7, Jan. 1901		6	5	
Lammers, C.M.	23, July 1887		15m	1	
Lammers, Henry	16, Aug. 1901		54	8	
Lammers, John W.	9, Sept 1893		3	5	
Lammers, Joseph	29, Sept 1894		17	5	
Lammers, Philomena	9, June 1897	8, June	64- 8m	5	
Lammert, Joseph	2, Mar. 1900	1, Mar.	73	4	
Lammert, Louisa	30, Nov. 1892		90	5	
Lammeyer, John	30, Nov. 1887		61	4	
Lampe, August	14, Apr. 1891		3w	4	
Lampe, Carrie	20, May 1893		22	5	
Lampe, Frances	13, Apr. 1896	12, Apr.	61	5	
Lampe, Harry A.	10, May 1901		5m	8	
Lampe, Heinrich Joseph	8, Apr. 1896	6, Apr.	17- 5m	5	
Lampe, John	1, Nov. 1892		20	5	
Lampe, Katharine	13, July 1896	12, July		5	
Lampe, Louise	31, Dec. 1891		34	1	
Lampe, Philip	21, Aug. 1891		43	4	
Lampe, William	5, June 1895		56	5	
Lampers, Carolina	6, Jan. 1892		34	5	
Lampert, Catharine	2, July 1901		41	8	
Lamping, Augusta	5, Mar. 1891		29	4	
Lamping, Bernard Heinrich	24, Nov. 1896	23, Nov.	73- 2m	5	
Lamping, Carl	24, July 1895		7m	5	
Lamping, Lillian	6, June 1895		9m	5	
Lamping, Lizzie	1, Aug. 1887		13m	1	
Lamping, Mathilda	21, Aug. 1888		1	1	
Lamping, Winifred	12, May 1895		5m	5	
Lampke, Rosa	5, Aug. 1898	3, Aug.	28- 1m	5	Schnueck
Land, Louise C.	28, Mar. 1893		31	5	
Landeberg, Maggie	3, May 1892		24	5	
Landenvitch, Alois	5, Mar. 1901		8	5	
Lander, Anna	25, June 1901		42	8	
Landheidel, Florence	17, June 1888		5w	1	
Landmann, B.G.	18, July 1887		38	1	
Landmeier, Mary	25, Feb. 1901		22	8	
Landwehr, Catharine L.	10, July 1887		6- 6m	1	
Landwehr, Dietrich W.	17, 21, Mar. 1893	15, Mar.	67- 7m	5	
Landwehr, E.J.	28, Dec. 1891		1	4	
Landwehr, Freddy	4, Aug. 1900		5	8	
Landwehr, Heinrich	24, Oct. 1887		33- 3m	1	
Landwehr, Herman	16, Apr. 1901		36	8	
Lane, Charles	10, June 1901		53	8	
Lane, Lena	22, Mar. 1901			8	
Lanfer, Annie	16, May 1901		13	5	
Lanfersiek, Heinrich	18, Aug. 1896	17, Aug.	50-11m	5	
Lang,	1, Aug. 1887		18d	1	
Lang, Amalia	30, Aug. 1888		9m	1	
Lang, Anna	18, Mar. 1889		34	1	
Lang, Anna	25, May 1893	24, May		5	Becker
Lang, Annie	22, May 1894		3	5	
Lang, Bertha	9, July 1887		10m	1	
Lang, Caroline	1, Aug. 1891		57	4	
Lang, Catharine	19, July 1893		5m	5	
Lang, Catharine	27, Apr. 1897	26, Apr.	73	5	
Lang, Clara M.	27, Sept 1888		5m	2	
Lang, Fanny	8, Apr. 1891		72	4	
Lang, Fred.	13, Jan. 1891		1d	1	

Name	Notice Date	Death Date	Age	Page	Maiden Name
****	****** ****	***** ****	***	****	****** ****
Lang, George	21, Sept 1887		9m	1	
Lang, George	8, Nov. 1893	7, Nov.	36- -11d	5	
Lang, Henry	6, July 1895		17m	5	
Lang, John	4, Jan. 1893		58	5	
Lang, John	9, Mar. 1893		63	5	
Lang, John	12, Dec. 1900		16m	8	
Lang, John F.	6, Mar. 1891		31	4	
Lang, Josephine	27, May 1901		28	8	
Lang, Leo	13, Mar. 1890		3m	4	
Lang, Louis	25, Sept 1891		40- 4m	4	
Lang, Louis	13, Mar. 1894		2	5	
Lang, Louis	6, Feb. 1896	4, Feb.	17- 1m	5	
Lang, Louis	2, Nov. 1900		60	8	
Lang, Louisa	17, Dec. 1900		71	8	
Lang, Mary	21, Mar. 1891		23	4	
Lang, Rose May	12, Oct. 1899	10, Oct.		5	
Lang, William A.	10, June 1889		30	1	
Langan, James	21, May 1901		23	8	
Langdon, Eunice M.	14, Sept 1901		76	1	
Lange, Agnes	21, Mar. 1898	19, Mar.	71-10m	5	Rolfzen
Lange, Alma	12, Feb. 1888	11, Feb.	77- -23d	5	
Lange, Aloysius	12, Aug. 1895	11, Aug.	23- 4m	5	
Lange, Anna	6, Aug. 1897	4, Aug.	72	5	
Lange, Anna Katharina	5, Apr. 1900	4, Apr.	66	5	Ruebusch
Lange, Anton	29, Nov. 1889		56	1	
Lange, Charles	30, Dec. 1899	29, Dec.	39- 6m-20d	5	
Lange, Christian	12, Mar. 1892		62	5	
Lange, Elisabeth	5, Jan. 1897		69	5	Surenkamp
Lange, Elisabeth	28, Mar. 1898	27, Mar.	76	5	
Lange, Erhardt	5, July 1888		35	1	
Lange, Franz	27, Oct. 1898	25, Oct.	86- - 9d	5	
Lange, Johan Heinrich	21, Nov. 1898	19, Nov.	53- 5m-17d	5	
Lange, John	17, Jan. 1890		36	1	
Lange, Joseph	5, Oct. 1896	4, Oct.	57- 8m	5	
Lange, Kate	5, Jan. 1901		76	8	
Lange, Maria	26, 27, Sept 1895	25, Sept	63	5	Piepper
Lange, Maria Elisabeth	26, May 1898	25, May	75	5	Niehaus
Lange, Mary	3, Mar. 1891		63	4	
Lange, William	23, June 1893		55	5	
Langebier, Millie	7, Dec. 1887		28	1	
Langeland, J.J.	2, Dec. 1895	1, Dec.	65	5	
Langemeier, Clemens F.	2, Apr. 1897	31, Mar.	25- 5m	5	
Langemeier, Gertrude	6, Dec. 1895	4, Dec.		5	Roth
Langen, Mary G.	28, June 1888		2	1	
Langenbach, Catharina	1, Feb. 1900	31, Jan.	70	5	Behrens
Langenbalm, P.	7, Dec. 1887		47	1	
Langenbein, G.	24, Apr. 1891		2	4	
Langenbrunner, Louis A.	9, Mar. 1900	8, Mar.	28	8	
Langenbucher, Ad.	22, June 1889		5m	1	
Langenbucker, Ernst	4, Feb. 1893		67	5	
Langendorfer, Fritz	23, Mar. 1895		40	5	
Langenstroer, Anna Josephina	29, Mar. 1898	27, Mar.	64- 5m	5	Hammes
Langermann, Emma	13, Nov. 1896	12, Nov.	29-10m	5	
Langermann, Karl	23, Apr. 1898	22, Apr.	64- 6m	4	
Langforter, Frank	30, May 1901		32	8	
Langhaus, Edward	3, July 1897	30, June	7m-11d	5	
Langhauser, Lotta	1, June 1892		39	5	
Langhorn, Emma A.	8, Dec. 1887		13	1	
Langhorst, Ed.	8, Aug. 1900		7m	8	
Langhorst, Henry	7, July 1891		8	1	
Langhorst, Louisa K.	22, Mar. 1893		10m	5	
Langhorst, William	18, Mar. 1890		73	1	
Langhurst, William	1, Aug. 1887		9w	1	
Langmead, William	22, May 1894		46	5	
Langmeyer, Ida	14, Aug. 1897	12, Aug.	34- -24d	5	Grundhöfer
Langmeyer, Mary	2, June 1891		27	4	
Lannon,	22, July 1887		3d	1	
Lannon, Robert	7, July 1888		39	4	
Lannspach, Elizabeth	16, Apr. 1889		57	1	
Lanser, Clara	17, Oct. 1888		55	1	
Lapaire, Maggie	6, Aug. 1901		49	8	

Name ****	Notice Date ****** ****	Death Date ***** ****	Age ***	Page ****	Maiden Name ****** ****
Lapley, Charles W.	5, May 1895		5m	5	
Lapp, Jacob	4, Oct. 1894		38	5	
Lapple, Elmer A.	21, Nov. 1891		21d	4	
Lappold, Carolina	9, Nov. 1893		40	5	
Lapthorn, Elsie	11, Oct. 1894		6m	5	
Lapthorn, S.	30, Jan. 1888		20	1	
Larbus, Joseph	16, Aug. 1901		2	8	
Larkins, Harry	17, Dec. 1900		2m	8	
Larkins, John	20, Oct. 1887		7	1	
Larney, Rose	28, Jan. 1901		32	8	
Lary, Theresa	8, Nov. 1887		44	1	
Lasance, Bernard	7, Mar. 1896	6, Mar.	82	5	
Lasch, Frederick	1, Mar. 1901		78	8	
Lasker, Henrietta	17, Dec. 1900		9	8	
Lassig, Theodor	22, Aug. 1892		59	5	
Lasy, William	6, Jan. 1892		49	5	
Latimer, Walter F.	15, Jan. 1901		3m	8	
Latosinsky, Vincent	8, Aug. 1890		6m	1	
Latostuski, Walter	30, Oct. 1891		3m	4	
Lattner, Joseph	22, Feb. 1893		7m	5	
Lauber, Josephine	11, Apr. 1891	10, Apr.	34	* 4	Maier
Laubernds, Henry	27, Nov. 1889		60	1	
Lauck,	20, June 1895		1d	5	
Laudenbach, Franz	19, Dec. 1899	18, Dec.	25-10m	4	
Lauderbach, Elizabeth	9, Dec. 1893		64	5	
Laudon, Mary	3, Jan. 1889		63	1	
Lauer, Garnetta	29, Dec. 1900		3	8	
Laufer, Adam	10, Apr. 1894		49	5	
Laufersiek, Louis G.	28, Apr. 1900	26, Apr.	49- 4m	5	
Laughlin, James	20, Sept 1887		28	1	
Laughlin, Michael	30, Nov. 1900		48	8	
Laughlin, Rebecca	21, Sept 1900			5	
Laumann, Anton	15, June 1901		30	8	
Laumann, Frank H.	21, June 1894		3- 6m	5	
Laumann, George	9, Apr. 1891		1	4	
Laumann, M.M.	31, July 1901		75	8	
Laumann, William	26, Feb. 1888		50	4	
Laurel, Helen	2, Feb. 1901		3m	8	
Laurens, Maria	26, Dec. 1900		52	8	
Laurer, Barbara	9, Apr. 1890		4	1	
Laurer, Sophia	18, June 1889		22m	1	
Laurier, F.	20, July 1897	19, July		5	
Laurier, Lulu	30, June 1897	28, June	6-11m	5	
Lauser, Rosa	11, July 1891		11m	1	
Lausing, Anton	5, June 1895		24	5	
Lautenberger, George	6, Apr. 1889		16	1	
Lautenschlaeger, E.	1, May 1901		68	8	
Lautenschlaeger, Ed.	23, Mar. 1901		37	8	
Lautenschlager, Mary E.	18, Feb. 1890		55	1	
Lautenschläger, B.	28, Sept 1901		69	5	
Lautenschläger, Jakob	20, Jan. 1890		32	1	
Lauterback, Cecilia	6, Feb. 1901		1	8	
Lauther, Caroline	4, Apr. 1901		75	8	
Lauther, Charles	16, Feb. 1899	15, Feb.	47- 2m	5	
Lautz, John	12, Oct. 1894		59	5	
Lauxtermann, Lauretta	5, Aug. 1898	3, Aug.	2- 6m	5	
Lauxtermann, Louis D.	17, Aug. 1899	16, Aug.	29-11m	4	
Lavamia, Alois	11, June 1891		4	4	
Lavin, John	11, July 1887		29	1	
Lawhorn, Charles	24, Dec. 1900		23	8	
Lawler, Anna	2, Jan. 1901		68	5	
Lawrence,	17, July 1901		12d	8	
Lawrence, A.L.	16, Aug. 1887		2w	1	
Lawrence, Lisetta	18, June 1896	17, June	53	5	Gildehaus
Laws, Emma	10, June 1901		34	8	
Lawson, Cagee	22, July 1901		39	8	
Lawson, John	30, Mar. 1901		51	8	
Layens, Elizabeth	27, Jan. 1891		62	4	
Layritz, Philipp	12, May 1891	10, May	47	1	
Layton, John	8, May 1901		1	8	
Lazarus, Barbara	20, Apr. 1896	19, Apr.		5	

Name ****	Notice Date ****** ****	Death Date ***** ****	Age ***	Page ****	Maiden Name ****** ****
Lazarus, Betty	2, July 1891			4	
Lazarus, Henry	25, Jan. 1892		25	5	
Laß, Josepha	8, June 1899	7, June	66-11m	4	Schürer
LeBoutillier, Mary	22, Aug. 1900		22	5	
Leahey, James	28, Nov. 1900		29	8	
Leahy, Elizabeth	25, Dec. 1891		55	2	
Learn, John	5, July 1888		5m	1	
Lebeau, Catharine	16, Jan. 1897	14, Jan.		5	
Lebeau, Jacob	28, Jan. 1889		60	1	
Lebherz, Johanna	4, Apr. 1894		61	5	
Lebmann, Charles G.	19, Dec. 1893		53	5	
Lechleitner, Anton	5, Dec. 1900		69	8	
Lechner, Mary	18, Apr. 1893		29	5	
Lecker, Clara Louise	20, July 1893		20	5	
Leder, August	5, July 1888	4, July	1- 3m	1	
Leder, Elsie	27, Mar. 1894		4m	5	
Lederer, Arthur	6, July 1901		6d	8	
Lederer, Clarence	29, Aug. 1891		4m	4	
Lederer, Elisabeth	26, Aug. 1895	25, Aug.	45- 6m	5	Krauser
Lederer, Henry	9, Aug. 1887		3m	1	
Lederhaus, Wilhelm H.	2, Sept 1898	1, Sept	44	4	
Ledge, May Jane	26, Sept 1901		81	8	
Ledig, Lulu	20, Oct. 1888		13	1	
Lee, Edna	2, Oct. 1900		3m	8	
Lee, Edward	8, Oct. 1900		3m	8	
Lee, Eliza	31, July 1901		37	8	
Lee, Ellen	4, Feb. 1888		74	4	
Lee, Jessie	31, Oct. 1900		32	8	
Lee, Joseph	23, July 1887		15m	1	
Lee, Mary E.	28, Apr. 1888		6d	1	
Leedle, Emma	11, Sept 1901		35	8	
Leek, Alb.	10, May 1888		9m	1	
Leeper, James	30, Aug. 1900		89	5	
Leers, Hubert	11, Oct. 1894		49	5	
Leesmann, Amelia	2, Sept 1897	1, Sept	63- 1m	5	Maier
Leesmann, Minnie	23, Jan. 1901		35	8	
Leewe, Bernhard H.	12, Apr. 1893		47	5	
Leewe, Caroline	2, Jan. 1890		7	1	
Lefeber, Mary E.	4, July 1887		73	1	
Legel, Louis	13, Apr. 1892		68	5	
Legge, Charity	25, June 1888		80	1	
Legner, Franziska	29, July 1901	29, July	73- - 7d	* 8	Burger
Legner, Mary	4, July 1901		73	8	
Lehan, John	22, Sept 1900		55	5	
Lehkamp, William	14, Nov. 1893		71	5	
Lehker, Joseph	5, Mar. 1901		3- 6m	5	
Lehman, Fred. A.	17, Mar. 1893		18	5	
Lehman, Nathan	13, Mar. 1896	12, Mar.	66	5	
Lehmann, Anna	8, June 1894		34	5	
Lehmann, Caroline	22, Aug. 1888		2	1	
Lehmann, Charles H.	10, 11, Mar. 1898	8, Mar.	21-11m	5	
Lehmann, Heinrich	13, Apr. 1896	9, Apr.	59- 8m	5	
Lehmann, Jacob	10, Sept 1901		53	1	
Lehmann, Joseph	24, Sept 1900		35	5	
Lehmann, Margaret	20, Mar. 1895		32	5	
Lehmann, Moritz	19, May 1899	18, May	3m	4	
Lehmann, Rebecca	16, Apr. 1891		36	4	
Lehmann, William	9, May 1894		36	5	
Lehmeier, August	3, Aug. 1887		6m	1	
Lehmkuhl, Henry	20, Mar. 1901		72	1	
Lehmkuhl, John H.	17, Aug. 1887		1d	1	
Lehmuth, Fred.	20, Mar. 1895		79	5	
Lehnhoff, Barbara	30, Jan. 1901		52	8	
Lehnhoff, Therese	10, May 1889		44	1	
Lehr, Emma	16, Aug. 1887		17d	1	
Lehr, Ida	11, Aug. 1887		13d	1	
Lehr, Margaretha	22, Jan. 1899	19, Jan.	69	5	
Leibbrand, Maria Louis	29, Mar. 1894	28, Mar.	40- 7m-14d	* 5	
Leibman, Selma	4, Mar. 1889		3	1	
Leibold, Anton	20, Mar. 1889		59	1	
Leibold, Magdalena	22, Jan. 1891		73	4	

Name	Notice Date	Death Date	Age	Page	Maiden Name
****	****** ****	***** ****	***	****	****** ****
Leich, Catharine	18, June 1889		61	1	
Leichnam, George	19, Apr. 1889		18	1	
Leicht, Margaretha	5, May 1896	4, May	46- 4m	5	
Leichtle, Alexander	11, Jan. 1889		21	1	
Leichtle, G.A.	21, Mar. 1888		2m	1	
Leidenheimer, Katie	21, Jan. 1894		79	5	
Leidlein, Kate	15, Mar. 1890		73	1	
Leifling, Anna M.	16, May 1893		73	5	
Leighton, H.M.	14, Feb. 1888		43	4	
Leikauf, Katharina	16, Feb. 1899	15, Feb.	72- 7m	5	Strobel
Leikauf, Leonhard	30, Nov. 1897	28, Nov.	79- -13d	5	
Leil, Georg	14, Jan. 1893		66	5	
Leimann, Caroline	7, Aug. 1897	5, Aug.	75	4	Morsch
Leimberger, Christina	10, May 1900	9, May	52- 5m- 9d	8	Leichtfuß
Leindecker, Josephine	1, Aug. 1887		13m	1	
Leinen, Katie	6, May 1889		24	1	
Leininger, Philomena	21, 23, Mar. 1894	19, Mar.	59-11m-22d	5	Hartlaub
Leisenbach, Joseph	3, Oct. 1891		14- 3m	1	
Leiser, Ida May	21, Oct. 1891		1m	4	
Leiser, Katharine	20, 21, Oct. 1896	17, Oct.	41- 1m	5	Eichenlaub
Leiser, Lizzie	28, Sept 1888		2w	2	
Leist, Andreas	17, Apr. 1891	16, Apr.	40- 7m	1	
Leist, Caroline	11, Aug. 1887		74	1	
Leist, Carrie	21, July 1891		1d	4	
Leist, George	24, July 1894		52	5	
Leist, Otto	7, May 1891		7m	4	
Leist, Walter	29, July 1887		1m	1	
Leitsch, Robert	14, Jan. 1893		66	5	
Leitz, Mathias	5, Jan. 1901		69	8	
Leive, Annette	27, June 1896	25, June	22- 7m	5	
Leive, Clara	19, July 1894		23	5	
Leive, Johan	15, Sept 1898	12, Sept	32- 2m	5	
Leive, Lizzie S.	7, June 1895		3	5	
Leivs, Charles	29, May 1901		53	8	
Lell, Georg	10, June 1898	8, June	51	4	
Lemberg, Henry	28, Oct. 1889		48	1	
Lembert, Alma	29, July 1888		18m	1	
Leming, James Alfred	29, Mar. 1897	27, Mar.	28	5	
Leming, William W.	30, Jan. 1891		5	4	
Lemke, Edna	28, May 1891		3w	4	
Lemmel, Anna	1, July 1891		2m	1	
Lemmel, Barbara	29, Sept 1893		54	5	
Lemmel, Catharina	22, July 1893		20	5	
Lemmel, George	28, Jan. 1892		6m	5	
Lemmel, Ottillia	22, Feb. 1896	21, Feb.	55- 1m	5	Zwick
Lemmer, John	10, May 1895		11m	5	
Lemmon, J.F.	16, Aug. 1887		4w	1	
Lemmonds, Carrie	15, July 1887		22m	1	
Lemper, Anna	18, May 1894		66	5	
Lemperle, Heinrich	15, Jan. 1896	14, Jan.	15-10m	5	
Lemuel, Sabina	26, Aug. 1901		26	8	
Lena, Joseph	18, Apr. 1890		8m	1	
Lender, Frederick B.	19, Feb. 1895		80	5	
Lenfurt, Heinrich	4, Nov. 1895	3, Nov.	62-11m	5	
Lengers, Philomena	20, Feb. 1895		3m	5	
Lenhart, Charles	22, May 1894		1	5	
Leni, Yetta	13, Aug. 1891		68	4	
Lennon, Carolina	19, Oct. 1900		43	5	
Lenthold, Rudolph S.	26, July 1895		48	5	
Lentz, Heinrich	25, Oct. 1898	24, Oct.	55-11m- 9d	5	
Lenzer, George H.E.	27, Sept 1890		2m	1	
Leonard, Anna	16, Oct. 1901		64	1	
Leonard, Augusta	14, Dec. 1893		14d	5	
Leonard, Catharine	3, Dec. 1900		56	8	
Leonard, George	3, Mar. 1888		1m	1	
Leonard, J.J.	21, Feb. 1888		1- 2m	1	
Leonard, James	4, Oct. 1888		67	4	
Leonard, Joseph A.	21, June 1888		3m	1	
Leonard, Margaret	14, June 1901		67	5	
Leonard, Maria	21, Apr. 1891		2m	4	
Leonard, Mary	8, Sept 1887		36	1	

Name	Notice Date	Death Date	Age	Page	Maiden Name
****	****** ****	***** ****	***	****	****** ****
Leonard, Sarah	21, July 1887		87	1	
Leonard, Thomas	30, Aug. 1888		47	1	
Leonhardt, Georg	4, June 1889		4	1	
Leonhardt, Georg	3, May 1895		81	5	
Leopold, Mary	30, Dec. 1891		56	4	
Lepper, W.	1, Oct. 1901		23	1	
Leppert, Friedricka	13, 14, Dec. 1888	13, Dec.	73- 7m-21d	* 1	Hohnstein
Leppert, Genevieve	26, Mar. 1901		3	8	
Leppert, Karl	4, Jan. 1898	3, Jan.	46- 2m	5	
Leppert, W.J.	21, Jan. 1889		3	1	
Lerch, Augusta	6, Aug. 1895	5, Aug.	68- 3m	5	Vonhof
Lerch, Charles	28, Jan. 1889		2m	1	
Lerch, L.	2, Mar. 1901		65	5	
Lerche, Margaretha	28, Dec. 1897	26, Dec.	64- 1m	4	Appel
Lertz, J.	2, Nov. 1894		68	5	
Lesmann, Fred.	2, Oct. 1891		5	4	
Lessel, Elizabeth	11, Aug. 1887		65	1	
Letch, Augustin	15, Sept 1900		14	5	
Leteche, Louis	12, May 1891		6	1	
Letom, Anna	26, Jan. 1901		1	8	
Letsche, Carl T.	27, June 1895		4m	5	
Letsche, Louis	9, Jan. 1894		35	5	
Lettersch, William	25, Aug. 1890		7m	1	
Letzler, Elisabeth	26, Feb. 1900	25, Feb.	56- 8m	8	
Letzler, Friedrich H.	28, Dec. 1900		30	8	
Letzler, Jakob	2, Apr. 1891		70	4	
Letzler, Jinnie	17, June 1889		3	1	
Letzler, Mary	27, Apr. 1900	26, Apr.	56	5	
Leucht, Josephine	7, June 1898	5, June	21- 2m	5	
Leuchtenberg, Emilie	19, May 1896	18, May		5	
Leuckering, William	21, Dec. 1892		14	5	
Leuermann, Bernard	6, June 1891		1d	4	
Leuk, Katharina	9, Mar. 1897	8, Mar.	78-10m	5	Czerwinski
Leutenegger, George	3, Sept 1901		30	8	
Leutner, Carl	5, Sept 1894		38	5	
Leutz, Henry	10, May 1889		19m	1	
Levandowski, Mary	7, Sept 1900		1	5	
Leveling, Joseph E.	19, June 1895		2	5	
Leverman, Maria	7, June 1890		6m	1	
Levermann, Theodor	12, Apr. 1892		22	5	
Levi, Leopold	11, Dec. 1891		73	4	
Levi, Louis	27, Nov. 1900		83	8	
Levi, Samuel	12, Nov. 1887		3- 2m	1	
Levi, Samuel	24, June 1893		12	5	
Levi, Theresa	14, Apr. 1893		1	5	
Levitt, Edward (Rev)	23, June 1888		58	1	
Levy, Fred.	18, Feb. 1891		38	4	
Levy, Isaac	1, Oct. 1890		67	1	
Levy, Jacob	21, July 1900		64	8	
Levy, Joseph	30, Oct. 1891		12d	4	
Levy, Mary	11, May 1889		46	1	
Lewing, Elisabeth	7, Aug. 1900		20	8	
Lewing, Gerhard	19, Dec. 1898	18, Dec.	79	4	
Lewis,	15, May 1895		3	5	
Lewis, Anna	21, Sept 1901		86	8	
Lewis, Aubrey	12, Dec. 1900		1m	8	
Lewis, Emma	22, Dec. 1900		60	8	
Lewis, Frank	2, Oct. 1888		4m	1	
Lewis, Fred. N.	17, Aug. 1901		51	8	
Lewis, Joseph	23, July 1901		6m	8	
Ley, Heinrich	19, Sept 1889	18, Dec.	80	* 1	
Ley, Margaretha	12, Nov. 1900		66	5	
Leyendecker, Peter	13, June 1900	12, June	69- 6m	8	
Lezer, Cunigunde	13, Mar. 1890		70	4	
Liable, Fred.	3, Sept 1891		4m	4	
Libean, William F.	21, Apr. 1895		47	5	
Licar, Bernard	23, Apr. 1896	22, Apr.	78	5	
Lichner, Josephine	10, July 1889		15m	1	
Licht, Jacob Heinrich	26, Jan. 1888		80	* 4	
Lichtenberg, August	3, July 1901		78	8	
Lichtendall, Fenne	8, Mar. 1892		74	5	

Name	Notice Date	Death Date	Age	Page	Maiden Name
****	****** ****	***** ****	***	****	****** ****
Lieb, Andreas	13, Mar. 1901		4	8	
Lieb, Johan	31, Oct. 1896	30, Oct.	59	5	
Liebelt, Adolf	14, Dec. 1898	13, Dec.	45- 1m	5	
Liebenstein, Isaac	18, Feb. 1890		70	2	
Lieber, Bernhard	10, May 1888		8m	1	
Liebermann, Theresa	24, Mar. 1896	18, Mar.	67	5	
Liebhulz, Isaac	28, Apr. 1891		8m	4	
Liebing, Christine	28, Jan. 1899	26, Jan.	55- 9m	5	
Lieblag, Geneva	3, Jan. 1901		14m	5	
Liebman, Louis	2, May 1901		19d	8	
Liebmann, Babette	2, June 1898	1, June	60- 6m	4	
Liebmann, Jacob L.	7, Oct. 1893		49	5	
Liebmann, Leop.	17, Sept 1889		58	1	
Lieboner, Anna	7, Sept 1895	6, Sept	28- 8m	5	
Liebrecht, William	28, Sept 1901		69	5	
Liebschütz, S.	22, July 1893		1d	5	
Lieman, Elmer	26, June 1891		2m	4	
Lienhardt, F.	28, Feb. 1888		8m-12d	1	
Lienhart, Maria Carolina	20, Feb. 1891	19, Feb.	2m- 6d	1	
Liest, Phillip	11, Nov. 1891		3m	1	
Lietemeyer, Elizabeth	24, Sept 1901		55	1	
Lieteren, P.H.	3, July 1894		13	5	
Lietz, Fred	6, Apr. 1892		36	5	
Lietze, Charlotte	10, Nov. 1896	7, Nov.	58	4	Fahrendorff
Liggins, Louisa	17, July 1901		90	8	
Light, Loretta A.	12, Mar. 1901		3	8	
Ligowsky, August	27, July 1899	26, July	73	5	
Liller, Michael	4, Apr. 1899	3, Apr.	74- 3m	5	
Lilley, John	22, Dec. 1900		2m	8	
Lillie, H.B.	26, Apr. 1898	25, Apr.	67- 1m	5	
Lilling, John B.	3, Mar. 1891		69	4	
Limbach, Fred. N.	19, Aug. 1893		2	5	
Limberger, Joseph	1, Mar. 1898	28, Feb.	52- - 8d	5	
Limbert, Albert	12, Feb. 1889		29	1	
Limbert, Anna Margaretha	9, Mar. 1900	7, Mar.	81	8	
Limer, Lizzie	6, Aug. 1901		66	8	
Lind, Christoph	5, June 1897	4, June	70- 6m	5	
Lind, Margaret	30, May 1901			8	
Lindauer, Louis	12, Aug. 1893		37	5	
Lindeman, Robert H.	17, Aug. 1899	16, Aug.	43	4	
Lindemann, Albert J.	26, Apr. 1895		1	5	
Lindemann, Aloysius	17, July 1895		20	5	
Lindemann, Anton	4, Dec. 1891		57	4	
Lindemann, Carrie Lulu	23, Aug. 1897	21, Aug.	8-11m	5	
Lindemann, Charlotte	11, 12, Sept 1895	10, Sept	82- 4m	5	Niemann
Lindemann, Christine	12, May 1893		76	5	
Lindemann, Georg W.	3, Oct. 1898	2, Oct.	37- 8m	5	
Lindemann, George	16, Jan. 1891		65	4	
Lindemann, George	16, July 1895		49	5	
Lindemann, Karl Frank	16, Apr. 1891		11m	4	
Lindemann, Lida	18, June 1901		18	8	
Lindemann, Paul J.	28, July 1887		2- 6m	1	
Lindemann, Ray Etta	10, Mar. 1893		3	5	
Lindemann, Sophia B.	29, Apr. 1896	28, Apr.	23	5	Meier
Linden, Mary	25, Mar. 1901		72	8	
Lindner, Fred.	28, Aug. 1890		73	1	
Lindner, Louise	11, July 1898	9, July	45	5	Weiß
Lindsay, Alice G.	9, May 1895		12d	5	
Lindsay, Bertie M.	14, Jan. 1891		9	4	
Lindsay, Jessie G.	14, Jan. 1891		8	4	
Lindsay, John	1, Oct. 1887		65	1	
Lindsey, Henry	15, Oct. 1900		14	5	
Linfert, Bernardina	17, Mar. 1891	15, Mar.	71	4	Thesing
Linfin, John Jacob	16, Dec. 1891		60	4	
Ling, Emiline	27, Mar. 1894		56	5	
Lingenfelter, Jesse	2, Jan. 1901		64	5	
Linger, Lillie	20, Sept 1901		14	1	
Lingers, Elizabeth	22, Jan. 1892		63	5	
Lingers, Maria	17, Dec. 1895	16, Dec.	63- 3m	4	Klostermann
Link, Anna	29, July 1890		50	1	
Link, Elisabeth	6, July 1897	5, July	76	5	

Name	Notice Date	Death Date	Age	Page	Maiden Name
****	****** ****	***** ****	***	****	****** ****
Link, Franziska	11, Feb. 1897	10, Feb.	66- 3m	5	
Link, Helen	5, Jan. 1892		41	5	
Link, Jakob	4, May 1898	2, May	82- 9m	5	
Link, Johan	28, May 1891	27, May	56- 4m	4	
Link, William	8, Oct. 1891		18	4	
Linke, Julius	22, Feb. 1893		56	5	
Linke, Louisa	17, Dec. 1892		78	5	
Linke, Maria M.	4, June 1892		2- 4m- 2d	5	
Linkenbach, Carl	19, Mar. 1889		7m	1	
Linkenbach, Josie A.	6, July 1893		31	5	
Linkenbach, Rosa	2, Aug. 1901		68	8	
Linkenstein, Jacob	25, May 1901		76	8	
Linko, Maria	2, 4, Apr. 1895	1, Apr.	73	5	
Linnebaum, Frank	6, Feb. 1899	5, Feb.	26	4	
Linneen, Kate	12, Sept 1900		50	5	
Linnemann, Alois	10, May 1895		10m	5	
Linnemann, Anna	11, Jan. 1893		72	5	
Linnemann, Francis	3, Feb. 1891		38	4	
Linnemann, John	12, Mar. 1889		1d	1	
Linnemann, John	30, Mar. 1901		82	8	
Linnemann, Leo	1, Sept 1900		2	5	
Linnemann, Maria	11, Feb. 1896	10, Feb.	42- 7m	5	Ortmann
Linnemeier, Louisa	9, Apr. 1891		62	4	
Linnenkamp, Henry	3, July 1901		39	8	
Linnenkohl, Edward	18, Nov. 1891		1	4	
Linning, Josephine	14, July 1891		25	4	
Lins, Andreas	8, Nov. 1887		8w	1	
Linskey, M.	6, Mar. 1901		22	5	
Linstey, Bessie	8, Jan. 1901		12d	8	
Linthume,	6, Jan. 1888		8d	1	
Linz, John	28, June 1895		28	5	
Linz, Martin	13, July 1892		4	5	
Linz, Mathias	23, Dec. 1891		52	4	
Linz, Vinzens	19, May 1900	17, May	78- 1m	8	
Lipke, Nathan	3, Sept 1891		76	4	
Lipman, Louisa	28, May 1901		73	8	
Lipmann, Edward	9, May 1895		7m	5	
Lipmann, Meier	5, Feb. 1895		44	5	
Lipp, Belle	16, Dec. 1891		37	4	
Lipp, Louise	23, May 1893	22, May	34- 3m-16d	5	Allinger
Lipp, Wilhelm	26, July 1890	24, July	30	* 1	
Lippelman, Lizzie	2, Feb. 1892		2	5	
Lippelmann, Elisabeth	27, July 1893		57	5	
Lipper, John	13, Mar. 1891		45	4	
Lippert, Ada H.	12, July 1893		4m	5	
Lippert, Clara	10, Feb. 1896	8, Feb.	18- 8m	5	
Lippert, Francis	20, Oct. 1900		74	8	
Lippert, Frank G.	19, Dec. 1900		3	8	
Lippert, Johan	6, June 1899	4, June	65- 1m	5	
Lippert, Louis	11, Aug. 1891		1	4	
Lippert, Regina	6, Apr. 1892		21	5	
Lippert, Rosa B.	21, Mar. 1893		43	5	
Lippold, Gabriel	21, Nov. 1891		79	4	
Lipps, Carolina	27, Dec. 1899	26, Dec.	61- 9m- 1d	4	Mayer
Lipps, Katharina	18, Jan. 1897	16, Jan.	72- 1m	5	Grebner
Lippscomb, Emily	18, June 1895		40	5	
Lipscomb, Daniel	4, Oct. 1901		58	8	
Lischer, C.J.	22, Aug. 1898	20, Aug.	38-10m	5	
Lischer, George	26, May 1900	24, May	71- 5m	8	
Lisker, Anna	7, Apr. 1891		66	4	
Lister, Emma F.	16, Apr. 1891		68	4	
Liston, Bridget	10, Aug. 1900		60	8	
Litmann, Bernard	24, July 1895		28	5	
Littel, Michael	16, Jan. 1897	14, Jan.	79- 4m	5	
Littell, Edward	15, Aug. 1900			5	
Littelle, Clifton A.	19, Nov. 1900			8	
Littelman, Emma	26, June 1894		13	5	
Little, Alexander L.	17, Aug. 1893		19	5	
Little, Elizabeth	11, Aug. 1888		9	1	
Little, John	26, Feb. 1901		82	8	
Little, Mary E.	5, Apr. 1901		52	8	

Name	Notice Date	Death Date	Age	Page	Maiden Name
****	****** ****	***** ****	***	****	****** ****
Litzel, Mary Katharina	17, Jan. 1899	16, Jan.	78- 7m	5	
Litzenberger, Jacob	28, Oct. 1891		69	4	
Litzenberger, Theodore	13, Oct. 1891		75	4	
Livermann, William	1, Aug. 1887		20	1	
Liß, Israel	17, Jan. 1901		42	8	
Liß, Lizzie	12, July 1895		6	5	
Lloyd, Hannah H.	27, Aug. 1901		60	1	
Lloyd, Samuel	15, Mar. 1901		76	8	
Loards, Harriet	19, Sept 1888		51	2	
Lobeck, Barney	10, May 1895		75	5	
Lobeck, Franz	16, Aug. 1894		9	5	
Lobenstein, Mina	30, Sept 1901		45	8	
Lochner, Charles	1, Feb. 1897	31, Jan.	52	5	
Lockmann, Thomas	14, Nov. 1891		2w	4	
Lockwood, Charles A.	4, Aug. 1887		48	1	
Lockwood, Margaret	1, Feb. 1901		94	8	
Lockwood, Samantha	10, Apr. 1895		61	5	
Lodwick, Elizabeth	31, Dec. 1890		1	4	
Lodwick, Preston	19, Jan. 1888		77	4	
Lodwick, Sarah C.	16, June 1894		68	5	
Loeb, Herman	9, Dec. 1897	6, Dec.	67	5	
Loeb, Jacob	29, June 1894		43	5	
Loeb, Jeanette	23, Sept 1893		69	5	
Loeb, Lisette	23, Feb. 1899	22, Feb.	73	5	
Loeb, Solomon	2, July 1901		80	8	
Loebitz, Estella	25, July 1901		2	8	
Loebker, Alma	26, Nov. 1892		4	5	
Loebker, Henry	11, Apr. 1893		1d	5	
Loebker, John	23, May 1901		1	8	
Loebker, Lena	11, July 1895		1	5	
Loebrecht, Annie	28, Sept 1901		51	5	
Loechel, Charles	30, Apr. 1895		52	5	
Loechtenfeldt, Norah	13, Dec. 1898	12, Dec.		5	Crotty
Loehle, Sophia	3, Feb. 1894		10m	5	
Loehrlein, John	23, Mar. 1894		33	5	
Loesche, Lina	8, Nov. 1898	6, Nov.	25- 7m	4	Hinnenkamp
Loew, J. George	20, Feb. 1896	19, Feb.	65- 8m	5	
Loewenstein, August	22, Dec. 1898	21, Dec.	71	5	
Loffink, G.	13, Sept 1900		15	5	
Lofler, Alfred	4, July 1887		35	1	
Loftus, Sussie A.	13, Sept 1888		9d	1	
Logan, Ben	15, June 1901		39	8	
Logan, Benjamin	27, Aug. 1901		45	1	
Logan, Frank	16, Apr. 1901		6m	8	
Logan, Ida	25, Feb. 1901		44	8	
Logan, Maggie	15, May 1901		2	8	
Logan, O.J.	3, Oct. 1901		76	8	
Loge, Marg.	15, July 1890		78	1	
Logue, Philipp	25, June 1888		39	1	
Loh, Charles	4, Aug. 1890		2	1	
Lohans, William	19, July 1887		9d	1	
Lohaus, Adolph	24, June 1896	21, June	70- 9m	5	
Lohbauer, William	19, Aug. 1893		18m	5	
Loheider, Bernard	2, Feb. 1901		62	8	
Lohmacher, Louisa	5, Aug. 1891		6w	4	
Lohman, John H.	3, Jan. 1893		73	5	
Lohman, Theresa	12, Aug. 1887		52	1	
Lohmann, Alph.	26, Nov. 1891		1	1	
Lohmann, Caroline	1, Dec. 1892		82	5	
Lohmann, Elisabeth	16, 17, July 1897	15, July	70- 6m	5	
Lohmann, Fred	16, July 1898	13, July	33- 7m	5	
Lohmann, John	19, July 1887		40	1	
Lohmann, Lucy	6, Jan. 1893		3	5	
Lohmiller, Joseph	5, Apr. 1901		30	8	
Lohr, J.H.	20, Feb. 1891		64	4	
Lohr, Michael	28, Jan. 1889		48	1	
Lohr, Phillip	11, Apr. 1899	10, Apr.	50-10m	5	
Lohrer, Amalie M.	12, Dec. 1896	9, Dec.	19- 4m	5	
Lohrer, Jacob	22, Nov. 1895	21, Nov.	49- 9m	5	
Lohrer, Karoline	10, Jan. 1893		48	5	
Lohrer, Katharina	25, Feb. 1897	23, Feb.		5	

Name ****	Notice Date ****** ****	Death Date ***** ****	Age ***	Page ****	Maiden Name ****** ****
Lohrer, Louise	28, Apr. 1890		46	1	
Lohri, Anna L.	8, July 1889		2m	1	
Londkuhl, Harry	2, July 1895		2	5	
Long, Elsie May	3, Jan. 1901		2	5	
Long, Fannie	4, June 1901		35	8	
Long, Francis	10, Apr. 1901		52	8	
Long, George	13, Nov. 1893		36	5	
Long, John	26, Mar. 1901		39	8	
Long, Kate	3, Apr. 1888		4- 6m	4	
Long, Mamie	10, Dec. 1888		4	1	
Long, William	13, Nov. 1893		14m	5	
Longdon, George F.	19, July 1887		26	1	
Longenecker, Margaret	11, Dec. 1893		74	5	
Longland, Joseph	3, July 1901		29	8	
Looker, Elisabeth	23, Oct. 1900		84	8	
Loos, Elisabeth	19, July 1887		69	1	
Loper, Frederick M.	28, Oct. 1891		30	4	
Lore, Henry	28, June 1888		43	1	
Lorentz, Jacob	8, Feb. 1894		79	5	
Lorentz, John	7, Sept 1887		5w	1	
Lorentz, Mary	30, Dec. 1890		5	4	
Lorentz, Michael	14, July 1891		83	4	
Lorenz, Anna	8, Oct. 1888		38	1	
Lorenz, Basilius	27, July 1893		73	5	
Lorenz, Euphrofina	29, May 1894		17m	5	
Lorenz, Gertrude	3, July 1895		10m	5	
Lorenz, Harry M.	4, Feb. 1901		35	8	
Lorenz, Joseph C.	12, Aug. 1887		18w	1	
Lorenz, Theresa	11, Dec. 1900		76	8	
Lorenz, Wenzel	4, June 1895		3	5	
Loring, Mary	17, Apr. 1894		50	5	
Lory, Mabel	14, Sept 1901		14	1	
Losacker, Catharina	13, Mar. 1890		5m	4	
Losekamp, Johan Heinrich	23, Dec. 1896	21, Dec.	80- 1m	5	
Loser, Isadore	9, Jan. 1901			5	
Loth, Ada	3, Aug. 1887		16	1	
Loth, Eddie	8, Mar. 1890		9	1	
Loth, Heinrich	8, Feb. 1896	7, Feb.	58- 5m	5	
Loth, Karolina	29, May 1889		61	1	
Loth, Katie	21, July 1887		1	1	
Loth, Louise	14, Dec. 1887		26	4	
Loth, Sarah	23, Sept 1898	22, Sept	49-11m	4	Beckert
Lothel, Mary	14, Feb. 1888		32	4	
Lother, Barbara	6, Dec. 1894		9d	5	
Lothes, Magdalena	2, Sept 1896	1, Sept	71-11m	5	Vogel
Lott, Sophie	7, Oct. 1899	6, Oct.	85- 8m	8	Eichler
Lottman, Johan Bernard	21, Jan. 1897	20, Jan.	73- 8m	5	
Lotz, Barbara	22, May 1899	21, May	85	4	Vogel
Lotz, Eduard M.	17, May 1898	15, May	41-10m	4	
Lotz, George	29, Mar. 1889		36	1	
Lotz, Louisa	20, Jan. 1894		70	5	
Lotz, Maria	4, Mar. 1897	3, Mar.	50- 2m	5	Mesloh
Louis,	1, Oct. 1900		1d	5	
Louis, Fred.	1, Feb. 1892		16d	5	
Louis, Robert	21, Dec. 1897	20, Dec.		5	
Louis, Samuel	14, July 1891		14d	4	
Lowderback, Charlotte A.	31, July 1900		17d	5	
Lowe, Stella	4, Sept 1888		4m	2	
Lowenstein, David	7, Jan. 1901		14	5	
Lowndes, Edward	8, Dec. 1900		36	8	
Lowry, Ed. N.	7, May 1901		43	1	
Lowther, Wilford M.	13, Apr. 1901		32	8	
Lowton, Sarah	31, July 1900		56	5	
Lubbers, Elisabeth	15, Feb. 1897	13, Feb.	26-10m	5	
Lubbers, Elmer	16, July 1901		2m	8	
Lubbers, Gertrude	17, July 1895		11m	5	
Luben, Augusta	31, Aug. 1901		47	8	
Lubernds, Harry	8, June 1895		1	5	
Lubke, John F.	1, May 1894		5	5	
Lucas, Angelina	12, Feb. 1891		32	4	
Lucas, Anna	23, Feb. 1901		72	8	

Name	Notice Date	Death Date	Age	Page	Maiden Name
****	****** ****	***** ****	***	****	****** ****
Lucas, Annie M.	23, May 1895		11m	5	
Lucas, Anton	16, Aug. 1899	15, Aug.	10	5	
Lucas, Maria A.	23, Sept 1895	22, Sept	16- 2m	5	
Lucas, Vernon	16, May 1901		3w	5	
Luck, Joseph	27, Oct. 1900		48	8	
Lucke, Bernhard	22, July 1889		49	1	
Luckens, H.	19, Aug. 1895	17, Aug.	44- 6m	5	
Lucker, Christ.	1, Mar. 1893		74	5	
Luckermann, Frank	1, Feb. 1892		10m	5	
Luckert, Charlotte	13, July 1892		12	5	
Luckey, George M.	1, May 1895		71	5	
Luckey, William	25, Mar. 1901		29	8	
Luckman, Albert	21, Mar. 1892		1	4	
Luckmann, Angela	26, Apr. 1898	25, Apr.	77- 4m	5	Klönne
Luddecke, George	27, Feb. 1892		6	5	
Ludecke, Friedrich	25, Dec. 1894		60	5	
Luderung, Albert	11, Dec. 1891		78	4	
Ludington, Mary	4, May 1895		17m	5	
Ludwig, Charles	14, Apr. 1893		49	5	
Ludwig, Delius	1, Aug. 1898	30, July	42	5	
Ludwig, Ed.	13, June 1901		20	8	
Ludwig, Gertie	29, May 1888		4	2	
Ludwig, Heinrich	10, Dec. 1895	9, Dec.	65-10m	5	
Ludwig, Katharina	22, Jan. 1898	20, Jan.	62-10m	5	Sprenger
Ludwig, Lane	1, Mar. 1893		48	5	
Ludwig, Maria J.	16, Dec. 1891		62	4	
Ludwig, Ottilia	22, Nov. 1898	21, Nov.	58- 3m	5	
Ludwig, Regina	8, Mar. 1889		5m	1	
Luebben, Josephine M.	8, Apr. 1891		26	4	
Luebbert, Harry	14, June 1895	13, June	3- 4m-15d	5	
Luebbert, Ida	29, Sept 1899	28, Sept	41-11m	5	Rengel
Luebbing, Frank W.	6, Feb. 1894		35	5	
Luebke, Alfred	21, Nov. 1891		1d	4	
Lueble, William	2, Nov. 1888		52	1	
Lueckert, Chr.	3, May 1901		64	8	
Lueddecke, Ella	26, Aug. 1889		13m	1	
Luedeke, Friedrich Heinrich	6, Dec. 1898	4, Dec.	20- 5m	5	
Lueders, Dorothea	7, June 1901		49	8	
Lueders, Pauline U.	1, Feb. 1901		23	8	
Luegding, Mamie	3, Nov. 1892		14	5	
Lueger, Elsie	27, Sept 1900		4	8	
Luegering, Albert	26, June 1891		10m	4	
Luegering, B.H.	18, Dec. 1891		47	2	
Luegering, Mary	2, Jan. 1901		52	5	
Luehrmann, Anna	24, Feb. 1894			5	
Luehrmann, Marie	21, Feb. 1901		65	8	
Lueke, Heinrich J.	18, Dec. 1899	16, Dec.	36- 3m-23d	5	
Luekens, Lotta	3, Sept 1889		6	1	
Lueker, Alvina	7, June 1890		8	1	
Luers, Herman	24, Apr. 1901		59	8	
Luesenhop, Mathilde	28, May 1892		7	5	
Luessing, Francis	17, Aug. 1894		4m	5	
Luetkenhaus, William	22, May 1890		5	1	
Lugik,	18, July 1887		1d	1	
Luhn,	25, Mar. 1893		1d	5	
Luhn, Anna M.	12, June 1899	11, June	77	4	
Luhn, Johan Georg	10, May 1899	8, May	22-10m	5	
Luhn, Margaretha O.	24, Nov. 1896	23, Nov.	67	5	
Luhn, Mary E.	27, Apr. 1894		63	5	
Luhr, Philippina	14, Nov. 1893		58	5	
Luhring, Alice	28, Jan. 1894		1	5	
Luhring, H.W.	2, Dec. 1899	1, Dec.	84	4	
Luhring, Sophie	31, July 1900		75	5	
Luhrman, George	1, Dec. 1891		3	4	
Luhrmann, Clarence	24, Dec. 1900		6d	8	
Luhrmann, Herman	27, Mar. 1896	25, Mar.	66	5	
Luhrmann, John	19, Dec. 1891		71	4	
Luigart, Joseph	24, June 1896	23, June	68	5	
Luitmeiser, Mary	8, July 1891		19	4	
Luken, Annie	8, July 1891		18	4	
Luken, Barney	1, Feb. 1888		81	4	

Name ****	Notice Date ****** ****	Death Date ***** ****	Age ***	Page ****	Maiden Name ****** ****
Luken, Frank	1, Nov. 1892		34	5	
Luken, George	9, Sept 1900		7m	5	
Luken, J.G.	3, Dec. 1897	2, Dec.	83	5	
Luken, John B.	12, Feb. 1891		72	4	
Luken, Mary Ann	23, Oct. 1900		83	8	
Luken, Mathilda Mary	20, Jan. 1898	19, Jan.	44- 9m	5	Going
Lukop, John	15, Oct. 1901		35	8	
Lullen, Edward	28, July 1888		1	1	
Lumen, Matthias	1, Nov. 1892		9	5	
Lummel, Christ.	16, Oct. 1894		38	5	
Lummel, Nickolaus	10, Feb. 1900	8, Feb.	48	5	
Lunan, Maggie	25, Aug. 1900			5	
Lundrigan, Michael	6, Sept 1900		33	5	
Lung, Bertha	11, July 1888		6w	1	
Lung, Bertha	25, Mar. 1901		26d	8	
Lunkenheimer, Louise M.	7, Jan. 1891		23	4	
Lurbes, Henrietta	4, May 1893		2	5	
Lureck, Catharina	24, Oct. 1890		42	1	
Lurie, Harris	13, Sept 1901		48	8	
Lurker, Mary	16, Apr. 1901		58	8	
Lurker, Rosa	20, Mar. 1890		21	1	
Lurking, Julius G.	6, Sept 1894		1	5	
Lurzer, John	10, Oct. 1890		73	4	
Lusch, Katie	26, July 1889		8m	1	
Lush, H.	14, Feb. 1888		8w	4	
Lusher, Charles J.	3, Apr. 1889	3, Apr.		1	
Luskey, Fred. J.	4, June 1895		42	5	
Lusky, H.	18, Aug. 1896	17, Aug.	45	5	
Lust, Charles	13, July 1887		27	1	
Luther, Charles	19, Nov. 1900		67	8	
Luthringer, Theresa	21, Aug. 1888		79	1	
Lutkehaus, Frank	11, Nov. 1894		75	5	
Lutkehaus, Katharine	21, July 1894		77	5	
Lutmer, Regina	30, Jan. 1891		1m	4	
Lutowitz, Julius	30, Sept 1891		9- 5m	4	
Lutters, Mary A.	23, Jan. 1894		9m	5	
Luttmann, Anna	5, Sept 1891		2	1	
Luttmann, Elizabeth	13, July 1894		59	5	
Luttmann, Emilia Magdalena	29, Oct. 1898	27, Oct.	14- 4m-18d	4	
Luttmann, Herman	21, Apr. 1895		85	5	
Luttmann, John A.	17, Jan. 1901		9d	8	
Luttmann, Mary	3, Apr. 1888		26	4	
Luttmer, Anna Maria	4, Jan. 1899	3, Jan.	79- 8m	5	Taebbing
Luttmer, Joseph	11, Oct. 1900		85	8	
Lutz, Catharine	8, Feb. 1901		83	8	
Lutz, Dora	30, Jan. 1894		7m	5	
Lutz, Ellie	31, Dec. 1888			1	
Lutz, Friedrich	22, June 1891	22, June	60	1	
Lutz, Gertrud	8, Sept 1900		1	5	
Lutz, Gertrude	17, June 1896	16, June	68- 2m	5	
Lutz, Katie	14, Feb. 1895		6	5	
Lutz, Marie	8, Sept 1899	7, Sept	86	4	
Lutz, Mathilda Katharina	19, June 1893	18, June	10m-13d	5	
Luxenberger, Josephine	11, Apr. 1892		9d	5	
Luxenberger, Katharina	16, May 1892		68	5	
Luz, Mollie	4, Dec. 1888		28	1	
Lyford, John	7, July 1896	6, July	65	4	
Lyhe, Jacob	13, Nov. 1900		86	8	
Lyman, Charles E.	2, May 1895		4m	5	
Lynch, Annie	7, May 1901		19	1	
Lynch, Frank	12, Sept 1891		2m	1	
Lynch, James	17, Oct. 1900		69	8	
Lyns, Alice	26, Apr. 1901		1	8	
Lyon, Charles	14, Mar. 1888		1m	1	
Lyon, George W.	25, Apr. 1888		19	1	
Lyon, K.L.	18, Feb. 1888		20	1	
Lyon, Wilbur	9, July 1887		3w	1	
Lyons, Harriet E.	26, Dec. 1900		76	8	
Lyons, W.	30, Sept 1901		69	8	
Läbly, Salome	8, Nov. 1895	6, Nov.	72- 1m	5	
Lösch, Arthur J.	3, Apr. 1891		2	4	

Name	Notice Date	Death Date	Age	Page	Maiden Name
****	****** ****	***** ****	***	****	****** ****
Lösche, Wilhelm	23, Dec. 1899	22, Dec.	21-10m	5	
Löwenstein,	11, July 1891		1d	1	
Löwenstein, Heinrich	2, Nov. 1896	31, Oct.	56	5	
Löwenstein, Marianne	26, Mar. 1896		80	5	
Löwenstein, Mina	12, July 1890		16	1	
Löwenstein, William	2, Feb. 1893		37	5	
Lübbe, Helene	3, Nov. 1896	31, Oct.	38- 9m	5	Peters
Lübbermann, Henry	9, Feb. 1894		1	5	
Lübbert, Gustav	4, Nov. 1895	3, Nov.	25- 2m	5	
Lübbing, Franz	28, Jan. 1897	27, Jan.	72- 9m	5	
Lückener, Agnes	26, Sept 1899	25, Sept	78-11m	5	Kordes
Lückmann, Johan Gerhardt	21, Apr. 1897	20, Apr.	77-10m	5	
Lüders, Margaretha G.	16, Aug. 1894		7m	5	
Lülf, H.W.	29, Oct. 1896	27, Oct.	58- 7m	5	
Lüning, Maria Anna	27, Nov. 1899	26, Nov.	74- 8m	5	Hülsmann
Lütmer, Joseph	10, Feb. 1896	7, Feb.	73- 6m	5	
Lütmerding, Ferdinand	27, Dec. 1899	26, Dec.	71- 1m	4	
Maag, H.	31, May 1889		61	1	
Maas, Irene	6, Dec. 1892		21d	5	
Maas, Ralph Sidney	13, July 1896	11, July	9- 3m	5	
Mabor, Louis	12, Sept 1890		7w	1	
MacKenzie, Catharine (Sr.)	6, Dec. 1900		68	8	
Mack, Bernard J.	20, Sept 1901		2m	1	
Mack, Clara	23, Dec. 1891		2	4	
Mack, Eva	28, Feb. 1901		1	8	
Mack, Henry	26, Dec. 1896	23, Dec.	76	5	
Mack, Herman	1, Apr. 1889		44	1	
Mack, Isaak H.	7, Aug. 1894		53	5	
Mack, James	23, Oct. 1888		66	1	
Mack, Jennie	5, Apr. 1901		55	8	
Mack, John	4, Mar. 1890		48	1	
Mack, Joseph	29, Sept 1897	28, Sept	48	5	
Mack, Julia	29, Dec. 1892		7	5	
Mack, Maggie	27, Apr. 1901		48	8	
Mack, Martin	30, July 1891		62	4	
Mack, Mary A.	6, Oct. 1900		90	5	
Mackably, Susan	27, Feb. 1901		1	8	
Macke, Angela	27, Sept 1900		84	8	
Macke, Angela	29, Sept 1900		84	8	
Macke, B.H.	29, Oct. 1896	28, Oct.	86	5	
Macke, Bernard Heinrich	18, May 1900	17, May	76- 9m	5	
Macke, Clara	22, Sept 1891		43	1	
Macke, Joseph H.	4, Aug. 1891		12	4	
Macke, Maria Anna	31, Mar. 1898	30, Mar.	81-10m	5	Elsche
Macke, Mary	31, Aug. 1889		6m	1	
Mackentepe, Maria	16, Dec. 1891		64	4	
Mackle, Edna M.	15, Apr. 1888		6m	5	
Mackle, Luetta	18, Feb. 1892		21	4	
Madden, Annie	16, July 1901		59	8	
Madden, Frank J.	9, Aug. 1888		5	1	
Madden, Patrick	18, May 1901		41	1	
Maden, Ben.	26, Mar. 1891		24	4	
Mader, Roger	28, Apr. 1888		18	1	
Madisne, Joseph	29, Aug. 1900		60	5	
Madison, George	28, Apr. 1888		62	1	
Madison, Robert	20, Sept 1887		39	1	
Maegher, J.	5, Oct. 1888		21	1	
Maegly, Abraham	16, Aug. 1895	14, Aug.	62- 9m	5	
Maehner, Rosie	30, Apr. 1895		1	5	
Maehringer, Lena	23, Apr. 1895		11	5	
Maerki, Rudolph	14, July 1889	14, July	16- 2m- 9d	5	
Maerray, M.	14, Dec. 1888		31	1	
Maess, John	31, July 1901		78	8	
Maeß, H.L.S.	14, Sept 1900		10m	5	
Mageley, Norma	18, Feb. 1901		4m	8	
Mageoney, Catharine	28, Jan. 1901		40	8	
Mager, Samuel	6, Mar. 1891		34	4	
Magie, E.C.	3, Apr. 1888		21	4	
Magly, Appolonia	28, Jan. 1898	26, Jan.	72-10m	5	
Magnus, Cecile	16, July 1901		3m	8	

Name	Notice Date	Death Date	Age	Page	Maiden Name
****	****** ****	***** ****	***	****	****** ****
Magnus, Clara	1, Aug. 1891		1	4	
Maguer, James	12, July 1895		39	5	
Maguire, John	31, July 1901		34	8	
Maher, Cecilia A.	16, May 1891		32	2	
Maher, John	13, June 1891		3m	4	
Maher, Margaret	11, Feb. 1891		17	4	
Maher, Pat.	30, Sept 1901		67	8	
Maher, William	29, Aug. 1900		61	5	
Mahley, Andrew	17, June 1899	16, June	72	5	
Mahlmeister, Anna Theresa	31, Mar. 1898	29, Mar.	1- 5m	5	
Mahoney, Agnes	16, Nov. 1899	14, Nov.	23- 1m	5	Foll
Mahoney, Dennis	11, Apr. 1901		73	8	
Mahoney, Jeremiah	15, Aug. 1900		45	5	
Mahoney, John	24, Oct. 1900		70	8	
Mahoney, Mary	31, May 1901		47	8	
Mahr, Margaret A.	23, Apr. 1891		8w	4	
Maibaum, K.	19, Nov. 1888		38	1	
Maier, Anton Joseph	13, Aug. 1896	13, Aug.	57- 6m	5	
Maier, Carolina	24, Dec. 1898	23, Dec.	17	5	
Maier, Ida	24, Nov. 1898	24, Nov.	20-10m	5	Kuntz
Maier, Joseph	28, June 1889		30	1	
Maier, Margaretha	4, Feb. 1893		67	5	
Maier, Simon	10, Feb. 1893		63	5	
Maier, Wilhelm	23, Dec. 1893		4m	5	
Maifield, Frank	17, Dec. 1891			4	
Maile, David	21, Nov. 1898	20, Nov.	25-11m	5	
Main, Clara	14, July 1900		1	8	
Mains, John W.	3, Apr. 1888		72	4	
Maithee, Gertrude	16, Mar. 1901		62	8	
Majowsky, Charles L.H.	16, Feb. 1895		5	5	
Make, Catharine	5, Sept 1900		60	5	
Malchus, Andrew	2, Oct. 1899	1, Oct.	34- 3m	4	
Malecky, Joseph	20, Sept 1901		2w	1	
Maley, Elisabeth	4, July 1901		72	8	
Malkmus, Barbara	8, Dec. 1900		23	8	
Malkums, Mary	23, Sept 1887		68	2	
Malkus, Henry	21, Nov. 1898	20, Nov.		5	
Malkus, Louisa	17, May 1901		55	8	
Mallet, Henry	26, Apr. 1901			8	
Malloy, Lawrence	7, Sept 1887		107	1	
Malloy, Lillie	10, Sept 1887		17m	2	
Malloy, Rose	19, Apr. 1895		45	5	
Malone, Ed.	8, Aug. 1892		2	5	
Malone, John	5, June 1901		31	8	
Malone, Kate	15, May 1901		32	8	
Malone, Maggie	29, Aug. 1900		8	5	
Maloney, John	19, Sept 1900		50	8	
Maloney, John	10, Oct. 1900		10m	8	
Maloney, Michael	20, Oct. 1900		75	8	
Malony, Margaret	20, Apr. 1888		2	4	
Maltauer, Joseph F.	3, Aug. 1901		76	8	
Mandell, Mina	17, June 1898	16, June	86-11m	4	
Mandery, Catharina	6, July 1899	5, July	80- 9m	5	
Mandery, Katharina	6, Feb. 1899	5, Feb.	55-11m	4	
Mandler, Jacob	7, Dec. 1893		49	5	
Mangold, Carl	19, Dec. 1900		2	8	
Mangold, Catharine	29, Sept 1893		66	5	
Mangold, Elizabeth	25, Sept 1891		33	4	
Mangold, Elizabeth	2, Aug. 1900		43	8	
Mangold, J.	6, Mar. 1889		1	1	
Mangold, Mathias	8, June 1895		23	5	
Manheimer, B. (Mrs)	6, Feb. 1891		68	4	
Manichewitz, Michael	11, July 1895		7w	5	
Manley, Charles	10, Aug. 1887		1	1	
Manley, William	5, Dec. 1900		53	8	
Mann, George	11, Oct. 1900		87	8	
Mann, Louisa	25, Feb. 1901		4	8	
Mannbeck, Emma	24, June 1899	23, June	9- 3m	4	
Manngold, Johan	15, Sept 1900		71	5	
Manning, Elizabeth	21, Mar. 1901		3	8	
Manning, Mary	1, June 1892		56	5	

Name	Notice Date	Death Date	Age	Page	Maiden Name
****	****** ****	***** ****	***	****	****** ****
Manns, Ellen	4, Aug. 1888		56	4	
Mansard, Theodor	2, Dec. 1899	1, Dec.	72	4	
Mansfeld, Ella	30, Dec. 1891		31	4	
Mansfield, Lucy	8, Aug. 1900		13	8	
Manshard, John G.	16, July 1895		9	5	
Manthy, Anna	26, Feb. 1891		33	4	
Mantz, Thomas	1, June 1894		74	5	
Manß, Karl	27, Feb. 1901		5m	8	
Mappes, Christina	10, Dec. 1898	9, Dec.	67- 4m	5	Wolf
Mara, Kate	1, Sept 1887		21	1	
Marahren, Therese	23, Nov. 1895	20, Nov.		5	Nold
Marahrens, Maria	3, July 1897	2, July	47- 5m-25d	5	Böhmer
Maratte, David	16, Apr. 1901		51	8	
Marazzi, Caroline	29, Oct. 1897	28, Oct.	60	5	Kurz
Marazzi, Lucia	25, Aug. 1899	23, Aug.	51- 8m	5	
March, Katharine	28, Mar. 1893		2	5	
Marcks, Maria	4, Mar. 1891		76	4	
Marcus, Eva	21, July 1891		73	4	
Marcus, H. Bernard	28, June 1895		75	5	
Marcus, Herman	24, June 1901		73	8	
Marcuse, Esther	2, Mar. 1896	29, Feb.	4-11m	5	
Margette, Joseph	13, Feb. 1901		24	8	
Margileth, Pauline	8, Mar. 1901		23	8	
Maringer, Sophia	5, Nov. 1900		17	8	
Mark, Ella D.	13, Apr. 1901		14	8	
Markbreit, Jane	31, Mar. 1891	30, Mar.	80	1	
Markgraf, Amelia	11, June 1891		28	4	
Markgraf, Anna	6, Mar. 1900	5, Mar.	11	8	
Markhofer, Jakob	12, Sept 1890		1m	1	
Marklein, Fred.	5, Dec. 1893		38	5	
Markley, Lillian	23, Mar. 1901		41	8	
Markowitz, Robert	3, Jan. 1893		4	5	
Marks, Alice	6, Dec. 1888		31	1	
Marks, Gertie	19, Mar. 1891		3	4	
Markus, Herman	14, July 1891		79	4	
Marmet, Florence	16, Nov. 1887	14, Nov.	56- 8m	* 1	
Marmet, Marie	21, Oct. 1899	19, Oct.	54	5	
Marmet, Otto	5, Oct. 1899	3, Oct.	71- 3m- 9d	5	
Marr, Joseph	9, Apr. 1891		31	4	
Marrahrens, Maria	2, Jan. 1901		34	5	
Marriott, Emma	22, Nov. 1888		38	1	
Marsbach, Eva	31, Mar. 1891		37	4	
Marsch, Harriet M.	8, Mar. 1901		83	8	
Marsch, Johan	13, Dec. 1893		50	5	
Marsh, Edward R.	2, Feb. 1888		18	4	
Marsh, John F.	17, Sept 1891		73	1	
Marshal, Robert	7, Aug. 1900		1m	8	
Marshall, Elisabeth	25, Sept 1900		4m	5	
Marshall, Emma	12, Dec. 1900		8m	8	
Marshall, Maria	29, Aug. 1901		62	8	
Marshall, William	27, Nov. 1900		64	8	
Marshmeyer, Lena	17, Jan. 1888		10	4	
Marten, Henry	14, Feb. 1900	13, Feb.	45	8	
Marten, Sophie	6, Aug. 1901		77	8	
Marthein, Elizabeth	23, Dec. 1890		41	1	
Martin,	2, Feb. 1901		6d	8	
Martin, Amelia	21, July 1887		90	1	
Martin, Amelia	13, Aug. 1891		4m	4	
Martin, Anna	10, Apr. 1891		27	4	
Martin, Anna	16, July 1900	15, July	81	8	
Martin, Anna Barbara	22, Jan. 1897	20, Jan.	75- 9m	5	
Martin, Anna Maria	10, Nov. 1896	9, Nov.	71- 8m- 2d	4	Schmidt
Martin, Annie	22, July 1891		35	4	
Martin, August	16, Aug. 1899	14, Aug.	6- 2m	5	
Martin, Catharina S.	10, July 1887		2m	1	
Martin, Catharine	12, May 1891		62	1	
Martin, Catharine	7, Aug. 1891		62	4	
Martin, Christ.	18, May 1892		3d	5	
Martin, Elisabeth	2, Feb. 1901		25	8	
Martin, Elizabeth	22, June 1889		30	1	
Martin, Ethel	8, Aug. 1901		4	8	

Name ****	Notice Date ****** ****	Death Date ***** ****	Age ***	Page ****	Maiden Name ****** ****
Martin, Fannie	26, Jan. 1888		17m	4	
Martin, Gottlieb	12, Nov. 1896	10, Nov.	51	5	
Martin, Helena	10, Aug. 1887		16m	1	
Martin, Henry	8, July 1891		45	4	
Martin, Herman	16, May 1892		7m	5	
Martin, J.	4, Aug. 1900		78	8	
Martin, J.N.	21, Feb. 1888		18m	1	
Martin, Jennie	11, Aug. 1891		3m	4	
Martin, John	8, Jan. 1891		30	4	
Martin, John	5, Feb. 1892		65	5	
Martin, John	15, July 1901		38	8	
Martin, John M.	28, Jan. 1893		7m	5	
Martin, Laura	3, Sept 1890		44	1	
Martin, Lil	5, Mar. 1901		1	5	
Martin, Marie	8, Nov. 1887		38	1	
Martin, Martha	21, Apr. 1888		58	1	
Martin, Mary	7, Oct. 1901		47	1	
Martin, Mary A.	16, Aug. 1894		72	5	
Martin, Michael	30, Jan. 1891		70	4	
Martin, Nora	17, Mar. 1891		17	4	
Martin, Phil.	2, Mar. 1901		69	5	
Martin, Rufus L.	14, Feb. 1901		54	8	
Martin, Sarah	17, Apr. 1901		60	8	
Martin, Thomas	5, Mar. 1891		2	4	
Martin, Valentine	4, Mar. 1891		56	4	
Martin, William	5, Jan. 1901		2	8	
Martin, William	26, Mar. 1901		80	8	
Martin, Zacharius	17, Nov. 1888		35	1	
Marty, Margaretha B.	27, Aug. 1895	26, Aug.	79	5	
Marx, Gottfried	23, Jan. 1894		83	5	
Marx, Hannah	11, Feb. 1891		77	4	
Marx, Johan	18, Nov. 1895	17, Nov.	37- 4m	5	
Marx, Josephine	24, June 1901		1	8	
Marx, Maria Antoinette	17, Jan. 1899	16, Jan.	6m-25d	5	
Marx, Nicolaus	10, Aug. 1892		69	5	
Marx, Peter	30, Nov. 1887		31	4	
Marx, Simon	15, Jan. 1901		69	8	
Marzinzek, Laura	5, Jan. 1897	3, Jan.	21- 5m	5	
Maschin, Franziska	15, Jan. 1892		18	5	
Maschmeier, Margaretha Char.	24, Apr. 1896	22, Apr.	2- 3m	5	
Maschmeyer, Dorothea A.	28, Dec. 1891		63	4	
Mason,	20, Sept 1887		1d	1	
Mason, Bertha	2, Aug. 1888		5	2	
Mason, E.H.	2, Oct. 1888		22	1	
Mason, Mary F.	15, Sept 1888		58	2	
Mason, William	1, Aug. 1901		8m	8	
Massath, Melchior	26, Feb. 1901		71	8	
Masset, Martin	2, Apr. 1901		48	8	
Massett, Franziska	7, June 1898	5, June	4- 9m	5	
Massey, Albert	22, Mar. 1901		4d	8	
Massmann, Joseph E.	27, Dec. 1893		11m	5	
Mast, Luella	18, Nov. 1894		1m	5	
Mastney, Fr.	25, June 1888		5	1	
Masur, Magdalena	27, Nov. 1889		10d	1	
Masur, Maria	18, Feb. 1890		2- 3m	1	
Matacia, G.	19, Jan. 1888		2w	4	
Matecia, Lena	18, Feb. 1901		3m	8	
Materna, L.	9, Sept 1889		26	1	
Mathaei, Frank	27, Aug. 1891		49	1	
Mathers, Eddie	10, Oct. 1891		24d	4	
Mathes, Jacob	19, June 1896	18, June	56- 5m	5	
Mathes, John	28, July 1890		40	1	
Mathias, Theobald	21, July 1891		71	4	
Mathis, Catharine	20, Feb. 1889		76	1	
Mathäß, Rosina	7, Apr. 1897	6, Apr.	72	5	Baron
Matre, Aloysius	5, Apr. 1895		40	5	
Matre, Victoria	26, Oct. 1899	25, Oct.	38	8	
Matrey, M.	6, Jan. 1888		10m	1	
Matt, Albert	29, June 1894		6m	5	
Matt, John	2, May 1901		58	8	
Matten, Rudolph	3, Oct. 1887		30	1	

Name ****	Notice Date ****** ****	Death Date ***** ****	Age ***	Page ****	Maiden Name ****** ****
Matthauser, Louis	10, Sept 1890		27	1	
Matthew, John	12, Nov. 1900		25d	5	
Matthews, Elvada	27, June 1888		6m	1	
Matthews, Mary	29, May 1901		29	8	
Matthiar, Catharine	20, Oct. 1888		1	1	
Matthiesen, Soncker	28, Aug. 1895	26, Aug.	68	5	
Mattler, George R.	28, Oct. 1893		2m	5	
Matz, Isabella	15, July 1901		51	8	
Matz, Victoria	3, Feb. 1899	2, Feb.	55- 3m	4	Wahlher
Matzmohr, Frieda	31, Aug. 1900		1	5	
Mauch, Karl	22, June 1889	21, June	4m-10d	1	
Maue, Winnie C.	17, Apr. 1899	15, Apr.		5	
Mauer, Virginia	18, July 1895		21d	5	
Mauller, M.A.	14, Dec. 1887		14m	4	
Mauntel, Chr.	31, Aug. 1895	30, Aug.	42	5	
Maurer, Bessie	27, June 1900	26, June	23	8	
Maurer, Edward R.	18, July 1893		1	5	
Maurer, Elisabeth	1, Mar. 1899	28, Feb.	64	5	
Maurer, Johan	30, July 1891		34	4	
Maurer, Louise	22, Sept 1893	21, Sept	22- 5m	5	
Maurman, Joseph	19, July 1893		1	5	
Maus, Annie	27, Oct. 1891		6m	1	
Maus, Charles E.	21, Feb. 1894		21	5	
Maus, Lorenz	27, Apr. 1889		49	1	
Maus, Ludwig	3, Dec. 1889		84	1	
Maus, Peter	16, Apr. 1891		15	4	
Maus, Wendel	5, Sept 1899	4, Sept	76- - 9d	5	
Mauser, Rebecca	17, Mar. 1893		74	5	
Mauthe, Alma	24, June 1893		3m	5	
Mauthe, Clarence	23, Nov. 1893		1	5	
Mautz, George	6, Feb. 1891		43	4	
Mauz, Johanna	11, May 1896	10, May	73	5	
Mauß, Karoline Becker	7, July 1897	6, July	43- 4m	5	
Mavors, Johanna	17, June 1896	15, June	35	5	
May, Babette	11, Dec. 1899	10, Dec.	57	4	
May, Thomas	24, Feb. 1894		67	5	
Mayborg, Maria	1, Dec. 1899	30, Nov.	35-10m	5	Bloemer
Mayer, Amelia	25, Feb. 1891		48	4	
Mayer, Andy	3, Feb. 1896	1, Feb.	59- 9m	5	
Mayer, Anna	11, Nov. 1887	10, Nov.	26	4	Boeniker
Mayer, Eva	26, Apr. 1895		71	5	
Mayer, Helene	13, July 1887		5m	1	
Mayer, Kunigunda	29, May 1901		13w	8	
Mayer, Louis	15, July 1898	13, July	60	5	
Mayer, Maria	7, Jan. 1899	5, Jan.	36	5	Nägele
Mayer, Peter Georg	1, Apr. 1891	1, Apr.	3- 7m-12d	1	
Mayerhofer, Edward	28, June 1894		1	5	
Mayhew, Jadock D.	2, Oct. 1900		64	8	
Mayhew, Leavitt	19, Mar. 1901		14	8	
Mayhugh, C.A.	13, Aug. 1888		67	1	
Mayrisch, James	17, July 1895		27	5	
Mays, Goldie	5, Jan. 1888		6m	1	
Maytum, Emma	15, Mar. 1888		29	4	
Mazer, George	10, June 1891		9	4	
Mazzer, Fr.	28, July 1888		30	1	
Maß, Emma L.	30, Dec. 1895	28, Dec.	67- 3m	5	
Maßbaum, Norma	4, Sept 1890		7w	1	
Maßmann, Karl	10, Apr. 1896	8, Apr.	51- 7m	5	
Maßmann, Louis	24, Feb. 1893		75	5	
Maßmann, Theodor	9, May 1894		44	5	
McAdams, Thomas	21, July 1900		7m	8	
McAllister, Ellen	1, Oct. 1901		60	1	
McAllister, Ettie	5, Jan. 1901		32	8	
McAndrew, Lillie	14, Aug. 1888		15	1	
McAnliff, Mary	29, Dec. 1900		30	8	
McArthur, J.	13, June 1888		22	1	
McAvoy, Edward	19, July 1900		1	8	
McBride, John	23, Aug. 1888		38	1	
McBride, Thomas	12, July 1901		59	8	
McCabe, Catharine	25, July 1900		38	5	
McCabe, William P.	21, Aug. 1888		32	1	

Name ****	Notice Date ****** ****	Death Date ***** ****	Age ***	Page ****	Maiden Name ****** ****
McCaffery, Margaret	3, Oct. 1901		55	8	
McCaffrey, Mary	14, Nov. 1900		69	8	
McCanny, A.	7, July 1888		78	4	
McCarter, Anna B.	12, Sept 1887		35	1	
McCarthy, Bridget	20, Aug. 1901		53	8	
McCarthy, Dan	7, Sept 1888		49	1	
McCarthy, Edna	31, Aug. 1901		5	8	
McCarthy, Ellen	21, Feb. 1901		6m	8	
McCarthy, James	26, Feb. 1901		30	8	
McCarthy, Joanne	21, Oct. 1887		73	1	
McCarthy, Maria	15, Mar. 1888			4	
McCarthy, Mary	26, Nov. 1900		53	8	
McCarthy, Mary	13, Feb. 1901		70	8	
McCarthy, Mary	2, Mar. 1901		72	5	
McCarthy, Mary (Sr.)	23, Mar. 1901			8	
McCartney, William	22, Nov. 1887		35	1	
McCarty, Mary	17, Oct. 1900		3	8	
McCauley, Thomas	26, Aug. 1887		62	1	
McChordy, Mary	5, July 1901		55	8	
McClain, Nana	1, Feb. 1888		11m	4	
McClain, S.	7, July 1888		66	4	
McClarn, James	5, Feb. 1901		43	8	
McClellan, Esther	31, Jan. 1901		42	8	
McClellan, M.H.	5, July 1887		36	1	
McClelland, Earl	8, Aug. 1900		6m	8	
McCloskey, Catharine	3, Nov. 1887		68	4	
McCollough, Harry	13, Dec. 1900		1	8	
McConnell, Anna	16, Feb. 1888		31	4	
McConnelty, Margaret	29, Sept 1900		7m	8	
McCormack, A.	11, July 1901		2m	5	
McCormick, Henry	11, Apr. 1895		50	5	
McCormick, Katharine	5, Mar. 1901		72	5	
McCoskell, Ed.	15, Nov. 1887		7- 2w	4	
McCourt, Edward	13, Oct. 1900		65	8	
McCove, Mercy	12, June 1901		60	8	
McCoy, John H.	3, Aug. 1901		12	8	
McCready, Laura B.	23, June 1888		18	1	
McCronen, Thomas	9, Oct. 1900		33	8	
McDenough, John	11, Aug. 1887		62	1	
McDermott, George C.	10, May 1901		53	8	
McDermott, Mary	8, Aug. 1891		82	4	
McDermott, Peter	27, May 1901		71	8	
McDermott, Walter	25, July 1888		5m	4	
McDonald, Henry	1, Sept 1887		3d	1	
McDonald, James	14, July 1900		10	8	
McDonald, Sarah	5, June 1888		24	4	
McDonald, W.	30, Nov. 1887		24	4	
McDonald, William	3, Nov. 1887		33	4	
McDonaugh, Mary	26, Feb. 1901		69	8	
McDonnell, Ellen	23, Apr. 1895		64	5	
McDonnell, Margaret	25, Oct. 1887		66	1	
McDonough, Anna E.	22, June 1895		4	5	
McDonough, Hanna	23, Aug. 1887		32	1	
McDonough, Mary	27, Nov. 1900			8	
McDonough, Michael	20, Nov. 1900		1	8	
McDowall, Lot	22, Mar. 1901		48	8	
McDowell, Carl	4, June 1895		7m	5	
McDowell, Eliza	8, Oct. 1901		59	1	
McDowell, Wiley	24, Oct. 1900		36	8	
McElroy, William	12, Dec. 1900		38	8	
McEvoy, Marie Antonie (Sr.)	4, July 1901		80	8	
McFarland, P.	22, Dec. 1887		1- 9m	4	
McFarland, William	13, June 1901		9	8	
McFlorine, Thomas	8, May 1897	4, May	72	5	
McGann, Catharine	27, Mar. 1901		53	8	
McGarigle, Maria E.	23, Oct. 1900		54	8	
McGarry, Edmond	28, Nov. 1900		89	8	
McGarvey, Lizzie	24, Mar. 1888		34	1	
McGeachy, Harry	26, Apr. 1895		22	5	
McGee, Charlotte	24, Jan. 1888		8	1	
McGee, James	1, Oct. 1887		17	1	

Name ****	Notice Date ****** ****	Death Date ***** ****	Age ***	Page ****	Maiden Name ****** ****
McGeorge, Robert	22, June 1901		39	8	
McGinn, Mary	12, Mar. 1901		45	8	
McGinnis, J.P.	26, Mar. 1888		15m	4	
McGinnis, Katie	4, Apr. 1895		2- 6m	5	
McGrand, Mary	2, Mar. 1901		62	5	
McGrane, Katie	27, Feb. 1901		40	8	
McGrane, Lawrence	15, Apr. 1888		73	5	
McGrath, Daniel	10, Oct. 1900		62	8	
McGrath, Ed.	4, Dec. 1900		77	8	
McGreehan, Owen	27, Feb. 1901			8	
McGreevy, Thomas	1, Dec. 1900		1	8	
McGregor, James	18, Jan. 1896	17, Jan.	27- 5m	5	
McGroarty, Eliza H.	2, Nov. 1900		52	8	
McGuff, Bridget	15, Mar. 1888		57	4	
McGuillan, Anna	10, Aug. 1900		20	8	
McGuire, Barney	4, June 1901		63	8	
McGuire, M.	26, Nov. 1900		28	8	
McGuire, Nannie	22, Mar. 1901		22	8	
McGuire, Patrick	12, Mar. 1901		26	8	
McGurren, Patrick	21, July 1887		79	1	
McGurrin, Patrick	8, Dec. 1891		71	4	
McHugh, Francis	14, July 1900			8	
McHugh, Mary	25, Mar. 1901		11	8	
McHugh, Patrick	22, Mar. 1901		55	8	
McHuh, P.J.	29, June 1901		7m	8	
McIntosh, Ida	11, Dec. 1900		5	8	
McIntosh, Mary	13, July 1901		52	8	
McIntyre, Mary	14, Feb. 1901		24	8	
McKee, Sidney	19, Sept 1900		58	8	
McKeever, Ella	29, Aug. 1901		46	8	
McKelvey, Grace	22, May 1888		6	1	
McKenna, George	27, Sept 1900		58	8	
McKenzie, Emma	12, Mar. 1901		17	8	
McLaine, Elizabeth	6, Sept 1901		61	8	
McLaughlin, Ann	19, Oct. 1900		36	5	
McLaughlin, Ellen M.	31, Aug. 1887		1d	1	
McLaughlin, Frank	10, Mar. 1888		11	1	
McLaughlin, Hannah	12, July 1901		61	8	
McLaughlin, Harriet	19, Mar. 1901		60	8	
McLaughlin, James T.	17, Apr. 1895		6m	5	
McLaughlin, M.	13, Jan. 1888		30	1	
McLaughlin, Mary	16, Apr. 1901		45	8	
McLean, Mary	23, Mar. 1901		53	8	
McLean, Rob. L.	5, Dec. 1887		70	1	
McLeod, Clara	24, Sept 1900		21	5	
McMahan, Harry	2, Mar. 1901		27	5	
McMahon, Edward	18, Dec. 1900		22	8	
McMakin, Mary	22, May 1888		62	1	
McManey, Bridget	29, Jan. 1901		81	8	
McManus, Elisabeth	9, Sept 1900		36	5	
McManus, Ellen	9, Aug. 1900		60	8	
McManus, John	4, Oct. 1900		2m	8	
McManus, John	22, Dec. 1900		32	8	
McMillan, Albert	6, Sept 1900		17	5	
McMillan, Anna	5, Mar. 1901		46	5	
McMillan, Q.A.	30, June 1888		40	1	
McMillan, Thomas	27, Oct. 1887		24	1	
McMillen, Galan S.	26, July 1887		1	1	
McMullen, John	10, Dec. 1900		48	8	
McNamara, Olga	26, July 1887		2	1	
McNary, Margaret	4, Jan. 1901		50	5	
McNay, Mary E.	10, May 1895		18	5	
McNulty, Magnolia	4, Feb. 1901		65	8	
McNulty, Mary	1, Mar. 1888		67	4	
McPheters, Robert	6, Apr. 1895		40	5	
McPhillips, Edwin T.	10, Oct. 1900		1	8	
McShane, Eddie	4, Aug. 1887		16m	1	
McVey, Frances	8, Jan. 1901		5m	8	
Mead, Cora	16, July 1895		11	5	
Meade, Dollie R.	8, Jan. 1901		7	8	
Meade, Lizzie	2, July 1901		40	8	

Name ****	Notice Date ****** ****	Death Date ***** ****	Age ***	Page ****	Maiden Name ****** ****
Meade, Mary	25, Feb. 1901		3m	8	
Meader, Nathan B.	4, May 1895		53	5	
Meagher, John	4, Sept 1901		66	8	
Meagher, Louise	18, July 1887		3m	1	
Meara, Thomas	12, July 1895		59	5	
Mebel, William	20, Feb. 1894		2	5	
Mechel, Marie	11, Apr. 1890		51	1	
Mechle, Cecil J.J.	31, Jan. 1891		7w	4	
Mechtenseimer, Elisabeth	1, Oct. 1887		64	1	
Mechtensiner, Jacob	25, Aug. 1900		45	5	
Meckeboeck, Theresa	29, Mar. 1888		1d	1	
Mecker, Catharine	4, Feb. 1888		4d	4	
Mecklenberg, Fred.	11, June 1895		57	5	
Meckner, Ben.	5, Sept 1900		48	5	
Medary, John	6, Mar. 1901		75	5	
Medeke, Lulu	23, Feb. 1893		1	5	
Meder, Anna	3, July 1889		28	1	
Meder, Joseph	7, Jan. 1901		3	5	
Mederhofer, John	17, Aug. 1900		5d	5	
Meecham, Harvey	23, Sept 1901			8	
Meechan, Bridget M.	12, Dec. 1891		101	4	
Meehan, Philomena	13, Apr. 1901		2m	8	
Meeker, Walter	1, Dec. 1900		2	8	
Meese, John	10, Apr. 1901		90	8	
Mehaus, Walter	25, Mar. 1901		28	8	
Mehlein, Mamie	11, Jan. 1888		3	4	
Mehmert, Lisette	18, June 1897	17, June	54	4	
Mehrmann, Adelheid	11, Dec. 1893		68	5	
Meicorsky, Aaron	22, July 1887		5	1	
Meidel, Franz	26, Oct. 1897	25, Oct.	37	5	
Meier, Adam	2, July 1898	1, July	56	5	
Meier, Anna	15, Nov. 1887		80	4	
Meier, Anna Marie	8, June 1889		56	1	
Meier, Anton	14, July 1899	13, July	46	4	
Meier, Bertha	17, Oct. 1893		41	5	
Meier, Caroline	1, Nov. 1895	31, Oct.	26- 3m	5	Karcher
Meier, Ed.	19, May 1896	17, May	10- 2m	5	
Meier, Ed. J.	13, Jan. 1894		7m	5	
Meier, Elmer M.	2, Dec. 1892		11m	5	
Meier, Heinrich	23, Aug. 1895	22, Aug.	22- 4m	5	
Meier, Herman	19, Sept 1900		69	8	
Meier, Katie	4, Oct. 1894		17m	5	
Meier, Louis	5, July 1887		6m	1	
Meier, Louis	31, May 1901		37	8	
Meier, Martina	4, Aug. 1887		37	1	
Meiler, Edward	26, Apr. 1893		2m	5	
Meimann, Caroline	24, June 1901		68	8	
Meinburg, Andrew	8, May 1889		22	1	
Meinecke, Charles A.	15, Aug. 1896	9, Aug.	17- 5m	5	
Meinecke, Rudolph	12, Aug. 1887		55	1	
Meineke, George Ed.	18, Sept 1901		29	8	
Meinerding, Anna	20, Feb. 1895		22	5	
Meiners, Catharine	8, Oct. 1901		73	1	
Meiners, Dietrich	15, Oct. 1900		33	5	
Meiners, Gerhard	3, Dec. 1897	2, Dec.	47-11m	5	
Meiners, H.	19, Nov. 1888		4	1	
Meiners, Mary Ann	17, Feb. 1888		87	4	
Meinhardt, Albert J.	16, July 1891		12	4	
Meinhardt, Barbara	30, July 1891		35	4	
Meinhardt, Ernst	22, Feb. 1890		17	4	
Meinhardt, Kate	1, Feb. 1899	31, Jan.		5	
Meinhardt, William	8, Nov. 1888		1d	1	
Meining, August	1, Mar. 1894		57	5	
Meining, Harry	27, Oct. 1900		30	8	
Meinking, Henry	17, Aug. 1894		20	5	
Meinsbeck, Lizzie	1, June 1892		25	5	
Meinshall, George	10, Aug. 1901		54	8	
Meinze, Mary	28, Jan. 1892		9m	5	
Meirner, Frank	24, May 1901		43	8	
Meis, Louis	18, Aug. 1892		14m	5	
Meis, William	29, Jan. 1891		52	4	

Name ****	Notice Date ****** ****	Death Date ***** ****	Age ***	Page ****	Maiden Name ****** ****
Meisberger, Mary	29, Oct. 1888		52	1	
Meise, Elisabeth	12, Dec. 1896	11, Dec.	61- -14d	5	
Meise, Gertrude	10, Jan. 1896	9, Jan.	2- 7m	5	
Meise, Viola	5, Apr. 1892		1	4	
Meisel, Georg	17, Feb. 1895		57	5	
Meister, Barbara	8, Dec. 1900		86	8	
Meister, Elma	19, Aug. 1890		4	1	
Meister, Everett E.	21, Feb. 1894		20m	5	
Meister, Frank	13, Jan. 1897	11, Jan.	23- 9m	5	
Meister, Leodegarine	25, Feb. 1897	24, Feb.	66	5	
Meister, Mathilda	3, July 1896	2, July	32	5	Wiegand
Meistermann, Henry	11, Dec. 1893		69	5	
Melage, Joseph	18, Sept 1894		75	5	
Melcher, Anna	1, May 1897	30, Apr.	22- 1m	5	Wähaus
Melcher, Carl Louis	25, Oct. 1898	24, Oct.	38-11m	5	
Melcher, Charles	12, Feb. 1890		30	1	
Melcher, Charles William	22, Feb. 1890		60	4	
Melcher, Edward	16, Feb. 1901		34	8	
Melcher, Wilhelm	25, July 1896	24, July	72- 5m- 3d	5	
Melchior, Bernhard Anton	29, Oct. 1889		64	1	
Melitta, Perina	10, Mar. 1889	9, Mar.		5	
Melkmeier, Fr.	17, July 1890		68	1	
Mellerding, Maria	9, Aug. 1900		12m	8	
Mellohe, Wilhelm Friedrich	24, Mar. 1897	23, Mar.	56- 2m	5	
Meltenbrink, Willie	2, Dec. 1887		6d	4	
Meltzer, Mary	3, Sept 1895	1, Sept		5	
Melz, Stella A.	16, July 1888		7d	1	
Melzer, Friedrich W.	15, June 1898	14, June	66	4	
Memmel, Auguste	19, Sept 1896	17, Sept	30- 4m	5	Prehn
Mench, Edward	22, July 1901		12	8	
Menchen, Ed. L.	18, Nov. 1889		30m	1	
Menchen, Mary	13, Feb. 1901		86	8	
Mende, Gottfried	8, Aug. 1869	6, Aug.	79-10m	5	
Mene, Frank	28, May 1901		5m	8	
Menge, B.J.M. (Fr.)	21, Nov. 1897	21, Nov.	66- 2m	4	
Menge, Frank	20, Apr. 1895		8	5	
Menge, L.E.	4, Oct. 1900		23	8	
Menge, Marcella	23, Aug. 1894		2	5	
Menger, Elisabeth	28, Oct. 1895	26, Oct.	42- 8m	5	Krucke
Menger, Max	4, Jan. 1890		10	1	
Menger, Myrtle	22, June 1895		1	5	
Menges, Georgia	8, July 1901		7m	8	
Menges, Margaret	3, Dec. 1900		29	8	
Menges, Valentine	17, Oct. 1893		45	5	
Menke, Angela	28, Feb. 1891		5	4	
Menke, Arnold	22, Feb. 1893		53	5	
Menke, Arnold	2, June 1899	31, May	45	5	
Menke, Bernard	17, July 1891		30	1	
Menke, Bernard	30, Nov. 1892		53	5	
Menke, Bertha	30, Apr. 1900	29, Apr.		4	Jark
Menke, Caspar	20, Feb. 1894		59	5	
Menke, Eduard	30, Mar. 1896	29, Mar.	27	5	
Menke, Emma	26, May 1894		30	5	
Menke, Franz A.	10, Jan. 1893		35	5	
Menke, Fred.	25, Mar. 1890		68	1	
Menke, Henry	1, Dec. 1892		51	5	
Menke, Johan Bernard	2, May 1896	1, May	83- 2m	5	
Menke, Johan H.	2, Sept 1898	1, Sept	47- -10d	4	
Menke, Johan Wilhelm	22, Feb. 1898	21, Feb.	43- 8m	5	
Menke, Josephine	8, Dec. 1891		1	4	
Menke, Josephine	7, Jan. 1897	5, Jan.	71	5	
Menke, Louis	6, July 1889		6m	1	
Menke, Rosa	26, Sept 1895	25, Sept	20- 2m	5	
Menke, Theresa	13, Dec. 1892		37	5	
Menker, Maria	22, Oct. 1889		70	1	
Menkhaus, F.H.	23, Feb. 1889		3	1	
Menle, Edwin	21, Feb. 1888		7	1	
Menne, Catharine	4, Jan. 1893		72	5	
Menner, Carolina	5, July 1899	2, July	50	4	Lott
Menner, Louis M.	6, July 1895		4	5	
Mennett, F.	5, Jan. 1888		62- 1m	1	

Name ****	Notice Date ****** ****	Death Date ***** ****	Age ***	Page ****	Maiden Name ****** ****
Mense, Fred. W.	2, Aug. 1893		1m	5	
Mensel, G.	25, Feb. 1901		72	8	
Mensing, Henry	9, June 1892		12	5	
Menson, Theresa	25, Apr. 1901		68	8	
Mente, Herman	18, Sept 1893	17, Sept		5	
Mentel, Amalia A.	15, Dec. 1896	12, Dec.	76	5	
Mentel, Charles E.	24, Apr. 1894		35	5	
Mentz, Edward	8, Dec. 1891		71	4	
Mentz, F.M.	31, July 1894		50	5	
Menz, Ludwina	16, Sept 1891		17	4	
Menz, Maria	11, Dec. 1895	10, Dec.	44- 4m	5	
Menz, Wilhelm	16, Jan. 1896	15, Jan.	43- 2m	5	
Menze, Elizabeth	16, Apr. 1891		76	4	
Menzel, Alwina	13, Aug. 1901		45	8	
Menzel, Caroline	26, Aug. 1901		74	8	
Menzel, Elsie	24, July 1895		6m	5	
Menzell, Susan	24, Feb. 1891		69	4	
Menzer, Josephine	3, Sept 1901		1	8	
Menzer, Margaretha	27, Dec. 1893		62	5	
Menzinger, Gottlieb	11, Feb. 1893		28	5	
Merchen, Theresa	29, Sept 1893		17	5	
Merckle, Emma	20, Dec. 1900		32	8	
Mercuris, Georgia	13, June 1891		8m	4	
Mergard, Henry	1, Feb. 1892		50	5	
Merke, Ernst	11, Aug. 1888		1	1	
Merkel, Anna	25, Sept 1888		27	1	
Merkel, Florien C.	28, Apr. 1894		3	5	
Merkel, John	13, Jan. 1890		64	1	
Merkens, Henry	11, 13, Jan. 1890		40	1	
Merkhofer, Barbara	14, Nov. 1899	13, Nov.	83- - 9d	4	Koch
Merkhofer, George	6, Sept 1901		46	8	
Merkl, Georg	26, Aug. 1897	25, Aug.	47	5	
Merkle, John	13, May 1901		19	8	
Merland, Anna	19, Dec. 1891		66	4	
Merland, August	29, Aug. 1892		3- 6m	5	
Merle, Balthasar	22, June 1889		50	1	
Merling, Katharine	19, June 1895		35	5	
Mermann, Kate	26, June 1894		7m	5	
Merren, William	29, May 1901		44	8	
Merring, Edwin	27, Sept 1900		47	8	
Merritt,	26, Aug. 1887		2m	1	
Merritt, Eliza B.	19, July 1887		18	1	
Merrs, George Henry	26, Feb. 1889		1	1	
Merry, William	7, Feb. 1901		7	8	
Mersch, August	7, Mar. 1900	6, Mar.	58	5	
Mersch, Joseph	20, Apr. 1896	18, Apr.	43- 5m	5	
Mersfelder, Katharine	21, Feb. 1894		40	5	
Mersmann, Anna Adelheid	29, Jan. 1898	28, Jan.	72-10m	4	Sütthoff
Mersmann, Belle	15, Nov. 1899	13, Nov.	26	5	Staley
Mersmann, Maria	6, July 1899	5, July	39	5	
Mertens, Joseph	5, July 1890		15m	1	
Mertens, Margaretha	27, Aug. 1890		38	1	
Mertz, Peter	31, Mar. 1891		35	4	
Merz, Alex	7, May 1891		11m	4	
Merz, Amalia	25, Apr. 1892		40	5	
Merz, Anna	1, Aug. 1890		7	1	
Merz, Eva	18, Apr. 1893		5	5	
Merz, Frank	14, Jan. 1901		4	8	
Merz, Harry	11, Sept 1889		18m	1	
Meschmeyer,	27, Aug. 1890		52	1	
Mese, Clara	13, Mar. 1888		58	1	
Mesloh, Maria	25, Apr. 1897	22, Apr.	63	5	
Messe, William	24, June 1891		7m	4	
Messer, Louis	25, June 1901		29	8	
Messerschmied, Bertha	11, July 1901		20	5	
Messerth, Sophia	23, Aug. 1901		43	8	
Messick, Emma	3, Mar. 1891		39	4	
Messick, Sallie A.	21, June 1895		69	5	
Messing, Alexander Wilhelm	28, Nov. 1899	27, Nov.	28-11m	8	
Messing, Charles	21, Feb. 1901		34	8	
Mestel, Frank	11, Sept 1888	11, Sept		1	

Name ****	Notice Date ****** ****	Death Date ***** ****	Age ***	Page ****	Maiden Name ****** ****
Mete, William	23, Sept 1901			8	
Meteler, Aloysius	11, Apr. 1893		22	5	
Mettey, Henry	30, Apr. 1901		60	8	
Mettmann, Rosa	7, Feb. 1894		2	5	
Metz, Alice	28, Aug. 1899	27, Aug.	26	4	
Metz, August P.	9, Nov. 1898	8, Nov.	46- 8m- 7d	4	
Metz, Charles M.	10, Jan. 1894		24d	5	
Metz, Elizabeth	19, Oct. 1891		29	1	
Metz, Johan J.	17, Apr. 1899	15, Apr.	57-11m	5	
Metz, Josephine	31, Aug. 1896	30, Aug.	79- 4m	5	Repberger
Metz, Katharine	29, May 1901		32	8	
Metz, Lizzie	18, June 1901		39	8	
Metz, Louisa	28, Dec. 1892		32	5	
Metz, Nic.	2, Dec. 1887		32	4	
Metz, Pauline	12, Jan. 1893		90	5	
Metze, Eliza	10, Jan. 1893		1m	5	
Metzger, Agnes C.	8, July 1891		8m	4	
Metzger, Dora	24, Sept 1891		82	1	
Metzger, Fred	30, Apr. 1901		57	8	
Metzger, Friedricka Dora	12, Mar. 1900	11, Mar.		8	Rosch
Metzger, Gottlieb	5, Sept 1894		67	5	
Metzger, Johan	20, June 1900	18, June	59	5	
Metzger, Jonas H.	18, June 1891		30	4	
Metzger, Joseph	6, Apr. 1889		54	1	
Metzger, Joseph	3, Nov. 1891		4d	4	
Metzger, Michael	20, Jan. 1890		54	1	
Metzger, Ollie	14, Feb. 1899	13, Feb.	22	5	
Metzger, Tillie	11, Apr. 1893		20	5	
Metzker, Mary A.	5, Feb. 1895		57	5	
Metzler, Anna	5, May 1898	2, May	73- 3m	5	Schalcher
Metzler, Gerhardt	24, Oct. 1891		1	4	
Metzler, Karl A.	1, June 1899	30, May	46- 8m	4	
Metzler, Katie	7, Sept 1887		11	1	
Metzler, Paul	30, July 1898	29, July	71- 1m	5	
Metzner, Rosalia	17, Mar. 1891		53	4	
Meville, Katie	16, Apr. 1890		28	1	
Mey, Catherine	17, Mar. 1896	15, Mar.	61-11m	5	
Meyer,	16, Dec. 1891		1d	4	
Meyer,	24, Apr. 1901			8	
Meyer, Ada	1, Sept 1900		26	5	
Meyer, Adele	1, Sept 1899	31, Aug.		5	Wedekemper
Meyer, Adolph	12, Sept 1888		6m	1	
Meyer, Albert	18, Dec. 1893		9m	5	
Meyer, Alberta K.	13, Sept 1901			8	
Meyer, Alfred	19, Mar. 1900	18, Mar.		5	
Meyer, Alice	26, Aug. 1895	25, Aug.		5	
Meyer, Alma	29, Oct. 1888		4	1	
Meyer, Aloradia	10, Oct. 1888		6	1	
Meyer, Anna	27, Dec. 1888		34	2	
Meyer, Anna	27, Feb. 1894		61	5	
Meyer, Anna	17, Aug. 1899	16, Aug.	48- 8m-25d	4	
Meyer, Anna	22, Dec. 1900		72	8	
Meyer, Anna	7, June 1901		62	8	
Meyer, Annie	15, Mar. 1889		3d	1	
Meyer, Annie	26, Aug. 1901		30	8	
Meyer, Anton	21, Dec. 1896	19, Dec.	74- 8m	5	
Meyer, Anton	7, Aug. 1900		62	8	
Meyer, August	25, Mar. 1893		30	5	
Meyer, Barbara	17, Feb. 1895		73	5	
Meyer, Bernard	27, Dec. 1897	26, Dec.	21- 7m	4	
Meyer, Bernard	30, Apr. 1901		50	8	
Meyer, Bertha	29, July 1887		16d	1	
Meyer, Bertha M.	28, July 1888		9m	1	
Meyer, C.J.	2, Dec. 1896	1, Dec.	63	5	
Meyer, Carl	27, Oct. 1894		36	5	
Meyer, Caroline	1, Sept 1898	31, Aug.		4	Funke
Meyer, Caroline R.	25, Dec. 1891		33	2	
Meyer, Charles	10, Dec. 1891		47	4	
Meyer, Charles	6, July 1901		46	8	
Meyer, Charlotte	27, July 1892		28	5	
Meyer, Chr.	30, June 1888		44	1	

Name ****	Notice Date ****** ****	Death Date ***** ****	Age ***	Page ****	Maiden Name ****** ****
Meyer, Chr. S.	20, July 1887		5m	1	
Meyer, Christ.	6, Jan. 1892		92	5	
Meyer, Christian	14, Sept 1887		6m	1	
Meyer, Christian	7, May 1891		64	4	
Meyer, Christian	8, May 1891		27	4	
Meyer, Christine	24, Feb. 1893		71	5	
Meyer, Clara	22, Apr. 1891		1	4	
Meyer, Conrad	8, Feb. 1894		63	5	
Meyer, Dina	3, Dec. 1889		90	1	
Meyer, Dorothy	10, Dec. 1891		58	4	
Meyer, E.	19, Sept 1900		30	8	
Meyer, Ed.	14, Jan. 1892		1	1	
Meyer, Edward	31, Dec. 1888		3	1	
Meyer, Elenora	29, Aug. 1900		6m	5	
Meyer, Elisabeth	12, Sept 1901		82	5	
Meyer, Elizabeth	9, Mar. 1901		64	8	
Meyer, Emma	23, Dec. 1891		19	4	
Meyer, F.	22, Dec. 1887		5	4	
Meyer, F.	20, Feb. 1891		4	4	
Meyer, Fannie	1, Nov. 1892		46	5	
Meyer, Florentine	14, Feb. 1899	13, Feb.	60	5	
Meyer, Francis	12, June 1901		39	8	
Meyer, Frank	20, Oct. 1888		66	1	
Meyer, Frank	2, Sept 1891		2m	4	
Meyer, Frank	17, Mar. 1894		2	5	
Meyer, Frank	1, May 1901		51	8	
Meyer, Frank	10, May 1901		61	8	
Meyer, Frank A.	11, June 1895		5	5	
Meyer, Franz	7, July 1890		74	4	
Meyer, Franz	6, May 1899	5, May	76	4	
Meyer, Fred.	27, Feb. 1890		60	1	
Meyer, Fred.	6, Feb. 1901		45	8	
Meyer, Frederick	24, Nov. 1900		69	8	
Meyer, Friedrich	1, Oct. 1895	30, Sept	37	5	
Meyer, Fritz	20, Oct. 1888		38	1	
Meyer, G.L.	11, Jan. 1888		74	4	
Meyer, George	25, Sept 1890		49	1	
Meyer, George	24, Oct. 1890		62	1	
Meyer, George	4, Jan. 1893		57	5	
Meyer, George J.	19, July 1894		11m	5	
Meyer, Golie	24, May 1889		4w	1	
Meyer, Grover C.	23, June 1894		15m	5	
Meyer, H.	23, Dec. 1893		5m	5	
Meyer, H.H.	20, Jan. 1899	17,Jan.	84- -16d	5	
Meyer, H.H.	28, Sept 1901		76	5	
Meyer, H.W.	24, Jan. 1888		1m	1	
Meyer, Hannah	25, June 1888		8m	1	
Meyer, Harry Fred.	28, Mar. 1893		4	5	
Meyer, Heinrich	26, Aug. 1897		61- 9m	5	
Meyer, Heinrich Bernard	13, Aug. 1887	12, Aug.	35	4	
Meyer, Heinrich Wilhelm	21, Dec. 1896	19, Dec.	58- 3m	5	
Meyer, Henry	3, Aug. 1887		7w	1	
Meyer, Henry	26, July 1888		1	2	
Meyer, Henry	9, Apr. 1891		69	4	
Meyer, Henry	13, Apr. 1893		48	5	
Meyer, Henry	13, Mar. 1894		79	5	
Meyer, Henry	21, Mar. 1901		69	8	
Meyer, Henry B.	14, Aug. 1887		35	1	
Meyer, Henry C.	29, Mar. 1898	27, Mar.	68	5	
Meyer, Herman	28, July 1890		33	1	
Meyer, Herman	13, June 1901		75	8	
Meyer, Jacob	18, July 1887		44	1	
Meyer, Jakob	21, Jan. 1890		56	1	
Meyer, Jakob	13, Oct. 1892		42	5	
Meyer, Johan	6, July 1897	5, July	67- 5m	5	
Meyer, Johan E. (Dr.)	17, Jan. 1899	16, Jan.	74- 4m	5	
Meyer, Johanna	8, Mar. 1892		81	5	
Meyer, John	28, Dec. 1891		68	4	
Meyer, John	15, Aug. 1892		26	5	
Meyer, John	8, Mar. 1894		17m	5	
Meyer, John	17, Feb. 1895		65	5	

Name ****	Notice Date ****** ****	Death Date ***** ****	Age ***	Page ****	Maiden Name ****** ****
Meyer, John	12, June 1901		75	8	
Meyer, John H.	28, Feb. 1901		60	8	
Meyer, John Henry	17, Dec. 1891		39	4	
Meyer, John Henry	3, Dec. 1893	3, Dec.	72- 5m- 1d	* 5	
Meyer, Joseph	11, July 1895		2	5	
Meyer, Joseph	10, Apr. 1899	7, Apr.		5	
Meyer, Joseph	24, May 1901		73	8	
Meyer, Joseph	5, Aug. 1901		3	8	
Meyer, Josephine	14, Jan. 1889		13m	1	
Meyer, Josephine	17, Aug. 1900		40	5	
Meyer, Karoline	29, June 1893		2m	5	
Meyer, Katharina	23, Dec. 1893		60	5	
Meyer, Katharina	8, Aug. 1896	7, Aug.	62- 6m	5	
Meyer, Katharine E.	14, Apr. 1891		49	4	
Meyer, Katie	26, Nov. 1892		5m	5	
Meyer, Klara	28, Mar. 1898	27, Mar.	53- 5m	5	Kratze
Meyer, Lawrence J.	4, Aug. 1888		14m	4	
Meyer, Leo	15, Feb. 1895		2	5	
Meyer, Leonard	30, Aug. 1888		1	1	
Meyer, Lilly	4, Apr. 1890		7m	1	
Meyer, Lizzie	5, Aug. 1887		15m	1	
Meyer, Louis	30, Apr. 1891		4m	4	
Meyer, Louis F.	22, Nov. 1889		1	1	
Meyer, Louisa	20, Apr. 1898	19, Apr.	48- 3m	4	
Meyer, Louise	15, Jan. 1890		32	1	
Meyer, Louise	30, May 1899	29, May	76	4	Wincke
Meyer, Marg.	2, Apr. 1890		1d	1	
Meyer, Margaret	12, Sept 1887		73	1	
Meyer, Margaret	18, Nov. 1891		4	4	
Meyer, Marie Adele	11, Sept 1896	9, Sept	2	5	
Meyer, Martin	27, Feb. 1894		73	5	
Meyer, Mary	15, Sept 1892		1	5	
Meyer, Mary A.	29, May 1894		82	5	
Meyer, Mary C.	3, Aug. 1887		14w	1	
Meyer, Mary E.	24, Jan. 1901		82	8	
Meyer, Mathilda	31, Dec. 1890		48	4	
Meyer, Minnie	18, Feb. 1889		30	1	
Meyer, Nathaniel	31, May 1892		36	5	
Meyer, Nicolaus	25, Apr. 1896	24, Apr.	67- 2m	5	
Meyer, Paulina	12, July 1890	12, July	5-11m- 7d	4	
Meyer, Peter G.	2, Apr. 1891		3	4	
Meyer, Phil.	2, Aug. 1901		61	8	
Meyer, Phil. A.	12, Nov. 1900		3d	5	
Meyer, Philipina	10, Apr. 1894		63	5	
Meyer, Rosa	29, May 1889		5w	1	
Meyer, Rosa	9, Nov. 1894		24	4	
Meyer, Rosa Huber	17, May 1898	16, May	59	4	
Meyer, Rosalia	23, July 1887		7m	1	
Meyer, Rudolf	17, Sept 1901		15	8	
Meyer, Rudolph	21, Feb. 1893		4m	5	
Meyer, Rudolph	20, Feb. 1895		26	5	
Meyer, Sebastian	6, July 1895		46	5	
Meyer, Sophia	18, Dec. 1899	19, Dec.	76-11m	4	Lübke
Meyer, Sophia	31, Aug. 1900		43	5	
Meyer, Theresa	27, Nov. 1894		18	5	
Meyer, Valentine	16, Nov. 1900		51	8	
Meyer, Walter	20, Apr. 1896	18, Apr.	11- 7m	5	
Meyer, William	19, Oct. 1889		60- 6m	1	
Meyer, William	9, July 1890		1	1	
Meyer, William	20, Jan. 1891		32	4	
Meyer, William	10, Dec. 1892		18	5	
Meyer, William	21, Jan. 1901		35	8	
Meyer, William	20, June 1901		30	8	
Meyerfeld, Wolf	13, Sept 1897	12, Sept		5	
Meyerhofer, G.	5, Jan. 1888		27	1	
Meyerhofer, J.	10, Feb. 1888		15	1	
Meyerott, Magdalena	26, Jan. 1892		3m	5	
Meyers, Amelia	14, Feb. 1891		10m	4	
Meyers, Barney	21, Mar. 1895		46	5	
Meyers, Catharine	28, Nov. 1900		68	8	
Meyers, Catharine M.	14, Jan. 1901		84	8	

Name ****	Notice Date ****** ****	Death Date ***** ****	Age ***	Page ****	Maiden Name ****** ****
Meyers, Charles	22, July 1887		40	1	
Meyers, Elizabeth	5, Feb. 1901		74	8	
Meyers, Elmer C.	5, Nov. 1891		3m	1	
Meyers, Fannie	8, Mar. 1901		62	8	
Meyers, Henry	1, July 1891		6m	1	
Meyers, James	21, Apr. 1891		70	4	
Meyers, Katharina	23, Dec. 1897	22, Dec.	74	5	Horstmann
Meyers, Lilly	23, July 1895		2	5	
Meyers, Lizzie C.	25, Feb. 1891		85	4	
Meyers, Louise	11, Jan. 1899	8, Jan.	31-10m	5	Brockmann
Meyers, Mabel	13, July 1901		16	8	
Meyers, Margaret	16, May 1894		54	5	
Meyers, Margaret	6, Mar. 1901		5m	5	
Meyers, Martin	31, Oct. 1895	30, Oct.	61	5	
Meyers, Mary	5, Mar. 1901		4m	5	
Meyers, Nellie	30, July 1890		3m	1	
Meyers, Romer	11, Sept 1900		1	5	
Meyersieck, Carrie	5, June 1890		40	4	
Meyrahl, Emma	3, Feb. 1890		13	1	
Meßmann, Maria	7, Aug. 1895	6, Aug.	3- 3m	5	
Meßmer, G. Rudolph	13, Dec. 1899	11, Dec.	39- 2m	5	
Meßmer, Louisa	21, Dec. 1892		3	5	
Meßmer, Marie J.	18, Dec. 1891		84	2	
Meßmer, William	1, Oct. 1891		1d	1	
Meßner, Louise	21, May 1889		4	1	
Meßner, Mattie	23, May 1895		22	5	
Mibben, Anna M.	24, June 1891		1d	4	
Michael, Bernard	27, Oct. 1898	26, Oct.	18- 8m	5	
Michael, Frederick	18, July 1895		2d	5	
Michael, John H.	13, July 1895		49	5	
Michael, Katharina	10, June 1892	8, June	74-11m	5	Hanhauser
Michael, Mamie C.	6, Feb. 1891		5	4	
Michaels, Charles	25, Jan. 1888		2	1	
Michaels, Clara	7, Jan. 1888		3	1	
Michaels, Kurt	23, Feb. 1891		73	4	
Michel, C.	1, Feb. 1889		54	1	
Michel, Johan Heinrich	17, Aug. 1896	16, Aug.	70- 6m	5	
Michel, Margaret	13, Feb. 1901		77	8	
Michel, Mary	21, July 1890		73	1	
Michel, William	4, Dec. 1900		25	8	
Michelbacher, Louis	16, July 1888		3	1	
Michele, Joseph	15, May 1894		25	5	
Michels,	20, Dec. 1900		1d	8	
Michie, Ann	8, Jan. 1891		73	4	
Mickelson, Jake	11, Aug. 1900		10	8	
Mickens, Robert	15, Jan. 1892		29	5	
Middelberg, Mary	5, Aug. 1887		7	1	
Middelhoff, Elizabeth	21, Mar. 1895		68	5	
Middendorf, F.	24, Aug. 1898	22, Aug.	41	5	
Middendorf, Harry	21, June 1900	19, June	7m	6	
Middendorf, Josephine	30, Oct. 1891		45	4	
Midendorff, Maria Anna	1, Mar. 1898	27, Feb.	67- 7m	5	Mersch
Mider, Georg	28, Dec. 1896	26, Dec.	63-10m	5	
Midgelay, John	7, Sept 1887		10w	1	
Midgley, Jeannette	25, Jan. 1901		18	8	
Miechers, Dietrich	19, Apr. 1889		77	1	
Miele, Marie	1, May 1901		20d	8	
Mierenfeld, Frederick	23, 24, Mar. 1893		7	5	
Mierle, Waldberger	1, Mar. 1893		66	5	
Millenberger, Mary	26, Dec. 1890		1d	1	
Miller, (Mrs. Henry)	27, May 1899	24, May	61- 9m	4	
Miller, Abraham	5, Feb. 1898	4, Feb.	76	5	
Miller, Adam	12, Aug. 1887		4w	1	
Miller, Adam	3, Nov. 1887		18	4	
Miller, Agnes	18, Oct. 1894		54	5	
Miller, Agnes	17, Oct. 1894	16, Oct.	51- 9m-16d	5	Urbanowski
Miller, Albert	4, Aug. 1888		7w	4	
Miller, Alfred A.	2, Aug. 1901		4m	8	
Miller, Anna	3, Apr. 1891		10m	4	
Miller, Anna	19, Dec. 1891		50	4	
Miller, Anna	6, July 1901		26	8	

Name ****	Notice Date ****** ****	Death Date ***** ****	Age ***	Page ****	Maiden Name ****** ****
Miller, Anna	12, Aug. 1901		64	8	
Miller, Annie	4, Apr. 1891		5	4	
Miller, Annie	29, Oct. 1891		45	4	
Miller, August	15, Mar. 1901		10	8	
Miller, Barbara	4, Aug. 1893		38	5	
Miller, Barbara	18, Aug. 1900		19	8	
Miller, Bernard	20, Jan. 1891		47	4	
Miller, Carrie	8, Dec. 1900		12	8	
Miller, Carrie S.	1, Nov. 1892		21	5	
Miller, Catharina Franziska	14, Nov. 1898	12, Nov.	72-11m-18d	5	Sidel
Miller, Charles	11, Dec. 1890		39	1	
Miller, Charles	12, Apr. 1892		3	5	
Miller, Charles	19, Apr. 1895		28	5	
Miller, Charles	28, Feb. 1901		30	8	
Miller, Charles A.	23, Mar. 1893		1	5	
Miller, Ed.	27, Aug. 1889		22	1	
Miller, Edmund	30, Mar. 1898	28, Mar.	22- 7m	5	
Miller, Edwin	23, May 1895		3m	5	
Miller, Edwin P.	14, Mar. 1891		3	4	
Miller, Elisabeth	25, Mar. 1891		61	4	
Miller, Elisabeth	27, Aug. 1891		58	1	
Miller, Elisabeth	12, Jan. 1898	10, Jan.	41- 5m	4	Schreiner
Miller, Eliza	22, Jan. 1892		75	5	
Miller, Elizabeth	16, Jan. 1891		82	4	
Miller, Ella	27, Apr. 1892		6	5	
Miller, Emil H.	17, July 1895		3m	5	
Miller, Eugen	12, Dec. 1900		26	8	
Miller, Eva	16, Dec. 1891		7m	4	
Miller, Francisca	15, Aug. 1891		2	4	
Miller, Frank	21, July 1888		1	1	
Miller, Frank W.	25, Mar. 1889		7m	1	
Miller, Franz Joseph	15, Oct. 1895	14, Oct.	28-10m	5	
Miller, Fred	17, Jan. 1901		34	8	
Miller, Georg	5, June 1896	2, June	9m	4	
Miller, George	30, Dec. 1891		1	4	
Miller, George	16, Oct. 1894		20	5	
Miller, George	5, June 1901		46	8	
Miller, Hannah	6, Mar. 1901		72	5	
Miller, Heinrich	7, Jan. 1899	5, Jan.	54	5	
Miller, Heinrich	18, Feb. 1899	16, Feb.	63	5	
Miller, Helen	3, Oct. 1888		18m	1	
Miller, Helen	10, Feb. 1891		5d	4	
Miller, Helen	11, Oct. 1900		3	8	
Miller, Helene	13, Mar. 1901		67	8	
Miller, Henry	1, Aug. 1887		24	1	
Miller, Henry	7, May 1891		35	4	
Miller, Henry	17, Feb. 1892		10m	5	
Miller, Henry	3, June 1892		53	5	
Miller, Henry	29, Oct. 1894		24	5	
Miller, Herman	6, June 1891		21	4	
Miller, Howard	2, Dec. 1887		1m	4	
Miller, Hubert	2, Aug. 1901		7m	8	
Miller, Isabella	12, Sept 1891		2	1	
Miller, J.	17, Jan. 1888		19	4	
Miller, J.J. (Dr.)	26, Oct. 1898	23, Oct.	38	5	
Miller, Jakob	15, Apr. 1889		49	1	
Miller, Jane	27, Mar. 1901		68	8	
Miller, Jennie M.	20, Dec. 1893		2m	5	
Miller, John	23, Aug. 1887		27	1	
Miller, John	21, Apr. 1888		1d	1	
Miller, John	1, May 1888		3m	2	
Miller, John	15, Aug. 1891		37	4	
Miller, John	17, Apr. 1894		33	5	
Miller, John	6, Nov. 1900		24	8	
Miller, John	13, Sept 1901		39	8	
Miller, John	4, Oct. 1901		35	8	
Miller, John B.	23, Jan. 1901		75	8	
Miller, John E.	18, Feb. 1901		70	8	
Miller, Joseph	17, Mar. 1891		41	4	
Miller, Joseph	9, July 1895		7	5	
Miller, Joseph	8, Oct. 1900		67	8	

Name ****	Notice Date ****** ****	Death Date ***** ****	Age ***	Page ****	Maiden Name ****** ****
Miller, Joseph C.	3, Feb. 1900	1, Feb.	27	5	
Miller, Julia	20, Mar. 1901		64	1	
Miller, Karl	14, Jan. 1893		5m	5	
Miller, Karoline	10, Mar. 1897	7, Mar.	52-11m	5	Dittmann
Miller, Katharina	2, Mar. 1893		64	5	
Miller, Katie	9, July 1887		4m	1	
Miller, Katie	24, Sept 1888		2	1	
Miller, Lena	26, July 1887		63	1	
Miller, Leroy	18, Feb. 1901		2	8	
Miller, Lizzie	13, Mar. 1891		18m	4	
Miller, Magdalena	11, Apr. 1896	10, Apr.		5	
Miller, Maggie M.	20, Jan. 1891		1m	4	
Miller, Margaretha	13, May 1901		55	8	
Miller, Maria	27, Oct. 1891		1	1	
Miller, Mary	27, Oct. 1891		3	1	
Miller, Mary	1, June 1892		65	5	
Miller, Mary	29, Dec. 1892		75	5	
Miller, Mary	29, Sept 1894		33	5	
Miller, Mary	24, Nov. 1900		53	8	
Miller, Mary	6, Aug. 1901		39	8	
Miller, Michael	14, July 1891		38	4	
Miller, Michael	31, July 1901		23	8	
Miller, Milo	25, Mar. 1891		30	4	
Miller, Missouri	4, Dec. 1891		38	4	
Miller, Mollie	13, Oct. 1900		25	8	
Miller, Nanna	13, Aug. 1891		2m	4	
Miller, Nicholas	9, Aug. 1892		33	5	
Miller, Nicholas	30, Nov. 1900		5m	8	
Miller, Nora	14, Aug. 1890		3w	1	
Miller, Otto	13, Apr. 1901		3m	8	
Miller, Patty	7, Sept 1887		22	1	
Miller, Pauline	3, Nov. 1891		4	4	
Miller, Richard	26, Mar. 1901		1	8	
Miller, Robert L.	1, Mar. 1893		2	5	
Miller, Sam.	20, Dec. 1897	18, Dec.	61	5	
Miller, Theodor	17, May 1901		3m	8	
Miller, Thomas	14, Sept 1887		2	1	
Miller, W.	15, May 1895		26	5	
Miller, Walburga	28, Oct. 1897	26, Oct.	56- 9m	5	Lingle
Miller, Wilhelm	11, Apr. 1898	10, Apr.	67	5	
Miller, William	22, Aug. 1888		46	1	
Miller, William	28, Sept 1888		30	2	
Miller, William	2, Sept 1891		41	4	
Miller, William	22, July 1893		85	5	
Miller, William	2, July 1901		1	8	
Miller, William H.	22, Nov. 1887		21	1	
Miller, William L.	28, July 1887		50	1	
Milliaan, Bernard	8, Dec. 1900		3m	8	
Millord, Benjamin	24, Sept 1901		75	1	
Mills, Anna F.	23, Sept 1887		49	2	
Mills, Clara	11, Jan. 1901		37	5	
Mills, Clarence	10, Sept 1887		8m	2	
Mills, Cordelia	13, Mar. 1901		21	8	
Mills, Helen	31, Oct. 1900		1m	8	
Mills, William	4, Apr. 1895		62	5	
Milroy, Elizabeth	13, Dec. 1900		75	8	
Minces, Aaron	24, July 1890		8	1	
Minces, Sam.	24, July 1890		39	1	
Minces, Sarah	24, July 1890		29	1	
Minderholdt, Katie	23, Jan. 1889		4	2	
Miner, George	15, July 1901		29	8	
Miner, Louisa J.	2, Apr. 1901		72	8	
Miner, May E.	21, June 1901		27	8	
Mingel, Lillie	3, Feb. 1892		25	5	
Minges, Lena	16, July 1895		22	5	
Mink, Katharine	25, June 1895	23, June	38- 7m- 2d	5	Griesser
Minkowsky, Anna	5, Mar. 1901		67	5	
Minneschläger, George	2, Dec. 1887		48	4	
Minnich, Paul	28, July 1888		17m	1	
Minning, Edna	16, Mar. 1892		2	1	
Minning, Johan Wilhelm	1, July 1899	29, June	90	5	

Name ****	Notice Date ****** ****	Death Date ***** ****	Age ***	Page ****	Maiden Name ****** ****
Minning, John	7, May 1891		42	4	
Minning, Louisa	31, Mar. 1891		82	4	
Minshall, Elisabeth	23, Nov. 1891		72	1	
Minstermann, E.	3, Aug. 1901		1	8	
Minstermann, William	16, July 1892		33	5	
Mintin, Henry	20, July 1889		58	1	
Mistler, Joseph	3, Aug. 1887		5m	1	
Mitchell, Ann	1, Oct. 1887		54	1	
Mitchell, Blanche	16, Apr. 1890		1	1	
Mitchell, Charles	23, Oct. 1900		1	8	
Mitchell, Jethro	7, Apr. 1895		77	5	
Mitchell, Lucy	25, June 1901		13	8	
Mitchell, Michael	14, Aug. 1887		34	1	
Mithave, Herman	27, Apr. 1901		53	8	
Mithoefer, Alma	5, Mar. 1901		7	5	
Mithoefer, Charlotte	5, July 1898	5, July	11m	5	
Mithoefer, Maria	28, Sept 1893		29	5	
Mitsch, Anna	5, Jan. 1888		5m	1	
Mitsch, Elizabeth	30, Aug. 1887		40	1	
Mitte, Charles	15, Feb. 1892		5	5	
Mittendorf, Emma	13, Sept 1895	12, Sept	27	5	Schmudde
Mittendorf, Herman	26, Nov. 1891		71	1	
Mittenzwei, Rachel	13, Sept 1900		60	5	
Mixus, Albert	5, Apr. 1901		54	8	
Moch, David	1, Aug. 1901		10m	8	
Mode, Sophia	30, Apr. 1895		90	5	
Moder, Charles	8, Mar. 1893		6	5	
Moedrocke, Joseph	22, July 1887		38	1	
Moehlmann, Carl	1, Sept 1888		1d	1	
Moellenkamp, Conrad	19, Nov. 1898	17, Nov.	73-11m	5	
Moellenkamp, Henry	12, Sept 1891		54	1	
Moellenkamp, Wilhelm	23, Oct. 1899	22, Oct.	72	* 5	
Moeller, Bernard	30, Sept 1901		80	8	
Moeller, Clara	14, Dec. 1893		3	5	
Moeller, Edmund	19, Aug. 1891		3d	4	
Moeller, Henry	16, Feb. 1888		14	4	
Moeller, Henry	17, Feb. 1891		69	4	
Moeller, Joseph	26, July 1898	25, July	17-10m	5	
Moeller, Joseph F.	14, Jan. 1892		40	1	
Moeller, Kate	21, June 1895		47	5	
Moeller, Linus	13, Apr. 1895		3	4	
Moeller, Maria Elisabeth	5, Aug. 1898	3, Aug.	40- 2m-23d	5	Fleddermann
Moeller, Mathilda	13, Nov. 1900		9m	8	
Moeller, Robert	30, Dec. 1893		2	5	
Moeller, Theodor	5, Apr. 1899	3, Apr.	27- 4m	4	
Moemke, John R.	1, Mar. 1893		22	5	
Moering, Willie	9, Aug. 1887		1- 9m	1	
Moerlein, Barbara	14, 15, Dec. 1893	14, Dec.	15- 8m-24d	5	
Moerlein, Christian	15, May 1897	14, May	79	4	
Moerlein, Ed.	16, Apr. 1890		1	1	
Moerlein, George	1, 2, Sept 1891	31, Aug.	39- 2m-23d	1	
Moerlein, Johan	19, Feb. 1900	18, Feb.	44- 8m	4	
Moerlein, Josephine	7, Feb. 1901		42	8	
Moerlein, Magdalena	23, 24, Jan. 1894	22, Jan.	40- 7m-11d	5	Zimmermann
Moerlein, Marg.	5, Aug. 1887		62	1	
Moerlein, Wilhelm	17, 19, Sept 1896	17, Sept	30-10m	5	
Moerlmann, Bernard	15, Apr. 1888		8d	5	
Moersch, Appolonia	9, Apr. 1890		51	1	
Moerschel, Conrad	11, Feb. 1893		1	5	
Moertl, Loretta	7, Aug. 1901		2	8	
Moeschl, Frank	29, July 1896	28, July	47	5	
Moeschl, Frank	22, Mar. 1897	20, Mar.	48- -16d	5	
Moeschl, Joseph H.	27, July 1893	24, July	79	* 5	
Moeser, Christ.	28, Jan. 1892		78	5	
Moeser, F.	5, Jan. 1888		2	1	
Moest, John F.	8, Aug. 1891		34	4	
Moesta, Richard	18, Feb. 1890		1- 9m	1	
Moffatt, Charl.	13, Jan. 1888		88	1	
Mogg, Charles C.	29, Aug. 1887		2	1	
Mohe, Fritz Wilhelm	12, Apr. 1897	10, Apr.	59	5	
Mohlenkamp, Gerhard	15, June 1889		3	1	

Name ****	Notice Date ****** ****	Death Date ***** ****	Age ***	Page ****	Maiden Name ****** ****
Mohlenkamp, Maria	12, Sept 1887		83	1	
Mohlenkamp, Philomena	12, Mar. 1900	11, Mar.	25	8	Berg
Mohnlein, Eva	20, Feb. 1895		76	5	
Mohr, Eleonora Rosa	29, Sept 1897	28, Sept	5m	5	
Mohr, Heinrich Johan	15, Feb. 1899	13, Feb.	30- 7m	5	
Mohr, Mary	20, July 1893		44	5	
Mohr, Oskar	18, Mar. 1890		30m	1	
Mohr, Oskar C.	14, Mar. 1895		3m	5	
Mohr, Ottilia C.	25, Dec. 1891		17d	2	
Mohr, Peter	20, June 1901		29	8	
Molder,	27, Mar. 1888		1d	4	
Moll, Jennie	25, July 1893		47	5	
Mollenkamp, Louisa	15, Dec. 1887		40- 1w	1	
Moller, Katharine	22, Feb. 1897	20, Feb.	52- 6m	5	Humbert
Moller, Margaret F.	5, June 1895		1m	5	
Molleran, Gertrud	3, May 1899	2, May	75-10m	5	Wessel
Molleran, Joseph	30, Aug. 1901		53	8	
Mollmann, Annie	11, Aug. 1887		5w	1	
Mollmann, Henry B.	21, Sept 1887		62	1	
Mollmann, Katharina	9, Feb. 1897	8, Feb.	43	5	Hollenden
Molloy, Charles	29, Jan. 1892			5	
Molloy, Francis J.	24, Jan. 1901		21	8	
Molloy, Michael	8, Nov. 1887		84	1	
Molloy, Thomas	13, June 1901		71	8	
Molters, Elizabeth	6, Aug. 1896	4, Aug.	30-11m	5	
Momberg, A.E.	8, Feb. 1898	6, Feb.	85- 3m	5	
Momberg, Elisabeth	12, Feb. 1898	9, Feb.	51- 6m	5	Rühl
Momberg, John Henry	1, Oct. 1891		85	1	
Momberg, Louise	20, Nov. 1897	19, Nov.	46-10m	5	
Momberg, Marie	15, June 1899	12, June	39- 4m-12d	5	Scheurer
Momberg, Victoria	31, July 1901		61	8	
Moming, William	19, Dec. 1888		21	1	
Monaghan, Sarah	19, Mar. 1901		57	8	
Monahan, Elizabeth	31, July 1901		67	8	
Mond, Heinrich	16, July 1888		64	1	
Mongan, Cecilia	27, Mar. 1901		20d	8	
Monheimer, Sophia	15, July 1887		29	1	
Monig, Mary	6, Mar. 1889		4m	1	
Monkedick, John	24, Feb. 1893		54	5	
Monnig, Henry	20, Oct. 1887		5w	1	
Monning, Henry	11, Feb. 1897	10, Feb.	53- 4m	5	
Monohan, Cilia	7, Apr. 1888		42	4	
Monroe, Alice	2, May 1895		15m	5	
Monroe, John	24, Nov. 1900		59	8	
Monsler, Harry	23, Nov. 1892		17m	5	
Montag, Magdalena	29, Mar. 1900	28, Mar.	42	4	Merz
Montegarri, Maria Agostina	3, Mar. 1888		15m	1	
Montgomery, Ann	26, July 1887		13d	1	
Montgomery, Sam.	3, Oct. 1901		43	8	
Montgomery, W.	6, July 1901		4	8	
Montjone, Clara	18, June 1901		21	8	
Montow, Charles	25, Nov. 1887		3	1	
Mooney, Mary	15, Aug. 1901		67	8	
Moor, Maria	4, Aug. 1896	3, Aug.	75	5	Henn
Moorbrink, John F.	23, July 1895		54	5	
Moore, Addie	6, May 1892		6	5	
Moore, Carrie	18, Sept 1901		25	8	
Moore, Cicero	12, Nov. 1900		68	5	
Moore, Clara E.	20, July 1901		64	8	
Moore, Ellen	7, Apr. 1888		33	4	
Moore, Frances	3, Nov. 1887		35	4	
Moore, James	13, July 1895		36	5	
Moore, Louis	25, July 1901		39	8	
Moore, Mollie B.	17, Apr. 1888		45	1	
Moore, Moses	6, Aug. 1901		48	8	
Moore, Sadie	8, Nov. 1900		4	8	
Moore, Sarah	4, May 1895		91	5	
Moore, T.G.	15, Mar. 1888		50	4	
Moore, Thomas	10, Apr. 1901		83	8	
Moore, William	30, Jan. 1901		18	8	
Moorherm, August	3, Apr. 1895		55	5	

Name ****	Notice Date ****** ****	Death Date ***** ****	Age ***	Page ****	Maiden Name ****** ****
Moormann, Bernard	27, Apr. 1894		63	5	
Moormann, Bernard H.	5, Aug. 1899	4, Aug.	76- - 1d	4	
Moormann, Dorothea	7, Feb. 1899	6, Feb.	68- 3m	5	Schulte
Moormann, Ed.	22, July 1901		2	8	
Moormann, Fred. H.	11, Feb. 1891		26	4	
Moormann, Henry	19, July 1887		47	1	
Moormann, Henry	5, Sept 1891		1d	1	
Moormann, Henry	4, Feb. 1901		48	8	
Moormann, J.J.	23, Apr. 1900	21, Apr.		8	
Moormann, Joseph	13, Nov. 1900		8m	8	
Moormann, Mary	20, Feb. 1901		78	8	
Moormann, Philomena	18, Dec. 1893		52	5	
Moormann, Wilhelm	23, Nov. 1897	22, Nov.	47- 9m	4	
Moran, Mary C.	8, Dec. 1887		10m	1	
Moran, Rose	8, Nov. 1887		55	1	
Mordloh, F.B.	18, Sept 1895	17, Sept	66- - 9d	5	
Mordman, George	1, Aug. 1901		33	8	
Morety, Gottfried	27, June 1888		67	1	
Morford, Alice	28, Sept 1901		16	5	
Morgan, Carrie	29, Dec. 1900		30	8	
Morgan, James	8, May 1896	7, May	60	5	
Morgan, John	10, Dec. 1900		36	8	
Morgan, Lucie	12, July 1901		5	8	
Morgan, Samuel	7, Dec. 1887		32	1	
Morgenroth, F.	21, Feb. 1888		57	1	
Morgenroth, Minnie	2, May 1901		82	8	
Morgenschweis, John	16, Jan. 1891		56	4	
Morgenthal, Casper	4, Feb. 1893		79	5	
Morgenweis, Adam	27, Feb. 1899	26, Feb.	38- 2m	5	
Moriarity, Hannah	24, Nov. 1900		65	8	
Moritz, E.	21, Jan. 1889		65	1	
Moritz, Sophie	23, Oct. 1897	22, Oct.	57	4	Tremmel
Morl, Mary	10, Sept 1890		1	1	
Morley, Harold R.	29, Aug. 1887		2- 3m	1	
Morrell, William	2, Oct. 1900		37	8	
Morris, Edw.	28, Jan. 1889		64	1	
Morris, Helen	26, Apr. 1901		37	8	
Morris, Nellie M.	11, Aug. 1887		20m	1	
Morrison,	3, Jan. 1901		2d	5	
Morrow, J.R.	16, Aug. 1887		10d	1	
Mors, Clarence	23, Sept 1901			8	
Morsch, A.	13, Mar. 1901		4m	8	
Morsch, Fred.	30, Aug. 1901		76	8	
Morsch, John	19, Mar. 1901		62	8	
Morsch, Margaret	11, Apr. 1901		69	8	
Morton, J.T.	29, Dec. 1900		75	8	
Morton, Santha	22, May 1888		63	1	
Mosbacher, Anton	20, Feb. 1899	18, Feb.	55- 9m	5	
Mosbacher, Julia	21, Apr. 1896	20, Apr.	15- 4m	5	
Mosbacher, Peter	16, Sept 1891		53	4	
Moschel, Jacob	13, Nov. 1900		62	8	
Mosenmeier, B. (Dr.)	30, Jan. 1896	28, Jan.	78- 4m	5	
Moser, Casper C. (Rev.)	27, June 1900	26, June	70- 6m-11d	8	
Moser, Christ.	17, Dec. 1887		36	1	
Moser, John F.	22, Apr. 1891		72	4	
Moser, Maria	4, Dec. 1897	2, Dec.	80- -14d	5	Friedmann
Moser, Minna	16, Feb. 1897	14, Feb.	38- 9m	5	Scholz
Moser, R.M.	14, June 1889		30	1	
Moser, Susanna	8, Aug. 1896	6, Aug.	68- 8m	5	Conrady
Moser, Vincenz	16, Jan. 1899	14, Jan.	84	5	
Moser, W.	16, Jan. 1893		82	5	
Moses, Joseph	8, Aug. 1893		40	5	
Mosler, Herman	24, July 1901		71	8	
Mosser, Lizzie	1, Mar. 1899	27, Feb.		5	
Mosser, Susanne	6, 7, Dec. 1895	5, Dec.	64- 8m	5	
Moster, Arthur R.	13, Feb. 1894		18m	5	
Mosz, Lizzie	19, Oct. 1892		77	5	
Motsch, Johan	1, Mar. 1898	28, Feb.	90-11m	5	
Mott, Katharina	14, July 1897	13, July	71- 5m	5	Bös
Motz, Agathe	17, May 1901		81	8	
Motz, Frank	14, Feb. 1891		41	4	

Name	Notice Date	Death Date	Age	Page	Maiden Name
****	****** ****	***** ****	***	****	****** ****
Motz, Louise	9, Aug. 1888		43	1	
Mouillett, Andrew	24, Apr. 1901		5	8	
Mouran, Fannie	10, Oct. 1901		42	8	
Mowaritz, (Mrs)	13, Sept 1900		30	5	
Moß, Frank	19, July 1900		82	8	
Moß, Henry J.	25, Mar. 1891		1d	4	
Moß, Johanna	7, Sept 1893		2	5	
Muchmore, Fanny B.	26, Dec. 1900		21	8	
Muchmore, George	23, May 1901		15	8	
Muchmore, Morris	15, Nov. 1900		60	8	
Muchmore, Stephen	4, Apr. 1901		54	8	
Muehe, John	8, Nov. 1895	6, Nov.	42-11m	5	
Muehring, Conrad	16, July 1901		84	8	
Mueller, Adoline H.	19, July 1894		1	5	
Mueller, Amalia	31, Jan. 1898	29, Jan.	67	5	Kretschmar
Mueller, Amelia	7, Mar. 1896	5, Mar.	58	5	
Mueller, Anna	30, June 1888		5m	1	
Mueller, Anna	20, Feb. 1900	19, Feb.		5	Heckert
Mueller, Anton	25, Mar. 1901		68	8	
Mueller, Arthur E.	14, Nov. 1893		24	5	
Mueller, B.	25, Jan. 1888		2m	1	
Mueller, Caroline	11, Apr. 1898	10, Apr.	67- 8m	5	Thiele
Mueller, Carrie	8, Feb. 1892		6m	4	
Mueller, Christian	3, Sept 1898	2, Sept	67- 6m	4	
Mueller, Conrad	19, Mar. 1901		40	8	
Mueller, Dora	31, May 1901		8m	8	
Mueller, Edna	22, Oct. 1894		5m	5	
Mueller, Frank	18, Feb. 1901		6d	8	
Mueller, Fred	27, Mar. 1901		72	8	
Mueller, Frederick	24, Nov. 1891			4	
Mueller, Frieda	11, Apr. 1890		1	1	
Mueller, G.A.	18, Feb. 1896	16, Feb.	4	5	
Mueller, George	20, Nov. 1900		38	8	
Mueller, George F.	16, Nov. 1894		24	5	
Mueller, Helene	4, Oct. 1894		29	5	
Mueller, Henry	25, Feb. 1897	23, Feb.	66	5	
Mueller, J.H.	10, Oct. 1893		68	5	
Mueller, Jacob Frank	21, Sept 1897	19, Sept	19	5	
Mueller, Johan M.	7, Jan. 1899	6, Jan.	86- 5m	5	
Mueller, John	3, Aug. 1892		68	5	
Mueller, John	26, Aug. 1901		66	8	
Mueller, John C.N.	14, Jan. 1901		79	8	
Mueller, Katharine B.	18, July 1895		58	5	
Mueller, Lorenz	21, July 1897	20, July		5	
Mueller, Louis	1, Sept 1888		27	1	
Mueller, Louis	16, Jan. 1899	14, Jan.		5	
Mueller, Louis P.	27, Jan. 1894		6	5	
Mueller, Louisa	7, July 1891		2	1	
Mueller, Marie	30, Apr. 1891		28d	4	
Mueller, Mary	7, July 1891		2m	1	
Mueller, Mary	3, Jan. 1901		78	5	
Mueller, Mary	7, June 1901		20	8	
Mueller, Mathilde	7, Feb. 1901		77	8	
Mueller, Nicholaus	2, Mar. 1896	29, Feb.	62-11m	5	
Mueller, Philip	12, June 1901		55	8	
Mueller, Regina	13, Oct. 1892		78	5	
Mueller, abby	18, Sept 1900		50	5	
Muellerschoen, Gottlieb	11, July 1895		56	5	
Muench, Adelina	17, Mar. 1897	15, Mar.	46- 3m	5	Kitt
Muench, Anna B.	28, Sept 1893		46	5	
Muench, Liebrath	18, June 1901		48	8	
Muenchen, Edmund	26, June 1895		10m	5	
Muenzenmeier, E.A.	30, Oct. 1891		15	4	
Mugler, Nicholas	22, Dec. 1893		45	5	
Muhle, Bernad	16, Dec. 1891		80	4	
Muhleisen, H. Ch.	17, Jan. 1888		18d	4	
Muhlhäuser, Johan G.	9, Jan. 1897	8, Jan.	25- 9m	5	
Muhlmann, John	8, July 1901		31	8	
Muir, Cacilia	1, Oct. 1897	30, Sept	81	5	
Muir, James	24, July 1891		24	1	
Muke, Minnie	7, Aug. 1894		18	5	

Name ****	Notice Date ****** ****	Death Date ***** ****	Age ***	Page ****	Maiden Name ****** ****
Mulcahy, Clara	11, Jan. 1901		2	5	
Muldoon, Bridget	20, Oct. 1887		26	1	
Muldoon, Peter	14, Oct. 1901		43	5	
Muleahy, William	13, Nov. 1893		82	5	
Mulholland, Mary	6, Dec. 1892		60	5	
Mullaley, Michael	26, Nov. 1900		55	8	
Mullally, Johanna	2, Nov. 1900		98	8	
Mullan,	12, Sept 1887		2d	1	
Mullane, Henrietta G.	12, Dec. 1891		38	4	
Mullaney, Hugh	9, Aug. 1900		84	8	
Mullaney, Virginia	17, Jan. 1901		36	8	
Mullen, Blanche	22, Mar. 1901		20	8	
Mullen, James W.	21, Aug. 1887		21	5	
Mullen, Thomas	26, Dec. 1900		11	8	
Mullen, W.	24, Aug. 1888		24	1	
Muller, Laura Rosa	16, Dec. 1891		2	4	
Muller, Louis	9, Feb. 1898	8, Feb.		5	
Muller, Maria	21, Feb. 1896	20, Feb.		5	
Mulligan, Alma	23, Apr. 1895		14	5	
Mullin, Elisabeth	13, Oct. 1892		76	5	
Mullinger, Harry J.	1, Aug. 1887		17d	1	
Mullins, Abby	19, Sept 1900		50	8	
Mullmeier, John	10, Oct. 1891		11m	4	
Mullmer, Esther	27, May 1901		8m	8	
Mullut, Frank	7, July 1887		2	1	
Mulsman, Tresia	3, May 1892		63	5	
Multner, Elizabeth	14, Feb. 1901		83	8	
Mulvihill, Clara E.	23, Apr. 1895		29	5	
Mulvihill, M.	16, Feb. 1888		54	4	
Mumer, George	15, June 1900	13, June	76- 7m	8	
Mummert, Philipp	24, Jan. 1900	22, Jan.	74	4	
Mund, (boy)	19, Oct. 1887		3m	1	
Mund, Catharine	15, 16, Nov. 1895	15, Nov.	38 -14d	5	Vester
Mund, Charles	2, Sept 1890		3	1	
Mund, Herman	30, Aug. 1887		71	1	
Mund, William	23, May 1894		54	5	
Mundhenk, Wilhelmine	5, Jan. 1892			5	
Munson, George R.	30, Nov. 1892		61	5	
Munster, Bernard	18, Jan. 1892		63	5	
Muntel, Johanna Carolina	28, Jan. 1896	27, Jan.	40-11m	5	
Munz, Anna S.	14, Jan. 1889		2	1	
Munzebrock, Bernard	13, Mar. 1895		38	5	
Murdoch, Earruth	2, Apr. 1901		5d	8	
Murdoch, Mary	7, Apr. 1888		75	4	
Murdock, Fannie	22, Mar. 1901		55	8	
Murdock, Henry	19, July 1901		69	8	
Murdock, Paul S.	5, June 1888		9	4	
Murphy, Ellen	28, May 1901		51	8	
Murphy, Genevieva	27, Oct. 1900		4	8	
Murphy, Hannah	1, Oct. 1887		35	1	
Murphy, James	8, June 1901		69	8	
Murphy, Lillian	31, May 1901		2m	8	
Murphy, Mary	27, Aug. 1901		29	1	
Murphy, N.	20, Jan. 1888		3- 5m	4	
Murphy, Philipp	1, Dec. 1900		29	8	
Murphy, Wilford	7, Dec. 1887		53	1	
Murr, Fannie	17, Dec. 1900		79	8	
Murr, Jost	19, Nov. 1900		81	8	
Murray, Anna	12, Aug. 1887		24	1	
Murray, Elenora	8, May 1901		4	8	
Murray, Ellen	19, Oct. 1900		56	5	
Murray, Francis	23, Apr. 1895		50	5	
Murray, Hattie Mabel	20, Oct. 1887		5w	1	
Murray, M.E.	17, Jan. 1888		1w	4	
Murray, Maria	15, Oct. 1900		1m	5	
Murray, Michael	24, Feb. 1888		65	4	
Murray, Nellie	18, July 1887		19	1	
Murray, Thomas	28, Apr. 1888		55	1	
Muschler, George B.	28, Mar. 1889		20	1	
Muschler, Mary	3, June 1901		7d	8	
Muscoft, C.S.	7, May 1888		68	1	

Name ****	Notice Date ****** ****	Death Date ***** ****	Age ***	Page ****	Maiden Name ****** ****
Mushaben, Wilhelmina	17, Oct. 1887		26	1	
Mussack, Mary	22, June 1892		48	5	
Musselmann, Emily S.	7, Jan. 1893		4	5	
Mussia, Anthony	18, July 1887		14m	1	
Muter, Joseph	15, July 1901		1m	8	
Muth, August	1, Sept 1890	30, Aug.	78- 2m	4	
Muth, Carl Friedrich	18, May 1898	16, May	65	4	
Muth, Carolina	9, Feb. 1899	8, Feb.	85	5	Eitelgeorge
Muth, Edward C.	6, Nov. 1891		11d	4	
Muth, Katie L.	13, July 1895		25	5	
Muthert, John	20, May 1893		24	5	
Mutschler, Maria Magdalena	24, Feb. 1900	23, Feb.		8	Armbrust
Mußmann, Henry	19, Sept 1888		75	2	
Myer, Margaret	29, Sept 1900		72	8	
Myerfeld, Hertz	28, May 1901		85	8	
Myers, Lillie M.	13, Nov. 1900		2	8	
Myers, Torney A.	17, June 1888		10	1	
Myrick, Mary E.	26, Aug. 1891		2m	2	
Myroß, Mariah	24, Aug. 1900		92	5	
Mähtenkamp, Bernard	21, Nov. 1897	21, Nov.	74- 2m	4	
März, Anna	5, Jan. 1892		59	5	
März, Jakob	11, June 1891		69	4	
Möhlmann, Charles A.	24, July 1889		2w	1	
Möhlmann, H.W.	24, Aug. 1888		4w	1	
Möhlmann, Ida Lena	19, Dec. 1891		15	4	
Möller, Annie M.	11, Jan. 1890		9m	1	
Möller, Carl	21, Oct. 1896	19, Oct.	67	5	
Möller, Fred.	11, Jan. 1892		4m	4	
Möller, Ida	26, July 1900		20	5	
Möller, John H.	7, Oct. 1891		1d	4	
Möller, Mary	13, Jan. 1890		49	1	
Möller, Theresa	17, Jan. 1898	15, Jan.	75	5	
Möllmann, Joseph	2, Sept 1891		4m- 4d	4	
Mörlein, George	31, Aug. 1891	31, Aug.	39- 2m-23d	1	
Mühlenhard, Sophie	26, Feb. 1898	24, Feb.	77- 2m	5	Barg
Mühlhauser, Joseph	16, Mar. 1889		5	1	
Mühlhäuser, A.G.	27, July 1888		10d	1	
Mühlhäuser, Henry	29, July 1888		12d	1	
Mühlhäuser, Lizzie	27, July 1888		26	1	
Mühlhäuser, William	29, July 1888		12d	1	
Müller, Adam	14, June 1897	12, June	42- 6m	5	
Müller, Agatha	20, Sept 1898	19, Sept	83	5	
Müller, Amelia	14, Aug. 1900		17	5	
Müller, Anna	26, Feb. 1890		9m	1	
Müller, Anna Christine	7, Nov. 1899	5, Nov.	63-11m	5	Stemer
Müller, August	6, Jan. 1893		1d	5	
Müller, Barbara	25, June 1891		50	4	
Müller, C.	25, Mar. 1892		2	5	
Müller, Charles F.	26, Oct. 1894		52	5	
Müller, Charles J.	25, July 1893		1	5	
Müller, Christian	25, Mar. 1890		35	1	
Müller, Clara	9, July 1887		4m	1	
Müller, Ed.	24, Aug. 1892		45	5	
Müller, Elise	26, Nov. 1891		4	1	
Müller, Elizabeth	19, Feb. 1889		45	1	
Müller, Elizabeth	17, Feb. 1892		10d	5	
Müller, Emma	5, Sept 1899	3, Sept	52- 1m	5	Bartels
Müller, Emma	9, July 1900	7, July	24- 5m	8	
Müller, Emma Katharina	21, Sept 1896	20, Sept	16- 7m-11d	5	
Müller, F.W.	26, Aug. 1895	24, Aug.	76-11m	5	
Müller, Florentina M.	24, Jan. 1891		13	4	
Müller, Florenz	4, Nov. 1896	2, Nov.	61	5	
Müller, Franziska	19, Mar. 1890		63	1	
Müller, Fred.	19, Feb. 1891		62	4	
Müller, Gabriel	30, Dec. 1890		78	4	
Müller, Georg	3, Dec. 1895	2, Dec.		5	
Müller, Georg Adam	2, Nov. 1896	31, Oct.	66- 7m	5	
Müller, George	8, Oct. 1889		5- 3m	1	
Müller, George F.	10, May 1894		20	5	
Müller, Gordan	28, June 1897	26, June	4m-16d	5	
Müller, Henrietta	19, Sept 1895	18, Sept	12	5	

Name ****	Notice Date ****** ****	Death Date ***** ****	Age ***	Page ****	Maiden Name ****** ****
Müller, Henrietta	15, Feb. 1899	13, Feb.	55- 7m	5	
Müller, Henry J.	16, July 1895		4	5	
Müller, Herman	19, Sept 1888		1m	2	
Müller, Honorina	6, Feb. 1896	5, Feb.	84- 1m	5	
Müller, Josephine	6, Feb. 1890		5	1	
Müller, Josephine	14, July 1890		29	1	
Müller, Josephine	26, Nov. 1892		29	5	
Müller, Julia	15, Dec. 1892		69	5	
Müller, Katharina	11, Aug. 1896	10, Aug.	61- 1m	5	Kraus
Müller, Lillie	15, Feb. 1890		9m	4	
Müller, Louisa	8, Aug. 1893		2	5	
Müller, M.	17, Jan. 1888		5m	4	
Müller, Mary	21, Mar. 1892		53	4	
Müller, Mary A.	29, Mar. 1894		79	5	
Müller, Mathilda	13, Mar. 1896	12, Mar.	3- 2m	5	
Müller, Mathilda M.	22, July 1887		18m	1	
Müller, Michael	14, May 1896	11, May	61- 5m	5	
Müller, Minnie	19, Mar. 1895		59	5	
Müller, Reinhard	26, Sept 1898	25, Sept		4	
Müller, Theodor	8, May 1889		15m	1	
Müller, Ulrich	16, Jan. 1891		52	4	
Müllerschoen, Josef	4, June 1891		23	4	
Münch. J. Henry	21, Dec. 1896	19, Dec.	63	5	
München, Fred.	2, June 1893		8m	5	
München, George	18, Aug. 1890		5m	1	
Münich, George	14, Sept 1897	13, Sept	42- 4m	5	
Münsch, Phil. Jak.	1, Sept 1891		47	4	
Münzenmaier, Amanda Elisabeth	30, Dec. 1897	28, Dec.	10m-17d	5	
Naber, Anna Katharina	4, Aug. 1896	3, Aug.	15- 2m	5	
Naberhaus, Catharine	23, Sept 1891		1	4	
Naberhaus, Elisabeth	4, Mar. 1893		59	5	
Nabig, Lawrence	9, Nov. 1893		57	5	
Nachtmann, Charles	24, Feb. 1893		2	5	
Nachtmann, Herman	17, Dec. 1892		3d	5	
Nachtmann, William	17, Dec. 1892		4d	5	
Nacke, Maria	20, Apr. 1896	18, Apr.	39	5	König
Nackenhorst, Charles	23, Aug. 1900		28	8	
Nadand, Anna	20, July 1901		60	8	
Nadler, Ferdinand	10, May 1889		72	1	
Naegel, Annie	18, Nov. 1893		30	5	
Naegel, Herman W.	4, Apr. 1891		23d	4	
Naegel, Katharina	5, Mar. 1898	4, Mar.	73	5	
Naegele, Hieronymus	28, Aug. 1895	27, Aug.	74-11m	5	
Naegle, Richard	10, Aug. 1901		4	8	
Naesen, John	18, May 1892		69	5	
Naeser, Margarethe	26, Mar. 1901		79	8	
Nagel, Barbara	9, Sept 1896	7, Sept	29	5	Lenhoff
Nagel, Emma	23, Oct. 1899	22, Oct.	45	5	
Nagel, Frank J.	2, Dec. 1893		74	5	
Nagel, G.	8, Mar. 1888		30- 6m	1	
Nagel, Heinrich	5, June 1899	3, June	59- 5m	5	
Nagel, John	20, Aug. 1888		43	1	
Nagel, Lizzie	14, Jan. 1891		1d	4	
Nagel, Louis	4, May 1896		57- 1m	5	
Nagel, Louise Sophie	29, Jan. 1900	27, Jan.	24- 1m	5	Thiele
Nagel, Margaretha	30, Jan. 1901			8	
Nagel, Michael	30, Mar. 1895		22	5	
Nagel, Wilhelmina	6, Oct. 1900		72	5	
Nagele, Alice	30, Oct. 1895	29, Oct.	23- 8m	5	
Nagele, Catharine R.	13, July 1894		8m	5	
Nagele, Heinrich	16, Sept 1895	15, Sept	69- 7m	5	
Nagele, Jakob	4, June 1896	2, June	21- 2m	5	
Nagg, John W.	8, Feb. 1901		47	8	
Nagle, George	22, Feb. 1890		8- 6m	4	
Nagle, John	10, Oct. 1889		35	1	
Nagle, John	29, June 1893		52	5	
Nagle, Lenora	14, Apr. 1891		31	4	
Nahrung, N.J.	24, Sept 1901		78	1	
Nahrup, Heinrich	30, Jan. 1896	28, Jan.	21- 8m	5	
Nahs, S.	13, Jan. 1888		57	1	

Name ****	Notice Date ****** ****	Death Date ***** ****	Age ***	Page ****	Maiden Name ****** ****
Nailor, Anna	30, May 1888		46	1	
Naltz, Pat. M.	29, Dec. 1887		59	4	
Nanjoks, Herman	8, July 1901		43	8	
Napf, Albert	16, June 1891		13m	4	
Narjes, Charles	3, June 1901		29	8	
Nary, Patrick	23, Feb. 1901		68	8	
Nasch, A.C.	17, July 1890		64	1	
Nassery, Nellie M.	10, Aug. 1887		9m	1	
Nast, Margareth	5, Sept 1898	4, Sept		5	
Nast, Margarethe	1, Dec. 1899	28, Nov.	62	5	Herancourt
Natting, Mathilda	15, May 1895		21m	5	
Nau, Michael	28, Jan. 1893		1m	5	
Nauerth, Lizzie	30, Oct. 1891		60	4	
Nauerth, Valentine	12, May 1895		35	5	
Nead, Alma	20, Oct. 1900		10	8	
Neagle, Minnie	1, Dec. 1891		21	4	
Nealans, Mary	15, Mar. 1901			8	
Nealon, Joseph	29, Jan. 1901		29	8	
Nebel, Barbara	19, July 1889		42	1	
Nebel, George	23, Nov. 1892		25	5	
Nebel, Heinrich	22, Feb. 1897	20, Feb.	78- -27d	5	
Neber, Anton	4, Nov. 1894		72	5	
Neberhaus, Bernard	19, Jan. 1894		70	5	
Neburhaus, Edwina	20, July 1893		7m	5	
Neckerauer, William	9, Mar. 1893		27	5	
Neddermand, William Fr.	10, Feb. 1892		1	5	
Neddermann, Charles H.	10, Jan. 1893		2m	5	
Nederhelman, Louise	3, Oct. 1887		36	1	
Nee, Ellen	24, Dec. 1900		26	8	
Neeb, Appollona	21, Aug. 1888		92	1	
Neeb, Johan B.	19, Sept 1898	17, Sept	63	5	
Need, Gertrude	17, Dec. 1900		2	8	
Needham, Anna	7, July 1887		11m	1	
Neer, Nora	3, Apr. 1901		38	8	
Nees, Anna	17, Aug. 1899	14, Aug.	17-11m	4	
Nees, Johan	23, Aug. 1898	22, Aug.	43- 6m	5	
Neff, Alice	17, Aug. 1901		10	8	
Neff, Carl Robert	17, Nov. 1896	16, Nov.	52	5	
Neff, Frank	8, Mar. 1897	5, Mar.	37- -22d	5	
Neff, William D.	20, June 1891		1d	1	
Neggermann, Elizabeth	19, Nov. 1900		15	8	
Nehls, John	1, June 1901		78	8	
Neil, Anna	29, Aug. 1900		60	5	
Neil, John	1, May 1888		78	2	
Neilan, Felix	1, Sept 1900			5	
Neilsen, Christ.	19, Nov. 1900		2m	8	
Neilson, Elizabeth	18, Dec. 1900		88	8	
Neimeister, Alice	4, Dec. 1891		55	4	
Neimeyer, Fred.	9, July 1889		68	1	
Neising, Johan Gerhard	4, Mar. 1896	2, Mar.	69- 3m	5	
Neithen, Conrad	1, July 1891		33	1	
Neldmann, Frank	9, Aug. 1901		2	8	
Nelle, Henry	10, Apr. 1889	9, Apr.	2- 6m	1	
Nelle, Johan	6, Dec. 1887	14, Nov.	72	* 4	
Nelle, John	28, 29, Jan. 1892	28, Jan.	3-10m	5	
Nelle, Joseph	11, Apr. 1889		3	1	
Nellon, Elisabeth	6, Aug. 1890		55	1	
Nelson, Albert	12, May 1895		2	5	
Nelson, Bessie	8, Oct. 1900		19	8	
Nelson, J.	19, July 1901		2m	8	
Nelson, Lilly	21, July 1888		2m	1	
Nelson, Rachel	26, Sept 1901		59	8	
Nelter, Laura	1, July 1891		34	1	
Nenner, Josephine	6, July 1895		66	5	
Nenold, Laura	4, Apr. 1901		1	8	
Nepper, William	20, Feb. 1901		43	8	
Nerceus, Eddie	5, July 1887		1	1	
Nerpel, Katie	3, June 1893	2, June	5- 3m-10d	5	
Nestler, Alwine	6, Feb. 1896	4, Feb.	38-11m	5	
Neteler, Herman	10, Nov. 1891		26	1	
Netterfield, Mary	3, Jan. 1889		18	1	

Name ****	Notice Date ****** ****	Death Date ***** ****	Age ***	Page ****	Maiden Name ****** ****
Neu, Freda	16, May 1894		11m	5	
Neu, Minnie	4, July 1887		21	1	
Neubacher, Franz	31, Mar. 1900	30, Mar.	58	5	
Neubauer,	11, June 1891		7d	4	
Neubauer,	8, Mar. 1894		1d	5	
Neubauer, Albert F.	3, July 1895		4	5	
Neubauer, Freda P.	13, July 1895		3	5	
Neubauer, M.	22, July 1901		3m	8	
Neuenkirch, George	21, Mar. 1893		31	5	
Neuer, H.	30, May 1898	27, May	65	4	
Neuer, Harry	10, Aug. 1893		12d	5	
Neufarth, Fred.	2, Sept 1891		28- 7m-16d	4	
Neugebauer, Arline	25, Oct. 1900		1	8	
Neugebauer, Edna	5, July 1888		9m	1	
Neugebauer, George	4, Dec. 1888		40	1	
Neuhaus, Edward	4, Apr. 1893		30	5	
Neuhaus, Katharina Ida	31, Dec. 1891		4d	1	
Neuhaus, Mary	31, July 1901		50	8	
Neuhaus, Wilhelmine	11, Apr. 1891		66	4	
Neulist, Reinmund	1, Nov. 1897	31, Oct.	72- 3m	5	
Neulman, Howard A.	7, May 1888		2	1	
Neumann, Charles	22, Dec. 1893		64	5	
Neumann, Joseph	8, Nov. 1888		48	1	
Neumann, Louis	1, Aug. 1888		2	2	
Neumeister, Alice	28, Dec. 1891		35	4	
Neumeister, Carolina	22, June 1897	21, June	47- 8m	5	Kischner
Neureiter, Rosa	16, July 1890		46	1	
Neustadt, John	5, June 1890		75	4	
Neustiel, Nicholas	14, Apr. 1897	12, Apr.	72	5	
Nevin, Hattie	12, Nov. 1887		20	1	
Nevin, Thomas	28, Mar. 1901		32	8	
Nevins, Charity	21, Nov. 1900		3	8	
Newman, Edward	27, Mar. 1901		37	8	
Newman, Herman	30, Oct. 1891		1m	4	
Newman, William	5, June 1901		71	8	
Newmann, Amelia	1, May 1900	29, Apr.	34- 9m	5	Frank
Newmann, Lisette	4, June 1896	2, June	75- 2m	5	
Newson, Louisa	20, Nov. 1900		4m	8	
Neyer, Kate	29, Sept 1887		61	4	
Neynes, Waldib't	6, July 1901		5m	8	
Nibby,	14, Sept 1887		1d	1	
Nicholans, Margaret	30, Apr. 1895		67	5	
Nicholl, Margaret	10, Feb. 1891		53	4	
Nicholson, Frank	15, Nov. 1894		36	5	
Nicholson, John	3, June 1891		59	4	
Nichting, Alois	4, Nov. 1891		2	1	
Nickels, Herman	1, Nov. 1890	31, Oct.	33	* 1	
Nickels, Lucretia	5, Sept 1894		70	5	
Nickens, David	27, Oct. 1891		24	1	
Nickey, Mary A.	5, Nov. 1900		83	8	
Nickles, William E.	18, Aug. 1891		25	4	
Nickum, Helen	12, Aug. 1901		2	8	
Nickum, Jakob	28, Feb. 1900	27, Feb.	80	5	
Nickum, Martha	6, Dec. 1900		11	8	
Nicola, Rosina	30, Dec. 1898	28, Dec.	68- -14d	5	Heit
Nicolay, Heinrich	21, Mar. 1898	19, Mar.	79- 6m	5	
Nicolay, Louis	22, Oct. 1900		70	8	
Nicoll, Emma	25, June 1888		9m	1	
Niderhellman, Ida	13, July 1887		5m	1	
Niebaum, J.H.	26, Feb. 1896	25, Feb.	65-10m	5	
Niebert, Elisabeth	29, Aug. 1891		81	4	
Niebruegge, Ben H.	27, Aug. 1901		69	1	
Nieddermann, Sophia	13, May 1901			8	
Nieder, George	16, Oct. 1890		71	1	
Nieder, Magdalena	15, Sept 1898	13, Sept	70- 6m	5	
Niederhaus, Gottlieb	19, Feb. 1889		34	1	
Niederhausen, Gottlieb	5, June 1894		68	5	
Niederhauser, Charles	28, Apr. 1894		21	5	
Niederhauser, Philipp	1, May 1895		17	5	
Niederhelman, Ed. A.	10, July 1888		3m	1	
Niederhelman, Elisabeth	30, Sept 1899	29, Sept	68- 6m	4	

Name ****	Notice Date ****** ****	Death Date ***** ****	Age ***	Page ****	Maiden Name ****** ****
Niederlehner, John	31, Aug. 1900		68	5	
Nieding, Katharina	18, Feb. 1897	16, Feb.	75	5	
Niehart, Theresa	16, Dec. 1889		4	1	
Niehaus,	29, Mar. 1889		1d	1	
Niehaus, Addie	19, Dec. 1889		2	1	
Niehaus, Adolph	21, Oct. 1899	19, Oct.	49	5	
Niehaus, Angelina	3, Apr. 1888		78- 6m	4	
Niehaus, Bernhard	23, Apr. 1889		57	1	
Niehaus, Catharina	3, Feb. 1894		77	5	
Niehaus, Catharine	7, Nov. 1895	6, Nov.	76- 5m	5	
Niehaus, George	21, Jan. 1893		74	5	
Niehaus, Henry	15, Mar. 1892		8	5	
Niehaus, Henry M.	15, May 1896	14, May	10	5	
Niehaus, J.H.	6, Dec. 1895	4, Dec.	9-11m	5	
Niehaus, John	17, Mar. 1891		69	4	
Niehaus, Joseph	26, Feb. 1900	24, Feb.	76	8	
Niehaus, Joseph L.	3, Jan. 1893		13d	5	
Niehaus, Mary	29, Jan. 1892		59	5	
Niehaus, Minnie	18, June 1895		9	5	
Niehaus, William	28, May 1901		42	8	
Niehenke, Caspar	10, Oct. 1893		77	5	
Niehoff, Bernardine	12, July 1901		46	8	
Niehoff, Bernhard	17, Jan. 1888		6d	4	
Niehoff, Heinrich	11, Jan. 1898	9, Jan.	42- 2m- 2d	5	
Niehoff, J.G.	5, May 1899	4, May	88- 6m	5	
Niehoff, John B.	2, Mar. 1889		76	1	
Niehoff, Josephine	11, Apr. 1892		2	5	
Niehus, Lillian	14, Nov. 1900		10d	8	
Nielen, Harry	12, Sept 1901		17	5	
Nieman, Clara	11, Aug. 1891		64	4	
Nieman, Herman R.	3, Mar. 1898	2, Mar.	19-11m	5	
Nieman, Joseph	10, May 1889		14m	1	
Niemann, Alwine	21, Mar. 1890		3	1	
Niemann, Amelia	19, Aug. 1901		18	8	
Niemann, Anna L.	15, Dec. 1892		12	5	
Niemann, Anna Maria	28, Mar. 1898	27, Mar.	65- 7m	5	Dulle
Niemann, Catharine	20, Jan. 1891		49	4	
Niemann, Charlotte	22, Mar. 1889		71	1	
Niemann, Frank H.	16, Apr. 1895		46	5	
Niemann, H.	6, Jan. 1888		59	1	
Niemann, Henry	26, Feb. 1890		23	1	
Niemann, Henry A.	25, Apr. 1888		1d	1	
Niemann, Lizzie	25, July 1900		33	5	
Niemann, Louise	1, Sept 1900		54	5	
Niemann, M.	27, Dec. 1887		75	1	
Niemann, Mary	11, Feb. 1889		1w	1	
Niemann, Theodor F.	28, June 1889		47	1	
Niemann, William	22, Apr. 1891		80	4	
Niemann, Wm.	17, Oct. 1891		80	4	
Niemeier, Caroline	1, July 1901		71	8	
Niemeier, Theodor	6, Mar. 1896	4, Mar.	44- 6m	5	
Niemer, F.	9, Mar. 1895		58	5	
Niemer, George W.	22, Feb. 1895		1	5	
Niemes, Margaretha	30, Mar. 1899	29, Mar.	29- 2m	5	Leindecker
Niemes, Rosa	1, Dec. 1888		21	4	
Niemeskern, Elisabeth	12, Mar. 1889		25	1	
Niemeyer, Elisabeth Theresia	22, Sept 1897	21, Sept	28-10m	5	Borgemenke
Niemeyer, Franz	20, Feb. 1896	17, Feb.	84	5	
Niemeyer, Fred	25, Oct. 1898	23, Oct.	24- 9m-21d	5	
Niemeyer, Justina	15, Feb. 1898	13, Feb.		5	
Niemeyer, Mary	24, Feb. 1888		74	4	
Niemeyer, Nettie	12, Jan. 1892		23	5	
Niemeyer, William	18, July 1895		25	5	
Niemeyer, William	2, July 1901		7	8	
Niemöller, Heinrich	2, July 1892		84- 8m- 4d	5	
Niemöller, Marie	29, June 1894		18	5	
Niemüller, Christine Regine	30, Dec. 1896	28, Dec.	72- 7m	5	Westermeier
Nienaber, Heinrich	16, Apr. 1889		11	1	
Nienaber, Margaretha	16, Oct. 1900		77	8	
Nienaber, Maria Anna	3, Oct. 1899	1, Oct.	83- 4m	5	Hehslenfeld
Niepage, Ernst	11, Oct. 1899	10, Oct.	45	5	

Name ****	Notice Date ****** ****	Death Date ***** ****	Age ***	Page ****	Maiden Name ****** ****
Nieper, Margaret	2, Aug. 1901		34	8	
Nieperte, Gerty L.	9, July 1895		10m	5	
Nieporte, Johan A.	14, May 1900	11, May	30- 6m	8	
Nieporte, Stella	30, Oct. 1891		1	4	
Niermann, George	8, July 1890		64	4	
Niermann, Joseph F.	22, June 1895		6m	5	
Niermann, Maria	30, Jan. 1896	28, Jan.	59-11m	5	
Nies, Emma	10, Aug. 1901		2	8	
Nieser, Henrietta	17, 18, Nov. 1891	6, Nov.	58- 9m	1	
Nieter, August H.	9, Dec. 1892		10m	5	
Nieters, Katharina	20, Mar. 1896	19, Mar.	45	5	Lamott
Niewedde, Catharine	2, Aug. 1897	1, Aug.	72	5	Stuckenberg
Ninson, Amanda	9, July 1887		13	1	
Nipper, Laurentius	7, July 1896	6, July	26-11m	4	
Nippert, Elise	22, July 1898	21, July		4	
Nippert, Louis	21, Aug. 1894		69	5	
Nitzel, F.W.	10, Aug. 1895	8, Aug.	64	5	
Nitzschmann, Bertha	27, June 1891		11m	1	
Noakes, Harvey	31, Aug. 1900		2m	5	
Nobel, George	17, Apr. 1888		65	1	
Nobel, Henry	16, Sept 1897	15, Sept	36- 9m	5	
Noble, Harry	14, Aug. 1888		29	1	
Noctor, Elizabeth	4, Feb. 1901		40	8	
Noeding, Valentin	29, Oct. 1896	27, Oct.	64- 6m	5	
Noel, Luella	9, Jan. 1894		1	5	
Noell, Anna	28, June 1897	25, June	29- 9m	5	Frey
Noell, Charles A.	1, May 1901		17	8	
Noell, Friedrich	16, May 1899	15, May	54- 6m	5	
Noell, Mathilda	26, Feb. 1896	25, Feb.	28	5	Raible
Noell, Philipp	21, June 1888		3m	1	
Noell, Prima	5, Jan. 1888		50	1	
Nofer, Katharine	31, Jan. 1896	30, Jan.	46- 4m	5	Schick
Nohl, Esther	11, Dec. 1891		77	4	
Nolan, James	4, Apr. 1895		74	5	
Nolan, Peter	8, Dec. 1891		76	4	
Nole, Katie	23, Aug. 1887		4w	1	
Nolker, Frederick L.	24, Mar. 1894		12d	5	
Noll, Elizabeth	21, Mar. 1890		2m	1	
Noll, Imgard	8, Aug. 1901		2	8	
Noll, John	13, Nov. 1900		82	8	
Noll, John A.	2, Nov. 1894		52	5	
Nolte, Anna M.	28, Dec. 1900		73	8	
Nolte, August	8, Oct. 1889		77	1	
Nolte, Elisabeth	14, Apr. 1897	12, Apr.	59	5	Herbert
Nolte, Heinrich Ferdinand	12, Sept 1896	11, Sept	74- 5m	5	
Nolte, Henry	27, Mar. 1901		79	8	
Nolte, Hermine	24, Nov. 1896	21, Nov.	66- 9m	5	
Nolte, Joseph B.	14, Feb. 1901		17	8	
Nolte, Mary	7, Jan. 1896	6, Jan.	66	5	Blanke
Nolte, Pauline	2, Apr. 1891		20	4	
Nolte, Wilhelm	26, Feb. 1895		63	5	
Nolty, J.P. Marat	6, Sept 1889		6w	1	
Nolty, James	12, 13, July 1895	10, July	41	5	
Nonamaker, William	4, June 1895		38	5	
Nonweiler, Margarethe	16, Mar. 1897	14, Mar.	69	5	Dietrich
Noppenberger, Anna Marie	2, Dec. 1896	1, Dec.	63	5	Göller
Nordeman, E.	6, Aug. 1901		31	8	
Nordeman, Esther	25, July 1900		4m	5	
Nordhorst, Dora H.	30, Apr. 1891		24	4	
Nordloh, F.B.	19, Sept 1895	17, Sept	66- - 9d	5	
Nordlohne, Henry	6, Nov. 1889		17	1	
Nordman, John H.	9, July 1887		53	1	
Nordmann, Rosalie	28, Apr. 1900	26, Apr.	52	5	
Nordmann, Sophie	7, Jan. 1901		58	5	
Normann,	9, July 1887		1d	1	
Norres, Mary	22, July 1901		1	8	
Norris, Edward	23, Jan. 1901		45	8	
Norten, Durene	6, June 1901		68	8	
Nortmann, Joseph	15, Mar. 1901		79	8	
Norton, Lena	8, Feb. 1901		1m	8	
Norton, Mary	27, Feb. 1901		58	8	

Name	Notice Date	Death Date	Age	Page	Maiden Name
****	****** ****	***** ****	***	****	****** ****
Noth, Alfred	19, Mar. 1895		2m	5	
Noth, Frank J.	23, June 1888		2m	1	
Noth, George	19, July 1895		1m	5	
Nothring, Walter T.	20, Feb. 1894		8m	5	
Notsch, Emma	22, July 1893		1	5	
Novitzky, Emilie	27, Jan. 1898	26, Jan.	46- 3m	5	Baum
Noyes, Mabel	22, June 1901		2m	8	
Nuebling, Anna	12, July 1901		69	8	
Nueblung, Christine	21, Mar. 1893		74	5	
Nueneker, Edward C.	26, Mar. 1895		2	5	
Nuernberger, Johan	21, Aug. 1896	19, Aug.	83- 4m	5	
Nugant, C.	22, Dec. 1887		24	4	
Nugert, Edward J.	21, Sept 1901		2	8	
Nulander, Henry	13, Mar. 1895		20	5	
Nulle, Minnie	22, Mar. 1893		22	5	
Nurnberg, Sophia	14, Mar. 1893		59	5	
Nurre, Elizabeth	17, Sept 1891		70	1	
Nurre, J. Joseph	7, Apr. 1900	6, Apr.	52- 3m	5	
Nurre, Joseph	27, Apr. 1895		76	5	
Nurre, Katharina Maria	7, July 1896	6, July	79- 2m	4	Feldmann
Nuser, Gertrude	8, Aug. 1896	7, Aug.	11-10m	5	
Nutting, Louis	9, Feb. 1901		43	8	
Nuttle, James	28, July 1887		27	1	
Nuttle, Mary	23, Sept 1887		54	2	
Nuxold, Marie Ann	28, Sept 1888		52	2	
Nuß, George Peter	19, Oct. 1889		54	1	
Nuß, Margaret	30, Nov. 1899	29, Nov.	62	5	Herancourt
Nußbaum, Catharina	17, Dec. 1889		77	1	
Nußbaum, John	27, Oct. 1887		57	1	
Nägle, Bertha	9, Jan. 1897	7, Jan.	20- 4m	5	
Nägle, May E.	4, May 1895		1d	5	
Nüsekabel, J. Heinrich	13, Feb. 1896	11, Feb.	70	5	
Nüslin, George	1, Sept 1891		34	4	
O'Bannie, M.	13, Jan. 1888		30d	1	
O'Barr, Fannie	15, 18, Sept 1900		56	5	
O'Brien, Annie	20, Oct. 1887		38	1	
O'Brien, Honora	4, Feb. 1901		58	8	
O'Brien, J.	17, Oct. 1901		61	8	
O'Brien, John	15, July 1887		45	1	
O'Brien, John	8, Apr. 1901		10	8	
O'Brien, Michael	21, Feb. 1901		55	8	
O'Brien, Michael	31, July 1901		35	8	
O'Brien, Patrick	15, Dec. 1900		80	8	
O'Brien, Rose	16, Nov. 1900		1	8	
O'Brien, Thomas	21, July 1887		66	1	
O'Brien, William S.	21, Jan. 1901		33	8	
O'Connell, Ann	23, Apr. 1895		58	5	
O'Connell, Joseph	5, Apr. 1895		8d	5	
O'Connell, Kate	30, Aug. 1887		17m	1	
O'Connell, Mary	16, Mar. 1888		23	1	
O'Connell, May B.	21, Oct. 1887		37	1	
O'Connell, P.	2, Mar. 1901		78	5	
O'Conners, Alma	1, Feb. 1888		21- 6m	4	
O'Connor, Catharine	23, Nov. 1900		53	8	
O'Connor, Catharine	3, Aug. 1901		4	8	
O'Connor, Charles	24, Jan. 1901		22d	8	
O'Connor, Ed.	11, July 1901		2m	5	
O'Connor, Ellen	20, Sept 1887		14	1	
O'Connor, Jane	7, Mar. 1901		65	8	
O'Connor, John	8, Apr. 1901		35	8	
O'Connor, Timothy	26, May 1888	25, May		4	
O'Connor, William	19, July 1900			8	
O'Donnel, Mary Amour	3, July 1887		72	4	
O'Donnell, Arthur	15, Dec. 1900		40	8	
O'Donnell, Ellen	15, Jan. 1901		52	8	
O'Donnell, James J.	2, Feb. 1901		12d	8	
O'Donnell, Joseph	12, Aug. 1887		63	1	
O'Donnell, Joseph	22, Aug. 1900		21	5	
O'Donnell, Kate	30, May 1888		49	1	
O'Donnell, William	17, Oct. 1901		25	8	

Name ****	Notice Date ****** ****	Death Date ***** ****	Age ***	Page ****	Maiden Name ****** ****
O'Dwyer, Mary Gertrud (Sr.)	21, June 1901		81	8	
O'Hara, Michael	2, Nov. 1900		65	8	
O'Hara, William G.	4, June 1895		19m	5	
O'Hare, Sarah	8, Jan. 1901		48	8	
O'Hearn, M.	26, Feb. 1901		38	8	
O'Hearn, Richard	21, Sept 1900			5	
O'Kane, George N.	21, Sept 1900		1	5	
O'Keefe, James	26, Aug. 1887		3w	1	
O'Konere, Dennis	18, July 1887		40	1	
O'Mara, Anna A.	23, July 1887		8m	1	
O'Neal, Ann	20, Sept 1887		52	1	
O'Neal, Michael	15, June 1901		23	8	
O'Neil, Cornelius	7, July 1887		6w	1	
O'Neil, Elizabeth	22, Oct. 1900		44	8	
O'Neill, Elizabeth	13, Aug. 1888		3w	1	
O'Niel, James	4, Apr. 1895		52	5	
O'Regan, William	26, July 1900		4m	5	
O'Reily, Margaret	30, Sept 1901		70	8	
O'Ryan, Anna	15, Oct. 1900		82	5	
O'Shea, Dennis	6, July 1901		59	8	
Oakley, Rebecca	14, Dec. 1900		5	8	
Oaks, George	20, July 1895		82	5	
Obenauer, Edna	8, Feb. 1894		1m	5	
Obenauer, Katie	24, Oct. 1887		2w	1	
Obenauer, Minnie	31, Mar. 1891		43	4	
Obenbach, Joseph	31, Mar. 1891		36	4	
Oberding,	28, June 1892		3d	5	
Oberding, Anna	26, July 1889		24	1	
Oberding, F.	25, Feb. 1901		3m	8	
Oberding, Louise	11, June 1898	9, June	84	5	
Oberer, Minna May	14, 18, Sept 1900		23	5	
Oberhelman, William	10, July 1891		43	4	
Oberhelmann, Mary	28, Mar. 1891		20	4	
Oberhelmann, Wilhelm	17, Jan. 1888		65	4	
Oberheu, Dorothea	17, Mar. 1894		90	5	
Oberhuber, Carl O.	27, Apr. 1894		6m	5	
Oberjohann, Margaretha	30, June 1898	29, June	53- 8m	5	
Oberklein, George H.	27, Nov. 1889		42	1	
Oberklein, Wilhelmina	2, Dec. 1893		83	5	
Oberlander,	14, Nov. 1893		8d	5	
Oberlander, Frances	17, Feb. 1895		5w	5	
Oberle, Lenhardt	22, Dec. 1892		4	5	
Oberly, William	25, Apr. 1901		22	8	
Obermeyer, Anna Maria	13, July 1897	12, July	82- 5m	5	Vedder
Obermeyer, August	22, July 1887		16	1	
Obermeyer, Barling	28, Oct. 1891		1	4	
Obermeyer, George	15, Dec. 1892		38	5	
Obermeyer, Henry	22, Mar. 1895		65	5	
Obernastheide, Sophia Mary	22, Jan. 1892		37	5	
Obernette, Louis	11, Jan. 1899		19m	5	
Oberst, John B.	22, Mar. 1893		73	5	
Obert, Franz Xaver	16, July 1896	14, July	76- 6m-14d	5	
Och, Samuel	3, Mar. 1891		2m	4	
Ochs, Abel	20, Oct. 1887		1	1	
Ochs, Annie	22, Dec. 1891		3	4	
Ochs, Christian	29, Oct. 1888		34	1	
Ochs, Christian	12, July 1890		65	1	
Ochs, Emilia	6, Dec. 1888		2	1	
Ochs, J.H.	18, Apr. 1888		16m	1	
Ochs, Sebastian	3, Jan. 1898	2, Jan.	30- 7m	5	
Ochs, Sophia	7, Sept 1893		2	5	
Ocker, Alphonse O.	4, Jan. 1894		1	5	
Ockerly, Andreas	4, May 1898		75	5	
Odenbach, Charles	3, Feb. 1893		3	5	
Odenbach, William	16, Feb. 1901		39	8	
Oechsle, Kunigunde	5, Feb. 1901		79	8	
Oechsle, William	14, Sept 1901		47	1	
Oeder, Frederick	5, Feb. 1895		67	5	
Oeh, Fred.	3, Mar. 1890		76	1	
Oeh, Karoline	17, May 1889		68	1	
Oehler, Anna Maria	20, Sept 1899	19, Sept	80	8	

Name	Notice Date	Death Date	Age	Page	Maiden Name
****	****** ****	***** ****	***	****	****** ****
Oehler, Charlotte C.	31, July 1896	30, July	19- 2m	5	
Oehler, David J.	7, May 1891		24	4	
Oehler, Maria	24, Oct. 1899	23, Oct.	56- - 8d	5	Becht
Oehler, Rosa	18, Jan. 1897	16, Jan.	64	5	Auer
Oehlmann, Clara	16, Feb. 1897	15, Feb.	78	5	
Oehlschlägel, Ida	3, July 1889		5m	1	
Oehlschläger, G.H.	22, Jan. 1890		56	1	
Oehs, John	23, May 1888		69	1	
Oelgeklas, Henry	25, Feb. 1901		69	8	
Oelgeschlaegel, Edward	30, Nov. 1900		4d	8	
Oelrich, George	23, May 1901		41	8	
Oelschlaeger,	26, June 1895		3m	5	
Oepen, Peter	11, Apr. 1900	10, Apr.	74	5	
Oertel, Fr.	22, Dec. 1900		1d	8	
Oerthel, Andrew	19, Dec. 1893		2	5	
Oescher, Peter	1, Aug. 1887		3m	1	
Oesper, Charlotte	25, Dec. 1899	24, Dec.	83	5	
Oesthger, Faustine	29, July 1887		38	1	
Oestricher, Adolph	10, June 1891		30	4	
Oetting, Heinrich	14, Aug. 1896	13, Aug.	77	5	
Oetting, Katie	20, Dec. 1897	20, Dec.	35	5	Loesch
Oetting, Minnie	24, Mar. 1894		57	5	
Ogden,	5, July 1887		9d	1	
Ohl, Anna Maria	7, Aug. 1899	5, Aug.	66- 2m	5	Langenbahn
Ohl, Wendelin	7, Mar. 1889		72	1	
Ohl, William	16, Mar. 1893		27	5	
Ohler, George	24, Oct. 1890		2	1	
Ohlhauser, Richmond O.	6, Aug. 1895	5, Aug.	66- 2m	5	
Ohlsen, Harold	5, June 1895		10m	5	
Ohlsen, Henry	2, Oct. 1896	30, Sept	71- 9m	5	
Ohmann, Wilhelm	31, Dec. 1898	30, Dec.	68	5	
Ohmer, John A.	5, Dec. 1893		2	5	
Oken, Elizabeth	17, Mar. 1890		70	1	
Olberding, Anton	1, Mar. 1899	27, Feb.	74- 5m	5	
Olbert, Maria	10, June 1901		8m	8	
Olbum, Gerschen	16, Mar. 1893		9d	5	
Olden, Peter	23, Aug. 1901		38	8	
Oldenbuettel, Meta	18, Feb. 1890		6	1	
Oldendick, Maria A.	17, Jan. 1893		40	5	
Oldendick, Mary	2, Oct. 1894		6m	5	
Oldendick, Mary R.	31, Dec. 1892		1	5	
Olding, Bernard August	22, Sept 1899	20, Sept	40- 7m	5	
Olding, William August	22, June 1889		8m	1	
Oliver,	12, Aug. 1887		6w	1	
Oliver, Griffin	11, Sept 1901		68	8	
Oliver, William	13, June 1901		45	8	
Olivier, Johanna F.	27, June 1899	26, June	72- 5m	5	Leive
Olleidiße, Anna	26, July 1900		28	5	
Ollier, Wilhelmina	20, Sept 1887		44	1	
Ollin, M.E.	13, Oct. 1892		48	5	
Olschlaeger, Susan	28, Jan. 1901		55	8	
Olsen, Eduard	15, Feb. 1895		30	5	
Olver, Edmund W.	9, Mar. 1901		73	8	
Omraker, Mary A.	26, Aug. 1891		44	2	
Ony, Joseph	11, Oct. 1901		47	5	
Opferkuch, Ernestine	8, Jan. 1892		3	5	
Opner, Rose	27, Mar. 1888		16	4	
Oppel, Elsa	15, June 1894		3m	5	
Oppenheimer, George	31, Mar. 1891		1	4	
Oppenheimer, H.	24, Jan. 1889		82	1	
Oppenheimer, Harry H.	15, Apr. 1893		57	5	
Orauska, Frank	8, Nov. 1888		3	1	
Orcatt, George C.	29, Dec. 1900		28	8	
Orenske, Charles	15, Aug. 1893		3m	5	
Orleman, Charlotte	18, Aug. 1894		18	5	
Ormston, George	20, Dec. 1900		4	8	
Orr, Anna	26, Dec. 1900			8	
Orr, Emma	21, June 1901		9	8	
Orr, Robert	8, Jan. 1892		86	5	
Orr, Thomas	15, Jan. 1892		38	5	
Orr, Thomas J.	25, Feb. 1891		43	4	

Name ****	Notice Date ****** ****	Death Date ***** ****	Age ***	Page ****	Maiden Name ****** ****
Orrett, Julia	2, Dec. 1894		30	4	
Ortgies, Catharine	31, Oct. 1900		58	8	
Orth, August	9, July 1890		25	1	
Orth, Edward H.	9, July 1895		2	5	
Orth, J.A.	25, June 1888		65	1	
Orth, John	13, July 1892		43	5	
Orth, Lorenz	10, Mar. 1897	9, Mar.	68- 3m	5	
Orth, Peter F.	7, Sept 1901		41	8	
Orthlipp, Bertha	28, Jan. 1891		54	4	
Ortman, William J.	29, Sept 1900		76	8	
Ortmann, Adolph	7, May 1901		81	1	
Ortmann, Anna	17, Oct. 1899	16, Oct.	14- 9m-11d	8	
Ortmann, Anna B.	14, Aug. 1887		1- 9m	1	
Ortmann, John P.	1, Aug. 1893		22d	5	
Ortmann, Joseph Wilhelm	30, Nov. 1899	28, Nov.	47- 3m	5	
Ortscheid, Anthony	26, Sept 1891		38	4	
Ortwein, Katie	18, Apr. 1888		78	1	
Osborn, William	27, Dec. 1888		65	2	
Osborne, M.	22, Dec. 1887		22- 5m	4	
Oser, Emma	27, Sept 1897	24, Sept	37-11m-14d	5	Ziesler
Osfeld, Edna	15, Jan. 1901		3m	8	
Oskamp, Marie A.	22, July 1898	21, July	73	4	
Osmus, Catharine	5, Dec. 1891		77	4	
Ossenbeck, Barney	15, May 1889		53	1	
Ossendorf, T.	3, Jan. 1888		69	1	
Ossenschmidt, Wilhelm	1, Feb. 1894		31	5	
Ossenschmied, Chririan	15, Feb. 1901			8	
Ost, John Anton	27, Aug. 1888		60	1	
Ostendarp, Maria	20, Apr. 1899	18, Apr.	81- 3m	4	
Ostendorf, August	26, Feb. 1894		63	5	
Ostendorf, Elisabeth	2, Dec. 1899	1, Dec.	67- 2m	4	Kreinborg
Ostendorf, Maria	7, Feb. 1901		75	8	
Ostendorp, Frank	25, Nov. 1895	24, Nov.	69-10m	5	
Ostenfeld, Philomena	8, Aug. 1896	6, Aug.	39	5	Thinnes
Ostenkamp, Catharine	4, Mar. 1893		1m	5	
Ostenkamp, Elizabeth	23, Apr. 1895		60	5	
Oster, John A.	29, May 1894		22	5	
Osterbrink, Anna Maria	13, Dec. 1898	12, Dec.	72- -16d	5	Toerner
Osterbrock, Dora	8, Mar. 1901		66	8	
Osterbrook, Fred.	8, May 1901		2	8	
Osterbrook, Minnie	27, Feb. 1894		5m	5	
Osterdorf, Katharine	29, Mar. 1888		71	1	
Osterfeld, August	26, Jan. 1900	25, Jan.	56- 8m	5	
Osterfeld, Charles	2, May 1890		3	1	
Osterfeld, Ida	22, May 1901		5	8	
Osterhaus, Aggie	18, Dec. 1889		5w	1	
Osterhaus, Herman	25, Feb. 1889		70	1	
Osterhaus, Mary	26, Dec. 1889		76	1	
Osterhaus, Mary	20, Sept 1901		16	1	
Osterhold, Lizzie	2, Aug. 1900		40	8	
Osterkamp, Clara	16, Jan. 1894		8m	5	
Osterman, Clara	1, Mar. 1901		3m	8	
Ostermann, Frank	22, Aug. 1895	21, Aug.		5	
Osterroth, A.F.	22, Aug. 1900		71	5	
Osterroth, Christian	3, Aug. 1897	2, Aug.	61- -12d	5	
Osterwick, William	1, Nov. 1892		30	5	
Osterwisch, John	12, Oct. 1889		3m	1	
Osting, Clemens	4, Apr. 1889			1	
Ostmeyer, Elizabeth	25, Feb. 1891		29	4	
Oswald, Bertha	27, Dec. 1897	26, Dec.		4	Schwer
Oswald, Ed.	30, July 1892		9m	5	
Oswald, Franziska	6, Nov. 1891		68	4	
Oswald, Nich.	15, Sept 1900		62	5	
Oswald, Nicholas	10, May 1895		31	5	
Oswaldt, August	20, Nov. 1896	19, Nov.	73-10m	5	
Oswaldt, Maria C.	30, Jan. 1894		9m	5	
Ott, Christoph	21, June 1895		37	5	
Ott, Henry	1, Aug. 1901		26	8	
Ott, John Henry	27, Aug. 1888		72	1	
Ott, Joseph	11, July 1901		45	5	
Ott, Lizzie	16, Feb. 1888		2w	4	

Name	Notice Date	Death Date	Age	Page	Maiden Name
****	****** ****	***** ****	***	****	****** ****
Ott, Mary	17, Jan. 1894		4d	5	
Ott, Mary	15, July 1901		84	8	
Ott, Valentin	24, May 1901		47	8	
Ott, William	10, Oct. 1893		2	5	
Otte, Bernard	19, Oct. 1897	17, Oct.	74	4	
Otte, Edward	6, Jan. 1894		13d	5	
Otte, Elisabeth	8, Sept 1891		6-	4	
Otte, Gerhardt H.	20, Dec. 1893		76	5	
Otte, Herman Ludwig	4, July 1891	3, July	3-11m-24d	4	
Otte, Maria Magdalena	24, Oct. 1898	22, Oct.	62- 1m-15d	5	Kinne
Otte, Myrtle	3, May 1892		8m	5	
Otten, Arthur H.	19, Apr. 1894		30	5	
Otten, Bernard	22, July 1901		36	8	
Otten, Lena	2, Aug. 1895	31, July	70- 4m	5	
Otten, Otto	5, Mar. 1897	4, Mar.	87	5	
Ottenheimer, S.	19, Oct. 1888		67	1	
Ottens, Herman	10, Dec. 1892		1	5	
Ottenschulte, Agnes	26, June 1900	24, June	67	8	Ahaus
Ottermann, Engel M.	7, Jan. 1891		77	4	
Otting, John L.	15, Apr. 1893		3	5	
Otting, Joseph W.	2, Feb. 1901		21	8	
Otting, Wilhelm	29, Mar. 1898	28, Mar.	78- 9m	5	
Ottke, Herman	30, Dec. 1890		66	4	
Ottke, Johan P.	23, Sept 1895	21, Sept	23- 6m	5	
Ottke, Maria	15, June 1896	13, June	26-11m	5	
Ottmann, Eva R.	25, July 1893		77	5	
Otto, Addie	7, Sept 1893		4	5	
Otto, Edmund	13, Feb. 1894		64	5	
Otto, Emma	4, Nov. 1895	2, Nov.	38	5	
Otto, Georg B.	22, Oct. 1891		50	1	
Otto, Ida	23, Apr. 1888		4m	1	
Otto, Norma	18, Dec. 1891		6m	2	
Otto, Tillie	8, Sept 1887		18	1	
Otto, William	25, July 1893		34	5	
Ovelgoermer, Maria	20, July 1887		76	1	
Overback, Marie	31, July 1900		3	5	
Overbeck, Ayres	10, Mar. 1896	9, Mar.	73- 4m	5	
Overbeck, B.	30, Jan. 1888		51	1	
Overbeck, Charles	17, May 1894		3	5	
Overbeck, Ed.	23, Aug. 1901		33	8	
Overbeck, Edw.	29, Aug. 1892		6m	5	
Overbeck, Florence	30, Sept 1893		2	5	
Overbeck, Franz	25, Jan. 1896	24, Jan.	43	5	
Overbeck, George	5, July 1890		7w	1	
Overbeck, George	5, Jan. 1901		20	8	
Overbeck, John	7, May 1895		69	5	
Overbeck, William	29, Mar. 1889		39	1	
Overbeck, William	12, Aug. 1889		48	1	
Overberg, Amalia	14, May 1900	12, May	70- 3m	8	Witte
Overberg, Catharine	4, Mar. 1892		63	1	
Overberg, Catharine	12, Feb. 1901		73	8	
Overberg, Henry	4, Jan. 1893		38	5	
Overdieck, L.A.	1, Nov. 1898	31, Oct.		5	
Overdiek, Henrietta	15, Feb. 1899	13, Feb.	76	5	Dunker
Overmann, Henry	28, Dec. 1893		64	5	
Overmann, Joseph	3, June 1889		65	1	
Overmann, William	23, Jan. 1891		58	4	
Overmoeller, August	6, 7, Dec. 1895	4, Dec.	28- 1m	5	
Overwater, Klara	18, Jan. 1897	16, Jan.	72-10m	5	Meistermann
Ovitz, A. Maria	1, July 1891		40	1	
Owen, Elisabeth	26, June 1901		68	8	
Owen, George	3, July 1901		62	8	
Owen, John W.	1, Oct. 1887		45	1	
Owens, Matthew	12, Aug. 1887		30	1	
Owens, Rebekka J.	1, Nov. 1887		45	1	
Owens, Thomas	7, Sept 1900		66	5	
Owerwater, Cornelius	1, July 1891		8m	1	
Pabst, Clifford	17, Apr. 1901		5w	8	
Pabst, Louisa	6, Mar. 1889		50	1	
Packer, Annie	8, Oct. 1891		16m	4	

Name ****	Notice Date ****** ****	Death Date ***** ****	Age ***	Page ****	Maiden Name ****** ****
Paebel, William P.	18, Mar. 1890		25	1	
Page, Josephine	19, Apr. 1895		35	5	
Pagel, John	12, June 1891		64	4	
Pahls, Angelina	10, May 1901		72	8	
Pahls, George	24, July 1895		71	5	
Pahner, Ed.	13, Mar. 1901		40	8	
Paine, Alonzo B.	26, Sept 1887		3m	1	
Pallock, Granville	11, Oct. 1901		64	5	
Palm, Henry	6, Nov. 1900		80	8	
Palm, Herbert	13, Apr. 1892		1	5	
Palmer, Elliott	13, Dec. 1900		30	8	
Palmer, George	30, May 1898	28, May	64- 4m	4	
Palmer, George W.	7, Jan. 1888		75	1	
Palmisano, G.	5, Mar. 1901		9	5	
Pancero, Clifford	8, Nov. 1887		5- 7m	1	
Pandorf, Charles	6, May 1896	4, May	69	5	
Pandorf, Erma M.	8, Aug. 1893		1	5	
Pandorf, Robert	22, Feb. 1899	21, Feb.	34- -14d	5	
Panhorst, J.	24, Jan. 1889		38	1	
Panhorst, Louisa	13, Sept 1888		4	1	
Pannhausen, F.	31, July 1901		56	8	
Panter, Barbara	18, Oct. 1895	15, Oct.	50- -15d	5	Huschle
Pape, Karolina	10, Feb. 1896	8, Feb.	45	5	Fox
Pape, Katharina	11, Apr. 1899	10, Apr.	68- -11d	5	
Papenheimer, Marie	12, May 1891		56	1	
Papst, Hilda	13, Feb. 1901		2	8	
Parchmann, Lena	31, Mar. 1898	28, Mar.	24- 9m	5	
Pardi,	17, Dec. 1887		5w	1	
Pardieck, Matthias	21, Nov. 1899	20, Nov.	62	5	
Parducci, Vlorda	17, July 1901		15m	8	
Paris, Charles	10, Oct. 1891		65	4	
Park, Ben.	21, July 1890		1m	1	
Park, Florence	6, July 1901		2m	8	
Park, Maria E.	16, Feb. 1901		2	8	
Parker, Bertha M.	3, Oct. 1900		1	5	
Parker, Carl W.	8, Nov. 1887		17	1	
Parker, Charles	11, May 1892		16	5	
Parker, Elijah	15, Mar. 1901		70	8	
Parker, Esther	1, June 1901		9m	8	
Parker, Nellie Ann	2, Aug. 1888		1	2	
Parker, Rosa	7, July 1891		3m	1	
Parkinson, Arthur	23, May 1901		4	8	
Parks,	19, Dec. 1900			8	
Parling, Mary C.	3, Aug. 1887		1	1	
Parmerton, Frances	28, Jan. 1901		69	8	
Parnell, William	17, Sept 1901		28	8	
Parr, Elliot H.	29, July 1887		2m	1	
Parth, Katharine	21, Sept 1901		62	8	
Partymiller, Charles Joseph	11, Sept 1889		37	1	
Pasche, Eleonore	28, Oct. 1895	27, Oct.	15m	5	
Pashen, Arnold	6, Apr. 1893		55	5	
Paslick, Henry	10, Jan. 1893		26	5	
Passauer, Albert	25, Sept 1888		6	1	
Passeckel, Rudolph	7, Apr. 1895		31	5	
Patberg, Mary	7, Apr. 1895		62	5	
Patlis, Joseph L.	18, Jan. 1901		51	8	
Patrick, Charles R.	26, Feb. 1888		45	4	
Patten, E.	3, Jan. 1888		8m	1	
Patterson, Adam	10, Mar. 1888		28	1	
Patterson, Carl E.	23, Apr. 1895		2m	5	
Patterson, Frances	18, Oct. 1900		59	8	
Patterson, Louise E.	20, Feb. 1891		33	4	
Patterson, W.	17, Sept 1901		39	8	
Pattimann, Louise	8, Apr. 1889		19	1	
Patton, David	20, Dec. 1900		68	8	
Patton, N.	22, Sept 1900		73	5	
Paul, E.	14, Dec. 1887		29	4	
Paul, Joseph	9, Sept 1889		25	1	
Paul, Lorenz	24, Aug. 1900		40	5	
Paul, Richard	3, July 1901		67	8	
Paul, Robert J.	16, Dec. 1891		43	4	

Name	Notice Date	Death Date	Age	Page	Maiden Name
****	****** ****	***** ****	***	****	****** ****
Paul, William H.	8, Oct. 1900		37	8	
Paulach, John	8, July 1891		7	4	
Paulesko, Rosalia	13, Oct. 1892		12d	5	
Pauli, Georg	27, Nov. 1897	26, Nov.	18- 2m	4	
Pauli, Herman	4, Apr. 1901		17	8	
Pauls, Helen	4, July 1901		5	8	
Paulus, Joseph	3, Nov. 1893		33	5	
Pauly, Frank	6, July 1901		11m	8	
Pautsh, H.M.	3, Jan. 1888		3m	1	
Paver, Carrie	11, May 1901		55	8	
Paxton, Eddie	24, July 1901		4m	8	
Payne, David	25, May 1895		67	5	
Payne, Elmer	5, Jan. 1892		7	5	
Payne, Hannah	30, Jan. 1901		84	8	
Payne, Thomas	2, Feb. 1901		53	8	
Peabody, Harriet	5, Mar. 1901		68	5	
Peabody, Rena	29, May 1901		50	8	
Peak, Harry	16, Nov. 1900		25	8	
Peaker, Robert	9, Aug. 1900		57	8	
Peale, Margaret A.	12, Mar. 1901		82	8	
Pearce, Sarah	13, Apr. 1901		75	8	
Pearl, S.	17, Jan. 1888		54	4	
Pearlman, Katie	29, May 1894		14m	5	
Pearne, Thomas	5, June 1901		82	8	
Pearson, Elizabeth	11, Nov. 1891		73	1	
Peaslee, John B. (Mrs)	19, 20, July 1894	18, July		5	
Pecht, John	18, July 1887		11m	1	
Pecht, Josephine	23, Dec. 1890		1	1	
Peck, Maria Elisabeth	14, Jan. 1898	13, Jan.	73- 1m	4	Burlage
Peck, Solomon	10, Aug. 1900		78	8	
Peebles, Harry L. (Mrs)	15, May 1895		33	5	
Peele, Mary	11, Sept 1900		6m	5	
Peetz, Rosa	5, Sept 1900		1	5	
Pehner, John	7, July 1891		4	1	
Peiler, Magdalena	17, Dec. 1891		75	4	
Peine, John	12, Dec. 1900		42	8	
Peiper, Clara	2, July 1895		1m	5	
Peitz, John	19, July 1900		1m	8	
Pelinko, Oscar	16, Feb. 1888		13- 2m	4	
Pelk, Bernhard	2, Oct. 1888		79	1	
Pelk, George	19, June 1889		3m	1	
Pelle, Ernst	6, Nov. 1900			8	
Pellens, Adolph J.	26, Jan. 1892		8	5	
Pellmann, Alfons	28, Jan. 1889		11d	1	
Pellmann, Mary E.	9, July 1891		19	4	
Pellmann, S.	1, Apr. 1889		27	1	
Pelstring, Ruth	29, Dec. 1900		2d	8	
Pelzer, Bernard	3, June 1901		80	8	
Pelzer, Mary T.	18, July 1893		72	5	
Pence, Edith	9, Feb. 1901		21	8	
Pendable, Maurice	28, Jan. 1901		83	8	
Penell, John	5, June 1888		33	4	
Penn, Peter	26, July 1895		35	5	
Penning, Johan	28, Nov. 1898	27, Nov.	47	5	
Penning, Johanna	23, Aug. 1900			8	
Penter, Herbert	25, Mar. 1899	24, Mar.	1- 6m	5	
Peoples, Essie	20, July 1895		13	5	
Pepert, Frank	8, July 1891		2	4	
Pepper, Sophie	18, Jan. 1901		79	8	
Pepper, Tillie	26, Dec. 1900		44	8	
Percival, Charles	12, June 1901		2m	8	
Perim, Catharine	16, July 1901		49	8	
Perin, Reuben	26, Nov. 1900		17	8	
Peroffky, Ladislaus	2, Aug. 1888		10m	2	
Perrant, Magdalena	6, Apr. 1895		25	5	
Perrin, Sarah	27, Feb. 1901		59	8	
Perry, B.C.	17, Mar. 1888		37- 6m	4	
Perry, Cornelia	26, June 1901		71	8	
Perry, Delia	26, Feb. 1901		20	8	
Perry, George	4, June 1895		93	5	
Perry, John	2, Feb. 1888		58	4	

Name ****	Notice Date ****** ****	Death Date ***** ****	Age ***	Page ****	Maiden Name ****** ****
Perschmann, Karl	17, May 1900	16, May	77	5	
Peter, Anton J.	9, Aug. 1888		3m	1	
Peter, Barbara	13, July 1896	11, July	66- 7m	5	Schrimi
Peter, Carrie	23, Dec. 1890		26	1	
Peter, Elmer B.	28, June 1895		3	5	
Peter, Eugenie	29, Dec. 1900		81	8	
Peter, Franzis	19, Aug. 1889		9m	1	
Peter, John	24, July 1890		10m	1	
Peter, John	12, Sept 1891		27	1	
Peter, Louis	16, Sept 1889		38	1	
Peter, Wilhelm	28, Mar. 1898	26, Mar.	28- -18d	5	
Petermann, Adolph	24, June 1893		54	5	
Petermann, Agnes	18, Apr. 1893		68	5	
Petermann, Karoline	17, Oct. 1888		76	1	
Peters, Bernard	19, Mar. 1895		76	5	
Peters, Carrie	26, Feb. 1891		24	4	
Peters, E.H.	24, Aug. 1887		88	1	
Peters, Ed.	23, Dec. 1890		4	1	
Peters, Edward	19, Jan. 1888		3w	4	
Peters, Edward	4, Sept 1889		53	1	
Peters, Frank	6, July 1901		71	8	
Peters, G. William	4, Mar. 1893		35	5	
Peters, Geneva	10, May 1888		5m	1	
Peters, Jakob	25, Mar. 1891		68	4	
Peters, John	19, Mar. 1889	18, Mar.	55	1	
Peters, Louis W.	19, Oct. 1888		2m	1	
Peters, Lucy	29, Jan. 1892		72	5	
Peters, Maggie Sophia	25, Sept 1891		30- 6m	4	
Peters, Mary	21, June 1894		75	5	
Peters, Nikolaus	22, Mar. 1888		74	1	
Peters, Sophie	29, May 1895		57	5	
Peters, Stephen	11, Apr. 1901		73	8	
Peters, William N.	6, July 1893		1	5	
Peters, Winfield	8, Aug. 1900		47	8	
Petersmann, Joseph	5, May 1891		74	1	
Petersmann, K.	9, Aug. 1888		8m	1	
Petersmann, Maria Engel	14, Jan. 1899	12, Jan.	73- -14d	5	Wulfeck
Peterson, Anna Maria	15, June 1900	14, June	25- 2m	8	Abbing
Peterson, Catharine	27, Oct. 1900		71	8	
Peterson, Charles	3, Nov. 1891		5	4	
Peterson, Henry	26, Jan. 1901		7m	8	
Peterson, Louis	5, June 1895		6m	5	
Peterson, W.	27, Jan. 1896	25, Jan.	17-10m	5	
Peterson, William	5, Nov. 1891		1	1	
Peterson, William	17, Oct. 1900		32	8	
Peths, Thomas	15, June 1894		57	5	
Petit, Tabetha	5, June 1901		52	8	
Petre, Anton	6, July 1893		34	5	
Petri, Christian	31, July 1894		41	5	
Petri, Conrad	10, Jan. 1896	9, Jan.	23- 1m	5	
Petri, Fritz	27, Feb. 1896	26, Feb.	2	5	
Petri, Katharine	17, Oct. 1893		48	5	
Petri, Philippina	27, July 1899	26, July	14-10m	5	
Petrusch, Franz	11, Sept 1894		68	5	
Petry, Alfred	17, May 1901		43	8	
Petry, Nick	12, June 1901		76	8	
Petzhold, Ewald	8, Oct. 1900		64	8	
Peyser, Dora W.	22, Feb. 1895		59	5	
Pezold, Heinrich	7, Oct. 1897	5, Oct.	47	5	
Pfadt, Carrie	31, Dec. 1892		14	5	
Pfaff, Johan P.	24, Feb. 1897	22, Feb.		5	
Pfaff, Katharine	31, Dec. 1895	29, Dec.	18- 2m	5	
Pfaffenberg, Elisabeth	22, Dec. 1891		10m	4	
Pfaffmann, Lena	2, May 1894		20	5	
Pfahler, Allen G.	31, Jan. 1891		5	4	
Pfahler, Clara	10, Mar. 1888		29	1	
Pfahler, Clara	1, May 1888		1	2	
Pfannstiel, Louise	11, Apr. 1889		66	1	
Pfau, Elisabeth	13, Apr. 1893		63	5	
Pfau, Jacob	4, Jan. 1898	3, Jan.	68- 1m	5	
Pfeffer, Agnes	21, Oct. 1889		36	1	

Name ****	Notice Date ****** ****	Death Date ***** ****	Age ***	Page ****	Maiden Name ****** ****
Pfeffer, Agnes	2, July 1892		72	5	
Pfeffer, John	24, Oct. 1891		60	4	
Pfeffer, John F.	21, Dec. 1892		47	5	
Pfeffer, Margaret	21, Feb. 1901		46	8	
Pfeifer, Anna Mary	4, Dec. 1894		63	5	
Pfeifer, Augusta	15, July 1893		73	5	
Pfeifer, Emilie	10, Sept 1901		10	1	
Pfeifer, Katie	18, June 1889		8m	1	
Pfeiffer, B.	12, Dec. 1900		6m	8	
Pfeiffer, Elisabeth	30, Jan. 1894		60	5	
Pfeiffer, Elisabeth	13, Apr. 1894		68	5	
Pfeiffer, Freda	9, Dec. 1893		14d	5	
Pfeiffer, George	14, Apr. 1893		10m	5	
Pfeiffer, George W.	15, Jan. 1901		80	8	
Pfeiffer, Jessie G.	6, Jan. 1890		3	1	
Pfeiffer, Jodocus	3, Feb. 1899	1, Feb.	69- 2m	4	
Pfeiffer, John	8, July 1891		60	4	
Pfeiffer, Otto	6, Feb. 1901		60	8	
Pfeiffer, Sylvester	6, Jan. 1893		4m	5	
Pfeiffer, Walter	14, Aug. 1895	13, Aug.	15-10m	5	
Pfingstag, Clara	11, July 1889		10m	1	
Pfirman, Oscar	22, July 1891		10m	4	
Pfirmann, Andrew	14, Apr. 1892		64	5	
Pfister, Barbara	30, May 1888		55	1	
Pfister, Charles	7, May 1901		42	1	
Pfister, Edward E.	19, July 1895		8m	5	
Pfister, Emma	12, Oct. 1889		15m	1	
Pfister, Ernst	5, July 1889	4, July	9m	1	
Pfister, Louis	12, June 1901		2	8	
Pfister, Paul	5, July 1889	30, June	9m	1	
Pfisterer, John	28, May 1892		64	5	
Pfitzer, Louisa L.	20, Jan. 1894		5m	5	
Pfitzer, Marie E.	2, July 1901		1	8	
Pflaum, Simon	28, Aug. 1889		55	1	
Pfleiderer, Agnes L.	14, Nov. 1893		1	5	
Pflueger, Jacobina	28, Feb. 1901		75	8	
Pflum, Karoline	23, Apr. 1889		75	1	
Pfläffle, Fritz	28, Feb. 1891		49	4	
Pfohl, Michael	6, Apr. 1894		70	5	
Pfrommer, Elisabeth	4, Apr. 1901		9m	8	
Pfäfflin, William F.	10, Mar. 1891		34	4	
Pförtner, Fred.	27, Apr. 1892		38	5	
Pförtner, Friedrich	26, 27, Apr. 1892	25, Apr.	38	* 5	
Phares, John H.	4, Aug. 1887		36	1	
Phiermann, Susanna	22, Mar. 1901		76	8	
Philhower, William	4, Apr. 1895		36	5	
Philipp, Elisabeth	30, Aug. 1898	27, Aug.	67	4	Baer
Philipps, Emma	4, May 1893		43	5	
Philipps, Henry	20, Jan. 1899	19, Jan.	62- 4m- 8d	5	
Philips, Charles W.	25, Oct. 1887		34	1	
Philips, Lillie	24, May 1893		12m	5	
Philipss, August	14, Jan. 1889		35	1	
Phillipps, Laura	10, July 1888		7m	1	
Phillipps, Robert	16, Apr. 1891		55	4	
Phillips,	2, June 1891		1d	4	
Phillips, Carrie	16, May 1901		70	5	
Phillips, Henry	26, June 1891		53	4	
Phillips, Reuben	24, Sept 1891		30	1	
Phillips, Sarah	3, Jan. 1901		88	5	
Philston, William	1, July 1901		21	8	
Phister, Lina	25, Feb. 1898	24, Feb.	31	5	
Phorwarth, George	24, Apr. 1891		3w	4	
Picher, A.K.	16, Mar. 1888		11d	1	
Pichler, B.M.	1, Sept 1888		53	1	
Pick, Eva	6, Nov. 1900		58	8	
Pickelheimer, L.L.	24, Dec. 1900		3	8	
Pickers, Laura	4, Dec. 1900		17	8	
Pieczonska, Edwin	10, Sept 1901		3	1	
Pieke, Mary	29, July 1887		48	1	
Pielage, Catharine	25, Mar. 1891		57	4	
Pielage, Frank	2, Jan. 1901		21	5	

Name	Notice Date	Death Date	Age	Page	Maiden Name
****	****** ****	***** ****	***	****	****** ****
Pielage, Katharina	25, Feb. 1898	23, Feb.	44- -21d	5	Reckers
Piepenbrink, George F.	20, July 1895		41	5	
Pieper, Frederick	15, Feb. 1895		46	5	
Pieper, Gerhard	17, Jan. 1896	16, Jan.	75	5	
Piepho, Amelie	25, Aug. 1897	23, Aug.	43- 1m	4	Ihle
Pierce, Hattie	1, Nov. 1887		21	1	
Piersall, Charles	11, Dec. 1900		21	8	
Pierson, James	8, Apr. 1901		65	8	
Pierson, Joseph	19, July 1887		25	1	
Pierson, Nellie	17, Sept 1901		41	8	
Piesche, Adolf	2, May 1900	1, May	32	8	
Pietsch, Oswald	1, June 1898	31, May	71- 2m	5	
Piker, Pesha	6, Dec. 1900			8	
Pille, Johan Herman	6, Mar. 1900	5, Mar.	51- 8m	8	
Pilman, Mary E.	14, July 1891		10	4	
Pines, Samuel	20, June 1901		15	8	
Pinger, Viola M.	27, June 1889		2	1	
Pingterhaus, Katharina	28, Dec. 1891		72	4	
Pink, Sarah	1, Aug. 1887		24	1	
Pinney, Lester M.	9, Aug. 1887		6	1	
Pinning, John	8, Jan. 1901		68	8	
Pinsenschaum, Albert	19, Mar. 1890		18d	1	
Pinsenschaum, M.	18, July 1887		27	1	
Pinßenschaum, Michael	15, 16, Mar. 1899	14, Mar.	52-10m- 3d	5	
Piott, Lulu	22, Sept 1891		10	1	
Pipp, Joseph	28, Feb. 1891		32	4	
Pipper, Conrad	20, Aug. 1888		71	1	
Pipps, Katharine	23, Aug. 1894		35	5	
Pirkin, Maria	13, Feb. 1901		73	8	
Pister, Carolina Columbia	7, Sept 1894	5, Sept	11m-10d	5	
Pister, George	15, June 1889		8	1	
Pister, Ottilia J.	13, Apr. 1893		10	5	
Pister, Walter A.	3, May 1893		5m	5	
Pistner, Christopher	30, Mar. 1889		75	1	
Pistor, Carl	5, Sept 1899	3, Sept	45- 7m	5	
Pistor, Ida	15, Feb. 1897	14, Feb.	18- 2m	5	
Pistor, Jacob	18, July 1893		57	5	
Pistor, Jacob	7, Aug. 1897	6, Aug.	33- -28d	4	
Pistor, Katharine	3, Feb. 1896	2, Feb.	60- 1m	5	Hust
Pitman, Emerson	26, Dec. 1900		16	8	
Pittman, Isaac A.	7, Apr. 1895		80	5	
Pittman, Robert	27, Sept 1900		3	8	
Pittmann, Adelaide N.	14, Sept 1893		33	5	
Pittner, Hilda K.	11, Nov. 1891		1m	1	
Pitts, Mary A.	22, Nov. 1888		40	1	
Plagemann, Bonfield	14, Sept 1893		3	5	
Plagemann, Gertrude	14, Sept 1893		8	5	
Plagemann, John	7, Sept 1893		5	5	
Plagge, Georg	1, Nov. 1898	31, Oct.	26	5	
Plagge, Henry	23, Jan. 1901		80	8	
Plaggemann, Harry	9, Sept 1893		6	5	
Plagsted, Theodore	7, Feb. 1891		11m	4	
Plankenhorn, Mary	4, Apr. 1893		81	5	
Plant, Sophie	13, Dec. 1900		79	8	
Plantenkamp, Gerhard H.	7, Aug. 1894		31d	5	
Plantholt, Henrietta M.	23, Feb. 1893		2d	5	
Plantholt, Josephine	2, Mar. 1893		35	5	
Planz, Susanna	21, Nov. 1898	19, Nov.	75- 9m	5	Seibert
Plappert, Elisabeth	17, July 1894		58	5	
Plappert, George	29, Dec. 1888		60	1	
Plaspohl, Lizzie	3, July 1901		76	8	
Platen, Mary	5, Sept 1889		2w	1	
Platt, Joshua	5, Dec. 1891		38	4	
Platter, Houston	27, Apr. 1901		30	8	
Plautholt, Franz Joseph (Dr.)	3, Feb. 1900	2, Feb.	79- 9m	5	
Pleasant, Theresa	7, Oct. 1901		20	1	
Pleiter, Annie	27, June 1895		5m	5	
Plester, Fred.	16, July 1892		32	5	
Plettner, Theodor	1, June 1896	31, May	72- 4m	5	
Pletzing, Angela	20, June 1888		11d	1	
Plint, Thomas	29, May 1901		77	8	

Name	Notice Date	Death Date	Age	Page	Maiden Name
****	****** ****	***** ****	***	****	****** ****
Ploehs, Catharine	1, Mar. 1894		65	5	
Ploehs, John P.	26, Mar. 1895		49d	5	
Plogman, Henry	18, Feb. 1901		45	8	
Plogmann, Henry	25, Dec. 1891		4m	2	
Plogsted, Friedrich J.	28, Aug. 1899	27, Aug.	22	4	
Plogstedt, Lillian Anna	2, Mar. 1898	1, Mar.	2m-17d	5	
Plogstedt, Marie E.	8, Apr. 1896	7, Apr.	67- 5m	5	Nordmann
Plogstedt, Walter Friedrich	7, May 1900	6, May	6	8	
Plonsk, G. (Mrs)	24, Feb. 1896	22, Feb.		5	
Ploog, Albert	1, Sept 1900		17	5	
Ploß, George	3, Nov. 1887		16- 2m	4	
Pluemer, Mary	5, June 1893		3	5	
Pluemer, Willie J.	16, Jan. 1890		1	1	
Plumb, John	15, Aug. 1901		60	8	
Plummer, Elisabeth C.	23, Dec. 1893		76	5	
Plump, Ben.	26, Apr. 1895		51	5	
Plump, Elisabeth C.	7, Aug. 1896	6, Aug.	50-11m	5	
Plunky, Herman	14, Aug. 1890		53	1	
Plünneke, Bertha	9, July 1890		1	1	
Pneumiar, Raymond R.	10, July 1891		11m	4	
Poage, George	19, Sept 1900			8	
Poardzinska, Roman	15, Jan. 1891		8m	4	
Pobertge, Charles	23, Apr. 1890		6	4	
Pockraudt, Louisa Johanna	8, Apr. 1896	6, Apr.	62	5	
Podesta, John	13, Aug. 1901		36	8	
Poehl, Albert	20, May 1890		70	1	
Poeller, J.B.P.	18, Feb. 1888		11m	1	
Poemerl, Catharine	15, July 1901		1	8	
Poetker, Edna	22, June 1898	21, June	10m	5	
Pogeler, Willie	26, Aug. 1891		3m	4	
Poggemann, Georg	5, Apr. 1897	4, Apr.	25- 1m	5	
Poggendick, Christ.	29, Sept 1891		58	4	
Pogue, Caroline H.	8, Aug. 1901		75	8	
Pohl, Catharine	6, June 1895		67	5	
Pohl, Johan Bernard	6, Mar. 1896	5, Mar.	35- 5m	5	
Pohlmann, Agnes	26, Dec. 1896	25, Dec.	72-11m	5	Rusche
Pohlmann, Alice	29, Nov. 1898	28, NOv.		5	Huber
Pohlmann, Emilie	30, Mar. 1901		68	8	
Pohlmann, Fred.	20, Mar. 1891		16	4	
Pohlmann, Henry	19, July 1887		35	1	
Pohlmann, Herman	6, June 1901		77	8	
Pohlmann, Hilda	27, Sept 1900		3	8	
Pohlmann, Maria Adelheid	30, Nov. 1896	28, Nov.	69	5	
Pohlmann, Phil.	18, May 1901		72	1	
Pohlmeyer, H.R.	20, Sept 1898	15, Sept	33- 2m	5	
Pohlmeyer, Henry	30, Mar. 1894		65	5	
Pohlmeyer, Katie	23, Mar. 1901		50	8	
Pohls, Joseph	4, Mar. 1892		38	1	
Poindexter, Carrie	3, Jan. 1901		40	5	
Poiskey, Anna Maria	24, Oct. 1887		63	1	
Poland, Lena	3, June 1891		43	4	
Poland, Lizzie	5, Dec. 1888		24	1	
Poland, Peter	9, Feb. 1901		48	8	
Poll, Caroline	19, Mar. 1891		52	4	
Poll, Ferdinand	16, Feb. 1901		5	8	
Pollak, Theresa	19, Nov. 1900		52	8	
Pollar, William	3, Aug. 1887		53	1	
Pollick, Arval	5, Aug. 1901		8m	8	
Pollitz, Jacob	28, Apr. 1891		62	4	
Pollmüller, E.	29, Dec. 1887		1- 9m	4	
Polman, Melinda	17, Apr. 1891		35	4	
Pons, Philomena	11, Oct. 1900		23	8	
Pontins, Mary C.	4, June 1895		41	5	
Ponzo, Stella L.	8, Jan. 1901		4	8	
Poog, Mary	20, Mar. 1901		2	1	
Poole,	21, Oct. 1891		1d	4	
Poole, Harvey W.	12, May 1895		2	5	
Poor, Mary	21, Jan. 1901		86	8	
Pope, Minnie	8, May 1901		37	8	
Popp, Maria	3, Feb. 1897	2, Feb.	24- 2m	5	Brinker
Popp, Viola	14, Dec. 1900		3	8	

Name ****	Notice Date ****** ****	Death Date ***** ****	Age ***	Page ****	Maiden Name ****** ****
Poppe, Sophia	18, Jan. 1899	17, Jan.	72	5	Speckmann
Poppe, William	22, Oct. 1894		69	5	
Poppitz, Herman	20, Oct. 1893		49	8	
Porter, Agnes E.	20, Mar. 1901		39	1	
Porter, Anna E.	18, Feb. 1901		61	8	
Porter, Anna Jane	28, Jan. 1901		75	8	
Porter, Wise	7, May 1895		2m	5	
Posey, Asbury	19, June 1901		60	8	
Posner, Henrietta	16, June 1893		9m	5	
Post, Aloisia	12, Jan. 1897	11, Jan.	70- 6m	5	Pfeil
Post, Ella	5, Nov. 1891		5	1	
Post, Henry S.	28, Mar. 1901		77	8	
Post, Lulu	17, Apr. 1901		21	8	
Postel, Barbara	6, Apr. 1888		80	4	
Postel, Charlotte	5, Dec. 1900		57	8	
Postel, Frank	17, Feb. 1900	16, Feb.	35- 3m	5	
Postel, Ida	4, Apr. 1891		8m	4	
Postel, Louisa	30, June 1893		40	5	
Postel, Mathilda	14, May 1900	12, May		8	
Posthorn, Rachel	15, Feb. 1901		5d	8	
Postle, Christine	31, July 1894		15	5	
Postler, George	1, Feb. 1894		43	5	
Poth, Georg	20, Oct. 1887		1	1	
Poth, John	3, Nov. 1887		4	4	
Pott, Clara	23, July 1901		8m	8	
Pottebaum, Fred. H.	22, Feb. 1895		12	5	
Pottebaum, Olinda L.	26, Nov. 1892		9d	5	
Potter, Henry	22, May 1888		29	1	
Pottinger, Mary	14, Nov. 1893		31	5	
Pottmann, Emma	4, June 1901		6m	8	
Pottmann, Sophia K.	30, Sept 1898	28, Sept	23- 9m	4	Koester
Potts, Christina	19, Aug. 1898	18, Aug.	74- 5m	5	
Potts, Sarah	25, July 1900		60	5	
Pounath, George H.	3, Apr. 1890		75	1	
Powell, D.B.	17, July 1901		50	8	
Powell, Ed.	24, Sept 1901		45	1	
Powell, John D.	14, Jan. 1901		58	8	
Powell, William	27, Feb. 1901		51	8	
Power, G.B.	6, Jan. 1899	31, Dec.		4	
Power, John	8, Aug. 1900		60	8	
Powers, Ray	26, Feb. 1901		6m	8	
Powers, Thomas	26, Mar. 1901		50	8	
Powers, Willie	12, Mar. 1901		2	8	
Pracht, Adam	1, Sept 1896	31, Aug.	29- 9m-12d	5	
Pracht, Katharina	24, Apr. 1900	22, Apr.	31- 5m	8	
Praechter, Willie	10, July 1888		8m	1	
Praschill, Frank	13, Apr. 1895		74	4	
Prasse, F.H.	14, May 1896	13, May	38	5	
Prasse, Rube	30, Aug. 1888		3	1	
Prater, Della	24, July 1901		21	8	
Prather, Malinda	10, Feb. 1891		52	4	
Preaffer, Thomas C.	9, May 1895		5m	5	
Precht, Nettie	29, Oct. 1894		12	5	
Prehn, Adelia	29, July 1888		25	1	
Prehn, Wilhelmina	6, Nov. 1896	5, Nov.	69- 2m	5	Borkenhagen
Preising, Charlotte	16, Oct. 1897	14, Oct.	25- 1m	5	Schwindt
Preising, Frederick	7, Jan. 1891		3d	4	
Preising, Regina	7, Jan. 1891		3d	4	
Prell, Charles	3, Mar. 1894		4	5	
Prell, Charles	30, Dec. 1898	29, Dec.	35- - 2d	5	
Prell, Katie	28, Feb. 1891		2	4	
Prell, Lilly	23, June 1893		2	5	
Prendergast, C.	20, Apr. 1888		20	4	
Prendle, Henry	11, June 1895		49	5	
Pressler, Edw.	17, Aug. 1901		5d	8	
Preuth, Marie Chr.	5, July 1888		9m	1	
Price, Eliza	21, Mar. 1901		47	8	
Price, Joseph B.	29, July 1887		2	1	
Price, Samuel	12, Sept 1901		29	5	
Price, Sarah	16, Feb. 1901		73	8	
Price, William S.	21, Sept 1901		72	8	

Name ****	Notice Date ****** ****	Death Date ***** ****	Age ***	Page ****	Maiden Name ****** ****
Priefer, Barbara	9, Dec. 1888	8, Dec.	18- 9m-22d	5	Metz
Pries, Conrad W.	26, Mar. 1897	24, Mar.	78- 4m	5	
Prieshoff, Maria Anna	14, Mar. 1899	12, Mar.	78- 4m-11d	5	Zumberger
Prietsch, Otto	8, Nov. 1888	7, Nov.	42	* 1	
Prilling, Peter	16, Oct. 1891		65	1	
Prima, (Sr.)	7, May 1891		26	4	
Prince, John	28, June 1893		2	5	
Pringle, Nellie	28, June 1888		9w	1	
Printz, Lucy	15, Nov. 1900		51	8	
Prinz, Julia	31, Mar. 1896	30, Mar.		5	
Prinz, Valentine	20, Feb. 1895		65	5	
Prior, Maria E.	15, Jan. 1901		82	8	
Priper, Amalie	17, Dec. 1889		3m	1	
Priton, Alma	17, Apr. 1888		4d	1	
Probasco, Henry	19, July 1901		11	8	
Probst, Bernardina	12, Sept 1891		2	1	
Procher, Harry	3, July 1888		14m	1	
Proches, Anna	14, July 1889	13, July		5	
Proctor, Bettie	4, Dec. 1900		40	8	
Procurian, Phyllis N.	15, Feb. 1901		2	8	
Proehl, Charles H.	29, May 1888		2	2	
Propheter, Adam	26, Sept 1896	25, Sept	58-11m	5	
Propheter, Margaret	31, Jan. 1891		82	4	
Propheter, William	2, Feb. 1888		5d	4	
Pruellage, Herman	9, Aug. 1897	7, Aug.	43	5	
Prues, Anna Wilhelmina	13, Apr. 1896	11, Apr.	66-10m	5	Hülskamp
Prues, B.H.	4, Apr. 1900	3, Apr.	79- 7m	8	
Prues, Catharine	2, Dec. 1893		71	5	
Prues, Edward H.	8, Dec. 1891		2	4	
Prues, Joseph	11, Dec. 1900		47	8	
Prues, Nellie	19, Aug. 1893		22	5	
Prueth, Johan Bernard	10, Mar. 1896	9, Mar.	41	5	
Pruhs, Anna	11, May 1889		18m	1	
Prullage, Joseph	2, Oct. 1899	1, Oct.	51- 9m	4	
Prutfeld, Tillie	19, June 1891		4	1	
Pruß, Clara	19, Apr. 1889		14	1	
Pryer, Alexander	5, July 1887		21	1	
Pröppermann, Catharine	5, Dec. 1891		50	1	
Pucking, Elizabeth	31, Aug. 1887		10m	1	
Puff, Frederike	11, Dec. 1895	9, Dec.	71	5	
Pugh, Charles	17, Sept 1901		45	8	
Pugh, Richard	28, Feb. 1888		81	1	
Pugh, William	3, July 1901		56	8	
Pulpeppen, Frank	8, July 1891		1	4	
Puls,	26, Nov. 1900		6m	8	
Puls, Anna	2, Aug. 1895	1, Aug.	75- 8m	5	
Puls, Sophia	28, Sept 1889		45	1	
Pulsing, Therese	29, Aug. 1892		21d	5	
Pumhofer, Richard	6, Oct. 1900		9d	5	
Pumill, L.H.	4, Apr. 1890		7m	1	
Pumpfrey, Samuel	10, Oct. 1891		41	4	
Punch, Harriet H.	14, Jan. 1901		68	8	
Pund, Anna M.	25, Nov. 1899	24, Nov.		5	Willenborg
Pund, Frederick	10, Mar. 1891		41	4	
Pund, Katharine	26, Sept 1895	24, Sept		5	Hackmann
Pund, Lizzie	1, Aug. 1891		4	4	
Pundsack, Mary	21, Oct. 1889		89	1	
Pundsack, T.	17, Nov. 1888		28	1	
Punshon, Ruth L.	19, Mar. 1901		66	8	
Purcell, Michael	19, Apr. 1888		46	1	
Purlein, Napoleon B.	15, Oct. 1891		58	4	
Purlier, M.	13, Feb. 1901		82	8	
Purner, George	26, Mar. 1891		1m	4	
Purnhagen, William T.	4, Oct. 1900		2m	8	
Purrell, N.F.	29, Dec. 1887		34	4	
Pursinger, Mary	10, Aug. 1901		35	8	
Pusatexe, Antonia	23, Oct. 1887		1m	4	
Puthoff, Mary Margaret	3, Oct. 1891		72- 7m	1	
Puttemeyer, J.	25, Mar. 1893		44	5	
Putthoff, Anna	16, Dec. 1889		2	1	
Putthoff, Bernard Johan	8, Mar. 1888		7m	1	

Name	Notice Date	Death Date	Age	Page	Maiden Name
****	****** ****	***** ****	***	****	****** ****
Putthoff, Henry	5, Aug. 1890		14	1	
Pölker, Maria P.	3, June 1889		6w	1	
Pöpper, Angela Maria	14, June 1898	12, June	67-11m	5	Heidt
Pörter, Frank	13, Sept 1897	10, Sept	61	5	
Pötker, Catharina	15, June 1898		61- 3m	4	Sextro
Pötker, Joseph E.	5, Apr. 1900	4, Apr.	16- -15d	5	
Pötter, Adelheid	17, Feb. 1897	16, Feb.	33- 7m	5	Moormann
Quadling, Theresa	27, Feb. 1894		61	5	
Qualtlander, C.	1, Aug. 1901		67	8	
Quarles, Willie	30, Apr. 1891		2	4	
Quartes, Robert	30, Dec. 1891		4	4	
Quartmann, Henry	2, Dec. 1887		1	4	
Quartmann, Theresa	2, Jan. 1889		25	1	
Quatkemeier, Ella	10, Apr. 1895		48	5	
Quatkemeyer, Rosa	11, Jan. 1901		14d	5	
Quatman, Joseph	25, Aug. 1900		69	5	
Quattländer, Emslie	30, Aug. 1887		10m	1	
Quebe, Mary	8, Jan. 1901		79	8	
Queberman, Frank	10, Sept 1891		1d	4	
Quebermann, Rosa	29, July 1890		1	1	
Quenser, Frida	25, Sept 1895	24, Sept	9m-10d	5	
Querengasser, Edward	7, Aug. 1895	4, Aug.	49- 8m	5	
Querner, Gussie	17, Apr. 1894		6	5	
Querngasser, Carl	1, July 1901		25	8	
Quigley, M.	4, June 1901		27	8	
Quillan, John	27, July 1895		71	5	
Quinlan, Eliza J.	16, Feb. 1901		63	8	
Quinn, Ellen	8, Dec. 1891		65	4	
Quinn, James	24, Oct. 1900		61	8	
Quinn, John Henry	15, Sept 1888		2	2	
Quinn, Thomas	1, May 1888		1	2	
Quinn, William	9, Aug. 1900		25	8	
Quitter, Anthony	18, May 1901		80	1	
Quittman, Hazel	18, Sept 1900		7m	5	
Raab, Magdalena	8, Jan. 1890		55	1	
Raabe, Martha	13, Dec. 1892		61	5	
Rabbe, Louis Walter	23, Nov. 1899	22, Nov.	26	5	
Rabe, Aldena	28, Feb. 1891		7m	4	
Rabe, B.H.	19, Aug. 1895	18, Aug.	79- 7m	5	
Rabe, Della	31, Mar. 1888		2- 3m	4	
Rabe, Ed.	10, Oct. 1890		1	4	
Rabe, Fred.	18, Feb. 1889		13	1	
Rabe, Henry	15, Apr. 1888		57- 6m- 7d	5	
Rabe, Leo H.	14, Apr. 1893		1	5	
Rabe, Lillie	20, Apr. 1889		17m	1	
Rabe, Walter E.	16, May 1893		8d	5	
Rabe, William	10, May 1889		6m	1	
Rabens, Dorothea	23, Dec. 1899	21, Dec.	71	5	Benning
Rabenstein, Louise	1, Mar. 1901		61	8	
Rachel, Carrie	22, June 1892		48	5	
Rachel, Joseph	30, Jan. 1901		2	8	
Rachel, William	21, Apr. 1892		41	5	
Rack, Eduard	4, June 1898	2, June	16-10m- 2d	5	
Racke, Berhard	12, Nov. 1891		4	4	
Radcliffe, Grace	26, Aug. 1901		82	8	
Radel, Frank	9, Sept 1891		8d	4	
Rademacher, Charles	12, Jan. 1892		2	5	
Rademacher, Henry	27, June 1889		17m	1	
Radermacher, George	8, Mar. 1892		38	5	
Radius, Alois	21, Apr. 1895		4d	5	
Radle, Mary	19, Nov. 1888		64	1	
Raemmich, Charles	10, July 1887		35	1	
Raffenberg, William	15, June 1894		4	5	
Rafferty, John	6, Apr. 1895		74	5	
Ragendorf, Moritz	7, Aug. 1899	6, Aug.	79	5	
Rahe, Adelheid	11, Apr. 1899	10, Apr.	1-10m	5	
Rahe, Herman	15, Dec. 1897	14, Dec.	58- 9m	4	
Rahe, J.H.	24, Mar. 1898	22, Mar.	34	5	
Rahe, Johan Heinrich	19, Dec. 1893		74	5	

Name	Notice Date	Death Date	Age	Page	Maiden Name
****	****** ****	***** ****	***	****	****** ****
Rahe, Louisa	22, Feb. 1890		1	4	
Rahenkamp, Alma	3, Feb. 1891		4	4	
Rahm, Henry	5, Mar. 1901		54	5	
Raible, Paul	21, Apr. 1899	20, Apr.	67	5	
Raichle, Fred. G.	3, Feb. 1890		1w	1	
Raimer, Otto	13, June 1901		2d	8	
Rake, Bernardina	9, July 1896	8, July	2- 2m- 8d	5	
Rake, John	28, Oct. 1895	26, Oct.	29- -20d	5	
Rakel, Bernard	27, Apr. 1895		40	5	
Rakel, Harry	10, Aug. 1900		9m	8	
Rakel, Magdalena	12, Oct. 1899	12, Oct.	37- 9m-21d	5	Strull
Rakel, Marie	3, July 1901		66	8	
Ralfer, George	18, Aug. 1900		61	8	
Rall, Josephine	9, Dec. 1897	7, Dec.	73-11m	5	
Ralston, Rebecca	8, July 1901		41	8	
Rambarts, Mary	19, Nov. 1900		22	8	
Ramey, Ada	4, Oct. 1900		1m	8	
Rammer, Frank	29, Oct. 1891		4	4	
Ramozotto, Virginia	12, Nov. 1887		35	1	
Ramsey, Amanda M.	21, Apr. 1895		71	5	
Ramsey, Mary F.	13, Nov. 1893		55	5	
Ramseyer, Christian	20, Jan. 1891		54	4	
Ramstetter, Alb.	7, Jan. 1888		50	1	
Rand, Margaret A.	10, Mar. 1891		60	4	
Randall, Hilah A.	14, Nov. 1900		86	8	
Randall, W.H.	20, Aug. 1888		76	1	
Randle, John A.	22, Nov. 1887		3m- 7d	1	
Ranly, Johan	29, Aug. 1896	28, Aug.	81- 1m	5	
Ransell, William	18, Feb. 1901		37	8	
Ransick, Hugo C.	15, June 1898	11, June	9-10m	4	
Ransohoff, Esther	13, June 1894		81	5	
Ransom, Eliza	17, Apr. 1901		63	8	
Ranus, Abram	6, Apr. 1895		35	5	
Ranz,	4, Apr. 1888		24d	1	
Ranz, Anna	1, Nov. 1887		3m- 3d	1	
Ranz, Oscar	24, June 1901		8	8	
Ranzhof, Edward R.	16, July 1890		5m	1	
Rapaport, Baer	21, Jan. 1891		23	4	
Rapier, Henry Leo	6, Apr. 1893		8m	5	
Rapking, Marie	1, July 1901		2	8	
Rapp, Barbara	24, Aug. 1887		82	1	
Rapp, Christian	29, 30, July 1901	24, July	62- 9m-20d	5	
Rapp, Emil	25, Jan. 1901		24	8	
Rapp, Ida	11, Mar. 1890		5w	1	
Rapp, Jacob	25, Apr. 1892		68	5	
Rapp, Jacob	9, Feb. 1898	8, Feb.	27- 6m	5	
Rapp, Jakob	15, May 1896	13, May	32- 4m	5	
Rapp, James	8, July 1891		74	4	
Rapp, Joseph	30, Apr. 1901		37	8	
Rapp, Julia C.	4, June 1891		63	4	
Rapp, Lena	28, Mar. 1893		48	5	
Rapp, Louis	29, Jan. 1890		39	1	
Rapp, Nicholas	21, Oct. 1891		37	4	
Rapp, Walter	3, Feb. 1891		4m	4	
Rappel, John A.	15, Apr. 1889		5m	1	
Rappold, Wilhelmina	26, Mar. 1901			8	
Rappsilver, Eliza	21, Dec. 1891		4m	4	
Rasch, Fred.	5, Aug. 1887		13m	1	
Rasenfelder, Erna T.	20, Mar. 1894		1	5	
Raster, Wm.	22, Feb. 1890		3m	4	
Rastert, Nicholaus	2, Apr. 1897	1, Apr.	23	5	
Ratermann, Frank	5, Oct. 1894		2d	5	
Ratermann, Paul H.	12, Aug. 1893		3m	5	
Rath, Mathilda	17, June 1888		8	1	
Rath, Mathilda Rosine	16, June 1888	15, June	3	4	
Rath, Rowena	29, June 1901		44	8	
Rather, Valentine	12, July 1899	11, July	58-10m	5	
Rathkamp,	12, Sept 1891		2d	1	
Rathkamp, Frieda	4, Nov. 1896	2, Nov.	9- 4m	5	
Rathmann, Fred.	13, Dec. 1893		16	5	
Rathring, Ella	4, Nov. 1891		3	1	

Name ****	Notice Date ****** ****	Death Date ***** ****	Age ***	Page ****	Maiden Name ****** ****
Ratrliff, William	5, Nov. 1900		48	8	
Rattermann, Dorothea	19, Aug. 1896	18, Aug.	60	* 4	Müller
Rattermann, Elisabeth	29, Sept 1891		75	4	
Rattermann, Emma	3, Mar. 1899	2, Mar.		4	Buscher
Rattermann, H.G.	3, Dec. 1895	2, Dec.	54	5	
Rattermann, Marie L.	1, Aug. 1894		51	5	
Rattermann, Paul	22, July 1901		17	8	
Rattermann, Philomena	3, Aug. 1893		49	5	
Rattermann, Theresa	3, Mar. 1898	2, Mar.	69- 4m	5	Bohmann
Rattermann, William F.	19, Nov. 1898	16, Nov.	31- 2m-10d	4	
Rau, Anna Maria	27, Feb. 1897	26, Feb.	70- 3m	5	Frantz
Rau, Charles	2, June 1892		20d	5	
Rau, Fredericka	15, Mar. 1897	14, Mar.	74- 9m	5	
Rau, George	14, Mar. 1893		54	5	
Rau, Therese	1, Dec. 1888		54	4	
Rau, Wilhelmina Barbara	27, Apr. 1897	26, Apr.	65- 5m	5	Rau
Rauch, Carl	29, Jan. 1900	28, Jan.	58-10m	5	
Rauch, Dorothy	23, Sept 1901			8	
Rauch, Florence	28, July 1893		4m	5	
Rauch, Francis	11, July 1888		77	1	
Rauh, Clara	9, Oct. 1889		3	1	
Rauh, Francis	22, Apr. 1891		63	4	
Rauh, Michael	3, Aug. 1896	1, Aug.	74- 6m	5	
Raum, John	10, Sept 1891		2	4	
Raum, Margaret	19, July 1900		80	8	
Raup, Fred.	13, Sept 1890		1	1	
Raus, Maria Agatha	21, Aug. 1894		76	5	
Rauscher, Mary	15, Oct. 1898	14, Oct.	76- 9m	4	
Rautenstrauch, Charles	23, Jan. 1901		34	8	
Ravey, Anthony	21, Mar. 1895		59	5	
Rawbings, James C.	5, May 1895		75	5	
Raweet, Henry	16, July 1895		56	5	
Rawlea, Stanley	17, May 1901		9m	8	
Ray, William H.	28, Mar. 1901		49	8	
Raye, Anna	11, Dec. 1899	9, Dec.	61- 2m-12d	4	Hechstede
Raymond, Daniel	12, Mar. 1901		68	8	
Raymond, Grace	3, Oct. 1887		7w	1	
Reardon, Catharine	15, July 1901		76	8	
Reardon, Daniel	4, Apr. 1901		83	8	
Reardon, L.E.	30, July 1901		41	8	
Reardon, Mary	5, Apr. 1901		67	8	
Reardon, Michael	26, Nov. 1900		32	8	
Reber, Andrew	12, Aug. 1901		38	8	
Reber, Anna	5, Dec. 1900		58	8	
Rebert, Herbert L.	24, Apr. 1891		7	4	
Rebholz, Amanda	28, May 1891		13d	4	
Rebmann, John	5, Oct. 1898	4, Oct.	35-10m	5	
Rebmann, Kunigunda	25, Jan. 1893		80	5	
Rebmann, Rosa	15, Feb. 1898	14, Feb.	30- 8m	5	Runk
Rebold, John F.	24, Mar. 1894		40	5	
Rebold, Michael Anton	27, Mar. 1897	25, Mar.	34- 4m	5	
Rebstock, Wilhelmina	23, Nov. 1897	23, Nov.	44	5	Greaser
Rech, Heinrich	24, Feb. 1897	23, Feb.	47-10m	5	
Rech, J.	13, Aug. 1895	11, Aug.	34	5	
Rech, John W.	21, Sept 1887		8m	1	
Rech, Philippina	3, Mar. 1900	2, Mar.	77-10m	5	
Rechel, Katharina	4, Oct. 1897	3, Oct.	88	5	
Rechtin, Anna Maria	28, Jan. 1896	26, Jan.	83- 9m	5	Buck
Rechtin, Bernard	28, June 1892		61	5	
Rechtin, Eleonora	25, May 1895		11m	5	
Rechtin, Henry	10, Feb. 1893		20	5	
Rechtin, Wilhelm	29, Nov. 1899	28, Nov.	31	8	
Reckerd, Amanda M.	30, Mar. 1894		65	5	
Recklingloh, Lizzie C.M.	30, Jan. 1894		2m	5	
Reclamus, A.	30, Jan. 1901		25	8	
Rectanus, Peter	13, Mar. 1896	12, Mar.	52- 1m	5	
Reddehouse, Charles	13, Sept 1901		40	8	
Redder, Mary	11, Oct. 1900		7	8	
Reddermann, Joseph	5, June 1895		14	5	
Reddert, Rosa	10, July 1889		13m	1	
Reddington, Arthur	14, Dec. 1900		4	8	

Name ****	Notice Date ****** ****	Death Date ***** ****	Age ***	Page ****	Maiden Name ****** ****
Reddy, Nicholas P.	2, Feb. 1901		33	8	
Reddy, Sarah	9, July 1895		2	5	
Redecker, Bernard	12, Mar. 1901		50	8	
Redecker, Maria E.	17, 20, Jan. 1890		95	1	
Redelsheimer, Samuel	20, Feb. 1891		29	4	
Reder, Heinrich	8, Mar. 1890		45	1	
Redfield, Ida	27, Oct. 1894		20	5	
Redginski, Joseph	21, July 1891		7m	4	
Redman, Lorenz	15, Feb. 1892		3	5	
Redman, Thomas	5, June 1894		10	5	
Redmann, Charles	16, Nov. 1889		4	1	
Redmont, Peter J.	28, June 1895		1	5	
Redrow, Charity	10, Dec. 1900		71	8	
Redwood, James	15, July 1887		19m	1	
Reeb, Joseph	26, May 1900	24, May	71- 1m	8	
Reeber, Joseph	26, Nov. 1892		32	5	
Reece, Catharine	13, Oct. 1900		4	8	
Reed, Alice M.	5, Aug. 1887		17	1	
Reed, Edward A.	7, June 1895		22	5	
Reed, Florence	7, Aug. 1901		30	8	
Reed, James R.	24, Aug. 1887		39	1	
Reed, John	1, May 1895		18	5	
Reed, London	30, Apr. 1895		65	5	
Reed, Raymond	6, Apr. 1888		8w	4	
Reed, Winifred	7, Feb. 1901		47	8	
Reeder, Alaric	23, Apr. 1895		37	5	
Reeder, Henry	23, May 1888		30d	1	
Reese, Ellen	30, May 1894		6	5	
Reese, Henry V.	7, May 1901		38	1	
Reese, Raymond	10, May 1895		9m	5	
Regan, Barney	26, Aug. 1901		68	8	
Regan, John	29, Dec. 1900		68	8	
Regan, Margaret	8, Aug. 1901		60	8	
Regan, William	22, Mar. 1888		24	1	
Regenburger, August	6, Mar. 1894		42	5	
Regenfunz, John	28, Dec. 1891		2	4	
Regensberger, Henry	16, Nov. 1900		17	8	
Regensperger, Engelbert	13, Feb. 1890		36	1	
Reger, Joseph	7, June 1888		28	1	
Rehbaum, Hanna	3, May 1897	30, Apr.		5	
Rehbaum, Willard	18, Sept 1891		4	1	
Rehbock, H.F.	21, Nov. 1895	20, Nov.	73-10m	5	
Rehe, Eduard A.	6, June 1900	5, June	33- 2m	8	
Rehe, Henry	19, Dec. 1890		64	1	
Reher, Anna	2, Mar. 1901		69	5	
Rehfuß, Hortense M.	22, Nov. 1888		1	1	
Rehm, Katie	7, July 1898	6, July	31- 5m	5	
Rehn, Clara Louisa	9, July 1900	7, July	12- 6m	8	
Rehn, George	16, Apr. 1901		9	8	
Rehn, John	4, Mar. 1890		2	1	
Rehn, Tillie F.	16, Jan. 1889		3	1	
Rehn, W.V.	23, Jan. 1900	22, Jan.	17	4	
Rehse, Ed. J.	17, Feb. 1892		4m	5	
Rehse, Emil	25, June 1895		36	5	
Rehstock, Mary	6, Dec. 1894		4d	5	
Reib, Maria	3, June 1897	2, June	82	5	Reichler
Reiber, Fred.	5, Jan. 1892		1	5	
Reiber, Wilhelmina	26, June 1900	24, June	32-11m	8	
Reibold, Henriette	12, Jan. 1889		59	1	
Reich, Emil	4, Apr. 1900	3, Apr.	68- 8m- 3d	8	
Reich, M.	20, Dec. 1900		64	8	
Reichard, Edward	5, Aug. 1889		13m	1	
Reichart, Edwin	10, July 1889		3	1	
Reiche, Fanny L.	5, Dec. 1898	3, Dec.	70	5	
Reichel, Laura	7, May 1895		3m	5	
Reichenbach, G.	14, Aug. 1888		55	1	
Reichenberger, Michael	8, July 1893		57	5	
Reicher, Samuel	18, Mar. 1889		39	1	
Reichers, Paul	19, Oct. 1892		4m	5	
Reichert, Adolph	18, 20, Apr. 1895	17, Apr.	54	5	
Reichert, Adonea	12, June 1889		68	1	

Name	Notice Date	Death Date	Age	Page	Maiden Name
****	****** ****	***** ****	***	****	****** ****
Reichert, Albert	13, Dec. 1893		2	5	
Reichert, Magdalena	6, May 1897	5, May	69-11m	5	Lippert
Reichert, Maria Magdalena	8, May 1900	6, May	69- 6m	5	Blank
Reichert, Richard	22, Dec. 1893		15m	5	
Reiching, Bob	16, Apr. 1891		42	4	
Reichle, Christ.	24, Sept 1892	23, Sept		5	
Reichmann, Albert	31, Oct. 1888		21	1	
Reick, Emma W.	18, July 1895		13m	5	
Reick, Karl	25, Nov. 1895	23, Nov.		5	
Reickelmann, H.H.	16, Sept 1897	15, Sept		5	
Reidfeld, Joseph	6, Oct. 1891		1m	4	
Reif,	1, Dec. 1891		1d	4	
Reif, Edward H.	29, Nov. 1893		13	5	
Reif, Maria G.O.	18, Aug. 1892		1m	5	
Reifenberger, Maggie	7, Aug. 1894		2	5	
Reiger, August	18, July 1893		10m	5	
Reiling,	6, May 1893		1d	5	
Reilly, Florency	22, July 1887		14m	1	
Reilmann, George	22, Feb. 1899	21, Feb.	42- 9m	5	
Reilmann, Henry	16, Apr. 1901		39	8	
Reilmann, J.F.	20, Feb. 1897	13, Feb.	65- 5m	5	
Reilmann, Mamie	3, Aug. 1893		2	5	
Reimer, Adolph	29, Mar. 1894		41	5	
Reimer, Paulina	21, Aug. 1894		1	5	
Reimer, Wilhelm F.	9, Mar. 1895		11d	5	
Reimers, Charles	4, Mar. 1889		20m	1	
Reimers, Charles	12, July 1893		4m	5	
Reimesche, Catharine	30, Mar. 1894		39	5	
Reimeyer, Albert	9, Jan. 1894		1	5	
Reimler, Elizabeth	27, June 1895		43	5	
Rein, Lena	27, Aug. 1891		5m	1	
Reinach, Rachel	17, Apr. 1891		24	4	
Reinbold, Peter	31, Mar. 1893		71	5	
Reinecke, A.	26, Feb. 1901		27d	8	
Reinecke, F.W.	18, Oct. 1889		69	1	
Reinecke, Hildreth	11, July 1901		8m	5	
Reineke, Hattie M.	21, Jan. 1893		1m	5	
Reineke, Nellie	22, Sept 1888		1w	1	
Reiner, Charles	18, Sept 1901		7m	8	
Reiner, Fred.	24, Dec. 1893		62	5	
Reinert, Jakob	10, June 1901		74	8	
Reinhard, Adam	6, Jan. 1890		38	1	
Reinhard, Anderson	15, Aug. 1892		20	5	
Reinhard, F.F.	19, Dec. 1895	16, Dec.	53-11m	5	
Reinhard, Ignatz	23, June 1894		67	5	
Reinhard, John	29, Aug. 1901		46	8	
Reinhard, Mary	6, Feb. 1889		9m	1	
Reinhard, Theodore	19, Aug. 1891		46	4	
Reinhardt, Bessie	3, Aug. 1887		9m	1	
Reinhardt, John C.	23, May 1894		4m	5	
Reinhardt, Otto C.	24, Dec. 1900		10	8	
Reinhart, Ellen J.	10, Mar. 1894		33	5	
Reinhart, Emil	5, July 1901		63	8	
Reinhart, Friedrich	28, Feb. 1900	27, Feb.	85- 2m	5	
Reinhart, Friedrich W.	1, Mar. 1898	28, Feb.	40- 4m	5	
Reinhart, Joseph	30, Jan. 1891		41	4	
Reinhart, Wilhelm	8, Feb. 1894		44	5	
Reinke, Adeline J.	22, July 1893		24	5	
Reinke, Emilie	3, Oct. 1895	1, Oct.	40- 4m	5	
Reinke, Henry A.	1, Nov. 1887		25d	1	
Reinke, Louisa	26, Apr. 1892		27	5	
Reinmuth, George	21, Feb. 1894		8m	5	
Reinsberg, Caroline	29, Sept 1891		76	4	
Reinserink, J.	20, May 1893		64	5	
Reinstatler, Rosa	27, Dec. 1888		17	2	
Reiring, Louise	17, Feb. 1891		31	4	
Reis, Caroline	3, Nov. 1887		13- -14d	4	
Reis, Catharine	19, June 1891		50	1	
Reis, Christine	31, Dec. 1891		31	1	
Reis, Cora	1, Nov. 1888		18	1	
Reis, Daniel	23, Nov. 1897	22, Nov.	51	4	

Name ****	Notice Date ****** ****	Death Date ***** ****	Age ***	Page ****	Maiden Name ****** ****
Reis, Elisabeth	28, Jan. 1891		51	4	
Reis, George J.	11, Jan. 1890		50	1	
Reis, Jakob	1, May 1894		70	5	
Reis, John B.	9, Sept 1889		61	1	
Reis, Katharine	13, Aug. 1888		66	1	
Reis, Lillian	26, Aug. 1901		3	8	
Reis, Oscar	5, June 1890		3m	4	
Reisch, John H.	23, July 1887		3m	1	
Reisenber, Rob G.C.	20, July 1887		1- 6m	1	
Reiser, Otto	24, Nov. 1896	23, Nov.	32- 1m	5	
Reisigen, Mathilde	15, Jan. 1890		7m	1	
Reising, Anna	13, Mar. 1901		50	8	
Reisingen, Elisabeth	29, Apr. 1899	27, Apr.	42-10m	5	Kenfer
Reisinger, Charles	11, Dec. 1888		33	1	
Reisinger, Christian Eduard	1, Dec. 1897	29, Nov.	2- - 5d	4	
Reisinger, G.	15, Mar. 1900	14, Mar.	10m-30d	5	
Reisinger, George E.	23, Sept 1893		38	5	
Reisinger, Herman	22, Mar. 1893		39	5	
Reisinger, Jackson	30, Sept 1901		64	8	
Reisner, Lillian	1, Feb. 1901		6	8	
Reister, John	10, May 1888		4m	1	
Reiter, John	12, Feb. 1890		26	1	
Reitmann, Cora	23, June 1893		3m	5	
Reitze, Sophia	7, Aug. 1901		60	8	
Reitzel, Rosa	28, July 1893		16	5	
Reizer, Elizabeth	17, Sept 1901		85	8	
Reling, Joseph	4, Aug. 1893		28	5	
Relse, Leland	5, Aug. 1901		6m	8	
Rembold, Clifford	23, May 1888		4m	1	
Rembold, Elsa	19, Dec. 1889		5m	1	
Remden, Ella	9, July 1887		5m	1	
Remer, Claretta M.	10, Nov. 1891		1m	1	
Remgers, Elisabeth	26, Mar. 1897	24, Mar.	49- 5m	5	Gauthmann
Remke, Edwin	16, Mar. 1894		14d	5	
Remke, Geschen Margaretha	13, Feb. 1899	10, Feb.	68- 8m	5	Dannemann
Remke, Louise F.	7, Oct. 1897	6, Oct.		5	Dierkes
Remking, Harry	9, Aug. 1887		2- 6m	1	
Remle, Jacob	24, Dec. 1896	23, Dec.	50	5	
Remle, Jakob	8, Sept 1897	7, Sept	78- 8m	5	
Remlin, Jakob	13, Mar. 1889		66	1	
Remling, Emil	20, Oct. 1887		42	1	
Remlinger, Margaret E.	21, Oct. 1895	19, Oct.		5	
Remmers, Clifford	23, Feb. 1891		5d	4	
Remmert, Heinrich	11, Aug. 1896	9, Aug.	77	5	
Remmy, Christian	24, Dec. 1898	23, Dec.	42- 8m-26d	5	
Rempe, Heinrich	16, Dec. 1896	14, Dec.	64-11m	5	
Rempe, Margaretha	13, June 1899	11, June		4	
Rempler, L.	6, Jan. 1888		2- 6m	1	
Renau, Nellie	23, Dec. 1897	21, Dec.	46	5	
Render, George	22, Dec. 1900		76	8	
Rendigs, Johan H.	30, Mar. 1896	29, Mar.	76- 2m	5	
Rendigs, Rosie	2, Dec. 1889		2m	1	
Renesch, Alba	5, Mar. 1901		31	5	
Renesch, Marie	6, July 1901		39	8	
Renfrow, Lulu	27, July 1895		13	5	
Rengans, Minna	17, Aug. 1887		11m	1	
Rengers, William	11, Dec. 1890		18	1	
Renker, Norma M.	21, June 1895		4m	5	
Renkert, Eva	12, July 1897	10, July	64- 4m	5	Bauer
Renkert, Wilhelm Otto	31, Jan. 1899	29, Jan.	35	5	
Renley, Josephine	9, Sept 1892		40	5	
Renn, Wolfgang	13, May 1901		69	8	
Renneberg, Ida	25, May 1900	24, May	49- 5m	8	Anschutz
Renneberg, Louis	8, Apr. 1901		53	8	
Rennekamp, Anton	8, Apr. 1901		76	8	
Rennekamp, Franziskus Jos.	8, Feb. 1896	7, Feb.	66	5	
Rennekamp, Georg August	11, Dec. 1899	9, Dec.	72- 9m-19d	4	
Rennekamp, Josephine	3, Dec. 1897	2, Dec.		5	Griese
Rennekamp, Maria Elisabeth	10, June 1896	9, June	67	5	Krüger
Renneker, Heinrich	8, Dec. 1896	7, Dec.	74- 4m	5	
Renneker, J. Heinrich	25, Feb. 1896	24, Feb.	36- 6m	5	

Name ****	Notice Date ****** ****	Death Date ***** ****	Age ***	Page ****	Maiden Name ****** ****
Rennemeyer, Herman	26, Nov. 1888		67	1	
Renner, Caroline	28, Oct. 1897	27, Oct.	64- 2m	5	Schmidt
Renner, Catharine	26, Sept 1887		39	1	
Renner, Edward	21, Jan. 1892		23	5	
Renner, Elizabeth	3, Feb. 1888		66	4	
Renner, Eva Margaretha	4, Feb. 1896	2, Feb.	86	5	
Renner, F.	19, July 1898	17, July		5	
Renner, Friedrich	19, July 1898	17, July		5	
Renner, George	14, Dec. 1887		64	4	
Renner, William A.H.	19, Feb. 1891		3	4	
Rennick, George N.	29, Aug. 1891		88	4	
Rensch, Emma	7, June 1895		1m	5	
Renschen, Sarah	5, Oct. 1894		50	5	
Rentner, Katharina	21, Feb. 1898	20, Feb.	79	5	
Rentrup, Sophia	9, Jan. 1896	7, Jan.	83	5	
Rentschler, Fred.	18, Aug. 1890		80	1	
Rentschler, George	13, Aug. 1888		11m	1	
Rentschler, Michael	15, Feb. 1899	14, Feb.	29	5	
Renz, Maria	31, July 1896	30, July	79-10m	5	Kraus
Renzelmann, Charlotte	22, Aug. 1900		64	5	
Renzelmann, Christ. F.	11, Oct. 1900		69	8	
Renzinger, Alma	13, Mar. 1894		6m	5	
Renß, Minnie	20, Mar. 1895		18m	5	
Resch, Alb.	23, Apr. 1888		83	1	
Retallic, Margaret	30, Mar. 1901			8	
Rethmann, Frank	24, Mar. 1894		24	5	
Rettich, Magnus	10, May 1900	9, May	73	8	
Rettig, Anna B.	24, Jan. 1901		35	8	
Rettig, John E.	7, Dec. 1889		5m	1	
Rettig, Katharina	19, Mar. 1890		9m	1	
Rettig, Leon F.	24, Mar. 1893		5m	5	
Reubusch, Henry Franz	1, Apr. 1898	31, Mar.	47- 5m	5	
Reuhl, Peter	8, Mar. 1901		57	8	
Reulmann, Adolph	17, May 1897	15, May	62- 9m	5	
Reuper, H.	30, Oct. 1889		12	1	
Reusch, Maggie	1, Nov. 1892		1	5	
Reuss, Herman C.	20, Aug. 1901		53	8	
Reuter, Alma W.	6, Apr. 1892		6m	5	
Reuter, Anna R.	18, July 1890		10m	1	
Reuter, August	22, Feb. 1896	20, Feb.	63	5	
Reuter, Bertha	6, Apr. 1894	6, Apr.	63-10m	5	Gaehde
Reuter, Elma	6, Dec. 1892		4m	5	
Reuter, Elmer E.	21, Feb. 1893		2	5	
Reuter, W.G.	19, Sept 1896	17, Sept	66- 7m	5	
Reuwer, Caroline	6, Apr. 1898	5, Apr.	53	5	
Reuß, Barbara	1, Nov. 1892		1	5	
Reuß, Louis	1, July 1891		2	1	
Reuß, Nannie	8, July 1891		5	4	
Rewald, Sophie	17, Feb. 1894		54	5	
Rewwer, Christian	21, Jan. 1901			8	
Reyering, Mary Agnes	31, Jan. 1893		13	5	
Reynolds, Andrew	22, Dec. 1900		1m	8	
Reynolds, John	3, Apr. 1888		17	4	
Reynolds, Lillian	1, Aug. 1887		13m	1	
Reynolds, Sophia	22, May 1888		28	1	
Rhein, Johan	30, June 1898	28, June	60	5	
Rhein, John P.	29, Dec. 1891		63	4	
Rhein, Joseph	14, Dec. 1900		67	8	
Rhein, Robert P.	11, Jan. 1894		2	5	
Rheinbold, Mary	6, June 1901		70	8	
Rheinhardt, Edna	22, Mar. 1888		14m	1	
Rhodes, Estella	10, Apr. 1888		32	4	
Rhomberg, Max	1, Aug. 1901		2m	8	
Rias, Peter	29, July 1890		14d	1	
Rice, Alverce	21, Jan. 1901		9m	8	
Rice, Anna	26, Nov. 1900		76	8	
Rice, Charles	23, Nov. 1900		21	8	
Rice, George	11, July 1895		38	5	
Rice, John L.	8, Aug. 1901		25	8	
Rice, Julia	21, Nov. 1900		59	8	
Rich, Alice	4, Oct. 1887		34	1	

Name ****	Notice Date ****** ****	Death Date ***** ****	Age ***	Page ****	Maiden Name ****** ****
Rich, Harry	13, Sept 1901		23d	8	
Richard, Christina M.	31, Mar. 1900	29, Mar.	67	5	Schuppert
Richard, Estella A.	1, Mar. 1893		8	5	
Richard, John	2, Aug. 1888		13	2	
Richard, Mary P.	1, Feb. 1892		96	5	
Richards, Edith	5, July 1901		7	8	
Richards, Elizabeth M.	1, Mar. 1893		2	5	
Richards, John	7, Dec. 1893		80	5	
Richardson,	30, June 1888		1d	1	
Richardson, Charles S.	21, Jan. 1894		44	5	
Richardson, J.F. (Dr)	28, Apr. 1888		52	1	
Richardson, J.W.	13, Nov. 1900		41	8	
Richardson, John	15, Dec. 1887		45	1	
Richardson, Robert Carter	29, June 1896	28, June	69	5	
Richardson, Samuel	20, Sept 1887		72	1	
Richey, Harriet A.	22, Aug. 1891		33	4	
Richt, Margaret	27, Aug. 1891		19	1	
Richter, Albert	4, Mar. 1891		5	4	
Richter, Alwin F.	21, Mar. 1893		2	5	
Richter, Amelia	2, May 1895		70	5	
Richter, Barbara	10, Mar. 1888		77- 7m	1	
Richter, Bernhard	18, Sept 1891		4	1	
Richter, Frank	7, Nov. 1898	6, Nov.	58-10m	5	
Richter, Friedrika Sophia	23, Jan. 1896	22, Jan.	39-11m	5	Gießler
Richter, George	2, May 1901		57	8	
Richter, Harry E.	10, Dec. 1891		3d	4	
Richter, Herman Ed.	9, Dec. 1898	8, Dec.	65- 2m	5	
Richter, Herman F.	14, Mar. 1891		39	4	
Richter, J.F.	18, Jan. 1897	17, Jan.	3- 1m	5	
Richter, Joseph	28, Sept 1888		4	2	
Richter, Lorenz	28, Jan. 1889		1	1	
Richter, Lotte	9, Oct. 1894		24	5	
Richter, Louise	31, Oct. 1900		65	8	
Richter, Louise S.	21, June 1899	20, June	38	4	Blume
Richter, Madeline	6, Oct. 1898	5, Oct.	28	5	
Richter, Mathilda	3, Aug. 1887		13m	1	
Richter, Michael	4, Apr. 1891		6	4	
Richter, W.	22, Dec. 1887		19- 5m	4	
Richter, Wilhelmina	22, Dec. 1898	21, Dec.	60-10m	5	Uhlmann
Richter, William	24, Apr. 1894		2	5	
Rickard, William	26, Dec. 1900		52	8	
Ricke, Bernardina	5, Mar. 1901		37	5	
Ricke, F.	7, June 1890		6	1	
Ricke, J.H.	1, July 1891		56	1	
Rickel, Elisabeth	1, Aug. 1894		33	5	
Rickel, William	19, Oct. 1892		69	5	
Rickert, Adline	2, Apr. 1901		66	8	
Rickert, Charles	2, Sept 1891	2, Sept	6m	1	
Rickert, Jacob	31, May 1892		49	5	
Ricking, Lizzie	6, Mar. 1891		56	4	
Rickmann, John	2, Dec. 1887		5	4	
Riddy,	8, Aug. 1891		13d	4	
Rideman, John	23, Apr. 1890		2	4	
Ridemann, Herman	22, Apr. 1889		6m	1	
Rider, Fannie	9, Mar. 1901		29	8	
Ridge, John	30, Jan. 1901		59	8	
Ridge, Pearl	26, July 1900		4	5	
Ridimann, Maria	20, Dec. 1895	19, Dec.	75- 3m	5	
Ridley, Samuel	9, Apr. 1891		29	4	
Ridman, Joseph	11, Sept 1889		39	1	
Ridzel, Georg	4, Jan. 1897	3, Jan.	89- 2m	5	
Riebel, Margaretha	25, Mar. 1897	24, Mar.	50- 5m	5	Greulich
Rieche, Frank	18, Aug. 1891		65	4	
Rieck, Charles	10, Aug. 1894		42	5	
Rieck, Erwin E.E.	30, Sept 1891		2	4	
Riecke, F.W.	8, Feb. 1889		46	1	
Riecke, Friedrich Wilhelm	24, June 1899	23, June	73- 3m	4	
Rieckelmann, Alice	9, Jan. 1901		1	5	
Rieckhoff, Christian	3, July 1887		20	4	
Rieddell, William	13, Oct. 1891		8	4	
Riedel, Eliza	21, June 1888		10m	1	

Name ****	Notice Date ****** ****	Death Date ***** ****	Age ***	Page ****	Maiden Name ****** ****
Riedel, Elizabeth	17, Aug. 1901		76	8	
Riedel, William	8, Feb. 1889		2m	1	
Riedemann, J.H.	2, Aug. 1901		49	8	
Riedemann, Philipp	18, Jan. 1894		3	5	
Rieder, John	21, Dec. 1893	21, Dec.	58- 2m-15d	5	
Rieder, John August	5, Oct. 1889		1- 6m	1	
Riedinger, Charles F.	27, Nov. 1899	26, Nov.	39- 2m	5	
Riedinger, G.	7, Sept 1899	5, Sept	37- 1m	5	
Riedmann, William	29, Oct. 1891		6m	4	
Riedmatter, B.	21, Mar. 1889		53	1	
Riedy, Andrew	5, Mar. 1901		36	5	
Rief, Viola	2, Feb. 1888		1	4	
Riefenstahl, Christ.	11, Sept 1900		71	5	
Riefenstuhl, Edna	6, Jan. 1892			5	
Riefle, Jakob	30, Mar. 1895		59	5	
Rieg, Fred.	1, 2, Apr. 1898	1, Apr.	50-11m	5	
Riegel, George	10, Jan. 1893		36	5	
Riegel, Hans	2, June 1897	31, May		5	
Riegel, Henry	1, Aug. 1901		36	8	
Riegel, Mary	20, May 1890			1	
Rieger, Alb.	5, Dec. 1900		1d	8	
Rieger, Dora	30, Nov. 1900		36	8	
Rieger, George S.	13, Apr. 1896	11, Apr.	20- 1m	5	
Rieger, Heinrich	17, Dec. 1898	15, Dec.	10- 7m	5	
Rieger, Ida	5, July 1887		9w	1	
Rieger, Rosa	26, Nov. 1892		17	5	
Rieger, Theresa	27, Apr. 1901		75	8	
Riegereger, Mary	29, Dec. 1891		50	4	
Riegert, Louisa	5, May 1895		11m	5	
Riegger, Sebastian	7, Nov. 1899	6, Nov.	73	5	
Riegler, Fritz	13, Mar. 1889		2	1	
Riehle, John	19, Aug. 1890		4m	1	
Riehle, Loretta	8, May 1901		4	8	
Riehmann, Johan	1, Feb. 1888		23	4	
Rieker, Charles	3, Sept 1891		6m	4	
Rieker, Fred.	6, June 1888		27	1	
Rieker, Jakob F.	21, Apr. 1891		70	4	
Rieker, Margaret	18, Sept 1900		58	5	
Riel, Francis	2, Aug. 1900		6m	8	
Rielag, Mary	19, July 1901		25	8	
Rielley, Violet	17, Dec. 1900		24	8	
Rieman, Charles W.	18, Jan. 1901		2m	8	
Rieman, Friedrich	11, Feb. 1898	9, Feb.	19- 9m	5	
Riemenschneider, Hildagart	5, Mar. 1892		1	5	
Riemenschneider, Rosa	13, Apr. 1893		23	5	
Riemeyer, Alvina	30, Apr. 1900	28, Apr.	27- 7m	4	
Riemeyer, C.A.	18, Jan. 1898	17, Jan.	6d	5	
Riemeyer, Harry	17, Dec. 1891		4	4	
Riemold, Johan Ulrich	29, Apr. 1898	27, Apr.	75- 8m	5	
Ries, Daniel	4, Dec. 1897	2, Dec.	65- 2m	5	
Ries, Frank	7, June 1888		63	1	
Ries, H.V.	9, July 1887		4	1	
Ries, John	11, Jan. 1888		4d	4	
Ries, Joseph	19, Jan. 1894		5m	5	
Ries, Katharine	30, Dec. 1895	28, Dec.	34	5	Gallagher
Ries, Louisa	12, Dec. 1900		53	8	
Ries, Nicholas	28, Jan. 1891		74	4	
Riesenberg, Maria Anna	8, Mar. 1897	6, Mar.	66	5	Gibbe
Riesenberger, George	14, Jan. 1892		5m	1	
Rieser, Catharine	25, June 1901			8	
Rieskamp, Henry	4, Jan. 1893		48	5	
Riesse, Dora	7, Dec. 1889		82	1	
Riestenberg, Anna Maria	24, Aug. 1897	22, Aug.	26	5	
Riestenberg, Elisabeth	25, Aug. 1897	24, Aug.	37- -27d	4	
Riestenberg, Henry	20, Apr. 1899	17, Apr.	29- 7m	4	
Rietenbach, John B.	11, Dec. 1893		62	5	
Rietman, Anna Jeanette	23, Mar. 1900	21, Mar.	59- 6m	8	Stockbrink
Rietmann, Herman	8, Sept 1898	7, Sept		4	
Rieß, Augusta	20, July 1895		18	5	
Rießer, Michael	2, Jan. 1901		74	5	
Rigger, Gerhardt J.	12, May 1893		1	5	

Name	Notice Date	Death Date	Age	Page	Maiden Name
****	****** ****	***** ****	***	****	****** ****
Rigney, Margaret	5, July 1887		43	1	
Rigney, Maria	29, May 1895		52	5	
Rigney, Michael	29, Dec. 1900		63	8	
Riley,	29, Mar. 1888		1d	1	
Riley, Austin	23, Feb. 1889		30	1	
Riley, Celia	8, Sept 1900		11m	5	
Riley, Eleonor	24, Feb. 1888		75	4	
Riley, Elizabeth	17, Apr. 1895		30	5	
Riley, Joseph	22, July 1887		76	1	
Riley, Nelson	6, Oct. 1900		13	5	
Riley, Phoebe	12, Dec. 1900		66	8	
Riley, Ruth	24, Jan. 1901		8	8	
Riley, Thomas	21, Aug. 1887		26	5	
Riley, William H.	13, Nov. 1900		43	8	
Rimpler, John	23, May 1901		55	8	
Rinck, Fred.	16, May 1893		64	5	
Rinck, George	17, Sept 1891		1m	1	
Rinckenberger, Lena	11, Mar. 1896	10, Mar.	27- 2m	5	Ziegler
Rind, Joseph	8, June 1895		73	5	
Rindsberg, Sarah	17, Dec. 1892		9m	5	
Rindsburg, S.	22, July 1893		16d	5	
Rinehardt, William	24, July 1901		42	8	
Ring, Alice May	18, Jan. 1894		4m	5	
Ring, Anna Maria	14, July 1900	12, July	80	8	
Ring, Herbert	3, Apr. 1901		6	8	
Ring, Mary	11, Oct. 1901		2	5	
Ringel, Norma	22, May 1901		10	8	
Ringel, Rosa	8, May 1894		22	5	
Ringwalt, Mary	11, Aug. 1900			8	
Rink, Daniel	11, Jan. 1888		4w	4	
Rinke, Charles	21, Jan. 1890		17	1	
Rinkenberger, Lewis	31, May 1897	30, May	43	5	
Rinner, Frank	11, May 1889		27	1	
Rinner, Friedrich	13, Feb. 1899	11, Feb.	24- 2m	5	
Rinner, Henry	28, Sept 1893		61	5	
Rinninsland, Rosa	14, Jan. 1901		44	8	
Rinthner, Charles	25, July 1901		58	8	
Riordan, James	20, Oct. 1900		29	8	
Ripley, Katie	14, Mar. 1891		2	4	
Rippe, G.	15, Dec. 1887		6m	1	
Rippe, Henry	2, Apr. 1897	1, Apr.	39- 6m	5	
Rippe, John B.	7, Mar. 1893		73	5	
Rippert, Maria L.	19, July 1894		3m	5	
Rippman, David	11, Nov. 1894		62	5	
Rippmann, Rosa	17, Oct. 1893		15	5	
Risale, Giovanni	12, Feb. 1891		60	4	
Risk, Harriet	26, June 1901		60	8	
Rissel, Carrie	16, May 1891		5	2	
Ritchie, Mattie	14, July 1900		24	8	
Ritlin, Lucy	28, Sept 1895	27, Sept	16	5	
Ritsch, Henry A.	26, Sept 1891		3	4	
Ritschard, Adele	17, Feb. 1899	15, Feb.	52- 4m	5	Miller
Ritsche, Annetta	25, Apr. 1892		1	5	
Ritter, Amalie	16, Mar. 1889		28	1	
Ritter, Edna	19, Sept 1891		8m	4	
Ritter, Genevieve	9, Sept 1900		79	5	
Ritter, Gottfried	14, Sept 1895	13, Sept	57- 4m	5	
Ritter, John	22, Dec. 1887		52	4	
Ritter, John	11, Jan. 1888		53	4	
Ritter, John O.	2, Aug. 1887		32	1	
Ritter, Joseph	2, July 1891		5m	4	
Ritter, Louise	5, Dec. 1893		69	5	
Ritter, Luessia	22, Oct. 1894		54	5	
Ritter, Mary A.	1, Dec. 1891		68	4	
Ritter, Rosa	5, Sept 1888		3m	2	
Ritter, Theresa	30, Dec. 1889		1	1	
Ritter, Wilhelm	12, Sept 1899	11, Sept	25	5	
Ritter, William	12, Dec. 1891		63	4	
Rittman, John	11, Feb. 1889		47	1	
Ritza, Philip	10, June 1891		11m	4	
Ritzel, Adam	2, Feb. 1894		68	5	

Name	Notice Date	Death Date	Age	Page	Maiden Name
****	****** ****	***** ****	***	****	****** ****
Ritzer, Joseph	8, Sept 1891		26	4	
Ritzler, Mary	8, Mar. 1901		32	8	
Ritzold, Rachel	12, Jan. 1893		62	5	
Ritzy, Sarah	10, Sept 1891		2	4	
Rizzo, Anna	5, July 1901		5m	8	
Roa, Anna	15, Mar. 1901		67	8	
Roa, Jennie	23, Mar. 1901		7d	8	
Roach, John	14, Nov. 1900		30	8	
Robard, Johan	17, Oct. 1891		92	4	
Robben, August	23, Nov. 1892		3m	5	
Robelath, John	28, Mar. 1891		41	4	
Robensberg, John	20, Mar. 1891		30	4	
Robers, Anna	13, Mar. 1889		5	1	
Robert, Christina	27, Sept 1889		50	1	
Roberts, Catharine E.	23, Sept 1887		78	2	
Roberts, Elizabeth	25, Jan. 1901		80	8	
Roberts, F.A.	11, Jan. 1888		73	4	
Roberts, Henry	29, May 1895		58	5	
Roberts, Joseph L.	27, Apr. 1895		64	5	
Roberts, Julia	22, Mar. 1901		16	8	
Roberts, Katie	21, June 1888		10	1	
Roberts, Thomas	29, July 1888		64	1	
Roberts, William H.	19, Oct. 1900		24	5	
Robertson, Arthur	15, Dec. 1899	13, Dec.		5	
Robinson,	8, Mar. 1888		1	1	
Robinson, Albert	12, Mar. 1901		20	8	
Robinson, Bartholomew	25, July 1888		43	4	
Robinson, Ben.	27, Aug. 1888		61	1	
Robinson, Ella	18, Feb. 1901		23	8	
Robinson, Harry	10, Aug. 1887		13m	1	
Robinson, John	25, Sept 1900		50	5	
Robinson, Mary	28, Aug. 1901		78	8	
Robinson, Robert	7, Mar. 1901		2	8	
Robinson, Samuel	1, Mar. 1892		24	5	
Robinson, Thomas	31, Aug. 1900		69	5	
Robinson, Van	12, Feb. 1901		19	8	
Robinson, William	17, Apr. 1895		22	5	
Robinson, William L.	19, Sept 1888		50	2	
Robisch,	10, Dec. 1900		4d	8	
Robison, Mary	13, Jan. 1888		45	1	
Rocel, R.	21, Oct. 1889		69	1	
Roche, Mamie C.	11, Mar. 1893		24	5	
Rocke, Julia	2, Nov. 1900		59	8	
Rockenfield, Ed.	29, Jan. 1901		11	8	
Rockhold, Flora M.	23, July 1887		39	1	
Rockwood, Charles A.	26, Jan. 1892	24, Jan.		5	
Rodamer, Barbara	14, Apr. 1899	13, Apr.	70- 8m	5	König
Rodde, Edmund Wilhelm L.	21, Mar. 1898	20, Mar.	33-10m	5	
Rodenberg, Carolina	30, Sept 1889		1- 6m	1	
Rodenberg, Carrie	28, Jan. 1891		29	4	
Rodenberg, Dora	8, Nov. 1889		66- 8m	1	
Rodenberg, H.	18, Apr. 1888		30	1	
Rodes, Irene	29, Dec. 1891		4	4	
Rodgers, Bridget	30, Jan. 1891		66	4	
Rodgers, J.J.	13, Jan. 1888		49	1	
Rodgers, Margaret	30, Mar. 1901		46	8	
Rodgers, Thornton	19, June 1901		71	8	
Rodicher, James H.	25, Feb. 1891		42	4	
Rodler, Christina	17, Jan. 1896	16, Jan.	32	5	
Roebling, Herman	28, Nov. 1900		56	8	
Roeder, Esther	10, May 1894		1m	5	
Roeder, Karl F.	15, June 1894		1d	5	
Roeder, Theresa	5, Feb. 1895		5	5	
Roedig, Frank	19, Aug. 1893		3	5	
Roehas, Christian	18, Aug. 1887		36	1	
Roehl, Dora	27, June 1891		3m	1	
Roehl, Henry	6, Oct. 1897	5, Oct.	76	5	
Roehling, Anna	23, Oct. 1895	21, Oct.	5- 1m	5	
Roehm,	1, Feb. 1901		1d	8	
Roelker, Anna	22, Dec. 1900		66	8	
Roell, Charles	12, Oct. 1889		7	1	

Name ****	Notice Date ****** ****	Death Date ***** ****	Age ***	Page ****	Maiden Name ****** ****
Roell, Christoph	15, Feb. 1896	14, Feb.	71	5	
Roeller, Elisabeth	16, Nov. 1900		37	8	
Roeller, Mary	11, May 1901		57	8	
Roelly, Henry	1, Dec. 1891		14d	4	
Roenker, Bernard	6, Jan. 1893		70	5	
Roepking, Catharine	3, Dec. 1900		75	8	
Roesch, George	21, June 1895		69	5	
Roesch, Henry	2, July 1901		42	8	
Roesch, Ignatz	18, Nov. 1893		3m	5	
Roesch, Johan	15, Jan. 1897	14, Jan.	64	5	
Roesch, Josephine	10, Nov. 1891		3	1	
Roesch, Josephine	12, Sept 1894		34	5	
Roesch, William	30, May 1901		3	8	
Roesche, Carl F.G.	31, Dec. 1892		65	5	
Roescher, Katharine	29, Mar. 1888		70	1	
Roeschke, Emma	10, May 1901		66	8	
Roese, Mary	8, June 1900	7, June	66	8	Wolf
Roesl, Marga	3, Aug. 1901		86	8	
Roesner, Mary	23, Apr. 1895		67	5	
Roethig, Emilia Theresa	31, Jan. 1898	30, Jan.	55- 4m	5	
Roetker, Fred.	20, Mar. 1895		18	5	
Roett, Joseph	18, July 1887		30	1	
Roettger, Anna	15, June 1894		84	5	
Roettger, Charles	19, Dec. 1900		26	8	
Roettger, Edward F.	22, Dec. 1891		33	4	
Roettger, Karl	25, Feb. 1901		90	8	
Roettinghaus, Elisabeth	1, Feb. 1893		57	5	
Roettker, Francis	14, Apr. 1892		7m	5	
Roewekamp, Josephina	11, Feb. 1899	9, Feb.	40	5	Nieporte
Roewekamp, Mary	1, Feb. 1892		79	5	
Rogan, Agnes	16, July 1901		4m	8	
Rogan, Arthur	1, Aug. 1887		10w	1	
Roger, George	25, Apr. 1888		46	1	
Rogers, F.	8, July 1901		10m	8	
Rogers, Her.	31, July 1890		52	1	
Rogers, John	16, Dec. 1892		86	5	
Rogers, Michael	3, Jan. 1888		66	1	
Rogers, Patrick	8, June 1901		56	8	
Rogers, Robert	15, June 1895		2	5	
Rogers, Warren C.	30, Apr. 1895		62	5	
Rogg, Emma	25, June 1888		18m	1	
Rogle, Maria L.	22, July 1891		3m	4	
Rohde, Frida B.	15, Jan. 1891		21d	4	
Rohde, Johann	16, Dec. 1889		1w	1	
Rohdenberg, Johanna F.	23, Sept 1893		1	5	
Rohe, Albert	6, Oct. 1891		25m	4	
Rohe, Anna	24, July 1890		26	1	
Rohe, Annie	3, Apr. 1901		82	8	
Rohe, Henry	26, Feb. 1888		28	4	
Rohe, Henry	23, Sept 1891		68	4	
Rohe, Joseph	7, Oct. 1890		70	1	
Rohe, Juliana	7, Jan. 1891		69	4	
Rohe, Maria	24, Apr. 1900	22, Apr.	35	8	
Rohe, Theodor H.	15, Feb. 1895		4m	5	
Rohe, William	8, July 1901		2	8	
Roher, Margaret	27, Feb. 1888		53	4	
Rohling, Frank	16, Dec. 1891		40	4	
Rohlmann, Leo	10, July 1888		30	1	
Rohmann, Agnes	26, Apr. 1889		9m	1	
Rohmann, Anna M.	21, Mar. 1901		57	8	
Rohmann, F. Joseph	20, Jan. 1888			4	
Rohmann, Francis	30, May 1901		15	8	
Rohmann, Henry	10, Apr. 1895		45	5	
Rohmann, Johan	3, Aug. 1896	1, Aug.	44	5	
Rohmann, Joseph	7, June 1895		4	5	
Rohmann, Louise	18, Dec. 1895	18, Dec.		5	
Rohner, Richard C.	27, Apr. 1894		56	5	
Rohr, Elizabeth	17, Oct. 1901		76	8	
Rohr, Frankie	25, July 1896	23, July	5w- 4d	5	
Rohr, Katie	1, June 1899	31, May	34	4	Siegrist
Rohrer, Anton	20, July 1901		78	8	

Name	Notice Date	Death Date	Age	Page	Maiden Name
****	****** ****	***** ****	***	****	****** ****
Rohrer, Frank	12, Jan. 1894		58	5	
Rohrer, Jacob	5, Mar. 1890		6	1	
Rohrer, Magdalena	7, Mar. 1893		67	5	
Rohrkasse, Margaretha D.	19, Oct. 1896	17, Oct.	83- 6m	5	
Rohrkaße, Frederick G.	4, Apr. 1895		80	5	
Rohs, Saloma	7, Oct. 1891		79- 4m	4	
Rohs, Theresa	7, May 1895		11m	5	
Rolf, Anna	9, July 1887		19	1	
Rolf, Anna Elisa	8, July 1887	7, July	19- 9m	1	
Rolf, Anton	3, Mar. 1896	20, Feb.	38	5	
Rolf, Edwin	16, July 1901		2	8	
Rolfes, Heinrich G.	15, Apr. 1898	14, Apr.	78	5	
Rolfes, Henry	11, Mar. 1893		32	5	
Rolfes, John H.	28, Jan. 1901		55	8	
Rolfes, Joseph	4, May 1893		3	5	
Rolfes, Maria Elisabeth	22, Apr. 1896	20, Apr.	73- 5m	5	Ruiter
Rolfes, Theodor Heinrich	19, Aug. 1898	17, Aug.	56- 1m	5	
Rolfing, Johan Heinrich	13, Oct. 1899	11, Oct.	37-10m	5	
Rolfson, Margarethe	15, Nov. 1887		1d	4	
Roling, Bernard	23, Feb. 1900	21, Feb.	51	5	
Roling, Pauline	22, May 1901		1	8	
Roll,	11, July 1901		1m	5	
Roll, Henry V.	13, Apr. 1893		77	5	
Roll, Johan Heinrich	16, Jan. 1899	15, Jan.		5	
Rollhoff, August Fred.	13, Dec. 1890		1m	1	
Rollins, Ella	4, May 1895		30	5	
Rollins, Joseph	1, May 1895		46	5	
Rollmann, Elizabeth	6, Apr. 1893		65	5	
Rollmann, George W.	5, Aug. 1891		18	4	
Rolls, Earl	17, May 1901		2	8	
Rollwage, Alfred S.	25, July 1898	23, July		4	
Rollwagen, Louis	18, Feb. 1896	17, Feb.	70	5	
Rombach, Ed. C.	18, Dec. 1888		1m	2	
Rombach, Joseph	28, Jan. 1889		10m	1	
Rombach, Lena	9, Feb. 1893		72	5	
Rombach, Mattie C.	11, Aug. 1891		9d	4	
Romeiser, Gertrude	2, Aug. 1888		51	2	
Romeiser, Peter	11, Jan. 1898	8, Jan.	62- 3m	5	
Romer, Elsie	2, Apr. 1891		6m	4	
Romer, H.	26, Sept 1895	25, Sept	69- 1m	5	
Romer, Herman H.	26, Dec. 1896	25, Dec.	41- 2m	5	
Rommel, Henry	20, June 1892		24	5	
Ronan, Nettie	25, Jan. 1892		26	5	
Ronan, Veronica	25, Oct. 1900		5	8	
Ronfer, Eugene	17, July 1901		8m	8	
Ronnebaum, Anna Minna	24, Sept 1896	22, Sept		5	
Ronnebaum, Mary	24, Jan. 1901		73	8	
Ronse, Arthe	22, Aug. 1888		7m	1	
Ronsheim, Isadore	5, Dec. 1893		21	5	
Ronsheim, Joseph	24, Dec. 1900		79	8	
Ronsheim, Minnie	11, Dec. 1900		25	8	
Room, William	12, July 1895		6	5	
Rooney, James	30, Aug. 1900			5	
Roosa, Nicolaus R.	7, July 1887		51	1	
Rop, A.H.	25, Jan. 1888		43	1	
Roppelt, B.J.	16, Aug. 1887		17m	1	
Roschenkemper, Lizzie	4, Nov. 1891		22	1	
Roschenkemper, Mary	23, Mar. 1900	21, Mar.	69	8	
Rose, America	4, Oct. 1887		65	1	
Rose, Anna	5, Jan. 1901		1m	8	
Rose, Annie	19, Oct. 1887		57- 2m	1	
Rose, Betty	24, Dec. 1900		32	8	
Rose, John A.D.	16, Feb. 1894		27	5	
Rose, Joseph	23, Aug. 1887		52	1	
Rose, Ludwig	5, Aug. 1897	3, Aug.	68	5	
Rose, Margaret	14, May 1891		18	4	
Rose, Richard	16, Mar. 1893		30	5	
Rose, Solomon	30, May 1888		79	1	
Rose, William	25, Jan. 1888		37	1	
Roseberry, James	29, Sept 1900			8	
Roseboom, Mary W.	2, Oct. 1900		73	8	

Name	Notice Date	Death Date	Age	Page	Maiden Name
****	****** ****	***** ****	***	****	****** ****
Roseboom, William	10, Aug. 1900		61	8	
Rosenbach, Esther	13, Apr. 1901		20	8	
Rosenbaum, Babette	15, Dec. 1899	14, Dec.	83	5	
Rosenbaum, Emma	28, Apr. 1894		3m	5	
Rosenbaum, Ida	31, Mar. 1892		34	5	
Rosenbaum, William	2, Apr. 1891		52	4	
Rosenberg, Alexander	20, Jan. 1890		81	1	
Rosenberg, Hannah	9, Mar. 1896	8, Mar.		5	
Rosenberg, Lester	4, Jan. 1901		24d	5	
Rosenbloom, Jane	26, Feb. 1891		57	4	
Rosenfeld, Albert (Dr.)	9, Jan. 1897	8, Jan.		5	
Rosenfelder, Wilhelmina	13, Dec. 1899	12, Dec.	38-11m	5	Willinger
Rosenheim, Lizzie	25, Feb. 1901		76	8	
Rosenstiel, Katharina	9, Oct. 1899	8, Oct.	56	5	Backmann
Rosenthal, John	20, Mar. 1901		42	1	
Rosenthal, Katharina	1, Nov. 1898	31, Oct.	66- 8m	5	
Rosenthal, Sophia	2, Feb. 1893		68	5	
Rosenzweng, Moses	1, Mar. 1893		10	5	
Rosewich, Emma	3, Apr. 1901		25	8	
Rosfelder, Frank	18, Sept 1900		7m	5	
Rosin,	14, Feb. 1891		1d	4	
Rost, Conrad	14, Feb. 1890		84	1	
Rost, Georg	5, Feb. 1897	4, Feb.	67- 2m	5	
Rost, J.	20, Apr. 1888		1- 2w	4	
Rost, Mary	13, July 1887		30	1	
Roswitz, Moritz	15, Oct. 1901		74	8	
Rotelle, Peter	22, Mar. 1901		31	8	
Rotert, Christ.	20, Jan. 1894		49	5	
Rotert, Henry	21, July 1897	18, July	32- 9m	5	
Rotert, Herman	21, June 1894		23	5	
Roth, Abraham	13, Mar. 1901		65	8	
Roth, Balthasar	24, Jan. 1888		72	1	
Roth, Barbara	24, Aug. 1895	23, Aug.	47- 6m	5	Weier
Roth, Benjamin	19, Dec. 1900		1m	8	
Roth, Bertha	4, Feb. 1893		7w	5	
Roth, Conrad	29, Apr. 1897	27, Apr.	54- 8m-19d	5	
Roth, Daniel H.	29, Apr. 1891		59	4	
Roth, Elisabeth	17, Dec. 1896	15, Dec.	66- 8m	5	
Roth, George	8, Dec. 1891		1	4	
Roth, George Harry	4, Jan. 1898	3, Jan.		5	
Roth, Gustav Peter	18, Dec. 1893		1	5	
Roth, Harry	18, Oct. 1897	16, Oct.	28	5	
Roth, Johan C.	14, Nov. 1898	12, Nov.	66	5	
Roth, John	21, Oct. 1889		78	1	
Roth, John	13, 14, Mar. 1890	13, Mar.	56	4	
Roth, John	14, Jan. 1892		4	1	
Roth, K.	14, Dec. 1888		3m	1	
Roth, Karl	6, Jan. 1892		1-10m	5	
Roth, Karoline	30, Sept 1888		33	4	
Roth, Katie	27, July 1888		45	1	
Roth, Lawrence	23, Sept 1887		8m	2	
Roth, Lawrence	29, Apr. 1897	27, Apr.		5	
Roth, Louis	15, Feb. 1892		23	5	
Roth, Louisa	28, Mar. 1894		26	5	
Roth, Margaretha	21, Mar. 1892		3	4	
Roth, Minnie	27, Oct. 1891		2m	1	
Roth, Otto (Mrs)	2, Dec. 1895	1, Dec.	6- 1m	5	
Roth, Peter	23, Dec. 1889		66	1	
Roth, Robert	22, Feb. 1890		30- 6m	4	
Roth, Thekla	15, Apr. 1900	12, Apr.	75	8	
Roth, Tilly L.	18, June 1890	17, June	1	4	
Roth, Valentin	28, Jan. 1897	26, Jan.	75	5	
Roth, William	31, July 1900		15d	5	
Rothaas, Alma	27, July 1892		3m	5	
Rothaker, Emma	11, Apr. 1890		7m	1	
Rothan, Gertrude	20, Jan. 1891		74	4	
Rothaus, Fred. H.	3, Feb. 1891		3m	4	
Rothe, Benno C.	8, Jan. 1888	6, Jan.	32- 2m	5	
Rothe, Emil	1, May 1895		68	5	
Rothenbusch, August	30, June 1897	28, June	43-10m	5	
Rother, Alfred	13, Nov. 1899	12, Nov.	18- 3m	5	

Name ****	Notice Date ****** ****	Death Date ***** ****	Age ***	Page ****	Maiden Name ****** ****
Rothert, A.T.	6, Apr. 1889		75	1	
Rothert, August J.H.	21, Nov. 1897	21, Nov.	63- 1m	4	
Rothert, Caroline	20, July 1896	19, July	28-10m	5	Temming
Rothert, J.F.	18, Aug. 1892		62	5	
Rothert, Louisa	8, Dec. 1900		71	8	
Rothert, Maria	23, 24, June 1896	22, June	61	5	
Rothfuß, Augusta C.	2, Dec. 1892		59	5	
Rothfuß, George	21, Feb. 1893		12	5	
Rothman, Mary D.	12, Apr. 1893		4m	5	
Rothschild, Maier	29, Dec. 1895	28, Dec.	72	4	
Rotinghaus, Frank	1, May 1895		61	5	
Rott, J.W.H.	5, Sept 1890		64	4	
Rotte, George	26, Aug. 1901		1	8	
Rottman, Mary	8, Aug. 1890		65	1	
Rottmann, B.H.	24, Mar. 1894			5	
Rottmann, Carolina	1, Mar. 1898	27, Feb.	65- 4m	5	Kaufmann
Rottmann, Elizabeth	13, Mar. 1901		40	8	
Rottmann, George	24, Dec. 1900		51	8	
Rottmann, Louisa	29, Apr. 1898	28, Apr.	67- 1m	5	
Rottmueller, Eva	14, Dec. 1893		19	5	
Rottmüller, Eva	13, Dec. 1893	11, Dec.	19- 5m-11d	* 5	
Rottmüller, Karl Heinrich	29, Jan. 1893	28, Jan.	1- 2m-21d	5	
Rottner, Henry	19, Aug. 1891		20	4	
Rouse, B.L.	3, Oct. 1887		32	1	
Rouse, Joseph	1, Dec. 1888		4	4	
Rouster, William	14, Sept 1901		21	1	
Rout, Richard	8, Oct. 1888		8	1	
Rovekamp, Mary	15, Sept 1892		5m	5	
Rover, Clara Louise	26, Dec. 1895	24, Dec.	14- -28d	4	
Rover, G.H.	3, Sept 1895	2, Sept	50	5	
Rover, Lillie A.	1, May 1891		4m	4	
Rowan, William	27, Mar. 1888		29	4	
Rowekamp, Catharine	9, June 1898	7, June	62- 6m	5	
Rowekamp, Ellen	1, May 1901		3m	8	
Royce, Jennie	3, May 1901		34	8	
Roß, Anna	5, June 1888		54	4	
Roß, Anna M.	2, Apr. 1895		59	5	
Roß, Eliza N.	21, Jan. 1894		72	5	
Roß, George	13, July 1887		24	1	
Roß, George	24, Sept 1900		58	5	
Roß, Hattie	30, Apr. 1895		57	5	
Roß, John	5, Aug. 1891		7	4	
Roß, John	15, Aug. 1900		40	5	
Roß, Josephine	18, Aug. 1891		1m	4	
Roß, Katharine	7, Mar. 1901		50	8	
Roß, Mary A.	30, Mar. 1895		59	5	
Roß, Thomas	13, Feb. 1901		68	8	
Roß, William	29, Aug. 1891		70	4	
Roß, Willie	17, June 1888		38	1	
Roßkopf, Ed. C.	14, Dec. 1887		6m	4	
Rubenow, Anna	29, Oct. 1900		66	8	
Rubenstein, Oscar	17, July 1901		6m	8	
Ruber, Catharina	27, Feb. 1892		45	5	
Ruberg, Elizabeth	5, Sept 1891		75	1	
Ruberg, Harry	19, Feb. 1900	17, Feb.	16-11m	4	
Ruberg, Herman	12, Aug. 1887		47	1	
Ruberg, Kate	5, Aug. 1901		39	8	
Ruberg, Maria Therese	13, Dec. 1898	11, Dec.	29- 6m	5	
Ruberg, Norbert	17, Oct. 1893		9m	5	
Ruby, Louise	27, Aug. 1901		54	1	
Ruck, Freddie	11, Jan. 1901		3	5	
Ruckelhausen, George L.	19, Sept 1891		1	4	
Ruckstuhl, Albert F.	5, June 1894		2	5	
Ruckstuhl, Peter	4, Nov. 1895	3, Nov.	58- 7m	5	
Ruckstäschel, Willie	28, July 1891	26, July	1	4	
Rudd, Alice M.	25, July 1901		4m	8	
Ruder, Josephine W.	5, June 1901		10	8	
Rudisell, John	29, July 1888		18	1	
Rudisell, Lusanna	18, July 1890		68	1	
Rudler, Louise	3, June 1901		70	8	
Rudolf, Joe	5, Nov. 1900		42	8	

Name ****	Notice Date ****** ****	Death Date ***** ****	Age ***	Page ****	Maiden Name ****** ****
Rudolph, A.	29, Oct. 1895	26, Oct.	63	5	
Rudolph, Charles	1, Aug. 1888		8m	2	
Rudolph, G.A.	17, Oct. 1896	11, Oct.		5	
Rudolph, Georgiana	28, Feb. 1891		42	4	
Rudolph, Helen Clara	27, Oct. 1891		2m	1	
Rudolph, Richard	21, July 1894		2m	5	
Rudolph, Stella	16, Mar. 1893		1d	5	
Rueble, John C.	23, Jan. 1901		4m	8	
Ruebusch, Margareth	23, Mar. 1894		34	5	
Rueger, Henry	16, Jan. 1890		45	1	
Ruehl, Christina E.	25, May 1900	24, May	74- 3m	8	Weigld
Ruehl, George	1, July 1901		3m	8	
Ruehl, Johan	15, Apr. 1896	14, Apr.	63	5	
Ruehl, Margarethe	26, Mar. 1901		59	8	
Ruehl, Mary	24, July 1895		3m	5	
Ruehlmann, Louisa	14, Nov. 1896	13, Nov.	46- 3m	5	Dorst
Ruehner, Gustav	8, July 1893		3	5	
Ruehrwein, Fr.	3, July 1896	1, July	45- -21d	5	
Ruesch, William R.	4, Apr. 1893		3m	5	
Ruesse, Louisa A.	10, July 1891		24	4	
Ruether, Walter J.	17, Aug. 1901		4	8	
Rueting, Elizabeth	26, Jan. 1892		72	5	
Rueve, Henry	13, Mar. 1901		55	8	
Rueß, Rosina	31, Dec. 1890		83	4	
Ruf, Frank	13, Jan. 1891		7d	1	
Ruf, Friedrich Wilhelm	20, Feb. 1896	19, Feb.	1-10m	5	
Ruf, Mary A.	28, June 1894		52	5	
Ruf, Theresa	8, Sept 1891		7	4	
Ruff, Flora Elma	15, Apr. 1889		3m	1	
Ruff, Grace	12, Apr. 1889		11	1	
Ruff, James	23, Mar. 1901		32	8	
Ruff, John	18, July 1890		45	1	
Ruff, Margaretha	8, Feb. 1890		7	4	
Ruffler, Katie	11, Aug. 1887		1	1	
Ruge, George	11, Jan. 1894		25	5	
Ruger, Johan Georg	14, Apr. 1896	13, Apr.	40-11m	5	
Rugg, Abigail	26, Apr. 1895		2d	5	
Ruggles, Charles	13, Nov. 1900		22	8	
Ruh, Henry P.	28, Dec. 1888		4m	1	
Ruhe, Theodore	17, Aug. 1893		72	5	
Ruher, Elizabeth	10, July 1891		8m	4	
Ruhl, Bertha G.	18, Apr. 1893		5	5	
Ruhlmann, Anna	27, Oct. 1900		66	8	
Ruhstaller, Anna	22, Feb. 1893		53	5	
Rulle, Mathilde	27, July 1894		64	5	
Rullkoetter, Mary	12, Aug. 1901		6m	8	
Rumbt, Frank	19, Aug. 1889		2	1	
Rumig, Wilhelmina	2, Oct. 1896	1, Oct.	33	5	
Rumig, William	26, June 1891		10m	4	
Rummel, Johannes	5, May 1899	3, May	57- 3m	5	
Rump, M.	19, July 1901		2m	8	
Rumpke, Edna	20, Apr. 1896		2- 3m	5	
Rumpke, Frida	30, June 1896	29, June	16m- 1d	5	
Rumpke, Katie	5, Dec. 1900		7m	8	
Rumpler, Viola L.	30, Dec. 1891		14m	4	
Runck, Catharine	26, Apr. 1901		72	8	
Runck, George	3, July 1901		45	8	
Runck, Philip	9, Feb. 1898	7, Feb.	51- 4m	5	
Runck, Sophia	22, July 1899	20, July	25- 6m	5	
Runck, Walter L.	17, Apr. 1894		2	5	
Runde, W.	22, Nov. 1887		4- 2m	1	
Runge, Anna Engel	2, Dec. 1895	30, Nov.	83	5	Ruesse
Runge, Emilie	13, Sept 1900		17	5	
Runge, Herman	11, Mar. 1899	8, Mar.	35	5	
Runge, Minnie	25, Jan. 1896	23, Jan.		5	
Runkel, Chesterfield	18, Dec. 1893		52	5	
Runnebaum, Clara	11, Mar. 1893		62	5	
Runnebaum, Herman	17, Jan. 1894		62	5	
Runnebaum, Josephine	1, Aug. 1894		1	5	
Runte, Lizzie	10, Mar. 1893		8m	5	
Runtz, Julia	5, Mar. 1901		61	5	

Name	Notice Date	Death Date	Age	Page	Maiden Name
****	****** ****	***** ****	***	****	****** ****
Runyan, Henry	11, Aug. 1887		30d	1	
Runyon, Martha	28, May 1901		70	8	
Runyon, Thomas M.	26, Dec. 1900		58	8	
Ruoff, Johanna	13, Dec. 1897	12, Dec.	78- 8m	5	Hafner
Rupien, John	27, Oct. 1888		7m	1	
Rupp, Elisabeth Barbara	26, July 1897	25, July	66-10m	5	Sohn
Ruppel, Johan	21, Nov. 1896	19, Nov.	75-10m	5	
Rupper, Marie	26, July 1900			5	
Ruppert, Agnes	22, Oct. 1895	20, Oct.	78	5	
Ruppiler, Julian	25, June 1888		35	1	
Ruprecht, Henrietta	22, Oct. 1894		3m	5	
Ruprecht, Louis	6, Apr. 1894		15m	5	
Ruröde, Katharina	19, Dec. 1898	18, Dec.	72-11m	4	Hellmers
Rusche, Addie	30, Aug. 1901		19	8	
Rusche, Alma	23, Sept 1893		4	5	
Rusche, Bernard	9, Sept 1895	7, Sept	45- 9m	5	
Rusche, Rose	14, Nov. 1891		6	4	
Ruschenbach, Elisabeth	3, Aug. 1887		67	1	
Ruschenbeck, Frank	28, Mar. 1891		69	4	
Ruschkorowski, August	15, July 1890		30	1	
Ruschulte, Anna Maria Clara	7, Dec. 1887		53	1	
Rush, James	5, Dec. 1887		82	1	
Rusher, Charles	3, Apr. 1889	3, Apr.	36	1	
Russe, Fred.	25, Aug. 1890		39	1	
Russe, Louise	22, Nov. 1893		59	5	
Russel, Eva	11, Oct. 1900		1m	8	
Russell, Bartley	27, Mar. 1901		56	8	
Russell, Harry W.	20, July 1887		8m	1	
Russell, William	5, Feb. 1901		40	8	
Rust, Annie Jane	3, Aug. 1887		51	1	
Rust, Harry	12, Apr. 1892		40	5	
Rustler, Lena	12, Aug. 1887		5m	1	
Rustmeier, Wilhelm	28, July 1893		14d	5	
Ruth, Eliza	23, Jan. 1901		80	8	
Ruth, John	12, Feb. 1901		32	8	
Ruther, John H.	23, Mar. 1889		16	1	
Ruthman, Henry	17, Feb. 1892		6m	5	
Ruthmann, August	15, Feb. 1890		3	4	
Ruthmeyer, Clara	1, June 1894		5m	5	
Ruths, Carrie	26, Nov. 1891		28	1	
Ruths, Nellie	1, Dec. 1891		2d	4	
Ruthven, Eather	13, Apr. 1895		71	4	
Rutke, Alma	29, Mar. 1892		7	5	
Rutman, Lena	17, Oct. 1900		5	8	
Rutner, Lilly	25, Nov. 1887		13	1	
Rutsche, Wilhelm	22, July 1899	21, July	75- 3m	5	
Rutterer, Mary L.	15, July 1891		6w	1	
Rutz, John	23, Nov. 1893		30	5	
Ruwe, F.L.	2, Feb. 1888		2- 3m	4	
Ruwe, H.	10, Mar. 1888		65	1	
Ruwe, Henry	3, Nov. 1891		47	4	
Ruwe, Theodor Heinrich	8, Dec. 1896	6, Dec.	83- 1m	5	
Ryan, Beatrice G.	1, Oct. 1887		18	1	
Ryan, Edward	14, Aug. 1887		11m	1	
Ryan, Edward	23, Sept 1887		30	2	
Ryan, Elizabeth	23, May 1901		31	8	
Ryan, Helen	30, Jan. 1901		58	8	
Ryan, James	7, Sept 1900		13m	5	
Ryan, James	30, May 1901		19	8	
Ryan, John M.	26, Apr. 1901		55	8	
Ryan, Joseph	9, July 1887		19	1	
Ryan, Joseph M.	4, Aug. 1888		32	4	
Ryan, Julia	29, Aug. 1901		56	8	
Ryan, M.V.	16, Oct. 1901		28	1	
Ryan, Mamie	31, July 1900		27	5	
Ryan, Thomas	6, June 1888		50	1	
Ryder, Alex.	1, Oct. 1900		101	5	
Ryeburn, Harry M.	11, Dec. 1900		2	8	
Ryling, John	1, May 1901		87	8	
Räbenstein, Henry	7, Dec. 1888		9m	1	
Räck, Anna Margaretha	18, Jan. 1897	16, Jan.	33- 5m	5	Ries

Name	Notice Date	Death Date	Age	Page	Maiden Name
****	****** ****	***** ****	***	****	****** ****
Räck, Anna Maria	15, Mar. 1897	14, Mar.	34- 5m	5	Focke
Räther, John H.	22, Mar. 1889		16	1	
Röck, Henry	14, Feb. 1889		51	1	
Röder, Valentine	13, July 1899	11, July	58-10m	5	
Röhling, Christian F.	30, Dec. 1893		11m	5	
Römer, J.H. August	11, May 1897	10, May	50- 2m	5	
Röpking, Elisabeth	2, Apr. 1898	1, Apr.	36	5	
Rösch, Mary	10, May 1889		10m	1	
Röthlisberger,	14, Feb. 1888			4	
Röttcher, Georg C.	1, Feb. 1899	31, Jan.	26- 1m	5	
Röttker, Annie	1, Aug. 1887		11m	1	
Röttker, Wilhelmina	1, Nov. 1898	31, Oct.	43	5	
Röttler, Martin	29, Nov. 1889		2	1	
Röwekamp, Franz Ludwig	28, Apr. 1898	27, Apr.	59-11m	5	
Rübke, Adelina	27, Aug. 1888		4m	1	
Rückert, Alexander	8, Mar. 1894			5	
Rühe, Jolly	5, Sept 1888		19	2	
Rühl, Lully	9, Aug. 1890		8d	1	
Rühlmann, Valentin	4, Dec. 1895	3, Dec.	46- -12d	5	
Rührwein, Catharine	14, Sept 1901		87	1	
Rührwein, Catharine C.	26, Mar. 1900	24, Mar.	48	8	Ponnoth
Rümelin, Karl	17, Jan. 1896	16, Jan.	82	5	
Rümmele, Lina	4, Aug. 1894	3, Aug.	26	5	Weyand
Saagmellar, Edward G.	27, June 1895		6m	5	
Saal, Caroline	18, May 1898	17, May		4	
Saalwaechter, Mina	29, June 1894		10m	5	
Saarbrück, Sophia	4, Jan. 1893		42	5	
Sabbert, Ida	5, Jan. 1897	4, Jan.	24-11m	5	
Sabin, Karl	1, Dec. 1897	30, Nov.	65	4	
Sabin, Louis	18, Nov. 1897	15, Nov.	19	5	
Sacher, Carolina	3, Jan. 1896	2, Jan.	65- 3m	5	Warner
Sachs, Isaac	21, Feb. 1895		5d	5	
Sachs, Louis	28, May 1890		46	1	
Sachs, Rosa	15, May 1901		14m	8	
Sachs, Simon	1, Aug. 1893		24	5	
Sachteleben, Anna M.	13, Nov. 1895	12, Nov.	57- 4m	5	
Sachteleben, Harry	4, June 1895		4d	5	
Sack, Bernard H.	16, Dec. 1891		54	4	
Sack, Jacob J.	28, May 1900	26, May	86	8	
Sackett, Nathaniel	15, Mar. 1901		60	8	
Sackriede, Johanna Dorothea	7, Dec. 1897	6, Dec.	66- 4m	5	Finkler
Sadler, George N.	7, May 1901		70	1	
Saeger, Joseph	10, May 1898	8, May	31- 5m	5	
Saeger, Josephina	25, Jan. 1892		6	5	
Saenger, Yetta	19, July 1901		19	8	
Saerger, Joseph	18, Dec. 1893		44	5	
Saeyer, William	8, Feb. 1890		18m	4	
Saffern, Francis	28, Dec. 1892		57	5	
Sagmartin, Steven	7, Aug. 1900		5d	8	
Sahre, William	11, Jan. 1888		1- 6m	4	
Saider, Frank	21, Feb. 1901		9m	8	
Sailer, Joseph	21, Jan. 1892		2	5	
Saldinberger, Willie	2, Dec. 1887		19m	4	
Sales, Carter	14, Aug. 1888		44	1	
Salinsky, Sophie	18, Aug. 1891		9m	4	
Sallady, Margaret	23, May 1895		77	5	
Sallee, Ida M.	29, Sept 1887		13	4	
Salmon, Pauline	31, Dec. 1893		33	5	
Salter,	7, May 1891		27d	4	
Salwächter, Louis	6, Mar. 1891		31	4	
Salzer, Emma	13, Jan. 1891		20	1	
Salzer, Mary	7, Dec. 1889		32	1	
Salzmann, Edward	29, Mar. 1889		10m	1	
Sambenea, Emil	17, Dec. 1900		53	8	
Sammet, Gertrud	15, Nov. 1895	14, Nov.	2- 4m	5	
Sammet, Samuel	30, Jan. 1896	29, Jan.	26-10m	5	
Sampfer, O.	13, Aug. 1901		9m	8	
Sampson, Gertrude	26, 27, Jan. 1893	25, Jan.	2- 3m	5	
Samring, Clara	11, Aug. 1887		27	1	
Sams, Joseph B.	21, Jan. 1892		51	5	

Name ****	Notice Date ****** ****	Death Date ***** ****	Age ***	Page ****	Maiden Name ****** ****
Samuels, Bessie	27, July 1888		2	1	
Samwehr, Theresa	5, Apr. 1892		64	4	
Sand, Anna Margaretha	30, NOv. 1899	29, Nov.	74-10m	5	Awerdunk
Sand, Bernard H.	2, Oct. 1899	1, Oct.	32- - 5d	4	
Sand, C.S.	9, Aug. 1888		10m	1	
Sand, Edward	18, Sept 1900		16m	5	
Sand, Maria Anna	13, Nov. 1896	11, Nov.	74- 4m	5	Ruwe
Sand, Mary	13, Mar. 1895		69	5	
Sand, Walter	4, Dec. 1894		1	5	
Sandau, C.E.	21, Aug. 1901	19, Aug.	46	5	
Sandau, Christian	11, July 1898	8, July	77	5	
Sandau, Christian	20, Aug. 1901		46	8	
Sandau, F.H.	1, July 1896	30, June	56	5	
Sandbrink, Frank	2, Aug. 1893		1	5	
Sander, Albert	5, June 1897	3, June	20	5	
Sander, Alexander	11, June 1895		67	5	
Sander, Alphonso	7, July 1891		4m	1	
Sander, Anna M.	9, Jan. 1891		75	4	
Sander, Charles	18, Dec. 1889		63	1	
Sander, Dora	21, Feb. 1896	20, Feb.	57	5	
Sander, George	10, Sept 1887		2- 9m	2	
Sander, Maria Adelheid	25, Oct. 1899	23, Oct.	78	5	
Sander, Marie	25, July 1900		68	5	
Sandera, John	13, May 1901		6	8	
Sanderlin, Mary E.	7, May 1891		38	4	
Sanders, Anna	10, June 1891		11m	4	
Sanders, Anton	31, Aug. 1901		27	8	
Sanders, Bella	23, Apr. 1890		2w	4	
Sanders, Benjamin	31, May 1889		45	1	
Sanders, Edward	17, Oct. 1887		2m	1	
Sanders, Friedrich G.	14, Sept 1899	12, Sept	42	5	
Sanders, H.	19, Sept 1900		46	8	
Sanders, John	14, June 1889		10m	1	
Sanders, John	5, Mar. 1901		24	5	
Sanders, Katharina	23, Aug. 1899	21, Aug.	43	5	Kiefer
Sanders, Louis	15, May 1895		28	5	
Sanders, Scott	14, Jan. 1901		30	8	
Sanders, William A.	26, Dec. 1889		19	1	
Sanderson, Abigail	4, July 1901		16	8	
Sandes, Fritz	28, Apr. 1890		40	1	
Sandfried, Irene	8, May 1901		2	8	
Sandmann, Anna	6, Sept 1900		48	5	
Sandmann, Charlotte W.	17, 18, Jan. 1898	16, Jan.		5	
Sandmann, J.F.	24, Dec. 1893		74	5	
Sandmann, Josephina	13, June 1891		24	4	
Sandt, Elisabeth	9, July 1889		7m	1	
Sang, J.J.	17, Jan. 1888		3	4	
Sanger, Albert	21, Feb. 1901		14	8	
Sanger, Fred.	1, July 1901		66	8	
Sanker, Frank	2, Dec. 1889		36	1	
Sanning, Kate	4, Sept 1888		16	2	
Sanning, Theodora	19, Aug. 1897	17, Aug.	24-10m	5	
Sansom, John	8, Feb. 1901		76	8	
Santers, M.	17, Jan. 1888		1m	4	
Sarage, Henry	1, Oct. 1901		63	1	
Sardasky, Frank	1, Nov. 1892		1d	5	
Saremba, Frank	7, July 1887		48	1	
Sartor, Ida	24, Mar. 1893		2	5	
Sasse, August	25, Apr. 1901		58	8	
Satter, Mary	29, Aug. 1892		67	5	
Sattier, Nicholas	2, Nov. 1900		40	8	
Sattler, Ernst	10, Oct. 1888		74	1	
Sattler, J.	19, Aug. 1897	18, Aug.		5	
Sattler, Marjorie	28, Nov. 1900		15	8	
Sauder, Johan Heinrich	5, Dec. 1899	4, Dec.	46- 2m	4	
Sauer, Agnes E.	4, Feb. 1891		1	4	
Sauer, Alexander	22, Jan. 1899	20, Jan.	64- 4m	5	
Sauer, Amelia C.	4, Feb. 1891		5w	4	
Sauer, Anna Gertrud	28, May 1896	27, May	68	5	Ring
Sauer, Anna H.	1, June 1893		66	5	
Sauer, August	1, Dec. 1892		12	5	

Name	Notice Date	Death Date	Age	Page	Maiden Name
****	****** ****	***** ****	***	****	****** ****
Sauer, Caroline	3, July 1894		68	5	
Sauer, Clifford	14, Jan. 1901		16	8	
Sauer, Conrad	8, Mar. 1901		81	8	
Sauer, Emma	22, July 1887		1	1	
Sauer, Florentina	6, Dec. 1892		2m	5	
Sauer, Gottlieben	28, Dec. 1896	26, Dec.	76- 6m	5	Kübler
Sauer, Lizzie	18, Jan. 1893		45	5	
Sauer, Maria	21, Jan. 1894		80	5	
Sauerbeck, Charles	28, Mar. 1891		21	4	
Sauerbeck, Mary	12, Jan. 1893		67	5	
Sauerhöfer, Peter	13, Apr. 1895		32	4	
Sauerwein, W.	9, Sept 1889		28	1	
Saul, Stella	7, Mar. 1893		3	5	
Saunders, Abraham Jefferson	28, Jan. 1893		10m	5	
Saunders, Charlotte	7, Feb. 1890		76	1	
Sauning, Clara	18, Aug. 1887		3w	1	
Saure, Gertrud	20, Oct. 1899	18, Oct.		8	
Southern, Sm.	14, May 1891		2	4	
Sautlans, J. Louis	17, Feb. 1888		2	4	
Savage, Anna	11, May 1901		70	8	
Savage, Richard	12, Feb. 1901		84	8	
Sawyer, Charles	26, Jan. 1901		23	8	
Sawyer, Charlotte N.	1, May 1888		88	2	
Sawyer, Margaret L.	19, Apr. 1895		88	5	
Sayers, Georgetta	31, July 1900		40	5	
Scanlan, Eliza	18, Sept 1901		70	8	
Scarlett, Mary J.	24, July 1901		45	8	
Scars, Georgianna	21, Feb. 1901		70	8	
Schaack, Henry	21, Jan. 1893		76	5	
Schaaf, Anna	22, Aug. 1890		1	1	
Schaaf, Kunigunde	29, Jan. 1898	27, Jan.	59	4	Trageser
Schaaf, Peter W.	18, Oct. 1895	18, Oct.	23- 1m	5	
Schaaf, Stella	15, July 1901		6m	8	
Schaaf, William	1, May 1888		48	2	
Schaar, Edward	4, May 1899	3, May	55	5	
Schacht, William	21, Mar. 1901		4d	8	
Schaedle, Louis	1, Aug. 1887		9m	1	
Schaefer, Adam	30, Nov. 1887		41	4	
Schaefer, Alma	12, Dec. 1891		8m	4	
Schaefer, Anna	19, Mar. 1901		70	8	
Schaefer, Annie M.	24, Apr. 1891		61	4	
Schaefer, Arthur	23, July 1887		13m	1	
Schaefer, Bernard	13, Feb. 1901		23	8	
Schaefer, Carrie	3, May 1901		24	8	
Schaefer, Charles F.	7, July 1891		21d	1	
Schaefer, Clara	24, Oct. 1891		1	4	
Schaefer, Elisabeth	23, Oct. 1895	21, Oct.		5	Sievering
Schaefer, Emil	30, Nov. 1896	28, Nov.		5	
Schaefer, Emma	21, Nov. 1900		1m	8	
Schaefer, Esther	12, Nov. 1900		23	5	
Schaefer, Florence	16, Dec. 1891		3	4	
Schaefer, George	11, July 1892		35	5	
Schaefer, Harry	27, June 1888		4	1	
Schaefer, Johan R.	20, Oct. 1898	18, Oct.	39- 9m-18d	5	
Schaefer, John R.	28, Feb. 1891		64	4	
Schaefer, Josephine	24, May 1893		11m	5	
Schaefer, Katie	11, Dec. 1900		27	8	
Schaefer, Lisette	23, Dec. 1893		68	5	
Schaefer, Louis R.	24, Apr. 1900	23, Apr.		8	
Schaefer, Ludwig	17, Oct. 1899	15, Oct.	63- 8m-13d	8	
Schaefer, Margarethe	15, July 1901		55	8	
Schaefer, Marie	20, Apr. 1896	18, Apr.		5	
Schaefer, Peter	24, Dec. 1900		26	8	
Schaefer, Reinhold	18, Jan. 1893		42	5	
Schaefer, Rosa	5, May 1893		31	5	
Schaefer, Rosa	3, June 1901		10d	8	
Schaefer, Rose	4, June 1901		50	8	
Schaefer, Ruth	23, Oct. 1900		5d	8	
Schaefer, Susan B.	14, Sept 1887		47	1	
Schaeffer, Jakob A.	13, June 1894		5	5	
Schaeffer, John W.	11, Jan. 1893		15d	5	

Name ****	Notice Date ****** ****	Death Date ***** ****	Age ***	Page ****	Maiden Name ****** ****
Schaeffer, Margaretha	22, Dec. 1891		54	4	
Schaeffler, Louisa	29, June 1901		27	8	
Schaeperklaus, John	2, Feb. 1892		68	5	
Schafer, Bernard Ludwig	23, Dec. 1897	22, Dec.	27- 8m	5	
Schafer, Henry	20, May 1890		2	1	
Schafer, Nora Maria M.	24, July 1899	22, July		5	
Schaffer, John H.B.	29, Dec. 1887		5	4	
Schaffner, John	13, Jan. 1890		53	1	
Schaffner, Katharina	22, Apr. 1898	20, Apr.	77- 2m	5	Bellermann
Schafstall, Oliver C.	16, Aug. 1887		4	1	
Schafstall, Wilhelm	18, Aug. 1899	17, Aug.	22-10m	4	
Schaibach, William	12, Aug. 1892		43	5	
Schaich, Joseph	3, Apr. 1901		51	8	
Schalk, Elizabeth	11, June 1895		52	5	
Schalk, Frank	19, Mar. 1901		20	8	
Schalk, John	28, Feb. 1889		6m	2	
Schalk, Lulu	16, Dec. 1891		7	4	
Schall, Anna M.	22, Feb. 1890		37	4	
Schaller, Albert	17, Oct. 1887		7w	1	
Schaller, Joseph	27, June 1888	25, June	77	1	
Schaller, Michael	11, Mar. 1899	10, Mar.	55- 5m-10d	5	
Schaller, William	4, May 1895		48	5	
Scham, Elisabeth	18, Apr. 1893		54	5	
Schamberg, Gustav	25, July 1900		35	5	
Schanpp, Alfaus	10, Feb. 1891		4	4	
Schanz, Theresa	30, July 1891		1d	4	
Scharat, August	17, Sept 1890		5	1	
Scharer, Mary M.	9, Jan. 1891		3w	4	
Scharf, Anthony	24, July 1894		14	5	
Scharfheide, Henry W.	5, May 1894		69	5	
Scharges, Louis	22, Oct. 1891		42d	1	
Scharnhorst, Henry	25, May 1889		1	1	
Scharrer, Anna	24, Apr. 1901		72	8	
Scharrer, Rosa Regina	23, Mar. 1900	22, Mar.	7	8	
Scharringhausen, Friedrich	11, Nov. 1899	10, Nov.	62- 9m	4	
Schartz, Mary	18, Jan. 1893		75	5	
Schaten, Georg	20, Aug. 1888		69	1	
Schaten, Oliver G.	10, July 1891		1	4	
Schath, Tillie M.	15, Mar. 1897	13, Mar.	25	5	Myers
Schatz, Dorothea	28, Feb. 1890		42	1	
Schatz, Fred.	11, May 1892		71	5	
Schatz, Johan	6, May 1899	4, May	81- 3m	4	
Schatzele, Albert T.	11, July 1893		12d	5	
Schatzmann, Fred.	14, Jan. 1892		71	1	
Schatzmann, Jacob	28, Jan. 1894		91	5	
Schaub, Anni	11, Feb. 1889		7w	1	
Schaub, Henriette	7, June 1890		58	1	
Schaufert, Albert	18, Aug. 1894		2m	5	
Schaufert, Ida	7, Oct. 1890		10m	1	
Schaufle, Jennie	23, Jan. 1894		5m	5	
Schaumberger, Louisa	10, Nov. 1896	9, Nov.	73- 4m	4	
Schaupert, F.	15, Jan. 1897	13, Jan.	61- 1m	5	
Schaurer, Michael	11, July 1893		84	5	
Schaurer, Michael	26, Apr. 1901		59	8	
Schauser, Margaretha	15, Dec. 1893		81	5	
Schawe, Johan Heinrich	25, May 1898	24, May	70- 3m	5	
Scheben, Charlotte	2, Apr. 1891		85	4	
Scheben, Eva	7, Aug. 1894		65	5	
Scheben, Katharina	15, Apr. 1896	14, Apr.	40-10m	5	
Schedel, Martha	13, July 1895		11m	5	
Schedel, William	8, July 1888		4m	1	
Scheeben, William	1, Dec. 1892		46	5	
Scheer, Alfred	1, June 1892		9m	5	
Scheer, Herman	28, Nov. 1896	27, Nov.	54	5	
Scheerer, Catharine	2, Feb. 1893		84	5	
Scheeve, John D.	15, Apr. 1889		75	1	
Schefer, Elmer	9, Jan. 1901		2m	5	
Scheffel,	9, Aug. 1887		1d	1	
Scheffel, Nancy F.	22, July 1893		3m	5	
Scheffel, Peter	4, Aug. 1898	3, Aug.	64	5	
Scheffer, Franz	15, Apr. 1893		77	5	

Name	Notice Date	Death Date	Age	Page	Maiden Name
****	****** ****	***** ****	***	****	****** ****
Schefflen, John	1, July 1891		4m	1	
Scheffler, Michael	11, June 1900	9, JUne	71	5	
Scheffling, Lottie	24, Feb. 1888		1m	4	
Schefler, Elizabeth	11, Apr. 1891		62	4	
Scheg, John	20, Dec. 1900		56	8	
Schehl, Frances	9, Dec. 1891		17	2	
Schehl, J. Friedrich	25, Apr. 1898	24, Apr.	38- 1m	5	
Scheiber, Adolph P.	7, Apr. 1891		33	4	
Scheible, Walter	11, Apr. 1899	9, Apr.	14	5	
Scheid, Katharine	23, Sept 1895	20, Sept	46-10m	5	
Scheidel, Carl	28, Jan. 1896	27, Jan.	42-10m	5	
Scheideman, Christ.	27, Apr. 1894		50	5	
Scheidemantel, Magdalene	31, Dec. 1897	29, Dec.	84	5	
Scheider, Charles	23, July 1895		83	5	
Scheiderer, Martin	9, Jan. 1899	7, Jan.	72-11m- 5d	5	
Scheidermann, Louise	26, Oct. 1897	23, Oct.	67- 2m	5	Göbel
Scheidt, H.	12, Aug. 1895	11, Aug.	31	5	
Scheidt, John	12, Nov. 1900		84	5	
Scheidt, Josephine	6, June 1895		17	5	
Scheidt, Maurice	20, Apr. 1894		37	5	
Scheillen, Mary Ann	14, May 1891		58	4	
Scheipers, Leo	25, Oct. 1900		22	8	
Scheit, Anna	11, Apr. 1893		5m	5	
Scheit, John Jacob	26, Sept 1887		2m	1	
Scheitlin, William	5, Dec. 1900		69	8	
Scheits, Katharina	28, Sept 1893		54	5	
Scheiß, Jacob	5, May 1894		64	5	
Schele, Caroline	25, Dec. 1894		54	5	
Schell, Karl	12, Aug. 1895	10, Aug.	42- 6m	5	
Schell, Louis	24, Oct. 1890		7m	1	
Schell, Margaretha	29, Apr. 1891		62	4	
Schell, Maria	28, July 1898	28, July	46	5	Rothe
Schellenbaum, Wilhelmina	30, June 1890	29, June		* 1	Gassenschmidt
Schellhammer, Clara	12, Mar. 1889		24	1	
Schellig, Henry A.	11, June 1895		22	5	
Schelling, Anna	14, Dec. 1887		38	4	
Schellinger, Eugene	12, July 1901		55	8	
Schellinger, William O.	16, Oct. 1889		17d	1	
Schencke, Maria A.	28, Jan. 1891		64	4	
Schencker, Julia	13, Apr. 1895		9m	4	
Schenk, George A.	7, Jan. 1891		62	4	
Schenk, Mary	16, Aug. 1887		25	1	
Schenke, Anton	4, Feb. 1899	1, Feb.	77- 7m	4	
Schenkel, Charles	28, Feb. 1890		31	1	
Schenkel, Maria	1, Sept 1898	31, Aug.	63	4	
Schepe, Carl	20, Jan. 1890		5	1	
Scheper, Henry	18, Dec. 1893		69	5	
Schepman, J.F.	6, Dec. 1892		54	5	
Schepmann, Alice	6, Aug. 1901		4	8	
Schepmann, Carrie S.	24, Feb. 1898	23, Feb.		5	
Scher, Jakob	20, 21, Feb. 1896	18, Feb.	59- 4m	5	
Scherder, Mamie	18, Aug. 1891		20m	4	
Scherehr, Irene	12, Feb. 1901		2	8	
Scherer, Anna M.	24, Feb. 1890		1	1	
Scherer, Charles	25, Apr. 1892		10m	5	
Scherer, Christian	3, Mar. 1900	1, Mar.	60- 7m	5	
Scherer, Elisabeth	22, Mar. 1894		47	5	
Scherer, Helen	30, Mar. 1894		1	5	
Scherer, Helena	2, Mar. 1901		1	5	
Scherer, Joseph	13, Apr. 1901		67	8	
Scherer, Magdalene	15, May 1894		29	5	
Scherer, Mary	20, Mar. 1891		57	4	
Scherer, Minnie	6, Apr. 1893		3	5	
Scherf, Otto	18, July 1895		49	5	
Scherff, Hannah	8, Sept 1890		76	4	
Scherm, Mary	30, Dec. 1892		53	5	
Schernbeck, Josephine	24, Jan. 1901		43	8	
Scherrer, Hilarius	31, Jan. 1896	30, Jan.	51- -18d	5	
Scherrer, Peter	23, Jan. 1899	21, Jan.	39- 1m	5	
Scherrer, Romi	10, Feb. 1898	9, Feb.		5	
Schertel, Leonard	13, Oct. 1892		52	5	

Name	Notice Date	Death Date	Age	Page	Maiden Name
****	****** ****	***** ****	***	****	****** ****
Schertler, Marie	12, May 1893		67	5	
Scherzer, Leonhard	11, Dec. 1893		31	5	
Scherzinger, Eleonore	10, Mar. 1895		67	5	
Scheton, Mamie	28, Apr. 1890		9m	1	
Schetter, Johann	6, June 1888		3m	1	
Scheu, Georg	17, 19, Aug. 1896	16, Aug.	74	5	
Scheu, Katie	27, Aug. 1898	26, Aug.		5	
Scheublein, Andreas	30, Aug. 1900		11m	5	
Scheuer, Theresa	21, Mar. 1898	20, Mar.		5	
Scheuerer, Lorenz	3, May 1899	2, May	69- 8m	5	
Scheuermann, Bertha	31, May 1890		4	1	
Scheufert, Jakob	13, Sept 1901		48	8	
Scheurer, Catharina	11, Mar. 1891		33	4	
Scheurer, Rosina	30, Mar. 1899	27, Mar.	71	5	Wiedmeyer
Scheve,	19, Aug. 1889		5w	1	
Scheve, Ed.	1, Aug. 1901		31	8	
Scheve, Joseph	28, Jan. 1898	27, Jan.	78	5	
Scheve, Joseph	6, Sept 1900		41	5	
Scheve, Joseph J.	16, Feb. 1895		21d	5	
Schewe, Henry	14, Mar. 1891		45	4	
Schewe, Henry E.	28, Mar. 1891		68	4	
Schewene, Edna C.	9, Jan. 1894		1m	5	
Schick, Bessy	30, July 1889		2	1	
Schick, Charles	2, Dec. 1889		9d	1	
Schick, K.M.	30, Jan. 1888		3	1	
Schickling, John	29, Aug. 1901		67	8	
Schickling, Michael	17, Jan. 1898	15, Jan.	73- 4m	8	
Schiebel, Gottfried	1, Feb. 1888		61	4	
Schiedler, Mary	5, Dec. 1893		49	5	
Schiefer, Elmer A.	10, July 1891		8	4	
Schiefer, Johan Heinrich	29, Jan. 1900	27, Jan.	66- - 2d	5	
Schieferdecker, Julius	28, May 1891		42	4	
Schiel, Francis	9, Aug. 1887		73	1	
Schiel, Julia	1, June 1894		33	5	
Schields, John	28, July 1891		24	4	
Schierberg, Bernard	15, June 1889		49	1	
Schierberg, Charles	12, Feb. 1901		46	8	
Schiereck, Christ	31, Jan. 1898	29, Jan.	48-11m	5	
Schierenbeck, Johan D.F.	8, 9, May 1900	7, May	44	5	
Schierling, Johan B.	17, Feb. 1900	14, Feb.	52- 6m	5	
Schierz, Harry	24, Oct. 1887		2m	1	
Schieß, George	4, Feb. 1889		2w	1	
Schiffel, Eva	16, Jan. 1894		13d	5	
Schiffmann, Minnie	17, June 1889		55	1	
Schiffmeier, Joseph	13, June 1891		7m	4	
Schiffmeyer, John	10, Mar. 1891		71	4	
Schild, Philipp	23, July 1887		28	1	
Schilderink, Anthony	9, June 1892		68	5	
Schilderink, Johanna	11, May 1901		8	8	
Schilderink, John Henry	14, Aug. 1896	13, Aug.	11m- 8d	5	
Schildknecht, Mary	3, Oct. 1895	2, Oct.	57- 6m	5	
Schildmann, William	24, Dec. 1893		62	5	
Schildmeyer, Herman Heinrich	7, June 1898	6, June	62- 1m-29d	5	
Schilferth, Josephine	16, May 1893		1	5	
Schilherbrink, Herman	8, Mar. 1901			8	
Schill, Anna	13, Mar. 1894		39	5	
Schille, Crescentia	27, Oct. 1898	25, Oct.	85- 4m	5	Seiler
Schillen, Caecilia	13, Jan. 1891		67	1	
Schiller, Catharine	20, Mar. 1901			1	
Schiller, Elizabeth	21, Jan. 1894		8d	5	
Schiller, Gabriel	4, Nov. 1887		16- 6m- 6d	1	
Schiller, Gustav	19, Aug. 1891		69	4	
Schilling, Agatha	2, Dec. 1892		80	5	
Schilling, Catharine	20, July 1887		75	1	
Schilling, Henry	17, Aug. 1887		11	1	
Schilling, Katie	18, Oct. 1897	16, Oct.	32	5	Sudkamp
Schilling, Margarethe	26, Mar. 1895		66	5	
Schilly, Wendelin	29, June 1893		83	5	
Schiltzberger, Elisabeth	15, Dec. 1892		58	5	
Schimanski, Anna	18, Mar. 1890		63	1	
Schimmel, Creszenzia	14, Jan. 1899	12, Jan.	72	5	Müller

Name ****	Notice Date ****** ****	Death Date ***** ****	Age ***	Page ****	Maiden Name ****** ****
Schimmelpfennig, George	15, Oct. 1900		80	5	
Schimmer, Jacob	28, Sept 1901		51	5	
Schimmrock, Karl	15, 16, Mar. 1899	14, Mar.	39- 5m	5	
Schimp, Edith	22, July 1901		9	8	
Schimpf, J.A.	13, Jan. 1888		11m	1	
Schindeldecker, Reinhart	8, Apr. 1897	7, Apr.	25- 9m	5	
Schindler, Henry	31, May 1901		78	8	
Schindler, John A.	10, Sept 1887		10m	2	
Schindler, William	13, Aug. 1901		30	8	
Schinel, Kate	10, Aug. 1901		42	8	
Schinner, Helena Magdalena	27, Apr. 1897	25, Apr.	58- 7m	5	Heyl
Schinner, Theresa	11, Nov. 1897	10, Nov.		4	
Schippee, Albert	10, Apr. 1901		2	8	
Schirm, Anna	27, July 1888		32	1	
Schirmbeck, Willis	14, Apr. 1891		1	4	
Schlacke, Johan Dietrich	15, Jan. 1897	13, Jan.	82	5	
Schlafer, Gerhardt	2, Aug. 1887		77	1	
Schlamann, Christina	3, Apr. 1891		59	4	
Schlanser, Alois	18, June 1889		3	1	
Schlatter, Christina	6, Sept 1900		16	5	
Schlauch, Charles	8, Oct. 1889		1	1	
Schlauch, W.	10, Apr. 1889		31	1	
Schlaxmann, Christofer A.	4, June 1891		3d	4	
Schlecht, Charles	6, Sept 1893		40	5	
Schlecht, William	13, Feb. 1901		63	8	
Schledron, Caroline	21, June 1900	19, June	57- 6m	6	Bischoff
Schlegel, Alfred	13, July 1901		10m	8	
Schlegel, Auguste	18, Sept 1900		38	5	
Schlegel, Bertha	3, Aug. 1893		69	5	
Schlegel, Gustav	26, June 1901		8	8	
Schlegel, Rachel	19, Aug. 1889		58	1	
Schlegel, Valentine	19, Sept 1900		38	8	
Schleicher, (child of Leopold)	1, Nov. 1887		1d	1	
Schleicher, Lena	14, Dec. 1888		28	1	
Schleichter, William	25, July 1893		17	5	
Schleid, Theresa	23, July 1887		6m	1	
Schleitler, Anna	2, Mar. 1893		7m	5	
Schlemmer, May	6, June 1888		3w	1	
Schlenbach, Johann	24, Mar. 1893		34	5	
Schlenker, Jacob	20, Apr. 1888		43	4	
Schlenker, Johan	14, July 1898	12, July	80- 4m	5	
Schlenker, Kate	13, Nov. 1893		24	5	
Schlenker, William E.	19, Mar. 1895		19	5	
Schlensker, Wilhelm Heinrich	15, Feb. 1900	14, Feb.	78- 1m	5	
Schlenther, Henry	13, May 1891		1	2	
Schlereth, Barbara	29, Nov. 1893		68	5	
Schlesinger, Charles	7, June 1895		1	5	
Schlesinger, Fred.	16, May 1891		9m	2	
Schleter, William	30, Jan. 1891			4	
Schlett, Mary	6, Dec. 1888		75	1	
Schleuter, Hattie	20, Nov. 1889		3	1	
Schleuter, John	24, Sept 1901		32	1	
Schleutker, Emma Emilie	25, Jan. 1897	23, Jan.	40	5	
Schleutker, John	7, Dec. 1888		13m	1	
Schleweir, Emma	2, Apr. 1891		4	4	
Schleyer, Margaretha	10, Mar. 1894		58	5	
Schlichte, John	11, Oct. 1894		70	5	
Schlichte, Maria Elisabeth	8, Dec. 1896		57- 9m	5	
Schlichte, Rose	6, June 1900	4, June		8	Ringemann
Schlichter, George E.	15, Mar. 1893		9m	5	
Schlittler, Josephine	17, Aug. 1893		61	5	
Schlitz, Katharine	3, Mar. 1897	1, Mar.	79- 1m	5	
Schlitzberger, Elisa	14, Dec. 1892		58- -23d	5	Hoffmann
Schlitzberger, Heinrich	5, 6, Dec. 1890	3, Dec.	69	1	
Schloemer, Anna	30, Nov. 1900		59	8	
Schloemer, George	23, Dec. 1890		51	1	
Schloemer, Margaret E.	6, Dec. 1900		72	8	
Schlosser, Gottfried	19, July 1887		33	1	
Schloterbeck, Gertie B.	4, Sept 1891		10m	4	
Schlothaus, John H.	30, June 1893		49	5	
Schlotterbeck, Dorothea	14, Feb. 1899	12, Feb.	52- 8m-13d	5	Benkering

Name ****	Notice Date ****** ****	Death Date ***** ****	Age ***	Page ****	Maiden Name ****** ****
Schlotterbeck, Fred.	23, Mar. 1894		15	5	
Schlotterbeck, Rosine	14, Feb. 1901		67	8	
Schlottmann, Elizabeth	12, Feb. 1889		40	1	
Schloß, Emilie	18, Dec. 1888		16m	2	
Schloß, Frank	10, July 1887		10m	1	
Schloß, Joseph M.	19, Dec. 1891		68	4	
Schloß, Ruth	24, Feb. 1894		1m	5	
Schluecker, Frederick J.	26, Feb. 1891		1	4	
Schlueter, Bernard	10, July 1901		10	5	
Schlumberger, Magdalena	25, Aug. 1899	23, Aug.	78- 7m	5	Schüler
Schluter, Chr. H.	6, June 1888		3m	1	
Schluter, Herman H.	11, Jan. 1890		3	1	
Schlächter, Elen	14, Apr. 1892		4m	5	
Schlüter, Rudolph	24, Sept 1888		3	1	
Schlüter, William H.	4, July 1895		1m	5	
Schlüther, John W.	25, May 1895		23m	5	
Schmacher, Earl	19, July 1901		1d	8	
Schmadel, Johan	17, Jan. 1896	15, Jan.	54	5	
Schmader,	4, Aug. 1888		5m	4	
Schmall, Ida C.	24, Dec. 1900		15d	8	
Schmall, Sophie	14, Feb. 1900	12, Feb.	65	8	
Schmalstieg, Maria	1, Oct. 1895	30, Sept	9m-11d	5	
Schmalz, Anton	14, May 1900	12, May	66	8	
Schmalz, Charles	27, Aug. 1888		8m	1	
Schmatz, Lester	30, Mar. 1901		6m	8	
Schmear, Peter	24, May 1892		51	5	
Schmecker, Wilhelm	13, Sept 1893		59	5	
Schmeer, Emma	23, Nov. 1900		12	8	
Schmees, Bernhard	23, Feb. 1889		2m	1	
Schmeig, Edward	14, Nov. 1893		1	5	
Schmeiser, Arthur E.	17, July 1894		6m	5	
Schmeiser, Ernst	28, Dec. 1888		62	1	
Schmeker, Wilhelm	13, Feb. 1894		32	5	
Schmelz, Albert L.	18, Apr. 1900	17, Apr.	34- 4m	8	
Schmelz, Katharine	26, July 1900		75	5	
Schmelz, Michael	7, July 1896	6, July		4	
Schmelzer, Libbie	14, Nov. 1895	11, Nov.		5	
Schmelzle, Tillie	25, Dec. 1891		3	2	
Schmerr, Katharina	16, Apr. 1901		63	8	
Schmesing, Caroline	10, Jan. 1888		3m	4	
Schmich, Johan	10, Aug. 1898	9, Aug.	73	5	
Schmid, C.S.	4, July 1900	3, July	62	8	
Schmid, Charlotte	14, Sept 1897	13, Sept	69- 8m	* 4	Melchior
Schmid, Emil	1, Dec. 1891		5m	4	
Schmid, Emil	22, May 1894		20m	5	
Schmid, Emil	20, Apr. 1899	18, Apr.	46	4	
Schmid, Johan M.	5, Nov. 1896	4, Nov.	19	5	
Schmid, L.	12, May 1895		79	5	
Schmidel, Ida	15, Mar. 1890		36	1	
Schmidlapp, Rudolph O.	30, Jan. 1894		4m	5	
Schmidlin, Joseph	24, Mar. 1888		86	1	
Schmidlin, Katharina	8, May 1889		3	1	
Schmidt, Adam	2, Dec. 1887		31	4	
Schmidt, Adam	25, July 1888		6w	4	
Schmidt, Adam	5, Aug. 1892		7m	5	
Schmidt, Adolph	21, June 1895		35	5	
Schmidt, Albert	26, 27, Oct. 1892	26, Oct.	5-11m- 9d	5	
Schmidt, Alice	12, Sept 1900		45	5	
Schmidt, Amelia C.	4, Sept 1891		2	4	
Schmidt, Andreas E.	6, Nov. 1895	5, Nov.	23- 4m	5	
Schmidt, Andrew	18, Feb. 1890		60	2	
Schmidt, Anna	31, Jan. 1891		2	4	
Schmidt, Anna	4, May 1893		66	5	
Schmidt, Anna	17, Apr. 1899	15, Apr.	84- 3m	5	
Schmidt, Anna B.	23, Jan. 1901		63	8	
Schmidt, Anna Eleonora	15, Aug. 1896	13, Aug.	17- 3m	5	
Schmidt, Anna Maria	27, Feb. 1899	25, Feb.	80	5	
Schmidt, Annie	21, Jan. 1890		47	1	
Schmidt, Arthur Emil	17, Jan. 1888			4	
Schmidt, Bertha	25, Aug. 1890		3m	1	
Schmidt, Bertha	27, June 1891		30	1	

Name	Notice Date	Death Date	Age	Page	Maiden Name
****	****** ****	***** ****	***	****	****** ****
Schmidt, Caroline	16, Jan. 1893		27	5	
Schmidt, Carrie	17, Dec. 1887		11m	1	
Schmidt, Carrie	2, Oct. 1888		6	1	
Schmidt, Casper B.	20, Feb. 1894		36	5	
Schmidt, Catharina	24, Jan. 1891		66	4	
Schmidt, Catharine N.	13, Oct. 1892		42	5	
Schmidt, Charles	1, June 1892		42	5	
Schmidt, Charles	21, June 1895		35	5	
Schmidt, Charles	23, Apr. 1896	22, Apr.	74	5	
Schmidt, Charles	4, May 1898	2, May	24- -16d	5	
Schmidt, Charles	22, Mar. 1901		40	8	
Schmidt, Charlotte	10, Jan. 1896	9, Jan.	56-11m	5	Laggemann
Schmidt, Charlotte	14, Sept 1897	13, Sept	69- 8m	5	Melchior
Schmidt, Christ.	31, Mar. 1888		3m- 8d	4	
Schmidt, Christian	7, May 1891		77	4	
Schmidt, Clara C.	6, Dec. 1899	5, Dec.	82- 2m	5	Breitholdt
Schmidt, Dorette	12, Apr. 1897	10, Apr.	67	5	
Schmidt, Dorothea A.	28, Mar. 1901		2m	8	
Schmidt, Edward	6, July 1897	5, July		5	
Schmidt, Elisabeth	25, Sept 1896	24, Sept	81	5	
Schmidt, Elisabeth	15, Nov. 1899	12, Nov.	60-11m	5	Gramann
Schmidt, Elise Maria	19, 21, Feb. 1894	19, Feb.	3m	5	
Schmidt, Elizabeth	30, Oct. 1889		55	1	
Schmidt, Ella	22, Apr. 1898	20, Apr.	22	5	
Schmidt, Elmer	15, July 1901		3m	8	
Schmidt, Emanuel	19, June 1901		69	8	
Schmidt, Emilie	14, Nov. 1898	13, Nov.	48	5	
Schmidt, Emma	21, July 1888		5m	1	
Schmidt, Emma	24, Jan. 1900	23, Jan.	31-10m	4	Waldvogel
Schmidt, Emma H.	14, June 1894		39	5	
Schmidt, Eugene	23, Dec. 1890		45	1	
Schmidt, Eugenie	23, Dec. 1893	21, Dec.	16- 7m	5	
Schmidt, F.	24, July 1901		66	8	
Schmidt, Ferdinand	8, Apr. 1896	7, Apr.	43	5	
Schmidt, Frances	16, July 1895		20m	5	
Schmidt, Franz	11, July 1887		2m	1	
Schmidt, Fred.	23, Mar. 1893		54	5	
Schmidt, Fred. S.	19, Mar. 1891		11d	4	
Schmidt, Frederick H.	5, Mar. 1891		20	4	
Schmidt, Friedrich	21, June 1888		3m	1	
Schmidt, Friedrich	20, Apr. 1898	19, Apr.	51- 8m	4	
Schmidt, George	19, 20, Aug. 1896	19, Aug.	55- 6m	5	
Schmidt, George	13, Nov. 1900		3	8	
Schmidt, Gottfried	27, Feb. 1897	24, Feb.	65- 9m	5	
Schmidt, Harry	4, Jan. 1893		19m	5	
Schmidt, Harry	23, June 1894		21m	5	
Schmidt, Heinrich	20, July 1896	18, July	60	5	
Schmidt, Helena	21, Oct. 1891		6	4	
Schmidt, Helene	29, Oct. 1891		4	4	
Schmidt, Henry	24, Oct. 1887		13	1	
Schmidt, Henry	29, Oct. 1889		20	1	
Schmidt, Henry	3, Feb. 1891		53	4	
Schmidt, Henry	17, Feb. 1894		44	5	
Schmidt, Henry	13, Apr. 1896		62	5	
Schmidt, Henry	17, Apr. 1901		80	8	
Schmidt, Henry J.	27, Jan. 1895		55	5	
Schmidt, Herman	29, Sept 1893		63	5	
Schmidt, Hubert	1, Dec. 1900		1	8	
Schmidt, Jacob	27, July 1888		31	1	
Schmidt, Jacob	10, Apr. 1895		73	5	
Schmidt, Jane	28, July 1891		3	4	
Schmidt, Jeanette	15, Feb. 1892		59	5	
Schmidt, Johan	21, Mar. 1893		40	5	
Schmidt, Johan	19, Aug. 1896	18, Aug.	27- 4m	5	
Schmidt, Johanna	9, Jan. 1889		8	1	
Schmidt, John	3, Aug. 1893		46	5	
Schmidt, John A.	13, June 1894		4	5	
Schmidt, John F.	19, June 1891		53	1	
Schmidt, John Henry	12, Oct. 1894		53	5	
Schmidt, Joseph A.	11, Oct. 1897	9, Oct.	81- 8m	5	
Schmidt, Karl	17, Apr. 1900	16, Apr.	40- 8m	5	

Name ****	Notice Date ****** ****	Death Date ***** ****	Age ***	Page ****	Maiden Name ****** ****
Schmidt, Karl L.	15, Feb. 1896	14, Feb.	2m-19d	5	
Schmidt, Karl Philip	18, May 1899	17, May	77- 1m	5	
Schmidt, Katharina Anna	15, Dec. 1896	14, Dec.	66	5	Müller
Schmidt, Katharine	7, Dec. 1893		37	5	
Schmidt, Katharine	19, July 1894		53	5	
Schmidt, L.	31, Mar. 1888		23- 7m- 2d	4	
Schmidt, Lambert	25, Mar. 1889		29	1	
Schmidt, Lizzie	1, July 1891		11m	1	
Schmidt, Lizzie	28, May 1901		21	8	
Schmidt, Louis	10, Jan. 1894		67	5	
Schmidt, Louis	16, May 1900	14, May	44	5	
Schmidt, Louisa	29, July 1887		9m	1	
Schmidt, Louise	30, Mar. 1895		32	5	
Schmidt, Louise	16, July 1897	15, July	79	5	
Schmidt, Ludwig	4, Aug. 1888		2	4	
Schmidt, Luisa	5, July 1898	4, July	21- 1m	5	
Schmidt, Margaretha	29, Jan. 1897	27, Jan.	76	5	Wagner
Schmidt, Maria Gertrud	28, Feb. 1896	26, Feb.	80	5	
Schmidt, Marie Elisabeth	21, Apr. 1897	20, Apr.	58- 9m	5	
Schmidt, Mary	6, Feb. 1894		66	5	
Schmidt, Mathilda	23, Sept 1887		14m	2	
Schmidt, Mathilde	8, Apr. 1896	7, Apr.	30- 1m	5	Jahn
Schmidt, Matilda	7, Mar. 1891		19	4	
Schmidt, Matilda S.	7, Jan. 1891		21	4	
Schmidt, Otto	19, Feb. 1891		10m	4	
Schmidt, Otto	2, Feb. 1892		12	5	
Schmidt, Peter	22, Mar. 1890		74	1	
Schmidt, Peter George	14, Aug. 1888		17m	1	
Schmidt, Philipp	18, Nov. 1891		44	4	
Schmidt, Philippina	21, Dec. 1899	20, Dec.		4	
Schmidt, Philomena	4, May 1894		37	5	
Schmidt, R.A.	6, May 1896	4, May	5- 3m	5	
Schmidt, Regina	23, Dec. 1893		16	5	
Schmidt, Robert Emil	2, May 1894		52	5	
Schmidt, Rose	31, Dec. 1890		77	4	
Schmidt, Salome	30, Oct. 1891		73	4	
Schmidt, Sophia	23, Sept 1891		5	4	
Schmidt, Sophia	18, Oct. 1895	15, Oct.	31	5	
Schmidt, Sus.	8, Nov. 1887		79	1	
Schmidt, Theodor Arnold Walter	25, June 1891	25, June	23- 2m-18d	* 4	
Schmidt, Wilhelmina	20, Apr. 1889		5	1	
Schmidt, Wilhelmine	21, Sept 1896	20, Sept		5	
Schmidt, William	30, May 1888		70	1	
Schmidt, William	8, Nov. 1889		10m	1	
Schmidt, William	12, Sept 1891		1	1	
Schmidt, William	5, July 1901		2	8	
Schmidt, William	10, Aug. 1901		79	8	
Schmidt, William C.	15, Jan. 1901		36	8	
Schmidt, William John	28, Dec. 1892		2	5	
Schmidt, Willie	3, Aug. 1887		11m	1	
Schmidter, Mary Anna	24, Apr. 1895		81	5	
Schmidthorst, Norma	7, June 1888		2	1	
Schmidthorst, Reuben	19, Mar. 1891		62	4	
Schmiech, Joseph	26, May 1892		35	5	
Schmied, C.	27, Dec. 1887		17m	1	
Schmiedeberg, Maria	2, June 1900	1, June		5	
Schmieder, Clarence O.	16, Mar. 1888		2m	1	
Schmieg, Caroline	25, Jan. 1898	23, Jan.	71	4	
Schmieg, Joseph	12, Dec. 1891		55	4	
Schmiesing, J.H.R.	22, June 1896	20, June	40- 2m	5	
Schmiesing, Louis	20, June 1888		5m	1	
Schmiesing, Lulu	27, June 1888		5m	1	
Schmit, Maria	17, Feb. 1894		70	5	
Schmitger, Emma	2, May 1895		38	5	
Schmitker, Adam W.	3, Apr. 1895		78	5	
Schmitker, Charles	10, July 1887		6m	1	
Schmitker, Heinrich	24, July 1899	23, July		5	
Schmits, Johan	22, Aug. 1898	21, Aug.	42- 6m	5	
Schmitt, A.	4, Apr. 1888		17	1	
Schmitt, Alma	27, July 1889		6	1	
Schmitt, Angelin	18, Jan. 1892		43	5	

Name	Notice Date	Death Date	Age	Page	Maiden Name
****	****** ****	***** ****	***	****	****** ****
Schmitt, Catharine	26, July 1895		66	5	
Schmitt, Conrad P.	21, July 1900	20, July	46	8	
Schmitt, Cornelius	20, July 1887		1	1	
Schmitt, Dora	1, Aug. 1888		11m	2	
Schmitt, Frank C.	20, July 1895		9m	5	
Schmitt, George	2, May 1901		73	8	
Schmitt, George J.	17, Feb. 1894		27	5	
Schmitt, Hilda F.	29, Dec. 1892		2m	5	
Schmitt, Johan	11, June 1898	10, June	72	5	
Schmitt, Johannes	9, Feb. 1899	7, Feb.	73- 5m	5	
Schmitt, Katharina	2, Aug. 1899	31, July	48	5	Schwank
Schmitt, Katharina Ursule	4, Mar. 1896	3, Mar.	75- 7m	5	Flick
Schmitt, Marie E.	24, 25, June 1896	23, June	42	4	Kauffmann
Schmitt, Philipp	6, Mar. 1896	5, Mar.	78	5	
Schmitt, Rosa	17, Aug. 1900		47	5	
Schmittker, Christina	15, Apr. 1892		10m	5	
Schmitz, Bernard	24, May 1892		50	5	
Schmitz, Bernhard	11, Jan. 1888		66	4	
Schmitz, Conrad	22, July 1898	21, July	11m-11d	4	
Schmitz, Francisca	12, Aug. 1899	11, Aug.	68- 9m	5	
Schmitz, George	11, Aug. 1900		21d	8	
Schmoll, Maria Anna	28, Apr. 1896	27, Apr.	69	5	Hellmann
Schmolt, Charles	3, July 1901		70	8	
Schmolt, Elisabeth	13, Nov. 1899	12, Nov.	60-11m	5	Gramann
Schmudde, Amelia	8, July 1898	7, July	45- 1m	4	Garnhauser
Schmuddl, Annie	5, Oct. 1889		26	1	
Schnabel, Anna	30, July 1892		70	5	
Schnabel, Anna Mathilda	21, Oct. 1895	18, Oct.	69	5	Meiering
Schnabel, C.E.	18, Oct. 1895	17, Oct.	51- 4m	5	
Schnabel, Norma C.	11, Jan. 1894		1	5	
Schnable, Edward	21, Jan. 1892		9m	5	
Schnedler, Anna	13, Feb. 1894		3	5	
Schnee, Peter Elmer	3, Mar. 1892		1m	5	
Schneebeck, Elisabeth	2, Feb. 1894		70	5	
Schneebeck, Martha	23, Mar. 1892		1	5	
Schneeberger, G.	25, Feb. 1901		43	8	
Schneemann, Henry F.	10, Mar. 1895		40	5	
Schneiboth, A.	29, Dec. 1887		3	4	
Schneider, Abraham	1, May 1901		36	8	
Schneider, Albert G.	8, June 1895		3	5	
Schneider, Amelia	2, Apr. 1898	1, Apr.	21- 9m-11d	5	
Schneider, Anna	16, Dec. 1891		55	4	
Schneider, Anna	5, Jan. 1892		33	5	
Schneider, Anna	18, Dec. 1900		39	8	
Schneider, Anna M.	15, July 1891		58	1	
Schneider, August F.	9, Sept 1893		24	5	
Schneider, Augusta	27, Nov. 1896	26, Nov.	75	5	Laile
Schneider, Balthasar	31, Jan. 1898	30, Jan.	79	5	
Schneider, Barbara	7, Feb. 1894		60	5	
Schneider, Ben	24, Nov. 1891		42	4	
Schneider, Bernard	22, Jan. 1898	21, Jan.	59	5	
Schneider, Bessie	2, Oct. 1888		21m	1	
Schneider, C.	11, Apr. 1900	10, Apr.	82	5	
Schneider, C.A. (Dr.)	13, Dec. 1895	12, Dec.	91	5	
Schneider, Caroline	21, Jan. 1893		32	5	
Schneider, Carrie J.	29, May 1894		4	5	
Schneider, Catharine	1, July 1896	29, June	71-11m	5	
Schneider, Clara	24, Apr. 1895		5	5	
Schneider, Clara	3, July 1901		1	8	
Schneider, Crescentia	27, June 1899	26, June	64- 2m	5	Jost
Schneider, David	27, July 1895		74	5	
Schneider, Edward	12, Dec. 1891		19	4	
Schneider, Edward	13, Apr. 1894		60	5	
Schneider, Edward	14, Nov. 1900		10m	8	
Schneider, Emma	3, Feb. 1891		7	4	
Schneider, Emma Katharine	11, July 1898	10, July	51	5	Kruse
Schneider, F.A.	3, Dec. 1888		63	1	
Schneider, Ferdinand	28, June 1893		7m	5	
Schneider, Fred.	23, Dec. 1893		21	5	
Schneider, Georg	22, July 1899	20, July	79- 2m	5	
Schneider, George	23, June 1888		14m	1	

Name ****	Notice Date ****** ****	Death Date ***** ****	Age ***	Page ****	Maiden Name ****** ****
Schneider, George	9, Mar. 1895		37	5	
Schneider, Gertrude	15, Mar. 1889		61	1	
Schneider, Gustav	30, Nov. 1887		30	4	
Schneider, H.	25, Nov. 1887		3- 9m	1	
Schneider, Harry	11, Apr. 1890		8m	1	
Schneider, Helena	2, July 1901		71	8	
Schneider, Helene	2, Oct. 1895	1, Oct.	1- 3m	5	
Schneider, Henry	7, May 1891		40	4	
Schneider, Henry	23, May 1895		59	5	
Schneider, Isaac	27, Feb. 1901		47	8	
Schneider, J.	10, May 1895		14m	5	
Schneider, J.	21, Nov. 1900		82	8	
Schneider, Jacob	11, Aug. 1900		49	8	
Schneider, Jakob	24, Oct. 1900		55	8	
Schneider, John	17, Sept 1889	16, Dec.	32- 6m	* 1	
Schneider, John	25, Mar. 1890		72	1	
Schneider, John	7, May 1895		17m	5	
Schneider, Karl	5, Oct. 1896	5, Oct.	68-11m	5	
Schneider, Katharine	7, Feb. 1899	5, Feb.		5	Geller
Schneider, Kunigunda	7, May 1891		80	4	
Schneider, Leopoldine	19, Aug. 1889		25	1	
Schneider, Lorenz	8, Nov. 1898	6, Nov.	76	4	
Schneider, Louis	26, Aug. 1891		1	4	
Schneider, Maggie	20, Mar. 1901		6m	1	
Schneider, Margaret	7, Dec. 1887			1	
Schneider, Margaretha	1, Aug. 1890			1	
Schneider, Margaretha	26, Sept 1895	25, Sept	64- 9m	5	
Schneider, Maria	13, 14, Nov. 1895	12, Nov.	77- 5m	5	Hack
Schneider, Marie	1, June 1893		8m	5	
Schneider, Mary	2, June 1893		54	5	
Schneider, Mary	10, Aug. 1901		52	8	
Schneider, Mary D.	16, Jan. 1890		66	1	
Schneider, Mary G.	8, May 1889		65	1	
Schneider, Oswald	23, Oct. 1900		41	8	
Schneider, P.W.	11, July 1898	9, July	58	5	
Schneider, Peter	11, Apr. 1889		62	1	
Schneider, Rachel	21, Nov. 1891		8m	4	
Schneider, Richard	30, Nov. 1898	28, Nov.	28- 5m	4	
Schneider, Rudolf	2, Feb. 1901		39	8	
Schneider, William	21, July 1891		6m	4	
Schneider, William H.	9, July 1887		2	1	
Schneiders, Anna	17, Sept 1901		2m	8	
Schnell, Anna	18, July 1887		6m	1	
Schnell, Charles	21, July 1888		21	1	
Schnell, Charles	23, Nov. 1893		25	5	
Schnell, Elisabeth	16, May 1891		30	2	
Schnell, Frederick K.	27, Mar. 1894		44	5	
Schnell, George	25, Jan. 1892		2	5	
Schnell, Henry	9, Mar. 1900	7, Mar.	45- 5m	8	
Schnell, Mary F.	17, Mar. 1891		29	4	
Schnelle, Fred.	28, July 1890		30	1	
Schneller, Charles	27, July 1888		43	1	
Schneller, Milton	29, Aug. 1900			5	
Schnerbrock, Gustav	21, Nov. 1900		62	8	
Schnier, Friedrich Johan	27, Jan. 1898	26, Jan.	57-10m	5	
Schnittger, Johan Herman	2, Aug. 1897	31, July	87	5	
Schnittger, L.H.	29, Aug. 1895	27, Aug.	21- 5m	5	
Schnotz, Val.	23, Apr. 1888		56	1	
Schnuck, Henry	11, Aug. 1891		1d	4	
Schnuck, Herman	8, Dec. 1900		59	8	
Schnuck, Michael	20, July 1893		42	5	
Schnun, Peter	3, Apr. 1895		38	5	
Schnöpfer, Josephine	11, June 1895		4m	5	
Schobbe, Catharina Maria	13, Sept 1899	12, Sept	74- 1m	4	Kampmeyer
Schobe, John	16, Sept 1887		62	1	
Schobel, A.	30, Sept 1889		4- 6m	1	
Schobel, Emma	8, Aug. 1893		1	5	
Schobel, William	4, Jan. 1893		46	5	
Schober, Katharine	24, Apr. 1900	23, Apr.	70- 6m	8	Steinert
Schober, Margaret A.	23, Jan. 1901		65	8	
Schoch, Antonia	1, May 1894		65	5	

Name ****	Notice Date ****** ****	Death Date ***** ****	Age ***	Page ****	Maiden Name ****** ****
Schock, Pauline	10, Dec. 1892		53	5	
Schock, Rosa	28, Mar. 1890		59	1	
Schodrowsky, Fannie	12, Apr. 1889		35	1	
Schoech, Peter	4, Sept 1891		44	4	
Schoeffer, Alma	25, Jan. 1894		4m	5	
Schoek, Benedict	24, Dec. 1895	22, Dec.	63- 2m	5	
Schoellhammer, Babette	22, July 1898	21, July	76	4	
Schoelwer, Karl	8, Nov. 1900		1m	8	
Schoemer, F.W. (Dr)	1, Oct. 1901		46	1	
Schoenberger, J.A.	29, Jan. 1898	28, Jan.		4	
Schoenberger, Phil.	12, Jan. 1898	9, Jan.	60- - 4	4	
Schoenebaum, John	27, Sept 1890		16	1	
Schoeneberger, G.F.	4, Sept 1901		72	8	
Schoenecker, Rosa	12, Sept 1896	11, Sept	7- 9m	5	
Schoenfeld, Betty	10, Feb. 1891		4m	4	
Schoenfeld, Rose	15, Sept 1900		21	5	
Schoenhals, Charles	7, Oct. 1891		64- -15d	4	
Schoenhoft, Mary	9, Aug. 1887		43	1	
Schoenkopf, Adelheid	11, July 1892		1	5	
Schoenleben, Tilly	28, May 1892		15	5	
Schoensiegel, Margaret	14, Jan. 1892		3	1	
Schoenstedt, Henriette L.	1, Aug. 1893		70	5	
Schoepperklano, Stella	7, Mar. 1901			8	
Schoettekotte, J.G.	14, Apr. 1891		79	4	
Schoettger, Fred.	15, July 1892		34	5	
Schoettinger, Anna	1, Oct. 1887		6m	1	
Schoettinger, Charles	18, Dec. 1893		3	5	
Schol, Jacob	13, Dec. 1900		45	8	
Scholl, Daniel Otto	6, Aug. 1896	5, Aug.	17- 6m	5	
Scholl, Marg.	26, Apr. 1889		58	1	
Scholle, Arthur	6, Sept 1893		2m	5	
Scholle, Elisabeth	20, July 1895		76	5	
Scholle, Franz	31, May 1892		70	5	
Scholle, Harry	3, Feb. 1893		1	5	
Scholle, Mary	2, Aug. 1893		64	5	
Scholz, George	14, Feb. 1893		5	5	
Schomaker, Elisabeth Josephine	26, June 1900	25, June	52- - 9d	8	Richter
Schomaker, Frank B.	10, Aug. 1889		4m	1	
Schomberg, Bernard	25, Oct. 1900		35	8	
Schone, Gerhard Heinrich	21, Apr. 1897	20, Apr.	41- 5m	5	
Schonhoft, Marie	21, Nov. 1893		37	5	
Schooby, George	5, Aug. 1890		5m	1	
Schooley, Mary E.	22, May 1888		60	1	
Schoonover, Anna	11, Dec. 1891		14	4	
Schopmeier, Alfred B.	23, July 1895		2m	5	
Schopmeyer, Herman	11, May 1889		21m	1	
Schopper, Charles	11, Mar. 1890		24	1	
Schopper, Philippine	4, May 1898	3, May	78	5	
Schorr, Herman A.	12, Jan. 1889		21m	1	
Schorr, Johan	8, Aug. 1895	7, Aug.	73-11m	5	
Schorr, William	18, June 1901		21	8	
Schott, Alice E.	15, May 1889		16m	1	
Schott, Anthony	2, July 1892		31	5	
Schott, Charles	1, Nov. 1892		33	5	
Schott, Christ.	29, Apr. 1889		7m	1	
Schott, Elisabeth	23, Jan. 1896	22, Jan.	64- 4m	5	Volz
Schott, Elsie	27, May 1899	27, May	5m-20d	4	
Schott, Frida	10, June 1889		2	1	
Schott, George	7, Dec. 1887		29	1	
Schott, Isabella	11, Nov. 1891		2m	1	
Schott, Johan	30, Jan. 1897	29, Jan.	69-10m	5	
Schott, John C.	30, June 1888		80	1	
Schott, Joseph	23, Jan. 1896	22, Jan.	40- 9m	5	
Schott, Karl	26, Nov. 1895	25, Nov.	64	5	
Schott, Lillie	25, July 1894		1m	5	
Schott, Nora M.	5, Sept 1888		5m	2	
Schott, Thomas J.	24, Dec. 1893		1	5	
Schott, William	25, Jan. 1894		41	5	
Schottenfels, John	29, July 1887		47	1	
Schottmiller, Elise	24, Feb. 1895	22, Feb.	34- 3m	5	
Schottmüller, Julia C.	5, July 1887		5w	1	

Name ****	Notice Date ****** ****	Death Date ***** ****	Age ***	Page ****	Maiden Name ****** ****
Schouder, Charles	28, Apr. 1891		2	4	
Schrader, Adolphine	20, Jan. 1899	18, Jan.	86	5	
Schrader, Carrie	10, Mar. 1888		13m	1	
Schrader, Christian	1, Mar. 1893		64	5	
Schrader, Clara	19, Oct. 1891		3	1	
Schrader, John A.	9, Oct. 1901		76	5	
Schrader, Kate	3, Oct. 1901		78	8	
Schrader, Leopold	22, July 1901		2	8	
Schrader, Otto	19, Aug. 1895	17, Aug.	11- 6m	5	
Schrader, Wilhelm	6, Jan. 1899	5, Jan.	72	4	
Schradski, Alexander	14, May 1895		35	5	
Schraeder, Catharina	11, Apr. 1900	9, Apr.	82	5	
Schraer, Carolina E.	8, June 1894		10m	5	
Schraffenberger, Adam	6, Nov. 1894		11m	5	
Schraffenberger, Katharine	12, Feb. 1896	11, Feb.	66- 4m	5	Vöster
Schraffenberger, Tillie	9, Nov. 1893		8	5	
Schrage, Mary	19, Nov. 1889		7m	1	
Schramm, Gertrud	17, July 1890		16	1	
Schramm, Magdalena	9, Feb. 1898	8, Feb.	28- 5m	5	
Schramm, Maggie	16, Aug. 1890		1	1	
Schramm, Mary	5, Jan. 1901		22	8	
Schramm, Philipp	28, Mar. 1893		49	5	
Schrand, Henry	20, May 1893		24	5	
Schrank, Frank	2, Sept 1891		1- -16d	4	
Schrantz, Emma	31, July 1900		9	5	
Schrantz, William	3, Dec. 1888		4	1	
Schraud, Gertrud	13, May 1897	11, May	71- 4m	5	Sanders
Schraud, Thekla	9, Apr. 1889		2	1	
Schraud, Tilly	12, June 1891		11m	4	
Schrauder, John	3, Feb. 1894		6	5	
Schray, Barbara	21, Apr. 1895		61	5	
Schreiber, Andreas	13, Mar. 1894		64	5	
Schreiber, Carrie	20, Feb. 1894		4d	5	
Schreiber, Charlotte	1, Oct. 1887		3w	1	
Schreiber, Charlotte	14, Feb. 1891		17	4	
Schreiber, Emma	26, Aug. 1889		15m	1	
Schreiber, G.M.	4, Mar. 1889		7	1	
Schreiber, J.	26, Apr. 1889		4	1	
Schreiber, Joseph	28, Apr. 1897	27, Apr.	68- 8m	5	
Schreiber, Louisa	17, July 1895		18m	5	
Schreiber, Mary	16, July 1892		6m	5	
Schreiber, Therese	1, Mar. 1889		23	1	
Schrencker, Joseph	11, Dec. 1891		5	4	
Schrenker, Ruther	1, Mar. 1894		1m	5	
Schreve, Ada	23, Dec. 1893		24	5	
Schriewer, J.H.	26, Apr. 1900	25, Apr.	39- 7m	5	
Schrimp, Archibald	25, June 1895		19	5	
Schrimper, George G.	24, Apr. 1896	22, Apr.	37	5	
Schrist, Alice M.	9, June 1891		31	4	
Schriver, Raymond	31, Oct. 1900		3	8	
Schroder, August	23, Aug. 1890		46	1	
Schroder, Dora	9, Aug. 1897	8, Aug.	72	5	
Schroeder,	19, July 1887		11d	1	
Schroeder, Anna	21, Nov. 1897	20, Nov.	12	4	
Schroeder, August	27, Sept 1890		45	1	
Schroeder, August	8, May 1901		42	8	
Schroeder, Bernard	27, July 1894		77	5	
Schroeder, Bernhard	28, May 1892		67	5	
Schroeder, Catharine	7, Aug. 1901		78	8	
Schroeder, Charles	3, July 1901		6	8	
Schroeder, Clifford C.	14, Nov. 1893		14	5	
Schroeder, Edward	15, Nov. 1887		3- 4m	4	
Schroeder, Elisabeth	10, Apr. 1895		64	5	
Schroeder, Emma	30, Apr. 1891		10	4	
Schroeder, F.	24, Jan. 1901		8m	8	
Schroeder, Frederick	1, Aug. 1891		60	4	
Schroeder, Heinrich	28, July 1898	27, July	61	5	
Schroeder, Henry	4, Apr. 1895		31	5	
Schroeder, Herman	8, June 1895		74	5	
Schroeder, Johan	13, Nov. 1899	11, Nov.	74- 7m	5	
Schroeder, John	26, Feb. 1901		73	8	

Name	Notice Date	Death Date	Age	Page	Maiden Name
****	****** ****	***** ****	***	****	****** ****
Schroeder, John	19, Aug. 1901		43	8	
Schroeder, Lillie	18, Feb. 1891		4	4	
Schroeder, Magdalena	2, July 1892		2	5	
Schroeder, Sophie	1, Oct. 1900		47	5	
Schroer, Anna	9, Feb. 1894		29	5	
Schroer, Barbara	3, Sept 1890		58	1	
Schroer, John H.E.	22, July 1893		2m	5	
Schroer, Leonie	24, July 1894		7m	5	
Schroer, Maria	8, May 1900	5, May	75- 4m	5	Klinkhammer
Schroer, Ruth H.	28, May 1891		18	4	
Schroerlucke, Carl L.	28, Oct. 1891		2	4	
Schroeter, Fred	1, Aug. 1887		39	1	
Schrohenlohler, Joseph	15, Aug. 1891		4	4	
Schrorr, George	19, Oct. 1901		27	8	
Schrotel, Charles	10, Dec. 1891		47	4	
Schroth, Friedrich H.	18, Oct. 1899	17, Oct.	29- 7m	7	
Schroth, G.	24, July 1894		45	5	
Schroth, Gottl.	18, Dec. 1888		79	2	
Schroth, Johan Georg	2, Apr. 1900	1, Apr.	84- 5m	8	
Schroth, Katharine	24, Feb. 1894		73	5	
Schroth, Minnie	11, July 1887		17m	1	
Schrott, Charles	27, July 1889		15m	1	
Schrout, Nicholas	22, June 1901		77	8	
Schruer, Harry	28, May 1891		3	4	
Schruntz, Mary	29, Sept 1887		62	4	
Schrätz, H.	7, Dec. 1887		28	1	
Schrödel, Charles	21, Mar. 1890		8m	1	
Schröder, Alma	20, July 1893		3m	5	
Schröder, Anna	6, July 1896	5, July	30-	5	Gerdes
Schröder, Caroline	30, Nov. 1892		5	5	
Schröder, Charles	21, July 1891		30	4	
Schröder, Christina	16, Mar. 1893		40	5	
Schröder, Ed.	3, Sept 1901		8	8	
Schröder, Fred.	22, Nov. 1887		83	1	
Schröder, Fred.	9, Feb. 1894		34	5	
Schröder, Henry	19, Mar. 1890		56	1	
Schröder, J.B.	25, July 1894		61	5	
Schröder, Joseph	11, Apr. 1891		2	4	
Schröder, Karl	22, June 1897	21, JUne	54	5	
Schröder, Liolo	25, June 1891		1m	4	
Schröder, Louis	10, May 1888		9m	1	
Schröder, Mathilda Eugenia	24, Mar. 1896	23, Mar.	16	5	
Schröder, Peter	19, July 1887		4w	1	
Schröder, Sophia	23, Oct. 1889		73- 6m	1	
Schröder, Wendel	15, June 1896	14, June	49- 2m	5	
Schröter, Herman	17, May 1889		39	1	
Schubach, Phil.	31, Mar. 1897	30, Mar.	67	5	
Schuber, Jakob	15, Aug. 1891		27	4	
Schubert, Edw.	11, July 1901		6d	5	
Schubert, John	13, Sept 1888		68	1	
Schubert, Marie Mollie	28, Sept 1897	27, Sept	13-10m	5	
Schubert, Theodore C.	23, Mar. 1900	23, Mar.	37- 7m	8	
Schubert, Willi	17, July 1889	16, July	17m	4	
Schuch, Johan Valentin	11, Feb. 1897	10, Feb.	46- 9m	5	
Schuchard, Fred.	14, Apr. 1891		79	4	
Schuchardt, Anna	1, May 1901			8	
Schuchardt, August	16, June 1898	15, June	17m-23d	5	
Schuchardt, Herman	21, Aug. 1894		35	5	
Schuchardt, Otto	18, Nov. 1895	16, Nov.	6- 8m	5	
Schuchart, Katharine	30, Aug. 1897	27, Aug.	18- 9m	5	
Schuchart, Michael	12, June 1889		3	1	
Schuchart, Phil.	17, May 1889		56	1	
Schucht, Ethel	11, Aug. 1900		2	8	
Schucht, Sitta	22, Sept 1891		43	1	
Schuck, Margaret	25, Jan. 1889		45	1	
Schuckmann, Angela	6, July 1898	4, July	68- 6m	5	Steinke
Schuckmann, George	11, June 1901		40	8	
Schuehler, David	24, 25, Oct. 1887	23, Oct.	56- 3m	4	
Schueler, Mary M.	17, Feb. 1894		4m	5	
Schuermann, Anna	14, Dec. 1888		74	1	
Schuermann, Caroline	29, Sept 1897	29, Sept		5	Rethmann

Name	Notice Date	Death Date	Age	Page	Maiden Name
****	****** ****	***** ****	***	****	****** ****
Schuermann, Franz	5, July 1898	4, July	82- 9m	5	
Schuermann, Fred.	3, Jan. 1893		26	5	
Schuermann, Theodor	23, Apr. 1891		1	4	
Schuermann, Wilhelm	4, Apr. 1899	3, Apr.	1- 3m	5	
Schuesler, M.	17, Oct. 1900		54	8	
Schuette, Auguste	30, Nov. 1897	29, Nov.		5	Groen
Schuette, Bernhard	7, May 1891		55	4	
Schuetz, Thekla (Sr. Sylvester)	17, Sept 1901		20	8	
Schuetze, Adolph	8, Feb. 1901		78	8	
Schuetze, Anna	18, July 1887		50	1	
Schueßler, Caroline	23, June 1894		7m	5	
Schugarmann, Jakob	6, June 1889		8m	1	
Schuh, Anton	25, Mar. 1898	24, Mar.	50	5	
Schuh, August	7, Aug. 1901		1m	8	
Schuh, Clara	25, May 1901		24	8	
Schuh, Henry	7, Feb. 1890		28	1	
Schuh, Johan Matthaus	19, Jan. 1899	17, Jan.	56- 5m	5	
Schuhmacher, Dietrich	7, Feb. 1890			1	
Schuhmacher, Henry	19, Mar. 1890		56	1	
Schuhmacher, Rosa	2, Dec. 1889		3	1	
Schuhmacher, Theresa	20, Mar. 1889		55	1	
Schuhmann, Andreas	22, Nov. 1899	20, Nov.	40	5	
Schuhmann, Elisabeth	5, Oct. 1896	4, Oct.	57-10m	5	Gärtner
Schuk, Thomas	6, Feb. 1896	4, Feb.	37- 1m	5	
Schule, Gertrude	3, Apr. 1895		3	5	
Schuler, Alois	30, Aug. 1900		48	5	
Schuler, Anna	22, Feb. 1899	20, Feb.	66- 3m	5	
Schuler, Elizabeth	2, Feb. 1892		58	5	
Schuler, Erich R.	24, July 1896	23, July	52	5	
Schuler, George	11, Sept 1894		26	5	
Schuler, H.	18, Apr. 1888		35	1	
Schuler, Joseph	22, Oct. 1891		33	1	
Schulhof, Henry	18, Nov. 1891		38	4	
Schulhoff, Henry E.	26, Dec. 1900		17	8	
Schuller, John	4, Aug. 1890		48	1	
Schullmeyer, August	1, Aug. 1888		39	2	
Schulmann, Henry	7, Mar. 1894		45	5	
Schulmeyer, Wilhelm	27, Nov. 1896	26, Nov.		5	
Schulte, (twins)	22, Oct. 1900		1d	8	
Schulte, Albert	19, Mar. 1901		30	8	
Schulte, Anna H.	28, Feb. 1891		59	4	
Schulte, Anna M.	23, July 1895		71	5	
Schulte, Anna N.	21, Nov. 1893		69	5	
Schulte, Bernard	23, Aug. 1887		11d	1	
Schulte, Bernard	30, Jan. 1901		32	8	
Schulte, Caroline	22, June 1895		29	5	
Schulte, Charles	22, Aug. 1900		2	5	
Schulte, Christine	13, June 1901		5m	8	
Schulte, Edward	12, July 1893		21d	5	
Schulte, Eugene	12, May 1895		9d	5	
Schulte, Flora	22, Feb. 1893		5m	5	
Schulte, Francis	6, July 1893		16d	5	
Schulte, Georg Heinrich	9, Nov. 1898	8, Nov.	82- 6m	4	
Schulte, H.	28, Mar. 1898	27, Mar.	49- -25d	5	
Schulte, Heinrich	2, Apr. 1896	1, Apr.	32- 2m	5	
Schulte, Heinrich	5, Jan. 1901		21	8	
Schulte, Heinrich Wilhelm	9, Apr. 1900	7, Apr.	74- 3m	4	
Schulte, Henry	11, Nov. 1892		43	4	
Schulte, J.A.	2, Aug. 1898	1, Aug.	90- 6m	4	
Schulte, Johan	27, Apr. 1896		73- 5m	5	
Schulte, Johan H.	8, June 1893		72	5	
Schulte, John	10, Jan. 1888		1- 3m	4	
Schulte, John	16, Oct. 1891		33	1	
Schulte, John H.	14, Apr. 1893		52	5	
Schulte, Joseph	27, Feb. 1894		61	5	
Schulte, Joseph	25, Dec. 1894		31	5	
Schulte, Joseph G.	14, Jan. 1901		82	8	
Schulte, Kate	7, June 1890		30	1	
Schulte, Katharina	19, Sept 1898	17, Sept	45- 6m	5	Schmidt
Schulte, Lizzie	20, May 1893		17	5	
Schulte, Louis Heinrich	25, Dec. 1899	23, Dec.	5- 4m	5	

Name	Notice Date	Death Date	Age	Page	Maiden Name
****	****** ****	***** ****	***	****	****** ****
Schulte, M.	15, Dec. 1887		13	1	
Schulte, Maria	16, Feb. 1901			8	
Schulte, Mary	5, June 1891		26	1	
Schulte, Mina A.	24, Feb. 1888		69	4	
Schulte, Rob.	4, Sept 1901		28	8	
Schulte, Theodor	5, Jan. 1892		48	5	
Schulte, Thomas	5, Feb. 1896	4, Feb.	38- 1m	5	
Schulte, Wilhelmine Regina	4, Apr. 1900	3, Apr.	70- -14d	8	Ahlert
Schulten, Adelheid Maria	12, July 1899	11, July	61- 2m	5	Heile
Schulten, Franziskus Johan	21, Oct. 1895	18, Oct.	2	5	
Schulten, Johan Gerhard	27, Jan. 1896	26, Jan.	80	5	
Schultheis, Anna	9, Mar. 1894		15m	5	
Schultheis, Michael	13, Apr. 1896	12, Apr.		5	
Schultheis, Peter	13, Mar. 1901		51	8	
Schultian, Bernhardt H.	29, Dec. 1892		36	5	
Schults, Katie	24, Feb. 1894		11	5	
Schulty, Christine	1, Dec. 1900		42	8	
Schultz, Agnes	22, Apr. 1891		66	4	
Schultz, Dora	3, Mar. 1891		62	4	
Schultz, Frank	25, June 1896	24, June	74	5	
Schultz, Franz	17, June 1896	15, June	77-10m	5	
Schultz, Friedrich (Dr.)	28, Oct. 1897	27, Oct.	57-10m	5	
Schultz, George	27, Nov. 1894		1m	5	
Schultz, Henry	18, Nov. 1894		3w	5	
Schultz, Laura	2, Aug. 1893		13m	5	
Schultz, Mary	17, Jan. 1893		22	5	
Schultz, Rudolph	18, July 1891		14d	1	
Schultz, Theresa	27, Oct. 1888		67	1	
Schultze, Charles	1, Nov. 1892		20	5	
Schultze, Elizabeth W.	23, Jan. 1891		59	4	
Schultze, Gustie	17, Feb. 1891		6m	4	
Schultze, Laura	22, July 1887		1	1	
Schulz, Alfred	10, Aug. 1894		5m	5	
Schulz, Ernst	12, July 1899	1, July	38-10m	5	
Schulz, Franz	2, July 1896	1, July	65	5	
Schulz, Johanne	23, Mar. 1893		69	5	
Schulz, Joseph R.	1, June 1893		5m	5	
Schulz, Julia	4, Apr. 1890		28	1	
Schulz, Julia	4, Jan. 1893		2	5	
Schulz, Julius	20, July 1893		11	5	
Schulz, Katie	23, June 1897	22, June	37- 3m	5	Moesta
Schulz, Louisa	27, Nov. 1894		51	5	
Schulz, Pauline	27, Feb. 1896	26, Feb.	73	5	Roesler
Schulz, Wilhelm F.	6, Apr. 1896			4	
Schulze, Anna	6, Sept 1901		39	8	
Schulze, Anna D.	18, June 1889		4	1	
Schulze, Christian	4, Nov. 1895	1, Nov.	59- 7m	5	
Schulze, E.A.	3, Dec. 1896	1, Dec.	20-10m	5	
Schulze, Frank	11, Mar. 1890		48	1	
Schulze, Louis	25, Jan. 1892		3	5	
Schulze, Martin	23, July 1890		70	1	
Schulzen, Elizabeth	14, Mar. 1891		105	4	
Schum, Henry	21, Jan. 1894		49	5	
Schum, Lizzie	10, Dec. 1892		8	5	
Schumacher, Alexander	10, Oct. 1889		58	1	
Schumacher, Casper	24, May 1901		70	8	
Schumacher, Charles	4, Sept 1890		69	1	
Schumacher, Dietrich	6, Feb. 1890	6, Feb.	11m-24d	1	
Schumacher, Ferdinand	27, Feb. 1894		43	5	
Schumacher, Johannes	23, June 1896	22, June	85- 9m	5	
Schumacher, John T.	12, May 1893		68	5	
Schumacher, Louis	29, Dec. 1892		32	5	
Schumacher, Thomas	13, Sept 1900		45	5	
Schumacher, W.	19, Dec. 1898	17, Dec.	56-11m	4	
Schumaker, Bertha	26, Dec. 1900		12d	8	
Schumann, Charles P.H.	22, Dec. 1892		1	5	
Schumann, Elisabeth	29, Oct. 1894		77	5	
Schumann, Fred. E.	8, July 1891		61	4	
Schumann, Fridolin	23, May 1894		63	5	
Schumann, William	23, Aug. 1887		27	1	
Schunthorst, Henry	16, May 1892		55	5	

Name	Notice Date	Death Date	Age	Page	Maiden Name
****	****** ****	***** ****	***	****	****** ****
Schupping, Ferd.	30, July 1890		20	1	
Schurbrook, Joseph	25, Feb. 1901		31	8	
Schurmann, Henrietta	28, May 1900	25, May	62- 1m	8	Möller
Schurmann, Joseph	23, Feb. 1893		24	5	
Schurtz, Maria	12, Jan. 1897	10, Jan.	76	5	
Schurtz, Thomas	24, July 1890		1	1	
Schuster, Alfred	10, Sept 1887		22	2	
Schuster, Catharine	26, Jan. 1894		18	5	
Schuster, Ed.	7, June 1888		11m	1	
Schuster, Elizabeth	1, Apr. 1890		31	1	
Schuster, Fred. J.	22, Nov. 1893		1m	5	
Schuster, Georg	20, Aug. 1888		10m	1	
Schuster, Henricke	12, May 1893		71	5	
Schuster, Ida	24, Feb. 1892		4m	5	
Schuster, John	27, May 1889		2	1	
Schuster, Karoline	12, Sept 1888		31	1	
Schuster, Lawrence	4, July 1901		82	8	
Schuster, Louise	9, Nov. 1896	8, Nov.	6- 5m	5	
Schuster, Mary	18, Aug. 1890		2	1	
Schuster, Veronica	23, Aug. 1890		3m	1	
Schutt, Charles F.	12, July 1889		8m	1	
Schutt, Elisabeth M.	4, July 1895		37	5	
Schutt, Ethel	27, Mar. 1901		3m	8	
Schutte, George	26, Feb. 1888		30	4	
Schuttenhelm, Andreas	4, Dec. 1895	3, Dec.	55-10m	5	
Schutz, Johan Matthaeus	18, Jan. 1899	17, Jan.	56- 5m	5	
Schwab, Bertha	7, June 1901		15	8	
Schwab, Catharine	10, Dec. 1891		52	4	
Schwab, Cecilia	17, Apr. 1894		18	5	
Schwab, Clara	15, Jan. 1890		16d	1	
Schwab, Ed.	20, July 1901		45	8	
Schwab, Emeline	4, Jan. 1901		82	5	
Schwab, Fannie H.	8, May 1891		34	4	
Schwab, Gottlieb	20, 22, Dec. 1892	19, Dec.	70- 8m-19d	* 5	
Schwab, Gottlieb	30, Nov. 1900		25	8	
Schwab, Joel	19, July 1893		64	5	
Schwab, Katharine	27, Jan. 1896	25, Jan.	79	5	
Schwab, Mary M.	17, Apr. 1891		78	4	
Schwab, Solomena	3, Feb. 1894		74	5	
Schwab, Susanne	19, Dec. 1895	16, Dec.	72- 2m	5	
Schwab, Wihelm	8, Aug. 1891		10m	4	
Schwabdis, August	30, Dec. 1891		68	4	
Schwach, Margaret	19, Dec. 1900		41	8	
Schwager, Margaretha	17, Mar. 1896	16, Mar.	36	5	Winkelbach
Schwaibold, Gustav	3, Nov. 1896	2, Nov.	14- 7m	5	
Schwan, Lorenz	24, June 1889	23, June	10m- 3d	1	
Schwan, Lotta	24, Mar. 1888		10	1	
Schwander, Louise	10, Aug. 1900		1d	8	
Schwaner, Philip	30, May 1894		64	5	
Schwank, Catharine	2, Apr. 1891		86	4	
Schwank, Margaretha	22, Nov. 1893		83	5	
Schwann, Elisabeth	11, May 1897	10, May	52	5	Heid
Schwarb, Crescentia	28, Jan. 1901		84	8	
Schwartz, Anna Katharina	15, Feb. 1897	12, Feb.	70	5	
Schwartz, Fredericka W.	10, Sept 1887		68	2	
Schwartz, George	13, Dec. 1893		85	5	
Schwartz, Gottlieb	20, June 1888		12	1	
Schwartz, Helena	21, Jan. 1891		65	4	
Schwartz, Jacob	3, May 1897	2, May	53	5	
Schwartz, John B.	9, Aug. 1887		8m	1	
Schwartz, Josie	16, Aug. 1890		5	1	
Schwartz, Katharine	14, Aug. 1887		63	1	
Schwartz, Lena	29, May 1888		63	2	
Schwartz, Marie	25, Aug. 1900		5m	5	
Schwartz, Martin	25, Sept 1889		55	1	
Schwartz, Rose A.	6, Mar. 1889		6	1	
Schwartz, Theodor E.	9, Mar. 1895		2m	5	
Schwartz, Yetta	10, Dec. 1900		88	8	
Schwartzen, M.	22, Aug. 1900		68	5	
Schwartzrauber, Joseph	12, Feb. 1901		55	8	
Schwarz, Emma	24, May 1889		10	1	

Name	Notice Date	Death Date	Age	Page	Maiden Name
****	****** ****	***** ****	***	****	****** ****
Schwarz, Friedricka	29, May 1889		3	1	
Schwarz, H.	9, Mar. 1895		2m	5	
Schwarz, J.	3, Dec. 1888		21	1	
Schwarz, Jacob	19, Sept 1898	16, Sept	53-10m	5	
Schwarz, Johan	23, Aug. 1900		70	8	
Schwarz, Katharine	25, May 1900	22, May	68- 3m	8	
Schwarz, Maria	23, Aug. 1900		6m	8	
Schwarz, Otto G.	17, Mar. 1891		18	4	
Schwarz, Philippine	28, May 1896	27, May	70- 9m	5	
Schwarz, Rose	31, Jan. 1891		92	4	
Schwarz, Sophia	18, Nov. 1893		1	5	
Schwarz, William J.	11, Mar. 1889		24	1	
Schwatty, Ben.	22, June 1892		13m	5	
Schwebel, Louis F.	25, Jan. 1893		59	5	
Schweeting, Christina	11, Apr. 1899	9, Apr.	76- 8m	5	Brandt
Schwegel, Dan.	2, Feb. 1888		65	4	
Schwegemann, Anna	22, Jan. 1892		31	5	
Schwegmann, Henry	29, May 1901		68	8	
Schwegmann, J.	29, Sept 1887		60	4	
Schweier, William	25, Jan. 1893		70	5	
Schweigert, Johanna	19, Nov. 1889		46	1	
Schweigh, George	29, Apr. 1891		82	4	
Schweighart, Frank	8, Feb. 1901		6d	8	
Schweikert, Anna J.	8, Mar. 1894		5	5	
Schwein, Barbara	11, July 1893		61	5	
Schwein, Frank J.	3, July 1889		17	1	
Schwein, Friederika	6, July 1899	4, July	60	5	
Schwein, Georg	10, Sept 1896		34-10m	5	
Schwein, Harry	14, Aug. 1887		9m	1	
Schwein, Julia	13, Jan. 1891		1d	1	
Schwein, Margaret	27, June 1891		2m	1	
Schweitzer, Albert	29, Apr. 1891		19	4	
Schweitzer, Henry	28, May 1890		4m	1	
Schweitzer, J.J.	11, Apr. 1893		75	5	
Schweitzer, Johanna	16, Aug. 1894		66	5	
Schweitzer, John	10, Mar. 1893		52	5	
Schweitzer, Louis	16, May 1891		51	2	
Schweitzer, Marie	14, May 1900	12, May	54	8	
Schweitzer, Rosina	14, July 1892		6m	5	
Schweizer, Adolf	18, July 1887		34	1	
Schweizer, Harry	30, Aug. 1888		6m	1	
Schweizerdorf, Fred. J.	30, Sept 1893			5	
Schwend, Louis	28, Nov. 1900		26	8	
Schwener, Elenora	22, June 1895		1	5	
Schwening, J.	13, Aug. 1888		2	1	
Schweninger, Emma	4, Mar. 1897	3, Mar.	54- 3m	5	
Schweninger, Maximilian	15, Dec. 1896	13, Dec.	35-10m	5	
Schwenker, Eliza	25, June 1895		74	5	
Schwenkhaus, Adolph	27, July 1888		51	1	
Schwer, Dorothea Theresa	21, Feb. 1893		1d	5	
Schwerdfeger, Anna Maria	15, Nov. 1899	14, Nov.	70- 3m	5	Thielen
Schwerdfeger, George	4, June 1891		19m	4	
Schwerdt, John	3, Sept 1901		57	8	
Schwerin, Henriette	28, Apr. 1888		2	1	
Schwerin, Otto	18, Aug. 1899	17, Aug.	3- 6m	4	
Schwertmann, Mary	21, July 1890		29	1	
Schwessinger, Mary A.	4, July 1887		35	1	
Schwietering, Bernard	18, Jan. 1898	16, Jan.	24- 8m	5	
Schwietering, Herman	14, Nov. 1896	12, Nov.	25- 8m	5	
Schwieters, Mary	23, July 1895		23	5	
Schwill, Ferdinand A.	30, Sept 1898	28, Sept	61	4	
Schwind, Arthur	7, Oct. 1890		5	1	
Schwind, Mary L.	16, Sept 1891		22d	4	
Schwind, Oskar E.	18, 19, July 1894	17, July	31- 4m-10d	5	
Schwing, George	4, July 1901		82	8	
Schwing, John	10, Aug. 1901		45	8	
Schwinker, Eric H.	23, July 1895		5	5	
Schwinn, Katharina	23, Mar. 1894		3m	5	
Schwinn, Peter	18, July 1893		61	5	
Schwitzer, Hannah K.	8, Oct. 1900		52	8	
Schwitzer, Louise	28, Oct. 1893		89	5	

Name ****	Notice Date ****** ****	Death Date ***** ****	Age ***	Page ****	Maiden Name ****** ****
Schwitzgabel, Catharina	15, July 1892		64	5	
Schwoerer, Alma	15, Mar. 1894		3	5	
Schwoerer, B.	13, Mar. 1888		68	1	
Schwoerer, Christine	16, May 1900	14, May	73-10m	5	Steimle
Schwoerer, Karolina	10, Mar. 1897	9, Mar.	65- 9m	5	Laumann
Schwoerer, Kate	11, Feb. 1891		39	4	
Schwull, Ph.	3, Jan. 1888		82	1	
Schwäber, A. (Mrs)	10, Jan. 1888		31	4	
Schwägerle, Regina	25, Oct. 1887		63- 7m- 7d	1	
Schwäppe, Albert	25, Mar. 1892		1	5	
Schwörer, Johan M.	18, Feb. 1899	16, Feb.	80- 3m	5	Grossius
Schädel, Adam	25, July 1888		72	4	
Schädle, Anton	15, Nov. 1887		32	4	
Schäfer, A.	5, July 1887		4m	1	
Schäfer, Addie	23, Apr. 1891		5	4	
Schäfer, Agnes	13, Feb. 1899	11, Feb.	70- 3m	5	
Schäfer, Alexander	12, Feb. 1890		3	1	
Schäfer, Andrew	31, Mar. 1891		2	4	
Schäfer, Anna Elisabeth	4, June 1898	2, June	75	5	Volkmann
Schäfer, Arthur	2, Apr. 1891		1	4	
Schäfer, Barbara	25, Mar. 1889		38	1	
Schäfer, Catharine Mary	11, Mar. 1893		8d	5	
Schäfer, Christ	5, Jan. 1888		63	1	
Schäfer, Elisabeth	16, Apr. 1895		73	5	
Schäfer, Eva	7, Dec. 1887		65	1	
Schäfer, Frank	2, Dec. 1890		70	1,4	
Schäfer, Friedrich	3, Mar. 1898	1, Mar.	55	5	
Schäfer, Georg	4, Jan. 1890		27	1	
Schäfer, Gertrud	9, Oct. 1888		17m	1	
Schäfer, Gottlieb	20, Dec. 1899	18, Dec.		4	
Schäfer, Hugo	4, Mar. 1889		2	1	
Schäfer, Maggie	19, Jan. 1899	18, Jan.	37- 3m	5	
Schäfer, Margaretha Katharina	1, Mar. 1897	28, Feb.	4- 9m	5	
Schäfer, Phillipina	24, Apr. 1894		34	5	
Schäfer, Theodor	10, June 1889		3	1	
Schäfer, William	15, May 1889		52	1	
Schäfer, William F.	31, Dec. 1890		44	4	
Schärges, Lewis	20, Jan. 1890		6w	1	
Schätzle, Albert	7, July 1887		43	1	
Schätzle, Theodor	21, Feb. 1893		15	5	
Schöffer, Johan C.	27, Sept 1897	26, Sept	45	5	
Schöllhammer, Johan Lorenz	20, Jan. 1897	18, Jan.	74-10m	5	
Schöllhammer, John	7, June 1888		69	1	
Schöllhammer, Oscar	21, Mar. 1893		11m	5	
Schöls, L. Rebekka	15, Mar. 1893		66	5	
Schöltinger, Katie	22, July 1891		22d	4	
Schön, Charles	28, Dec. 1891		50	4	
Schöne, Wilhelm	5, Jan. 1892		61	5	
Schönenberger, Marcellus J.	23, July 1897	22, July	4m	5	
Schönfeld, Wilhelm	21, Nov. 1899	19, Nov.	66	5	
Schönlant, William	18, Aug. 1890		2	1	
Schönle, Wolfgang	4, Jan. 1892	3, Jan.		1	
Schöttinger, Conrad	25, Mar. 1889		75	1	
Schöttinger, K.	22, Apr. 1889		65	1	
Schöttkar, Fred.	11, Feb. 1889		15m	1	
Schöttker, Heinrich	7, Oct. 1896	6, Oct.	34-10m	5	
Schöttmer, Anna Maria	23, Dec. 1898	21, Dec.	60- 4m	5	Schmedding
Schüler, Agatha	20, Jan. 1890		5	1	
Schüler, William	14, June 1889		64	1	
Schürmann, Anna	15, June 1889		72	1	
Schürmann, Jakob	20, Oct. 1899	19, Oct.	32- 7m	8	
Schürrer, Friedrich	16, 17, Nov. 1893	15, Nov.	48-11m-20d	5	
Schüttenhelm, Jakob	25, Oct. 1898	24, Oct.	62- 2m	5	
Schüttler, Elisabeth	19, Mar. 1897	18, Mar.	72- 2m	5	
Scofield, Odelia	10, May 1901		4m	8	
Scott, Amelia	31, Aug. 1887		51	1	
Scott, B.	27, Dec. 1887		5	1	
Scott, Clarissa	4, Oct. 1900		67	8	
Scott, James W.	4, May 1895		3	5	
Scott, Katharine	15, Aug. 1900		74	5	
Scott, L.	20, June 1888		78	1	

Name	Notice Date	Death Date	Age	Page	Maiden Name
****	****** ****	***** ****	***	****	****** ****
Scott, Louis	8, July 1901		79	8	
Scott, Melissa	27, May 1901		25	8	
Scott, Ollie	18, July 1887		12m	1	
Scott, Samuel	6, Oct. 1900		44	5	
Scott, Sarah	22, Aug. 1888		52	1	
Scott, Winfield	24, June 1901		58	8	
Scruggs, Fanny	29, Jan. 1901		31	8	
Scull, Minnie	20, Nov. 1900		38	8	
Scully, Jas.	19, Dec. 1888		45	1	
Scully, Ruth	24, Apr. 1895		20m	5	
Scultetus, Karl Ludwig	14, Jan. 1899	13, Jan.	74	5	
Seader, Charles	15, June 1901		29	8	
Seaffert, E.J.	19, Feb. 1898	18, Feb.	28	5	
Seals, Charles A. (Dr)	1, Dec. 1888		71	4	
Seamann, R. Fulton	15, Dec. 1887		37	1	
Sears, Annie G.	7, July 1888		1	4	
Sease, Carrie	10, Oct. 1891		1- 7m	4	
Sease, Louis F.	4, Jan. 1890		4	1	
Seasongood, S.	15, Nov. 1900		27	8	
Sebastian, Ida	25, Sept 1888		1	1	
Sebastiani, Robert E.	23, Jan. 1901		13	8	
Sechier, Mary J.	30, Nov. 1900		41	8	
Secrist, Mary E.	5, Dec. 1891		68	4	
Sedler, Christian C.	11, Dec. 1893		31	5	
Sedler, Julia	27, May 1901		2	8	
Seebauer, Clara	10, Aug. 1900		41	8	
Seefer, Georg	18, May 1897	17, May	80- 1m	5	
Seegar, Christina	26, Apr. 1895		41	5	
Seegars, Mabel C.	5, May 1895		16d	5	
Seeger, George	15, Feb. 1901		34	8	
Seeger, Kate	8, July 1901		33	8	
Seegers, Elizabeth	23, Jan. 1901		79	8	
Seegers, Elizabeth	20, Sept 1901		75	1	
Seegers, F.	13, Mar. 1888		74	1	
Seegers, Philipp E.	9, July 1895		43	5	
Seegers, Walter	31, Aug. 1900		6d	5	
Seegers, William	1, Oct. 1887		27	1	
Seekin, Mary	16, Apr. 1901		50	8	
Seel, Appolonia	6, Apr. 1889		54	1	
Seep, Johan Bernard	7, July 1898	6, July	63-11m	5	
Seers, John	10, Oct. 1890		49d	4	
Seery, B. Teresa	27, Aug. 1901		70	1	
Seewald, Julius	5, Nov. 1889		37	1	
Seffer, John	14, July 1900		20d	8	
Seger, Ella	2, Oct. 1891		3m	4	
Seger, John	14, Feb. 1891		14m	4	
Seger, Maria E.	16, Sept 1887		4d	1	
Seib, Rob. L.	10, Oct. 1895	7, Oct.	10	5	
Seibel, Henry	17, Dec. 1891		47	4	
Seibel, Lenora	22, Sept 1891		7m	1	
Seibel, Sophia	1, Nov. 1895	30, Oct.	22	5	Stille
Seibert, Amelia	25, July 1901		53	8	
Seibert, Barbara	17, Aug. 1898	16, Aug.		4	
Seibert, Christian	4, May 1893		30	5	
Seibert, Clara	10, Aug. 1893		51	5	
Seibert, Daniel	3, Aug. 1887		16m	1	
Seibert, Gottlieb	6, June 1895		38	5	
Seibert, Katharine	15, May 1895		31	5	
Seibert, Minna	9, Apr. 1897	7, Apr.	34- 3m	1	
Seible, Jakob	12, May 1891		34	1	
Seidel, Arthur	8, June 1889	7, June	8	1	
Seidel, Helene	16, June 1889		2- 4m	5	
Seidel, Louise	30, Dec. 1899	30, Dec.		5	
Seidel, Margaretha	31, Dec. 1898	30, Dec.	59	5	
Seidel, Walter	24, June 1891	23, June	6m	1	
Seidenspeier, Annie	16, Sept 1887		32	1	
Seidenspinner, Caroline	20, Mar. 1894		36	5	
Seidenspinner, Charles	25, Feb. 1901		35	8	
Seidenspinner, Goldie	21, Oct. 1891		3w	4	
Seidenspinner, J.G.	1, Oct. 1897	30, Sept	5- 9m	5	
Seidenspinner, Jakob	25, Mar. 1889		32	1	

Name ****	Notice Date ****** ****	Death Date ***** ****	Age ***	Page ****	Maiden Name ****** ****
Seidenspinner, Lena	14, Sept 1895	13, Sept		5	Dohrmann
Seidling, Johanne	2, Aug. 1901		65	8	
Seifer, John	25, Mar. 1901		53	8	
Seifer, Junes	18, Dec. 1889		5	1	
Seifert, Stephan	1, Apr. 1890		69	1	
Seifreit, Bernardine	27, Oct. 1900		52	8	
Seifried, Joseph	26, Nov. 1892		22	5	
Seifried, Mary	1, June 1901		76	8	
Seigel, George J.	5, July 1901			8	
Seilacher, Henry	15, June 1894		69	5	
Seiler, Charles	23, July 1901		59	8	
Seiler, F.J.	2, Oct. 1900		2m	8	
Seiler, Ferdinand	5, Dec. 1891		1	4	
Seiler, Joseph	2, May 1894		5m	5	
Seiler, Joseph	20, Sept 1901		41	1	
Seilkop, Ernst F.	23, Nov. 1899	22, Nov.	63- 3m	5	
Seilkopf, Sophia	15, Sept 1892		76	5	
Seimer, Bernard	3, Dec. 1891		60	4	
Seinecke, Adolph	25, 26, Feb. 1890	24, Feb.		1	
Seinsheimer, Bernard	20, Apr. 1896	19, Apr.	78	5	
Seip, Ed.	24, May 1892		8m	5	
Seip, Emil (Dr.)	16, May 1900	14, May	72	5	
Seip, Florence	19, Jan. 1894		7	5	
Seip, Frank	3, Dec. 1887	2, Dec.	24	4	
Seip, Sarah E.	10, Jan. 1893		39	5	
Seistner, George J.	28, May 1891		1m	4	
Seiter, Marie T.	7, Sept 1893		66	5	
Seiter, Parker	8, Apr. 1891		4m	4	
Seitz, G.	27, Dec. 1887		75	1	
Seiwert, Peter	8, Jan. 1896	7, Jan.	35	5	
Seiz, Anna	27, Jan. 1890		80	1	
Seißinger, Clara M.	1, July 1891		11m	1	
Selcer, Annie C.	28, Dec. 1892		1m	5	
Selig, Martin	17, July 1895		52	5	
Seling, Johan Heinrich	1, Feb. 1898	31, Jan.	92	5	
Sell, Jessie	6, Sept 1900		21	5	
Sellenings, Fred.	13, Aug. 1901		46	8	
Seller, Robert	3, Oct. 1888		5	1	
Seller, Robert	23, Nov. 1894	22, Nov.	44- 8m- 2d	5	
Sellers,	4, Apr. 1888		26d	1	
Sellers, Nettie	17, Sept 1891		35	1	
Selm, Anna Maria	27, Jan. 1896	25, Jan.	72	5	
Selm, Henry	14, Feb. 1890		64	1	
Selman, Harry	17, June 1891		40	4	
Selzer, Aaron	14, Jan. 1889		7w	1	
Semme, Michael	7, Feb. 1901		21	8	
Senburt, Herman C.	25, Mar. 1891		3	4	
Sendelbeck, Margaret	31, Oct. 1891		66	4	
Seneff, John	10, Nov. 1891		74	1	
Senft, Andreas	8, Feb. 1899	7, Feb.	22-11m	5	
Sengenberger, John	3, Feb. 1891		32	4	
Senholzi, Ernst	5, June 1901		58	8	
Senior, Willie	5, Oct. 1888		6w	1	
Senkbeil, Gertrude	30, July 1892		6m	5	
Senteff, Henry	22, Oct. 1900		19	8	
Seppel, Jacob	26, Dec. 1890		1	1	
Serodino, Bertha	10, June 1898	9, June	66	4	
Sertel, Magdalena	19, Apr. 1889		87	1	
Setters, William H.	27, Feb. 1894		20d	5	
Seubert,	10, Apr. 1891		6m	4	
Seubert, Elizabeth	10, July 1889		71	1	
Seubert, Joseph	28, Jan. 1893		42	5	
Seuer, Charles	5, May 1892		29	5	
Seufferle, Charles C.	4, Apr. 1893		25	5	
Seufferle, Christian	11, Nov. 1899	10, Nov.	69- 9m- 4d	4	
Seufferle, Clara	13, Oct. 1896	12, Oct.	10- 3m	5	
Seufferle, John	21, Mar. 1891		45	4	
Seufferle, Rachel	9, June 1897	7, June	67- 2m	5	Deck
Seurkamp, Alfred H.	17, Mar. 1891		14d	4	
Seurkamp, Hannah	13, June 1901		38	8	
Severin, Ludwig	12, Sept 1899	11, Sept	3- 1m	5	

Name	Notice Date	Death Date	Age	Page	Maiden Name
****	****** ****	***** ****	***	****	****** ****
Seward, Donna D.	30, Jan. 1894		2	5	
Seward, Leslie	2, Feb. 1901		16m	8	
Sexton, Rebecca	20, July 1901		76	8	
Sextro, Adelheid	10, Feb. 1900	9, Feb.	23- 7m-21d	5	
Sextro, Christina	16, Aug. 1890		3m	1	
Seybert, Wilhelm Johan	28, Aug. 1894	26, Aug.	3	5	
Seyberth, Anna M.	6, Nov. 1891		38	4	
Seybold, Clara	24, Dec. 1892		24	5	
Seyfried, John	10, Jan. 1888		28	4	
Seyfried, Robert A.	8, Apr. 1891		18d	4	
Seyler, Anna Louisa	27, Feb. 1888		2	4	
Seyler, F.W.	8, Oct. 1897	8, Oct.	22	4	
Seß, Friedricka	9, Nov. 1893		61	5	
Seß, Julia	10, May 1901		52	8	
Seß, Rudolph	8, June 1894		55	5	
Seßmann, Anton	25, May 1901		75	8	
Shaerli, James	11, Feb. 1891		30	4	
Shafer, Ann	18, Feb. 1891		72	4	
Shafer, George	6, Mar. 1901		32	5	
Shafer, John C.	17, May 1901		4m	8	
Shanahan, David J.	15, Jan. 1901		50	8	
Shank, Clara M.	15, May 1895		9	5	
Shannon, John	8, Feb. 1901		55	8	
Shannon, Katharine	11, Oct. 1901		59	5	
Shannon, Maggie	15, Jan. 1901		17	8	
Shannon, Sophia	12, Dec. 1900		60	8	
Sharp, John	17, Apr. 1895		28	5	
Sharp, Selden	19, July 1887		9m	1	
Sharrs, R.	14, July 1900		88	8	
Shau, Georg	18, Feb. 1890		47	2	
Shau, John	11, Nov. 1891		19	1	
Shaw, Estella	14, Mar. 1888		1	1	
Shaw, Lonnie	9, Aug. 1900		29	8	
Shaw, Thomas	1, Dec. 1900		34	8	
Shay, Anna	29, July 1887		59	1	
Shay, Catharine	19, Dec. 1900		10	8	
Shea, Annie M.	8, Aug. 1901		1	8	
Shea, John J.	2, Oct. 1900		41	8	
Shea, Margaret	18, Sept 1901		59	8	
Shea, Mary	10, Nov. 1900		32	8	
Sheahan, Anna	13, July 1901		2	8	
Sheahan, Thomas	20, July 1901		1	8	
Shear, Rudolph	1, Feb. 1901		44	8	
Shearer, Susan	9, Oct. 1900		73	8	
Sheehan,	17, Oct. 1887		19	1	
Sheehan, Mary Bernardin (Sr.)	17, Oct. 1887		26	1	
Sheehan, Sophia	30, July 1901		65	8	
Shehy, John	20, July 1887		1	1	
Shelt, Fanny	14, May 1895		49	5	
Shelton, Benney	20, Aug. 1888		11m	1	
Shengi, Jakob	15, 16, Nov. 1900		64	8	
Shenk, John	21, Aug. 1887		45	5	
Shepler, Fay	13, Oct. 1892		5m	5	
Shepman, John	19, Aug. 1901		56	8	
Sheppard, Hattie	1, June 1901		8	8	
Sherer, George	12, June 1901		2d	8	
Sheridan, Agnes	4, Aug. 1888		4m	4	
Sheridan, Anna	14, Aug. 1900		54	5	
Sheridan, Barbara	28, Aug. 1901		62	8	
Sheridan, James	11, Aug. 1887		65	1	
Sheridan, John	17, Oct. 1900		70	8	
Sheridan, John	21, Jan. 1901		39	8	
Sheridan, William	2, May 1895		26	5	
Shetke, John	8, Mar. 1892		74	5	
Shields,	27, Dec. 1887		3m	1	
Shields, Cora	27, July 1888		3	1	
Shields, Robert	3, May 1901		23	8	
Shifford, Charles	16, Apr. 1895		6	5	
Shipp, Thomas	11, Apr. 1901		43	8	
Shipper, John	17, Jan. 1894		31	5	
Shoemaker, Herman	8, Mar. 1901		60	8	

Name	Notice Date	Death Date	Age	Page	Maiden Name
****	****** ****	***** ****	***	****	****** ****
Shoemaker, J.N.	7, Feb. 1899	7, Feb.	67	5	
Shoomaker, Nicolaus	1, Aug. 1887		90	1	
Short, David	15, 18, Sept 1900		30	5	
Short, Mary	17, May 1901		49	8	
Shott, Katie	3, Dec. 1891		4	4	
Show, William	14, Mar. 1901		20	8	
Shran, Anna	5, Apr. 1901		30	8	
Sibille, August	20, Aug. 1888		46	1	
Sibley, Kasper	29, July 1896	28, July		5	
Sichrist, Mary	30, Nov. 1887		74	4	
Sick, Alex.	23, Nov. 1889		3m	1	
Sickbert, Elisabeth	8, Oct. 1900		70	8	
Sicking, Anna	12, Oct. 1899	10, Oct.	68-11m-20d	5	Meekers
Sicking, Frank	7, Sept 1893		8	5	
Sickinger, Ed.	22, June 1892		46	5	
Sickinger, Maria	19, Aug. 1889		6m	1	
Sickler, Kate	15, July 1901		32	8	
Sickles, Rosina	4, Mar. 1889		71	1	
Sickmann, Herman	23, Jan. 1891		56	4	
Siebenburger, William	1, Aug. 1894		28d	5	
Siebenthaler, Gottfried	3, Oct. 1898	1, Oct.	52	5	
Siebenthaler, Ida	22, Dec. 1887		19- 5m-12d	4	
Siebenthaler, Jacob Christian	9, Apr. 1896	8, Apr.	36	5	
Siebenthaler, Sophia	6, Apr. 1896	4, Apr.	52- 7m	4	Hoffmann
Sieber, Christina	29, June 1901		78	8	
Sieber, John	1, Mar. 1892	29, Feb.	60	5	
Sieber, Marguerite	7, Dec. 1893		62	5	
Siebern, H.W.	23, Feb. 1899	22, Feb.	53	5	
Siebert, John R.	3, Dec. 1900		1m	8	
Siedenfried, Goldie	22, Oct. 1891		3w	1	
Siefer, Elisabeth	28, Oct. 1891		42	4	
Siefer, Frank	19, Dec. 1889		5	1	
Siefert, Alexandrine	24, Aug. 1897	23, Aug.	77	4	
Siefert, Henry	28, Jan. 1891		43	4	
Siefert, Henry	6, Apr. 1894		3w	5	
Siefert, Joseph	9, Aug. 1894		84	5	
Siefert, Joseph	7, 9, Aug. 1894	7, Aug.	84	5	
Siefert, Peter D.	27, Mar. 1891		9m	4	
Siefke, Agnes	29, Jan. 1892		26	5	
Siefke, Catharine T.	4, Mar. 1893		69	5	
Siefke, Johan Heinrich	10, Oct. 1898	9, Oct.	62- 9m-14d	4	
Siefret, Addie	23, June 1897	22, June	20- 8m	5	
Siefried, Rosa	17, Sept 1890		36	1	
Siefte, Emma	21, May 1889		22	1	
Siegbert, John	28, June 1889		1	1	
Siegel, Charles	19, July 1887		18m	1	
Siegel, Leopold	10, Nov. 1900		21	8	
Siegel, Philip	2, June 1894		34	5	
Sieger, Maggie	2, Sept 1887		22	1	
Siegfried, Anna	6, May 1897	5, May	30-11m	5	Oeh
Siegler, Johan	24, May 1897	21, May	56- 8m	5	
Siehl, Anna Louisa	15, Oct. 1898	14, Oct.	26- 2m- 5d	4	
Siehl, Carl	8, Mar. 1893		49	5	
Siehl, Frederick	19, Dec. 1891		79	4	
Sieker, Casper H.	16, July 1895		84	5	
Sieker, Maria	25, Jan. 1890		81	1	
Sielschott, Carolina	6, Dec. 1892		75	5	
Siemer, Carsten	22, Oct. 1898	21, Oct.	76	5	
Siemer, J.H.	16, Aug. 1901		6m	8	
Siemer, Louise	11, May 1892		46	5	
Siemer, Michael	18, Aug. 1892		11m	5	
Siemüller, Mary	27, Oct. 1894		68	5	
Siepel, Thomas	9, Jan. 1891		6w	4	
Siermann, Hubert H.	25, Apr. 1898	22, Apr.	4- 2m	5	
Sieser, Mary	20, June 1892		82	5	
Sieve, Louis	15, Mar. 1901		3d	8	
Sieverding, J.	25, Nov. 1887		51	1	
Sievers, F.	24, Jan. 1888		7w	1	
Sievers, Heinrich	9, Aug. 1897	6, Aug.	46- 8m-24d	5	
Sievers, Mary	4, 5, Nov. 1895	2, Nov.	39- -23d	5	Sieger
Sieveveldt, Clarence Jacob	20, Oct. 1887		3w	1	

Name	Notice Date	Death Date	Age	Page	Maiden Name
****	****** ****	***** ****	***	****	****** ****
Sigbert, Heinrich	30, July 1898	28, July	68	5	
Sigmund, Fritz	2, Mar. 1889		36	1	
Sigolka, Thomas	3, Aug. 1893		1	5	
Sigwart, Eugen	9, Jan. 1901		47	5	
Sigwart, William	7, Dec. 1887		46	1	
Silas, Katharine	24, July 1890		65	1	
Silberberg, Augusta	26, 27, Mar. 1892	26, Mar.	6- 6m-12d	5	
Silberberg, Dora	18, Feb. 1901		55	8	
Silberberg, Otto	30, Mar. 1892	29, Mar.	4- 4m- 2d	5	
Silberman, Frank	13, Aug. 1891		3m	4	
Silbermann, M.	4, Dec. 1900		36	8	
Silbernagel, Mich.	29, Jan. 1901		70	8	
Silbersack, Clara	30, Jan. 1891		18	4	
Silcher, Caroline	8, Dec. 1891		37	4	
Siller, Philip	5, June 1901		65	8	
Siller, Tekla	10, June 1901		8	8	
Siller, William	3, June 1891		14	4	
Silstetter, Henry	25, Mar. 1901		53	8	
Silverman, Simon	8, Aug. 1900		81	8	
Silvey,	31, Jan. 1901		1d	8	
Silzer, Henry Harrison	21, Jan. 1893		4m	5	
Simme, John	15, May 1895		35	5	
Simmendinger, Willie Aug.	30, Oct. 1890	30, Oct.	5- 8m	1	
Simmons, Laura M.	26, July 1895		19m	5	
Simms, Isabella	20, Oct. 1887		35	1	
Simon, Adolf	13, July 1892		43	5	
Simon, Adolf	3, Apr. 1901		66	8	
Simon, Anna M.	29, Dec. 1892		3w	5	
Simon, August	25, Apr. 1896	23, Apr.	45	5	
Simon, B.	20, Nov. 1891		2	4	
Simon, Babette	21, Nov. 1900		71	8	
Simon, Beatrice	24, June 1901		2	8	
Simon, Bernard	16, May 1899	14, May	43- 5m-12d	5	
Simon, Caroline	19, Aug. 1891		52	4	
Simon, Clara	11, Sept 1888		7m	1	
Simon, E.	29, Nov. 1895	27, Nov.	77	5	
Simon, Edward	7, Nov. 1891		5	1	
Simon, Eugene	7, May 1901		1	1	
Simon, Isadore	30, July 1901		4	8	
Simon, Kate	18, July 1887		45	1	
Simon, Raymond	18, Dec. 1900		35	8	
Simon, Robert F.	29, Jan. 1901		3	8	
Simon, Sophia E.	13, July 1895		4m	5	
Simper, Alma C.	16, Jan. 1894		7m	5	
Simper, Catharine	23, May 1894		53	5	
Simpkinson, Anna	14, Sept 1887		47	1	
Simpkinson, John	5, Mar. 1901		88	5	
Simpson, Ella	26, Mar. 1892			1	
Simpson, Jerry	8, Aug. 1900		38	8	
Sims, Scott	9, Mar. 1901		38	8	
Singer, Christine	23, May 1901		75	8	
Singer, John	11, Sept 1895	9, Sept	58- 3m	5	
Singer, Samuel	19, Sept 1888		26	2	
Singler, Wilhelmine Elisabeth	23, 24, Nov. 1896	22, Nov.	42- 9m	5	
Singleton, William	9, May 1895		76	5	
Sinneberg, Marie	1, Sept 1888		70	1	
Sinnige, Henry C.	10, Mar. 1898	8, Mar.		5	
Sinter, Johan	9, Dec. 1899	6, Dec.	75- 8m	4	
Sividersky, Louis	9, Jan. 1891		4	4	
Skaats, George	23, Oct. 1900		46	8	
Skaats, Zeneca	13, July 1887		4	1	
Skahill, Mary	30, Apr. 1901		2m	8	
Skaken, J.H.	14, Feb. 1888		3w	4	
Skillbeck, Sophia L.	4, Jan. 1894		29	5	
Skinner, Isabella	10, May 1895		68	5	
Skinner, John A.	5, July 1887		79	1	
Skinner, S.W.	24, May 1901		42	8	
Slaab, Emma	23, Oct. 1888		27	1	
Slack, Mary	12, Sept 1887			1	
Slade, Corrine F.	16, June 1891		5m	4	
Slane, Anna	18, Aug. 1900		40	8	

Name	Notice Date	Death Date	Age	Page	Maiden Name
****	****** ****	***** ****	***	****	****** ****
Slattery, Ellen	18, May 1901		57	1	
Slattery, Michael	5, Dec. 1898	4, Dec.	36- -10d	5	
Slatzhofer, Gottlieb	6, Dec. 1892		45	5	
Slaughter, Maggie D.	4, Apr. 1895		39	5	
Slayter, Elwood	21, Apr. 1888		8m	1	
Sleery, Pauline	14, Oct. 1901		42	5	
Slemkamp, Henry	4, Aug. 1890		39	1	
Slicer, Emma	22, Oct. 1900		33	8	
Slicer, Fenner	22, Oct. 1900		26d	8	
Slimer, George	20, May 1893		73	5	
Slirus, Goerdmand	11, Feb. 1891		66	4	
Sloan, Alice	17, Aug. 1901		56	8	
Sloggeman, Annie M.	2, Apr. 1891		64	4	
Slomer, Johan H.	8, May 1900	7, May	68	5	
Slüter, F.H.	11, Dec. 1895	9, Dec.		5	
Small, Emma	10, Sept 1887		4	2	
Smalley, Camille	18, Feb. 1888		18	1	
Smallwood, Fannie	10, Aug. 1901		71	8	
Smallwood, Henry	11, June 1901		71	8	
Smargusky, John	18, Aug. 1891		8m	4	
Smiley, David	5, July 1901		3m	8	
Smith,	23, Oct. 1900		1d	8	
Smith, A.	13, Jan. 1888		3m	1	
Smith, Ada	14, Feb. 1901		18	8	
Smith, Ada	21, May 1901		33	8	
Smith, Albert B.	29, Dec. 1892		48	5	
Smith, Alice	11, June 1901		39	8	
Smith, Amanda	18, Sept 1900		25	5	
Smith, Anna	2, Apr. 1891		4m	4	
Smith, Anna	11, Aug. 1900		63	8	
Smith, Anna	12, Nov. 1900		58	5	
Smith, Anna	18, Dec. 1900		29	8	
Smith, Anna	30, Sept 1901		33	8	
Smith, Annie	2, Apr. 1901		33	8	
Smith, Barbara	3, June 1901		32	8	
Smith, Benjamin	15, June 1901		23	8	
Smith, Bessie	7, Sept 1887		45	1	
Smith, Bridget	22, Dec. 1900			8	
Smith, Buelah	11, Apr. 1901		4	8	
Smith, Calvin	15, Oct. 1900		43	5	
Smith, Catharine	30, Jan. 1901		91	8	
Smith, Catharine	10, May 1901		24	8	
Smith, Catharine	8, Aug. 1901		64	8	
Smith, Charles	4, Nov. 1887		30	1	
Smith, Charles	25, June 1888		6m	1	
Smith, Charles	2, Apr. 1891		32	4	
Smith, Charles	21, July 1900		15	8	
Smith, Charles	26, July 1900		57	5	
Smith, Charles	7, June 1901		25	8	
Smith, Charlotte	1, Oct. 1887		59	1	
Smith, Clara	8, Oct. 1900		18	8	
Smith, Cora	12, Nov. 1900		24	5	
Smith, Cyrus	23, Feb. 1901		51	8	
Smith, Delia	2, Feb. 1901		30	8	
Smith, Dietrich	28, Dec. 1899	26, Dec.		5	
Smith, E. (Mrs)	23, Jan. 1891		64	4	
Smith, Earl	6, Mar. 1901		1	5	
Smith, Elise	24, July 1901		38	8	
Smith, Elizabeth	11, Aug. 1890		79	1	
Smith, Elwood	24, Oct. 1900		29	8	
Smith, Emma E.	12, Aug. 1887		21	1	
Smith, Ethan B.	13, Apr. 1895		3	4	
Smith, Frank	13, Oct. 1900		36	8	
Smith, George	23, Nov. 1888		4	1	
Smith, Grace	5, July 1901		9m	8	
Smith, Grant	8, Dec. 1891		42	4	
Smith, Harriet H.	18, Oct. 1900		81	8	
Smith, Harrison	3, Jan. 1901		63	5	
Smith, Harry J.	23, Nov. 1892		42	5	
Smith, Henry	21, Mar. 1901		1m	8	
Smith, James	24, Dec. 1900		81	8	

Name	Notice Date	Death Date	Age	Page	Maiden Name
****	****** ****	***** ****	***	****	****** ****
Smith, James	28, Mar. 1901		19	8	
Smith, James	18, May 1901		21	1	
Smith, Jennie	15, May 1895		41	5	
Smith, John	30, Aug. 1888		74	1	
Smith, John	21, Oct. 1891		51	4	
Smith, John J.	24, Oct. 1887		37	1	
Smith, Joseph	11, Oct. 1901		52	5	
Smith, Josephine	23, July 1901		29	8	
Smith, L.L.	30, Sept 1901		27	8	
Smith, Leo	21, Feb. 1888		6d	1	
Smith, Lilly	17, Apr. 1891			4	
Smith, Lucy	14, June 1901		45	5	
Smith, Lydia	2, Nov. 1900		94	8	
Smith, Margaret	7, July 1887		87	1	
Smith, Margaret	4, Sept 1891		32	4	
Smith, Mary Elisabeth	10, Nov. 1900		58	8	
Smith, Mary M.	21, June 1901		1d	8	
Smith, Nellie	7, Jan. 1901		25	5	
Smith, Nicholas J.	24, Apr. 1895		4	5	
Smith, Nina Q.	21, Jan. 1891		2	4	
Smith, Nora	13, Aug. 1896	11, Aug.		5	
Smith, Oscar	10, Apr. 1895			5	
Smith, Peter M.	20, Apr. 1895		26	5	
Smith, R.W.	1, Aug. 1887		30	1	
Smith, Rob.	20, Apr. 1895		35	5	
Smith, Robertha	10, Oct. 1900		18	8	
Smith, Sarah	10, June 1901		30	8	
Smith, Sophie	25, Jan. 1901		42	8	
Smith, Sylvester	8, May 1901		2	8	
Smith, Willard	2, Mar. 1901		46	5	
Smith, William	26, Feb. 1901		69	8	
Smith, William	1, May 1901		33	8	
Smith, William H.	21, July 1893		27	5	
Smith, William P.	10, Aug. 1892		32	5	
Smother, Charles	23, Mar. 1901		7	8	
Smyth, Hugh	24, Sept 1901		67	1	
Sneider, Carl	24, Jan. 1894		38	5	
Snider, Carolina B.	24, Feb. 1894		37	5	
Snider, John R.	2, Sept 1887		78	1	
Snitker, Walter S.	10, Oct. 1893		6	5	
Snook, L.	25, Nov. 1887		16	1	
Snyder, Casper	2, Mar. 1901		41	5	
Snyder, G.M.	27, Dec. 1897	25, Dec.	38- 6m	4	
Snyder, Harry	30, May 1895		34	5	
Snyder, John W.	2, Mar. 1888		80	1	
Snyder, Mabel	10, Aug. 1901		6m	8	
Snyder, Maggie	27, Mar. 1888		2	4	
Sobotka, Ludwig	19, Dec. 1895	18, Dec.	78	5	
Soehner, Ferdinand	30, Dec. 1890		69	4	
Soellner, John	7, May 1898	6, May	46	* 5	
Solch, Charles	23, Aug. 1887		12m	1	
Sollm, Andrew	12, July 1895		77	5	
Sollmann, Hilda	31, July 1901		2	8	
Solomon, Jac.	17, July 1890		48	1	
Somhorst, Dina	17, Dec. 1887		45	1	
Somhorst, John	28, June 1893		67	5	
Sommer, Charles	26, Feb. 1889		2	1	
Sommer, Franziska	13, Jan. 1899	12, Jan.	79	4	Pitz
Sommerhalter, Rudolph	30, Jan. 1888		2	1	
Sommerkamp, C.H.	11, Apr. 1898	10, Apr.	77- 2m	5	
Sommerkamp, F.A.	18, Mar. 1898	15, Mar.	37- 3m	5	
Sommerkamp, M.	15, Dec. 1900		54	8	
Sommermann, Rudolph	29, Dec. 1891		3	4	
Sommermeyer, August	25, May 1899	23, May	57- 9m	5	
Sommers, Elisabeth	11, Jan. 1893		74	5	
Sommers, Gottlob	25, Jan. 1901		45	8	
Sommers, Richard	17, Oct. 1901		46	8	
Sonderhaus, Catharina	24, Apr. 1894		82	5	
Sonnentag, Frank	12, Feb. 1890		8	1	
Sonner, James	22, June 1901		34	8	
Sonntag, Charles	18, June 1901		39	8	

Name ****	Notice Date ****** ****	Death Date ***** ****	Age ***	Page ****	Maiden Name ****** ****
Sonntag, Elise	4, Oct. 1890	4, Oct.		1	
Sonntag, Heinrich	27, July 1892	26, July	30	5	
Sorbach, Sophia	20, Nov. 1888		12	1	
Sorg, Henry	2, Feb. 1893		35	5	
Sorg, Mary	31, May 1892		28d	5	
Sorg, Mary E.	21, June 1894		4m	5	
Sorg, Philip	13, July 1887		35	1	
Sorg, Philippine	8, July 1897	5, July	32	4	Koßmann
Sorgel, Catharine	20, Aug. 1896	19, Aug.		5	
Sorgel, Johan	9, Nov. 1897	8, Nov.	45	5	
Sorieth, Friedricka	20, Dec. 1892		84	5	
Sorsch, Frances	27, Oct. 1891		59	1	
Sostofski, Salomon	26, Jan. 1892		6m	5	
Sotanski, Armah	25, July 1900		30	5	
Sottung, Margaret K.	29, Dec. 1891		1	4	
Southard, Mathilda	8, Oct. 1900		78	8	
Southworth, Ralph	25, May 1895		3d	5	
Spaeth, Albert	18, Dec. 1899	16, Dec.	6m	4	
Spaeth, Barbara	16, May 1901		81	5	
Spaeth, E.H.	27, Aug. 1901		46	1	
Spaeth, Josepha M.E.	1, Feb. 1898	31, Jan.		5	
Spaeth, Michael	6, July 1897	5, July	49- 1m	5	
Spaeth, Michael	12, July 1899	12, July	82	5	
Spaeth, Samuel	27, Apr. 1896	26, Apr.	67	5	
Spalding, Thomas	11, Apr. 1890		48	1	
Spamer, Hugo	26, Mar. 1889		67	1	
Spangenberg, Caroline	7, Feb. 1901		40	8	
Spangenberg, Eugene	3, May 1901		61	8	
Spangenberg, Frank	10, Feb. 1892		32	5	
Spangler, Gottfried	17, Jan. 1893		57	5	
Spangler, Ida	21, Feb. 1901		22	8	
Spangler, Nellie	12, Sept 1900		2m	5	
Sparenberg, Maria F.L.	4, Mar. 1893		29	5	
Spark, Salathiel	27, Jan. 1895		2m	5	
Sparkman, Mabel	18, Feb. 1901		8m	8	
Sparks, Math.	27, July 1888		63	1	
Spaukuck, Mary	2, Dec. 1889		49	1	
Spaulding, John J.	2, Jan. 1889		58	1	
Spaulding, Richard	24, June 1901		37	8	
Specht, Daniel	4, Feb. 1893		37	5	
Specht, Joseph H.	24, Feb. 1894		12	5	
Specht, Lizzie	21, Apr. 1891		1	4	
Specht, Sophia	17, Mar. 1890		16m	1	
Speck, Mary	18, Jan. 1893		42	5	
Speckbauch, Catharine	23, Jan. 1891		36	4	
Speckbauch, Friedrich	3, Oct. 1888		60	1	
Specker, Johan Heinrich	29, Jan. 1896	28, Jan.	36- 3m	5	
Specker, M. Theresa	1, Apr. 1898	31, Mar.	68- 7m	5	Hellebusch
Speckmann, Katie E.	24, Feb. 1890		5	1	
Specter,	29, Dec. 1887		1d	4	
Specter, Ben	14, Sept 1900		1m	5	
Speidel, Clara	18, Mar. 1889		42	1	
Speies, Jacob	23, July 1901		34	8	
Speiser, Barbara	20, Jan. 1890		78	1	
Speiser, Harris O.	3, Nov. 1891		-0	4	
Speitz, John	10, July 1891		56	4	
Spellbring, Francis	18, Feb. 1901		28	8	
Spellbrink, E.	10, Aug. 1901		66	8	
Spellbrink, Fred	8, May 1901		66	8	
Speller, Emma	19, Mar. 1901		8	8	
Speller, John B.	5, Apr. 1901		45	8	
Spelling, Laura	23, May 1901		2m	8	
Spellmann, Dan.	25, July 1888		71	4	
Spellmann, Mary	21, Oct. 1895	18, Oct.	46	5	
Spellmeier, Adelaide	3, May 1901		67	8	
Spencer, Anna	30, May 1888		27	1	
Spencer, Magdalena	5, July 1901		47	8	
Spengel, John	9, July 1897	7, July		4	
Spengler, Katharina	7, Nov. 1899	6, Nov.	42- 8m	5	Kraemer
Sperber, Frank V.	3, Mar. 1897	2, Mar.	41- 8m	5	
Sperber, Nicholas	17, Feb. 1895		42	5	

Name	Notice Date	Death Date	Age	Page	Maiden Name
****	****** ****	***** ****	***	****	****** ****
Sperry, Carrie	8, Nov. 1889		4	1	
Sperry, Margaretha	13, Jan. 1897	12, Jan.	37	5	Ruehl
Speyer, Alma	3, Mar. 1890		6m	1	
Speyer, Theresa	3, Nov. 1887		54	4	
Spicer, Jim	11, Aug. 1888		12d	1	
Spicher, Otto	11, Aug. 1891		20	4	
Spicker, Helen	23, July 1895		5m	5	
Spicker, Johanna A.	24, Feb. 1890		24	1	
Spicker, Marie	9, July 1895		2	5	
Spiedel, Charles	14, Jan. 1892		7w	1	
Spiegel, Alma	19, Aug. 1890		2m	1	
Spiegel, George C.	18, Jan. 1894		77	5	
Spiegel, Margaretha	27, Aug. 1897	26, Aug.	78- -26d	4	Creppel
Spieker, John G.	5, Jan. 1892		74	5	
Spielberg, Ben.	28, Jan. 1891		21	4	
Spies, Elisabeth	13, Oct. 1892		2	5	
Spies, Jacob	13, July 1894		64	5	
Spies, Margaret	17, July 1894		1	5	
Spieß, Christina	22, Nov. 1898	21, Nov.	76- 6m	5	Brueckmann
Spieß, G.K.	19, Sept 1895	17, Sept	74-11m	5	
Spieß, Louisa M.	24, July 1895		16m	5	
Spieß, Peter	14, Mar. 1895		20	5	
Spigurza, Philip	7, Jan. 1891		9m	4	
Spilker, Bernard	9, Mar. 1901		38	8	
Spinger, Charles	25, Jan. 1888		52	1	
Spise, Callie	29, Sept 1900		38	8	
Spitaler, Joseph	19, Apr. 1889		14d	1	
Spitzle, Gertrude	1, Oct. 1891		64	1	
Spitzmüller, Louise	28, Feb. 1900	27, Feb.	70	5	Weldin
Spitznagel, Kate	4, Jan. 1894		14	5	
Splain, Annie	6, Sept 1901		24	8	
Splain, Willie	26, Feb. 1891		4	4	
Sponsel, Ellen M.	26, July 1889		27	1	
Sponsel, George F.	24, Apr. 1889		2	1	
Sponsel, Johan	9, 11, Jan. 1894	8, Jan.	43- 7m-15d	* 5	
Spottswood, Grace	13, Oct. 1900		17	8	
Spraehnle, Philipp	1, Apr. 1896	30, Mar.		5	
Sprague, T.W.	10, June 1898	8, June	38	4	
Sprahnle, Minna	7, Nov. 1895	5, Nov.	51- 6m	5	
Sprandel, Madeline	26, July 1893		16d	5	
Sprang, Robert	17, Apr. 1894		4	5	
Spranz, Catharine	25, Sept 1890		67	1	
Sprau, Charles	12, Feb. 1896	9, Feb.	27-11m	5	
Spraukel, John	9, Apr. 1891		66	4	
Spraul, Charles	26, Mar. 1891		26	4	
Spreen, Abraham F.	4, June 1898	4, June	32	5	
Spreen, Charles	24, May 1892		56	5	
Spreen, Elsie	23, July 1895		2	5	
Spreen, Friedrich W.	18, Oct. 1897	16, Oct.	82	5	
Spreen, Henry	16, Apr. 1889		37	1	
Spreen, Henry F.	23, June 1888		9m	1	
Spreen, Louis W.	2, May 1901		40	8	
Spreen, Louise	4, Apr. 1889		5m	1	
Sprengard, Jakob	5, Apr. 1895		29	5	
Sprengel, Christian	8, May 1891		71	4	
Sprengel, Mary	11, June 1901		32	8	
Sprenger, Ferdinand	27, Oct. 1900		45	8	
Spriggs, Willie	10, Aug. 1900		13d	8	
Springelmeier, Henry H.	6, May 1893		20	5	
Springer, Albert	5, June 1895		63	5	
Springer, Lina	24, Mar. 1893		9	5	
Springer, Louise	18, Dec. 1899	15, Dec.	19	4	
Springer, Maggie	30, Aug. 1901		43	8	
Springmeier, Henrietta	5, Oct. 1896	2, Oct.	81	5	Kollmeier
Springmeier, John	25, Mar. 1891		56	4	
Springmeier, Louis	8, Sept 1900		53	5	
Springmeier, Mary A.	8, Feb. 1895		48	5	
Springmeier, Sophie	6, June 1901		91	8	
Springmeyer, Wilhelm H.	9, June 1898	7, June	64- 1m	5	
Spritzky, Charles	7, May 1888		32	1	
Sprung, Johan Wilhelm	24, Sept 1896	23, Sept	75-10m	5	

Name	Notice Date	Death Date	Age	Page	Maiden Name
****	****** ****	***** ****	***	****	****** ****
Spuler, Tillie E.	17, Oct. 1900		38	8	
Späth, Jeremie	9, July 1887		41	1	
Späth, Philipp	11, July 1895		84	5	
Squire, Ida J.	21, Mar. 1889		18	1	
St.Benson, James	8, Aug. 1901		3m	8	
St.Mari, Edgar C.	20, Oct. 1891		44	1	
St.Roche, Michael	19, Nov. 1900		58	8	
Staab, Barbara	1, Feb. 1892		66	5	
Staab, Maria Anna	21, Dec. 1896	20, Dec.	77	5	
Staas, Emma	6, July 1889		16m	1	
Staas, John	1, Aug. 1893		10m	5	
Staatfeld, Henriette	18, Apr. 1889		54	1	
Stacey, William	19, June 1901		61	8	
Stach, Henry	28, Jan. 1901		57	8	
Stackers, B.H.	30, Jan. 1888		35	1	
Stadt, John J.	9, Feb. 1895		72	5	
Stadtlander, Fred.	18, May 1892		26	5	
Staetfeldt, George	22, June 1901		20	8	
Stagerel, Karl	28, Aug. 1897	25, Aug.	51- 6m	5	
Stagge, Caroline	6, Mar. 1890		44	1	
Stagge, Harry	29, Oct. 1896	28, Oct.	4-11m	5	
Stagge, Herman	5, Feb. 1901		86	8	
Stagge, Oscar	23, June 1894		5m	5	
Stagge, Wilhelm	9, Nov. 1899	6, Nov.	61- 9m	5	
Staggenberg, Katharine	28, Jan. 1901		86	8	
Stagmann, Rosa	11, Mar. 1891		58	4	
Stahl, Anna	23, Sept 1889		9m	1	
Stahl, August	22, Dec. 1893		1	5	
Stahl, Celilie G.	5, Nov. 1900		23	8	
Stahl, Elisabeth	6, Jan. 1893		38	5	
Stahl, Henry	26, Apr. 1892		69	5	
Stahl, Karl	13, Sept 1899	12, Sept	71- -14d	4	
Stahl, Mary	29, Aug. 1891		6	4	
Stahl, Mary	11, Apr. 1895		65	5	
Stahl, May J.	27, Aug. 1891		4	1	
Stahl, Peter	10, June 1901		44	8	
Stahlhaber, Joseph	31, July 1894		14d	5	
Stahlkamp, John M.	17, July 1895		73	5	
Stahllander, Addie	9, Feb. 1893		30	5	
Stahlmann, Henry	8, Dec. 1891		44	4	
Stahr, Laura	25, Aug. 1896	23, Aug.	28- 7m	5	Theis
Stalf, John P.	17, Feb. 1894		5m	5	
Stall,	29, Jan. 1891		1d	4	
Stall, Flora	17, Jan. 1888		38	4	
Stall, Johan Heinrich	25, Feb. 1898	23, Feb.	54- 7m	5	
Stall, Maria	22, Oct. 1889		7	1	
Stallmann, John	17, Mar. 1891		44	4	
Stallo, Eliza	15, Oct. 1900		57	5	
Stallo, Maria Elisabeth	2, Sept 1897	1, Sept	28-11m	5	Osterhaus
Stamen, Theodor	16, Aug. 1894		37	5	
Stamm, Carrie	10, Dec. 1896	9, Dec.	29- 6m	5	
Stamm, Christ.	2, Aug. 1890		32	1	
Stamm, Henrietta C.	23, Nov. 1891		15m	1	
Stamm, Mary	18, Dec. 1900		47	8	
Stams, E.	6, Oct. 1894		74	5	
Stanberg, Cecilia B.	4, May 1889		68	1	
Stanbridge, Wallace	31, July 1901		42	8	
Stanczewski, Franz	26, Nov. 1891	25, Nov.	33-11m	1	
Stand, Clara	24, Jan. 1901		5	8	
Stander, Joseph Edward	21, Oct. 1891		7m	4	
Standigel, John	4, Nov. 1887		3w	1	
Stang, Annie	2, Apr. 1890		35	1	
Stang, S.	19, Nov. 1888		32	1	
Stang, William	9, Dec. 1887		17- -23d	1	
Stanley, Elizabeth	11, Oct. 1901		24	5	
Stanley, M.	4, Dec. 1900		4m	8	
Stannah, August	2, July 1901		43	8	
Stansbury, H.	24, July 1901		1	8	
Stante, Bertha	4, Aug. 1893		7m	5	
Stapleton, Emma	8, Dec. 1887		96	1	
Stapp, Amalie	24, Sept 1900			5	

Name	Notice Date	Death Date	Age	Page	Maiden Name
****	****** ****	***** ****	***	****	****** ****
Starcher, Viola	15, Aug. 1900		14d	5	
Stark, August	1, Mar. 1894		6m	5	
Stark, Calvin W.	9, Aug. 1887		9	1	
Stark, Esther	30, Mar. 1901		76	8	
Stark, Henry	9, Nov. 1893		67	5	
Stark, John	4, July 1901		32	8	
Stark, Joseph	22, Dec. 1893		79	5	
Stark, Naomi	7, Sept 1893		20	5	
Stark, Ottilia	9, Dec. 1891		61	2	
Starke Amilie	15, May 1900	14, May	31- 6m	8	Bonn
Starkey, George H.	29, July 1888		40	1	
Starkon, John	7, June 1890		6m	1	
Starr, Dorothea F.	14, Sept 1893		69	5	
Starr, John	11, Jan. 1888		67	4	
Starr, Madeline	10, Nov. 1900		23	8	
Starrmann, J.	19, Oct. 1900		31	5	
Startzmann, William R.	10, Mar. 1893		6	5	
States, John	30, Oct. 1894		1	5	
Staub, Adam	23, June 1894		71	5	
Staub, Harold V.	15, July 1893			5	
Staub, Jacob	20, July 1897	19, July	68- 9m	5	
Staub, Maria	23, Sept 1898	22, Sept	60-10m	4	
Staubach, Louis	27, Feb. 1894		36	5	
Stauber, Elenore A.	3, Mar. 1894		1m	5	
Staubitz, Anna	16, July 1892		27	5	
Staubitz, Erwin	5, Sept 1901		1	8	
Stauder, Francis	8, Dec. 1893		60	5	
Staudigel, Rosina	17, Mar. 1897	15, Mar.	67- - 8d	5	Spankuch
Stauffer, Fred.	11, July 1893		49	5	
Stautberg, Anna	16, Aug. 1895	15, Aug.	85-11m	5	
Stautberg, Elizabeth	8, July 1901		51	8	
Stayton, John	4, June 1901		76	8	
Stead, Alfred	7, Sept 1887		32	1	
Stearns, Ellen	4, Oct. 1900		64	8	
Stecher, Auguste	18, Nov. 1896	17, Nov.	59	5	
Steckmeier, Eva	24, Apr. 1894		53	5	
Steel, Louis	28, Apr. 1888		3w	1	
Steele, Florence	29, Aug. 1900			5	
Steelmann, J.	17, Jan. 1889		81	1	
Steffel, Anna M.	27, Sept 1888		21	2	
Steffen, Margaret	24, Jan. 1901		68	8	
Steffens, A.	9, Nov. 1899	8, Nov.		5	
Steffens, Mary	7, Jan. 1901		57	5	
Steffens, Willie	4, July 1891		9m	4	
Stegeman, Ben	19, July 1887		37	1	
Stegemann, Elisabeth	27, Mar. 1895		31	5	
Stegemayer, August	8, Aug. 1895	7, Aug.	26- 6m	5	
Stegemeier, Heinrich	31, July 1900		14	5	
Stegemeier, J.	12, Aug. 1901		2m	8	
Stegemeier, Wilhelmine	3, Apr. 1890		64	1	
Stegemeyer, Ralph E.	27, Apr. 1894		8	5	
Steghemper, Henry C.	16, June 1891		42	4	
Stegman, Mary	4, Aug. 1888		28	4	
Stegmann, F.X.	19, Mar. 1890		72	1	
Stegmann, Henry	6, Apr. 1893		31	5	
Stegmann, Joseph	16, Mar. 1893		70	5	
Stegmenz, John	2, July 1892		40	5	
Stegner, Howard John	3, Nov. 1891		22m	4	
Stegner, Katharine	7, Aug. 1900		59	8	
Stegner, Lisetta	3, Sept 1901		26	8	
Stegner, William H.	2, Apr. 1891		15m	4	
Stehl, Wilhelm	4, Apr. 1900	3, Apr.		8	
Stehle, August	22, July 1891		64	4	
Stehle, Engelbert (Fr.)	29, July 1896	28, July	75	5	
Stehling, Joseph	25, Sept 1894		56	5	
Stehmann, Joseph B.	12, May 1893		10m	5	
Stehr, Louis	9, May 1894		9m	5	
Steidele, Abelon	8, Mar. 1888		8d	1	
Steidinger, Ruth	11, Dec. 1891		25d	4	
Steidle, Adolph	13, Dec. 1898	11, Dec.	64- 5m	5	
Steidle, Adolph	27, Nov. 1899	26, Nov.		5	

Name	Notice Date	Death Date	Age	Page	Maiden Name
****	****** ****	***** ****	***	****	****** ****
Steidle, Charles	28, Mar. 1891		6m	4	
Steidle, Theresia	6, July 1897	4, July	67- 8m	5	Hipp
Steidle, Theresia	6, Nov. 1897	5, Nov.		5	Kattus
Steigelmann, Carl N.	1, Apr. 1889		7m	1	
Steigelmann, Guy	21, Dec. 1891		10	4	
Steiger, Felix	29, Oct. 1898	28, Oct.	56	4	
Steigerwald, Isabella	18, Dec. 1900			8	
Steigleder, Andreas	14, May 1896	12, May	63- 2m	5	
Steigler, Louisa	10, Oct. 1894		39	5	
Steihe, Joseph	1, July 1891		11m	1	
Steiler, Carrie	7, July 1891		21d	1	
Steiler, Josie	11, July 1889		10m	1	
Steimer, Louis C.	10, Dec. 1900		29	8	
Steimer, Nellie	1, Dec. 1900		13	8	
Stein,	5, Oct. 1888		3w	1	
Stein, Frank	25, June 1895		23	5	
Stein, Friederike	2, Aug. 1893		31	5	
Stein, George	28, July 1887		10	1	
Stein, Ida	15, Apr. 1888		10d	5	
Stein, Johanna	20, Apr. 1900	19, Apr.	70-10m	5	Hohl
Stein, Louis	2, Apr. 1901		10d	8	
Stein, Louise	25, Mar. 1889		31	1	
Stein, Marie	23, Mar. 1895		38	5	
Stein, Nancy	24, Dec. 1893		95	5	
Stein, Wilhelm	1, Sept 1899	31, Aug.	72- 5m	5	
Stein, William	4, Feb. 1901		56	8	
Steinau, J.	14, Dec. 1888		71	1	
Steinauer, Hilte	5, Nov. 1900		6w	8	
Steinbach, Catharine	30, June 1888		16	1	
Steinberg, Adelheid	11, Mar. 1889		60	1	
Steinberg, Joel H.	25, Oct. 1898	24, Oct.	69	5	
Steinbicker, J.H.	6, Sept 1893		73	5	
Steinbrecher, Henry	28, June 1892		53	5	
Steinbrenner, John	10, Apr. 1901		37	8	
Steinecke, Bertha	18, Feb. 1889		16	1	
Steinecke, Gust.	23, July 1890		37	1	
Steinecke, Henry	11, Sept 1900		62	5	
Steinecke, Mary	30, Nov. 1887		1d	4	
Steinegeweg, Clara	8, Sept 1890		8	4	
Steiner, Edward	25, Feb. 1889		22m	1	
Steiner, Frank	17, Oct. 1887		45	1	
Steiner, Friedrich	1, June 1895		31- 9m	5	
Steiner, Fritz	6, Oct. 1899	6, Oct.	75	5	
Steiner, Jacob P.	4, Nov. 1887		29	1	
Steiner, John	18, Aug. 1900		10m	8	
Steiner, Louis	9, Sept 1895	7, Sept	57	5	
Steiner, Martin H.	20, July 1893		1m	5	
Steinert, Amalia	6, July 1889		4m	1	
Steinert, Ida E.	28, Jan. 1894		5	5	
Steinfels, Louis	29, Sept 1891		71	4	
Steinhauser, Elisabeth	11, Aug. 1898	10, Aug.	72	5	
Steinhilder, Konrad	9, Jan. 1901		22	5	
Steinhiller, Pauline	21, July 1891		51	4	
Steinhoff, C.E.	17, May 1897	16, May	22- 8m	5	
Steinkamp, Barbara	17, Feb. 1898	16, Feb.	41	5	Ritter
Steinkamp, Catharina Maria	6, Sept 1894		75	5	
Steinkamp, Charles	10, Dec. 1891		30	1	
Steinkamp, Fred.	8, Nov. 1900		66	8	
Steinkamp, H. Louis	7, Aug. 1900		57	8	
Steinkamp, Lisette	12, Nov. 1888		24	2	
Steinkamp, Margaretha	13, Feb. 1894		65	5	
Steinkamp, Robert	29, Jan. 1896	24, Jan.	21-11m	5	
Steinkamp, Robert	21, May 1901		9m	8	
Steinkamp, Theresia	10, Dec. 1891		66	1	
Steinker, Harry	17, Jan. 1901		7	8	
Steinker, Marie	13, Oct. 1899	11, Oct.	14- 1m	5	
Steinmann, Caroline	19, Dec. 1891		85	4	
Steinmann, Louis Eduard	11, Sept 1896	9, Sept	80	5	
Steinmeier, Augusta	13, July 1887		5m	1	
Steinmetz, Clara	2, Aug. 1900		40	8	
Steinmetz, Victoria S.	5, June 1895		5m	5	

Name	Notice Date	Death Date	Age	Page	Maiden Name
****	****** ****	***** ****	***	****	****** ****
Steinmeyer, Mine	22, Mar. 1890		8m	1	
Steinmueller, Katharina Barb.	24, Mar. 1897	23, Mar.	46	5	
Steinwart, Heinrich J.	25, Jan. 1896	23, Jan.	75	5	
Steinwart, William	15, Jan. 1901		25	8	
Steir, Carrie	7, May 1891		6m	4	
Steir, Carrie	28, Mar. 1893		41	5	
Steir, Gertrude	6, July 1893		3m	5	
Steiris, Clara F.	29, Jan. 1891		13	4	
Steller, Anna Maria	2, Mar. 1888		57	1	
Stelnauer, Herman	25, Dec. 1887	23, Dec.	54- 3m	5	
Steltenkamp, Frank	11, Aug. 1887		68	1	
Steltenpohl, Anton	28, Nov. 1893		91	5	
Steltenpohl, Bernard	19, Aug. 1889		29	1	
Steltenpohl, Caroline	12, June 1889		9d	1	
Steltenpohl, Clemens	22, Oct. 1891		8	1	
Steltenpohl, Henry J.	19, June 1895		69	5	
Steltenpohl, Johanna	31, Jan. 1890		44	1	
Steltenpohl, John	26, May 1892		3	5	
Steltenpohl, Maria	24, Aug. 1895	22, Aug.	63- 6m	5	Derrenkamp
Steltenpohl, Maria Agnes	8, July 1897	6, July	82-10m	4	
Steltenpohl, Maria Dorothea	6, Jan. 1899	5, Jan.	66	4	Bohlke
Steltenpohler, Leonard	29, Mar. 1898	27, Mar.	4- 3m	5	
Steltenpuhl, Anna	24, Jan. 1888			1	
Stelzer, Ernst Heinrich	15, July 1901	14, July	52- 6m	5	
Stelzer, Kate	31, Jan. 1891		63	4	
Steman, Bernardina	19, Jan. 1898	18, Jan.	67	5	Holt
Steman, Johan	8, Dec. 1898	8, Dec.	80- 1m-29d	5	
Steman, Maria Theresia	29, Sept 1897	28, Sept	71- 4m	5	Roosmann
Stembicker, Maria	8, Nov. 1895	7, Nov.	72- 4m	5	
Stemmer, Frank	28, May 1891		36	4	
Stemmer, Karl Franz	12, May 1895		16	5	
Stemmer, Theresa	18, Feb. 1891		66	4	
Stemmler, Karl	28, Apr. 1898	27, Apr.	57- -18d	5	
Stemmler, Wilhelm	9, 10, Dec. 1893	9, Dec.	4- 6m	5	
Stempfle, Maria	7, Jan. 1901		83	5	
Stender, Carl	2, Apr. 1896	30, Mar.	72- 6m	5	
Stengel, Albert	27, Apr. 1901		12	8	
Stengel, Emma	21, Mar. 1893		21	5	
Stengel, H.W.	11, May 1896	10, May	5m	5	
Stengel, Katharina	28, Jan. 1897	25, Jan.	75-11m	5	Nettermann
Stenger, George	15, Oct. 1901		24	8	
Stenger, Joseph	2, Nov. 1900		63	8	
Stenger, Margaretha	10, Sept 1887		23	2	
Stenger, Rosa	28, Dec. 1892		7d	5	
Stenglein, Kunigunde	31, July 1900		70	5	
Stenglein, Lorenz J.	1, Apr. 1896	31, Mar.	2	5	
Stenglein, Mary	24, May 1892		2	5	
Stenglin, Fred.	14, June 1901		38	5	
Stentz, George	30, May 1895		15m	5	
Stepeldy, Josepha Sophia	16, Jan. 1892		2	5	
Stephan, August	22, Aug. 1895	21, Aug.		5	
Stephan, Carolina	18, Sept 1901		66	8	
Stephan, Georg	9, Feb. 1895		72	5	
Stephan, Jennie	23, July 1895		20m	5	
Stephan, W.	3, Dec. 1888		5m	1	
Stephens, Elisabeth	15, Feb. 1901		74	8	
Stephens, Jeanette E.	9, July 1895		2	5	
Stephens, Mable R.	5, July 1887		5	1	
Stephens, Milton P.	19, June 1889		9	1	
Stephens, Rachel	24, Dec. 1900		83	8	
Stephenson, Arthur	19, June 1901		90	8	
Stephenson, Robert	13, Aug. 1901		28	8	
Stepp, Marie	20, July 1901		66	8	
Stepp, Wilhelm	28, Jan. 1897	27, Jan.	63	5	
Stepp, Wilhelm	10, Jan. 1898	9, Jan.	35	5	
Steptoe, William	6, July 1901		34	8	
Sterfer, Maria	30, July 1892		75	5	
Stern, A.M.	25, Sept 1891		74- 2m- 1d	4	
Stern, Alice	19, Sept 1891		51	4	
Stern, Fannie	15, Aug. 1901		74	8	
Stern, Gabriel	15, Apr. 1898	14, Apr.	86	5	

Name ****	Notice Date ****** ****	Death Date ***** ****	Age ***	Page ****	Maiden Name ****** ****
Stern, Henry	23, Dec. 1891		78	4	
Stern, Israel	27, July 1887		61	1	
Stern, Rosa	16, July 1891		6m	4	
Sternberger, Nathan	17, May 1894		6m	5	
Sterns, Simon	26, Jan. 1901		23	8	
Sterrith, Martha	6, June 1901		84	8	
Stertz, Joseph	25, July 1893		76	5	
Stetefeld, John	9, Jan. 1891		26	4	
Steuber, John	13, Apr. 1901		18d	8	
Steuer, William A.	28, Apr. 1894		29	5	
Steuernagel, Bernardina	1, June 1893		74	5	
Steuernagel, C.	11, Jan. 1888		75	4	
Steuernagel, Lorenz	29, May 1889		35	1	
Steuernagel, Valentin	7, Jan. 1897	6, Jan.	76	5	
Steven, Christ.	18, Feb. 1888		32	1	
Stevens, Alfred	29, June 1901		50	8	
Stevens, Amelia	26, Dec. 1900		37	8	
Stevens, Charles H.	27, Apr. 1898	26, Apr.	71	5	
Stevens, Ethel B.	18, Apr. 1895		2m	5	
Stevens, Frank	22, Mar. 1901		10	8	
Stevens, George	16, Sept 1891		8	4	
Stevens, Leonidas E.	15, Sept 1900		2	5	
Stevens, Nathan	7, Nov. 1891		3	1	
Stevens, Ollie	29, Sept 1887		19m	4	
Stevens, Phillis	27, Mar. 1901		62	8	
Stevens, Susie	17, Apr. 1888		4m	1	
Stevens, Thomas	30, Oct. 1895	29, Oct.	35	5	
Stevenson, Cassie L.	3, May 1895		3m	5	
Stevenson, Peter G.	17, Sept 1901		67	8	
Steves, Eleanor	12, Sept 1901		1	5	
Steves, Elisabeth A.	5, Oct. 1895	4, Oct.	1-11m	5	
Steves, William	12, Mar. 1901		1	8	
Stewart,	13, Feb. 1901		8d	8	
Stewart, Arthur	28, Feb. 1901		22d	8	
Stewart, Ephraim J.	12, May 1895		4m	5	
Stewart, George H.	5, Apr. 1895		2	5	
Stewart, John	15, Dec. 1900		41	8	
Stewart, Kate	28, May 1890		28	1	
Stich, Walburga	27, Mar. 1895		92	5	
Sticht, Casper	4, Mar. 1890		45	1	
Stichtenoth, George	10, July 1891		18	4	
Stick, Joseph	24, Apr. 1901		51	8	
Stickan, Elise	3, Feb. 1891		25	4	
Stickler, Hyronimus	2, Apr. 1890		87	1	
Stickler, Joseph	9, Mar. 1897	7, Mar.	69	5	
Stiebel, Jakob	1, Nov. 1887		31	1	
Stiefel, Edwin Graf	25, Aug. 1892		18d	5	
Stiefel, Minnie	30, June 1888		14m	1	
Stiefvater, Theodor	24, Oct. 1892	22, Oct.	33- 6m-22d	5	
Stiegelmann, Charles	4, July 1901		50	8	
Stiegler, Andreas	5, July 1890		9m	1	
Stiegler, Rosine	13, Sept 1890		40	1	
Stiel, Herman	20, July 1887		19m	1	
Stiemann, Minerva	13, Oct. 1894		71	5	
Stiemer, Rose	10, Apr. 1901		7m	8	
Stienker, Dietrich	18, May 1897	16, May	65- 5m	5	
Stiens, Alma A.	26, June 1894		2m	5	
Stiens, Edward	8, Jan. 1898	6, Jan.	31-10m	4	
Stiens, Emilie C.	16, July 1890		2- 6m	1	
Stiens, John H.	3, Feb. 1894		80	5	
Stiens, Maria	2, Oct. 1895	1, Oct.	46	5	
Stier, Catharine W.T.	27, Feb. 1894		35	5	
Stier, John	13, Mar. 1901		46	8	
Stier, Kate	11, Aug. 1887		3m	1	
Stier, William Joseph	29, Dec. 1891		11m	4	
Stierer, G.C.	6, Mar. 1899	5, Mar.	31	4	
Stieringer, John	21, Mar. 1901		31	8	
Stierle, Isabella	15, July 1887		7m	1	
Stierle, Melchior	27, Mar. 1899	26, Mar.	73- 5m	4	
Stiesel, William	3, Nov. 1891		46	4	
Stieß, Wilhelm L.	4, Feb. 1899	3, Feb.	39	4	

Name	Notice Date	Death Date	Age	Page	Maiden Name
****	****** ****	***** ****	***	****	****** ****
Stifel, Clara A.	29, Apr. 1893		28	5	
Stifel, Mary	20, Nov. 1891		51	4	
Stifel, Rosina	23, July 1887		74	1	
Stigelman, Robert	17, Apr. 1901		29	8	
Stigler, Albert	15, Jan. 1901		4	8	
Stigler, Walburga	27, Sept 1893		73	5	
Stilk, Mary	5, Apr. 1893		92	5	
Still, August	9, Dec. 1887		57	1	
Still, Benetha M.	25, June 1888		5m	1	
Stille, G.	31, Dec. 1891		30	1	
Stille, Mary	6, Apr. 1893		92	5	
Stillerich, Michael	23, June 1893		35	5	
Stillmann, George K.	28, Jan. 1891		70	4	
Stimker, Henrietta	13, May 1901		9	8	
Stimmer, Andrew	21, Apr. 1895		69	5	
Sting, Jacob	29, Sept 1898	28, Sept	77	5	
Stippish, Fred.	14, Mar. 1891		19	4	
Stirle, Louis	21, July 1893		70	5	
Stirn, Maria	19, Sept 1895	18, Sept	78	5	Stieve
Stirnkorb, Charles	4, Feb. 1901		43	8	
Stirnkorb, Jacob	15, July 1898	13, July	37- 2m	5	
Stirnkorb, Katie	17, Apr. 1888	16, Apr.	10m-26d	4	
Stitericht, J.	14, Dec. 1893		41	5	
Stith, Florence	19, Sept 1888		14m	2	
Stobler, J.D.	8, May 1889		47	1	
Stobley, Carrie	14, May 1895		3	5	
Stock, Anna	19, June 1901		63	8	
Stock, Barbara	1, Oct. 1890		76	1	
Stock, Henriette	30, Aug. 1898	30, Aug.	57- 3m	4	Mühlberger
Stocker, Geneva Georgia	29, Oct. 1898	28, Oct.	2m	4	
Stocker, Joseph	5, Apr. 1889		13m	1	
Stocker, Katharina	25, Apr. 1892		7	5	
Stocker, Mary C.	5, July 1887		11m	1	
Stocker, Michael	10, Mar. 1899	8, Mar.	62- 8m	5	
Stockhoff, Elisabeth	30, Sept 1889		69	1	
Stockhoff, Katharina	2, Nov. 1898	31, Oct.	100-11m	5	Takenberg
Stockhove, Katharine	3, Aug. 1901		55	8	
Stockman, Catharine	9, Feb. 1901		78	8	
Stockmann, Anna M.	21, Jan. 1891		75	4	
Stockmeier, Minnie	29, Oct. 1900		9	8	
Stockum, Johan	22, Jan. 1890		80	1	
Stockum, Mary	10, Nov. 1900		36	8	
Stoddard, Ida	30, Aug. 1900		51	5	
Stoebel, Henry G.	5, May 1897	3, May	72	5	
Stoecklin, Emma	20, July 1895		8m	5	
Stoecklin, Harry F.	28, Sept 1893		19m	5	
Stoehr, Leonard	28, Apr. 1891		73	4	
Stoehr, Paul	11, July 1896	10, July	17- 6m	5	
Stoehr, Seraphinus (Br.)	21, July 1898	20, July	50- 5m	5	
Stoehr, Willie P.	21, June 1894		8	5	
Stoes, Mathias	26, Mar. 1900	25, Mar.	49	8	
Stoeser, F.	13, Jan. 1888		10	1	
Stoever, Katharine	7, Aug. 1894		69	5	
Stoever, Richard	22, July 1887		55	1	
Stoffer, Konstantine	10, Apr. 1894		75	5	
Stoffregen, Amelia	28, Mar. 1893		33	5	
Stoffregen, Maria Katharina	10, Mar. 1896	9, Mar.		5	Theobald
Stohl, Katharine	6, Sept 1893		62	5	
Stohl, Margaret	27, Sept 1900		76	8	
Stohlmann, Bernard	28, Apr. 1891		3m	4	
Stokes, James	30, Aug. 1900		68	5	
Stoll, (son of Mathias)	23, Oct. 1889	17, Oct.	3- 8m	4	
Stoll, Jakob	3, Jan. 1890		15m	1	
Stoll, Maria	28, Nov. 1896	27, Nov.		5	
Stoll, William	3, Feb. 1891		1	4	
Stoll, William C.	11, Apr. 1893		2	5	
Stolla, John	24, May 1894		40	5	
Stollmann, Josephine	17, May 1901		6m	8	
Stolz, Bernard	14, May 1895		39	5	
Stolz, Bernard	24, July 1895		75	5	
Stolz, Ellie	9, July 1891		2w	4	

Name	Notice Date	Death Date	Age	Page	Maiden Name
****	****** ****	***** ****	***	****	****** ****
Stoman, Bernard	29, Nov. 1893		26	5	
Stone, Harvey	4, July 1887		33	1	
Stone, James	19, Nov. 1900		22	8	
Stone, M.	27, Dec. 1887		7w	1	
Stone, Olive C.	29, Dec. 1900		66	8	
Stoops, John L.	13, Nov. 1900		46	8	
Stoppelkamp, Catharine	19, June 1897	17, June	56	4	Roß
Storch, Adelheid	9, Dec. 1899	8, Dec.	72- 6m	4	Plagge
Storch, Anna M.	24, May 1894		17d	5	
Storch, Charles H.	29, May 1894		23d	5	
Storch, Eleanor	4, Feb. 1901		27	8	
Storch, L. Charles	11, Dec. 1893		32	5	
Storch, William	17, Aug. 1901		69	8	
Storck, Franz	9, Dec. 1891		64	2	
Storck, William	30, Apr. 1895		59	5	
Stordeur, Henry	20, Dec. 1889		78	1	
Storey, George	3, July 1901		6m	8	
Storey, Joseph Ed.	7, Sept 1901		31	8	
Storig, Louise	17, Feb. 1894		27	5	
Storing, Elizabeth	25, Dec. 1891		80	2	
Stork, Maria A.	4, June 1891		83	4	
Stortz, Helena	8, May 1891		74	4	
Story, Apollonia	10, Jan. 1899	9, Jan.	56- 9m	5	
Storz, Carl	29, June 1901		57	8	
Stothfang, Clifford	29, May 1894		13	5	
Stothfang, Fred.	14, Sept 1894		16m	5	
Stout, Ann	18, June 1901		89	8	
Stout, Ruth	16, Apr. 1895		9m	5	
Stover, Friedrich Johan	25, Apr. 1899	23, Apr.	65- 7m	4	
Stow, Daniel	20, Nov. 1900		78	8	
Stowers, Jerry	8, Mar. 1901		67	8	
Stoz, Fred. E.	23, Nov. 1892		43	5	
Stoß, Bertha	4, Jan. 1899	3, Jan.	40- 1m	5	Ochsle
Stradtmann, H.B.C.	27, July 1887		60	1	
Stralow, Charles	7, July 1888		65	4	
Straltmann, Adelheide	26, Jan. 1893		76	5	
Strankmeyer, Minnie	11, May 1889		7	1	
Stranon, John	24, Dec. 1893		51	5	
Strapemeyer, Mary	3, Apr. 1888		76	4	
Strassel, Nicolaus	24, Feb. 1896	23, Feb.	66- 4m	5	
Strasser, Ella	16, Nov. 1899	14, Nov.	10	5	
Strasser, Gilbert	13, July 1897	12, July	3	5	
Strasser, Joseph	8, July 1893		37	5	
Strasser, Margaretha	23, Jan. 1891		73	4	
Strategir, Heinrich	13, Jan. 1899	11, Jan.	43- 2m	4	
Strategir, Maria	17, Aug. 1898	16, Aug.	61- -25d	4	Gohs
Stratemeyer, Anna	24, Jan. 1901		75	8	
Stratemeyer, Charles	5, July 1901		26	8	
Stratemeyer, J.	25, Feb. 1901		74	8	
Stratemeyer, Minna	28, Sept 1895	27, Sept		5	
Stratmann, J.B.	5, May 1894		73	5	
Stratmann, Mary	24, Apr. 1895		29	5	
Strattan, Jennie	29, Aug. 1891		33	4	
Strattmann, Henry	11, Feb. 1889		38	1	
Straub, Louis	7, Aug. 1894		10m	5	
Straub, Theresa	1, Apr. 1889		7	1	
Straughter, Sarah	30, Aug. 1887		65	1	
Straukamp, Franz F.	20, May 1897	18, May	74	5	
Straus, Julian H.	24, Oct. 1891		30d	4	
Straus, Lena	5, May 1894		48	5	
Strautmann, H.F.	11, Oct. 1895	10, Oct.	86	5	
Strauß,	10, Jan. 1891		1d	4	
Strauß, Barbara	9, July 1896	8, July	73	5	Schettinger
Strauß, Hannah	12, Oct. 1894		47	5	
Strauß, Julius	5, Mar. 1901		20	5	
Strauß, Nettie	1, Dec. 1891		18	4	
Strauß, Rachel	8, Apr. 1891		87	4	
Strauß, Seligman	3, Mar. 1900	2, Mar.	76	5	
Strauß, Seligman	3, Mar. 1900	2, Mar.	7	5	
Strauß, Yetta	22, Feb. 1895		70	5	
Strawa, Emma	5, June 1888		45	4	

Name ****	Notice Date ****** ****	Death Date ***** ****	Age ***	Page ****	Maiden Name ****** ****
Straßburger, George	7, Sept 1900		58	5	
Straßburger, Philomena	3, Feb. 1896	1, Feb.	47- 3m	5	Kaiser
Straßer, Kasper	19, Oct. 1889		75- 9m	1	
Straßer, Theresa	21, Aug. 1888		6m	1	
Stredelmeyer, Christina	21, Oct. 1891		2m	4	
Streeter, G.	27, Dec. 1887		25	1	
Streetmeyer, Albert A.	15, Mar. 1892		27	5	
Strefelt, Gertrude	29, July 1893		85	5	
Streher, Peter	25, Dec. 1894		36	5	
Streif, Adelheid	20, Aug. 1888		4	1	
Streif, Fred. J.	19, Jan. 1888		34	4	
Streif, Rosa	26, July 1893		4m	5	
Streifel, William J.	28, Jan. 1891		16d	4	
Streiff, J.R.	24, Nov. 1898	21, Nov.		5	
Streit, Bertha	21, Aug. 1887		42	5	
Streit, Franz Joseph	21, June 1898	20, June	89- 9m	4	
Streng, Henry J.	22, May 1899		43- 9m	4	
Streng, Maria Henriette	16, Apr. 1898	15, Apr.	3- 9m	5	
Streng, Mary	26, May 1896	25, May	43	5	
Strettholt, Katharina J.	28, June 1889		7m	1	
Stretz, Elisabeth	31, Jan. 1893		1m	5	
Stretz, Mary	21, Mar. 1898	19, Mar.		5	
Streutker, Anna	22, Dec. 1891		75	4	
Streutker, Friedrich	3, Apr. 1890		82	1	
Streutker, Mina	7, Dec. 1887		67- 5m	1	
Stribley, George	8, July 1901		4m	8	
Strickenkamp, Emma	17, Oct. 1887		21d	1	
Stricker, Bernard F.	5, Feb. 1898	4, Feb.	32- 7m-14d	5	
Stricker, Edward	28, Aug. 1890		10m	1	
Stricker, Elizabeth	10, Sept 1890		41	1	
Stricker, Joseph	19, Apr. 1894		21	5	
Stricker, Katharine	24, June 1896	23, June	62- 5m	5	Worpenberg
Stricker, Leo	13, Feb. 1894		21	5	
Stricker, Mary	1, Feb. 1893		67	5	
Stricker, Peter	24, July 1899	23, July	51-10m-11d	5	
Stricker, Peter	11, May 1901		25	8	
Strickler, Friedricka	3, Mar. 1888		41	1	
Strickler, Michael	18, May 1899	17, May		5	
Stridle, John	25, Aug. 1900		40	5	
Strietelmeyer, Amelia	1, June 1893		5	5	
Strietmann, Johan Heinrich	21, 22, Feb. 1898	19, Feb.	76-10m	5	
Strietmann, John F.	28, Nov. 1893		70	5	
Striff, M.A.	3, Jan. 1888		82	1	
Strilley, Clarence	12, Mar. 1901		1	8	
Strittholt, Bernard	30, Apr. 1898	28, Apr.	16- 1m	4	
Strittholt, Maria Anna	23, July 1896	22, July	18- 5m	5	
Strobel, Lena M.	29, Mar. 1894		14m	5	
Strober, Mary	16, Apr. 1891		67	4	
Stroeher, Fred.	29, July 1893		44	5	
Strohbach, Georg	11, Nov. 1896	10, Nov.	50-11m	5	
Stroheim, Salo	12, Sept 1901		24	5	
Strohkamp, John	20, Mar. 1891		48	4	
Strohm, Fr.	18, Aug. 1890		34	1	
Strong, Ethel	16, Mar. 1892		5m	1	
Strong, M.	3, Sept 1901		32	8	
Strong, William	25, Aug. 1900			5	
Stroppel, Anna	20, Sept 1901		28	1	
Strothmann, George	8, Dec. 1891		47	4	
Strotmaier, B.	25, June 1888		19m	1	
Stroup, George D.	5, Jan. 1889		7w	1	
Strubbe, Katharine	10, Jan. 1893		54	5	
Strubbe, Lucy	31, July 1894		49	5	
Struck, Minnie	9, Feb. 1901		41	8	
Struden, H.	30, Jan. 1888		9	1	
Struke, Catharine	4, July 1901		2	8	
Strull, Margaret	18, Jan. 1901		72	8	
Strumpler, Henry W.	20, May 1893		72	5	
Strunk, Anna	29, Oct. 1900			8	
Strunk, Mary	9, Dec. 1892		72	5	
Strunk, Minnie	12, Aug. 1892		68	5	
Strunk, Simon H.	15, Nov. 1900		58	8	

Name	Notice Date	Death Date	Age	Page	Maiden Name
****	****** ****	***** ****	***	****	****** ****
Strunk, William	1, June 1901		5	8	
Strupe, Barbara	10, July 1888		37	1	
Strut, George	26, June 1891		2m	4	
Strübbe, Johan Heinrich	21, Dec. 1898	20, Dec.	44- 1m	5	
Stuart, G.L.	25, June 1888		14m	1	
Stuart, Leonard	2, July 1892		6m	5	
Stubbs, Quincy	8, Dec. 1891		6	4	
Stubenrauch, Jacob Franz	7, Aug. 1896	5, Aug.	73-11m	5	
Stuber, Johan	19, Mar. 1896	17, Mar.	58	5	
Stuck, Adam	7, Apr. 1891		19	4	
Stuck, George	16, July 1900		79	8	
Stuck, Mary	23, Oct. 1887		3w	4	
Stuckenberg, Georg	8, Feb. 1901		63	8	
Studelberg, Caroline	24, Feb. 1891		78	4	
Studerns, Jakob	25, Mar. 1901		8	8	
Stuebe, Lina	3, Feb. 1894		33	5	
Stueberger, Catharine	13, July 1887		49	1	
Stuesti, Anna	1, Jan. 1888			5	Tickuß
Stuewe, Isabella	11, Sept 1889		19	1	
Stuff, John	13, June 1901		1m	8	
Stuhlburg, Pauline	16, Apr. 1901		10	8	
Stuhlreyer, Hubert	29, Apr. 1897	28, Apr.	56- 7m- 7d	4,5	
Stuit, Otto (Rev)	4, Sept 1888		38	2	
Stukenborg, Elisabeth	20, Feb. 1899	18, Feb.	44-11m	5	Meyer
Stulz, George	11, Nov. 1891		1	1	
Stumininsko, Maria	22, July 1887		12m	1	
Stump, Catharine	29, Mar. 1888		60	1	
Stump, John	17, Sept 1901		50	8	
Stump, Sophia	4, May 1893		1	5	
Stumpf, Casper	2, Jan. 1896	1, Jan.	61	5	
Stumpf, Charles	12, Aug. 1889		30m	1	
Stumpf, Elisabeth	26, Nov. 1892		46	5	
Stumpf, George	8, Jan. 1901		81	8	
Stumpf, Jennie Lind	8, Dec. 1887		5m	1	
Stumpf, Louisa	9, Nov. 1896	8, Nov.	78	5	
Stumpf, Louise	1, Feb. 1890		32	1	
Stumpfmeyer, Conrad	16, Jan. 1897	15, Jan.	71- 9m	5	
Stuntebeck, Friedrich	31, Jan. 1898	29, Jan.	66- 8m-24d	5	
Stuntebeck, Maria	20, Apr. 1899	18, Apr.	65-10m	4	Dürstock
Sturgardt, Howard	23, May 1901		11d	8	
Sturle, Cate	1, July 1891		65	1	
Sturm, Andreas J.	23, Feb. 1900	22, Feb.	53	5	
Sturm, J.	20, Apr. 1888		53	4	
Sturm, Joseph	30, Sept 1901		66	8	
Sturm, Julius	15, July 1898	14, July		5	
Sturm, Karolina	16, Apr. 1896	15, Apr.	38- 4m	5	Bergmeier
Sturm, Philippina	27, June 1888		1	1	
Sturm, William	14, July 1892		10m	5	
Sturm, William	21, Jan. 1893		1	5	
Sturow, Philippine	11, Jan. 1898	9, Jan.	66- 7m	5	
Sturtz, William	4, Jan. 1901		70	5	
Sturwold, Rosa	26, Mar. 1896	24, Mar.	25- 1m	5	
Stute, W.	17, Jan. 1894		1m	5	
Stutfanth, Christoph	5, Sept 1889		64	1	
Stutzmann, Margaret	1, Dec. 1900		55	8	
Stöllender, Georg	16, May 1900	15, May	48	5	
Stöver, Sophia	24, Feb. 1888		29	4	
Stübing, Charles	12, Nov. 1887		45	1	
Stücke, Anna	7, Sept 1887		1d	1	
Stürmer, Anton	7, Dec. 1895	6, Dec.	47-11m	5	
Sudbeck, Franz A.	4, Mar. 1889		76	1	
Suddendorf, Frank J.	26, Feb. 1891		2m	4	
Suddendorf, Katie	11, Jan. 1892		2m	4	
Suddendorf, Walter J.	29, Mar. 1894		7d	5	
Suddon, Mary	5, Mar. 1901		8d	5	
Sudendic, Sophia	16, Mar. 1889		30	1	
Sudendorf, Ferdinand	19, July 1894		1d	5	
Sudor, E.H.	31, Mar. 1892		36	5	
Sudorius, Anna	19, Sept 1888		67	2	
Sueferle, Christina	22, Apr. 1891		56	4	
Suessdorf, Hugo	11, Aug. 1896	9, Aug.	43	5	

Name ****	Notice Date ****** ****	Death Date ***** ****	Age ***	Page ****	Maiden Name ****** ****
Suetholz, Elisabeth	21, June 1900	18, June	76	6	Arlinghouse
Sueß, Christine	7, Aug. 1896	7, Aug.	69	4	
Sueß, George	28, Sept 1897	27, Sept	44	5	
Suhr, Franz Xaver	16, Dec. 1897	15, Dec.	76	5	
Suhr, Mary	21, Feb. 1888		33	1	
Suhre, Karl W.	11, Aug. 1896	9, Aug.	34- -13d	5	
Suhrenbusch, Friedrich	23, Dec. 1891		32	4	
Sullinger, Addie	14, Dec. 1893		40	5	
Sullivan, Ben F.	30, Aug. 1901		24	8	
Sullivan, Catharine	25, Apr. 1888		44	1	
Sullivan, Charles	29, Dec. 1900		55	8	
Sullivan, Cornelius	2, Nov. 1900		26	8	
Sullivan, Daniel	20, July 1887		25	1	
Sullivan, Dennis	7, Aug. 1900		80	8	
Sullivan, Dennis	24, May 1901		36	8	
Sullivan, Ellen S.	5, Apr. 1895		53	5	
Sullivan, Florence	17, Dec. 1900		27	8	
Sullivan, Franziska	8, Jan. 1897	7, Jan.	38	5	Ruebusch
Sullivan, George	8, May 1888		10m	1	
Sullivan, Jennie	1, Feb. 1901		46	8	
Sullivan, Jeremiah	19, July 1887		1w	1	
Sullivan, John	30, Nov. 1887		10m	4	
Sullivan, John	7, Aug. 1901		5m	8	
Sullivan, Joseph	7, May 1888		1d	1	
Sullivan, Julia	6, Mar. 1901		62	5	
Sullivan, M.	31, Jan. 1901		64	8	
Sullivan, Maria	27, Nov. 1900		56	8	
Sullivan, Mary	25, Apr. 1901		52	8	
Sulser, Jessie	17, Apr. 1901		10	8	
Sultzer, Leona	27, Aug. 1901		36	1	
Summe, Theresa	27, Oct. 1891		20	1	
Summer, Emanuel	4, Apr. 1888		46	1	
Sumper, Cecil	29, June 1901		6m	8	
Sund, George	2, Aug. 1887		9m	1	
Sund, Gerhard Heinrich	7, Aug. 1897	5, Aug.	73- 2m	4	
Sund, Hilda	24, Sept 1894		1d	5	
Sunderbruch, August	14, Aug. 1896	12, Aug.	33	5	
Sunderbruck, Harry L.	7, Jan. 1897	6, Jan.	41	5	
Sundermann, Alwine	13, Oct. 1900		20	8	
Sundermann, M.	6, Feb. 1901		10	8	
Sundermann, Marie Louise	23, Aug. 1895	21, Aug.	56- 7m	5	
Suns, J.F.	20, June 1888		1d	1	
Supe, Caroline	3, Jan. 1896	1, Jan.	63- 8m	5	
Supplee, Emily Marie	27, Feb. 1901		82	8	
Suptus, Wilhelm G.	15, Aug. 1893		34	5	
Surbeck, Lena	10, Aug. 1894		1m	5	
Surkamp, Elisabeth	13, Feb. 1894		51	5	
Surmann, Anton	3, Nov. 1897	2, Nov.	79- 4m	5	
Surmann, Marie E.	28, Dec. 1891		72	4	
Suter, Emma	15, Jan. 1901		10	8	
Suter, J.L.	16, Aug. 1887		77	1	
Sutkamp, H.H.	10, Mar. 1897	8, Mar.	68- 3m	5	
Sutter, John L.	8, Aug. 1889		28	1	
Sutter, Therese	13, Feb. 1901		58	8	
Sutton, Mary Anna	9, Nov. 1896	8, Nov.	4- 8m	5	
Sutton, Pearl	10, Aug. 1901		29	8	
Svendsen, Rosa	15, June 1894		25	5	
Swedersky, Mary	13, Feb. 1901		25	8	
Sweeney, Amelia	2, Aug. 1901		48	8	
Sweeney, Andrew	2, Jan. 1901		67	5	
Sweeney, Honora	1, Sept 1888		1m	1	
Sweeney, Margaret	6, Oct. 1900		84	5	
Sweeney, Mary	8, Sept 1887		1d	1	
Sweeney, Pat.	11, Nov. 1891		63	1	
Sweeney, Rosa	23, Apr. 1895		34	5	
Sweers, Maria	23, Oct. 1896	22, Oct.	32-11m	5	
Swerdosky, Frank	5, Dec. 1889		56	1	
Swielan, John	7, July 1888		79	4	
Swietzer, Katie	28, Feb. 1891		9	4	
Swift,	8, Aug. 1901		1d	8	
Swift, Joseph	4, Nov. 1887		33	1	

Name ****	Notice Date ****** ****	Death Date ***** ****	Age ***	Page ****	Maiden Name ****** ****
Swis, Joseph	23, Sept 1896	22, Sept	24-11m	5	
Switzer, Jacob	5, Mar. 1892		32	5	
Swobland, William	4, Jan. 1893		9m	5	
Sylvester, (Mrs)	11, Sept 1888	11, Sept	72	1	
Sylvester, Eliza	31, July 1894		59	5	
Syms, Arthur	20, Feb. 1901		3m	8	
Synnestadt, Marie	6, June 1901		80	8	
Synneswelt, John C.	9, May 1895		75	5	
Syron, Julia	21, May 1901		40	8	
Szwirschina, Maria	16, 17, May 1893	16, May	78	5	
Säger, Cecilia	26, Mar. 1895		2m	5	
Sälinger, Anton	12, June 1889		60	1	
Söhngen, Tekla	23, Nov. 1889		2m	1	
Söllheim, Egmont	13, Dec. 1895	9, Dec.	2m	5	
Sönke, Gerhard	25, Mar. 1889		52	1	
Süßeling, Joseph	14, May 1891		3	4	
Tabben, Harry	28, May 1891		7	4	
Tabeling, Anna Maria	30, Jan. 1900	28, Jan.	71- 9m	5	Siemer
Tabeling, Bernard	16, Nov. 1899	14, Nov.		5	
Tache, Hen.	27, Feb. 1894		40	5	
Tacke, Wilhelmine	30, 31, Oct. 1895	29, Oct.	72	5	Hartmann
Tadloch, Stanley	17, Apr. 1890		2	1	
Tafel, Hugo A.	6, May 1897	30, Apr.	25	5	
Taft, Rebecca	13, Nov. 1900		79	8	
Tahse, Raymond W.	2, Feb. 1897	1, Feb.	5- 5m	5	
Taland, August	5, Aug. 1892		59	5	
Talbot, Peter	26, July 1900			5	
Talke, Fritz H.	4, June 1896	3, June		5	
Tams, Sophia	30, Apr. 1895		69	5	
Tandrop, Ulrich C.	20, July 1899	19, July	81	5	
Tanke, Katharine	9, 11, Nov. 1895	8, Nov.	78- 5m	5	
Taphorn, Elisabeth	23, Mar. 1894		66	5	
Taphorn, Frank J.	23, Mar. 1895		26	5	
Taphorn, John H.	14, Feb. 1891		50	4	
Taphorn, Kate	29, Jan. 1901		83	8	
Tapke, Joseph A.	27, Mar. 1900	26, Mar.		5	
Tapke, Maria Elisabeth	24, Jan. 1888		87- 9m	1	
Tappe, Doretta	13, Jan. 1891		2	1	
Tappe, Flora	22, June 1892		1	5	
Tappe, G.	24, Jan. 1888		79-10m	1	
Tappehorn, Jennie	5, Dec. 1893		49	5	
Tarbarg, Johanna C.	24, Feb. 1891		70	4	
Tarhardes, Rosa M.	17, July 1891		10m	1	
Tarrell, Kate	20, July 1887		55	1	
Tasce, Maggie	12, July 1890		9m	1	
Tate, George H.	25, Apr. 1890		76	1	
Tatgenhorst, Dora	2, Nov. 1900		52	8	
Tatgenhorst, Emilie	1, Aug. 1888		16m	2	
Tatman, Abbie	14, Mar. 1893		21	5	
Tatten, Mary Hazel	19, Aug. 1892		7d	5	
Tattlich, Lena	15, Aug. 1891		28	4	
Tatum, Sam. C.	8, Nov. 1887		31	1	
Taub, Francis	23, Mar. 1901		28	8	
Taubald, Charles H.	14, Feb. 1900	13, Feb.	42	8	
Tauchert, Bertha	17, Apr. 1899	16, Apr.	54	5	Thiel
Tavel, Annie	25, Sept 1890		1m	1	
Taylor, Clifford	13, Aug. 1901		7m	8	
Taylor, D.	3, Oct. 1901		36	8	
Taylor, George	7, Aug. 1900		60	8	
Taylor, George	19, Sept 1900		83	8	
Taylor, Harrey	23, Aug. 1887			1	
Taylor, Henry	12, Nov. 1900		55	5	
Taylor, James	7, Oct. 1901		65	1	
Taylor, John	19, July 1900		70	8	
Taylor, John C.	7, Feb. 1901		51	8	
Taylor, Joshua	26, June 1901		36	8	
Taylor, Lucinda	24, Jan. 1901		110	8	
Taylor, Maline	2, May 1901		57	8	
Taylor, Martha	20, Aug. 1901		81	8	
Taylor, Mary T.	19, July 1887		75	1	

Name ****	Notice Date ****** ****	Death Date ***** ****	Age ***	Page ****	Maiden Name ****** ****
Taylor, Melvin	30, Apr. 1901		3m	8	
Taylor, Thornton	9, Jan. 1901		8d	5	
Taylor, William F.	13, Nov. 1900		55	8	
TeLintels, Anthony	1, July 1891		1	1	
Tebb, Joseph	21, Oct. 1895	19, Oct.	37	5	
Tebbe, J.B.	17, Dec. 1895	16, Dec.	67- 7m	4	
Tebbe, John H.	24, Jan. 1891		68	4	
Tebbe, Lillian F.	26, Aug. 1893		33	5	
Tebbe, Mary E.	28, May 1891		5d	4	
Tebbenhoff, C.	27, Dec. 1887		3- 6m	1	
Tebbs, Cora	10, Feb. 1896	9, Feb.	10	5	
Tebhardt, William	12, Sept 1891		8m	1	
Techmeier, Sophia	9, Nov. 1896	8, Nov.		5	Fisbeck
Technow, Katie	1, Sept 1896	31, Aug.		5	
Teckel, John	7, June 1888		29	1	
Tedesche, Fanny	5, Sept 1888		65	2	
Tedtmann, Elisabeth	26, July 1893		44	5	
Tedtmann, Elisabeth	23, Sept 1896	22, Sept	74- 7m	5	Schmidt
Teepe, Louise	2, Apr. 1901		71	8	
Teepen, Bernard	24, Feb. 1894		1	5	
Teepen, Mary	3, Jan. 1898	31, Dec.	43- - 6d	5	Freking
Teesen, Joseph	20, Feb. 1901		37	8	
Teets, Cornelia	10, Aug. 1889		3m	1	
Tegeler, Carolina	3, Oct. 1898	1, Oct.	40	5	Becker
Tegeler, William	24, Oct. 1887		18	1	
Tegeler, William	19, Jan. 1894		2	5	
Tegge, Anna	10, Apr. 1889		96	1	
Tegtmeier, William	10, Oct. 1891		8	4	
Tehan, Cornelius	6, Nov. 1900		38	8	
Tehan, Mary	10, Oct. 1900		90	8	
Teigler, Ferdinand	14, Feb. 1891		71	4	
Teimer, Adolphine	13, July 1900		27	8	
Teipe, Gertrude	30, July 1896	27, July	48	5	
Tekuelve, Anna M.	16, July 1888		16	1	
Telgheder, Herman	25, Aug. 1887	24, Aug.	46- 4m-19d	* 1,4	
Telgheder, Katharina	22, Feb. 1897	21, Feb.		5	Mundorff
Telgheder, Mary	10, May 1889		1	1	
Telgmann, Else	24, Nov. 1896	22, Nov.		5	Dangers
Telychan, John	23, June 1888		14m	1	
Temmen, Johan Herman	23, Jan. 1899	21, Jan.	79	5	
Temmen, Robert	24, May 1895		3m	5	
Temple, Elisabeth	15, Oct. 1900		60	5	
Ten, Katie	3, July 1894		2m	5	
Tenant, L.B.	10, Oct. 1900		72	8	
Tenbrink, Anton	4, Feb. 1893		84	5	
Tenbusch, J.W.	11, Jan. 1888		72	4	
Tenger, Adeline	12, May 1895		69	5	
Tenhemfeldt, Christina	16, Apr. 1895		59	5	
Tenhenfeld, Josephine	7, May 1891		37	4	
Tenhunefeld, Herman	28, Sept 1888		80	2	
Tenkotte, Katharina	26, May 1898	24, May	47- -22d	5	Vandeneynden
Tennemann, Elise	21, May 1889		87	1	
Tennenbaum, Dinah	22, Jan. 1891		8w	4	
Tenner, Armin	22, June 1898	16, June	53	5	
Tenoever, Elisabeth	27, Mar. 1895		12	5	
Tenoever, Herman A.	7, Aug. 1894		64	5	
Teodale, Eliza	11, Aug. 1887		70	1	
Tepe, Chr.	17, Jan. 1888		2	4	
Tepe, Emma L.	25, Mar. 1899	24, Mar.	40- 1m-24d	5	Huntemann
Tepe, John B.	8, May 1889		5	1	
Tepe, Mary	14, June 1889		25	1	
Tepe, Wilhelm	7, Aug. 1900		25	8	
Tepie, J.H.	27, May 1897	25, May	71	5	
Terry, Cora	2, Mar. 1888		1- 6m	1	
Terstege, Mary	16, Apr. 1895		65	5	
Teski, Johan	3, July 1897	30, June		5	
Teufen, Frank	23, Feb. 1889		9m	1	
Teveluwe, Wilhelm	14, Dec. 1899	13, Dec.	50- 7m	5	
Tevlin, Mary	3, Apr. 1888		66	4	
Tewens, James	31, Jan. 1891		47	4	
Textor, Willie	14, Nov. 1896	13, Nov.	8m- 6d	5	

Name ****	Notice Date ****** ****	Death Date ***** ****	Age ***	Page ****	Maiden Name ****** ****
Thai, Betty	12, Aug. 1887		68	1	
Thale, Christoph	16, Aug. 1901		16	8	
Thalheimer, John	13, May 1901		16	8	
Tharp, Pet.	5, Aug. 1890		64	1	
Thatcher, John	8, Aug. 1900		25	8	
Thauwald, Christina	28, Dec. 1897	27, Dec.	72- 8m	4	Waechter
Thauwald, Friedrich Wilhelm	5, Mar. 1898	3, Mar.	59	5	
Thedick, Eliza	13, Dec. 1900		72	8	
Theil, Charles	14, Dec. 1893		44	5	
Theiler, Ben.	12, July 1889		77	1	
Theilmann, H.H.	18, Dec. 1895	17, Dec.	62- 2m	5	
Theis, Andy	21, May 1889		16m	1	
Theis, Charles	5, Sept 1900		49	5	
Theis, Heinrich	19, May 1896	17, May	23	5	
Theis, Helena	14, Feb. 1893		3m	5	
Theis, Henry	24, May 1892		4m	5	
Theis, Herbert H.	14, July 1891		20d	4	
Theis, Herman	31, July 1901		67	8	
Theis, J.V.	15, Dec. 1896	13, Dec.	48- 8m	5	
Theis, Jakob	23, Mar. 1901		48	8	
Theis, Rhoda	11, May 1901		2	8	
Theise, Dorothea H.	3, July 1887		5m	4	
Theise, Fred.	15, Feb. 1901		36	8	
Theising, Ben.	30, Dec. 1893		66	5	
Theler, Elizabeth	29, Dec. 1888		63	1	
Theman, Bernard	31, Mar. 1892		5m	5	
Theobald, Annie	25, Mar. 1901		45	8	
Theobald, Conrad	30, Dec. 1893		64	5	
Theobald, Conrad	23, Jan. 1900	20, Jan.	41-10m	4	
Theobald, Edna	27, Apr. 1901		6	8	
Theobald, Elisabeth	31, Mar. 1897	30, Mar.	69- 8m	5	Meider
Theobald, Emma Edith	17, Nov. 1896	16, Nov.	10- 5m	5	
Theobald, George	16, Oct. 1890		75	1	
Theobald, John	12, July 1890		65	1	
Theobald, John A.	14, Mar. 1893		59	5	
Theobald, Maggie	6, June 1901		26	8	
Theobald, Maria	15, May 1896	14, May	50-11m	5	
Theobald, Marie	9, Dec. 1896	7, Dec.	3- 2m	5	
Thering, Joseph	31, Oct. 1894		60	5	
Thesing, Johan Friedrich Wm.	8, Aug. 1896	6, Aug.	64- 4m	5	
Thesken, Catharine	24, July 1901		70	8	
Theurkauf, Anna W.	15, Feb. 1895		40	5	
Thicken, Clara	30, July 1898	29, July	8m- 4d	5	
Thie, William	12, Aug. 1901		2m	8	
Thiecken, Thekla E.	1, Nov. 1887		1- 7m-15d	1	
Thiede, Fred.	11, Feb. 1896	10, Feb.	64	5	
Thiel, Frank	24, Aug. 1888		40	1	
Thiel, Hannah	19, Mar. 1891		39	4	
Thiel, Nikolaus	24, Aug. 1900		57	5	
Thiele, Catharine	24, Dec. 1900		79	8	
Thiele, Edward A.	27, Jan. 1895		46	5	
Thiele, John H.	27, July 1888		67	1	
Thielen, Anna M.	27, Feb. 1894		63	5	
Thielen, Casper	16, Feb. 1895		67	5	
Thielen, Frida	23, Nov. 1888		1	1	
Thielen, Julius	4, Dec. 1897	2, Dec.	70- 9m	5	
Thiem, Anthony	3, June 1892		36	5	
Thiemann, Elisabeth	2, July 1901		90	8	
Thieme, Minna	20, Nov. 1889		33	1	
Thien, Henrietta M.	29, July 1887		1	1	
Thien, Louisa	26, Aug. 1887		19m	1	
Thiergartner, Mary	4, May 1893		2	5	
Thiermann, John	23, Sept 1891		18	4	
Thiersch, Frieda A.	13, Apr. 1895		11	4	
Thiersch, Theresa	26, Sept 1894		69	5	
Thiersing, Elisabeth	10, Oct. 1891		3	4	
Thiery, Bertha	3, July 1901		30	8	
Thiesch, Therese	23, Aug. 1894		1m	5	
Thiesing, Friedrich Heinrich	6, Jan. 1897	5, Jan.	73	5	
Thiesing, Katharine	7, Apr. 1895		61	5	
Thinnes, Phil.	2, Aug. 1898	30, July	27- 6m	4	

Name	Notice Date	Death Date	Age	Page	Maiden Name
****	****** ****	***** ****	***	****	****** ****
Thole, Joseph	10, Apr. 1888		8	4	
Tholen, Bernard Henry	11, Apr. 1898	10, Apr.	74-11m-25d	5	
Thomann, Anna	31, Dec. 1890		2	4	
Thomann, Antoinette Bernardina	17, Apr. 1899	15, Apr.	33	5	Packskamp
Thomas,	11, Apr. 1891		7m	4	
Thomas, Arthur	11, Feb. 1892		18	4	
Thomas, Benjamin O.	19, July 1887		6m	1	
Thomas, Charles E.	19, July 1887		12m	1	
Thomas, Clara	21, June 1888		2m	1	
Thomas, Elisabeth	14, Dec. 1887		3d	4	
Thomas, Elizabeth	20, Jan. 1891		7d	4	
Thomas, Ermine	6, June 1901		36	8	
Thomas, Francis	25, Sept 1900		69	5	
Thomas, Frank	16, Apr. 1901		4m	8	
Thomas, George W.	23, May 1888		40	1	
Thomas, Jac.	1, Aug. 1890		52	1	
Thomas, John	29, July 1890		89	1	
Thomas, John	14, May 1891		38	4	
Thomas, Joseph	15, Jan. 1901		44	8	
Thomas, Mamie	16, Sept 1895	16, Sept	37	5	
Thomas, Martha E.	15, Sept 1888		80	2	
Thomas, Martin	14, June 1901		49	5	
Thomas, Paul	22, Apr. 1891		13	4	
Thomas, Rebecca	28, Mar. 1901		80	8	
Thomas, Ruby	21, Jan. 1901		3m	8	
Thomas, Sarah	24, Apr. 1891		1m	4	
Thomas, Sherman	24, Aug. 1887		18	1	
Thomas, Stephen	29, June 1901		80	8	
Thomas, W.R.	8, Jan. 1891		86	4	
Thompkins, Garretson	13, Oct. 1900		76	8	
Thompson, Addie	30, Apr. 1901		56	8	
Thompson, Andrew C.	11, Apr. 1895		41	5	
Thompson, Anna	24, Sept 1900		69	5	
Thompson, Claude	18, July 1887		19m	1	
Thompson, Elisabeth	28, June 1895		48	5	
Thompson, G.	12, May 1895		60	5	
Thompson, Grace	17, Dec. 1900		15	8	
Thompson, Harry	28, July 1888		9	1	
Thompson, Herbert	23, Nov. 1900		50	8	
Thompson, Marie	30, May 1888		8	1	
Thompson, Mary	11, July 1887		36	1	
Thompson, Mary	25, June 1901		55	8	
Thompson, W.L.	3, Oct. 1901		79	8	
Thompson, Willis	5, Feb. 1901		43	8	
Thomson, Helen	16, Jan. 1891		51	4	
Thomson, John N.	10, Sept 1901		45	1	
Thomson, Lizzie	12, June 1901		33	8	
Thomwarth, Anna M.M.	18, July 1887		17	1	
Thonns, Oliver	8, May 1901		72	8	
Thormann, Henry	9, May 1894		56	5	
Thormöhle, Olga	16, May 1893		3	5	
Thornburg, Mary	5, Sept 1901		36	8	
Thornecker, Walter	20, Nov. 1891		3m	4	
Thorner, Max (Dr.)	28, Aug. 1899	26, Aug.	39	4	
Thornett, Thomas	5, Feb. 1901		23	8	
Thornton, Mary	12, Sept 1901		75	5	
Thorp, John	6, Oct. 1891		82	4	
Thorp, Julia A.	6, Sept 1901		75	8	
Thorp, Nelson	1, Oct. 1901		20	1	
Thorp, Sadie	13, Dec. 1890		7m	1	
Thorwarth, A.M.	13, Mar. 1888		2w	1	
Threm, Elisabeth	27, Aug. 1897	26, Aug.	64	4	Terranni
Threm, John	6, Dec. 1900		73	8	
Thuenemann, Anthony	5, Feb. 1891		1	4	
Thuenemann, Louise	22, Mar. 1901		80	8	
Thuener, Henry	24, Oct. 1894		45	5	
Thumann, Elsie M.	22, Nov. 1893		3m	5	
Thumann, J.G.	5, July 1888		81	1	
Thurnet, Elizabeth	18, Mar. 1889		54	1	
Thurrah, John	6, July 1901		3	8	
Thye, Elisabeth	26, Apr. 1900	23, Apr.	33-10m	5	Uhlenbrock

Name ****	Notice Date ****** ****	Death Date ***** ****	Age ***	Page ****	Maiden Name ****** ****
Thönges, George	8, June 1889		9m	1	
Tibbs, Sol.	14, Sept 1893		25	5	
Tic, Charles	14, Jan. 1889		5	1	
Tice, Elizabeth	7, Oct. 1901		82	1	
Tichle, Katharine	2, Feb. 1897	1, Feb.	83- 5m	5	Losche
Ticking, William K.	23, July 1895		5m	5	
Tiefe, Edward	23, Sept 1893		29	5	
Tiefenbach, Anna Maria	13, Aug. 1896	11, Aug.	71	5	
Tiefenbach, Fred.	12, Oct. 1889		64	1	
Tiefenbach, John	3, Nov. 1887		4	4	
Tiefhaus, Marg.	16, Aug. 1887		12m	1	
Tieking, Carl H.	29, Jan. 1901		4	8	
Tieman, Clemens	4, Aug. 1887		48	1	
Tieman, Elizabeth	25, Apr. 1888		65	1	
Tieman, Harry	12, Feb. 1889		5	1	
Tiemann, Harry	7, June 1901		1	8	
Tiemeyer, Mary L.	25, May 1901		24	8	
Tiemeyer, Wilhelm	29, Apr. 1899	26, Apr.	45- 3m	5	
Tiernan, Lillie A.	4, Nov. 1894		7m	5	
Tierney, B.	21, Apr. 1888		29	1	
Tierney, Eliza	30, Nov. 1887		19	4	
Tierney, William	8, Nov. 1887		31	1	
Tierney, William	28, July 1888		65	1	
Tiettmeyer, Herman George	9, Dec. 1897	7, Dec.	55- 3m	5	
Tietz, Emma	11, May 1901		48	8	
Tiffenbach, Joseph	4, Dec. 1889	3, Dec.	67- 8m-22d	4	
Tig, Hannah	2, Apr. 1901		33	8	
Tighe, Howard	5, Apr. 1901		7	8	
Tighe, Katharine	28, Nov. 1900		55	8	
Tilghmann, Nancy D.	28, Dec. 1893		48	5	
Tillar, Benjamin	24, Feb. 1893		43	5	
Tillar, Eleanore	8, Sept 1887		20m	1	
Tillar, Johan Herman	18, Jan. 1897	16, Jan.	56- 7m	5	
Tiller, Jacob	8, Apr. 1901		45	8	
Tillett, Anna	17, Aug. 1900		4m	5	
Tillinghaust, Jennie	23, Jan. 1901		29	8	
Tillman, Louis	31, Dec. 1892		9m	5	
Tillmann, Mathilda	1, Dec. 1900		55	8	
Tilly, Gustav Joseph	19, Aug. 1893		33	5	
Tilly, W.	5, Feb. 1896	3, Feb.	64	5	
Tilly, Wilhelm	4, Feb. 1896	3, Feb.	84	5	
Tilversen, Frank	7, Dec. 1887		43	1	
Timbermann, David	14, Sept 1901		48	1	
Timerding, George	30, July 1891		10d	4	
Timm, E.H.	23, Mar. 1899	22, Mar.	74- 5m	5	
Timmer, Henry	1, Dec. 1891		71	4	
Timmermann, Alb.	7, July 1888		5d	4	
Timmermann, Elise	1, Nov. 1893		27	5	
Timmermann, Ferd.	29, Nov. 1893		7d	5	
Timmermann, J.F.	10, Oct. 1900		49	8	
Timmermann, Lena	3, June 1901		70	8	
Timmermare, John H.	30, Sept 1891		75	4	
Timmers, William H.	25, May 1901		48	8	
Timmerwilke, Aloysius	29, Aug. 1891		1	4	
Timmich, Gustav	27, May 1901		47	8	
Tinschert, Rosa	28, Jan. 1899	27, Jan.	38	5	
Tioba, Mary (Sr.)	17, Apr. 1891		22	4	
Tirre, Wilhelm	26, Apr. 1900	24, Apr.	57	5	
Tischbein, Michael	9, July 1896	8, July	46	5	
Tischer, Bessie	24, Aug. 1889		8	1	
Tischner, Margaret	8, Apr. 1891		70	4	
Titinger, Ralph	1, May 1895		2m	5	
Titor, John	25, Apr. 1888		32	1	
Toal, James	27, Feb. 1889		32	1	
Toben, Hugh E.	11, June 1895		18	5	
Toberte, Edward	16, Dec. 1891		2	4	
Tobin, Julia	25, May 1895		75	5	
Tobin, Richard	5, Dec. 1900		17	8	
Todd, George	22, Aug. 1891		1	4	
Todd, Rebecca	26, Jan. 1901		67	8	
Toddy, Emma	24, June 1901		68	8	

Name	Notice Date	Death Date	Age	Page	Maiden Name
****	****** ****	***** ****	***	****	****** ****
Toelke, Amelia	9, Apr. 1890		5m	1	
Toenges, Johanna Louisa	25, Nov. 1899	24, Nov.	73- 1m	5	Siegmann
Toepfer, Sophia	10, Aug. 1894		5m	5	
Toerner, Anna	6, May 1898	4, May	36- 6m	5	Doerle
Toerner, Wilhelm	21, Aug. 1896	20, Aug.	34-10m	5	
Togt, George	7, Jan. 1901		36	5	
Tohermes, Adelheid	15, Mar. 1900	14, Mar.	68	5	
Toker, Elizabeth	13, Oct. 1894		38	5	
Tolley, Julia	12, Sept 1888		72	1	
Tollheis, Albert	15, June 1899	14, June	42-11m	5	
Tollmer, Barbara	19, Oct. 1901		20	8	
Tommies, Hans	29, June 1901		2	8	
Tompson, Hugh	26, Feb. 1901			8	
Tone, Chloe	20, Nov. 1900		80	8	
Tone, Clara	14, Dec. 1900		42	8	
Tonkotte, Marie	2, July 1895		14	5	
Tonnes, Laura	2, Mar. 1901		29	5	
Tonnes, Margaretha	18, Apr. 1895		62	5	
Tooker, Walter	1, Aug. 1890		4m	1	
Topie, George F.	5, Jan. 1889		25	1	
Topmoeller, Anna	15, June 1894		1m	5	
Topmoeller, Emma	15, June 1894		1m	5	
Topmöller, Elisabeth	19, Aug. 1899	17, Aug.	83	5	
Topp, Bertha	18, Aug. 1900		76	8	
Torbeck, H.H.	10, Dec. 1895	8, Dec.	8	5	
Tormey, John H.	5, July 1887		11	1	
Torrence, T.F.	1, Oct. 1887		73	1	
Tost, Hedwig	17, Oct. 1893		1	5	
Totino, Biagio	15, Feb. 1901		50	8	
Totten, Ellen	11, Jan. 1888		65	4	
Tottleben, William	2, Apr. 1891		47	4	
Touschardt, Carl H.	11, Apr. 1901		3	8	
Touschardt, Frieda	29, July 1899	28, July	35- 3m	5	Thoele
Towers, D.R.	30, Oct. 1899	28, Oct.		5	Ruettinger
Townsley, A.L.	17, Apr. 1895		77	5	
Tozzer, Susan	1, Sept 1900			5	
Tozzer, William S.	18, Aug. 1893		59	5	
Tracey, Eliza	21, July 1887		4m	1	
Tracey, Mary	4, Feb. 1901		61	8	
Tracey, Patrick	27, Nov. 1900		71	8	
Traegeser, Loretta	15, May 1901		4	8	
Trager, Herold	15, May 1901		8m	8	
Trageser, Helen	28, Aug. 1901		2	8	
Trainer, Pearl	7, Sept 1900		19	5	
Trame, Leonora	29, July 1888		41	1	
Trame, W.	29, Mar. 1900	27, Mar.	83- 4m	4	
Trankenberg, Maria Helena	23, June 1898	22, June	74- 2m	5	Splinters
Trapp, Margaret	27, July 1895		1m	5	
Trapp, Margaretha	6, Oct. 1897	4, Oct.	69-11m	5	Radler
Trarbach, Peter	28, Apr. 1898	27, Apr.	70- 8m-27d	5	
Traubach, Anna	4, Dec. 1891		23	4	
Trauermann, Milton	11, Sept 1895	9, Sept	15	5	
Trautmann, Anna	9, June 1893		83	5	
Trautmann, Charles	24, Sept 1896	23, Sept	60	5	
Trautmann, Franziska	28, Feb. 1900	26, Feb.	91	5	Werner
Trautvetter, Elizabeth	19, June 1891		57	1	
Travers, John	16, Nov. 1900			8	
Trawley, Bridget	8, May 1901		48	8	
Traxel, Henry	14, July 1890		37	1	
Traxel, Willa	5, June 1899	3, June	7-10m	5	
Trebs, Fr.	20, May 1890		4	1	
Trebs, Fred. C.	25, Feb. 1893		5m	5	
Treen, Charles	15, Aug. 1891		1	4	
Trefz, Gottlieb	27, July 1892		43	5	
Trefz, Louis	9, Jan. 1900	8, Jan.	58- 6m-22d	* 4	
Trefzger, Catharine	9, Nov. 1893		54	5	
Trefzger, Ollie	2, June 1893		31	5	
Tremmel, Xavier	1, Dec. 1891		22	4	
Trenary, Bertha	22, Oct. 1900		14	8	
Trendel, Charles A.	10, Oct. 1891		4	4	
Trentersheim, Joseph	28, Nov. 1893		53	5	

Name	Notice Date	Death Date	Age	Page	Maiden Name
****	****** ****	***** ****	***	****	****** ****
Trentmann, Bernard F.	17, Jan. 1898	17, Jan.	50-10m	5	
Trentmann, Franz	6, Aug. 1896	4, Aug.	77- 9m	5	
Trentmann, Herman	10, Oct. 1893		17	5	
Trenz, Anna M.E.	23, Feb. 1892		4m	5	
Trepohl, Herman	29, Sept 1900		34	8	
Trescher, Maggie	14, June 1895		2m	5	
Tresenius, Carolina	21, Feb. 1896	19, Feb.	62- 6m	5	
Treu, Eva	27, Feb. 1897	27, Feb.		5	
Treu, Fritz	3, Apr. 1899	2, Apr.	38	5	
Treßler, Heinrich	29, May 1900	28, May	64- 4m-24d	5	
Treßler, Margaret	2, Mar. 1901		49	5	
Treßler, Paul	14, Feb. 1895		3	5	
Tribs, Carrie	4, July 1887		20	1	
Tridel, Margaret	18, Jan. 1894		69	5	
Trieschmann, Fidel W.	7, Apr. 1893		1	5	
Trilarder, Pearl L.	14, Mar. 1891		4	4	
Trimbach, August	2, Aug. 1887		7m	1	
Trimble, Eleanor	24, July 1901		77	8	
Trimbur, Maria Magdalena	2, Apr. 1897	1, Apr.	87- 6m	5	Oliger
Trine, Frank	20, Mar. 1890		74	1	
Trinkle, August	20, Aug. 1901		62	8	
Trippel, Leo	15, Jan. 1901		68	8	
Trischlor, Phil.	3, Jan. 1888		1d	1	
Trischy, Margaret	15, Aug. 1891		64	4	
Trisham, Annie	30, Jan. 1888		34	1	
Trisler, Jennie	15, May 1901		60	8	
Tritow, Herman	29, Oct. 1889		2m	1	
Tritsch, Emma	30, Apr. 1895		4	5	
Tritschler, Alma	18, July 1895		16m	5	
Trivett, John	3, May 1901			8	
Trochelmann, Adolph	20, Aug. 1889		4m	1	
Trochelmann, August	19, June 1889		6	1	
Troeger, Kunigunda	31, Oct. 1891		70	4	
Troescher, Edward W.	26, Dec. 1900		56	8	
Troescher, William	3, Dec. 1900		40	8	
Trollmann, Mary E.	23, Dec. 1891		71	4	
Tromey, Jeremiah	21, Feb. 1901		55	8	
Tromey, Johan	2, July 1897	30, June	39- 6m	5	
Tromey, Rosa	15, May 1896	14, May	42- 5m	5	Algeier
Tronk, Franziska	10, Aug. 1894		70	5	
Tropf, Mathilda	15, Nov. 1895	12, Nov.	25- 4m	5	
Troskey, Henrietta	19, Dec. 1900		87	8	
Trost, Babetta	1, Dec. 1892		78	5	
Trost, Eduard	16, Jan. 1899	14, Jan.	43- 6m	5	
Trost, Emil	20, Mar. 1894		28	5	
Trost, John	5, Nov. 1891		35	1	
Trost, Margaretha	25, Apr. 1899	24, Apr.	46- 6m	4	
Trost, Theodora	27, June 1895		17m	5	
Trott, Michael	18, Feb. 1891		43	4	
Trounstine, Babette	22, June 1901		68	8	
Troussin, Delano	10, July 1887		3	1	
Troxel, Magdalena	2, May 1901		64	8	
Troy, Lillie	24, Sept 1900		26	5	
Truechter, Maria	7, Jan. 1893		33	5	
Trueter, Franz	24, Oct. 1899	22, Oct.	75- 7m	5	
Trum, Antoinette	28, Mar. 1898	26, Mar.	45- 3m	5	
Truman, Emma	4, Dec. 1891		29	4	
Trumbaugh, William	6, June 1888		20	1	
Trumeter, Georg	25, Jan. 1897	24, Jan.	50- 5m	5	
Trumiter, Hattie	24, June 1891		18	4	
Truschel, Emilie H.	2, Feb. 1893		10m	5	
Trusnau, Mary	29, Apr. 1891		47	4	
Tröger, Margaret	13, Aug. 1888		17	1	
Tschamber, Mary	18, Feb. 1890		2	1	
Tschampel, Christian	22, Nov. 1889		33	1	
Tschechtelin, Bertha Paulina	18, Aug. 1899	17, Aug.	55- - 7d	5	Cohr
Tschudi, Henry	19, Dec. 1895	18, Dec.	13- 9m	5	
Tschächtelein, Karl	26, Jan. 1893	25, Jan.	8- 9m-25d	5	
Tucker, Annie	1, Mar. 1888		54	4	
Tucker, Katharina	29, Jan. 1896	28, Jan.	76	5	
Tudor, Emma	31, July 1900		50	5	

Name	Notice Date	Death Date	Age	Page	Maiden Name
****	****** ****	***** ****	***	****	****** ****
Tuerck, John Ch.	24, Aug. 1889		42	1	
Tuerck, Katharina	5, Apr. 1898	3, Apr.	25- 8m	5	Zange
Tuergang, Magdalena	7, June 1890		1	1	
Tulby, John	7, June 1890		7	1	
Tully, Patrick	23, May 1895		48	5	
Tunhorst, William	24, June 1893		3m	5	
Turmoil, Maria	21, Dec. 1897	20, Dec.	55- 4m	5	Sander
Turner, Clara	5, Dec. 1891		24d	4	
Turner, Edna G.	29, Dec. 1900		4m	8	
Turner, Elisabeth	17, Apr. 1895		39	5	
Turner, Henry	19, Dec. 1890		57	1	
Turner, Leonora	27, Sept 1890		3	1	
Turner, Mary Alcott	13, Dec. 1900		72	8	
Turner, Rachel	22, Dec. 1891		36	4	
Turner, Rebecca	8, May 1891		2	4	
Turner, William	4, Aug. 1891		46	4	
Turner, William	7, Sept 1901		31	8	
Turrell, Francis	4, Apr. 1895		3- 6m	5	
Turwin, Leon	29, Aug. 1901		50	8	
Tuschner, Conrad P.	4, June 1889		3m	1	
Tuschner, Peter	7, Sept 1893		7d	5	
Tusting, Henry August	29, Mar. 1888		36	1	
Tuttle, Mary Anna	13, Sept 1888		81	1	
Twachtmann, Edna	5, Feb. 1896	4, Feb.	6- 5m	5	
Twachtmann, Elisabeth	21, Dec. 1898	20, Dec.	65-10m	5	
Twachtmann, L.	8, Dec. 1900		77	8	
Twachtmann, Sophia	9, July 1896	8, July	73	5	
Twehus, Joseph	6, Feb. 1901		68	8	
Twitchell, Jennie A.	1, Sept 1887		52	1	
Twohig, Edward	1, Oct. 1900		10m	5	
Tykotte, Euphonia M.	10, Dec. 1900		83	8	
Tyrell, Bridget	8, Apr. 1901		58	8	
Täger, Christian	17, Aug. 1893		26	5	
Täusen, Phil.	3, Dec. 1888		61	1	
Tönnies, Elisabeth	11, May 1889		-0	1	
Tönsing, Gottlieb	21, Apr. 1900	19, Apr.	74- 9m	5	
Töpfer, Christian	19, Feb. 1895		50	5	
Tüpker, Elizabeth	5, July 1890		41	1	
Ubel, Celia	15, Mar. 1901		19	8	
Ubrich, Katharina	21, Jan. 1889		55	1	
Ubrig, Herbert	29, Jan. 1892		11m	5	
Udwein, Eduard	2, Dec. 1892		9d	5	
Uerbel, Katie	6, June 1893		5	5	
Uetrecht, Christian	21, Mar. 1896	20, Mar.	65- 3m	5	
Uffmann, Heinrich	15, Jan. 1898	14, Jan.	37- 4m	5	
Uhl, Christian	26, Mar. 1898	25, Mar.	71- 3m	5	
Uhl, Christian	7, Sept 1901		45	8	
Uhl, Euphrofina	20, Nov. 1899	18, Nov.	71- -16d	5	Oswald
Uhl, Georg W.	23, Jan. 1901		18	8	
Uhl, Johann	12, Dec. 1900		44	8	
Uhl, Mary	14, Aug. 1890		4	1	
Uhland, Louis	11, Mar. 1890		26	1	
Uhlen, Nellie	1, Aug. 1901		5	8	
Uhlenbrock, Mary A.	6, July 1893		63	5	
Uhlhorn, John F.	17, Dec. 1891		86	4	
Uhlmann, Adolph	9, Dec. 1892		56	5	
Uhlmann, Albert	6, Sept 1893		6	5	
Uhlmann, Dora	26, Feb. 1895		12	5	
Uhlmann, Jacob	28, Jan. 1894		61	5	
Uhlmann, Walter	8, May 1889		2	1	
Uhlrich, Francis Joseph	27, Apr. 1897	25, Apr.	32-10m	5	
Uhrig, Martin	8, Aug. 1900		68	8	
Uihlein, Katharina	6, July 1897	4, July	79- 7m	5	
Ulland, Fred.	20, Sept 1889		20	1	
Ullmann, Bertha	15, Sept 1888		82	2	
Ullrich, Anna	13, Feb. 1894		7	5	
Ulmer, Anna Maria	30, Aug. 1887		66	1	
Ulmer, Dorothea	29, Mar. 1895		24	5	
Ulmer, Jacob	3, Mar. 1890		58	1	
Ulmer, Magdalena	9, Apr. 1900	8, Apr.	58- 4m	4	Postel

Name ****	Notice Date ****** ****	Death Date ***** ****	Age ***	Page ****	Maiden Name ****** ****
Ulmer, Mary	16, July 1888		21	1	
Ulmer, Wilhelmine	28, Dec. 1893		75	5	
Ulmer, William	22, Mar. 1894		15d	5	
Ulrich, Augustus	2, Dec. 1894		66	4	
Ulrich, Ellen	2, Sept 1891		1m	4	
Ulrich, George	18, July 1887		47	1	
Ulrich, John M.	1, Nov. 1892		5	5	
Ulrich, Leopold	12, Oct. 1896	11, Oct.	33-11m	5	
Ulrich, Louis	14, Jan. 1901		5m	8	
Ulrich, Sophia	30, Nov. 1895	29, Nov.	65- 3m	5	
Ulrich, W.P.	7, Sept 1893		11d	5	
Ulrich, William H.	10, Feb. 1891		34	4	
Ulrichs, Eugenia A.J.	25, Mar. 1893		5m	5	
Umgetter, Fred.	31, Dec. 1891		31	1	
Ummethum, G.W.	21, Sept 1895	19, Sept	62	5	
Umscheid, M.E.	18, Apr. 1888		20d	1	
Underwood, Dewitt	20, Feb. 1901		57	8	
Ungebühler, J.G.	23, Nov. 1896	22, Nov.	33- 9m	5	
Ungeheuer, Loretta	11, May 1899	10, May	5- 3m	4	
Unger, Adolph	27, Nov. 1889		1	1	
Unger, Caroline	18, Sept 1901		84	8	
Unger, Frank	18, Nov. 1894		1	5	
Unkraut, Lena	11, Apr. 1893		3m	5	
Unkraut, Stephanie	25, May 1889		9	1	
Unland, Andy	24, May 1889		5	1	
Unland, Mary	16, Sept 1887		72	1	
Unnewehr, Andreas	14, Feb. 1889		1d	1	
Unnewehr, Carrie Rose	27, Apr. 1896	25, Apr.	16-10m	5	
Unnewehr, Friedrich	14, Mar. 1891		65	4	
Untersinger, Sophie	27, Oct. 1899	26, Oct.	45- 4m	8	
Unverzagt, Friedricka	30, Nov. 1887		71	4	
Unverzagt, Ludwig F.	31, May 1890		2	1	
Unwine, Charles S.	25, June 1895		29	5	
Unzieher, Margaretha	15, Feb. 1892		70	5	
Uphaus, Mary	20, Jan. 1891		82	4	
Uppenrode, Alma	18, Sept 1889		1- 6m	1	
Uptmoor, Bernhard	31, Mar. 1891		6m	4	
Urban, John	29, Oct. 1889		45- 6m	1	
Urcheus, Carolina	30, July 1892		44	5	
Urner-Foote, Eloise	18, Aug. 1900		20	8	
Urweiler, George S.	7, Aug. 1894		50	5	
Usse, Louise J.	5, Apr. 1892		4m	4	
Uthe, Margaretha	19, Aug. 1898	18, Aug.		5	Gnüge
Utter, Lyon E.	28, Jan. 1901		27	8	
Utterich, Anna F.	16, Feb. 1889		33	1	
Utz, Carl	24, Sept 1901		75	1	
Utz, Clara	11, Feb. 1889		6m	1	
Utz, Lawrence M.	23, Mar. 1893		2	5	
Uzuber, Peter C.	1, Aug. 1887		10m	1	
Vahling, Frank	31, Mar. 1891		2	4	
Vahlung, Charles	19, Sept 1891		53	4	
Vaile, Edward E.	11, Jan. 1888		49	4	
Vaimmer, Mary	26, Sept 1900		72	5	
Valanda, Anna	19, Apr. 1895		35	5	
Valentine, Anna M.	2, Dec. 1892		69	5	
Valentiner, Clara	17, Apr. 1901		2	8	
Vallandingham, Esther	26, Feb. 1901		3	8	
Valleau, Emilie	20, Feb. 1901		76	8	
Vallo, F.A.	7, Aug. 1888		9m	1	
Van, Anna	27, Mar. 1901		59	8	
Van, Johan	2, Mar. 1896	1, Mar.	42	5	
Van, John	13, June 1891		88	4	
VanArnam, Martha M.	4, Feb. 1893		30	5	
VanAusdol, Daniel	9, Aug. 1887		1d	1	
VanBargen, Friedrich	10, July 1887		59	1	
VanBeulsen, Theodore	16, July 1891		11m	4	
VanBoemel, Herman	26, Apr. 1895		79	5	
VanBoemel, Raymond J.	5, Nov. 1891		1	1	
VanCleve, Margaret	4, June 1901		1d	8	
VanCluff, Babetta	22, Feb. 1895		56	5	

Name ****	Notice Date ****** ****	Death Date ***** ****	Age ***	Page ****	Maiden Name ****** ****
VanDyke, H.	3, Oct. 1901		53	8	
VanDyke, Netta	22, Dec. 1891		28	4	
VanDyke, Wilhelm Mandeville	16, July 1900	15, July	20	8	
VanFossen, Alfa	7, Feb. 1894		39	5	
VanFoster, Marie	10, June 1901		1	8	
VanHolle, Anna	17, Mar. 1891		50	4	
VanHolte, Henry	22, Mar. 1893		41	5	
VanHorn, Maria	16, Feb. 1895		20	5	
VanLeeuwee, Mary	14, Mar. 1901		72	8	
VanMourik, Theodor	9, Aug. 1901		65	8	
VanNes, Carl H.	20, Dec. 1889		36	1	
VanSant, Higbee	13, Feb. 1901		60	8	
VanTharen, G.	14, Feb. 1888		10m	4	
VanWormer, Wilhelm Erastus	25, Mar. 1896	24, Mar.		5	
VanWyck, E.	28, Oct. 1895	26, Oct.	64	5	
VanWyk, Maria	4, 5, Nov. 1895	3, Nov.	70- 7m	5	Verhagen
VanZan, Catharine	24, Nov. 1891		83	4	
Vanden, Ella	27, Apr. 1901		58	8	
VandenNiewenhuysen, Gerhard	17, Oct. 1894		43	5	
Vandenberg, Leonora	24, Feb. 1894		1	5	
Vanderberg, Katharina B.	2, Nov. 1896	30, Oct.	19- 9m	5	
Vandergrift, Katie	22, July 1887		14m	1	
Vanling, John H.	11, Aug. 1891		11m	4	
Vannice, Cornelius	3, Feb. 1891		82	4	
Varelmeier, Georg Heinrich	5, Dec. 1896	3, Dec.	19- 8m	5	
Varnau, Friedrich	1, Mar. 1897	26, Feb.	63-11m	5	
Varwick, Margaretha	26, June 1891			4	
Vasey, Mary	12, Nov. 1900		50	5	
Vaske, Doretta	7, Aug. 1901		81	8	
Vassen, Anna	12, July 1901		5	8	
Vatter, John	16, May 1893		26	5	
Vaucher, Jane	7, Jan. 1896	5, Jan.		5	
Vaughan, John	20, Nov. 1899	19, Nov.	92- - 2d	5	
Vaupel,	10, July 1887		1d	1	
Veeneman, John	28, Feb. 1889		7m	2	
Veerkamp, Frank	1, Sept 1887		12	1	
Vehlein, Willie	25, Mar. 1891		1	4	
Vehr, Harry	31, July 1901		43	8	
Vehr, Maria F.	25, July 1893		70	5	
Vehrenkamp, Heinrich	26, Aug. 1899	25, Aug.	67- 8m	4	
Veid, Chester	29, June 1893		1	5	
Veid, Michael	11, Jan. 1890		36	1	
Veigel, Fred	26, Aug. 1901		57	8	
Veinle, Christian	12, Apr. 1897	11, Apr.	66- 1m	5	
Veit, Christina	3, July 1896	2, July	58- 3m	5	
Veith, Daniel	30, Dec. 1891		2	4	
Veldman, Merinos	12, July 1901		67	8	
Velkle, Maria Rebecca	31, May 1899	29, May	73	4	Herter
Velmeier, Hilda	5, May 1895		5m	5	
Velter, Leopold	4, Oct. 1901		36	8	
Vendighaus, Henry	13, Dec. 1893		57	5	
Vennemann, Anton Johan	31, Oct. 1899	28, Oct.	88- 6m	5	
Vennemann, Eleanora	23, Apr. 1891		2m	4	
Verges, Eva	30, Jan. 1901		80	8	
Vergins, Laura	1, June 1892		27	5	
Verhage, Henry	12, Jan. 1897	10, Jan.	65	5	
Verkamp, Anton	24, Apr. 1901		42	8	
Verkamp, Gerhard Heinrich	30, June 1897	28, June	64	5	
Vernan, August	23, Mar. 1895		80	5	
Verwohlt, Charles Ferdinand	14, Feb. 1896	13, Feb.	36- 9m	5	
Verwohlt, Elizabeth	13, Mar. 1901		68	8	
Veser, John	27, May 1901		57	8	
Vester, Anna M.	1, June 1893		74	5	
Vester, Louis	15, Jan. 1898	13, Jan.	48- 6m	5	
Vester, Martha	27, Jan. 1894		65	5	
Vester, William	11, Aug. 1887		4w	1	
Vestner, Martina	2, Oct. 1888		56	1	
Vestring, Adelheid	11, Aug. 1890		9m	1	
Vestring, Anna	28, Feb. 1889		22	2	
Vestring, Anna	19, Mar. 1901		66	8	
Vestring, William	2, Dec. 1894		29	4	

Name	Notice Date	Death Date	Age	Page	Maiden Name
****	****** ****	***** ****	***	****	****** ****
Vestrup, Louise	3, Jan. 1898	31, Dec.	32-10m	5	Reiser
Vettel, George	17, Dec. 1900		52	8	
Vetter, Florentine R.	15, Jan. 1891		4m	4	
Vetter, George	21, Oct. 1895	20, Oct.	68	5	
Vetter, Ida	4, Feb. 1889		17d	1	
Vetter, Joseph	26, Dec. 1890		30m	1	
Vetter, Marie	8, Mar. 1901		81	8	
Vetter, Peter	10, Aug. 1900		73	8	
Vickers, Mary Ann	27, Sept 1888		67	2	
Vickroy, William	25, Sept 1900		3	5	
Victoire, (Sr.)	27, Mar. 1901		49	8	
Victor, Jacob	11, Jan. 1899	10, Jan.	72	5	
Vidoll, Edna	8, May 1891		18m	4	
Viehweg, Robert	7, Aug. 1895	5, Aug.	44- 5m	5	
Vienhage, Anna Maria	3, Apr. 1897	2, Apr.	83- 7m	5	Thiemann
Vietch, Elizabeth	19, Nov. 1900		55	8	
Vieth, Fred.	19, Sept 1900		8	8	
Vilein, Brahan	25, Mar. 1891		29	4	
Villing, Marie	8, Dec. 1900		28	8	
Vilzmann, Adolphine	11, Nov. 1895	10, Nov.	47	5	
Vimmer, Mary	24, Sept 1900		72	5	
Vincens, Nic.	11, Mar. 1891		40	4	
Vincent, Harry	21, Aug. 1887		8w	5	
Viner, Charles	27, Apr. 1895		60	5	
Virion, Henrietta	16, Apr. 1901		83	8	
Visser, Frank B.	28, June 1889		16m	1	
Vocke, Anna	5, Sept 1900		71	5	
Vocke, Anton	7, Dec. 1893		52	5	
Vocke, Friedrich	28, Apr. 1898	27, Apr.	55	5	
Voegth, Fred.	5, Aug. 1887		62	1	
Voelkel, Jakob	11, Nov. 1892		76	4	
Voelker, Anna	23, Aug. 1900		72	8	
Voelker, William	12, Nov. 1887		54	1	
Vogdes, J.H. (Fr.)	9, July 1896	8, July	27- 1m	5	
Vogel, Andrew	8, Apr. 1891		47	4	
Vogel, Charles	24, Apr. 1894		3	5	
Vogel, Frank	26, Sept 1891		4d	4	
Vogel, Frank	4, June 1900	3, June		8	
Vogel, Harry	29, Nov. 1893		14d	5	
Vogel, Ludwig	19, Nov. 1896	18, Nov.	53- 8m	5	
Vogel, Marie	4, Jan. 1898			5	Shock
Vogel, Philomena	19, Nov. 1895	18, Nov.	48	5	Meissemer
Vogel, Sophie	19, Feb. 1895		49	5	
Vogel, Wilhelm Anthony	19, Feb. 1898	18, Feb.	16	5	
Vogel, Wilhelmina	3, Apr. 1889		37	2	
Vogel, William	15, June 1901		60	8	
Vogele, John	23, Sept 1887		44	2	
Vogele, Peter	2, Oct. 1894		35	5	
Vogelsang, Catharine	17, June 1891		20	4	
Vogler, (Mrs.)	18, Jan. 1899	17, Jan.	82	5	
Vogler, George	23, May 1888		5m	1	
Vogler, Hannah	16, Apr. 1891		51	4	
Vogler, Joseph A.	18, Nov. 1897	16, Nov.	46- 8m- 6d	5	
Vogt, Albert	2, Apr. 1895		64	5	
Vogt, Blanche	25, July 1888		3m	4	
Vogt, Edwin	2, Mar. 1893		1m	5	
Vogt, Elizabeth	14, July 1892		36	5	
Vogt, Gustav	20, Sept 1887		13	1	
Vogt, Heinrich Johan	10, Jan. 1896	9, Jan.	64	5	
Vogt, Henry	12, Sept 1899	10, Sept	71- 9m-25d	5	
Vogt, John	16, Jan. 1891		64	4	
Vogt, John	11, Aug. 1891		5	4	
Vogt, Lottie	16, Feb. 1901		21	8	
Vogt, Margaret	11, Apr. 1893		42	5	
Vogt, Mary	21, Aug. 1887		37	5	
Vogt, Maximillian	23, Apr. 1900	22, Apr.	34-11m	8	
Vogt, Oskar	19, July 1894		19	5	
Vogt, Walburga	11, June 1901		9	8	
Vogt, William L.	15, Oct. 1900		44	5	
Voight, Carsten	20, Jan. 1894		72	5	
Voigt, Charles	8, Aug. 1893		27	5	

Name	Notice Date	Death Date	Age	Page	Maiden Name
****	****** ****	***** ****	***	****	****** ****
Voigt, F.W.	16, Dec. 1893		23	5	
Voigt, Heinrich	27, July 1896	25, July	52	5	
Volant, Lizzie	19, Sept 1894		50	5	
Volk, Albert F.	6, Aug. 1901		2m	8	
Volk, Charles	3, Oct. 1894		33-11m	5	
Volkart, Jennie	20, Nov. 1900		37	8	
Volker, J.B.	29, Oct. 1896	27, Oct.	71- 8m	5	
Volkerding, Mary	17, July 1901		8m	8	
Volkert, Albert	13, Sept 1890		1m	1	
Volkert, Catharine G.	23, Dec. 1893		78	5	
Volkmann, Ernst	13, Jan. 1896	10, Jan.	78	5	
Voll, Alma	22, Oct. 1894		3	5	
Voll, Anna M.	4, Nov. 1891		28	1	
Voll, Christian	17, Feb. 1894		32	5	
Voll, Frank A.	12, June 1891		30	4	
Voll, Jacob	20, Apr. 1894		80	5	
Voll, John	24, Apr. 1901		58	8	
Voll, Wilhelm	21, Mar. 1895		49	5	
Voller, William	3, Oct. 1896	1, Oct.	43	5	
Vollman, Fred.	23, Oct. 1887		3m	4	
Vollmer, Alma	3, Nov. 1887		6- 1m	4	
Vollmer, Edmund	10, Mar. 1888		7m	1	
Vollmer, Herman	24, May 1901		26	8	
Vollmer, Thomas J.	18, Dec. 1893		62	5	
Vollmer, W.	8, May 1888		9m	1	
Vollmer, William	27, Aug. 1891			1	
Vollweiler, Charles	20, July 1887		6m	1	
Volmer, Bernard	27, Apr. 1895		65	5	
Volmer, Margaret	11, Feb. 1893		53	5	
Voltermann, Henry	19, Aug. 1901		28	8	
Volz, Carolina	24, Feb. 1894		22	5	
Volz, Felicides	26, Dec. 1890		-5	1	
Volz, Flora	9, Nov. 1893		3	5	
Volz, George	29, Oct. 1888		55	1	
Volz, George	2, Dec. 1893		35	5	
Volz, George	14, May 1900	12, May	79	8	
Volz, Joseph	2, June 1892		27	5	
Volz, Leonard	30, Mar. 1894		40	5	
Volz, Sarah	8, Dec. 1891		55	4	
Volz, William	6, Oct. 1891		46	4	
Volzlogel, Clio	28, May 1891		22	4	
Volzmann, August	9, Nov. 1897	8, Nov.	62	5	
VomHidt, Mina	8, June 1899	6, June	49	4	
VonAhn, Louis	11, Sept 1894		69	5	
VonBargen, George	23, Aug. 1887		14m	1	
VonBargen, Otto	27, Apr. 1894		26	5	
VonBaumen, Dina	23, Feb. 1891		35	4	
VonBehren, Alwine	2, Dec. 1896	30, Nov.	14- 8m	5	
VonBehren, Dora	17, Feb. 1894		54	5	
VonBehren, Henry William	21, June 1901		67	8	
VonBrinken, Kate	21, Dec. 1891		3	4	
VonEye, William	20, Apr. 1894		34	5	
VonFelde, Elisabeth	16, Dec. 1898	14, Dec.	58	5	
VonFelde, George	16, Jan. 1897		64	5	
VonHagel, Gerhard	7, July 1896	6, July	56- 3m	4	
VonHagen, John	25, Feb. 1893		50	5	
VonHeis,	19, Feb. 1895		1d	5	
VonHoene, Walter	27, June 1895		3	5	
VonHolle, Amos	3, Mar. 1894		55	5	
VonHolle, Caroline	10, June 1889		2	1	
VonHolle, Frank	1, Feb. 1897	31, Jan.	23- 7m	5	
VonKeitz, Katharine	6, 7, Nov. 1899	5, Nov.	40	5	
VonKämmel, Samuel	1, Feb. 1893		51	5	
VonLahr, John H.	3, May 1895		51	5	
VonLehmden, Joseph	11, Dec. 1900		45	8	
VonMartels, Henry	17, June 1896	16, June	93	5	
VonPhul, Anna	19, Apr. 1893		11	5	
VonSeggern, Elsie	26, Feb. 1894		4	5	
VonSeggern, Franklin	20, Mar. 1901		28	1	
VonSeggern, Fred. H.	1, Feb. 1894		56	5	
VonStrohe, Mary E.	22, June 1889		3	1	

Name	Notice Date	Death Date	Age	Page	Maiden Name
****	****** ****	***** ****	***	****	****** ****
VonStrohe, Mary E.	18, Jan. 1893		44	5	
VonThare, Henry	5, Mar. 1890		43	1	
VonWahlde, Henry	1, Mar. 1893		20	5	
VonWahlde, Maria	2, Dec. 1899	1, Dec.	45	4	Hau
VonWalde, Herman	12, June 1889		4	1	
VondenBerger, Willie	14, Feb. 1901		1	8	
Vondenbrink, Christian	27, Oct. 1891		47	1	
VonderBank, Elizabeth	7, Sept 1893		53	5	
VonderBurg, Henry	3, Mar. 1892		60	5	
VonderHaar, Anton	28, Jan. 1901		47	8	
VonderHaar, Anton	7, July 1899	6, July	71-11m-28d	4	
VonderHaar, Carolina	14, Apr. 1892		37	5	
VonderHaar, Elisabeth	25, Nov. 1895	23, Nov.	70- 3m	5	Fraß
VonderHaar, Friedrich	31, Mar. 1898	30, Mar.	34- 8m	5	
VonderHaar, Henry	21, Mar. 1891		65	4	
VonderHaar, Louis	16, May 1901		47	5	
VonderHaar, Theresa	11, June 1901		68	8	
VonderHare,	10, Apr. 1888		1d	4	
VonderHeide, Charles	4, May 1889		4	1	
VonderHeide, Clara	9, Dec. 1887		21- 2m	1	
VonderHeide, Ethel	22, Feb. 1895		9m	5	
VonderHeide, Fritz	7, Sept 1900		60	5	
VonderHeide, H.	18, Feb. 1888		63	1	
VonderHeide, H.	3, Feb. 1891		51	4	
VonderHeide, Henry	31, Dec. 1891		43	1	
VonderHeide, J.	27, Dec. 1888		2m	2	
VonderHeide, Louis	26, Jan. 1894		29	5	
VonderHeide, Mary	29, Apr. 1891		56	4	
VonderHeide, Mary F.	21, Nov. 1891		38	4	
VonderHorst, Raymond	26, July 1895		10m	5	
Vonderahe, Elisabeth	26, June 1894		56	5	
Vonderahe, Lilly	2, June 1897	1, June	7-10m	5	
Vonderhaar, Elisabeth	3, May 1897	1, May	73- 2m	5	Overberg
Vonderheid, Anna	3, Feb. 1898	2, Feb.	27- 9m	5	
Vonderheid, Elisabeth	27, Aug. 1897	26, Aug.	30	4	
Vonderwische, Herman Heinrich	18, Nov. 1899	16, Nov.	68- 6m	4	
Vondriska, Cecilia	30, May 1901		2	8	
Vongardt, F.W.	23, Jan. 1896	21, Jan.	42- 9m	5	
Voots, Mary	9, Sept 1900		11m	5	
Vorbroker, Marie	13, Sept 1892	12, Sept	43	5	Kipp
VordemBerg, Edna	12, Feb. 1897	10, Feb.	2- 9m	5	
Vorderlage, Georg	3, Aug. 1897	1, Aug.	67- 7m	5	
Vorherr, John	15, Mar. 1898	14, Mar.		4	
Vorherr, John A.	17, June 1891		70	4	
Vorhouse, Charles	1, Mar. 1893		38	5	
Vormohr, Elisabeth	2, July 1901		31	8	
Vormohr, Frank	25, Feb. 1901		58	8	
Vornberg, Rosa	1, Feb. 1892		3m	5	
Vornberger, Anton	25, Sept 1889		3m	1	
Vorneder, William	30, Apr. 1901		10m	8	
Vornhorn, Helena	23, Mar. 1900	22, Mar.	73	8	Thole
Voskotter, Marie M.	5, Dec. 1896	3, Dec.	66- 6m	5	
Voslammer, Henry	11, Mar. 1891		49	4	
Voss, J.B.	11, Nov. 1896	10, Nov.	69- 2m	5	
Votel, Al.	6, Jan. 1892		4	5	
Voth, Henrietta	29, Dec. 1892		60	5	
Votteler, Fred	29, Sept 1900		75	8	
Voß, Agnes	13, Aug. 1891		46	4	
Voß, Elisabeth	24, Aug. 1898	23, Aug.	63-11m	5	
Voß, Henry	27, Dec. 1888		63	2	
Voß, John	15, Feb. 1889		52	1	
Voß, Joseph H.	27, Feb. 1899	25, Feb.	48- 4m	5	
Voß, Lilly	9, Aug. 1892		1- 9m	5	
Voß, Mary	29, Dec. 1900		59	8	
Voßler, Jakob	4, May 1897	2, May	44- 2m	5	
Voßmeyer, Minnie (Sr. Edwina)	6, Sept 1901		27	8	
Vägelon, Julius	29, June 1893		19	5	
Völker, Adam	31, Jan. 1899	30, Jan.	61- 7m	5	
Völker, John M.	18, Apr. 1893		4m	5	
Völkle, Joseph	6, Mar. 1891		57	4	
Vöster, Margaretha	27, Oct. 1896	25, Oct.	41- -16d	5	

Name ****	Notice Date ****** ****	Death Date ***** ****	Age ***	Page ****	Maiden Name ****** ****
Wachendorf, Minnie	15, Mar. 1889		29	1	
Wachmann, A.D.	7, Feb. 1890		81	1	
Wachsmann, Dora	28, Oct. 1893		57	5	
Wachtendorf, Fred.	15, Apr. 1888		55	5	
Wachtendorf, Friederika	14, Feb. 1900	12, Feb.	37	8	
Wachter, Peter	9, Dec. 1891		15	2	
Wack, Michael	20, May 1890		53	1	
Wackermann,C.	14, Feb. 1888			4	
Wade, Richard	25, Jan. 1897	24, Jan.	66	5	
Waehaus, Wilhelm	8, Mar. 1898	7, Mar.	25- 1m	5	
Waerdmann, Lizzie	4, Feb. 1891		46	4	
Waeser, Herman	14, Apr. 1895	11, Apr.	42	5	
Waffenschmidt, Margaretha	17, Jan. 1901		84	8	
Wagener, Frederick	4, Dec. 1891		2	4	
Wagener, Katharine	24, Feb. 1888		37	4	
Wagner,	31, Mar. 1888		1d	4	
Wagner,	6, Nov. 1891		1d	4	
Wagner,	2, July 1895		22d	5	
Wagner, Anna M.	17, June 1888		7m	1	
Wagner, Annie	26, Feb. 1888		28	4	
Wagner, Anton	12, Nov. 1887		69	1	
Wagner, Archie	10, Mar. 1895		7m	5	
Wagner, Barbara	3, Feb. 1888		28	4	
Wagner, Barbara	10, May 1888		52	1	
Wagner, Barbara	4, Jan. 1899	1, Jan.	35- 6m	5	Joachim
Wagner, Barbara	13, July 1901		77	8	
Wagner, Ben.	21, Feb. 1888		6m	1	
Wagner, Carrie	13, July 1900		7m	8	
Wagner, Edward	1, Nov. 1898	29, Oct.	31-11m	5	
Wagner, Edward	23, Nov. 1900		36	8	
Wagner, Elisabeth	29, July 1888		27	1	
Wagner, Ella	10, Feb. 1888		8m	1	
Wagner, Emil	11, Mar. 1899	10, Mar.	62- 1m- 2d	5	
Wagner, Ernst H.	2, July 1896	1, July	31- 6m	5	
Wagner, Franz	26, Apr. 1898	24, Apr.	41- 5m	5	
Wagner, G.W.	14, Aug. 1888		32	1	
Wagner, George	4, Aug. 1891		31	4	
Wagner, George H.	6, Oct. 1891		1m	4	
Wagner, H.	3, Oct. 1898	1, Oct.	69- 1m	5	
Wagner, H.T.	22, May 1899	21, May	63-10m	4	
Wagner, Henry	26, Feb. 1901		50	8	
Wagner, Ida R.	1, Aug. 1898	31, July	67	5	
Wagner, J.A.	16, Mar. 1888		48	1	
Wagner, J.A.	3, Nov. 1891		1m	4	
Wagner, John	11, Jan. 1892		14d	4	
Wagner, John	15, Nov. 1894		3	5	
Wagner, John	9, Nov. 1894		61	4	
Wagner, John V.	25, Nov. 1893		42	5	
Wagner, Julius J.	7, Mar. 1897	6, Mar.	67- 5m	* 4	
Wagner, Karl	18, June 1895		71	5	
Wagner, Katharine	19, Jan. 1888		58	4	
Wagner, Louis	15, Apr. 1892		41	5	
Wagner, Louisa	23, Nov. 1891		8	1	
Wagner, Lucy	10, Sept 1887		33	2	
Wagner, Maggie	8, Feb. 1889		3	1	
Wagner, Maria	26, June 1891		31	4	
Wagner, Maria	28, July 1899	27, July	66-10m	5	
Wagner, Maria Amelia	19, Jan. 1899	17, Jan.	25-10m	5	
Wagner, Martha E.	16, May 1894		3m	5	
Wagner, Mary	25, June 1901		35	8	
Wagner, Mary E.	8, Feb. 1901		5w	8	
Wagner, Mina	3, Oct. 1887		59	1	
Wagner, Myrtle	17, July 1901		4	8	
Wagner, Nik.	25, Mar. 1889		5d	1	
Wagner, Peter	20, Nov. 1891		84	4	
Wagner, Peter	1, Feb. 1901		64	8	
Wagner, Philipp	8, Dec. 1890	7, Dec.	43- 7m-20d	1	
Wagner, Regina	20, Dec. 1900		70	8	
Wagner, Tillie	24, July 1889		4m	1	
Wagner, Tobias	9, July 1900	8, July	64- 7m	8	

Name ****	Notice Date ****** ****	Death Date ***** ****	Age ***	Page ****	Maiden Name ****** ****
Wagner, Walter	16, Jan. 1893		14	5	
Wagner, Wesley	29, Oct. 1891		49	4	
Wagner, Wilhelmine	1, Sept 1900		59	5	
Wagner, William	24, Oct. 1887		17	1	
Wagoner, Walter	5, Sept 1894		1m	5	
Wahemann, Joseph	15, July 1897	14, July		5	
Wahl, Anna M.	31, Jan. 1901		77	8	
Wahl, Clemens	7, Sept 1901		47	8	
Wahl, Emma Weber	14, Jan. 1901		24	8	
Wahl, Joseph	29, Apr. 1896	28, Apr.	42- 1m	5	
Wahl, Philipp	30, 31, Oct. 1896	29, Oct.	33	5	
Wahle, Adelheid	13, June 1901		51	8	
Wahle, Anna	18, Nov. 1891		4	4	
Wahle, Bertha F.	22, May 1891		18	1	
Wahle, Emma A.	21, Aug. 1896	20, Aug.	22	5	
Wahle, Josephine M.	2, Sept 1897	31, Aug.	19	5	
Wahlers, Jakob	6, Mar. 1889		61	1	
Wahlicht, Martha	7, Aug. 1888	6, Aug.	4- 7m- 8d	4	
Wahlrauch, Jos.	11, Feb. 1893		2	5	
Wahlters, Aaron Max	9, Apr. 1890		60	1	
Wahmes, Bernard W.	15, Feb. 1901		28	8	
Wahoff, Maria	5, Oct. 1898	4, Oct.	75- 1m	5	Lambers
Wahoff, St. H.	25, June 1888		68	1	
Wahrenberger, John	29, Dec. 1888		18	1	
Wahrenberger, M.	9, Aug. 1901		53	8	
Waibel, Louisa	5, Mar. 1891		2m	4	
Wainright, John H.	23, Nov. 1888		52	1	
Waise, Anthony	27, July 1887		9m	1	
Wakemann, Joseph	16, July 1897	14, July	65- - 5d	5	
Walber, Edward	15, Aug. 1891		18	4	
Walbrech, Caroline	25, May 1901		77	8	
Walburg, Herman	9, Jan. 1894		65	5	
Wald, Louis	17, Dec. 1898	16, Dec.	67	5	
Waldhard, Louisa	28, Apr. 1891		4m	4	
Waldhaus, Diedrich Henry	18, Oct. 1899	16, Oct.	66- -27d	7	
Waldmann, Dorothea	14, Nov. 1895	12, Nov.	36-11m	5	Brinkmann
Waldner, Jenny	21, June 1895		9	5	
Waldner, Rosa	25, Nov. 1887		5w	1	
Waldron, Jane E.	1, May 1888		80	2	
Waldschmid, John	11, Apr. 1889		11	1	
Walkenhorst, Edna	11, June 1895		7	5	
Walker, Lucinda	8, Dec. 1887		49	1	
Walker, Samuel	6, June 1901		85	8	
Walker, William	2, Nov. 1888		6	1	
Walker, William	30, Nov. 1900		11m	8	
Wall, John	15, Mar. 1901		32	8	
Wall, Lorena	8, July 1888		9m	1	
Wall, Mamie	30, Apr. 1901		6m	8	
Wall, Thomas	13, Aug. 1901		2	8	
Wall, William	21, Mar. 1893		10	5	
Wallace, Charles	20, Dec. 1900		65	8	
Wallace, Margaret	26, Jan. 1901		14d	8	
Wallbrech, John Fred.	28, Dec. 1892		73	5	
Wallbrecht, Emilia	6, Oct. 1891		5m	4	
Wallbrecht, Rudolph	21, Jan. 1890		1	1	
Wallburg, Dorothea	12, Sept 1895	9, Sept		5	Laun
Waller, Benjamin	27, July 1887		21	1	
Waller, L.	18, Feb. 1888		58	1	
Walling, Frank	15, Jan. 1891		40	4	
Wallinger, Kate	18, Aug. 1891		17	4	
Wallingford, C.	24, Sept 1888		7m	1	
Wallrauch, Sebastian	11, Sept 1888		65	1	
Walls, Annie	24, Aug. 1887		43	1	
Walls, James P.	14, Feb. 1888		57	4	
Walmer, Dora	1, Aug. 1891		24	4	
Walpole, John M.	19, July 1901		4	8	
Walpole, William W.	25, Jan. 1894		56d	5	
Walsdorf, Arthur	14, Aug. 1900		9m	5	
Walsh, Agnes	6, Sept 1900		1	5	
Walsh, James	5, Aug. 1887		1d	1	
Walsh, Kate	26, July 1900		40	5	

Name	Notice Date	Death Date	Age	Page	Maiden Name
****	****** ****	***** ****	***	****	****** ****
Walsh, Mary	23, June 1888		59	1	
Walston, Martha	11, Aug. 1900		47	8	
Walt, Anna C.	3, Apr. 1895		69	5	
Waltemat, Lena	1, Aug. 1887		8m	1	
Walter, A.	24, Aug. 1888		9d	1	
Walter, Alma	6, Jan. 1892		2	5	
Walter, Amelia	10, Nov. 1900		73	8	
Walter, Andrew F.	2, Nov. 1900		37	8	
Walter, Caroline B.	22, July 1893		1	5	
Walter, Catharina	22, June 1889		85	1	
Walter, Charles	3, Feb. 1891		37	4	
Walter, Christian	19, Dec. 1890		4m	1	
Walter, Dora	9, Oct. 1901		72	5	
Walter, Eduard	29, Sept 1891		2- 4m	4	
Walter, Frank	8, Mar. 1901		73	8	
Walter, Frank	22, Mar. 1901		50	8	
Walter, Georg	27, Mar. 1892	25, Mar.	5- 3m-25d	5	
Walter, George	14, Mar. 1888		2	1	
Walter, J.	15, Dec. 1887		52	1	
Walter, Jacob F.	25, Oct. 1897	23, Oct.	56- 1m	5	
Walter, John	21, Nov. 1891		56	4	
Walter, John P.	2, Apr. 1891		19	4	
Walter, Joseph	23, Nov. 1888		13	1	
Walter, L.	27, Aug. 1889		68	1	
Walter, Laura	21, July 1887		19m	1	
Walter, Leopold	13, 14, Mar. 1896	12, Mar.	41	5	
Walter, Maggie	26, Dec. 1898	24, Dec.	31- -12d	5	Pfenning
Walter, Mary	11, Aug. 1900		70	8	
Walter, Sophie	27, Apr. 1895		74	5	
Walter, Wilber	10, Nov. 1898	8, Nov.		4	
Walter, Wilhelm	26, Sept 1899	24, Sept	41- -13d	5	
Waltering, Maria	13, Jan. 1896	12, Jan.	76	5	Robben
Walters,	2, Feb. 1888		3m	4	
Walters, Earl R.	26, Jan. 1901		2m	8	
Walters, Frances A.	27, July 1892		92	5	
Walters, George	17, Dec. 1887		26	1	
Walters, George	26, Mar. 1891		65	4	
Walters, Lena	26, Sept 1887		53	1	
Walters, Nellie	16, Oct. 1900		1	8	
Walther, Charles	16, Sept 1891		69	4	
Walther, Edwin B.	10, Dec. 1898	8, Dec.	2- -18d	5	
Walton, Albert	7, Mar. 1892		8m	5	
Walton, Clinton E.	26, Jan. 1901		35	8	
Walton, Willard	4, Aug. 1900		50	8	
Waltz, Karl	18, May 1900	16, May	62-11m	5	
Waltz, Ludwig F.	17, Feb. 1897	15, Feb.	2- 4m-15d	5	
Waltz, Melinda	17, Apr. 1891		11	4	
Waltz, Nannie E.	16, Jan. 1894		43	5	
Waly, Elisabeth	6, Feb. 1899	4, Feb.	63	4	Thalmann
Walz, Conrad	19, July 1887		32	1	
Walz, Fred. S.	5, Jan. 1901		49	8	
Walz, G.	29, Apr. 1889		41	1	
Walz, Wilbur	2, Feb. 1895		10m	5	
Walzer, Augusta	15, July 1887		28	1	
Walzer, John	30, Nov. 1887		70	4	
Wambold, Bertha	20, Aug. 1892	19, Aug.	26	5	
Wambold, Ida	23, July 1887		11m	1	
Wambsgans, Elisabeth	16, May 1899	15, May	63- 5m	5	
Waminger, Joseph	23, June 1893		3d	5	
Wandstrat, Louise	3, Feb. 1899	2, Feb.	25- 3m	4	Jordan
Wang, Otto	2, Feb. 1895		15	5	
Wanner, Edw. F.	4, Aug. 1888		7m	4	
Wanner, Ernst	13, Oct. 1899	13, Oct.	39	4	
Wanner, Marie	25, Dec. 1895	23, Dec.	53	4	
Wanner, Martin	17, Sept 1895	17, Sept	56	5	
Wanner, William	14, July 1891		7d	4	
Wanra, Ida	2, July 1895		2m	5	
Wanstrath, G.H.	16, Sept 1897	15, Sept	67	5	
Wanstrath, Johan Heinrich	16, Nov. 1897	15, Nov.	84-11m	4	
Warburg, George	3, July 1887		72	4	
Ward, Robert	16, Aug. 1890		59	1	

Name ****	Notice Date ****** ****	Death Date ***** ****	Age ***	Page ****	Maiden Name ****** ****
Ware, Lillian	25, Aug. 1900		3m	5	
Warfield, Annie	14, Feb. 1891		1	4	
Warfield, F.	1, Mar. 1888		2	4	
Warflinger, John	31, Dec. 1898	30, Dec.		5	
Warndorf, Franziska	20, Feb. 1897	19, Feb.	53- 7m	5	
Warneke, Dora	3, May 1892		10m	5	
Warneke, Gertie	26, Feb. 1891		65	4	
Warneke, Lizzie	28, Apr. 1888		5m	1	
Warner, Frank	25, May 1889		4w	1	
Warner, Jakob	6, Mar. 1895		70	5	
Warner, Josie	18, Mar. 1893		2	5	
Warner, Lottie	30, Aug. 1890		6m	2	
Warner, Melisse	15, Nov. 1887		36	4	
Warner, Theodor	13, May 1889		50	1	
Warner, William	8, Jan. 1901		1m	8	
Warning, W.	7, Nov. 1898	5, Nov.	53- 6m	5	
Warnking, Minnie	30, Mar. 1897	29, Mar.	28- 7m	5	
Warren, Michael	23, Apr. 1895		56	5	
Warrington, Eliza	10, May 1901		78	8	
Warrington, J.	12, Dec. 1900		1	8	
Warsel, Anna	19, Nov. 1895	18, Nov.	21	5	Rolf
Wart, Albert	17, Mar. 1890		5w	1	
Wartcke, Flora	19, Sept 1891		68	4	
Wartemann, Lorenz	8, June 1889		2	1	
Wartmann, Nora	16, Apr. 1896	12, Apr.	4- 5m	5	
Warwick, Mary	4, Feb. 1901		35	8	
Waseli, William	27, Sept 1897	26, Sept	57- 1m	5	
Washington, Albert	18, May 1901		21	1	
Washington, George	24, Apr. 1895		2m	5	
Wasteney, George W.	14, Feb. 1891		38	4	
Waterfield, J.C.	13, July 1900		55	8	
Waters, J.	13, Jan. 1888		21	1	
Watkins, Mary	2, Nov. 1900		8m	8	
Watkins, Walter	15, Sept 1888		3w	2	
Watman, Louis	10, May 1889		66	1	
Watman, William	27, Oct. 1888		28	1	
Watoff, Anna Maria	17, Apr. 1896	16, Apr.	71-11m	5	Wuebben
Watson, E.M.	9, Dec. 1887		30	1	
Watson, Ethel	19, Dec. 1900		4	8	
Watson, Ida	19, Aug. 1901		37	8	
Watterson, Elizabeth	30, Aug. 1888		56	1	
Wausbecher, Katharina	7, Feb. 1890		66	1	
Wayke, Joseph	7, Apr. 1893		14	5	
Waykind, R.E.	6, Mar. 1899	5, Mar.		4	
Waß, Thomas	22, Mar. 1894		14	5	
Weatherby, Hannah	14, Aug. 1887		67	1	
Weatherby, Maria S.	25, May 1895		61	5	
Weatz, Joseph	10, Oct. 1901		57	8	
Weaver, Lena	30, Mar. 1893		34	5	
Webb, Bessie W.	18, Jan. 1901		4	8	
Webb, Mary	4, Aug. 1888		34	4	
Webber, Augusta	3, Feb. 1891		67	4	
Webber, Margaret	3, Oct. 1888		40	1	
Webber, Mary	8, Nov. 1887		26	1	
Webbling, Anna	19, Apr. 1900	18, Apr.	54- 4m	4	Schoenebaum
Webe, Eddie	5, Jan. 1892		7	5	
Webeler, H.	14, Dec. 1897	11, Dec.	46- 4m	5	
Weber, Adam	11, Dec. 1891		79	4	
Weber, Albert	3, Dec. 1888		1	1	
Weber, Albert	17, Apr. 1890		2	1	
Weber, Albert	8, July 1891		5d	4	
Weber, Anna	15, Apr. 1893		37	5	
Weber, Anna	23, Apr. 1897	21, Apr.	78- 8m	5	Heddeke
Weber, Anna C.	4, Aug. 1888		9m	4	
Weber, Anna Maria	6, May 1893		53	5	
Weber, Annie	6, July 1889		6m	1	
Weber, Annie M.E.	9, Dec. 1892		68	5	
Weber, Anton	30, Mar. 1901			8	
Weber, August	2, Mar. 1889		39	1	
Weber, Barbara	30, Sept 1887		77	1	
Weber, Barbara	2, Mar. 1901		51	5	

Name ****	Notice Date ****** ****	Death Date ***** ****	Age ***	Page ****	Maiden Name ****** ****
Weber, Bernard	12, Sept 1891		34	1	
Weber, Bernhard	13, May 1891		68	2	
Weber, Carrie	23, Apr. 1888		18m	1	
Weber, Charles W.	10, Jan. 1891		24d	4	
Weber, Clara	5, June 1889		17m	1	
Weber, Clara	31, Dec. 1890		2m	4	
Weber, Clarence	28, Sept 1888		3	2	
Weber, Conrad	9, Apr. 1900	8, Apr.	75	4	
Weber, Edward	25, Sept 1889		20	1	
Weber, Elenora	21, May 1901		1	8	
Weber, Elisabeth	13, Jan. 1899	12, Jan.	80- 1m	4	Bockhorst
Weber, Elisabeth	18, Aug. 1900		62	8	
Weber, Elizabeth	16, Apr. 1891		54	4	
Weber, Elizabeth	21, Dec. 1891		58	4	
Weber, Elma	11, Sept 1888		13m	1	
Weber, Emilie	25, July 1898	23, July		4	
Weber, Emma	5, Oct. 1894		24	5	
Weber, Emma	4, Oct. 1894	3, Oct.	24- 3m-12d	5	
Weber, Ernst	10, May 1895		10	5	
Weber, Ernst W.	21, Jan. 1891		2	4	
Weber, Eva	2, Nov. 1896	31, Oct.	74-10m	5	Brandt
Weber, Fr.	22, Dec. 1900		46	8	
Weber, Fred.	16, Apr. 1889		61	1	
Weber, Fred.	1, Apr. 1890		2	1	
Weber, Fred.	13, Aug. 1901		58	8	
Weber, Fred. W.	1, May 1891		5m	4	
Weber, Fred. W.	25, Apr. 1892		4	5	
Weber, Frederika	3, Sept 1889		70	1	
Weber, George	13, Apr. 1892		17d	5	
Weber, George	16, May 1893		64	5	
Weber, Henrietta	5, Apr. 1893		33	5	
Weber, Henriette	13, Apr. 1896	9, Apr.	42- 3m	5	Niederhelmann
Weber, Henry	27, Sept 1890		29	1	
Weber, Henry	17, Jan. 1893		6	5	
Weber, Hester C.	15, July 1891		11m	1	
Weber, J.H.	30, Dec. 1895	27, Dec.	73- 2m	5	
Weber, Jacob	6, 7, May 1889	6, May	57- 7m	1	
Weber, Jakob	7, May 1891		77	4	
Weber, Johan	16, Mar. 1896	15, Mar.	60	5	
Weber, Johan	31, July 1899	30, July	55- 6m	4	
Weber, Johan Andy	7, Mar. 1900	5, Mar.	74- 4m	5	
Weber, John	30, Aug. 1887		5w	1	
Weber, John	22, Dec. 1892		48	5	
Weber, John	22, Dec. 1893		1	5	
Weber, Joseph	28, Oct. 1891		38	4	
Weber, Joseph A.	26, Mar. 1891		44	4	
Weber, Kate	28, Oct. 1891		80	4	
Weber, Katharina	21, Jan. 1893		57	5	
Weber, Katharine	12, Jan. 1897	9, Jan.	39	5	Gerhard
Weber, Leo J.	14, Nov. 1891		10m	4	
Weber, Louise	23, Aug. 1900		32	8	
Weber, Lucy	10, Jan. 1894		47	5	
Weber, Magdalena	30, Oct. 1891		41	4	
Weber, Margaret	8, July 1901		1d	8	
Weber, Margaretha	25, Sept 1888		70	1	
Weber, Maria	6, Oct. 1891		72	4	
Weber, Marie	25, July 1898	21, July		4	
Weber, Martin	4, Jan. 1897	3, Jan.	61	5	
Weber, Mary	27, Feb. 1892		38	5	
Weber, Peter	1, July 1899	28, June	77- 5m	5	
Weber, Philip	25, Mar. 1891		59	4	
Weber, Philip	10, Jan. 1898	9, Jan.	67	5	
Weber, Philipp	30, Dec. 1893		48	5	
Weber, Rosa	16, Nov. 1895	15, Nov.	61	5	
Weber, Sarah	30, Aug. 1901		36	8	
Weber, Selma	4, Oct. 1887		5w	1	
Weber, Sophia	11, July 1889		65	1	
Weber, Sophia	21, Sept 1898	19, Sept		4	
Weber, Susanna	27, July 1895		70	5	
Weber, Wilhelmina	2, June 1891		62	4	
Weber, Wilhelmina	23, Apr. 1897	21, Apr.	65- 7m	5	Vonderhaar

Name	Notice Date	Death Date	Age	Page	Maiden Name
****	****** ****	***** ****	***	****	****** ****
Weber, William	19, Mar. 1901		4d	8	
Webster, William	27, Feb. 1901		36	8	
Wechmann, John H.	17, Jan. 1893		39	5	
Wechter, Ida	5, Dec. 1891		7	4	
Weckenbrog, Anna	27, July 1888		18d	1	
Weckermeyer, George	9, Sept 1893		9m	5	
Weckermeyer, John E.	29, Sept 1887		20m	4	
Weddendorf, A.H.	26, Mar. 1888		3m	4	
Weddendorf, Adolph	19, May 1894		42	5	
Wedemeyer, Ferdinand	24, Mar. 1897	22, Mar.	14-10m	5	
Wedig, Dora	18, Aug. 1890		5	1	
Wedig, Emma	18, Aug. 1890		2	1	
Weekstein, Mary	10, Apr. 1888		6w	4	
Weffenstedt, Gertie	26, Feb. 1891		2	4	
Wegelein, Joseph	28, May 1892		36	5	
Weger, Casper	5, July 1890		72	1	
Weghorst, Henry	13, July 1900	12, July	70	8	
Weghorst, Ira	14, Aug. 1887		14m	1	
Wegmann, Peter	10, Oct. 1890		8	4	
Wegner, Mary	12, Nov. 1888		15m	2	
Wehe, H.	21, May 1897	19, May	77	5	
Wehkamp, Bernard	11, June 1901		3	8	
Wehlage, Gertrud	15, Oct. 1901		70	8	
Wehlfelder, Loeb	22, Apr. 1891		88	4	
Wehling, Rosalie	5, Mar. 1895		2	5	
Wehmann, Christina Louise	17, May 1900	15, May	64- 4m	5	Gerke
Wehmann, Louise	1, Feb. 1899	31, Jan.	58-11m	5	Moeller
Wehmeier, Edwin	1, Aug. 1893		11m	5	
Wehmeier, Louis	18, Jan. 1893		33	5	
Wehmer, Katharina	4, Jan. 1898	3, Jan.	89-10m	5	
Wehmeyer, A.H.	1, Mar. 1894		53	5	
Wehming, Bernhard	21, May 1889		75	1	
Wehming, Edward	29, Nov. 1889		18m	1	
Wehner, Casper	14, Nov. 1891		56	4	
Wehner, Leo J.	26, Jan. 1901		8m	8	
Wehr, Martin	31, Aug. 1896	30, Aug.	34- 1m	5	
Wehr, Wilhelmine	13, Jan. 1897	12, Jan.	70-11m-26d	5	Bittenbring
Wehrfritz, Anna	11, Dec. 1900		39	8	
Wehrfritz, Margaretha	15, Feb. 1895		48	5	
Wehrle, Theresa	13, July 1887		20m	1	
Wehrle, Valentin	8, Nov. 1899	7, Nov.	71- 8m	5	
Wehrmann, Dorothea	30, Apr. 1898	29, Apr.		4	
Wehrmann, Wilhelm F.	11, Feb. 1898	10, Feb.	50	5	
Wehrmeyer, Carrie	5, Feb. 1897	3, Feb.		5	Brenner
Wehrmeyer, F.	17, Dec. 1900		22	8	
Wehrmeyer, Walter	17, Feb. 1895		1	5	
Wehrung, John A.	31, Mar. 1891		70	4	
Wehry, Katharine	20, Mar. 1895		66	5	
Weibel, Fannie M.	2, Mar. 1893		21	5	
Weibers, Veronica	2, Nov. 1894		1m	5	
Weich, Clifford N.	12, Aug. 1887		2- 6m	1	
Weick, Catharina	5, July 1887		78	1	
Weid, Anna Katharine	17, Nov. 1888	15, Nov.	37- -27d	1	Meier
Weid, Elisabeth	18, Dec. 1891		37	2	
Weidelt, Charles F.	4, Feb. 1896	2, Feb.	15	5	
Weidenbacher, Friedrich Wm.	3, June 1897	2, June	9- 2m	5	
Weidenweber, Anna	15, Sept 1888		30m	2	
Weiderholt, Walter	2, May 1894		18m	5	
Weidgenant, Rosa	6, Apr. 1894		29	5	
Weidkampe, Bernard	23, Apr. 1891		53	4	
Weidner, Appolonia	29, Dec. 1888		59	1	
Weier, Carolina	27, Feb. 1901		42	8	
Weier, Dorothea	15, 16, May 1900	15, May	81- 6m	5	
Weier, Margaret	15, Sept 1892		8m	5	
Weier, Otto	11, July 1891	11, July	3	1	
Weigand, John	22, Oct. 1900		41	8	
Weigand, Mary	23, Sept 1893		22	5	
Weigand, Val.	1, June 1892		80	5	
Weigel, Bernardine	19, Jan. 1892		60	5	
Weigel, Catharina	30, Oct. 1893	29, Oct.	63	5	Kaiber
Weigel, Charles	23, July 1897	22, July	37- 6m	5	

Name ****	Notice Date ****** ****	Death Date ***** ****	Age ***	Page ****	Maiden Name ****** ****
Weigel, Clara	26, Jan. 1893		41	5	
Weigel, George	27, Mar. 1899	26, Mar.	64- 4m	4	
Weighaus, Flora	12, Sept 1891		2	1	
Weighaus, Henry	4, Apr. 1901		61	8	
Weihe, Alfred	31, Dec. 1890		6m	4	
Weihe, Arthur	23, July 1887		7m	1	
Weihe, Barbara	10, Mar. 1888		54	1	
Weihe, Emilia	11, Sept 1888		31	1	
Weihmann, L.	24, Feb. 1888		52- 6m	4	
Weihsel, Sarah	25, Dec. 1891		65	2	
Weik, Theresa	6, Oct. 1891		46	4	
Weil, A.	23, Nov. 1899	21, Nov.	90	5	
Weil, Amelia	21, Sept 1901		67	8	
Weil, Anna	5, Apr. 1895		63	5	
Weil, Anna	20, Mar. 1896	19, Mar.	32- 5m	5	Haverkamp
Weil, Anna	1, Sept 1900		74	5	
Weil, Anthony	19, Nov. 1900		47	8	
Weil, Carrie	12, Sept 1900		25	5	
Weil, Clarence A.	9, Mar. 1898	8, Mar.	10- 2m	5	
Weil, Frank X.	19, Feb. 1900	17, Feb.	70-11m-19d	* 5	
Weil, Freda	21, Feb. 1893		2m	5	
Weil, Hedwig	6, Apr. 1893		63	5	
Weil, Johan Allen	18, Mar. 1897	17, Mar.	22- 7m	5	
Weil, Johannes	10, Aug. 1900		78	8	
Weil, Mina	3, Aug. 1901		89	8	
Weil, Peter	31, Aug. 1889		6	1	
Weil, Sallie H.	18, July 1895		24	5	
Weil, Samuel	11, Sept 1901		74	8	
Weil, Sophia	25, May 1898	24, May	86	5	
Weiland, Christ.	7, Apr. 1888		58	4	
Weiland, Herman	21, Jan. 1892		15d	5	
Weild, Mathilde	15, Mar. 1889		6m	1	
Weilemann, Johan	10, Aug. 1898	8, Aug.	46- 2m-11d	5	
Weiler, Jette	28, Mar. 1889		65	1	
Weiler, Joseph	4, Feb. 1889		1	1	
Weiler, William J.	3, May 1893		2m	5	
Weiman, Theresa	2, Dec. 1887		75	4	
Weimann, Mary	18, Nov. 1891		16	4	
Weimann, Wilhelm	24, Feb. 1897	22, Feb.	14- 3m	5	
Weimer, Morris	5, Sept 1888		10m	2	
Weimer, Richard	20, Oct. 1891		1d	1	
Weinberg, Lizzie E.	27, Dec. 1890		45	2	
Weinberg, William B.	28, Jan. 1894		1	5	
Weinbrecht, Barbara	15, June 1889		1	1	
Weiner, Elisa	1, Feb. 1893		16	5	
Weiner, M.L.	28, Sept 1888		43	2	
Weiner, Regina	18, Aug. 1893		49	5	
Weinewuth, Harry	28, Dec. 1891		9d	4	
Weingart, Nickolas	14, Mar. 1896	11, Mar.	42- 9m	5	
Weingartner, Edw.	17, Dec. 1900		1d	8	
Weingartner, Joseph	30, Mar. 1896	29, Mar.	54	5	
Weingartner, Joseph R.	6, Jan. 1890		45	1	
Weingartner, Louisa F.	21, July 1894		1	5	
Weingartner, Rachel	3, Oct. 1888		1m	1	
Weingartner, Theodor	29, Aug. 1895	28, Aug.	61- 8m	5	
Weinheimer, Anton	11, July 1887		63	1	
Weinheimer, Evaline	2, Aug. 1893		8m	5	
Weinreich, G.	18, Feb. 1890		5	2	
Weinreich, John	4, June 1889		15m	1	
Weinrich, Mary E.	5, Feb. 1895		66	5	
Weintz, Anna	17, Feb. 1892		2	5	
Weinuß, Emma	5, July 1890		7	1	
Weir, Leo D.	29, June 1894		11m	5	
Weirecke, G.N.	7, Nov. 1898	6, Nov.	3- 9m	5	
Weirich, Barbara	5, Nov. 1896	4, Nov.	60-	5	Weber
Weirich, Ferdinand	8, Oct. 1897	8, Oct.	67-11m	5	
Weirich, Mary	26, Apr. 1889		25	1	
Weirick, Dora	13, Feb. 1894		52	5	
Weirman, George	9, Oct. 1900		21d	8	
Weis, Catharine	23, Sept 1901			8	
Weis, Ed.	11, Apr. 1892		26	5	

Name ****	Notice Date ****** ****	Death Date ***** ****	Age ***	Page ****	Maiden Name ****** ****
Weis, Ernst	7, Oct. 1893		27	5	
Weis, Jacob	11, Feb. 1891		24	4	
Weis, John	21, Dec. 1892		55	5	
Weis, Louis	10, July 1889		3	1	
Weis, Louis	5, Mar. 1901		28	5	
Weis, Maria	22, Feb. 1890		52	4	
Weis, Maria	4, Dec. 1891		69	4	
Weis, Therese	17, Feb. 1892		63	5	
Weis, William	6, Sept 1894		18m	5	
Weisberger, Frank E.	18, Aug. 1894		1m	5	
Weisbrod, George	19, July 1900		75	8	
Weise, Albert	18, Jan. 1892		2	5	
Weise, Bertha	5, May 1891		26	1	
Weise, Flora	7, Apr. 1895		3	5	
Weisel, Carolina	6, Jan. 1892		10d	5	
Weisenbach, Conrad	28, Dec. 1897	26, Dec.	49	4	
Weisenbach, John	27, June 1889		2	1	
Weisenberger, A.	5, Dec. 1900		51	8	
Weisenberger, Albert	15, June 1895		28	5	
Weisenberger, George	30, Sept 1887		68	1	
Weisenborn, H.	25, May 1897	24, May		5	
Weisenborn, Louise	14, Mar. 1895		20	5	
Weisgerber, Anna M.	31, Dec. 1891		78	1	
Weisgerber, Frieda A.	30, Dec. 1892		5m	5	
Weisgerber, Lizzie	8, Dec. 1891		1	4	
Weishaupt, Fred.	25, Aug. 1890		85	1	
Weishaupt, Kate	7, May 1901		70	1	
Weiskopf, Mary	28, Nov. 1900		36	8	
Weismeyer, William	21, Jan. 1893		2m	5	
Weismiller, Catharine	26, Mar. 1891		71	4	
Weisner, Alice	16, Jan. 1889		3	1	
Weisner, Andie	29, Jan. 1891		5w	4	
Weiss, Anna Maria	12, July 1897	10, July	89- 4m	5	
Weiss, Mary	14, Jan. 1899	12, Jan.	62	5	
Weissert, John J.	15, Nov. 1893		34	5	
Weist, Edward G.	19, Dec. 1891		5m	4	
Weist, Gustav	25, Jan. 1896	24, Jan.	38- 7m	5	
Weist, John	23, May 1894		35	5	
Weitenkamp, Mary	24, Mar. 1893		80	5	
Weitershagen, John	12, Jan. 1893		72	5	
Weitzel, Alice	26, Aug. 1891		17	4	
Weitzel, Elisa Margaretha	21, July 1894		88	5	
Weitzel, Elizabeth	9, June 1892		20	5	
Weitzel, Henry	8, Mar. 1889		54	1	
Weitzel, Johan S.	15, Feb. 1897	13, Fe.b	30- 2m	5	
Weitzel, Louis	3, Dec. 1896	28, Nov.	58	5	
Weiß, Adam	3, Apr. 1895		43	5	
Weiß, Albert	26, Mar. 1895		3m	5	
Weiß, Arthur Wilhelm	28, Dec. 1896	27, Dec.	11m-23d	5	
Weiß, Bernard	16, Mar. 1895		63	5	
Weiß, Catharine	22, Aug. 1898	21, Aug.	33- 4m	5	
Weiß, Charles	8, Mar. 1897	6, Mar.	32- 2m	5	
Weiß, Franziska	7, Mar. 1900	6, Mar.	71- 6m	5	Renner
Weiß, George	13, May 1898	12, May	75-10m	4	
Weiß, Hannah	10, May 1888		2	1	
Weiß, Herman	13, Mar. 1894		32	5	
Weiß, Jacob	11, Mar. 1889		25	1	
Weiß, Konrad	14, Aug. 1899	13, Aug.	81	4	
Weiß, Mary	28, Mar. 1891		50	4	
Weiß, Mathilde	7, June 1898	5, June	13- 6m	5	
Weiß, Minna	30, Sept 1899	29, Sept	74	4	
Weiß, Robert	2, Apr. 1895		3m	5	
Weiß, Wilhelm	27, Apr. 1897	25, Apr.	31- 7m	5	
Weiß, Wilhelm A.	31, Mar. 1898	29, Mar.		5	
Weiß, Wilhelm F.	29, July 1896	28, July	4m-16d	5	
Weiß, William	23, Apr. 1897	21, Apr.	33- 3m	5	
Weißgerber, Eleanora	9, Apr. 1890		8	1	
Weißhaar, Marcella	23, May 1894		6m	5	
Weißkopf, Margaret	17, Oct. 1888		2w	1	
Weißleder, Edward	1, May 1891		4	4	
Weißmann, Charles W.	10, Jan. 1891		54	4	

Name	Notice Date	Death Date	Age	Page	Maiden Name
****	****** ****	***** ****	***	****	****** ****
Weißmann, Clinton	20, Mar. 1901		40	1	
Weißmann, H.	20, Feb. 1901		6m	8	
Weker, Rosa	10, Mar. 1897	9, Mar.	37- 4m-28d	5	
Welch, Anna	28, July 1890		24	1	
Welch, John	30, May 1895		57	5	
Welch, John	5, Feb. 1901		30	8	
Welk, Frank W.	9, Aug. 1888		20	1	
Welking, G.	16, Oct. 1895	15, Oct.	48	5	
Wellbrock, Christian	15, July 1893		51	5	
Wellen, Johan Herman	17, Jan. 1899	16, Jan.	72	5	
Wellen, Mary E.	17, Nov. 1888		61	1	
Weller, George	1, June 1901		4m	8	
Weller, Raimond, Eduard	10, Feb. 1896	8, Feb.	8m-19d	5	
Weller, Samuel	18, July 1893		92	5	
Weller, Wilhelm	11, Feb. 1897		41	* 5	
Weller, William	18, July 1887		30	1	
Wellging, W.C.	17, Aug. 1887		2m	1	
Wellick, Frieda	26, Feb. 1890		27	1	
Welling, E.F.	13, Mar. 1888		2- - 6d	1	
Welling, Ella	9, June 1891		1d	4	
Wellman, William L.	11, Aug. 1887		6m	1	
Wellmann, F.H.	2, Feb. 1895		54	5	
Wellmann, Heinrich	13, Sept 1900		49	5	
Wellmann, Katharine	17, Mar. 1888		55	4	
Wellmann, Laura	8, Apr. 1901		27	8	
Wellmann, Maria Anna	29, Mar. 1898	28, Mar.	74- 6m	5	Fischer
Wellmann, Mary E.	20, July 1893		69	5	
Wellmann, R.	1, Oct. 1900		1m	5	
Wellmann, William	30, Dec. 1891		30	4	
Wellner, Ernst	25, Apr. 1888		2	1	
Wellner, Harry	5, Jan. 1892		3w	5	
Wellner, Thomas	11, Apr. 1890		3m	1	
Wellrock, Johan Bernard	27, Jan. 1898	27, Jan.	71- 5m	5	
Wells,	25, July 1888		10w	4	
Wells, Barbara	30, June 1898	27, June	66	5	
Wells, George A.	2, Aug. 1901		1	8	
Wells, Lida Coon	27, Oct. 1887		48	1	
Wells, M.	13, Jan. 1888		31	1	
Welp, Annie M.	21, Sept 1900		5m	5	
Welsch, Barbara	15, Aug. 1896	14, Aug.	80	5	
Welsch, Catharine	13, Jan. 1898	11, Jan.	77	5	
Welsch, Mary	25, Mar. 1901		47	8	
Welsch, Minnie	17, May 1901		37	8	
Welsch, William	18, July 1887		22	2	
Welscher, Johan	15, July 1897	13, July	28- -16d	5	
Welsh, Annie	11, Sept 1888		18	1	
Welsh, Bridget	9, May 1895		42	5	
Welsh, Celia	4, Oct. 1901		82	8	
Welsh, Delia	15, Dec. 1900		52	8	
Welsh, Dicey	17, Dec. 1900		44	8	
Welsh, George	27, Feb. 1901		39	8	
Welsh, Jennie	6, Apr. 1893		10m	5	
Welsh, Kate	15, July 1901		40	8	
Welsh, Martin	25, July 1901		50	8	
Welsh, Michael	3, Nov. 1887		32	4	
Welsh, Willis B.	5, Nov. 1900		56	8	
Welter, E.	4, Dec. 1888		2w	1	
Welzbach, Hilda	22, Aug. 1900		1	5	
Wemel, Friedrich	10, Jan. 1896	9, Jan.	79-11m	5	
Weming, Margaretha	23, Feb. 1892		7m	5	
Wempe, Clemens	31, Aug. 1887		65	1	
Wende, Julius	4, Mar. 1898	3, Mar.	85	5	
Wendebrock, William C.	31, Dec. 1891		2m	1	
Wendel, Elisabeth	26, Feb. 1896	25, Feb.	55	5	Seibert
Wendel, George	4, Jan. 1893		79	5	
Wendel, J.	23, Feb. 1901		81	8	
Wendels, Mary	11, Nov. 1891		26	1	
Wenderoth, Georg	24, Mar. 1896	23, Mar.	47	5	
Wendle, Karl	20, June 1888		10m	1	
Wendt, Anna	9, July 1895		2	5	
Wendt, Elsie	30, June 1896	29, June		5	

Name ****	Notice Date ****** ****	Death Date ***** ****	Age ***	Page ****	Maiden Name ****** ****
Wendt, Maria	21, Sept 1895	20, Sept		5	Lohmann
Wendte, Peter R.	22, Mar. 1897	20, Mar.	45- 1m	5	
Wenert, May	10, Feb. 1895		39	5	
Wenger, Anna M.	8, Dec. 1893		75	5	
Wengert, Paul	22, Feb. 1893		31	5	
Wenhoff, Mary	2, Apr. 1895		5m	5	
Wenholt, Friedricka	9, Feb. 1894		56	5	
Wenner, Ella	13, July 1895		30	5	
Wenning, Ada	1, Mar. 1899	28, Feb.		5	
Wenning, Bernard	30, Sept 1888		7	4	
Wenning, Bernard	10, Sept 1901		26	1	
Wenning, Gertrude	19, Oct. 1891		2d	1	
Wenning, John	7, Aug. 1891		37	4	
Wenning, Karoline	11, Apr. 1896	10, Apr.		5	
Wenning, Myra	1, Feb. 1899	31, Jan.	16- 2m	5	
Wenning, William V.	27, Feb. 1894		3m	5	
Wenninger, Francis Xavier (Fr)	30, June 1888	29, June	83	* 1	
Wente, Anna Carolina	9, Mar. 1898	7, Mar.	29- 2m- 9d	5	
Wentermann, Mary	5, May 1895			5	
Wentworth, Eliza	5, Jan. 1901		67	8	
Wenz, Lena	5, Feb. 1895		9m	5	
Wenzel, Joseph	15, Jan. 1901		66	8	
Wepinger, John	7, Dec. 1888		62	1	
Werdmann, John	16, Jan. 1891		23	4	
Werges, Stella	26, July 1900		12	5	
Werinel, Anthony	14, June 1895		21	5	
Werkmeister, Joseph	21, Mar. 1896	20, Mar.	61	5	
Werkner, Theresa	10, Apr. 1894		87	5	
Werks, Charlotte	28, Aug. 1901		68	8	
Werle, Andy	9, Aug. 1887		3	1	
Werlein, Frederike	4, Feb. 1897	3, Feb.	59	5	
Wermuth, Emma	22, June 1901			8	
Werner, Alfred	23, Mar. 1895		68	5	
Werner, Andrew	3, Mar. 1894		72	5	
Werner, Barbara	28, Jan. 1889		64	1	
Werner, Charles	1, July 1891		16m	1	
Werner, Christopher	1, Nov. 1897	30, Oct.	12- 3m	5	
Werner, Elisabeth	6, July 1897	4, July	65	5	Betz
Werner, Elizabeth	10, Aug. 1901		60	8	
Werner, Ella	11, July 1893		37	5	
Werner, Henry G.	23, Dec. 1891		4m	4	
Werner, Joseph	5, Dec. 1900		47	8	
Werner, Margaret	26, Apr. 1901		19d	8	
Werner, Margaret	10, July 1901		88	5	
Werner, Maria	6, Feb. 1896	5, Feb.	49- 4m	5	
Werner, Marie	27, Sept 1889		24	1	
Werner, Marie C.	6, May 1889		14	1	
Werner, Mary	10, Nov. 1900		87	8	
Werner, Theresa	4, Feb. 1894	3, Feb.	11- 5m-18d	5	
Werner, Theresa	23, Oct. 1899	22, Oct.	36-10m	5	
Werning, Henry	22, July 1887		38	1	
Wernke, Anna	1, June 1894		60	5	
Wernke, Frank	10, June 1901		43	8	
Wernke, John	13, Mar. 1895		8d	5	
Wernke, Maria Susanna	28, Feb. 1900	27, Feb.	62- 8m	5	Kneuven
Wernke, Mary C.	24, Oct. 1891		1	4	
Werreas, Francis	6, Sept 1900		72	5	
Werry, Elizabeth	9, July 1890		64	1	
Werschel, Emma	24, July 1890		9	1	
Werschmann, Joseph	13, May 1891		41	2	
Werse, Annie W.	26, Sept 1894		18m	5	
Wershag, Isabelle	15, Mar. 1901		81	8	
Wershy, Annie	4, Feb. 1888			4	
Werterbeck, Margaret	16, June 1891		14m	4	
Werth, Frank	31, July 1894		21m	5	
Werther, John	3, Jan. 1901		40	5	
Werthwein, Christiana	10, Apr. 1888		78- 7m	4	
Wertsch, Elise	9, 10, Aug. 1900		58	8	
Wertz, Adam	26, Apr. 1895		3	5	
Wertz, Joseph	22, Dec. 1900		3	8	
Wertz, William	14, May 1895		6m	5	

Name	Notice Date	Death Date	Age	Page	Maiden Name
****	****** ****	***** ****	***	****	****** ****
Wesanger, William A.	12, May 1891		4m	1	
Weschler, Joseph	23, July 1896	21, July	32	5	
Weschnefsky, Herman F.	24, July 1895		17m	5	
Wesdorp, John	12, Nov. 1900		70	5	
Wesker, Bernard	24, Nov. 1898	23, Nov.	18- 4m- 3d	5	
Weskilbach, Joseph	31, Dec. 1890		5m	4	
Wesley,	10, Jan. 1888		12w	4	
Wesley, Alfred	15, Aug. 1900		28	5	
Wessel, Adam	25, Apr. 1889		61	1	
Wessel, Bernard	20, Dec. 1900		85	8	
Wessel, Christopher F.	24, Dec. 1893		65	5	
Wessel, Doris	30, May 1894		11m	5	
Wessel, Edwin	17, Jan. 1901		6m	8	
Wessel, Emma	10, Mar. 1897	9, Mar.	2- - 4d	5	
Wessel, Fr.	25, July 1890		1	1	
Wessel, J.F.	9, Feb. 1899	8, Feb.		5	
Wessel, Johan	7, June 1899	6, June	29	5	
Wessel, Johan	18, Oct. 1899			7	
Wessel, Marie A.	11, Apr. 1893		83	5	
Wessel, Marie C.	20, Oct. 1891		82	1	
Wesselmann, Anna Theresa	15, Feb. 1899	14, Feb.	60-10m	5	Flinker
Wesselmann, August	2, Feb. 1899	1, Feb.	54	5	
Wesselmann, Edw.	24, Apr. 1889		1	1	
Wessels, Bernard	26, Apr. 1901		70	8	
Wessels, Eva B.	28, June 1900	27, June	73-10m	8	
Wessels, Frank E.	14, Feb. 1889		1	1	
Wessels, Hannah	30, May 1895		1m	5	
Wessels, John	11, Aug. 1892		50	5	
Wessels, Rose	13, Mar. 1894		1	5	
Wessels, Theodor	26, Nov. 1891		51	1	
Wessinger, Lena	30, Apr. 1897	28, Apr.	54	5	
West, Endora	4, Aug. 1900		30	8	
West, Frank	23, Dec. 1890		3	1	
West, Isaac E.	20, Sept 1887		63	1	
West, John	4, Sept 1890		40	1	
West, John	25, May 1901		42	8	
West, Thomas	4, Mar. 1891		20	4	
West, Viola	16, Mar. 1901		10m	8	
West, Walter	23, July 1887		2m	1	
Westcott, Emma	29, Nov. 1888		28	1	
Westehaus, Henry	21, Apr. 1888		86	1	
Westemacher, Ernst	16, Mar. 1892		6	1	
Westendorf, B.	23, Oct. 1895	22, Oct.	52- 3m	5	
Westendorf, George	26, June 1891		2	4	
Westendorf, Gerde	22, Apr. 1889		7w	1	
Westendorf, Herman Johan	25, Apr. 1898	23, Apr.	59- 8m	5	
Westendorf, Wilhelm	23, Mar. 1899	22, Mar.	25	5	
Westenhoff, H.	8, Sept 1899	7, Sept	71- 4m	4	
Westenhoff, Johan B.	14, Jan. 1896	13, Jan.	32-11m	5	
Wester, Bernard	20, July 1896	17, July	62- 9m	5	
Westerbeck, Clara	14, Sept 1893		3m	5	
Westerbeck, Clemens	16, May 1900	15, May	79	5	
Westerdorf, Kate	5, Feb. 1891		25	4	
Westerfreulke, Fred.	6, Feb. 1901		63	8	
Westerhaus, Joseph	17, Dec. 1891		58	4	
Westerhoff, Anton	23, Sept 1895	21, Sept	60	5	
Westerhoff, Elisabeth	25, Mar. 1893		51	5	
Westerhoff, Frida	20, Jan. 1891		1	4	
Westerhoff, H.J.	24, Nov. 1900		37	8	
Westerhoff, Josephine	29, Aug. 1892		17	5	
Westerhold, Edwin T.	22, Apr. 1896	21, Apr.	23	5	
Westerkamm, Anna	16, Aug. 1901		35	8	
Westerkamm, John	19, Sept 1900		76	8	
Westerkamp, Christian G.	17, July 1894		58	5	
Westerkamp, Eduard	17, Feb. 1896	16, Feb.	19- 2m	5	
Westerkamp, Franz Heinrich	12, Mar. 1896	11, Mar.		5	
Westermann,	3, Nov. 1891		2d	4	
Westermann, Caroline	29, Aug. 1895	27, Aug.	52-10m	5	Doecker
Westermann, Fred.	30, Jan. 1890		3	1	
Westermann, Friedrich	8, Mar. 1898	7, Mar.	79	5	
Westermann, H.G.	14, June 1898	12, June	4- 2m	5	

Name ****	Notice Date ****** ****	Death Date ***** ****	Age ***	Page ****	Maiden Name ****** ****
Westermann, Henry	16, Apr. 1895		44	5	
Westermann, Maria Elisabeth	2, Oct. 1899	30, Sept	66- 4m	4	Stübbe
Westermann, Thomas H.	16, Sept 1891		11m	4	
Westhaus, C.	14, Feb. 1888		2- 9m	4	
Westjohn, Frank	31, Oct. 1888		37	1	
Westjohn, Maria	17, Jan. 1894		80	5	
Westmeier, Anna	27, June 1891		45	1	
Westmeier, Anna Elisabeth	4, Apr. 1899	3, Apr.	72	5	Plogmann
Westmeier, Casper	19, Oct. 1892		9	5	
Westner, Margaret	24, Sept 1900		1m	5	
Weston, Joseph R.	4, July 1887		41	1	
Weston, Mary	16, Sept 1889		33	1	
Weston, Walter	13, Dec. 1900		2m	8	
Westphal, Charles	10, Sept 1887		56	2	
Westphal, John P.	16, Sept 1891		9m	4	
Westphalen, Anthony	12, May 1892		34	5	
Westrup, Mamie	24, Apr. 1891		1	4	
Wetling, Elisabeth	21, Dec. 1891		68	4	
Wetsell, Charles	12, Mar. 1901		27	8	
Wette, Albert	11, July 1892		2m	5	
Wette, John	22, Dec. 1891		60	4	
Wettengel, Frank	18, Aug. 1887		3w	1	
Wettengel, Jakob	22, Sept 1899	21, Sept	61	5	
Wettengel, Margaret	3, Dec. 1891		81	4	
Wetter, George	11, Feb. 1899	7, Feb.		5	
Wetter, Maria	27, Dec. 1890		20	2	
Wetterer, Arthur A.	23, Aug. 1887		4m	1	
Wetterer, John	25, Feb. 1901		25	8	
Wetterer, Severin	19, Nov. 1896	18, Nov.	52	5	
Wettering, August	2, Dec. 1893		26	5	
Wettering, John H.	26, Dec. 1890		66	1	
Wetzel,	28, July 1891		14d	4	
Wetzel, Emilie	19, July 1901		55	8	
Wetzel, Fred. J.	14, Nov. 1891		3m	4	
Wetzel, John	17, Mar. 1888		43- 6m	4	
Weuck, Paul H.	11, July 1887		13d	1	
Weyand, Walter F.	30, Jan. 1899	28, Jan.	18- 1m	4	
Weyer, Rosa	2, Mar. 1889		3	1	
Weyl, Emilie	27, July 1888		34	1	
Weyler, Charles	11, Apr. 1901		6m	8	
Weyler, Harry	15, June 1895		6	5	
Weynard, Joseph	31, Oct. 1900		75	8	
Weyrich, Anna M.	28, Oct. 1893		77	5	
Weß, Clara M.	30, Aug. 1888		1m	1	
Weßling, Dena	27, Sept 1893		63	5	
Weßling, Emma	28, Jan. 1889		18	1	
Weßling, George	7, June 1901		30	8	
Weßling, George H.	8, Jan. 1901		72	8	
Weßling, Maria Elisabeth	14, Mar. 1896	12, Mar.	66- 6m	5	Arning
Whalen, Bridget	2, Mar. 1888		29	1	
Whalen, James	13, Mar. 1901		22	8	
Whalen, Kate	12, Aug. 1887		45	1	
Whalen, William	4, July 1887		11m	1	
Whaley, James	28, Feb. 1888		27	1	
Wharton, Alma	28, July 1887		9m	1	
Whateley, Henry	5, Jan. 1901		76	8	
Wheeler, Anna	19, July 1887		36	1	
Wheeler, Caroline	2, Feb. 1899		50- 2m	5	Ehrhardt
Wheeler, George	26, July 1887		3w	1	
Wheeler, Harry E.	11, Oct. 1900		42	8	
Wheeler, K.	24, Sept 1888		73	1	
Wheeler, Ollie	10, May 1888		2w	1	
Wheeling, Henry	28, Dec. 1893		58	5	
Wheelright, Louisa	10, Oct. 1900		2	8	
Whelan, Marcus	5, Nov. 1900		31	8	
Whistler, Cornelia	6, Dec. 1900		4m	8	
Whitcher, Mary	4, Dec. 1900		52	8	
Whitcomb, George H.	15, Oct. 1900		1	5	
White, Blanche	17, Aug. 1901		7	8	
White, John R.	14, Sept 1900		60	5	
White, Leo	22, Feb. 1897	20, Feb.	35	5	

Name	Notice Date	Death Date	Age	Page	Maiden Name
****	****** ****	***** ****	***	****	****** ****
White, Martha L.	6, June 1895		52	5	
White, Mary	24, Sept 1890		67	4	
White, Myrtle	26, Nov. 1900		4m	8	
White, Thomas	21, May 1901		66	8	
White, Thomas	26, June 1901		45	8	
White, Timothy	5, Aug. 1887		11m	1	
White, William	4, Dec. 1900		43	8	
White, William B.	25, June 1888		3m	1	
Whiteman, H.C.	21, Aug. 1889	20, Aug.	72	1	
Whitford, Katharine	26, Dec. 1900		14	8	
Whitney, Henrietta	9, May 1895		33	5	
Whitney, M.C.	14, Dec. 1887		1w	4	
Whittacker, Thomas	11, Apr. 1890		35	1	
Whittaker, J.W.	31, Mar. 1888		65	4	
Whitteker, Gertrude F.	11, Feb. 1891		3	4	
Whitter, H.	17, Jan. 1888		26	4	
Whittlesy, Charles A.	23, Aug. 1887		3	1	
Wibben, Clara	12, May 1898	11, May	22	5	
Wibben, Philomena	20, Dec. 1895	18, Dec.	62- 9m	5	Wörmann
Wichelmann, Johan Clemens	2, Mar. 1896	29, Feb.	79-	5	
Wichering, Margarethe	5, Apr. 1895		46	5	
Wichmann, Arthur Gerhard	26, Feb. 1896	24, Feb.	2- 1m	5	
Wichmann, Bernard	10, Mar. 1894		78	5	
Wickemeyer, Grace	17, Apr. 1894		2m	5	
Wickering, Ettney	23, Feb. 1891		1	4	
Wickes, Robert	26, May 1892		10m	5	
Wicol, Maggie	5, Nov. 1889		4	1	
Widmann, Andreas	21, June 1888		18m	1	
Widmann, Peter	22, June 1895		66	5	
Widmann, Robert	24, July 1901		5d	8	
Widmer, Anna	3, Nov. 1891		65	4	
Widmer, Elizabeth	31, Oct. 1891		73	4	
Widmeyer, John	24, May 1901		41	8	
Widmeyer, Mary A.	29, July 1893		9m	5	
Widrig, Margaretha	31, July 1896	30, July	56	5	Feth
Wiebbebi, M.	27, Dec. 1887		6	1	
Wiebe, Alice W.	18, June 1895		15m	5	
Wiebe, Edna	22, June 1895		15m	5	
Wiebell, Margaretha	16, Sept 1898	15, Sept	51- 3m	5	Zumstein
Wiebke, Sophie	11, Nov. 1897	9, Nov.	70-10m	4	Schürmann
Wiebking, Herman	15, Feb. 1898	14, Feb.	32	5	
Wiebling, Fred.	11, July 1889		24	1	
Wiechand, John F.	9, Dec. 1891		61	2	
Wiechart, Henry	13, Aug. 1891		59	4	
Wiechelmann, J.W.	7, June 1893	5, June	49	5	
Wiechering, Theresa	11, Sept 1894		58	5	
Wiechers, J.F.	21, Mar. 1888		85	1	
Wiechmann, Flora	21, Jan. 1891		2	4	
Wiechmann, Heinrich	5, Aug. 1899	3, Aug.	34- 9m- 8d	4	
Wiechmann, Joseph	10, Apr. 1896	10, Apr.	7- 5m	5	
Wieck, Johan Bernard	15, May 1897	14, May	63- 9m	4	
Wieckering, Emma	17, Apr. 1895		3	5	
Wiede, William C.	16, Jan. 1889		6m	1	
Wiedemann, C.	21, Nov. 1900		1	8	
Wiedemann, Elise	14, Feb. 1900	13, Feb.	39	8	
Wiedemann, L.	19, Oct. 1900		65	5	
Wiedemann, Ludwig	19, Sept 1901	18, Sept	36- 8m-13d	5	
Wiedenroth, George	1, Sept 1891		54	4	
Wiederholt, Frank	9, July 1890		1	1	
Wiedersprung, Maria	5, Oct. 1888		71	1	
Wiedmann, Katharine	7, Dec. 1893		73	5	
Wiedmer, John H.	26, Apr. 1895		54	5	
Wiefermeier, Kate	6, Jan. 1892		2	5	
Wiegand, Elisabeth	20, Nov. 1899	18, Nov.	50- 6m	5	Finkelmeier
Wiegand, Katharine	20, Nov. 1900		46	8	
Wiegand, L.	15, Dec. 1887		25	1	
Wiegand, Mary E.	13, Jan. 1891		65	1	
Wiegand, Minnie	21, May 1901		28	8	
Wiegand, Philipp	21, Aug. 1894		52	5	
Wiegand, Stuart	18, June 1895		1d	5	
Wiegand, Sylvester J.	1, Aug. 1887			1	

Name ****	Notice Date ****** ****	Death Date ***** ****	Age ***	Page ****	Maiden Name ****** ****
Wiegert, Elisabeth	29, June 1893		66	5	
Wiegmann, Catharine	7, Sept 1888		80	1	
Wiehers, August	11, May 1889		5	1	
Wieland, Emilia	28, June 1895		1	5	
Wieland, Julia	13, July 1894		3m	5	
Wieland, William	22, May 1901		86	8	
Wielert, Amelia	30, Nov. 1887		23	4	
Wielert, Charlotte	15, Feb. 1899	14, Feb.		* 4	Meier
Wielert, Henry	30, 31, Aug. 1892	29, Aug.	57	5	
Wieman, Anna M.	11, June 1891		68	4	
Wiemann, Franziska	3, Jan. 1889		1	1	
Wiemann, Friedrich	13, May 1898	11, May	81- 4m	4	
Wiemann, Joseph H.	28, May 1891		84	4	
Wiemann, Maria Louisa	17, Nov. 1896	16, Nov.	37- 5m	5	
Wiemer, Annie M.	18, Aug. 1891		2m	4	
Wiemeyer, John H.	11, Jan. 1894		2m	5	
Wiening, Charlotte	17, Mar. 1897	16, Mar.	51- 9m	5	Schwetter
Wienke, Wilhelm	26, Jan. 1897	24, Jan.	71	5	
Wienning, Herman	1, Oct. 1900		38	5	
Wientz, Henriette Sophia	9, Dec. 1893		75	5	
Wiep, Fred	8, Dec. 1896	6, Dec.	23	5	
Wierhake, Jeanette M.	20, June 1895		23m	5	
Wierich, John	8, Dec. 1893		50	5	
Wiermel, George E.	22, July 1887			1	
Wiermel, J. Chr.	25, June 1888		6m	1	
Wiese, Christine	5, Jan. 1901		25	8	
Wiese, Heinrich Johan	30, Sept 1897	29, Sept	28- 1m	5	
Wiese, John C.	11, Feb. 1891		50	4	
Wiese, Joseph	14, June 1901		23	5	
Wiese, Marie M.	17, Dec. 1888		33	1	
Wiesenhahn, John	5, July 1888		36	1	
Wiesenthal, Hermine	31, Aug. 1896	29, Aug.	36	5	Wachsmuth
Wiest, Edward	20, June 1889		31	1	
Wiete, Nicholas	16, Aug. 1895	15, Aug.	20- 8m	5	
Wiethoff, Anna	22, Dec. 1900		68	8	
Wiethorn, Gertrude	29, Dec. 1891		75	4	
Wieß, Wilhelm	7, June 1898	6, June	19- 4m- 6d	5	
Wigbels, Bernard H.	21, Apr. 1900	20, Apr.	64- 6m	5	
Wigbels, Johanna	25, Jan. 1896	23, Jan.	71- -13d	5	Bese
Wiggermann, Lisette	3, Feb. 1900	2, Feb.	8	5	
Wiggers, Flora	16, Apr. 1901		4m	8	
Wiggers, Robert	17, Dec. 1900		7	8	
Wilberding, Ferd.	16, Apr. 1890		35	1	
Wilberding, Hy.	14, July 1900		81	8	
Wilberding, Laura	27, Oct. 1891		2	1	
Wilberding, Mary	11, Sept 1889		79	1	
Wilbering, Agnes	20, Mar. 1891		7	4	
Wilcox, Edwin M.	9, May 1895		6	5	
Wilcox, William	4, June 1901		54	8	
Wild, Barbara	13, Oct. 1898	12, Oct.	52- 7m- 8d	5	Bürger
Wild, Louisa	17, Oct. 1900		61	8	
Wild, Minnie	9, July 1891		23d	4	
Wilde, August Edward	13, Jan. 1893	12, Jan.	69	5	
Wilde, Emma	3, July 1887		2m	4	
Wilde, George	19, Sept 1894		23	5	
Wildel, Louise Marie	11, Nov. 1898	10, Nov.	47- 3m-16d	5	Vondemfange
Wilder, Angie L.	22, Jan. 1891		19	4	
Wildt, Charlotte	7, Oct. 1893		38	5	
Wildt, Christian	9, Oct. 1896	8, Oct.	80- 2m- 8d	5	
Wiles, Christ.	25, Aug. 1890		65	1	
Wiley, Harry	6, Nov. 1900		22	8	
Wiley, Josephine	12, Jan. 1898	11, Jan.		4	Wehrkamp
Wiley, Mary E.	23, Sept 1887		18	2	
Wilharm, Wilhel.	15, Dec. 1900		54	8	
Wilhelm, Franz	6, Nov. 1896	4, Nov.	11m-20d	5	
Wilhelm, George K.	22, July 1893		60	5	
Wilhelm, John C.	3, Feb. 1891		48	4	
Wilhelm, Joseph	25, June 1895		15d	5	
Wilhelm, Marion R.	19, Dec. 1893		33	5	
Wilke, August J.	29, May 1894		1	5	
Wilke, Ben	28, Aug. 1901		25	8	

Name	Notice Date	Death Date	Age	Page	Maiden Name
****	****** ****	***** ****	***	****	****** ****
Wilke, Caroline	27, Jan. 1895			5	
Wilke, Herman	27, Dec. 1890		51	2	
Wilke, Mattie E.	5, May 1895		9	5	
Wilke, Stella	9, Jan. 1901		10m	5	
Wilken, Helen	18, Jan. 1901		6m	8	
Wilkening, Floratina	22, Sept 1897	19, Sept	4- 4m	5	
Wilkening, Sophia	10, Mar. 1894		40	5	
Wilkening, W. Heinrich	17, June 1896	15, June	62- 2m	5	
Wilkens, Annie	18, June 1895		2	5	
Wilkens, Sophia L.	19, Oct. 1900		76	5	
Wilker, Heinrich J.	21, Apr. 1899	19, Apr.	35- 9m	5	
Wilkerson, William	2, Jan. 1901		36	5	
Wilkie, Marie	29, June 1901		19	8	
Wilking, Franciska	1, Nov. 1895	31, Oct.	28	5	Brinkmann
Wilking, Laura V.	3, July 1887		46	4	
Wilking, Mary	26, Nov. 1900		2d	8	
Wilkinson, Anna	6, Mar. 1901		54	5	
Will, Anna Franziska	8, June 1900	6, June		8	Ruby
Will, Anton	24, June 1899	23, June	37- - 8d	4	
Will, Georg	15, July 1897	14, July	25- 4m	5	
Will, Johan	1, Feb. 1900	30, Jan.	73- 6m	5	
Will, Katharine	4, Nov. 1896	3, Nov.	85	5	
Wille, Katharine	17, Aug. 1900		54	5	
Wille, Otto	3, Nov. 1887		27	4	
Wille, Werhardt	24, June 1901		81	8	
Willebrand, Margaretha	11, Sept 1888		1w	1	
Willeke, Bernard H.	15, July 1890		6w	1	
Willeke, Helen	29, May 1894		35d	5	
Willen, Elisabeth	10, Mar. 1899	9, Mar.	38	5	Gers
Willen, Frances	5, Sept 1891		3m	1	
Willen, George M.	12, Feb. 1891		76	4	
Willenberg, J.H.	24, Feb. 1888		63	4	
Willenberg, M.	27, Dec. 1887		23	1	
Willenborg, Francis H.	18, Jan. 1893		69	5	
Willenborg, John H.	6, Mar. 1891		32	4	
Willenborg, Margarethe	4, Oct. 1900		30	8	
Willenbrink, Frank J.	20, July 1895		9m	5	
Willenburg, Ida	4, May 1892		1	5	
Willering, Louis	25, Nov. 1895	24, Nov.	24- 9m	5	
Willert, Mary A.	27, July 1887		85	1	
Willet, Jakob	30, Dec. 1897	28, Dec.	53- 6m	5	
Willey, J.D.	14, Jan. 1898	11, Jan.		4	
William, Magdalena	31, May 1892		66	5	
William, N.	11, Jan. 1888		23	4	
William, W.H.	21, Jan. 1888	20, Jan.	48	4	
Williams,	21, Nov. 1900		23d	8	
Williams, Benjamin H.	13, May 1889		5m	1	
Williams, Birdie	7, Apr. 1888		12	4	
Williams, Clara	27, Feb. 1901		39	8	
Williams, Dennis	4, Feb. 1891		40	4	
Williams, Eleonore	18, Aug. 1887		30	1	
Williams, Fr.L.	27, Oct. 1900		81	8	
Williams, George H.	17, Aug. 1901		32	8	
Williams, Hattie	4, Aug. 1900		30	8	
Williams, Henry	10, July 1887		2	1	
Williams, J.	18, Dec. 1888		6m	2	
Williams, J.J.	30, June 1888		47	1	
Williams, John	19, Oct. 1894		33	5	
Williams, John	8, Oct. 1901		38	1	
Williams, Joseph	3, Dec. 1900		34	8	
Williams, Katie	27, Sept 1888		6	2	
Williams, Lee	29, Mar. 1888		21	1	
Williams, Lena	15, Aug. 1900		25	5	
Williams, Lulu M.	21, Mar. 1895		12d	5	
Williams, Maggie	21, Sept 1900		4m	5	
Williams, Mary	5, Aug. 1890		76	1	
Williams, Mary A.	19, June 1895		48	5	
Williams, Moses	13, Oct. 1900		38	8	
Williams, Moses	31, July 1901		44	8	
Williams, Myrtle H.	3, Oct. 1887		5	1	
Williams, P.	3, Jan. 1888		14m	1	

Name ****	Notice Date ****** ****	Death Date ***** ****	Age ***	Page ****	Maiden Name ****** ****
Williams, Patrick	7, Sept 1888		37	1	
Williams, Ruth	26, Apr. 1901		8m	8	
Williams, Sadler	10, Jan. 1899	7, Jan.	63- 7m	5	
Williams, Sarah B.	27, Aug. 1892		85	5	
Williams, Victoria	3, Oct. 1888		33	1	
Williams, W.	19, Dec. 1900		1m	8	
Williams, W.R.	8, Nov. 1887		18	1	
Williams, Walter	13, July 1887		6m	1	
Williamson, A.	30, Jan. 1901		53	8	
Williamson, Ethel	12, June 1901		21	8	
Williamson, Samuel	3, June 1901			8	
Willich, Maria	16, July 1897	15, July	25- 2m	5	Teufel
Willig, Friedrich Gottfried	20, Feb. 1899	19, Feb.	54-11m	* 5	
Willis, C.	10, Apr. 1888		4	4	
Willis, Martha J.	16, Feb. 1901		74	8	
Willis, Ruth	25, Feb. 1901		2	8	
Willman, Fred.	5, June 1890		37	4	
Willman, H.	20, Sept 1889		52	1	
Willman, Joseph	4, June 1895		1d	5	
Wills, Ellen	14, Feb. 1901		54	8	
Wilmare, Amanda	31, May 1901		40	8	
Wilmer, Bernard	20, Apr. 1894		66	5	
Wilmer, Charles	28, May 1892		9m	5	
Wilmes, August	30, Mar. 1894		23	5	
Wilmes, Joseph	10, Mar. 1891		40	4	
Wilmes, Joseph F.	6, Feb. 1899	5, Feb.	38	4	
Wilmes, Josephine	24, Feb. 1896	22, Feb.	71- 2m	5	Robeloth
Wilmes, Lawrence	9, July 1887		6w	1	
Wilmes, Maria Elisabeth	28, Apr. 1897	25, Apr.	70	5	Heinrichs
Wilmes, Marie	13, June 1901		3	8	
Wilmington, Belle	2, Apr. 1901		40	8	
Wilmink, Fredericka	16, July 1892		65	5	
Wilmot, Frank	9, Jan. 1901		40	5	
Wilms, Gustav	23, Aug. 1888		70	1	
Wilms, J.C.	20, Sept 1901		74	1	
Wilms, Joseph	15, Jan. 1892		12	5	
Wilp, Dina	30, June 1897	29, June	26- 8m	5	
Wilp, Henry	15, Apr. 1889		75	1	
Wilp, Henry	17, May 1901		76	8	
Wilp, Minnie	27, Feb. 1892		30	5	
Wilsemann, Heinrich	23, Sept 1896	22, Sept	24- 1m	5	
Wilson, A.	8, Mar. 1901		6	8	
Wilson, Agnes	11, Sept 1900		46	5	
Wilson, Alice	29, Aug. 1892		1m	5	
Wilson, Bridget	1, Sept 1900		40	5	
Wilson, Charles	29, Aug. 1891		5m	4	
Wilson, Cl.	5, Jan. 1888		15m	1	
Wilson, Ellen	27, Mar. 1901		9d	8	
Wilson, Florence	8, Nov. 1887		27	1	
Wilson, George A.S.	4, Feb. 1901		52	8	
Wilson, Gerhardina	1, June 1892		44	5	
Wilson, Hannah	20, Mar. 1901		77	1	
Wilson, Harry	5, Sept 1900		28	5	
Wilson, Howard	13, July 1900		21	8	
Wilson, J. (Dr)	29, Nov. 1888		80	1	
Wilson, John H.	10, Apr. 1888		58	4	
Wilson, Lotta	4, Aug. 1887		30	1	
Wilson, Mary M.	27, Oct. 1900		82	8	
Wilson, Nathan	21, Aug. 1887		19	5	
Wilson, Rose	29, Sept 1900		18	8	
Wilson, Sarah	8, Jan. 1901		59	8	
Wilson, William	12, June 1901		60	8	
Wilson, William E.	5, Feb. 1901		21	8	
Wilz, Mary C.	6, May 1889		18m	1	
Wilzbach, Charles	14, Nov. 1900		21	8	
Wimmer, Rosina	12, Feb. 1901		65	8	
Wimmers, Barbara	18, May 1894		4d	5	
Windau, Edward	6, Apr. 1893		1	5	
Windau, Rosie	23, Jan. 1889		2	2	
Windgassen, Theresa	15, Mar. 1901			8	
Windisch, Conrad	4, 5, July 1887	2, July	62	4	

Name ****	Notice Date ****** ****	Death Date ***** ****	Age ***	Page ****	Maiden Name ****** ****
Windisch, Georg Johan	11, Aug. 1896	10, Aug.	30- 4m	5	
Windisch, John V.F.	19, Mar. 1891	17, Mar.	35-10m	1	
Windisch, Philipp J.	16, May 1894		30	5	
Windley, Mary	13, Sept 1888		69	1	
Windmeyer, George	3, Mar. 1894		78	5	
Wingbermuhle, B.	5, Sept 1891		72	1	
Wingbermuhler, Joseph Wilhelm	28, Apr. 1890		44	1	
Wingeberg, Mary	14, June 1895		36	5	
Wingenberg, William	15, June 1889		8m	1	
Wingerberg, Helene	6, Mar. 1889		30m	1	
Wingerberg, Herman H.	18, Aug. 1891		77	4	
Wingerberg, Mary	1, Feb. 1888		78	4	
Wink, Katharine	25, June 1901		80	8	
Winkel, Henry	13, Sept 1893		39	5	
Winkelmann, Emma	19, Sept 1894		5	5	
Winkelmann, H.A.	22, Sept 1888		4w	1	
Winkelmann, Henry	13, Apr. 1894		52	5	
Winkelmann, Henry	26, June 1901		37	8	
Winkelmann, Henry W.	18, May 1901		72	1	
Winkelmann, T.	10, Mar. 1888		5w	1	
Winkelmann, William	28, Feb. 1888		56	1	
Winkenberg, Anna	9, Feb. 1895		6d	5	
Winkler, Anna Maria	5, 6, Mar. 1890	5, Mar.	69	* 1	
Winkler, Emil	10, June 1891		22	4	
Winkler, Emilie	5, Apr. 1901		3	8	
Winkler, George	10, Apr. 1891		2d	4	
Winkler, James J.F.	27, Apr. 1895		1	5	
Winkler, Maria	29, Jan. 1897	28, Jan.	30- 4m	5	
Winne, Sarah	11, July 1892		27	5	
Winners, Lillian	18, July 1895		7m	5	
Winnes, Harry	12, Sept 1900		2d	5	
Winnes, Jane Ann	8, May 1899	8, May	72	4	
Winslow, Harmon S.	10, Sept 1887		61	2	
Winslow, John A.	8, Dec. 1891		30	4	
Winsmann, Alma	26, May 1898	25, May	5m-12d	5	
Winstieg, Lawrence J.	16, May 1894		8m	5	
Winter, Alice	21, Nov. 1891		30	4	
Winter, Charles	28, Apr. 1888		38	1	
Winter, Elsa	25, Sept 1890		14m	4	
Winter, Ida	24, Jan. 1888		1- 1m	1	
Winter, Maria	7, Aug. 1896	4, Aug.	25	5	
Winter, Maria	30, Jan. 1897	28, Jan.	30- 4m	5	Büche
Winter, Nellie R.	14, Feb. 1891		15m	4	
Winter, Nicolas	28, Feb. 1891		53	4	
Winter, Raymond	11, Apr. 1896	10, Apr.	5- 7m	5	
Winter, William	5, Mar. 1901		4d	5	
Winterburn, John	15, Aug. 1901		72	8	
Winterfeld, James T.	30, Sept 1893		65	5	
Winterhalt, Lena	29, Mar. 1889		9m	1	
Winterhalter, Charles	26, Mar. 1889		8	1	
Winterhalter, George	7, Dec. 1889		80	1	
Winterhalter, Stephan	25, Aug. 1900		72	5	
Winterholter, Edward	10, July 1891		2m	4	
Wintering, Theodor	20, Dec. 1899	19, Dec.	63-11m	4	
Winters, August	26, Apr. 1901		63	8	
Winters, Barbara	26, Feb. 1900	24, Feb.	51- 2m-24d	8	Metzler
Winters, Edward	3, Oct. 1891		2m- 7d	1	
Winters, Elizabeth	3, Oct. 1901		55	8	
Winters, George W.	11, July 1895		4d	5	
Winters, Gust.	2, Aug. 1893		25	5	
Winters, Isabelle C.	8, Mar. 1894		36	5	
Winters, Sophia	26, Aug. 1889		65	1	
Wintzinger, Clara	7, 8, Nov. 1895	6, Nov.	27- 7m	5	Voigt
Wintzinger, Philip	7, Oct. 1901		65	1	
Winzelburger, Regina	3, Feb. 1888		26	4	
Winzerberg, Alois	3, July 1894		6d	5	
Winzig, Conrad	21, Mar. 1892		2m	4	
Winzig, Theresa	22, Mar. 1895		79	5	
Wipper, Fred.	20, Mar. 1901		59	1	
Wirmel, Charles	28, May 1891		85	4	
Wirmel, Jakob	18, Nov. 1897	17, Nov.	47- 3m	5	

Name ****	Notice Date ****** ****	Death Date ***** ****	Age ***	Page ****	Maiden Name ****** ****
Wirth, Andrew	22, Nov. 1893		86	5	
Wirth, Annie	1, Feb. 1888		11	4	
Wirth, Fr.	17, Dec. 1887		27	1	
Wirth, John	31, Oct. 1888		55	1	
Wirth, Julia	18, Oct. 1894		55	5	
Wirth, Louis	26, Aug. 1891		65	2	
Wirth, Maggie	5, Oct. 1888		3d	1	
Wirth, Mary	10, Apr. 1901		64	8	
Wirthwein, Annetta S.	18, Nov. 1891		2	4	
Wirthwein, J.A.	5, June 1888		48	4	
Wirthwine, Ethel R.	30, Dec. 1893		6m	5	
Wirtstefer, Anna	24, May 1889		88	1	
Wischmeyer, Anna	2, July 1895		70	5	
Wise, Isaac M. (Dr.)	27, Mar. 1900	26, Mar.	81	5	
Wise, John	22, July 1901		1	8	
Wise, Julia	25, Sept 1891		3m	4	
Wise, Julia A.	31, July 1901		56	8	
Wise, Lillie V.	10, Apr. 1891		12	4	
Wise, Margaretha	8, Mar. 1899	7, Mar.	74	5	Gresh
Wise, Sarah S.	13, Dec. 1900		59	8	
Wise, William J.	7, Mar. 1891		39	4	
Wiser, Otto	12, Nov. 1888		7m	2	
Wishman, Mathilda	28, Jan. 1892		3w	5	
Wisner, John	2, Sept 1891		49	4	
Wissel, Adam	29, Sept 1897	27, Sept	76- 1m	5	
Wissel, Albert	20, May 1893		26	5	
Wissel, John V.	26, July 1887		10m	1	
Wisser, Henry	11, Nov. 1889		57	1	
Wissing, Edward	29, July 1887		1	1	
Wissing, Elizabeth	17, Jan. 1890		59	1	
Wissing, Herman	4, Sept 1891		29	4	
Wissing, Marie E.	27, Sept 1900		3d	8	
Wissmann, Maria	16, July 1896	14, July	93- 9m	5	
Witherby, Georgie	26, Nov. 1900		6	8	
Witherspoon, Susie	21, Mar. 1901		30	8	
Witmer, Gottlieb	8, May 1891		1d	4	
Witschger, Dollie	10, Aug. 1900		3m	8	
Witsken, Maria	26, Aug. 1901		17d	8	
Witt, Charles	21, Nov. 1889		2d	1	
Witt, Frank	14, Sept 1887		1d	1	
Witt, Richard	31, Dec. 1890		4m	4	
Witte, Arthur	18, July 1891		7	1	
Witte, Bernardina	12, Nov. 1900		81	5	
Witte, Henry	2, July 1901		52	8	
Witte, John	28, May 1891		60	4	
Witte, Kate	20, June 1888		5m	1	
Witte, Minna	12, Aug. 1895	11, Aug.	14- 8m	5	Hülsing
Wittebrock, Johan B.	23, Dec. 1897	20, Dec.	67	5	
Wittekind, Carrie	13, Sept 1900			5	
Wittel, John C.	13, Oct. 1894		42	5	
Wittenberg, Carrie	27, July 1893		4m	5	
Wittenberg, Mary	17, Feb. 1892		1	5	
Wittenberg, Minnie	16, Nov. 1900		41	8	
Wittenborg, Lucilla	16, Mar. 1897	15, Mar.	3m-21d	5	
Wittereide, Emma	28, Mar. 1891		7	4	
Wittfeld, Richard	2, Oct. 1895	1, Oct.	56-11m	5	
Wittgenfeld, George	13, Feb. 1900	10, Feb.	33	8	
Wittkamp, E.	17, Jan. 1888		9m	4	
Wittkamp, Katharina	13, Dec. 1899	11, Dec.	68- 5m	5	Schmitt
Wittkamp, Theodor	7, Jan. 1901		72	5	
Wittlinger, Wilhelm	18, Aug. 1896	16, Aug.	57	5	
Wittmann, Barbara	12, Aug. 1893		74	5	
Wittmann, Mary E.	24, Aug. 1896	22, Aug.	76	5	
Wittrock, John	7, June 1901		66	8	
Witzens, Annie	17, Dec. 1892		83	5	
Wißler, Adolph	18, May 1894		52	5	
Wißling, Willie	7, Aug. 1888		10w	1	
Wißman, Frederick L.	10, Oct. 1901		53	8	
Wlake, Matilda	18, Aug. 1892		7m	5	
Wobrauch, Freddie	22, Nov. 1888		12d	1	
Wobst, August	19, Dec. 1898	18, Dec.	44- 4m	4	

Name	Notice Date	Death Date	Age	Page	Maiden Name
****	****** ****	***** ****	***	****	****** ****
Wochelmann, Terese	4, Dec. 1895	3, Dec.	66- 1m	5	
Wode, Ludwig	29, Sept 1891		75- 9m	4	
Woehler, Arnold H.	25, Jan. 1901		25	8	
Woehrlein, Jacob	22, June 1895		4m	5	
Woehrlein, Wilhelm	27, June 1895		4m	5	
Woelfel, F. Joseph	5, Nov. 1900		1	8	
Woelfle, Bertha	6, Jan. 1892		3	5	
Woelke, Anna	14, July 1891		5m	4	
Woeller, August	18, July 1890		54	1	
Woellner, Elise	30, Apr. 1895		79	5	
Woellner, Johanna	10, May 1898	9, May	72	5	
Woerz, Karl	25, Jan. 1889	24, Jan.	33	* 1	
Woeste, Bernard	30, Nov. 1900		11m	8	
Woeste, Margaret	26, June 1901		9	8	
Woeste, Mary	14, Feb. 1901		63	8	
Woestermann, Gertrude	30, Mar. 1895		65	5	
Woestmann, John	30, Apr. 1901		3m	8	
Wogenstahl, Harry	17, Dec. 1887			1	
Wohentarsky, Anna Maria	23, Nov. 1895	22, Nov.	68- 4m	5	
Wohlgemuth, Bertha	23, 25, Jan. 1890	22, Jan.	38	1	
Wohlgemuth, Christ.	6, Feb. 1901		54	8	
Wolf, Albert	2, Nov. 1894		39	5	
Wolf, Andreas	25, July 1898	23, July	76- 5m	4	
Wolf, Anna	9, Jan. 1891		38	4	
Wolf, Edward	20, Oct. 1900		47	8	
Wolf, Emma	25, Apr. 1892		21	5	
Wolf, Emma	29, Apr. 1893		20m	5	
Wolf, Florence	4, July 1891		7m	4	
Wolf, Fred. Henry	29, Dec. 1891		17m	4	
Wolf, George E.	11, Mar. 1889		40	1	
Wolf, Henry	28, Nov. 1900		48	8	
Wolf, Isidor	2, Oct. 1888		8m	1	
Wolf, Johan	25, May 1897	24, May	44- 1m	5	
Wolf, Johan F.	2, Feb. 1897	31, Jan.	84	5	
Wolf, Johan Rudolf	8, Jan. 1897		48	5	
Wolf, John	31, Aug. 1887		80	1	
Wolf, John	31, Dec. 1888		35	1	
Wolf, Josephina	18, Jan. 1892		2d	5	
Wolf, Karl	12, Mar. 1898	10, Mar.	56	5	
Wolf, Louisa	4, Aug. 1900		59	8	
Wolf, Louise	13, Aug. 1901		29	8	
Wolf, Magdalena	19, Dec. 1900		82	8	
Wolf, Margaretha	6, July 1896	4, July	59- 4m-	5	Kern
Wolf, Mary	5, May 1894		78	5	
Wolf, Moses	10, June 1889		54	1	
Wolf, Nicholas	11, July 1901		5	5	
Wolf, Nicholas	12, Aug. 1901		42	8	
Wolf, R.E.	6, Nov. 1889		43	1	
Wolf, Reichel	26, Feb. 1896	25, Feb.	82	5	
Wolf, Susanna	13, Sept 1889		45	1	
Wolf, W.	17, Oct. 1888		40	1	
Wolf, Wilhelmina	2, June 1898	1, June	45- 4m-14d	4	Meyerrose
Wolf, William H.	13, Sept 1894		4m	5	
Wolfe, James A.	22, Apr. 1891		1	4	
Wolfer, Amos	29, Dec. 1892		41	5	
Wolfer, Barbara O.	3, Mar. 1898	2, Mar.	69- 2m	5	Oehler
Wolfer, Georg	23, Sept 1889		34	1	
Wolfer, George	24, Mar. 1894		17	5	
Wolfer, John P.	3, Feb. 1890		1	1	
Wolfer, Katie	15, May 1894		2	5	
Wolfer, Martha	4, Jan. 1893		2	5	
Wolfer, Rosa	25, Mar. 1890		3	1	
Wolff, Barbara	18, Apr. 1893		79	5	
Wolff, Caroline	17, Dec. 1898	14, Dec.		5	
Wolff, Catharina B.	12, Aug. 1892		64	5	
Wolff, Charles	7, Apr. 1900	5, Apr.	83	5	
Wolff, Charles	2, Feb. 1901		65	8	
Wolff, Christian	25, Sept 1889		18	1	
Wolff, Edward	27, Mar. 1894		21	5	
Wolff, Leopold	3, Nov. 1891		53	4	
Wolff, Robert	16, May 1891		33	2	

Name ****	Notice Date ****** ****	Death Date ***** ****	Age ***	Page ****	Maiden Name ****** ****
Wolfhoefer, Benlina	6, Sept 1889		4	1	
Wolfram, Katie	10, Mar. 1888		5m	1	
Wolfsdorf, Frida	20, June 1889		30m	1	
Wolfsons, Walter	3, Dec. 1891		4	4	
Wolfstein, Josephine	21, Feb. 1901		69	8	
Wolke, Clemens	7, Feb. 1896	6, Feb.	57- 3m	5	
Wolke, Johan Clemens	10, June 1898	9, June	1- 4m	5	
Wolke, Mary	6, Apr. 1895		42	5	
Woll, Ludwig	24, Feb. 1888		22m	4	
Wollenhaupt, Michael	24, Aug. 1887		19m	1	
Wollerding, Franz	10, Jan. 1894		1m	5	
Wollering, Frank	12, Aug. 1887		6m	1	
Wollfrath, F.	13, July 1900		60	8	
Wollmann, William T.	14, Dec. 1893		15	5	
Wollton, Johanna	26, Nov. 1900		35	8	
Wolpert, Anna M.	11, Dec. 1891		65	4	
Wolpert, Kate	27, June 1889		2	1	
Wolpole, Harris	7, May 1901		9m	1	
Wolsifer, Aloysius R.	23, Sept 1891		2d	4	
Woltenberg, Henry	27, Nov. 1889		29	1	
Wolter, William	3, Nov. 1891		2	4	
Woltermann, Josephine	26, June 1894		75	5	
Wolters, George	24, Mar. 1888		10m	1	
Wolters, Pauline	19, July 1889		18m	1	
Woltz, Cora J.	6, Apr. 1893		4	5	
Wonn, Louis	2, July 1891		3w	4	
Wood,	5, Feb. 1901		4d	8	
Wood, Catharine	25, Mar. 1901		6m	8	
Wood, Jeannette	4, Apr. 1895		4d	5	
Wood, Mary	17, July 1901		65	8	
Wood, Mary A.	9, Aug. 1887		75	1	
Wood, Sallie	28, Apr. 1888		1	1	
Wooding, Kemp	7, Feb. 1901		25	8	
Woodley, Francis	2, Mar. 1901		68	5	
Woodley, Mamie	19, July 1901		21	8	
Woodrow, D.C.	16, Feb. 1901		60	8	
Woodruff, Eliza	20, Dec. 1900		74	8	
Woodruff, Harry	4, June 1901		1m	8	
Woods, A.	10, Mar. 1888		7d	1	
Woods, Anna	3, Apr. 1901		44	8	
Woods, Annie	5, June 1901		18	8	
Woods, Charles	5, Feb. 1901		16	8	
Woods, Ignatius	28, Jan. 1901		1d	8	
Woods, Laura	3, Mar. 1888		43	1	
Woods, Maria	27, Nov. 1900		56	8	
Woodside, Samuel	8, July 1901		68	8	
Wooley,	16, Aug. 1887		3w	1	
Woolford, Fred. P.	1, Nov. 1887		50	1	
Woolwine, Edith	7, Feb. 1901		28	8	
Woost, Johanna	25, Jan. 1890		46	1	
Wops, Fred.	20, July 1887		30	1	
Work, Katharine	17, Apr. 1901			8	
Workman, Cleveland	18, July 1887		4m	1	
Wormser, Lena	15, June 1894		80	5	
Worpenberg, Gerhard	17, May 1899	14, May	79	5	
Worpenberg, Johan	2, June 1899	1, June	51- 4m	5	
Worrell, Anna E.	24, Jan. 1901		37	8	
Worst, Ed.	18, July 1890		21	1	
Worstell, Beatrice	26, Mar. 1895		10d	5	
Worstell, Katie	19, July 1901		4d	8	
Worth, Catharine	2, Oct. 1894		72	5	
Worthington, Baby	10, Dec. 1900		1d	8	
Worthmann, Frederick W.	9, Mar. 1893		18	5	
Wortman, Mary	27, Oct. 1891		2d	1	
Wortman, William	30, Dec. 1890		71	4	
Wortmann, Friedrich	30, June 1896	29, June	54	5	
Wortmann, Heinrich	21, 22, Feb. 1898	20, Feb.	21- 5m	5	
Woster, Hattie	22, June 1895		15m	5	
Wrapelmeier, Fred	5, Oct. 1891	4, Oct.	72-10m	1	
Wraßmann, Friedrich Heinrich	7, Apr. 1900	4, Apr.	72- 3m	5	
Wraßmann, Maria Margaretha	7, Apr. 1900	5, Apr.	67- 7m	5	Carls

Name ****	Notice Date ****** ****	Death Date ***** ****	Age ***	Page ****	Maiden Name ****** ****
Wrede, Anna	18, Mar. 1899	17, Mar.	66	5	Vial
Wrede, Charles	3, Mar. 1891		5	4	
Wright, Anna	8, Jan. 1901		24	8	
Wright, David	8, Feb. 1895		2	5	
Wright, Hattie	18, Sept 1901		77	8	
Wright, Mary D.	13, Apr. 1895		73	4	
Wright, S.	25, Jan. 1888		2	1	
Wright, Sophia	9, Aug. 1900		30	8	
Wrin, Sarah	21, Jan. 1888		80	4	
Wubbolding, B.J.	25, May 1900	24, May	65- 6m	8	
Wubeler, Florence Bertha	6, June 1900	5, June	2- 5m	8	
Wuerges, August	13, June 1901		55	8	
Wuertz, Mary	26, Apr. 1893		34	5	
Wuest, Aloys	5, Dec. 1896	4, Dec.	26- 3m	5	
Wuest, Charles F.	28, Nov. 1896	27, Nov.	25- 1m	5	
Wuest, Fr. Christ.	28, Mar. 1888		74	1	
Wuest, Franz H.	26, Aug. 1891		5m	2	
Wuest, Helene	24, Apr. 1900	22, Apr.	50- 6m	8	Hahner
Wuest, Henry	2, Dec. 1894		3	4	
Wuest, Howard	12, Dec. 1900		5	8	
Wuest, Ida	21, Aug. 1891		15	4	
Wuest, Louisa	24, Nov. 1891		39	4	
Wuest, Margaretha	21, Nov. 1894		70	5	
Wuest, Michael	15, Mar. 1901		1	8	
Wuest, Michael	28, Mar. 1901		31	8	
Wuestefold, George	13, May 1901		16	8	
Wuestenfeld, Elise	21, Sept 1894		18	5	
Wulekuhl, Ella	16, Dec. 1891		8	4	
Wulf, Albert	20, Mar. 1895		40	5	
Wulf, William	25, Mar. 1901		33	8	
Wulfekotter, Ernst	30, July 1901		82	8	
Wulfekötter, Emma H.	9, Apr. 1897	7, Apr.	34- 5m	5	
Wulfhorst, Charlotte	1, Mar. 1897	27, Feb.	63- 4m	5	Nolte
Wulfhorst, Frank	16, Jan. 1890		2	1	
Wullner, Frank	13, July 1887		71	1	
Wund, Georg	10, Sept 1896		23	5	
Wunder, Julia	24, Sept 1900		59	5	
Wunder, Lucy F.	31, Dec. 1891		77	1	
Wunder, Ottilia	28, May 1901		81	8	
Wunderlich, Elsie	4, Apr. 1893		2	5	
Wuney, George Mac.	7, Oct. 1901		3m	1	
Wunker, Friedrich	9, Dec. 1896	7, Dec.	43	5	
Wurdeman, Johan Theodor	16, Oct. 1889		6	1	
Wurmser, R.	30, Sept 1888		72	4	
Wurst, Mary	6, July 1895		59	5	
Wursten, Oscar	21, Nov. 1894		4	5	
Wurster, Anna	30, Nov. 1897	27, Nov.	42	5	Blankenbühler
Wurster, Caroline	17, Feb. 1899	16, Feb.		5	Rieger
Wurster, Eduard	17, Dec. 1898		24	5	
Wurster, Katharina	23, Aug. 1899	22, Aug.	24- 5m	5	Brütsch
Wursthorn, William	14, Apr. 1891		29	4	
Wurth, Andrew	21, Jan. 1892		71	5	
Wurth, Elmer H.	6, Apr. 1894		5m	5	
Wurth, Theresa	8, July 1889		77	1	
Wurtz, William A.	13, Dec. 1892		1	5	
Wurz, Catharine	21, Feb. 1901		49	8	
Wurz, Katharine	26, Aug. 1889		17m	1	
Wust, Eugenia	16, Oct. 1889		31	1	
Wust, Frank E.	28, Mar. 1894		1	5	
Wust, George	22, Dec. 1891		3	4	
Wuth, W.	30, Jan. 1888		7	1	
Wyatt, James	28, Mar. 1888		20	1	
Wydman, Sam.	3, Oct. 1901		82	8	
Wyenandt, Elnora C.	26, July 1893		13d	5	
Wyisph, Eliza	26, Aug. 1887		25	1	
Wynant, Louisa	4, Aug. 1887		3m	1	
Wyß, Louis	26, July 1888		4m	2	
Wächter, Carolina	3, Apr. 1895		58	5	
Wächter, Jakob	19, Dec. 1893		5m	5	
Wöllner, Anna S.	6, Mar. 1891		61	4	
Wöllner, Johan	22, Feb. 1897	20, Feb.	72-10m	5	

Name ****	Notice Date ****** ****	Death Date ***** ****	Age ***	Page ****	Maiden Name ****** ****
Wöllner, Susanna	4, Mar. 1891	3, Mar.	61-11m- 5d	1	
Wübbeler, Frederick	15, July 1893		56	5	
Würdemann, Hermina	2, Feb. 1899	1, Feb.	71- 6m	5	Meier
Würsch, Elisabeth	27, Feb. 1894		54	5	
Würstle, Louisa	8, Sept 1887		10m	1	
Würtz, Anna	8, Sept 1887		4	1	
Wüst, Alois	20, Jan. 1890		4m	1	
Wüst, Anna	20, 21, Dec. 1895	19, Dec.	71- 8m	5	Walter
Wüst, Charles	12, Jan. 1889		53	1	
Wüst, Johan	31, Oct. 1899	30, Oct.	81- 1m-20d	5	
Wüst, John	4, July 1891		49	4	
Wüst, Margaretha	25, July 1898	23, July		4	Kramer
Yaeger, Elisabeth	15, Sept 1900		42	5	
Yaeger, Fred	1, Oct. 1900		44	5	
Yaeger, John C.	29, Dec. 1891		76	4	
Yaenhe, Edward	28, May 1891		62	4	
Yager, Walter	5, Nov. 1900		34	8	
Yalen, Alvine	17, Apr. 1900	15, Apr.	13m-24d	5	
Yalen, Johan	15, Apr. 1899	14, Apr.	4-10m	4	
Yantz, Edna	30, Nov. 1892		16m	5	
Yards, Anna	26, Dec. 1900		31	8	
Yaschka, William	22, May 1890		3	1	
Yates, Mary	24, July 1901		69	8	
Yauß, Rose	20, Feb. 1901		19	8	
Yeager, H.J. (Mrs.)	10, Mar. 1898	9, Mar.		5	
Yeager, John	8, Dec. 1900		52	8	
Yearley, Rebecca M.	29, May 1895		70	5	
Yelton, Morris	23, July 1901		26	8	
Yerger, Ignatius	15, Nov. 1899	14, Nov.	71- 3m	5	
Yetter, Mary	24, July 1896	22, July	26	5	
Yockey, William	28, Aug. 1890		35	1	
Yoerg, Clifford	20, July 1895		3m	5	
York, Andrew	29, Dec. 1900		57	8	
York, Dudley	24, Jan. 1901		3m	8	
Yost, George	3, Nov. 1893		49	5	
Yost, Heinrich	18, Feb. 1897	18, Feb.	73- 9m- 6d	5	
Yost, Magdalena	21, Jan. 1898	20, Jan.	71- 6m	5	Lich
Young, Andrew	14, Aug. 1900		52	5	
Young, Bertha	30, Aug. 1887		19	1	
Young, Blanche M.	2, Aug. 1887		10m	1	
Young, Clarence	13, July 1901		8m	8	
Young, Emily	7, Apr. 1888		5	4	
Young, Harry	5, Oct. 1888		4	1	
Young, Jennie	8, June 1895		41	5	
Young, John	21, Aug. 1888		16m	1	
Young, John	19, July 1900		25	8	
Young, John C.	26, Sept 1887		30	1	
Young, Lawrence	14, Aug. 1900		52	5	
Young, Marcus	17, Sept 1901		38	8	
Young, Mary	11, July 1895		38	5	
Young, Rosa	25, Sept 1900		39	5	
Young, Rosa C.	6, Oct. 1900		1	5	
Young, William	20, Oct. 1887		50	1	
Young, William	5, June 1888		5m	4	
Young, William	18, June 1901		29	8	
Young, William B.	26, Apr. 1895		88	5	
Young, Zacharius	29, Mar. 1888		21m	1	
Yowees, Ella	10, Oct. 1900		53	8	
Yowell, Clarence R.	7, July 1887		15	1	
Zabke, Alwine	1, Feb. 1888		40	4	
Zabke, Julius	13, Feb. 1900	12, Feb.	53	8	
Zacharias, Catharine	30, Mar. 1901			8	
Zachnitz, William	29, Jan. 1892		26	5	
Zacpal, Josephine	4, May 1896	2, May	71- 8m	5	
Zaenger, Laura	24, Dec. 1900		44	8	
Zahn, Anna	9, Feb. 1894		33	5	
Zahn, Flora	9, Feb. 1901		32	8	
Zahn, Joseph	18, Dec. 1893		34	5	
Zahn, Salome	27, Oct. 1900		41	8	

Name ****	Notice Date ****** ****	Death Date ***** ****	Age ***	Page ****	Maiden Name ****** ****
Zammert, Anna	15, Nov. 1893		5	5	
Zang, Ed.	29, June 1893		5w	5	
Zang, Elizabeth	18, Feb. 1889		4m	1	
Zanka,	17, July 1895		2d	5	
Zapf, Antonio	17, Jan. 1893		59	5	
Zapf, Ernst	20, June 1901		28	8	
Zapf, Pauline	21, Nov. 1891		3	4	
Zapp, Emil E.	10, Jan. 1896	9, Jan.	42	5	
Zapp, John	11, Apr. 1892		4m	5	
Zaus, George	14, Jan. 1898	12, Jan.	63-11m	4	
Zech, Katie	9, Jan. 1901		1m	5	
Zech, Margaretha	29, Dec. 1887		78-10m	4	
Zeeb, Jakob	3, Feb. 1897	1, Feb.	68- 4m	5	
Zegolka, Valentin	3, Dec. 1889		2	1	
Zeh, Eddie	29, July 1887		13m	1	
Zeh, Frank	5, May 1894		54	5	
Zeh, Joseph	27, Feb. 1894		10m	5	
Zehnder, Frank	2, Aug. 1893		46	5	
Zehrer, John	14, Sept 1887		76	1	
Zeidner, Anna	26, May 1894		5	5	
Zeileman, Edward	1, Aug. 1887		11m	1	
Zeiller, Joseph	10, Sept 1888	9, Sept	66	1	
Zeilman, Charles	6, July 1893		28	5	
Zeinz, Anna M.	25, May 1901		45	8	
Zeiser, John	15, Jan. 1901		53	8	
Zeisler, Adam	14, May 1897	13, May	62- - 3d	5	
Zeisler, Mary	3, June 1892		4m	5	
Zeiß, Charles J.	21, Nov. 1893		2	5	
Zeiß, George M.	18, Nov. 1893		4	5	
Zelina,	20, July 1887		4d	1	
Zell, Alice E.	22, Mar. 1888		21	1	
Zeller, Rosa	19, July 1887		25	1	
Zellner, Mary	22, Oct. 1900		28	8	
Zeltner, Georg Leonhard	11, Nov. 1899	10, Nov.		4	
Zeltner, Maria	19, Dec. 1898	17, Dec.	82	4	
Zengel, Margaretha	2, Aug. 1900		55	8	
Zenner, David	30, Dec. 1891		75	4	
Zentner, Barbara Z.	2, Jan. 1890		6	1	
Zentner, Joseph	1, May 1891		2	4	
Zentner, Julius	31, Mar. 1889		53	4	
Zepf, Eleonora	2, Aug. 1901		2	8	
Zepf, Frank	24, July 1901		6m	8	
Zepf, Juliana	22, Mar. 1888		3m	1	
Zepp, Christopher	24, Jan. 1894		36	5	
Zerr, Emma	3, Aug. 1897	2, Aug.	17- 1m	5	
Zestermann, Julius	8, 10, Nov. 1897	8, Nov.	58	5	
Zestermann, Selma L.	6, Dec. 1892		58	5	
Zeuner, Elisabeth	26, Feb. 1900	25, Feb.	79	8	
Zeverink, P.B. (Rev.)	11, Nov. 1894		31	5	
Ziebold, Richard	8, Feb. 1889		30	1	
Ziegelmeier, Louis A.	18, May 1901		18	1	
Ziegler, Barbara	16, Mar. 1893		72	5	
Ziegler, Ellen Xavier	17, Dec. 1891		15m	4	
Ziegler, Francisca	18, Feb. 1891		84	4	
Ziegler, Fred.	16, Dec. 1889		54	1	
Ziegler, Fredericka	15, Aug. 1901		79	8	
Ziegler, Katharine	27, Mar. 1889		56	1	
Ziegler, Laurence	19, Sept 1888		8	2	
Ziegler, Wilhelmina	17, Dec. 1889		5m	1	
Ziegler, Wilhelmina	3, Apr. 1891		45	4	
Ziek, Jeanette	4, May 1895		3m	5	
Zielke, Emma	5, Apr. 1890		1w	1	
Zier, Johan	21, Apr. 1896	20, Apr.	36	5	
Zierer, Georg	26, Mar. 1897	25, Mar.		5	
Zieres, (Mrs. Henry)	6, May 1889		36	1	
Zieres, Heinrich	30, Nov. 1897	28, Nov.	50- -12d	5	
Zies, Henry	7, July 1891		29	1	
Zievering, Adolph W.	11, July 1893		7m	5	
Zieverink, Kate	21, Jan. 1901		38	8	
Zimmer, Jacob	17, Feb. 1895		65	5	
Zimmer, M.	1, Sept 1898	30, Aug.	67- -12d	4	Fuchs

Name	Notice Date	Death Date	Age	Page	Maiden Name
****	****** ****	***** ****	***	****	****** ****
Zimmer, Pius	1, May 1894		41	5	
Zimmer, Therese	13, Feb. 1901		52	8	
Zimmerer, Elenora	19, Jan. 1894		6	5	
Zimmerer, Emma M.	19, Feb. 1895		1	5	
Zimmerer, Henry	5, Apr. 1901		86	8	
Zimmermann, Alb.	31, July 1890		5m	1	
Zimmermann, Andrew	24, Feb. 1894		44	5	
Zimmermann, Andy	20, Mar. 1891		58	4	
Zimmermann, Anna	4, Jan. 1890		32	1	
Zimmermann, Anton	8, Sept 1887		15m	1	
Zimmermann, Anton	26, Aug. 1895	24, Aug.	75- -12d	5	
Zimmermann, Auguste	12, Sept 1901		66	5	
Zimmermann, Charles	21, July 1890		11m	1	
Zimmermann, Elizabeth	18, July 1887		30	1	
Zimmermann, Emma	5, Sept 1888		14m	2	
Zimmermann, George	25, Jan. 1889		40	1	
Zimmermann, George	23, Jan. 1896	22, Jan.	9m	5	
Zimmermann, Henry	22, Mar. 1890		38	1	
Zimmermann, Irma	22, Feb. 1896	20, Feb.	1- 9m	5	
Zimmermann, J.	25, June 1888		1	1	
Zimmermann, John	3, Aug. 1901		53	8	
Zimmermann, Josephine	5, July 1887		5- 6m	1	
Zimmermann, Katharina	26, May 1900	25, May	77- 6m	8	Loui
Zimmermann, Laura	27, Feb. 1889		1w	1	
Zimmermann, Margarethe	8, Oct. 1900			8	
Zimmermann, Maria M.	2, Jan. 1897	1, Jan.	60- 7m	5	Feid
Zimmermann, Marie	7, Sept 1899	5, Sept	56	5	Kahle
Zimmermann, Mary	19, Mar. 1895		66	5	
Zimmermann, Nick.	7, Apr. 1893		5	5	
Zimmermann, Philipp	15, Dec. 1892		65	5	
Zimmermann, William	26, July 1900		1	5	
Zimpelmann, Peter	11, Apr. 1899	9, Apr.	65	5	
Zind, Minnie	26, June 1895		49	5	
Zind, Theresia	7, Mar. 1898	6, Mar.	71-10m	5	Junker
Zink, Amelia	6, May 1892		22	5	
Zink, Johan	3, Aug. 1895	2, Aug.	27- 4m	4	
Zinke, Wilhelmina	6, Nov. 1894		64	5	
Zinnkann, Louise	21, June 1895		25	5	
Zinser, August	7, Aug. 1894		54	5	
Zinsle, Mannie	4, Aug. 1888		1d	4	
Zinsle, Marie	18, Dec. 1891		24	2	
Zinsmeyer, August	19, Nov. 1900		33	8	
Zint, A. Carl	11, Jan. 1901		2m	5	
Zint, F.L.	13, Jan. 1888		2	1	
Zint, Michels A.	20, July 1901		14d	8	
Zirndorf, Henry	20, Dec. 1893		64	5	
Zischeck, Regula	4, May 1896	3, May	71- 7m	5	Pfister
Zitt, George	24, July 1891		2	1	
Zittinger, Jakob	2, Sept 1898	1, Sept	42	4	
Zittinger, Maria	12, Oct. 1896	11, Oct.	31- 2m	5	Kolb
Zitzelsberger, Johan	14, Sept 1897	12, Sept	59	5	
Zobel, Fred.	13, July 1901		59	8	
Zobel, Hulda	26, Jan. 1893		9m	5	
Zobel, Johan	15, Mar. 1900	14, Mar.	68	5	
Zobel, Louisa	1, Feb. 1892		11	5	
Zodekoff, Jacob	7, Sept 1893		11w	5	
Zoellner, Carl	2, Mar. 1901		78	5	
Zoellner, Henrietta	7, May 1891		70	4	
Zoll, Maria	10, Apr. 1891		1	4	
Zoller, Theresa	5, Mar. 1891		68	4	
Zoller, Elisabeth	21, Apr. 1895		50	5	
Zolois, Anna	14, Feb. 1891		69	4	
Zopf, Annie	23, June 1888		9m	1	
Zopfie, Carry	19, Apr. 1898	17, Apr.	59	5	
Zorb, Conrad	18, Jan. 1901		65	8	
Zorn, Elizabeth	11, Feb. 1896	10, Feb.	36- 2m	5	Schweitzer
Zuber, Anna	23, Feb. 1901		64	8	
Zubiller, Caroline	20, Feb. 1889		50	1	
Zucker, Philipp	17, May 1897	15, May	54- 5m	5	
Zueldorst, Carl	17, Jan. 1894		29	5	
Zuercher, Catharine	20, Mar. 1891		61	4	

Name ****	Notice Date ****** ****	Death Date ***** ****	Age ***	Page ****	Maiden Name ****** ****
Zuffy, Josephine	13, Sept 1899	12, Sept	61	4	Garas
Zuflucht, Isaac	11, Sept 1901		3	8	
Zugenhorst, Arthur	29, May 1894		7m	5	
Zulage, Katharine	3, Feb. 1888		4	4	
Zuleger, Barbara	26, Aug. 1891		54	2	
Zuleger, Joseph	2, Jan. 1896	1, Jan.	60- 4m	5	
Zumbahlen, Clemens	16, Nov. 1896	14, Nov.	58- 8m	5	
Zumbusch, Elisabeth	13, Aug. 1898	12, Aug.		5	
Zumkeller, Joseph	28, Sept 1889		3	1	
Zumkeller, Otto	30, Apr. 1901		59	8	
Zumstein, Christian	26, Aug. 1896	24, Aug.	70	5	
Zumstein, Georg	1, May 1901		34	8	
Zumwalde, Heinrich	6, July 1897	4, July	73-10m	5	
Zurborn, Ernest	17, Mar. 1896	16, Mar.	40	5	
Zurlage, Henry	2, June 1893		4	5	
Zurlage, Mary	14, Feb. 1891		2	4	
Zurlage, Theodor	17, Aug. 1887		14m	1	
Zurweiden, J. Otto	23, Nov. 1893		4	5	
Zurwelle, Augusta	6, Mar. 1899	5, Mar.	56	4	
Zusang, George	27, June 1889		26	1	
Zusang, John	4, Jan. 1893		30	5	
Zutt, Catharine	3, Oct. 1901		74	8	
Zwasta, Kunigunda	4, Apr. 1891		5	4	
Zwick, Ed.	31, May 1890		1	1	
Zwick, Kate	25, Apr. 1890		6m	1	
Zwick, Philipp	10, Jan. 1893		39	5	
Zwicker, August F.	30, Dec. 1899	28, Dec.	76	5	
Zwicker, Margarethe	19, Mar. 1897	18, Mar.		5	Jenner
Zwilling, Herman	10, May 1898	8, May	33	5	
Zwißler, Elisabeth	30, July 1889		35	1	
Zwißler, John	20, June 1901		77	8	
Zünkeler, Elisabeth	19, May 1896	17, May	73- 5m	5	Grieshaber
Zünkeler, Louise M.	21, Feb. 1898	19, Feb.	43-11m	5	Ahlers

Maiden Name		Married Name of Deceased
Abbing	---->	Peterson, Anna Maria
Adam	---->	Deschser, Louisa
Agnus	---->	Hener, Maria
Ahaus	---->	Ottenschulte, Agnes
Ahlers	---->	Jenkins, R.C. (Mrs)
Ahlers	---->	Zünkeler, Louise M.
Ahlers	---->	Feldkamp, Sophia Christin
Ahlert	---->	Schulte, Wilhelmine Regin
Alf	---->	Bollmann, Elisabeth Maria
Algeier	---->	Tromey, Rosa
Allinger	---->	Lipp, Louise
Alripp	---->	Held, Paulina
Aman	---->	Doerler, Christina
Anschutz	---->	Funk, Augusta
Anschutz	---->	Renneberg, Ida
Apke	---->	Hesse, Louise
Appel	---->	Doerr, Kunigunda
Appel	---->	Lerche, Margaretha
Apries	---->	Dickmann, Anna Maria
Arlinghouse	---->	Suetholz, Elisabeth
Armbrust	---->	Mutschler, Maria Magdalen
Armleder	---->	Hallermann, Emma
Arning	---->	Weßling, Maria Elisabeth
Attermeier	---->	Knollmann, Theresia
Auer	---->	Oehler, Rosa
Aufderheide	---->	Corbly, Emilia
Auzinger	---->	Dahms, Franziska
Awe	---->	Ader, Elisabeth
Awerdunk	---->	Sand, Anna Margaretha
Backer	---->	Knabe, Louisa K.
Backmann	---->	Rosenstiel, Katharina
Baer	---->	Philipp, Elisabeth
Bailer	---->	Kampel, Karolina
Balster	---->	Koring, Sophia Louise
Banner	---->	Bertsch, Rosine
Bansing	---->	Buns, Elisabeth
Barg	---->	Mühlenhard, Sophie
Baron	---->	Mathäß, Rosina
Bartels	---->	Müller, Emma
Bauer	---->	Renkert, Eva
Bauer	---->	Essel, Elisa Amalia
Baum	---->	Novitzky, Emilie
Becht	---->	Oehler, Maria
Beck	---->	Heß, Helena
Beck	---->	Gick, Elisabeth
Becker	---->	Egner, Maria
Becker	---->	Lang, Anna
Becker	---->	Hahner, Amelia
Becker	---->	Feiertag, Helena Barbara
Becker	---->	Tegeler, Carolina
Becker	---->	Heis, Catharina
Becker	---->	Hugo, Margaretha
Becker	---->	Arnold, Margaretha
Beckert	---->	Loth, Sarah
Beckschmidt	---->	Dunker, Maria
Beelmann	---->	Cook, Margaretha
Beerens	---->	Keim, Anna Christine
Behrens	---->	Doepke, Anna Katharina
Behrens	---->	Langenbach, Catharina
Beinert	---->	Dietrich, Louise
Bellermann	---->	Schaffner, Katharina
Bene	---->	Hambers, Maria Anna
Benecke	---->	Beelmann, Louise
Benkering	---->	Schlotterbeck, Dorothea
Benning	---->	Rabens, Dorothea
Benolken	---->	Homan, Katharina
Benter	---->	Kapauf, Sabina
Berg	---->	Mohlenkamp, Philomena
Bergmeier	---->	Sturm, Karolina
Berwanger	---->	Kilgenstein, Maria
Bese	---->	Wigbels, Johanna

Maiden Name		Married Name of Deceased
Bester	---->	Hoffmann, Eva
Betz	---->	Werner, Elisabeth
Beyer	---->	Füsser, Maria
Bezold	---->	Dorsch, Kunigunde
Bickel	---->	Gaßner, Eva
Bierbaum	---->	Dornette, Wilhelmina
Bikel	---->	Baum, Elisabeth
Bill	---->	Dießlin, Barbara
Binder	---->	Fritz, Maria Magdalena
Bischoff	---->	Schledron, Caroline
Bittenbring	---->	Wehr, Wilhelmine
Blank	---->	Reichert, Maria Magdalena
Blanke	---->	Nolte, Mary
Blankenbühler	---->	Wurster, Anna
Bloemer	---->	Mayborg, Maria
Blume	---->	Richter, Louise S.
Blymer	---->	Brenner, Katharina
Blömer	---->	Berting, Katharina
Blömer	---->	Bockhorst, Maria Katharin
Bockhorst	---->	Weber, Elisabeth
Bocklage	---->	Crone, Catharine
Bode	---->	Buddelmann, Katie
Boeh	---->	Fachler, Maria Anna
Boeniker	---->	Mayer, Anna
Boheim	---->	Froehlich, Margaretha
Bohler	---->	Blum, Elisabeth
Bohmann	---->	Rattermann, Theresa
Bohne	---->	Brunswick, Wilhelmine
Bold	---->	Brennan, Josephine
Bolland	---->	Hintereck, Emma M.
Bollicke	---->	Degenhorst, Wilhelmine
Bollstedt	---->	Carstens, Anna Dorothea
Boni	---->	Gaßner, Regina
Bonn	---->	Starke Amilie
Borgemenke	---->	Niemeyer, Elisabeth There
Borkenhagen	---->	Prehn, Wilhelmina
Born	---->	Keber, Susanna
Boulnois	---->	Königkramer, Hermine L.
Brand	---->	Anthe, Maria
Brandhove	---->	Burmann, Maria Anna
Brandt	---->	Weber, Eva
Brandt	---->	Schweeting, Christina
Braun	---->	Filser, Theresa
Breddermann	---->	Lackmann, Maria
Brehe	---->	Dieckmann, Maria Sophia
Breitholdt	---->	Schmidt, Clara C.
Brenner	---->	Wehrmeyer, Carrie
Brink	---->	Kempe, Elizabeth
Brinker	---->	Popp, Maria
Brinkmann	---->	Wilking, Franciska
Brinkmann	---->	Waldmann, Dorothea
Brinkmann	---->	Lammeier, Maria Angela
Brinkmann	---->	Gramann, Caroline
Brockmann	---->	Meyers, Louise
Brodbeck	---->	Kautz, Wilhelmina
Bruch	---->	Brückner, Anna M.
Brucker	---->	Glatz, Pauline
Brueckmann	---->	Spieß, Christina
Brunett	---->	Bleichner, Margaret
Brunnemeyer	---->	Ahlers, Katharina Marie
Brütsch	---->	Wurster, Katharina
Bucher	---->	Friedmann, Crescentia
Buck	---->	Rechtin, Anna Maria
Buermeier	---->	Buarmann, Clara Elisa
Bueter	---->	Heskamp, Margaretha
Buntschuh	---->	Kurrus, Katharina
Burbacher	---->	Geyer, Emma
Burger	---->	Legner, Franziska
Burkard	---->	Bruetting, Margaretha
Burlage	---->	Peck, Maria Elisabeth
Buscher	---->	Rattermann, Emma

Maiden Name ****** ****		Married Name of Deceased ******* **** ** ********
Busse	---->	Barnhorn, Amelia
Butler	---->	Dorse, Anna Maria
Butscha	---->	Diehl, Josephine
Böhmer	---->	Marahrens, Maria
Bös	---->	Mott, Katharina
Büche	---->	Winter, Maria
Bürger	---->	Wild, Barbara
Cahn	---->	Burckhardt, Carrie
Carls	---->	Wraßmann, Maria Margareth
Cawein	---->	Baum, Eva
Classen	---->	Bedinghaus, Antoinette
Clemens	---->	Hoffmann, Friedericka
Cohr	---->	Tschechtelin, Bertha Paul
Conrady	---->	Moser, Susanna
Cook	---->	Abeling, Louise
Creppel	---->	Spiegel, Margaretha
Crotty	---->	Loechtenfeldt, Norah
Czerwinski	---->	Leuk, Katharina
Daiker	---->	Braun, Barbara
Daller	---->	Appel, Eva
Dallmann	---->	Eppens, Elise Margaretha
Dangers	---->	Telgmann, Else
Dannemann	---->	Remke, Geschen Margaretha
Dater	---->	Klein, Franziska
Deck	---->	Seufferle, Rachel
Deibert	---->	Koch, Magdalena
Deiering	---->	Gunselmann, Louise
Deppen	---->	Ficker, Theresa
Derrenkamp	---->	Steltenpohl, Maria
Dickmann	---->	Kalvelage, Theresa
Diehl	---->	Hildwein, Magdalena
Diehl	---->	Hutzelmann, Catharine
Dieringer	---->	Bettinger, Elisabeth
Dierkes	---->	Remke, Louise F.
Dietinger	---->	Kuhn, Jakobine
Dietrich	---->	Nonweiler, Margarethe
Dittmann	---->	Miller, Karoline
Dodt	---->	Bunker, Anna Maria
Doecker	---->	Westermann, Caroline
Doerle	---->	Toerner, Anna
Dohrmann	---->	Seidenspinner, Lena
Donner	---->	Härtig, Emma Johanna
Dornberger	---->	Drees, Elisabeth
Dornbusch	---->	Freytag, Elisabeth
Dorrmann	---->	Dickescheid, Maria
Dorst	---->	Ruehlmann, Louisa
Dotzauer	---->	Kraus, Theresia
Drill	---->	George, Amelie Philomena
Druck	---->	Kiefer, Katharina
Dulle	---->	Niemann, Anna Maria
Dunker	---->	Lagnia, Treisa
Dunker	---->	Overdiek, Henrietta
Dürstock	---->	Stuntebeck, Maria
Ehrhardt	---->	Eckert, Elisabeth
Ehrhardt	---->	Wheeler, Caroline
Eichenlaub	---->	Leiser, Katharine
Eichenlaub	---->	Bobe, Maria A.
Eichler	---->	Lott, Sophie
Eilermann	---->	Krusemeyer, Maria
Eilermann	---->	Hagemeyer, Lizette
Eilers	---->	Klostermann, Maria Magdal
Eiserle	---->	Doescher, Barbara
Eitelgeorge	---->	Muth, Carolina
Elsche	---->	Macke, Maria Anna
Elsenheimer	---->	Kleine, B.C.
Engelhardt	---->	Hartung, Catharine
Enneking	---->	Emsieke, Anna Maria
Enneking	---->	Huermann, Maria Angela
Erpenstein	---->	Kolen, Rosa
Ewald	---->	Ante, Louise
Exner	---->	Kurtz, Maria Anna

Maiden Name ****** ****		Married Name of Deceased ******* **** ** ********
Fahrendorff	---->	Lietze, Charlotte
Faulhaber	---->	Huber, Theresia
Fehr	---->	Heckmann, Anna
Fehrenbach	---->	Kiesel, Friederika
Feick	---->	Goetz, Rosina
Feid	---->	Zimmermann, Maria M.
Feil	---->	Christmann, Elisabeth
Feitmann	---->	Hoffmann, Maria
Feldmann	---->	Nurre, Katharina Maria
Feldmann	---->	Klinckhammer, Elisabeth
Felix	---->	Bohnert, Anna
Fels	---->	Duebel, (Mrs. Heinrich)
Fern	---->	Coombs, Elizabeth
Feth	---->	Widrig, Margaretha
Fideldey	---->	Fromeyer, Elisabeth
Finkelmeier	---->	Wiegand, Elisabeth
Finkler	---->	Sackriede, Johanna Doroth
Firnkoetz	---->	Heine, Margaret
Fisbeck	---->	Techmeier, Sophia
Fischer	---->	Blandow, Caroline
Fischer	---->	Wellmann, Maria Anna
Fischer	---->	Gottman, Karoline
Flaspoehler	---->	Hüdepohl, Maria Gertrud
Fleddermann	---->	Moeller, Maria Elisabeth
Flinker	---->	Wesselmann, Anna Theresa
Focke	---->	Räck, Anna Maria
Folbert	---->	Köhler, Katharina
Foll	---->	Mahoney, Agnes
Fox	---->	Pape, Karolina
Frank	---->	Kempf, Eva
Frank	---->	Newmann, Amelia
Frantz	---->	Rau, Anna Maria
Fraß	---->	VonderHaar, Elisabeth
Freers	---->	Behlendorf, Sophia
Freibert	---->	Gehret, Margaretha
Freking	---->	Teepen, Mary
Frey	---->	Noell, Anna
Frey	---->	Bernauer, Elisabeth
Freytag	---->	Freytag, Elisabeth
Frie	---->	Eibeck, Elisabeth
Friedmann	---->	Moser, Maria
Froehly	---->	Gressi, Maria
Frone	---->	Fischer, Maria Gertrude
Fuchs	---->	Ernst, Agnes
Fuchs	---->	Zimmer, M.
Funke	---->	Meyer, Caroline
Fürste	---->	Kukehan, Henriette
Gaehde	---->	Reuter, Bertha
Gallagher	---->	Ries, Katharine
Garas	---->	Zuffy, Josephine
Garnhauser	---->	Schmudde, Amelia
Gassenschmidt	---->	Schellenbaum, Wilhelmina
Gauthmann	---->	Remgers, Elisabeth
Geers	---->	Kettmann, Anna Maria
Gehring	---->	Bernhard, Elisabeth
Geiger	---->	Fischer, Margaretha
Geller	---->	Schneider, Katharine
Gerdes	---->	Schröder, Anna
Gerding	---->	Koch, Margaretha Gesina
Gerhard	---->	Weber, Katharine
Gerke	---->	Wehmann, Christina Louise
Gerlach	---->	Kemmerer, Anna Maria
Gers	---->	Willen, Elisabeth
Gibbe	---->	Riesenberg, Maria Anna
Gießler	---->	Richter, Friedrika Sophia
Gildehaus	---->	Lawrence, Lisetta
Gimpel	---->	Kille, Anna Maria
Glöckler	---->	Fiedler, Anna Maria
Gnüge	---->	Uthe, Margaretha
Goas	---->	Helmig, Carolina
Gohs	---->	Strategir, Maria

Maiden Name		Married Name of Deceased
****** ****		******* **** ** ********
Going	---->	Luken, Mathilda Mary
Gottschalk	---->	Fromm, Auguste
Gottschalk	---->	Falk, Henriette
Gramann	---->	Schmolt, Elisabeth
Gramann	---->	Schmidt, Elisabeth
Grammer	---->	Höhlein, Paulina
Grammer	---->	Bühler, Elisabeth
Grapperhaus	---->	Böckmann, Katharina
Greaser	---->	Rebstock, Wilhelmina
Grebner	---->	Lipps, Katharina
Grefenkamp	---->	Käter, Anna Maria
Greiner	---->	Dauwalter, Katharina
Greiwe	---->	Kramer, Maria
Gresh	---->	Wise, Margaretha
Gressel	---->	Feuerstein, Margaretha
Greulich	---->	Riebel, Margaretha
Griese	---->	Rennekamp, Josephine
Grieshaber	---->	Zünkeler, Elisabeth
Griesinger	---->	Hüpel, Anna Maria
Griesser	---->	Mink, Katharine
Grimm	---->	Dumbacher, Maria Susana
Groen	---->	Schuette, Auguste
Grossius	---->	Schwörer, Johan M.
Gruener	---->	Endres, Barbara
Grundhöfer	---->	Langmeyer, Ida
Grüßer	---->	Hochstrasser, Karolina
Guenther	---->	Hoel, Franziska
Gutzwiller	---->	Heil, Elizabeth
Gärtner	---->	Esmann, Elisabeth
Gärtner	---->	Schuhmann, Elisabeth
Göbel	---->	Scheidermann, Louise
Göller	---->	Noppenberger, Anna Marie
Görlich	---->	Faith, Louise
Günther	---->	Geisler, Johanna
Haarmeyer	---->	Gott, Anna Maria
Hack	---->	Schneider, Maria
Hackmann	---->	Pund, Katharine
Haehn	---->	Bottenhorn, Malinda
Hafner	---->	Ruoff, Johanna
Hagemeister	---->	Kruse, Charlotte
Hahn	---->	Gerhardt, Katharina
Hahn	---->	Krebs, Maria
Hahner	---->	Wuest, Helene
Hammann	---->	Hammann, Elisabeth
Hammelmeyer	---->	Hartmann, Katharina
Hammer	---->	Gruener, Barbara
Hammes	---->	Langenstroer, Anna Joseph
Hammlert	---->	Gunkel, Caroline
Hanes	---->	Kurtz, Clara
Hang	---->	Heilmann, Anna
Hanhauser	---->	Michael, Katharina
Harsch	---->	Holzwart, Barbara
Hartke	---->	Eichhorn, Franziska
Hartlaub	---->	Leininger, Philomena
Hartmann	---->	Tacke, Wilhelmine
Hasselbacher	---->	König, Elisabeth
Hau	---->	VonWahlde, Maria
Hauck	---->	Heck, Elisabeth
Hauck	---->	Heck, Maria
Hauger	---->	Bruening, Catharina A.
Haverkamp	---->	Weil, Anna
Hechstede	---->	Raye, Anna
Heckert	---->	Blase, Maria E.
Heckert	---->	Mueller, Anna
Heddeke	---->	Weber, Anna
Heemann	---->	Hilgeman, Henrietta
Heger	---->	Boehm, Henriette
Hehslenfeld	---->	Nienaber, Maria Anna
Heid	---->	Schwann, Elisabeth
Heidelmann	---->	Graf, Elisabeth
Heidlage	---->	Enneking, Maria Agnes

Maiden Name		Married Name of Deceased
****** ****		******* **** ** ********
Heidt	---->	Pöpper, Angela Maria
Heidt	---->	Bedinghaus, Helena
Heile	---->	Schulten, Adelheid Maria
Heimkreider	---->	Heß, Elisabeth
Heinemann	---->	Knapmann, Frederike
Heinrichs	---->	Wilmes, Maria Elisabeth
Heins	---->	Bunselmeier, Anna
Heit	---->	Nicola, Rosina
Hellebusch	---->	Specker, M. Theresa
Hellmann	---->	Schmoll, Maria Anna
Hellmers	---->	Ruröde, Katharina
Helmig	---->	Etterer, Philomena Joseph
Henke	---->	Berting, Karolina Antonet
Henkel	---->	Herrmann, Johanna
Henkender	---->	Hunsche, Sophia
Henn	---->	Moor, Maria
Herancourt	---->	Nuß, Margaret
Herancourt	---->	Nast, Margarethe
Herbert	---->	Nolte, Elisabeth
Hersel	---->	Hebbig, Margaretha
Herter	---->	Velkle, Maria Rebecca
Herzog	---->	Kramer, Rosa
Hettinger	---->	Baur, Barbara Magdalena
Heyl	---->	Schinner, Helena Magdalen
Hick	---->	Haßlocher, Christine Elis
Hilf	---->	Horn, Anna Margaretha
Hinkender	---->	Afsprung, Katharine
Hinnenkamp	---->	Loesche, Lina
Hinninger	---->	Balz, Margaretha
Hipp	---->	Steidle, Theresia
Hock	---->	Kraemer, Elisabeth
Hoecker	---->	Barlag, Theresia
Hoelscher	---->	Grabo, Henriette
Hoffmann	---->	Schlitzberger, Elisa
Hoffmann	---->	Siebenthaler, Sophia
Hoffmann	---->	Güthlein, Barbara
Hohl	---->	Stein, Johanna
Hohnstein	---->	Leppert, Friedricka
Hollenden	---->	Mollmann, Katharina
Hollstein	---->	Bernhart, Margaretha
Holt	---->	Steman, Bernardina
Holtmeier	---->	Koehlke, Anna Maria Engel
Hormiller	---->	Heutle, Veronika
Horn	---->	Kuehnle, Elisabeth
Horstmann	---->	Meyers, Katharina
Huber	---->	Pohlmann, Alice
Humbert	---->	Moller, Katharine
Hunsche	---->	Huevelmann, Bernardina
Huntemann	---->	Tepe, Emma L.
Huschle	---->	Panter, Barbara
Hust	---->	Pistor, Katharine
Huß	---->	Hinkler, Elisabeth
Häring	---->	Blanken, Sabina
Höveler	---->	Böhmer, Charlotte
Hülsing	---->	Witte, Minna
Hülskamp	---->	Prues, Anna Wilhelmina
Hülsmann	---->	Lüning, Maria Anna
Hünemeier	---->	Frölke, Maria
Hüninghacke	---->	Hasselmann, Maria Anna
Hütte	---->	Holthausen, Henrietta
Ihle	---->	Piepho, Amelie
Intlekoffer	---->	Kroeger, Wilhelmine
Jahn	---->	Schmidt, Mathilde
Jakob	---->	Eckhardt, Theresa
Jark	---->	Menke, Bertha
Jenisy	---->	Hermerding, Amalia
Jenner	---->	Zwicker, Margarethe
Joachim	---->	Wagner, Barbara
Jochers	---->	Butz, Barbara
Johannes	---->	Hammel, Margaretha
Jordan	---->	Wandstrat, Louise

Maiden Name		Married Name of Deceased
****** ****		******* **** ** ********
Jost	---->	Schneider, Crescentia
Junker	---->	Zind, Theresia
Kaemmerling	---->	Grüßer, Maria
Kahle	---->	Zimmermann, Marie
Kaiber	---->	Weigel, Catharina
Kaiper	---->	Hoffmann, Mathilda
Kaiser	---->	Straßburger, Philomena
Kamphaus	---->	Grosquade, Anna
Kampmeyer	---->	Schobbe, Catharina Maria
Kappel	---->	Blumenbach, Henriette
Kappel	---->	Heck, Jennie
Karcher	---->	Meier, Caroline
Kassel	---->	Haake, Margaretha
Kattus	---->	Hammer, Maria
Kattus	---->	Steidle, Theresia
Kattus	---->	Henrich, Maria Magdalena
Kauffmann	---->	Schmitt, Marie E.
Kaufmann	---->	Rottmann, Carolina
Kaus	---->	Heim, Elisabeth
Keller	---->	Geiß, Louise
Kemper	---->	Gildehaus, Mina
Kenfer	---->	Reisingen, Elisabeth
Kern	---->	Wolf, Margaretha
Kichler	---->	Kapp, Lulu
Kiechler	---->	Johannes, Barbara
Kiefer	---->	Sanders, Katharina
Kinne	---->	Otte, Maria Magdalena
Kipp	---->	Vorbroker, Marie
Kirschner	---->	Clemens, Marie
Kischner	---->	Neumeister, Carolina
Kitt	---->	Muench, Adelina
Klein	---->	Hoffmeister, Rosalie
Klein	---->	Jung, Elisabeth
Klein	---->	Autenrieth, Margaretha
Klein	---->	Fritz, Katharina
Klinkhammer	---->	Schroer, Maria
Klostermann	---->	Lingers, Maria
Klostermann	---->	Dörger, Margaretha
Klostermann	---->	Gehring, Gesina
Klönne	---->	Luckmann, Angela
Knapke	---->	Kotter, Anna Maria Elisab
Knauber	---->	Böbinger, Maria
Knauber	---->	Hoffman, Anna Marie
Kneuven	---->	Wernke, Maria Susanna
Knorr	---->	Dornbusch, Barbara
Kobbe	---->	Bunker, Anna Maria Theres
Koch	---->	Frohle, Regina
Koch	---->	Merkhofer, Barbara
Kochmann	---->	Haders, Gertrud
Koehler	---->	Brand, Maria
Koehnken	---->	Bramsche, Anna
Koenig	---->	Daiber, Christiana
Koester	---->	Pottmann, Sophia K.
Kohake	---->	Bachherms, Emma
Kolb	---->	Zittinger, Maria
Kollmeier	---->	Springmeier, Henrietta
Kordes	---->	Lückener, Agnes
Kordes	---->	Doppes, Klara
Korzenborn	---->	Goetz, Louisa
Koske	---->	Brock, Katharina Margaret
Kostermann	---->	Brand, Margaretha Josephi
Kottkamp	---->	Ballmann, Eliza
Kotz	---->	Doerger, Anna
Kowener	---->	Farwick, Sophie
Koßmann	---->	Sorg, Philippine
Kraemer	---->	Spengler, Katharina
Kragler	---->	Bachmann, Katharine
Kramer	---->	Bauer, Maria
Kramer	---->	Wüst, Margaretha
Krans	---->	Busam, Magdalena
Kratze	---->	Meyer, Klara

Maiden Name		Married Name of Deceased
****** ****		******* **** ** ********
Kraus	---->	Renz, Maria
Kraus	---->	Müller, Katharina
Krauser	---->	Lederer, Elisabeth
Kreinborg	---->	Ostendorf, Elisabeth
Kretschmar	---->	Mueller, Amalia
Krieger	---->	Altevers, Anna Maria
Kriemberg	---->	Homberg, Anna
Krimpelbach	---->	Boehmer, Maria A.
Kroeger	---->	Hopmann, Eliza
Kroeger	---->	Frehse, Betty Regina
Krucke	---->	Menger, Elisabeth
Kruse	---->	Jahn, Katharine
Kruse	---->	Franke, Wilhelmine
Kruse	---->	Farmann, Anna
Kruse	---->	Schneider, Emma Katharine
Kruse	---->	Becker, Bernardina Maria
Kruse	---->	Heidenreich, Marie
Krämer	---->	Heis, Margaretha
Krüger	---->	Rennekamp, Maria Elisabet
Kudel	---->	Koch, Juliane
Kuehne	---->	Heuer, Wilhelmina
Kuhl	---->	Kuhl, Wilhelmina
Kuhlmann	---->	Giessler, Sophie
Kuhlmann	---->	Gilbert, Wilhelmine
Kukelhau	---->	Bruckmann, Sophie
Kunkel	---->	Draude, Gertrud
Kuntz	---->	Maier, Ida
Kurz	---->	Marazzi, Caroline
König	---->	Nacke, Maria
König	---->	Rodamer, Barbara
Kübler	---->	Sauer, Gottlieben
Lachtrip	---->	Hünefeld, Elise
Laggemann	---->	Schmidt, Charlotte
Laile	---->	Schneider, Augusta
Laing	---->	Kruthaup, L. Bernardina
Lambers	---->	Wahoff, Maria
Lamott	---->	Nieters, Katharina
Lampe	---->	Kuehte, Elisabeth
Lamping	---->	Kindt, Maria
Lampke	---->	Brinker, Adelheid
Lang	---->	Fitsch, Maria
Lange	---->	Kruthaup, Maria Anna
Langenbahn	---->	Ohl, Anna Maria
Lanz	---->	Heß, Maria Dorothea
Laubner	---->	Ceck, Katie
Laumann	---->	Schwoerer, Karolina
Laun	---->	Wallburg, Dorothea
Lebening	---->	Burghardt, Dorothea
Legner	---->	Espenscheid, Anna Barbara
Lehde	---->	Kunter, Henriette Maria E
Leichtfuß	---->	Leimberger, Christina
Leick	---->	Gerber, Theresa
Leindecker	---->	Niemes, Margaretha
Leive	---->	Olivier, Johanna F.
Lemmel	---->	Brink, Marie
Lenhoff	---->	Nagel, Barbara
Lenz	---->	Kupper, (Mrs. Frank)
Leonard	---->	Goertemoeller, Margarethe
Lergenmüller	---->	Bellem, Eva
Lich	---->	Yost, Magdalena
Lietemeyer	---->	Greiwe, Elisabeth
Lindauer	---->	Burger, Sophia
Lingle	---->	Miller, Walburga
Link	---->	Heinzmann, Ursula
Lippert	---->	Reichert, Magdalena
Lipps	---->	Barth, Sophia
Lischer	---->	Englert, Maria Emma
Loesch	---->	Oetting, Katie
Lohmann	---->	Wendt, Maria
Lorenz	---->	Boebinger, Margaretha
Losche	---->	Tichle, Katharine

Maiden Name ****** ****		Married Name of Deceased ******* **** ** ********
Lott	---->	Menner, Carolina
Loui	---->	Zimmermann, Katharina
Ludwig	---->	Grimmer, Dorothea
Luebke	---->	Germann, Augusta
Lurz	---->	Hümmer, Maria
Lyer	---->	Junker, Edeltraut Kathari
Lübke	---->	Meyer, Sophia
Lücken	---->	Borgemenke, Maria
Lütti	---->	Kutschkowsky, Catharine
Mager	---->	Bauer, Anna Maria
Maier	---->	Lauber, Josephine
Maier	---->	Leesmann, Amelia
Mang	---->	Claß, Carolina
Manzer	---->	Bepler, Maria
Markert	---->	Jacobi, Kunigunde
Martin	---->	Hartfinger, Anna Susanna
Mathes	---->	Anther, Katharina
Mayer	---->	Lipps, Carolina
McGregor	---->	Feitig, Katharina
Meekers	---->	Sicking, Anna
Meiburg	---->	Kruse, Anna Maria Kathari
Meider	---->	Theobald, Elisabeth
Meier	---->	Weid, Anna Katharine
Meier	---->	Lindemann, Sophia B.
Meier	---->	Würdemann, Hermina
Meier	---->	Helwig, Karoline
Meier	---->	Wielert, Charlotte
Meiering	---->	Schnabel, Anna Mathilda
Meimann	---->	Kempfer, Elisabeth
Meissemer	---->	Vogel, Philomena
Meistermann	---->	Overwater, Klara
Melber	---->	Bauer, Julia
Melchior	---->	Schmidt, Charlotte
Melchior	---->	Schmid, Charlotte
Mersch	---->	Midendorff, Maria Anna
Merz	---->	Kuhborth, Maria
Merz	---->	Montag, Magdalena
Mescher	---->	Kamp, Maria
Mese	---->	Bosandick, Anna
Mesloh	---->	Lotz, Maria
Metz	---->	Priefer, Barbara
Metzger	---->	Eschenbrenner, Johanna
Metzler	---->	Winters, Barbara
Meyer	---->	Stukenborg, Elisabeth
Meyer	---->	Eismann, Anna
Meyer	---->	Bauer, Lena
Meyer	---->	Engelke, Maria Elisabeth
Meyerrose	---->	Wolf, Wilhelmina
Middendorf	---->	Beckmann, Elisabeth
Miller	---->	Ritschard, Adele
Millern	---->	Goepfert, Maria Theresia
Moeller	---->	Wehmann, Louise
Moesta	---->	Schulz, Katie
Molitor	---->	Hiller, Victoria
Moormann	---->	Foß, Catharina Maria
Moormann	---->	Pötter, Adelheid
Morch	---->	Atzel, Margaretha
Morsch	---->	Leimann, Caroline
Mueller	---->	Häckel, Christina
Mueller	---->	Heß, Emma
Mundorf	---->	Braun, Margaretha
Mundorff	---->	Telgheder, Katharina
Mundorff	---->	Brown, Margaretha
Munter	---->	Huber, Elisabeth
Myers	---->	Schath, Tillie M.
Mäding	---->	Fischer, Pauline
Möller	---->	Brande, Rosina
Möller	---->	Schurmann, Henrietta
Mühlberger	---->	Stock, Henriette
Müller	---->	Rattermann, Dorothea
Müller	---->	Schmidt, Katharina Anna

Maiden Name ****** ****		Married Name of Deceased ******* **** ** ********
Müller	---->	Hoffmann, Dorothea
Müller	---->	Schimmel, Creszenzia
Müller	---->	Evers, Anna
Müller	---->	Kumpel, Amelia
Nagel	---->	Handrich, Anna
Nagel	---->	Dierkes, Elisabeth
Nageleisen	---->	Eckerle, Franziska
Nees	---->	Hienbuch, Theresa
Nettermann	---->	Stengel, Katharina
Newdorfer	---->	Kuhnell, Magdalena
Niederhauser	---->	Hoffman, Emma
Niederhelmann	---->	Weber, Henriette
Niehaus	---->	Lange, Maria Elisabeth
Niehaus	---->	Berding, Josephine
Niemann	---->	Lindemann, Charlotte
Nieporte	---->	Roewekamp, Josephina
Noeding	---->	Erbeck, Anna Catharina
Nold	---->	Marahren, Therese
Nolte	---->	Wulfhorst, Charlotte
Nordmann	---->	Plogstedt, Marie E.
Nordmann	---->	Cherdron, Amelia L.W.
Nägele	---->	Mayer, Maria
Oberhellmann	---->	Heine, Sophia
Obert	---->	Keßheimer, Franziska
Ochsle	---->	Stoß, Bertha
Oeh	---->	Siegfried, Anna
Oehler	---->	Wolfer, Barbara O.
Olberding	---->	Hofiger, Maria Josephina
Oliger	---->	Trimbur, Maria Magdalena
Ortmann	---->	Linnemann, Maria
Ostendorf	---->	Hehemann, Katharina
Osterhaus	---->	Stallo, Maria Elisabeth
Oswald	---->	Uhl, Euphrofina
Otten	---->	Knockeweisel, Olga
Overberg	---->	Vonderhaar, Elisabeth
Overberg	---->	Fisse, Christina
Packskamp	---->	Thomann, Antoinette Berna
Pahlmann	---->	Katenbrink, Katharina Mar
Pape	---->	Dinkelmann, Adelheid
Paust	---->	Hagedorn, Mary
Peters	---->	Lübbe, Helene
Pfeiffer	---->	Keller, Margaretha
Pfeiffer	---->	Baurittel, Karolina
Pfeil	---->	Post, Aloisia
Pfenning	---->	Walter, Maggie
Pfister	---->	Zischeck, Regula
Pfisterer	---->	Hauck, Eva
Philipp	---->	Holderbach, Maria
Piepper	---->	Lange, Maria
Pinger	---->	Diehm, Margaretha
Pitz	---->	Sommer, Franziska
Placke	---->	Lakamp, Margaretha Caroli
Plagge	---->	Storch, Adelheid
Plogmann	---->	Westmeier, Anna Elisabeth
Poggendick	---->	Eich, Anna Margaretha
Pohl	---->	Egbers, Helena Adelheid
Ponnoth	---->	Rührwein, Catharine C.
Popp	---->	Koellner, Elisabeth
Popp	---->	Bauer, Kunigunde
Postel	---->	Bitzer, Eva
Postel	---->	Ulmer, Magdalena
Pothoff	---->	Herzog, Christina
Prehn	---->	Memmel, Auguste
Rabbe	---->	Carpenter, Lillie
Radler	---->	Trapp, Margaretha
Raible	---->	Noell, Mathilda
Rapp	---->	Braun, Elisabeth
Rau	---->	Rau, Wilhelmina Barbara
Reche	---->	Binne, Anna
Reckers	---->	Hilbers, Maria
Reckers	---->	Pielage, Katharina

Maiden Name		Married Name of Deceased
****** ****		******* **** ** ********
Redder	---->	Groene, Anna Maria
Reichler	---->	Reib, Maria
Reiners	---->	Jutzi, Caroline
Reiser	---->	Vestrup, Louise
Rengel	---->	Luebbert, Ida
Rennecke	---->	Falke, Dorothea
Renner	---->	Weiß, Franziska
Renzelmann	---->	Embshoff, Emilie
Repberger	---->	Metz, Josephine
Rethmann	---->	Schuermann, Caroline
Reusing	---->	Evers, Elisabeth
Rhein	---->	Eichenlaub, Theresa
Richter	---->	Janson, Elisabeth
Richter	---->	Schomaker, Elisabeth Jose
Riederhauser	---->	Goldschmidt, Rosina
Rieger	---->	Wurster, Caroline
Ries	---->	Räck, Anna Margaretha
Rietmann	---->	Kottmann, Louise
Riley	---->	Jahn, Emma
Rinck	---->	Köhler, Anna Mary
Ring	---->	Sauer, Anna Gertrud
Ringemann	---->	Schlichte, Rose
Risser	---->	Hauenstein, Maria Cathari
Ritter	---->	Steinkamp, Barbara
Robben	---->	Waltering, Maria
Robeloth	---->	Wilmes, Josephine
Rober	---->	Herrmann, Anna Barbara
Roesler	---->	Schulz, Pauline
Rohling	---->	Fischer, Lena
Rohr	---->	Aebi, Maria Eva
Rohr	---->	Gellhaus, Katharina
Rolf	---->	Warsel, Anna
Rolfzen	---->	Lange, Agnes
Roosmann	---->	Steman, Maria Theresia
Rosch	---->	Metzger, Friedricka Dora
Roth	---->	Langemeier, Gertrude
Rothe	---->	Schell, Maria
Rover	---->	Bautz, Adam (Mrs)
Rover	---->	Bautz, Christine
Roß	---->	Stoppelkamp, Catharine
Ruby	---->	Will, Anna Franziska
Ruebusch	---->	Sullivan, Franziska
Ruebusch	---->	Lange, Anna Katharina
Ruehl	---->	Sperry, Margaretha
Ruesse	---->	Runge, Anna Engel
Ruettinger	---->	Towers, D.R.
Ruhe	---->	Brinkman, Maria Elisabeth
Ruiter	---->	Rolfes, Maria Elisabeth
Runk	---->	Rebmann, Rosa
Rupp	---->	Kreidler, Walburga
Rusche	---->	Pohlmann, Agnes
Rusche	---->	Hinderberger, Lillie
Ruwe	---->	Sand, Maria Anna
Ruwe	---->	Decke, Maria Elisabeth
Römmler	---->	Didie, Anna Babette
Rößner	---->	Hust, Anna Otilie
Rühl	---->	Momberg, Elisabeth
Salzmann	---->	Grunewald, Louise
Sander	---->	Turmoil, Maria
Sander	---->	Dunhoft, Anna Maria
Sanders	---->	Schraud, Gertrud
Sandroh	---->	Fratz, Helena
Sauerland	---->	Hoelscher, Henrietta
Schaefer	---->	Herman, Franziska
Schaettle	---->	Beck, Maria Theresia
Schaffstall	---->	Bosse, Alma M.
Schaible	---->	Bueckle, Christina
Schalcher	---->	Metzler, Anna
Scheeta	---->	Fangmann, Maria K.
Scheidt	---->	Kaney, Wilhelmina
Schettinger	---->	Strauß, Barbara

Maiden Name		Married Name of Deceased
****** ****		******* **** ** ********
Scheurer	---->	Momberg, Marie
Schick	---->	Nofer, Katharine
Schiele	---->	Bacharach, Theresa
Schildmeyer	---->	Knapke, Maria Adelma
Schmedding	---->	Schöttmer, Anna Maria
Schmidt	---->	Bettinger, Elisabeth
Schmidt	---->	Tedtmann, Elisabeth
Schmidt	---->	Martin, Anna Maria
Schmidt	---->	Kauffmann, Anna Barbara
Schmidt	---->	Renner, Caroline
Schmidt	---->	Kimmich, Rosina
Schmidt	---->	Schulte, Katharina
Schmidt	---->	Buschmiller, Bernardina
Schmidt	---->	Heck, Christine
Schmit	---->	Clodius, Henriette
Schmit	---->	Busch, Walburga Lutz
Schmitt	---->	Wittkamp, Katharina
Schmudde	---->	Mittendorf, Emma
Schmurr	---->	Koch, Margaretha
Schneider	---->	Becker, Anna M.
Schneider	---->	Kaiser, Klara Maria Agnes
Schneider	---->	Betzing, Anna Elisabeth
Schneiders	---->	Kerstiens, Anna Maria
Schneidhorst	---->	Deichman, Marie Elisabeth
Schnueck	---->	Lampke, Rosa
Schoell	---->	Faust, Frederika
Schoen	---->	Hoffmann, Fanny
Schoenauer	---->	Kettner, Juliana
Schoenebaum	---->	Webbling, Anna
Scholz	---->	Moser, Minna
Schopmeier	---->	Haverkamp, Wilhelmine
Schoppe	---->	Burrichter, Josephine
Schopper	---->	Huß, Paulina K.
Schorle	---->	DeRaay, Magdalena
Schrage	---->	Korte, Anna Christina
Schreick	---->	Brokate, Emma
Schreiner	---->	Miller, Elisabeth
Schrimi	---->	Peter, Barbara
Schroeck	---->	Conradi, Anna Maria
Schuler	---->	Eberhardt, Lena
Schuler	---->	Heinzelmann, Theresia
Schulte	---->	Moormann, Dorothea
Schulte	---->	Laing, Christina
Schumacher	---->	Boedker, Caroline
Schumacher	---->	Janszen, Elisabeth
Schuppert	---->	Richard, Christina M.
Schwank	---->	Schmitt, Katharina
Schwarz	---->	Good, Elisabeth
Schwarz	---->	Goetz, Christina
Schwarzkopf	---->	Brenner, Katharine
Schwecke	---->	Hindersmann, Mathilde
Schweigert	---->	Herrlinger, Rosina
Schweitzer	---->	Zorn, Elizabeth
Schwenlein	---->	Hartmann, Anna
Schwer	---->	Oswald, Bertha
Schwetter	---->	Wiening, Charlotte
Schwierjohann	---->	Gerversmann, Maria
Schwietert	---->	Gerwing, Adelheid
Schwindt	---->	Preising, Charlotte
Schäfer	---->	Hoffmann, Apollonia
Schönefeld	---->	Harff, Josephine Albert
Schönefeld	---->	Burg, Louisa
Schönhoff	---->	Kramer, Maria Katharina
Schüler	---->	Schlumberger, Magdalena
Schürer	---->	Laß, Josepha
Schürmann	---->	Wiebke, Sophie
Seibert	---->	Wendel, Elisabeth
Seibert	---->	Planz, Susanna
Seiler	---->	Schille, Crescentia
Seiter	---->	Beuttel, Amanda
Sextro	---->	Pötker, Catharina

Maiden Name ****** ****		Married Name of Deceased ******* **** ** ********
Shock	---->	Vogel, Marie
Sickmann	---->	Kramer, Marie Anna
Sidel	---->	Miller, Catharina Franzis
Sieger	---->	Sievers, Mary
Siegmann	---->	Toenges, Johanna Louisa
Siegrist	---->	Rohr, Katie
Siemer	---->	Tabeling, Anna Maria
Sievering	---->	Schaefer, Elisabeth
Sohn	---->	Ebert, Alma
Sohn	---->	Rupp, Elisabeth Barbara
Sonne	---->	Gauß, Amalia
Spankuch	---->	Staudigel, Rosina
Speckmann	---->	Poppe, Sophia
Spengler	---->	Gullner, Augusta
Splinters	---->	Trankenberg, Maria Helena
Sprenger	---->	Ludwig, Katharina
Sprung	---->	Kattmann, Maria
Staiber	---->	Klein, Louise
Staley	---->	Mersmann, Belle
Steffen	---->	Budde, Maria Elisa
Steffen	---->	Bardelmann, Maria Louisa
Stegemüller	---->	Bohn, Charlotte
Steidle	---->	Kattus, Katharina
Steimer	---->	Boland, Elisabeth
Steimle	---->	Schwoerer, Christine
Stein	---->	Gall, Caroline
Steinecke	---->	Bolofoha, Marie
Steineman	---->	Börger, Maria
Steiner	---->	Christophel, Barbara
Steinert	---->	Schober, Katharine
Steinke	---->	Schuckmann, Angela
Stemann	---->	Lambers, Louisa
Stemer	---->	Müller, Anna Christine
Stengel	---->	Galvagni, Justine Kathari
Stephan	---->	Bollinger, Marie M.
Stephens	---->	Kunkel, Margaretha
Stevens	---->	Drees, Maria Teckla
Stickworth	---->	Beckroeger, Elisabeth
Stieve	---->	Stirn, Maria
Stille	---->	Seibel, Sophia
Stockbrink	---->	Rietman, Anna Jeanette
Stoeser	---->	Abt, Magdalena
Stolz	---->	Dickmann, Louise
Stragegir	---->	Ahlering, Katharina Elisa
Strobel	---->	Leikauf, Katharina
Strull	---->	Rakel, Magdalena
Stuckenberg	---->	Niewedde, Catharine
Stübbe	---->	Westermann, Maria Elisabe
Sudkamp	---->	Schilling, Katie
Surenkamp	---->	Lange, Elisabeth
Susinger	---->	Frey, Katharina
Söllmann	---->	Hollenbeck, Hannah Sophia
Sütthoff	---->	Mersmann, Anna Adelheid
Taebbing	---->	Luttmer, Anna Maria
Tag	---->	Fesker, Emma
Takenberg	---->	Stockhoff, Katharina
Taphorn	---->	Kotte, Katharina
Tecklenburg	---->	Kayer, Emma Anna
Teipe	---->	Bruns, Carolina
Temming	---->	Rothert, Caroline
Terranni	---->	Threm, Elisabeth
Teufel	---->	Willich, Maria
Thalmann	---->	Waly, Elisabeth
Thein	---->	Brehm, Eva
Theis	---->	Stahr, Laura
Thels	---->	Bischoff, Catharina
Theobald	---->	Stoffregen, Maria Kathari
Thesing	---->	Linfert, Bernardina
Thiel	---->	Tauchert, Bertha
Thiele	---->	Mueller, Caroline
Thiele	---->	Nagel, Louise Sophie

Maiden Name ****** ****		Married Name of Deceased ******* **** ** ********
Thielen	---->	Schwerdfeger, Anna Maria
Thiemann	---->	Vienhage, Anna Maria
Thiemann	---->	Enneking, Johanna
Thinnes	---->	Ostenfeld, Philomena
Thoele	---->	Touschardt, Frieda
Thole	---->	Vornhorn, Helena
Tickuß	---->	Stuesti, Anna
Toerner	---->	Osterbrink, Anna Maria
Torner	---->	Büncker, Elisabeth
Trageser	---->	Schaaf, Kunigunde
Tremmel	---->	Moritz, Sophie
Trenkamp	---->	Joering, Elisabeth
Trickler	---->	Bley, Theresia Karolina
Uelzhöffer	---->	Kantz, Elisabeth
Ueschel	---->	Geier, Margaretha
Uhlenbrock	---->	Thye, Elisabeth
Uhlmann	---->	Richter, Wilhelmina
Uphues	---->	Exter, Karoline
Urbanowski	---->	Miller, Agnes
Vandeneynden	---->	Tenkotte, Katharina
Vedder	---->	Obermeyer, Anna Maria
Veit	---->	Eckert, Elisabeth
Verhagen	---->	VanWyk, Maria
Vester	---->	Mund, Catharine
Vial	---->	Wrede, Anna
Victor	---->	Gerbus, Katharina
Vogel	---->	Lothes, Magdalena
Vogel	---->	Lotz, Barbara
Voigt	---->	Wintzinger, Clara
Volck	---->	Dorenbusch, Maria
Volkmann	---->	Schäfer, Anna Elisabeth
Volz	---->	Schott, Elisabeth
VonDalkmann	---->	Biere, Wilhelmine
Vondemfange	---->	Wildel, Louise Marie
Vonderhaar	---->	Weber, Wilhelmina
Vonhof	---->	Lerch, Augusta
Vordermark	---->	Hilge, Katharina
Vöster	---->	Schraffenberger, Katharin
Wachsmuth	---->	Wiesenthal, Hermine
Waechter	---->	Thauwald, Christina
Wagner	---->	Schmidt, Margaretha
Wagner	---->	Dinnies, Margaretha
Wagner	---->	Heimbold, Katharine
Wagner	---->	Bardes, Louisa Mary
Wahlher	---->	Matz, Victoria
Wahoff	---->	Heink, Maria
Waldapfel	---->	Glandorf, Josephine E.
Waldvogel	---->	Schmidt, Emma
Walter	---->	Wüst, Anna
Warner	---->	Sacher, Carolina
Wasserfallen	---->	Jörg, Marie
Weber	---->	Weirich, Barbara
Wedekemper	---->	Meyer, Adele
Wehrkamp	---->	Wiley, Josephine
Weier	---->	Roth, Barbara
Weigld	---->	Ruehl, Christina E.
Weis	---->	Kimmich, Rosina
Weitmann	---->	Bader, Barbara
Weiß	---->	Lindner, Louise
Weldin	---->	Spitzmüller, Louise
Wellmer	---->	Eversmann, Maria Engel
Wenzler	---->	Hux, Anna Barbara
Werey	---->	Fuchs, Anna Maria
Wermuth	---->	Berger, Andrea Emilie Chr
Werner	---->	Trautmann, Franziska
Wessel	---->	Molleran, Gertrud
Westerkamp	---->	Blase, Louise
Westermeier	---->	Niemüller, Christine Regi
Weyand	---->	Rümmele, Lina
Weyler	---->	Haller, Susanna
Whde	---->	Hoffe, Johanna

Maiden Name ****** ****		Married Name of Deceased ******* **** ** ********
Whetoter	---->	Feldmann, Christina
Wiedmeyer	---->	Scheurer, Rosina
Wiegand	---->	Meister, Mathilda
Wiegand	---->	Deffren, Louise
Wielenberg	---->	Bannemeyer, Maria Agnes
Wilke	---->	Bockhorst, Bernardina
Willenborg	---->	Pund, Anna M.
Willer	---->	Hempel, Margaretha
Willinger	---->	Rosenfelder, Wilhelmina
Wills	---->	Buening, Alice Elizabeth
Wincke	---->	Meyer, Louise
Winkelbach	---->	Schwager, Margaretha
Winkelmann	---->	Boeck, Friedericka
Winn	---->	Gaßner, Bertha Elisabeth
Winter	---->	Eisenhart, Karolina
Wintz	---->	Fischer, Anna Barbara
Witte	---->	Overberg, Amalia
Woerner	---->	Brauner, Emilia
Wolf	---->	Döpke, Bertha Barbara
Wolf	---->	Mappes, Christina
Wolf	---->	Brown, Lillian A.
Wolf	---->	Roese, Mary
Wolfer	---->	Behling, Katharine
Wolff	---->	Kleinmann, Magdalena
Wolff	---->	Baker, Margaretha
Worpenberg	---->	Stricker, Katharine
Wuebben	---->	Watoff, Anna Maria
Wulf	---->	Ennebrock, Dora
Wulfeck	---->	Petersmann, Maria Engel
Wulfert	---->	Klostermann, Katharina
Wähaus	---->	Melcher, Anna
Wörmann	---->	Wibben, Philomena
Zange	---->	Tuerck, Katharina
Zehndick	---->	Fußhippel, Marie
Ziegler	---->	Rinckenberger, Lena
Ziegler	---->	Deubel, Theresia
Zier	---->	Kister, Elizabeth
Ziesler	---->	Oser, Emma
Zimmermann	---->	Moerlein, Magdalena
Zimmermann	---->	Graf, Barbara
Zinck	---->	Deramo, Karoline
Zumberger	---->	Prieshoff, Maria Anna
Zumstein	---->	Wiebell, Margaretha
Zurborg	---->	Klawest, Elizabeth
Zurliene	---->	Kabbes, Maria Anna
Zwick	---->	Lemmel, Ottillia
Zwick	---->	Bracher, Albertina

Other Heritage Books by Hamilton County Chapter of the Ohio Genealogical Society:

CD: Hamilton County, Ohio Burial Records, Volumes 1-9:

Hamilton County, Ohio Burial Records:
** Volume 1: Wesleyan Cemetery, 1842-1971 (1984)*
** Volume. 2: Anderson Township Cemeteries, 1800-1989 (1990)*
** Volume 3: Vine Street Hill Cemetery, 1852-1977 (1991)*
** Volume 4: Miami Township (Primarily Maple Grove) (1993)*
** Volume 5: Crosby and Whitewater Township Cemeteries (1993)*
** Volume 6: Colerain Township Cemeteries (1994)*
** Volume 7: Springfield Township Cemeteries (1994)*
** Volume 8: Sycamore Township Cemeteries (1994)*
** Volume 9: Union Baptist African American Cemetery (1997)*

Hamilton County, Ohio Burial Records:
Volume 4: Miami Township Cemeteries
Volume 5: Crosby and Whitewater Township Cemeteries
Volume 7: Springfield Township Cemeteries
Volume 8: Sycamore Township Cemeteries
Volume 9: Union Baptist African American Cemetery
Volume 10: Green Township
Volume 11: Columbia Township
Volume 12: Calvary Cemetery
Volume 13: First German Protestant Cemetery of Avondale and Martini United Church of Christ Records
Volume 14: Harrison Township

Hamilton County, Ohio Church Death Records, 1811-1849

Index of Death Lists Appearing in the Cincinnatier Zeitung, *1887-1901*

Index of Death Notices Appearing in the Cincinnati Daily Times, *1840-1879*

Index of Death Notices Appearing in the Cincinnati Volksblatt, *1846-1918, [Hamilton County]*

Restored Hamilton County, Ohio Marriages, 1808-1849

Restored Hamilton County, Ohio Marriages, 1850-1859

Restored Hamilton County, Ohio Marriages, 1860-1869

Restored Hamilton County, Ohio Marriages, 1870-1884

Other Heritage Books by Jeffrey G. Herbert:

Index of Death Notices and Marriages Notices Appearing in the Cincinnati Daily Gazette, *1827-1881*

Index of Death and Other Notices Appearing in the Cincinnati Freie Presse, *1874-1920*

Index of Death Notices Appearing in the Cincinnati Commercial, *1858-1899*

Restored Hamilton County, Ohio Marriages, 1808-1849

Restored Hamilton County, Ohio Marriages, 1860-1869

Restored Hamilton County, Ohio Marriages, 1870-1884

CD: Restored Hamilton County, Ohio Marriages, 1860-1869

www.ingramcontent.com/pod-product-compliance
Lightning Source LLC
Chambersburg PA
CBHW081430270326
41932CB00019B/3144

* 9 7 8 0 7 8 8 4 1 2 0 6 6 *